Propaganda in the Helping Professions

Propaganda in the Helping Professions

Eileen Gambrill

OXFORD
UNIVERSITY PRESS

OXFORD
UNIVERSITY PRESS

Published in the United States of America by Oxford University Press, Inc.,
198 Madison Avenue, New York, NY, 10016
United States of America

Oxford University Press, Inc., publishes works that further Oxford University's
objective of excellence in research, scholarship, and education

Oxford is a registered trademark of Oxford University Press
in the UK and in certain other countries

Copyright © 2012 Oxford University Press, Inc.

All rights reserved. No part of this publication may be reproduced, stored in a
retrieval system, or transmitted, in any form or by any means, without the prior
permission in writing of Oxford University Press, Inc., or as expressly permitted
by law, by licence, or under terms agreed with the appropriate reproduction
rights organization. Inquiries concerning reproduction outside the scope of the
above should be sent to the Rights Department, Oxford University Press, Inc., at
the address above

You must not circulate this work in any other form
and you must impose this same condition on any acquirer

___

Library of Congress Cataloging-in-Publication Data

Gambrill, Eileen D., 1934-
  Propaganda in the helping professions / Eileen Gambrill.
     p. cm.
  Includes bibliographical references and index.
  ISBN 978-0-19-532500-3 (hardcover : alk. paper) 1. Professional employees.
2. Consumer confidence. 3. Propaganda. 4. Persuasion (Psychology)
5. Consumer education. I. Title.
  HD8038.A1G36 2012
  650.101'4—dc23   2011033020
___

1 3 5 7 9 10 8 6 4 2

Typeset in Minion Pro
Printed in the United States of America
on acid-free paper

PREFACE

How can you tell a quack or a fraudster from the real thing? We all face this challenge. Indeed people have faced this challenge since the beginning of time as illustrated by the colorful and often tragic history of quackery and fraud confounding people's efforts to find happiness and to seek relief from suffering and misery. Making this important distinction is rendered more difficult by the lack of success in helping us all to become critical thinkers during our education. Some have even suggested that this lack of effectiveness is deliberate because of the enormous benefits to the ruling elite of a populace that cannot detect propaganda—material that encourages beliefs and actions with the least thought possible. The purpose of this book is to increase your awareness of how propaganda in the helping professions influences your decisions and to increase your skills in avoiding its unwanted effects. This book is for professionals, as well as clients. They also are often bamboozled by false claims in professional journals and textbooks, as well as in the media, about what is helpful and what is not. The helping professions include medicine, dentistry, psychiatry, psychology, social work, nursing, counseling, and related fields.

Only if professionals minimize the influence of the propaganda they encounter can they avoid propagandizing their clients. All parties are interconnected in a dance of competing realities. Propaganda in the helping professions includes inflated claims of knowledge and ignorance regarding: (1) the effectiveness of certain products, practices, and policies including assessment methods and frameworks; (2) what is a problem or risk; (3) alleged causes of concerns; (4) professional competence; and (5) what research methods can critically appraise a question. Perhaps even more often than greed, paternalism ("I/We know best what is good for you") encourages propaganda in the helping professions. This book will help readers to lift the curtains of mystifications and confusions created by propaganda in the helping professions and the many related enterprises described. Indeed you, as was I, may be amazed to learn about all the action hidden in the wings. It is almost as if one had a house infested with mites that one did not know about—but there they are, affecting our lives.

Professionals, as well as those they hope to help, are typically caught up in propaganda in the helping professions, for example, by accepting gifts and free dinners from pharmaceutical companies, attending continuing education programs funded by these companies, and by reading journal articles prepared by commercial writing firms hired by pharmaceutical companies. (I call these "marticles" as described in chapter 9.) It is only within the past few years that greater attention has been given to related subterfuges, mostly because they have become so "over the top," including creation of new maladies by pharmaceutical companies and fellow travelers such as the American Psychiatric Association. The framing of life's dilemmas (how to act in the world—e.g., whether to batter one's partner or not) as psychiatric maladies, ignoring moral and ethical aspects, provides endless opportunities for the helping profession industries to expand. But does it offer us opportunities to grow as thoughtful, responsible human beings who confront the effects of our behavior and experience the joys possible? Do we, as some ask, want to be a nation of "Charlie Chuckles"? Certainly, many people have problems that can be alleviated by the help of informed, caring professionals, including medication; but how many, and under what umbrella—psychiatric, or moral and existential? Are all the problems-in-living now framed as psychiatric a matter of brain diseases? How many are moral-ethical dilemmas that, if we confront, perhaps with the help of an expert guide, we can have a richer and perhaps still at times anxious life, rather than a tranquilized-zombie-like life? And who benefits from these different decisions?

In this book, propaganda is viewed as an epistemic and ethical concern—it concerns knowledge and ethics. Because propaganda is deceptive—it hides, confuses, distorts and distracts, perhaps even fabricates—it is a deeply ethical issue. It deprives us of opportunities to make up our own minds about what to believe and how to act. It diminishes our humanity and our agency—our freedom to make our own decisions. Decisions we think we have made are orchestrated by others, including public relations firms hired by pharmaceutical companies. I hope that this book helps readers to identify unknown influences on their decisions and to understand how we are all deceived in many ways and how we are complicit in this process. If propaganda is essential in the technological society in which we live, as Ellul (1965) suggests, then we cannot escape its influence. Our only recourse is to try to understand how it works, how it influences our lives, and, for professionals, how it influences the lives of clients, and how we may mute its effects.

Propaganda pitches often create an illusion of openness, while at the same time, obscuring competing views and questionable grounds for claims about what is true and what is not. They are carefully tailored to appeal to our self-interests and deepest motives (to be right, to be a member of the in group) in order to discourage critical appraisal. Chapters are included designed to help readers detect different forms of propaganda, for example, about bogus risks, unneeded screening tests that may do more harm than good, and unneeded interventions that may harm rather than help. Readers will learn what questions to ask about claims and recommendations made by professionals and others. And they will learn how to have fun unpacking clever persuasion tactics used in direct-to-consumer advertisements rather than being influenced by them in uncritical ways hoped for by the creators: "Ask your doctor for X." Do you really have irritable bladder? Is depression really a brain disease? Should you take a statin? Should you seek the radical method of treating cancer of taking out all your insides and pouring a harsh chemotherapy into your abdomen? Is this likely to do more harm than good? Thus, it is my hope that this book will not only inform and in this way expand your ability to make informed decisions, but be fun in the process. What seems innocent, such as taking a screening test, may lead to a cascade of events that may ruin your life such as a false positive test which results in further intrusive tests with adverse side effects.

You will have to decide whether you want to coast along with the tide directed by others or take your oars and make your own way. You may believe that you are now in charge—that your oars are securely in the water and you are forging your own path. This is exactly what manipulators want you to think. But, if there is one lesson to be learned from history, including the history of public relations and advertising, as well as the history of the helping professions, it is that we often think we are captains of our ship when we are not. This is the essence of manipulation—to make us believe that we are in charge when we are deck hands in ships steered by others toward goals that we may even despise if we were aware of them. When the curtain closes on a good play, the messages of the play continue. My hope is that this happens to you—that reading this book is not the end but the beginning of a new approach to propaganda, one that begins with increased recognition of propaganda and its many venues and scripts, one that expands your vision and possibilities, one that yields a reawakening of curiosity and belief in your own ability to arrive at well-reasoned decisions that you, not others, choose.

I owe much to all the writers who have contributed to the rich literature on propaganda. I have drawn on the masterful analysis of Jacque Ellul, which so well integrates the psychological and sociological in understanding what propaganda is, how it works, and how it affects us. I wish to thank Maura Roessner, Senior Editor at Oxford, for her support and interest in this area as well as Nicholas Liu, also of Oxford for his help. I thank Bruce Thyer, Brian Sheldon, and the remaining anonymous reviewers of earlier drafts who provided helpful feedback. I thank the Hutto Patterson Charitable Foundation for financial help with this project, as well as Sharon Ikami for her word processing skills. Thanks also to Gail Bigelow for her enduring support and caring about the world.

E.G.

CONTENTS

PART ONE Introduction

1. Propaganda in the Helping Professions: What Is It and Why Should You Care? 5

PART TWO Context, Actors, and Scripts

2. Introduction to the Players 29

3. Interactions Among the Players 63

4. Propaganda Analysis: Different Levels 90

PART THREE Consequences of Propaganda

5. A Rogue's Gallery of Harms Related to Propaganda in the Helping Professions 123

6. The Medicalization of Life 159

PART FOUR How They Reel Us In

7. Obscure Different Views of Knowledge and How to Get It 199

8. Appeal to Popular Grand Narratives and Metaphors 235

9. Disguise Advertisements as Professional Literature 278

10. Propagandistic Use of Language and Social Psychological Persuasion Strategies 297

11. Appeal to Our Psychological Vulnerabilities 326

PART FIVE What You Can Do

12. Enhance Your Argument Analysis Skills 351

13. Increase Your Skill in Spotting Fallacies 382

14. Increase Your Skill in Searching for Answers for Yourself 405

Notes 429
References 475
Index 541

Propaganda in the Helping Professions

PART ONE

Introduction

1

Propaganda in the Helping Professions

What Is It and Why Should You Care?

Professionals such as physicians, psychologists, and dentists affect our lives on a daily basis. We turn to certain kinds of professionals for help with particular problems. We may be forced to deal with social workers, psychologists, or psychiatrists as are parents accused of maltreating their children or adults alleged to be "mentally ill" and committed against their will. In countries without national health insurance in which all residents have access to health care, profit making is of keen interest spawning a cornucopia of related industries. Regardless of the kind of health services, claim making is a central activity. Claims are made about alleged risks, about problems that warrant attention and about causes and remedies. Such claims entail certain views of reality, for example, what is a problem? How should it be handled? Consider controversies regarding drinking alcohol and smoking marijuana. The essence of claims making is constructing realities—realities which forward a particular view. Both professionals and clients are often bamboozled by false claims in professional journals and textbooks, as well as in the media, about what is helpful and what is not. Such claims hide certain aspects of reality and/or assert realities that do not exist. False claims are a key form of propaganda—inflated claims about what works, what causes certain behaviors, what can keep us healthy, what a risk is, and how we can identify risks. False claims of ignorance are also common (hiding knowledge that is available). It was in part because of inaccurate statements in texts, editorials, and professional articles that evidence-based practice was developed (Gray, 2001a).

As propaganda methods have become more sophisticated, the influence of propaganda becomes more subtle, pervasive, and difficult to detect and resist. Misleading claims are often effective in influencing our behavior and beliefs because we do not critically appraise them. Rather, we are patsies for others' bogus claims because of our own inactions—our failure to ask questions—to be skeptical. The environments in which we work may discourage asking questions. Indeed the questioner may be drummed out of the organization. The importance of thinking carefully about claims of knowledge and ignorance and the means used to forward them is highlighted by harming in the name of helping. This book will increase your awareness of how you may be mislead in making life-affecting decisions and how you yourself may contribute to being mislead. It will help you to be more informed about what questions to ask about claims of what is true and what is not.

WHAT IS PROPAGANDA?

Propaganda "seeks to induce action, adherence and participation—with as little thought as possible" (Ellul, 1965, p. 180). This can be contrasted to critical thinking defined as arriving at well-reasoned beliefs and actions based on critical appraisal of related arguments and evidence and an understanding of relevant contexts. Propaganda is a topic of discussion in many different fields including theology, military history, and art. The word "propaganda" was first used in 1622. Pope Gregory XV created the Sacra Congredatio de Propaganda Fide. The purpose of this papal propaganda office was to encourage people to accept church doctrines via use of deliberate strategic persuasion. This illustrates that the word "propaganda" is not necessarily negatively viewed. The creation and diffusion of propaganda increased greatly with the invention of the printing press and the various forms of printed sources such as newspapers, bulletins, newsletters, and books and increased yet again with the development and wide use of electronic media such as radio and television. Another boost occurred during the two world wars; the dissemination of propaganda was viewed as a critical part of the war effort by the major countries involved in the world wars. The growth of the Internet provides another source of propaganda, as well as sources designed to counter it, such as <http://www.healthyskepticism.org/global/>. The examples below illustrate propaganda in the helping professions including overemphasizing the benefits of a favored alternative and hiding the possible costs including lost opportunities of receiving effective methods. There is a hiding of context, a partiality in the use of evidence, a promotion of distorted realities that is so integral to propaganda.

1. A brochure designed to encourage nonsymptomatic women to be tested for breast cancer by having a mammogram does not describe the high rate of false positives and resultant unnecessary biopsies.
2. Lilly, the pharmaceutical company, hid the fact that taking Zyprexa increased the risk of diabetes.[1]
3. An International Consensus Statement about ADHD (Attention Deficit Hyperactivity Disorder) was signed by 86 people but contains two pages of text with no well-reasoned responses to criticisms but many ad hominem attacks on critics. Consensus is promoted as a sound criterion on which to make claims when it is not (Barkley, Cook, Diamond, Zametkin, Thapar, Teeter et al., 2002).
4. A researcher does not describe key limitations in his research in a published article.
5. An instructor in a professional education program misrepresents a well-argued alternative view that competes with her favorite practice theory.
6. A continuing education instructor does not tell his audience that there have been no critical tests of his claim that a "new" therapy is effective.
7. A psychologist does not tell her client about alternative methods that have a better track record of success compared to the treatment she recommends.
8. A social work textbook misrepresents a major theoretical approach that has led to the development of effective programs for children and adults.

9. Authors of an article assert conclusions that cannot accurately be made based on the methods used. For example, based on a pre-post study, they claim that a program was responsible for changes (e.g., Rubin & Parrish, 2007).
10. Osteoporosis is described as a disease when it is a risk factor (not a disease).
11. Facilitated communication, designed to encourage speech in those who have never spoken, was developed in Australia and spread throughout the world, being promoted based on testimonials and research studies that cannot critically test the effectiveness of a service. (See Jacobson, Foxx, & Mulick, 2005.)
12. A psychiatrist at the University of Minnesota prescribed Risperdal (a powerful antipsychotic drug) to 12-year-old Anya Bailey to address her eating disorder (Harris, Carey, & Roberts 2007). She was not offered or informed about alternative treatments.
13. Doctors who accept money from drug companies prescribe more drugs. Some of these drugs result in more harm than good.[2]

Propaganda ploys are used to influence the choices we make while giving us the illusion that we freely make these choices. Consider the following:

- Taking a multivitamin everyday.
- Participating in a full-body diagnostic scan designed to catch and prevent illness.
- Placing a child on Ritalin.
- Taking Paxil to decrease anxiety.
- Drinking two cups of green tea a day to prevent colds.
- Attending a National Screening Day for Anxiety Disorder.

In each example, we can ask whether a choice is well reasoned or based on questionable grounds such as appeals to fear or popularity and engineered by others such as public relations firms employed by pharmaceutical companies or professional organizations. In each, we can ask, "How good is the evidence?" In each, we should ask whether the choice we make will result in more good than harm and how can we find out? We are not free to make choices if we are not informed. Assuring us that we are free in such circumstances is a propaganda ploy. Like optical illusions, propaganda offers illusions of explanation, risk, and remedies. Detecting them is rendered even more difficult today given the complexity and scale of interactions among the many different parties in many different locations, including governmental regulatory agencies facilitated by increasingly pervasive and sophisticated technologies (Applbaum, 2009a & b). These interactions are typically hidden unless brought to our attention by concerned journalists, politicians, academics, and consumer groups. We live in a sea of propaganda pitches, including propaganda in the helping professions and related industries. These include inflated claims of knowledge (what we know) and ignorance (what we do not know):

- About causes.
- About the accuracy of diagnostic tests.

- About the effectiveness of proposed remedies; about "what works."
- About problems and risks.
- About the prevalence of concerns—advocacy in place of evidence.

Propaganda in the media and in the professional literature interact with groupthink in organizations, as well as with self-propaganda, such as wishful thinking and confirmation biases (searching only for material that supports our views), to compromise decisions. Common propaganda ploys include the following:

- Hiding limitations of research.
- Preparing uncritical, incomplete research reviews related to a practice or policy.
- Ignoring counterevidence to favored views.
- Ignoring or misrepresenting well-argued alternative views and related evidence.
- Arguing ad hominem (attacking the critic) rather than ad rem (responding to the argument). (See also Table 1.1.)

Isn't one person's propaganda another person's carefully gathered evidence? Definitions of propaganda highlight its contrast to critical inquiry. For example, in the former, evidence against favored views is hidden. In critical appraisal, evidence related to claims is actively sought such as critical tests and open discussion of competing views. Interrelated kinds of propaganda in the helping professions include deep propaganda that obscures the political, economic, and social contingencies that influence problems claimed by a profession, such as alcohol abuse, and the questionable accuracy of related assumptions about causes such as labeling hundreds of (mis) behaviors as mental disorders requiring the help of experts. It includes inflated claims

Table 1.1 INDICATORS OF PROPAGANDA

- Discouraging critical appraisal of claims; avoiding opportunities to discuss views with others who favor alternative views.
- Inflated claims (puffery); excessive claims of certainty (We have "the way").
- Personal attacks/ridicule.
- Presentation of information/issues/views out of context; hiding context.
- Vagueness that obscures interests and arguments.
- Emotional appeals.
- Suppression of data unfavorable to views promoted.
- Distortion and suppression of competing well-argued views.
- Appeal to popular prejudices.
- Reliance on informal fallacies, such as unfounded authority and manner of presentation to support claims.
- Appeals to case examples and testimonials to support claims of effectiveness.
- Reliance on association and suggestion (e.g., negative innuendo).
- Transforming words to suit aims.
- Claiming one thing but doing another.
- Repetition.
- Oversimplification of complex topics.

of effectiveness regarding practices and policies that woo clients to professionals and professionals to professions. Propaganda hides influences on our decisions and information of value in making decisions. It uses false figures and misleading claims. It hinders our autonomy to make our own decisions based on accurate information.[3] We all try to influence other people—to persuade people to believe or act in a certain way. The question is how do we do so? We can persuade people via a clear description of arguments, including their premises and conclusions and related evidence, or via a variety of propaganda pitches that do not clearly describe arguments and related evidence and relevant contextual variables (such as special interests). Aristotle wrote the first detailed account of persuasion about 323 B.C. He argued that the purpose of persuasion was to communicate a point of view. This was the first book on rhetoric—the art of persuasion. *Reasoning* (true rhetoric) involves a *critical evaluation of claims* and their context. This is quite different from the manipulative rhetoric of propaganda. (See Table 1.2.) Bennett and O'Rourke (2006) note that people have suggested the need to use rhetoric to limit its potential for abuse (p. 57).

Table 1.2 RHETORIC AND PROPAGANDA: WHAT IS THE DIFFERENCE?

Rhetoric	Issues Relevant to Democratic Process	Propaganda
Participant in decision making; person worthy of equal respect	1. Other (Audience)	Target or recipient; instrument of propagandist's will
Significant and informed	2. Nature of Choice	Limited because not fully informed
Thinking, reasoned	3. Desired Response	Reactionary; thinking response is short-circuited
Effective and ethical appeals Reason is primary, supported with both logic and imagination to appeal to emotions	4. Appropriate Means Use of reason Use of emotion Use of imagination	Most effective appeals Emotional appeals designed imaginatively to produce the quickest action
Socially constructed; constituted and reconstituted in open debate	5. Determining Contingent "Truth"	Determined by primary goal; determined by propagandist; often irrelevant or glossed
Co-participant in decision making; seeks to engage others; post-Copernican; often less powerful	6. Self (Communicator)	More important than others; above, greater; pre-Copernican; often more powerful

SOURCE: B. S. Bennett & S. P. O'Rourke (2006). A prolegomenon to the future study of rhetoric and propaganda: Critical foundations. In G. S. Jowett & V. O'Donnell (Eds.), *Readings in propaganda and persuasion: New and classic essays* (pp. 51–71). Thousand Oaks, CA: Sage. With permission of Sage.

The examples in this book illustrate the ubiquitous nature of bogus claims of knowledge in the helping professions, typically for a profit to the purveyor including status as a researcher. There is selective use of evidence, such as ignoring studies showing lack of effectiveness or harms of intervention. Claims are promoted based on weak grounds, such as anecdotal reports and pre-post studies that do not consider rival explanations because there are no comparison groups. Although we may expect to find misleading claims in advertisements and on the part of quacks and fraudsters, we may be surprised to find them in professional education programs, even in prestigious universities, in our clinics and hospitals, and in professional journals and textbooks as illustrated in this book. Selection of interventions, including assessment methods, may be based on a faulty theory embraced due to exaggerated claims of accuracy. Promotion and use of procedures critically tested and found to be harmful or ineffective illustrate that propagandized professionals often interact with eager-to-be propagandized clients. Clients' hopes and wishes for happiness and redress from difficult circumstances such as chronic pain, or "out-of-control" teenagers, and professionals' interests in helping, combine in a potent, often mystical brew, that encourages uncritical belief in claims as to what will help and what will not, often resulting in the use of ineffective or harmful methods.

In propaganda, realities constructed are partial-tilted toward those that forward beliefs and actions favored by the claims maker. Other realties are shoved aside, ignored, or actively censored, such as adverse effects of medications promoted by pharmaceutical companies. Consider the assertion that smoking marijuana is a gateway drug to use of heroin. This (false) claim has been used to rationalize the criminalization of marijuana resulting in imprisoning tens of thousands of (mostly African American) men (Alexander, 2010). Much propaganda is "a set of methods employed by an organized group that wants to bring about the active or passive participation in its actions of a mass of individuals, psychologically unified through psychological manipulations and incorporated in an organization" (Ellul, 1965: p. 61).

Those who make claims may not care about the truth or falsity of a claim, just whether the claim is acted on. This is a key point in understanding propaganda in the helping professions. That is, truth may not be (and often is not) a concern to those who promote claims of knowledge (or ignorance). The goal is to create beliefs and encourage certain actions. "The genius of most successful propaganda is to know what the audience wants and how far it will go" (Johnson, 2006, p. A23). The goals emphasized in propaganda pitches (protecting your health) may not be those that the propagandizer is most interested in (making money from your purchases).[4] Even a cursory examination of newspapers and professional literature indicates that there is a continuing need to remind ourselves about the pervasiveness of propaganda and its effects.

> It is the emergence of mass media which makes possible the use of propaganda techniques on a societal scale. The orchestration of press, radio and television to create a continuous, lasting and total environment renders the influence of propaganda virtually unnoticed precisely because it creates a constant environment. Mass media provides the essential link between the individual and the demands of the technological society. (Ellul, 1965)

Propaganda methods include suppression of important information such as well-argued alternatives to a recommended practice, distortion of competing perspectives, and diversion from critical appraisal of claims. Marketing is disguised as education (Brody, 2007). Related methods are used to hide the lack of match between risks and problems and the remedies promoted and related evidence (e.g., to direct attention away from environmental causes of physical illness and psychological distress). Consider overlooking environmental causes of cognitive and behavioral problems due to parasitic diseases contracted through contaminated water.[5] Many efforts described as "scientific research" or "scholarly inquiry" do not reflect the values, aims, or methods of science such as self-correction. Inflated claims of knowledge are more the norm than the exception. In her essay review "Drug companies & doctors: A story of corruption" (2009), Marcia Angell concludes:

> It is simply no longer possible to believe much of the clinical research that is published, or to rely on the judgment of trusted physicians or authoritative medical guidelines. I take no pleasure in this conclusion which I reached slowly and reluctantly over my two decades as an editor of *The New England Journal of Medicine*. (p. 15)

Ioannidis (2005) argues that most research findings in biomedical research are false.[6] A variety of strategies are used to give the illusion of successful outcomes including focusing on surrogates (reducing plaque rather than mortality), data dredging (searching for significant findings unguided by specific hypotheses), describing only outcomes found to be positive and not reporting negative ones, folding outcome measures not found to be significant into a composite score and arguing that the composite is effective. Such ploys are common in the professional literature (e.g., Gorman & Huber, 2009). Inadequate education about what science is and what it is not, lapses in scholarship on the part of academics and researchers, as well as the daily barrage of propaganda in the media—often in the guise of "scientific research"—blur the distinction between science and pseudoscience, many times with serious consequences. Lack of historical knowledge fuels the process such as ignorance concerning use of coercion throughout the history of psychiatry (Szasz, 2002).

Those who have products to sell, including residential centers, pharmaceutical companies, and professional organizations, use sophisticated strategies to encourage purchase of their products. These range from the obvious, such as advertisements, to the hidden, such as offering workshops or conferences without identifying the funding source. It is estimated that pharmaceutical companies spend $61,000 per medical student per year to market their products to these individuals (Gagnon, 2010). A review of advertising on marketing brochures distributed by drug companies to physicians in Germany revealed that 94% of the content in these had no basis in scientific evidence (reported in Tuffs, 2004). In advertising we are usually aware of the purpose of the advertiser—to sell a service or product. (See Figure 1.1.)

In propaganda in other venues and forms, purposes are often hidden. Indeed, as Ellul (1965) emphasizes, propaganda is often presented as education. Presenting pitches for a product in an "article" form ("advertorials") may lull readers into uncritical acceptance of promotional material (Prounis, 2004), as may reading articles in professional journals. Drug companies promote common concerns such as social anxiety and premenstrual dysphoria as "mental illnesses" to increase profits from sales of drugs. (See chapter 3.) Continuing education programs in medicine are funded by pharmaceutical companies, as are screening days for anxiety and

Figure 1.1. Example of advertisement.
SOURCE: American Psychologist, 1998, 53 (6), right after p. 696.

depression. In 2003 the percentage of all commercial support for continuing medical education activities from pharmaceutical companies was 97% (Brody, 2007, p. 204).

Marketing values and strategies, prevalent throughout time in selling nostrums for our maladies, have increasingly entered the realm of professional education, as well as published literature. Needs and desires are created and promoted to sell products and services to satisfy these needs and avoid these risks. We are thus kept on tender-hooks, waiting to hear about the next avoidable risk, the next promised remedy to meet our needs, described not only in the media but also in professional journals and texts.

WHAT ARE THE HELPING PROFESSIONS?

The helping professions include (among others) psychiatry, medicine, nursing, dentistry, psychology, social work, counseling, podiatry, occupational therapy, physical therapy, and optometry. They have grown in influence over the past decades, fueled in part by grand narratives central in our culture, such as "progress," "cure," and "health" and related technologies. The helping professions and related enterprises are huge industries. Billions of dollars are consumed by those who try to improve or maintain the health of those who voluntarily seek or are coerced into contact with them and by training, research, and educational programs that purport to provide related values, knowledge, and skills, including the continuing education industry. Mental health services expanded during the community mental health movement, and the number of mental health professionals increased greatly.[7] In addition to practitioners, many others are involved in the helping industries including politicians, support staff in hospitals and clinics, and staff in related industries such as the insurance, medical supply, and pharmaceutical industries as described in chapter 3.

We often take professions for granted, as if they have always existed. However, professions such as social work, counseling, psychology, and psychiatry are relatively recent. Certain occupations have been transformed into professions, which Abbott defines as "exclusive occupational groups applying somewhat abstract knowledge to particular cases" (1988, p. 8). They became professions, not necessarily because they had a better track record of solving certain kinds of problems, but because they were successful in selling the view that they were most successful and therefore should have a unique right to address them (Abbott, 1988). For example, midwifery was officially discredited at the beginning of the twentieth century when it was replaced by obstetric care, even though midwives had lower rates of stillbirths and puerperal sepsis than did the (male) physicians (Ehrenreich & English, 1973). Abbott (1988, 2010) views professions as groups that "acquire jurisdiction (control) over an area of work." He argues that the structural shape they take, such as licensing and ethical codes, is determined by an interest in control of certain problems (not vice versa as others have argued). Each profession (or would-be profession) must "culturally constitute" certain problems, for example, "fatness must be turned into the disease of obesity" (p. 175). "Indeed, it is by competing in this way—via the cultural reconstitution of human problems—that an occupation identified itself as a profession" (p. 175). And, these framings and jurisdiction over them must be defended against competitors—"other would-be professions." Remedies must be created to address problems and theories offered to link "diagnosis" and treatment. Each profession must create a social structure that provides "legitimacy" to key audiences, including the public and the legal system. This view of the professions highlights the inevitabilities of ongoing conflict among different ones for control over certain "problems."

Claimed special knowledge supposedly makes those with certain degrees, training, and/or experience more effective in achieving certain outcomes than those without such "credentials." That is, certain kinds of professionals are supposed to be "experts" in solving certain problems. Professional organizations claim that expertise is acquired via special education and experience; this distinguishes professionals from technicians who use clear routinized skills.[8]

> The main instrument of professional advancement, more than the profession of altruism, is the capacity to claim esoteric and identifiable skills.... The claim of expertise aims at gaining social recognition and collective prestige which, in turn, are implicitly used by the individual to assert his authority and demand respect in the context of everyday transactions within specific role-sets. (Larson, 1977, p. 180)

Different professionals lay claim to different problems, although there is considerable overlap among some such as psychology, psychiatry, social work, and counseling. Each asserts success in doing good.[9] The special rights of professionals are protected by certificates and licenses that are claimed to protect the public from less effective interlopers. Professions have well-organized national and state organizations dedicated to maintenance and expansion of turf, based often not on claims of effectiveness that have survived critical tests, but on inflated claims of success and on questionable criteria such as consensus and appeals to fear—classic propaganda ploys (McCormick, 1996). Propaganda in the helping professions creates and maintains the belief that professionals are in possession of unique knowledge that can benefit those they claim to serve. In some cases this is true. In others it is not. Studies in medicine show that specialized content knowledge is vital to making sound decisions in many instances.[10] But in how many instances? Do licenses and credentials protect us from incompetent practices and harmful policies? Dawes (1994) argues that those without certain credentials, licenses, and experience are often as effective as those who have them in achieving a range of outcomes. He argued that licensing gives the public an illusion of protection, but serves the economic interests of professionals.[11]

The Role of the Helping Professions: Claimed and Hidden

Not all viewed the rise of the helping professions as good. George Bernard Shaw (1946) described all professions as "conspiracies against the laity." Critics argue that professionals often harm rather than help by promoting the deception that (mis-) behaviors are "mental illnesses" warranting intervention by professionals with the blessing of the state.[12] In addition to providing help with certain kinds of problems, professions have political, social, and economic functions and interests. "No matter how disinterested its concern for knowledge, humanity, art, or whatever, the profession must become an interest group to at once advance its aims and to protect itself from those with competing aims. On the formal association level, professions are inextricably and deeply involved in politics" (Friedson, 1973, pp. 29–30). The political, social, and economic functions of the helping profession accounts for the prevalence of propaganda in related venues, such as exaggerated claims of expertise and success (to gain public and legislative support). This can be seen in battles to protect and expand "turf," for example, between psychologists and psychiatrists. Professionals are integrally involved in defining problems and deciding what should be done about them: what is healthy (good) or unhealthy (bad) with the blessing of the government. Each promotes and appeals to popular goals such as "wellness" to justify its actions (and inactions) and to assure the public that it is working in its best interests; although, there is considerable overlap as seen in the area of "mental health" in which deviant behaviors and problems-in-living are labeled as mental illness in need of treatment by experts. Promotion of health as a valued commodity has become so prominent that some describe this as "health fascism" (Fitzpatrick, 2001). The creation of health scares and related state policies enrich health promoters and enhance politician's power to control the population (McCormick, 1996). The growth in the number of professionals is fueled by the creation of ever more alleged "diseases," and risks, for example, labeling common mood changes and anxieties as "mental disorders." An ever-lengthening list of behaviors are defined as mental illnesses requiring the help of "experts." The growth of the helping professions has also been fueled by new technologies such as neuroimaging methods used in mammograms, which can identify very small calcifications, and the proliferation of psychological measures claimed to accurately identify various dysfunctions and maladies including female sexual dysfunction.

Social control is a key function of the helping professions. This refers to encouraging adherence to social norms and minimizing, eliminating, or normalizing deviant behavior. Functions of social control include getting rid of troubling or disturbing people, protecting citizens from harm, and reaffirming standards of morality (Conrad, 2007; Conrad & Schneider, 1992, p. 7). Examples of social control include mental health laws and regulations and actions by governmental representatives such as police, psychiatrists, and social workers. Public health regulations are designed to protect others from the spread of disease and, in so doing, often limit our discretionary behavior. Institutions concerned with social control include the educational, social welfare, penal, public health, and biomedical systems and the mass media. The social control functions of professionals can be seen in their roles as probation and parole officers and as child protection workers when they remove children from neglectful or abusive parents, in protective services for the elderly when they arrange for conservatorship, and in mental health agencies when they recommend hospitalization.

Moral values are reflected in the design and practices of related institutions. Wacquant (2009) argues that the welfare and mental health systems are closely intertwined with the criminal justice system in punishing the nonconforming and the poor—"behavioral control of marginalized populations" (Wacquant, 2009, p. xix). Psychiatrists arrange for coerced outpatient commitment and commit people to hospitals against their will on the grounds that they are mentally ill (Morrisey & Monahan, 1999).[13] The history of institutional psychiatry reveals this to be a coercive social control enterprise designed to help family members and the state to deal with difficult behavior, for example, to get rid of relatives engaged in troubling behaviors (e.g., Szasz, 1987; Valenstein, 1986).

Handler and Hasenfeld (1991) argue that moral assumptions are reflected in the classification system designed to distinguish between clients who are required by social welfare legislation to participate in work activities (workfare) and those who are not. Since colonial times, social welfare policies have treated women differently, based on the extent to which their lives conformed to certain family ethics (Abramovitz, 1988, pp. 3–4). Katz argues that welfare has often been designed "to promote social order by appeasing protest or disciplining the poor" (1989, p. 33). A policy's social control function is not necessarily obvious. The language of caring and nurturance may obscure manipulative and coercive practices, such as institutionalizing people against their will in mental hospitals and keeping them under surveillance. In *Under the Cover of Kindness*, Margolin (1997) argues that social workers use strategies such as building empathy in manipulative ways in order to gain entry into the private homes of families. He contends that social work in public agencies is engaged mainly in political surveillance, keeping track of marginal people in their homes.[14] It is professionals who investigate and keep records that clients rarely see and thus cannot correct.

An interest in social reform can also be seen in the history of the helping professions. From the earliest days of social work, many social workers stressed the need for social reform, believing that the lack of food, housing, employment, and educational and recreational opportunities—not the unworthiness of individual persons—was responsible for social problems. Here too, political interests intrude. Katz (1989) argues that social reform efforts serve many functions, including gaining political advantage over opponents. Some efforts serve the needs of corporations (to protect and expand markets) and professional groups more effectively than the needs of the groups for which they were supposedly designed. For example, Katz suggested that in order to secure low-paid workers, fast food chains lobbied legislators to pass bills requiring women on welfare (even those with young children) to work. Appeals to professionalism are used to direct practitioner behavior in ways the organization (not necessarily the profession) deems appropriate.

> The appeal to professionalism most often includes the substitution of organizational for professional values; bureaucratic, hierarchical, and managerial controls rather than collegial relations; budgetary restrictions and rationalizations; and performance targets, accountability, and increased political control. In this sense, then, it can be argued that the appeal to professionalism is in effect a mechanism of social control at micro, meso, and macro levels. (Evett, Mieg, & Felt, 2006, p. 112)

Competing Goals in the Helping Professions

The different interests and functions of the helping professions highlight the potential for conflict, confusion, contradiction, and the play of propaganda. Conflicting goals stem from and lead to different opinions about what is viewed as a problem and how (or if) it should be addressed. Goals of control of unwanted behaviors by the state and by family members and profit making by those in the troubled persons industries compete with goals of helping clients and of accurate descriptions of research findings related to recommended methods (have they been critically tested and found to do more good than harm?). In state child welfare agencies, social workers are mandated both to protect children (e.g., remove them from their parents) and to help parents who have harmed (and may continue to harm) their children. Social control aims related to containing the marginal and related coercive acts are often disguised as "treatment" as illustrated by the history of institutional psychiatry, as well as by current practices such as forced outpatient commitment. Negotiating a balance between individual freedom and the protection of others has been the subject of treatises both small and large.

THE AIMS OF PROPAGANDA

Ellul (1965) suggested that the key purpose of propaganda is to encourage certain ways of acting. "The aim of modern propaganda is no longer to modify ideas, but to provoke action. It is no longer to change adherence to a doctrine, but to make the individual cling irrationally to a process of action. It is no longer to lead to a choice, but to loosen the reflexes. It is no longer to transform an opinion, but to arouse an active and mythical belief" (p. 25).[15] It relies on presuppositions and myths and hardens and sharpens them. Propaganda in the helping professions maintains and expands turf by obscuring mismatches between claims of effectiveness and their evidentiary status (have they been critically tested and, if so, with what results) and by rechristening ever more common variations in bodies, behaviors, feelings, and thoughts as risks or illnesses in need of expert attention.[16] It serves the function of integrating us into our society, as suggested in the earlier discussion of the social control functions of the helping professions. A key aim of all propaganda is to obscure contingencies (associations between our behavior and environmental consequences) that, if noticed, would result in countercontrol. Skinner (1953) has long advocated increasing our awareness of social, political, and economic contingencies to enable us to exert countercontrol to avoid unwanted influences, as have other authors such as Freire (1973) and Mills (1959).

MYTHS ABOUT PROPAGANDA

False beliefs about propaganda may get in the way of spotting propaganda in the helping professions:

1. We can avoid the effects of propaganda.
   We live in a technological society and its related propaganda pitches, which will fail unless they are compatible with our goals and deepest motives such as to stay healthy and have a happy life. There is no way we can avoid their effects, although we can become more aware of them and try to minimize their influence.
2. It is easy to avoid the effects of propaganda.
   Because of the persuasiveness of propaganda this is not possible.
3. Propaganda consists of lies.
   Propagandists go out of their way to avoid telling lies that may be discovered and so discredit the "liar."
4. The distribution of propaganda requires a conspiracy.
   Most propaganda may be unplanned.
5. Good intentions can protect us from propaganda, especially in the helping professions.
   One reason propaganda flourishes in related venues is because we assume that good intentions will protect us from harm. They have not, as the history of the helping professions shows, and they will not.
6. We learn how to avoid the effects of propaganda in our education.
   Not true, as shown for example in the dismal findings regarding the teaching of critical thinking values, knowledge, and skills (e.g., Paul,

Elder, & Bartell, 1997). What is presented as education is often indoctrination with the vital differences between these two endeavors obscured (Gambrill, 1997).

7. Professionals learn how to spot and avoid the effects of propaganda during their professional education including material that appears in professional journals and textbooks.
Although this may be true for some, including the few who take a special course designed to yield this outcome (e.g., Wofford & Ohl, 2005), it is not true for most professionals.

8. It appeals only to our emotions.
Appeals to "reasoning" are often used.

THE PLAY OF PROPAGANDA

We can use the metaphor of a stage when thinking about propaganda. Plays take place on a stage. "Staging" allows emphasis of different ideas, people, and backgrounds. This is the beauty of theater; we can create unique environments that create different realities. A stage (like an advertisement or published article) allows us to hide or mute certain features of reality and to display and emphasize others in order to attain certain effects—this is exactly what propaganda strategies do. There are front stage and back stage activities (Goffman, 1961).

> . . . medicine has for many decades now been betraying [the] public trust in the way that it has accepted various benefits from the pharmaceutical industry. Medicine and the [pharmaceutical] industry together have been very creative in thinking up rationalizations to make it seem as if all this behavior really serves the interest of the public after all. And medicine has also managed to convince itself that its world is divided into an on-stage and backstage portion. Patients, we imagine, see us on-stage but cannot peek behind the curtains and see us backstage. So long as some of the embarrassing exchanges between medicine and industry occur backstage, we think that no one will notice and public trust in the profession will not be compromised. (Brody, 2007, p. 5)

Stage designers (like propagandists) create varied ways to portray different "realities." In successful plays, we suspend disbelieve as we enter the world of the playwright, the actors, and the set designers who bring different realities to life. To understand propaganda in the helping professions, we must understand stories within stories and identify stories that remain hidden. What is offered to us as an explanation in the helping professions, such as an account of depression or breast cancer, is linked to a variety of other players and levels of activity of which we may be, and usually are, unaware, that may shape claims and limit our ability to make informed decisions.

The interrelationships among involved individuals and related institutions (such as profit-making treatment centers) may be (and typically are) hidden; they are not obvious and not described. With propaganda, we often do not realize that we have entered someone else's stage set, as in continuing education programs funded by pharmaceutical companies. Propaganda arranges a stage. It hides context and history.

It hides individual differences and experiences and flawed methodologies and environmental contributors to concerns. It presents a distorted view of reality. It hides other actors eager to present other views; they are hidden in the wings, their myths and scripts are rejected, perhaps not even acknowledged. Different kinds of propaganda may enter a storyline at different times. Self-propaganda, for example, wishful thinking and overconfidence, and propaganda from other sources are often closely entangled. Indeed Ellul (1965) suggests that unless propaganda appeals to our deep motives and goals, it will fail. The cast of characters and their venues are quite varied as described in chapters 2 and 3. Some players may surprise you, such as academics in prestigious universities who hide money paid by pharmaceutical companies and ghostwriters (staff in public relations firms who write articles that appear in professional journals with academics' names) (LaCasse & Leo, 2010).

THE CONSEQUENCES OF PROPAGANDA

Consequences of propaganda in the helping professions include:

- Labeling normal variations in behavior (or other conditions/indicators) as pathological, thereby creating avoidable worry and stigma.
- Creating bogus risks and related worries that drain life of its pleasures.
- Failing to receive effective services.
- Increased dependency on professionals, erosion of individual competence.
- Forcing clients to accept unneeded and excessively intrusive diagnostic tests and other interventions (e.g., forced commitment).
- Losing opportunities to minimize avoidable miseries such as death of children due to diarrhea caused by contaminated water because of attention to high-profile concerns such as AIDS.

Lumley (1933) suggested two distinguishable results of propaganda: the effects on particular individuals, such as being misled in an election or having one's mind closed, and effects on groups and societies. For example, a society may become capitalistic or socialistic economically, democratic or monarchistic politically. Residents may become pessimistic or optimistic. Some argue that the effects of propaganda may be positive, such as encouraging peace rather than war. In addition to the moralist view of propaganda, arguing that it encourages "belief without knowledge," is the "neutralist" view (Brown, 2006) traced to Aristotle and reflected in Harold Lasswell's book *Propaganda Technique in World War I* ([1927] 1971). Lasswell viewed propaganda as a "mere tool." In this neutralist view, propaganda is viewed as a practical process of persuasion and as such, inherently neutral (Taylor, 1992). Ellul (1965) argued that the effects of propaganda are always negative, especially in a democracy, because, whether intentional or not, rational propaganda creates an irrational situation and thus remains, propaganda "an inner control over the individual by a social force [typically unrecognized], which means that it deprives him of himself" (p. 87). Ellul (1965) views propaganda as "a direct attack against man—a menace which threatens the total personality." Effects he suggests can be seen in Table 1.3.

Lumley (1933) suggests that one of the gravest negative effects of propaganda is to encourage fear and suspicion, which decreases human happiness. He argues that

Table 1.3 CONSEQUENCE OF PROPAGANDA

- Alienates us from ourselves. We can no longer judge for ourselves. Encourages depersonalization, fragmentation.
- Creates an illusion of freedom (we feel free but are not).
- Creates resignation and inertia.
- Reduces critical judgment and experimenting on our own. "Man can no longer . . . decide for himself . . . he needs a guardian, a director of conscience, and feels ill when he does not have them" (p. 186).
- Creates an inability to distinguish ourselves from society, institutions, and groups.
- Destroys individuality, we are not at ease unless integrated into a mass. "Egocentricity is the product of the cessation of propaganda" (p. 185).
- Creates a dissociation between thought and action (e.g., we act without thinking and think without acting); dissociation between public and personal opinion.
- Encourages us to cling to certainties.
- Discourages the growth of knowledge.
- Encourages prejudice/hate; sets up in-groups and out-groups "for all propaganda is aimed at an enemy" (Ellul 1965, p. 152).
- Offers justification, for example, for dreadful deeds.
- Discourages open discussion so vital in a democracy.
- Decreases empathy for and understanding of others.
- Encourages a dysfunctional (to the person) standardization; conformity.
- Encourages an adaptation that deprives us of feedback and responsibility; propaganda "makes him into a 'thing,' and puts him where he is most desirable from the point of view of another technique, that is, where he is most efficient" (Ellul, 1964, p. 362).
- Encourages spectatorship (versus activity).
- Encourages specialization.
- Encourages separation from the natural world.
- Increases influence by tranquilizing abstractions.
- Encourages a defensive "flight into involvement" (e.g., into a political party or belief in a form of healing to escape the "opposing clash of propaganda" from different sources).
- Increases insensitivity to propaganda shocks; we react with indifference but are still subject to its effects.
- Creates a feeling of self-importance.

propaganda "awakens passion by confusing the issues (making the insignificant seem weighty and the important insignificant)" (p. 389). When propaganda is presented under the guise of education, it encourages a misplaced trust that is especially pernicious. Propaganda in the helping professions obscures the problematic nature of popular views and therefore hinders understanding of and active pursuit of well-argued alternative views (Boyle, 2002; Horowitz & Wakefield, 2007). It encourages coercive treatments in the name of alleged "scientific findings" that are conceptually and methodologically bogus. Harm includes removing valuable opportunities, locking people up against their will, stigmatizing them by means of negative diagnostic labels, and not fully informing clients, with the result that they make decisions they otherwise would not make. Historically, women have been the main unfortunate victims of bogus claims (Scull, 2005). Some view the history of psychiatry as a history of torture in the name of helping.[17] And, there is enormous hubris—false claims of cures. Given that claims do not match reality, they are a form of propaganda. If harms result from propaganda (e.g., choosing services that harm rather than help, removing opportunities for clients to help themselves), it is important to examine its nature and to develop ways to avoid its effects.

PROPAGANDA AS KEY IN QUACKERY, FRAUD, AND CORRUPTION

Quackery refers to the promotion and marketing, for a profit, of untested, often worthless and sometimes dangerous, health products and procedures, by either professionals or others (Jarvis, 1990; Young, 1992).[18]

> People generally like to feel that they are in control of their life. Quacks take advantage of this fact by giving their clients things to do—such as taking vitamin pills, preparing special foods. . . . The activity may provide a temporary psychological lift, but believing in false things can have serious consequences. The loss may be financial, psychological (when disillusionment sets in), physical (when the method is harmful or the person abandons effective care), or social (diversion from more constructive activities). (Barrett, Jarvis, Kroger, & London, 2002, p. 7)

Quackery takes advantage of a variety of propaganda methods designed to encourage beliefs and actions with the least thought possible. Barrett and his colleagues (2002) suggest that victims of quackery usually have one or more of the following vulnerabilities: (1) lack of suspicion; (2) desperation; (3) alienation (e.g., from the medical profession); (4) belief in magic; or (5) overconfidence in discerning whether a method works. Advertisers, both past and present, use the trappings of science (without the substance) to encourage consumers to buy products (Pepper, 1984). Indicators of quackery include the promise of quick cures, the use of anecdotes and testimonials to support claims, privileged power (only the great Dr. _____ knows how to _____), and secrecy (claims are not open to objective scrutiny). Natale (1988) estimated that in 1987 Americans spent $50 million on subliminal tapes, even though there is no evidence that they offer what they promise (Druckman & Bjork, 1991).

For every claim supported by sound evidence, there are scores of bogus claims making it a considerable challenge to resist their lures. McCoy (2000) describes a cornucopia of questionable medical devices. Reasons suggested by William Jarvis (1990) for why some professionals become quacks include the profit motive (making money) and the prophet motive (enjoying adulation and discipleship resulting from a pretense of superiority). Quacks probably existed as long as people did. (See Figure 1.2.) They may award themselves degrees or obtain degrees from bogus institutions.[19]

Fraud includes the intentional misrepresentation of the effect of certain actions, such as recommending unneeded treatment.[20] It does this by means of deception and misrepresentation, drawing on propaganda ploys such as hiding information about

Figure 1.2. Taking your chances.
SOURCE: J. Gillray (1801). Elijah Perkin's metallic tractors National Library of Medicine.

harmful side effects. Today, the pharmaceutical industry tops all industries in the total amount of fraud payments for actions against the federal government under the False Claims Act. Between 1991 and 2010 pharmaceutical companies paid $19.8 billion in penalties. This however is small change compared to global pharmaceutical profits. For example, this was $500 billion in 2003. (See Angell, 2004, p. 11.)[21] The *Merriam-Webster Dictionary of Law* defines fraud as:

> any act, expression, omission, or concealment calculated to deceive another to his or her disadvantage; specifically: a misrepresentation or concealment with reference to some fact material to a transaction that is made with knowledge of its falsity or in reckless disregard of its truth or falsity and with the intent to deceive another and that is reasonably relied on by the other who is injured thereby.

Legal aspects of fraud in this definition include: (1) misrepresentation of a material fact; (2) knowledge of the falsity of the misrepresentation or ignorance of the truth; (3) intent; (4) a victim acting on the misrepresentation; and (5) damage to the victim (Bosch 2008, p. 3).

A doctor, a businessman, and a journalist in Germany persuaded dying people that Galavit, a Russian food supplement could stop their cancer. Patients paid $13,500 for the treatment, which was administered in a rented ward of a hospital (Tuffs, 2008).

Fraudulent claims (often appealing to the trappings of science) may result in overlooking effective methods or being harmed by remedies that are supposed to help, as described in chapter 5. If we define fraud as the promotion of a product we know to be ineffective for a profit, that is, we lie about the consequences of using a product, then the promotion of practices and policies we know are not effective is a form not only of quackery but also fraud. For example, if I am a director of an agency offering a service that I know is not effective, yet I promote it as effective and my staff and I make money offering this, aren't I engaged in fraud? Consider the billions of dollars spent by state and local governments on contracted services. In child welfare, most services are contracted out to other agencies. There is little systematic investigation of the extent to which services offered match those most likely to be effective in achieving hoped-for outcomes. What research is available suggests that there is little match (e.g., Gorman, 1998).[22] Fraud is so extensive in some areas that special organizations have been formed, newsletters written, and Internet sites created to help consumers evaluate claims.[23] Fraud seems to have no limits to creative variation.

Corruption includes deceitful practices, such as dumping unsafe drugs in developing countries and misrepresenting evidence. It includes bribery of officials and kickbacks for referrals.[24] Krimsky (2003) argues that the lure of profit has corrupted biomedical research. (See also Elliott & Abadie, 2008.) Corruption in the health area is vast. Examples of corruption in the health area include selling or prescribing pills with no active ingredients or containing harmful substances. Corruption is so common that an international organization, Transparency International, was created to decrease it. Corruption, fraud, and quackery (and propaganda methods used in their service) compromise our "right-to-know" (Florini, 2007)—transparency and accuracy. Corruption and fraud are closely intertwined. In both, propaganda methods are used to forward self-interests in deceptive, manipulative ways.

CHOICES

Surely there must be benefits from propaganda in the helping profession. Indeed there are many, such as offering hope, saving time, avoiding struggle with existential problems, getting rid of obnoxious people by calling them mentally ill and medicating them, and escaping responsibility for avoidable harms to others because of "mental illness." Our desires for certainty and hope for relief from distress meet seductive offers of players who have a profit or "prophet" motive, illustrating the symbiotic interrelationship between buyers and sellers of propaganda. Benefits of the ADHD label (Attention Deficit Hyperactivity Disorder) suggested by Jacobs (1995) include: (1) pharmaceutical companies make money ($600 million annually for stimulant medication in the United States alone); (2) physicians want to be helpful and are trained in the medical model; (3) the diagnosis lets parents "off the hook" (removes concerns about inadequate parenting); and (4) overcrowded and underfunded schools can drug children to control misbehaviors. However, the downside is that options to alter circumstances related to hoped-for outcomes and "grow" in the process are surrendered. (See also Carey, 2011.)

We each must make up our own mind regarding propaganda and its consequences, particularly in relation to self-propaganda (how we deceive ourselves). Indeed one of the purposes of this book is to encourage you to explore interactions between "self" and "other" propaganda. We make decisions about how informed to be about choices we make. We may assume our decisions are those we have chosen for ourselves and, in one sense, this is correct. We have made them. But, we should ask: How good is the evidence for different views? Who has influenced our decisions? Who gains if we make certain choices? We may discover that professionals we trust to guard our interests have been influenced by biased material prepared by public relations firms hired by pharmaceutical companies, especially in countries without national health insurance in which related for-profit companies abound. Consider promotion of anxiety in social situations as a mental disorder described in chapter 3. You may know what questions to ask such as: What are alternative diagnostic procedures? But, if a physician to whom you are referred misinforms you, how can you discover the straight scoop? If you turn to the Internet, will you find accurate information? You will have to decide whether you want to be a more critical consumer of claims made in the helping professions. You will have to decide, for example, if the statement by your optometrist that your lens prescription cannot be improved so that you can see more clearly is true and accept his prescription, or consider whether he is influenced by propaganda acquired during a continuing education program. If you are a professional, you will have to decide what questions to raise that relate directly to the well-being of clients—such as "How good is the evidence?"

Reasons to read this book include: (1) you may avoid making decisions you later regret; (2) you may make more decisions that you are happy with; (3) you will not be a patsy for those who try to fool you for their own benefit; (4) you will increase your skills in critically appraising claims that affect your life; and (5) propaganda spotting can be fun as related ploys and often absurd premises become transparent. Reasons for not reading this book include: (1) you will be more aware of the uncertainty associated with decisions—this may be scary; (2) you will have to spend time and effort to seek out research findings to check out recommendations of "experts"; (3) you will have to take more responsibility for your decisions because you cannot blame bad behavior on a "brain" disease; and (4) you may have to be more assertive in interactions with professionals and raise more questions. Assuming that we are masters of our fate (even if untrue) allows us to bask in this ignorance, save time and effort, and avoid offending people by asking unwelcome questions, such as "Is there any evidence that lowering cholesterol increases longevity?"

A poor reason for not reading this book is the false belief that we are not influenced by propaganda in the helping professions, when in fact, we are surrounded by it. Indeed, if you try to avoid it by simply not paying attention to it, it is even more likely to influence you in ways you may not like because your "guard is down." Other poor reasons for not becoming more informed about propaganda in the helping professions and how it may influence you include the following:

- It will take too much time. As your skills and knowledge increase, propaganda spotting often takes little time.
- It will be a bore. To the contrary, learning to recognize propaganda ploys is fun and becomes more fun as your skills become more fluid.
- The belief that you are protected because you are a helping professional. Actually, you may be the most propagandized of all because you have spent years in classes and have read reams of secondary material that is propagandistic in nature.

- The belief that you can depend on consumer groups, professional organizations, and government bodies such as the FDA to protect your interests. Not so, as illustrated in this book.
- The belief that you will be alone in your quest for accurate information. Indeed today helpful tools and websites abound.

IN CONCLUSION

It is time to pay more attention to propaganda in the helping professions, including related venues such as professional journals and education programs. The stakes are high in terms of lost opportunities to make informed rather than "engineered" decisions, those that are yours, not those created by others, others who may not have your best interests at heart. Are your beliefs engineered by others based on bogus grounds promoted by staff in public relations agencies hired by pharmaceutical companies? That is, has an illusion of knowledge (or ignorance) been created? Are your beliefs about the prevalence and causes of normal variations in behavior influenced by psychiatrists on the payroll of pharmaceutical companies serving as "opinion leaders"? Are these beliefs accurate? Does it make any difference as long as you "feel free"—as long as you believe that you have made an informed choice (when actually you have been misinformed)? These questions are at the heart of this book.

Professional practice today includes practices and policies based on the latest research in which clients are involved as informed participants, as well as the continued use and dissemination of services that have been carefully evaluated and found to be harmful. Most interventions are of unknown effectiveness. This mix reflects the diverse, often conflicting, functions of the "helping professions," for example, helping clients versus social control functions and related social judgments. Distinctions among services of different degrees of effectiveness are obscured by propaganda. Propaganda permeates society, including the halls of "academia" and related venues such as professional journals as illustrated by the examples given at the beginning of this chapter. Some of these trends were predicted long ago by Veblan ([1918] 1993), who described the increasingly "business like" environment of higher education. That is, rather than the pursuit of truth wherever this may lead, economic interests and marketing concerns compromise this search. Fraud and corruption in the helping profession, as well as quackery and propaganda used in their service, are common as revealed by our daily newspapers and described in this book.

Understanding the nature and prevalence of propaganda, its aims and consequences, and keeping critical thinking skills well honed, will be useful in spotting and countering propaganda. The increased accessibility of critical appraisal skill programs and guidelines for reviewing content can help to counter this influence as described in later chapters. The philosophy and process of evidence-based practice is designed to weed out bogus claims and involve all interested parties as informed consumers (Gray, 2001b; Straus, Richardson, Glasziou, & Haynes, 2005). It is designed to increase transparency regarding the uncertainty associated with making life-affecting decisions (e.g., see DUETs website). Learning how to detect propaganda ploys will help you to make more informed decisions and to avoid being bamboozled by others, for example, about what is healthy and what is not and what makes no difference. You will have at hand questions that can help you to discover uncertainties related to decisions. You will understand the symbiotic relationship between our hopes for cures and relief from distress and professionals' wish to help or "sell us" on options that encourages both self and "other" propaganda. There are costs however. You will lose the option of depending on others to make choices for you because you take more responsibility for becoming informed about uncertainties related to life-affecting decisions. Recognizing uncertainties can be scary. You will have to confront self-deceptions such as wishful thinking. The examples in this book illustrate the costs and benefits of opening rather than closing your eyes. I invite you to write down two of your beliefs that have affected or do affect your life before you read the rest of this book. I also invite you to look back on the grounds for them after finishing it.

PART TWO

Context, Actors, and Scripts

2

Introduction to the Players

Understanding propaganda in the helping professions is easier when we are familiar with the players, venues in which they play their parts, and influences on them. This can help us to understand the strategies they favor, why they favor them by virtue of their different roles and the locations in which they play them, and the interactions among different players. Many players contribute to the enormous "advice industry" (Illouz, 2008). If behavior occurs for a reason, such as creating and distributing propaganda, then we must assume that it serves some or many purposes for involved parties. For example, psychiatrists are alleged to have special expertise as a result of their specialized education concerning use of medication. This background encourages a biochemical view of distress and promotion of related claims, such as the assertion that anxiety in social situations is a "mental disorder" caused by a chemical imbalance. Without critical reflection on content presented as true during professional education, professionals may acquire misleading beliefs and misinform clients about their concerns and related options.

Over the past years there has been an explosion of material calling attention to troubling practices in the helping professions and related industries. These include conflicts of interests between academic researchers and pharmaceutical and device manufacturing industries resulting in publication of biased research and use of ghostwriters to prepare articles published in academic journals; they are written by staff in a hired company, not by the academic whose name appears on the published article. (See Lo & Field, 2009.) This material has called attention to the many hidden players involved in propaganda in the helping professions, as well as to related venues, such as professional education and the varied strategies used, for example, giving gifts to create positive attitudes toward products such as drugs. In just a few years, we have moved from the funding of most continuing education in medicine being paid for by pharmaceutical companies to calls for the discontinuation of such funding. For example, the medical school of the University of Michigan has been the first to decide that it will not accept any funding from drug and device makers for continuing education (Singer & Wilson, 2010a & b; see also Tanne, 2008a). These decisions are informed by research showing the biased nature of such programs as described later in this chapter. Some professional schools now offer courses designed to help students to identify strategies used in pharmaceutical ads so they can avoid influence by these ploys, including recognizing disease mongering—the transformation of normal variations in behavior such as urinating more than eight times a day into "diseases"—irritable bladder disorder.[1]

A MARKETING PERSPECTIVE

Professionals and professions have products to sell to potential buyers. We can view the players and their products in relation to their position in this exchange: customers, sellers, and middlemen (and women) who mediate exchanges between buyers and sellers. (See Table 2.1.) Sellers, such as pharmaceutical companies, hire a variety of other players to encourage sales, including ghostwriters who work in medical communication companies such as Design Write who write articles for publication in professional journals. Sellers forge ties with clinicians and consumer groups to promote their products and related views in what is increasingly a global market (e.g., see Petryna, Lakoff, & Kleinman, 2006). A marketing perspective helps us to understand the hidden nature of many of the players. Middlemen (women) far outnumber clients and professionals in their variety, if not their numbers. Some are

Table 2.1 A Marketing View of the Helping Profession: Middlemen (Women)

Health care industry
Health insurance companies
Medical device manufacturers
Biotech industry
Pharmaceutical industry
Medical supply companies
Contract research organizations
Advertising and public relations companies
Publishing companies (books, journals, newsletters)
Professional organizations
Continuing education industry
Professional education programs
Charitable and not-for-profit organizations
Consumer organizations/advocacy groups
Bogus credential industry
State and federal regulatory agencies
Lobbyists
Politicians
Residential treatment care industry
Health products industry (e.g., vitamins)
Laboratory industry
Communications industry (e.g., newspapers, magazines, newsletters, TV, radio)
Risk management industry
Therapy aid industry
Academic researchers
Think tanks
Commercial research organizations
Lawyers
Licensing and accreditation boards or agencies
Social problem industry

parasitic, using their hosts simply to enrich themselves, while providing no benefit to their hosts. Some do so while also harming their hosts as discussed in chapters 5 and 6. Many players who contribute to propaganda in the helping professions are obvious—clients, practitioners, the insurance industry, the pharmaceutical, medical device, and biotechnology industries, and administrators in hospitals and mental health clinics. Other players are not obvious. Just as content may be hidden, such as adverse side effects of drugs, entire industries may be hidden, which are vital players in the propaganda game. Hidden players work in the public relations industry, are employed in companies to serve as "middle men" in the distribution of drugs, and populate companies like Design Write that "ghostwrite" articles published in professional journals.

Loeske (1999) includes all people whose work involves doing something about social problems such as the use of illegal drugs in the social problems industry. She points out that if drug abuse was not considered a problem, the manufacturer of Methadone would lose much of their business and employees of Methadone dispensing clinics would lose their jobs. She suggests that "the social problems industry in the United States probably employs more people and is more economically important than the automobile and airline industries put together" (p. 29).

> This troubled-persons industry includes all those places designed to help victims of social problems or to rehabilitate or punish offenders [and those who work in them]. In the United States today, this includes everything from prisons and jails to shelters for battered women, from psychiatric hospitals to programs for children at risk, from midnight basketball to programs of Methadone treatment, to programs for teenage mothers. (p. 31)

It includes industries that sell products to consumers and people who are paid to educate others about problems, such as educators in professional schools. It also includes social problem claims makers in government (local, state, regional, national, and international) including politicians and political lobbyists. Helping professionals are a key part of the personal and social problem industries. So are academics and researchers who study and write about social and personal problems. Advocacy groups, politicians, public relations firms, public interest and law firms are involved in the social problems industry (Hilgartner & Bosk, 1988) as are people who work for television and radio stations—"those who write plays or music with social problems themes, and people who write about social problems for newspapers and magazines" (Loeske, 1999, p. 30). She refers to these people as secondary claims makers. They translate and package claims made by others. They also may be primary claims makers (those who construct problems).

Different claims makers frame problems in different ways promoting different views of reality as described in chapter 8. The social and personal problems industries continue to grow as shown by the increasing number of psychologists, social workers, and counselors in the United States, as well as by the extent of related published literature. Millions of people are involved in these industries. Claims making regarding personal and social problems, alleged causes and remedies, is central to the helping professions. Examples include what are alleged to be problems and how they are framed (e.g., as a result of individual deficiencies or as economic and social inequalities). Related claims are integral to the personal "advice industry."

PROFESSIONALS

Thousands of different kinds of professionals occupy scores of different helping professions. (See Table 2.2.)[2] All licensed practitioners have been required to complete professional education programs and to pass licensing exams alleged to make them competent to offer certain services. Each agrees to abide by a professional code of ethics, which obligates them to help clients, avoid harm, involve clients and patients as informed participants, and to be competent to offer services they provide. Most have our best interests at heart and all say they do. Some believe they do but do more harm than good. Self-interests in making a living and helping others may "morph" into goals that do not help clients as can be seen in Jarvis's suggested reasons why professionals become quacks. (See Table 2.3.) Alarming examples of greed are exposed in our newspapers such as the New York eye doctor Shaul Debbi who performed unneeded eye surgery on clients in adult homes for the mentally ill, blinding some in the process and billing for treatment he never provided (Levy, 2003).

Lawyers who sue doctors, hospitals, and drug companies on behalf of their clients are yet other players. We see their role in reports in our daily newspapers, as well as in advertisements for legal services in the media.

There is a Proposed Settlement with GlaxoSmithKline ("GSK"), one of the Defendants in a class action lawsuit pending in the U.S. District Court for the District of Massachusetts. The name of the lawsuit is *In re: Pharmaceutical Industry Average Wholesale Price Litigation*, Docket No. 01-CV-12257-PBS, MDL No. 1456. (*Parade, San Francisco Chronicle*, February 18, 2007, p. 15)

Lawyers may try to cheat plaintiffs of money won in settlements:

LEXINGTON, KY, March 22—W. L. Carter knew there was something fishy going on when he went to his lawyers' office a few years ago to pick up his settlement check for the heart damage he had sustained from taking the diet drug combination fenphen.

The check was, for starters, much smaller than he had expected. And his own lawyers threatened to retaliate against him if he ever told anyone, including his

Table 2.2 Examples of Professionals

- Psychologists
- Psychiatrists
- Social Workers
- Counselors
- Marriage and Family Therapists
- Case Managers
- Educators
- Physicians
- Occupational Therapists
- Physical Therapists
- Nurses
- Nurse Practitioners
- Veterinarians
- Dentists
- Dental Hygienists
- Optometrists
- Podiatrists
- Life coaches
- Pharmacists

Table 2.3 WHY PROFESSIONALS BECOME QUACKS

- *"Boredom.* Daily practice can become humdrum. Pseudoscientific ideas can be exciting" (p. 5).
- *Low self-esteem.* Some professions such as social work are not the most highly regarded. Dissatisfaction with a limited scope of practice may encourage pursuit of grandiose goals and unwarranted claims of effectiveness.
- *Reality shock.* Professionals regularly see troubling situations. This may require psychological adjustments that some helpers are not up to.
- *Belief encroachment.* Science in its methodology is limited to dealing with problems that are possible to solve. This constraint may become burdensome and additional aims embraced, such as helping people with religious questions.
- *The profit motive.* Quackery can be lucrative.
- *The Prophet motive.* "Some clients experience uncertainty, doubt, and fear about the meaning and purpose of life. Others confront situations that may seem hopeless. The power over people provided by the prophet role is seductive. Egomania is commonly found among quacks. They enjoy the adulation and discipleship their pretense of superiority evokes. By promoting themselves, they project superiority not only to their clinical colleagues, but often to the entire scientific community" (p. 6).
- *Psychopathic traits.* "Psychopaths exhibit glibness and superficial charm, grandiose sense of self-worth, pathological lying, conning/manipulative behavior, lack of guilt, proneness to boredom, and lack of empathy often seen in quacks" (p. 7).
- *The conversion phenomenon.* Many professionals who become quacks have gone through emotionally difficult experiences such as a practice failure, midlife crisis, divorce, or life-threatening illnesses.

NOTE: Quackery refers to promoting services known to be ineffective, or which are untested, for a profit.

SOURCE: Based on William Jarvis (1990). *Dubious dentistry* (Part 4, pp. 1–29). Loma Linda, CA: Loma Linda University.

family, how much he had been paid. "You will be fined $100,000, you will go to jail and you will be sued," Mr. Carter recalled them saying.

Mr. Carter was right to have been suspicious. The lawyers defrauded their clients, a state judge has ruled in a civil case, when they settled fenphen lawsuits on behalf of 440 of them for $200 million but kept the bulk of the money for themselves. (Liptak, 2007)

Drug companies and professional organizations have lawyers on their staff to defend and promote their interests.

CLIENTS AND PATIENTS

Clients and patients are the largest group, comprising millions of people who seek the help of thousands of professionals for different kinds of concerns ranging from bunions to existential longings that diminish the quality of life. To maximize help and minimize harm a complex process of matching must take place between potential clients and those who offer services. Poor matches may occur in many ways. One is consulting the wrong kind of professional. Access to the right kind of professional may be blocked by managed health care policies or by lack of knowledge on the part of clients. Some ways in which matching can go awry are unavoidable. Others are avoidable but may be hard to detect by naive and uninformed clients. For example, professionals may deliberately misrepresent what they do, could do, or cannot do, to give the false appearance of a match. Favorite ploys include exaggerated claims of benefit and hiding alternatives. Lack of match may be masked by bold assertions such as "I can help you" (when this is not true), or "Don't worry about my lack of a degree in plastic surgery, I have lots of experience." Consumers play a vital role in acting on their beliefs about the kind of help that will be of value. They may pressure physicians for certain medications because of influence by pharmaceutical ads. Indeed, "Ask your doctor" is a key part of many pharmaceutical ads. In coercive situations, for example, protective services for children and the elderly, neither clients nor professionals may have a choice.

RESEARCHERS, ACADEMICS, AND UNIVERSITY ADMINISTRATORS

Researchers and academics are major players. They make decisions about what to investigate and how to do so and what to teach and how to do so. They cast research proposals within views favored by funding agencies. At the University of California at Berkeley there are scores of Organized Research Units (ORUs). Research centers are a key part of professional schools in universities. Those who work in them aggressively seek research funds. Bauer (2004) argues that the movement toward knowledge monopolies and research cartels makes innovation more difficult.

> Increasingly corporate organization of science has led to *knowledge monopolies*, which, with the unwitting help of uncritical mass media, effect a kind of censorship. Since corporate scientific organizations also control the funding of research, by denying funds for unorthodox work they function as *research cartels* as well as knowledge monopolies. (p. 643)

Cutbacks in public funding for universities has encouraged both researchers and university administrators to pursue collaboration with businesses and industries.[3] Marcia Angell (2004) notes that:

> Bayh-Dole enabled universities and small businesses to patent discoveries emanating from research sponsored by the National Institutes of Health (NIH), the major distributor of tax dollars for medical research, and then to grant exclusive licenses to drug companies. Until then, taxpayer-financed discoveries were in the public domain, available to any company that wanted to use them. But now universities, where most NIH-sponsored work is carried out, can patent and license their discoveries, and charge royalties. Similar legislation permitted the NIH itself to enter into deals with drug companies that would directly transfer NIH discoveries to industry. (p. 7)

COMMERCIAL RESEARCH ORGANIZATIONS

Commercial research organizations (CROs) are hired to conduct research for various parties including the government, as well as the pharmaceutical industry. There are hundreds of such research organizations. Some are owned by advertising and public relations firms. Some pharmaceutical companies own a number of contract research companies. Pharmaceutical companies, state agencies, and many other sources contract with such centers to conduct research or gather statistical information. As of 2002, 52% of clinical psychiatric research was funded by the pharmaceutical industry (Kelly, Cohen, Semple, Bialer, Lau, Bodenheimer, Neustadter, et al., 2006). Research organizations compete with each other to conduct trials but also cooperate in sharing important information. Thus, as Applbaum (2009) demonstrates, although it seems as if there is a free market economy, actually it is not.[4]

THINK TANKS

A think tank could be an organization, corporation, institute, or group that carries out research and advocates for certain policies. Large foundations or major companies usually fund them. They prepare public policy analysis and engage in research. Some are nonpartisan, others offer intellectual support to particular politicians or parties. They may be not-for-profit organizations or for-profit organizations. They may be centrist, conservative, liberal, or libertarian. Some, but not all, conduct research and provide consultation services. Some are primarily in the public relations business, for example, writing editorials and supplying experts for government. The purpose of most think tanks is to prepare material favorable to funding sources, including research reports. Names may be misleading.

> Another industry approach is to fund "think tanks" and nonprofit groups with innocuous sounding names to write reports and policy papers. These groups accept subsidies or grants from corporate interests to lobby or produce research when they normally might not, but too often fail to disclose the connection between their policy positions and their bank accounts. (This is not true of all industry-friendly think tanks; some, like the Progress and Freedom Foundation, disclose supporters on their websites.)
>
> These sorts of campaigns are dangerous for our democracy. They deliberately mislead citizens, and they deliberately mislead our lawmakers, who are already charged with the difficult task of making sense of complex telecommunications policies. Corporations that already have significant economic clout and influence are trying to co-opt the voices of everyday citizens and think tanks, and use them to their own advantage. In the end, that practice dilutes the power of true grassroots and nonprofit advocacy. (Wolves in sheep's clothing 2006) (<http://www.commoncause.org/site/pp.asp?>)

PROFESSIONAL ORGANIZATIONS

Each profession has an organization. These include national organizations such as the American Psychological Association, the American Psychiatric Association, the

National Association of Social Workers, as well as more specialized organizations such as the National Association of Cognitive-Behavioral Therapists (NACBT). These nonprofit organizations sponsor problems by initiating claims making, as well as by donating money and organizational skills to claims making initiated by others. Large professional organizations such as the American Medical Association and the American Psychological Association are a kind of mini industry with real estate and stock holdings. However, money is short and the pharmaceutical industry pays a portion of the costs of many medical organizations (Brody, 2007, p. 218). Staff in these organizations actively promote expansion of turf and seek to resist boundary intrusions from other professions.[5] Professional organizations hold conferences, which supports the conference-organizing industry. The conference industry is a huge business with airlines, hotels, conference centers, and restaurants gaining from money spent. Conference organizers have their own conferences with presentations on how to help sponsors market their products. Related advertisements highlight exotic locations and opportunities for entertainment and recreation.

Professional organizations accredit professional degree programs that provide education for entry into a profession. For example, the Council on Social Work Education accredits bachelor's and master's degree programs in social work. Each social work degree program must go through what is called a "reaffirmation" process every 10 years. This process requires the preparation of an exhaustive self-study and includes visits from selected individuals who interview students and faculty over a number of days and prepare a final report. There is no evidence that any of this activity contributes to the quality of social work programs even though it is claimed that it does. Such activity gives the appearance rather than the substance of critical appraisal of programs in terms of educating professionals who offer effective services to clients. State licensing boards and professional organizations take responsibility for dealing with ethical violations. However, there is relatively little activity in this area. Other accrediting bodies include the American Nurses Association, American Occupational Therapy Association, American Psychological Association, American Speech-Language-Hearing Association, Association of Social Work Boards, Commission on Dietetic Registration, National Board for Certified Counselors, and the National Association of Alcoholism & Drug Abuse Counselors.

Professional organizations have political divisions to raise money to forward interests of the organization.[6] They publish journals and newsletters and have websites that promote their views and interests. The 2004 catalog of publications of the American Psychiatric Association is 112 pages long. The American Psychiatric Association publishes *Psychiatric Services*, which contains many pharmaceutical ads in each issue. Pharmaceutical companies sponsor their conferences, as well as other "special symposiums" in which exhibits marketing medications play a prominent role (Brody, 2007). Professional organizations are also in the continuing education business offering certification and continuing education courses to thousands of professionals who must take a certain number of credits to be relicensed. They offer a variety of special credentials that require certain education requirements. This is another source of income. Continuing education opportunities, as well as seminars, are advertised in professional newsletters and on the Internet.

There are hundreds of specialized organizations. Examples include the National Council on Family Relations and the International Pauresis Association promoted "as a resource for people who find it difficult or impossible to urinate in the presence of others" (retrieved July 26, 2009, from <http://www.paruresis.org>).[7] The Association for the Treatment of Sexual Abusers (ATSA) held its 26th Annual Conference in Fall 2007. This Association:

> is a non-profit, interdisciplinary organization. ATSA was founded to foster research, facilitate information exchange, further professional education and provide for the advancement of professional standards and practices in the field of sex offender evaluation and treatment. ATSA is an international organization focused specifically on the prevention of sexual abuse through effective management of sex offenders. (34-page conference brochure, p. 2)

Some organizations exist mainly to make money by offering special certifications such as the American Board of Mental Health Specialists.[8] Increasing quality of care and educating the public is another goal many organizations claim to promote. Elected heads of professional organizations such as the British Medical Association play a role in framing how problems are viewed. Consider this from Michael Marmot (2010) in his acceptance speech as the new president of the British Medical Association: "We do have an ideology: health inequalities that are avoidable by reasonable means are quite wrong. Putting them right is a matter of social justice. But the evidence matters. The evidence suggests that action has to be on the conditions in which people are born, grow, live, work, and age."

PROFESSIONAL EDUCATION PROGRAMS

Professional education is a huge industry including advanced degrees offered online. Social work has 470 accredited bachelor's degree programs (the entry level degree required for social work licensure) and 200 accredited master's degree programs (retrieved on July 24, 2010, from <http://www.cswe.org>). Social workers provide most of the mental health services in the United States today. There are scores of accredited counseling and clinical psychology degree programs. There are hundreds of human service degree programs, including on-line programs. Do these programs produce professionals who provide effective services? There is no critical test of this question, although there are many claims that they do. Those who teach in professional programs are influenced by propaganda from the players described in this chapter. Educators who have not been trained to spot propaganda distributed by pharmaceutical companies or by professional organizations, such as the American Psychiatric Association, may indoctrinate rather than educate students concerning related topics such as framing problems-in-living as "mental illnesses" treatable by medication. For example, LaCasse and Gomory (2003) examined course outlines in social work on psychopathology and found that these typically followed the party line of framing troubled and troubling behavior as psychiatric disorders. Controversies received little attention, including Szasz's (1994, 2002) critique of institutional psychiatry. This is particularly ironic in professions such as social work, in which, historically, empowerment and social justice are emphasized including the role of environmental factors on poverty and child maltreatment. Yet, when we look at what social workers actually do, they often focus on the psychological, on the individual. Many have jumped on the psychiatric bandwagon in their zest for biochemical answers to "mental problems," and perhaps for status as well. Debates concerning controversial issues and values may be replaced with trying to force ideology on students. For example, a student in the Master's degree program in Social Work at Rhode Island College was penalized by a professor for refusing to lobby for progressive causes, which was a requirement in a course on social policy.[9]

Kozloff (2005) describes schools of education as a "primordial Soup of Fad, Folly, and Fraud."[10] In perhaps no other area than education, particularly at elementary and secondary levels, including services offered to those with developmental disabilities, does propaganda have such unfortunate effects in encouraging ineffective or harmful methods and hindering use of effective services. Examples can be seen in controversies regarding how language should be taught, what service should be offered to children with developmental disabilities, what books should be included, and whether evolution should be taught (e.g., Jacobson, Schwartz, & Mulick, 2005). Censorship of material in elementary and secondary education, including literature, is common as described by Ravitch (2003). Examples of books censored in elementary and secondary schools include the *Canterbury Tales* and *Tom Sawyer*.

THE CONTINUING EDUCATION INDUSTRY

Professionals have to satisfy continuing education requirements in order to maintain their licenses creating a huge continuing education industry.[11] Conferences for which credits can be obtained may last days. Certificates are offered via continuing education.[12] Do courses provided benefit clients? To what extent does information acquired in such programs change a professional's behavior back at the office or clinic? Often, outcomes promised are vague and typically the evidentiary status of methods promoted is not accurately described nor are controversies. Examination of what is offered and what can be taken to satisfy continuing education requirements raises concerns about whether fulfilling such obligations benefits clients. If continuing education requirements are mainly for the purpose of giving the appearance of competence, then they may satisfy this goal. If, on the other hand, there is a need for professionals to be up-to-date and accurately informed regarding both old and new practices and policies, some of which may have been found to be harmful, then we must be skeptical regarding related claims. Research suggests that popular formats such as didactic presentations are not effective in changing the practice of professionals (Forsetlund, Bjørndal, Rashidian, Jamtvedt, O'Brien, Wolf, et al., 2009). Indeed the finding that traditional methods of knowledge dissemination were not effective was a key reason for the development of problem-based learning using the process and philosophy of evidence-based practice (Gray, 2001). In the past pharmaceutical companies have funded most continuing medical education programs. Concerns about biased presentations have resulted in policies restricting such funding.

THE BOGUS CREDENTIAL INDUSTRY

There is a huge bogus credential industry fueled by the importance attributed to credentials and the assumption that they yield competence to practice. Here is an example from *Dubious Dentistry* (Jarvis, 1990, pp. 8–9):

> The most prolific producer of spurious nutrition diplomas has been Donsbach University in Huntington Beach, California. In 1983 Donsbach University

claimed to have over 3500 students enrolled, and gave more PhD's in nutrition than all of the recognized nutrition programs in the nation combined. Donsbach University was classified as an "authorized" institution under the laws of the State of California.

Dr. Donsbach claimed to study with "the world-famous Dr. Royal Lee" who "was a graduate dentist who never practiced. He was a vitamin products jobber and a manufacturer of engineering products who was a key source of nutritional quackery in the United States. Donsbach opened a clinic in Tijuana where he dispensed laetrile and other dubious remedies" (Jarvis, 1990, pp. 8–9).

CHARITABLE AND NOT-FOR-PROFIT ORGANIZATIONS

Thousands of charities and not-for-profit organizations raise funds for and promote "awareness" of scores of different kinds of personal and social problems. Many are multi-million dollar enterprises. All are tax-exempt. All engage in advocacy for certain problems/populations, which may result in biased research and reporting of results (e.g., Best, 2008). Consider bogus claims regarding dangers of osteoporosis:

> The organizers of Australia's "healthy bones week" have come under fire for making exaggerated and misleading claims about the dangers of osteoporosis— the loss of bone density that raises the risk of fracture with age.
> "Fact 1" on a poster sent to Australian general practitioners last week read: "More Australian women die from osteoporosis than all female cancers combined." There was no reference to back up the statement, and a search has been unable to find any evidence to support it. Sydney general practitioner Mark Donohoe, a government adviser on false health claims whose surgery was sent the poster, described the claim as "patent rubbish" and a "bald faced lie." (Moynihan, 2003a, p. 358; see also Alonzo-Coello et al., 2008)

Many nonprofits, including NARSAD (National Alliance for Research on Schizophrenia and Depression), promote a biological view of psychiatric disorders. NARSAD describes itself as "the leading donor-supported organization funding research on brain disorders." It claims that "one in five Americans suffers from a diagnosable mental illness in a given year" (p. 3). It has awarded more than $219 million dollars to research scientists. It is claimed that schizophrenia is "a severe, chronic and generally disabling brain disease" (retrieved on February 10, 2009, from <http://www.narsad.org>). There is no mention of alternative views (e.g., Boyle, 2002). Under GAD (generalized anxiety disorder) we read: "GAD is generally treated with medication." Cognitive-behavioral methods are not mentioned. ADHD is described as a "neurobehavioral condition." Of 10 myths described on their website, one is that "psychiatric disorders are not true medical illnesses like heart disease and diabetes." These 10 myths are also presented in test form (true/false).

Here too, we see increasing ties with corporations. For example, the King's Fund, a leading British charity interested in healthcare policy, recently created a partnership with Humana Europe, the regional subsidiary of the U.S. health insurer that bids for contracts with the National Health Service (NHS) (Dyer, 2007a). Critics of funding for charities highlight conflicts of interest. Consider this from <http://www.whale.to/w/quotes7.html> (retrieved on July 15, 2006):

> The American Cancer Society is one of the most powerful and corrupt organizations in American society. It operates as a behind-the-scenes force, influencing powerful politicians, imposing its views and prejudices on governmental research, instigating government suppression and harassment of independent researchers, making newspaper editors cower, and all the while asking the public for money through its public relations image as the leading cancer fighter—Barry Lynes (The Healing of Cancer p39).[13]

Fraud and corruption are common as seen by theft of $600,000 by a former United Way executive.[14]

THE GOVERNMENT

The helping professions are intimately concerned with behavior. Szasz has long highlighted that psychiatrists (and fellow travelers) are agents of social control who administer state policies. Both Foucault (1977) and Ellul (1965) emphasize the exercise of government control over individuals and populations by varied techniques/technologies. Foucault used the term "biopower" to refer to state power reflected in regulatory controls and various forms of discipline alleged to be used for the good of the individual and entire populations. (See discussion of the therapeutic state and related social control functions in chapter 8.) The psychiatric view of behavior promoted by the American Psychiatric Association in shaping what is normal and what is not, could not have occurred without the active participation of the government (Moncrieff, 2008; Szasz, 1994). Moral and political problems are defined as technical-scientific concerns to be handled by "experts."[15]

Politicians

Politicians play a key role in influencing public and social policies and related legislation both in positive and negative ways as illustrated by the recent passage of Obama's health initiative. Politicians influence the framing of problems, for example, as concerns of individuals and/or as obligations of the state to address. Examples include poverty, crime, quality of education, and access to health services. Battles over how resources are to be distributed to address certain problems are fought out in the political arena, as are battles about what problems to address and how to frame them. (See chapter 8.) It is in the national political arena that bills are introduced to limit "resource hoarding" (Tilly, 1998).[16] Politicians and their supporters, now including corporations viewed as individuals regarding financial contributions, play a key role in both hiding or showcasing certain problems and directing resources toward (or away from) them in a context of clashing values, agendas, and hoped-for outcomes.

Senator Charles E. Grassley of Iowa initiated inquiries into conflicts of interest created by ties between professional organizations such as the American Psychiatric

Association and Big Pharma (Gever, 2008). Senator Grassley also raised concerns about undeclared income from Big Pharma by psychiatrists promoting drugs. For example, Schatzberg, then president-elect of the American Psychiatric Association, was accused of failing to disclose $74,000 from Johnson & Johnson and Eli Lilly in filings with Stanford (Gever, 2008). At that time, he owned millions of dollars in stock in Concept Therapeutics, which promotes mifepristone as a treatment for depression. Schatzberg "has been doing research on a psychiatric application of the drug mifepristone—at the same time as he has been doing NIH-supported research on the drug and writing textbook chapters about it" (retrieved on August 7, 2008, from <http://www.brodyhooked.blogspot.com>). Schatzberg has claimed this drug is effective when data from trials do not support this claim. Politicians may intrude in harmful ways even in areas where an obligation of the office is to transmit accurate scientific findings regarding health concerns to the public as revealed in testimony by three past Surgeon Generals of the United States.[17] Pharmaceutical industries donate heavily to politicians who they hope will promote their industry, for example, by opposing regulations.

Lobbyists

Each industry has scores or hundreds of lobbyists in Washington and state capitals to foster their clients' interests.

> In the realm of government and politics there also are *political lobbyists* who just as clearly do the social problems work of making claims. These persons are paid by others (social change groups, segments of the economy such as health, real estate, cigarette manufacturers) to make claims about social problems to politicians in order to influence social policy. At times, these folks make claims to create social problems. So, for example, a lobbyist for the AARP (American Association for Retired People) might lobby (make claims to) congressional members that there *is* a social problem of elderly people not being able to afford increases in their medical insurance premiums. At other times these lobbyists may make claims that a social problem doesn't exist: A lobbyist for the cigarette industry might try to convince officials that there is *not* a problem of that industry targeting young children for their advertisements. Political lobbyists certainly are claims-makers. It's their job, they're paid to do it. (Loeske, 1999, pp. 29–30)

Professional organizations hire lobbyists to promote their interests to legislators. The Center for Responsive Politics lists top spenders on <http://www.opensecrets.org/>. There are 665 pharmaceutical lobbyists in Washington out of an estimated total number of 33,000. MaLAM is a medical lobby for appropriate marketing of pharmaceuticals. Residential facilities also hire lobbyists. "It is hardly an accident that the Empire State Association of Adult Homes & Assisted Living Facilities, the lobbying arm of the adult home industry, is among the leading 10 spenders in the state legislature, funneling more than $700,000 last year to lawmakers through top Democratic and Republican-connected firms" (retrieved on September 22, 2011, from <http://www.wsws.org/articles/2002/jul2002/ny-j10.shtml>). Pharmaceutical companies actively lobby legislators to increase health care drug budgets. Moncrieff (2006) notes that as early as the 1950s, Smith Kline French, manufacturers of Thorazine, targeted state legislators to lobby for an increase in the drug budget (Swazey, 1974).[18]

State and Federal Regulation Agencies

Both state and national regulatory agencies such as the Federal Trade Commission (FTC) and Federal Drug Administration (FDA) are mandated to keep track and monitor the quality and safety of foods and drugs offered for consumption. (For an in-depth view of the history of the FDA, see Brody, 2007; Hawthorne 2005.) The Federal Trade Commission (FTC) recently fined marketers of four weight loss pills $25 million for false advertising claims including rapid weight loss and decreased risk of cancer.[19] There are troubling interconnections between those with interests in the decisions made by staff in these agencies and pharmaceutical companies (Lenzer, 2004c). For example, the pharmaceutical industry contributes $300 million in annual fees to the financing of the drug approval and regulation process. In the past, experts serving on appeal panels have had significant financials ties to the pharmaceutical industry, in the form of speaking fees, consultantships, and research grants; few efforts were made to screen these individuals regarding conflicts of interest such as stock holdings in a company.[20] Recent alarms about aggressive marketing of drugs with adverse effects have brought increasing attention to oversight lapses on the part of regulatory agencies such as the FDA, including punishing or ignoring drug safety officers who uncover dangers of widely used medicine.[21] These include Dr. A. Mosholder who in 2003 discovered that antidepressants led some children to become suicidal, and Dr. D. Ross who in 2006 raised concern about reports of serious illness and death from patients taking the antibiotic Ketek, among others. Post-marketing surveillance to detect harms is typically lacking (Fontanarosa, Rennie, & DeAngelis, 2004). Dr. John B. Buse who testified about the safety of Avandia, the popular diabetes drug was threatened with a lawsuit by a drug company executive in 1999 after raising concerns about Avandia in a medical meeting. He said the executive called him a "liar" and a "scoundrel" in complaints about him both to his supervisor and the University of North Carolina.[22] Those who raise questions may be dismissed from their jobs.[23]

Governmental agencies mandated to protect consumers from abuse and neglect often fail to do so as seen by reports in our daily newspapers.[24] Journalists have revealed scams concerning home health aides, "The investigation found that at least two New York City contracting agencies allowed people to buy certificates for $400 or less showing that they had been trained as home health aides, despite receiving little or no instruction. Federal rules require that home care aides receive 75 hours of instruction in basic skills, like administering medication, taking temperatures and blood pressures, bathing and dressing." In another scam known as "50–50 split, companies persuaded patients to hire improperly certified aides, then caused Medicaid to be billed for help they never provided and split the payments with the patients."[25] In 2003 former New York State Attorney General, Spitzer, recommended passage of a state false claims act modeled on the federal False Claims Act, which authorizes treble damages against the perpetrators of frauds against state and local governments.[26]

The majority of medical devices have never been demonstrated to be effective. Promises to fix the problem have gone unfulfilled.[27]

Related Federal and State Government Departments

The National Institute of Mental Health (NIMH) is a key player in promoting biomedical view of problems. Depression is described as a brain disease in a brochure distributed by NIMH. NIMH conducts "education" programs, for example, regarding "anxiety disorders." This agency initiated an "anxiety disorders education campaign" October 1996 holding press conferences.

> several patients who had found relief through professional treatments for their anxiety disorders offered personal accounts. The various speakers, including Dr. Hyman, repeatedly mentioned the effectiveness of psychotherapy, as well as the role of medication, in treating these disorders.
>
> Unfortunately, APA [American Psychological Association] Practice Directorate staff who attended the event found that the NIMH press release about the program launch offered a less balanced presentation. "It emphasized brain mechanisms and genetic factors, while failing to convey the critical role of psychosocial factors in the development of anxiety disorders," said Randy Phleps, PH.D., the directorate's assistant executive director for professional issues. (Practitioner Update, 1996)

The National Institute on Drug Abuse publishes a newsletter *NIDA Notes*. *SAMHSA News* (Substance Abuse and Mental Health Service Administration) is published by the U.S. Department of Health and Human Services. Both promote a biomedical framing of problems. These institutes are key sources of research funds and grant proposals; grant seekers must typically problems within a biomedical narrative of mental illness. Bauer (2004) argues that reports such as UNAIDS/WHO (2004) reflect "mutual back-scratching rather than technically competent peer review" (p. 656). Preventative public health initiatives are widespread with considerable room for debate regarding whether some do more harm than good and whether it is ethical to coerce people to engage in or refrain from certain activities such as smoking or drinking alcohol. (See Skrabanek & McCormick, 1998.)[28]

To what extent do agencies such as the Center for Disease Control censor alternative well-argued views and hide lack of evidence for claims made? Are pressures placed on governmental representatives such as Surgeon Generals to parrot the party line? Are such individuals censored for blowing the whistle on harmful practices?[29] Past Surgeon General Joycelyn Elders was forced to resign for her suggestion that masturbation "is a part of human sexuality and it's a part of something that perhaps should be taught."[30] State publications promote biomedical framing of problems-in-living concerning children. For example, *Treatment of Children with Mental Disorders*, published by the New York State Department of Mental Health, shows a medication chart claiming appropriate uses of stimulants (Concerta, Adderall), antipsychotics (Haldol) for children three or older and mood stabilizing medications (Depakote) for children two and older. The National Resource Center on ADHD is "the CDC[Center for Disease Control]-funded national clearinghouse for evidence-based information about AD/HD." The National Institute of Mental Health (NIMH) conducts campaigns such as the National Anxiety Disorder Campaign, often with endorsements of professional organizations.[31] Such campaigns often have a self-serving function of increasing referrals.[32]

THE PUBLISHING INDUSTRY

Publishing companies such as Thompson Publications, Elsevier, and Oxford University Press are multi-billion dollar companies making millions on the publication of professional journals and books. Professional books are a huge industry. For example, Guilford Press has a 50-page catalog advertising hundreds of books for those in the helping professions. Related advertisements make claims such as:

> Now, at last, there's a positive and proven strategy to assist parents who come to you seeking advice in solving their children's or teenager's behavior problems—whether caused by school or family issues, ADD, fears, anger, adolescent conflict, drug use, trauma, or other factors. (Prentice Hall, letter to me, October 1996)

Profits are so large and costs to libraries in universities and colleges so great, especially for journals, that some universities have joined together to try to negotiate lower costs. The University of California system recently called on its scholars not to publish in *Nature* because of Elsevier's plan to increase costs to subscribers.[33] Most professional organizations have a large publication department, which brings in millions of dollars, such as the British Medical Association, the American Psychiatric Association, and the American Psychological Association. Scores of more specialized publishers also exist.[34]

CONSUMER ORGANIZATIONS/ADVOCACY GROUPS

There are hundreds of consumer organizations and advocacy groups, some more specialized than others. These range from financially independent groups to groups of consumers funded by pharmaceutical companies, which promote certain views, products, or services. They can be divided into four categories: (1) groups clearly funded by industry; (2) grassroots groups; (3) watchdog groups; (4) front groups (sources of initiation and funding hidden).

Groups Funded by Pharmaceutical Companies

The National Alliance for the Mentally Ill (NAMI) is primarily made up of family members of the "mentally ill." It received 75% of its total donations from 2006 through 2008 (23 million) from the pharmaceutical industry (Harris, 2009b). Children and Adults with Attention Deficit Disorder (CHADD) is a nonprofit membership organization founded in 1987 "in response to the frustration and sense of isolation expressed by parents and their children with AD/HD" (retrieved on September 6, 2007, from <http://www.chadd.org>). Most of its funding comes from pharmaceutical companies. Members are organized in 235 chapters in 43 states and Puerto Rico. This organization publishes a bi-monthly magazine *Attention! For Families & Adults with Attention-Deficit/hyperactivity Disorder*, which has a circulation of 86,000. The August 2005 copy is 56 pages long and contains six pages for pharmaceutical ads (for Adderall, Concerta, and Metadate). This organization, like most others, promotes a particular view of a problem.

> CHADD strives to implement the Surgeon General's report, **Mental Health: Culture, Race, Ethnicity** as well as the President's New Freedom Commission on Mental Health report, **Achieving the Promise: Transforming Mental Health Care in America.** (Mission and History, <http://www.chadd.org>)

Related material states that AD/HD "is a neurobiological condition that affects an estimated 3–7 percent of the population. In most cases AD/HD is thought to be inherited." This center "serves both professionals and the general public by providing information on the most relevant topics: diagnosis of AD/HD, treatment options, school and workplace challenges and guidelines, and tips on parenting, time-management, legal issues, social skills, coaching and more" (CHADD).

Grassroots Groups

Mind Freedom International is an international coalition of grassroots groups and individual members. Its mission is to protect the rights of people who have been labeled with psychiatric disorders. They aim to expose and decrease coercion in the name of helping, including forced medication. They publish *MindFreedom Journal* and hold annual conventions. Many view themselves as "survivors of human rights violations in the mental health system." The organization is also open to any individual who supports human rights.[35] Marius Romme and Sandra Escher initiated the Hearing Voices movement in the Netherlands in the late 1980s. A psychiatric framing of hearing voices is rejected and there is an emphasis on acquiring coping skills to live one's life with these voices. Hearing voices is considered common and is not viewed as requiring treatment (Romme & Escher, 1989). AbleChild: Parents for Label and Drug Free Education was founded in 2000 by parents who had personal experience with psychiatric labeling and drug coercion by the education system. Their website describes this nonprofit organization as a resource center and support network for parents faced with issues "surrounding subjective labels (ADD, ADHD, OCD, ODD and many others)," and drug "treatment" prescribed for children (retrieved July 13, 2008, from <http://www.ablechild.org>). The Moms Rising Organization is designed to bring people together who "share a concern about the need to build a more family-friendly America" (retrieved February 10, 2009, from <http://www.momsrising.org>).

Watchdog Groups

Other organizations focused on patient/client rights include the American Civil Liberties Union, Citizens Commission on Human Rights, PsychRights (Law Project for Psychiatric Rights), Alliance for Human Research Protection, Children's Rights Group, Advocacy for Children in Therapy, and the National Association for Rights Protection and Advocacy (NARPA). The Church of Scientology established the Citizens Commission on Human Rights in 1969 "to investigate and expose psychiatric violations of human rights." They argue that psychiatrists have become drug pushers and emphasize the harm done by psychotropic medication including illness and death (<http://www.cchr.org/)index.cfm>). The International Society for Ethical Psychology and Psychiatry is a nonprofit research and educational network of professionals and lay persons who are concerned with the impact of mental health theory and practice upon well-being, personal freedom, families, and communities, including the potential dangers of drugs, electroshock, psychosurgery, and the biological theories of psychiatry.[36]

Other organizations dedicated to transparency include the Fairness & Accuracy in Reporting (FAIR), healthyskepticism.org, Judicial Watch, Institute for Safe Medicine, Taxpayers Against Fraud, Project Censored (Sonoma State University), the National Council Against Health Fraud (NCAHF), Center for Science in the Public Interest, Transparency International, Public Citizens Health Research, and Consumers International.[37] The U.S. consumer group that publishes *Consumer Reports* calls attention to marketing practices, such as promotion of dangerous dietary supplements. The Commercial Free Childhood Organization advocates against corporate advertising to children. This organization argues against the commercial exploitation of children. The Center for Media Literacy promotes awareness of corporate influences. Revealing ties of scientists to industry is one interest of the U.S. Center for Science in the Public Interest.[38]

Some consumer organizations are dedicating to helping us to make a specific decision, such as whether to get a mammogram. A comparison of consumer websites, those initiated by the federal government, and those established by groups interested in increasing use of mammograms, showed that only the consumer site gave accurate information (Jørgensen & Gøtzsche, 2004). That is, both the website of the federal government and website of special interest groups designed to encourage women to get a mammogram overestimated the benefits of getting a mammogram and hid the harms of false positives and false negatives. Typically, they did not describe absolute risk; they described only relative risk. (See chapter 6.)[39]

Front Groups

Large industries, including the chemical, petroleum, pharmaceutical, insurance, health, and agricultural industries fund front groups with deceptive names that give the illusion that they provide the public with accurate information, when in fact, that is exactly the opposite of what they are about. A front group claims to forward one agenda while, in reality, it is serving some other interest whose sponsorship is hidden. (See SourceWatch.org.) Forging ties with grassroots organizations, indeed even creating them, is a favorite tactic of the pharmaceutical industry to promote sales of a drug and to lobby against governmental policies that may affect their profits. Ties may be forged by giving a grant to an organization. If no group exists, one may be created. The term "astroturfs" refers to bogus grassroots organizations created to promote sales of a product or view.[40]

THE HEALTH CARE INDUSTRY

Health care companies are regularly bought, sold, merged, and shed in the search for profit. Their executives are obligated first and foremost to stockholders. CEOs make multi-million dollar salaries. The explosive expansion of the term "health" to traditionally non-health concerns has fueled the growth in this industry. Concerns about company personnel blocking or trying to block information about adverse or negative effects of drugs are everyday news.[41] Mortality rates are higher in for-profit health care organizations compared to organizations that have no profit motive. Hospitals that had to make a profit had a higher death rate.[42] Clinics actively promote their services, boasting about the excellence of specialized centers such as cancer treatment centers and potential for back pain relief in national newspapers such as the *New York Times*, often in full-page ads. Hospitals also make money by offering continuing education programs.[43] Policies in managed care companies influence what is funded and what is not and the amount of help offered.[44]

The Pharmaceutical Industry

The pharmaceutical industry is a multi-billion dollar international industry characterized by cooperative competition (Applbaum, 2009b; Sorkin, 2006). Profits made by pharmaceutical companies in past years have exceeded those in most other industries. Selling one drug may bring in billions of dollars in one year. This profit has been compromised in recent years because of a series of revelations of harmful effects of widely advertised drugs and related cover-ups by drug companies resulting in lawsuits and damage awards. Pharmaceutical companies spend far more money on promoting their products than on research and development.[45] Big Pharma profits from tax-funded research. That is, results of research studies funded by tax dollars are then drawn on by Big Pharma to develop products to sell at a profit. Companies compete with each other, for example, by making minor adjustments in a blockbuster drug to which they own the patent rights so their rights do not expire and they can continue to profit from sale of the drug rather than have it sold less expensively as a generic. Aggressive marketing of products later shown to be useless or harmful have focused attention on marketing practices as illustrated in books such as *Selling Sickness* (Moynihan & Cassels, 2005), *The Truth About Drug Companies* (Angell, 2004, 2005), and *On the Take: How Medicine's Complicity with Big Business Can Endanger Your Health* (Kassirer, 2005).[46]

Sales representatives market drugs to professionals and distribute gifts and other perks such as dinners. Many physicians do not believe that gifts and other favors from pharmaceutical companies affect their behavior but studies show they do; for example, physicians who receive gifts (even a pen) from a company advocating the use of a certain drug prescribe this medication more often (see review in Brody, 2007). Giving gifts is designed to (and does) create reciprocal obligations as described in chapter 10. A review of gifts from drug companies to doctors in Vermont (for example, for lectures and other services) showed that psychiatrists topped the list.

> Vermont officials disclosed Tuesday that drug company payments to psychiatrists in the state more than doubled last year, to an average of $45,692

[to psychiatrists with the highest drug company earnings in 2006]. Antipsychotic medicines are among the largest expenses for the state's Medicaid program.

Over all last year, drug makers spent $2.25 million on marketing payments, fees and travel expenses to Vermont doctors, hospitals and universities, a 2.3 percent increase over the prior year, the state said.

The number most likely represents a small fraction of drug makers' total marketing expenditures to doctors since it does not include the costs of free drug samples or the salaries of sales representatives and their staff members. According to their income statements, drug makers generally spend twice as much to market drugs as they do to research them. (Harris, 2007c, p. A14)

Some medical schools, becoming alarmed about the influence of gifts from pharmaceutical companies on physicians and students now ban the taking of any gifts from pharmaceutical companies (Singer & Wilson, 2010a & b).

As of 1997, pharmaceutical companies can market directly to consumers in the United States. These ads encourage viewers, readers, and listeners to ask their doctors for certain drugs. (See Figure 2.1.) Pharmaceutical ads provide rich opportunities for propaganda spotting, including devices such as images designed to integrate us into our consumer-oriented society as happy, fulfilled human beings while at the same time hiding information such as adverse side effects, lack of follow-up studies regarding long-term effects of drugs, and the lower cost of alternative methods such as a daily walk.

The Medical Supply and Device Industry

The medical supply and device industries are other major players.[47] Full-page ads in the *New York Times* promote these companies with hypes such as "from apprehension to exhilaration."[48] They sell everything from $1,000.00 screws used in back surgery to multimillion dollar CT machines, MRIs, ultrasound equipment, screening devices used in mammograms, bandages, technologies for examining blood, urine, cells, surgical instruments, and furnishings for operating rooms. Primary obligations are to stockholders. They are in business to make money, and there is nothing wrong with this if they act ethically (for example, do not spread bogus information about their products).[49] Here too, what was once thought to be beneficial, for example, a screening device, may turn out to be harmful. Consider concerns regarding computer screening for breast cancer.[50] Here too, as with medications, controversies among different players including insurers, the FDA, and producers, are common.[51]

The Biotech Industry

The biotech industry is expected to become one of the most profitable industries. Stock in biotech companies is actively traded. Our daily newspapers note concerning practices such as unexpected uses of genetic analyses of blood samples from indigenous peoples.[52] The OncotypeDX test created by Genomic Health is used to determine the probability of recurrence of a breast tumor and to plan next steps regarding chemotherapy and/or hormone therapy. This test costs $3,800.00. Its use assumes a

Introduction to the Players

Figure 2.1. Example of pharmaceutical ad.
SOURCE: Women's Day: 5/5/09, p.31.

genetic cause of cancer. It scans 21 genes and claims a high accuracy rate. Internet descriptions include stock reports. Results have been disappointing (Lewontin, 2009). An alternative chromosomal theory of cancer (Duesberg et al., 2011) suggests a less expensive (about $250.00) and, some would argue, more accurate DNA cytometry to test for aneuploidy. This option is typically not offered.

The Malpractice Insurance Industry

Professionals take out insurance to protect themselves against lawsuits. Spirited controversies abound regarding how many malpractice claims are made and how many result in awards of large damages. Contrary to what we hear from those with ties to the insurance industry, it is estimated that relatively few (7%) of those with a plausible claim bring a lawsuit.[53]

> Indirect costs arise when the liability system causes physicians to supply more health care services than they would in the absence of a liability threat. Services that are provided primarily or solely for the purposes of protecting physicians against malpractice liability, rather than the medical benefit of the patient, are referred to as defensive medicine. True defensive-medicine costs are properly counted as indirect costs of the malpractice system, but the costs of additional appropriate (i.e., medically indicated) services should not be included in that estimate. (Mello, 2006)

Critics argue that the current system does a poor job compensating patients injured by medical malpractice, involves high transaction costs, and does little to deter negligent care. Other concerns include focusing on the misdeeds of individual providers, whereas errors are usually due to breakdowns in systems of care.[54]

The Health Insurance Industry

Health insurance companies are a key player in countries such as the United States that do not have national health insurance. America's Health Insurance Plans is a national trade association, which represents 1,300 companies that provide health care benefits to 200 million Americans.[55] Health care insurance companies regularly merge and their business dealings appear in our daily newspapers. Billions of dollars are at stake in these mergers and sheddings. Our newspapers report the adverse effects of aggressive and, in some case, fraudulent marketing practices.[56] Our newspapers, as well as movies such as "Sicko" by Michael Moore illustrate efforts to find ways to deny coverage. At the time of the recent restructuring of the health care system in the United States, 47 million people in the United States had no health insurance.

The Residential Treatment Center Industry

Psychiatric hospitals, residential settings for youth and group homes including addiction treatment residential centers are another big industry with daily rates and length of stay determined in part by insurance guidelines. A given setting may employ hundreds of people. What percentage of services offered are most likely to help residents? Are they offered with a high degree of fidelity? Brochures typically claim positive results.[57] Misleading graphics may be used to exaggerate benefits (Tufte, 2006).

The Health Products Industry

Here too, there is an enormous industry making use of propaganda methods such as bold assertions and glittering generalizations to sell their products. Appeals may be made to symbols such as people wearing white coats to establish credibility. Cartels have been implicated in price fixing.[58] William Jarvis (1990), an early critic of this industry, offered the following description in his book *Dubious Dentistry*:

> The Pseudonutrition Industry.
> A multibillion dollar industry [that] thrives upon nutrition pseudoscience. It is a multifaceted industry running counter to scientifically-based food and medicine. This sham industry is nearly complete in its scope. It has developed its own educational system, certification agencies, authorities, writers, publishers, retail stores, over-the-counter drugs component, trade associations, and even health care practitioners. It is well-entrenched politically and economically enjoying protection by business laws designed to encourage open competition.
> Health Foods.
> The pseudonutrition industry's retail outlet is primarily through so-called "health foods" stores (**Note:** This is not a universal condemnation of all health food stores since a few do make a serious effort to offer only sound products and information). The health foods industry is actually a specialty foods industry. It is the most profitable dimension of the overall food industry with a profit margin that is about 80% greater than conventional foods (1). In reality, health foods are not healthier. Health food snacks are often more carcinogenic than conventional varieties (2); are as apt to be contaminated with undesirable chemical residues (3,4,5) and filth (6,7). Health foods promoters simply create the illusion of health through clever marketing and labeling strategies. (Part 3, p. 7)

Related Publications

There are thousands of popular publications in which services and products related to the helping professions are advertised. For example, in California, the *Open Exchange: Healthy Living Magazine* describes hundreds of different services claimed to offer valued outcomes. These sources provide a wondrous source of propaganda ploys including testimonials and bold assertions used to promote dubious methods.

Newsletters. Scores of publications such as the *Harvard Health Letter* and *Psychiatry Drug Alert* promise to inform readers. Advertisements for these newsletters are mailed at nonprofit organization rates. Some are for professionals, many others are for consumers. Many are published to make money from subscriptions. Scare tactics are often used to lure subscribers: "If anyone suggests you take the 'health' supplement named inside . . . just say 'Not on your life!'" (latter in red, former in huge letters). We then see "Says who?" (in red) followed by: "The doctors at Harvard Medical School, that's who." Claims of valuable knowledge abound as illustrated on the back of the envelope for the *Harvard Women's Health Watch*: "What the physicians at Harvard Medical School now know to help you live healthier, happier and longer!"[59] The educational objective of *Psychiatric Drug Alert* is "to encourage participants to increase their knowledge of important advances in psychiatric drugs and to integrate this knowledge into clinical practice." More specifically the program participants "will be better able to 1) provide optimum pharmacotherapy for psychiatric disorders, 2) recognize, avoid, and manage psychiatric drug effects and psychiatric drug interactions, and 3) recognize the psychiatric consequences of drugs used in the other areas of medicine." No evidence is offered for any of these claims. Also, notice the grand narrative here; there is no questioning of the premise of psychiatric disorders and no mention of alternative grand narratives and related interventions. To what extent would a review of abstracts included in various newsletters show that claims are well reasoned? Some newsletters are quite specialized such as *The National Panic/Anxiety Disorder Newsletter* and the *OCD Newsletter* (published by the OC Foundation, Inc. to expand research, understanding, and treatment of obsessive compulsive disorders). Many of the consumer/advocacy groups, such as the International Center for the Study of Psychiatry and Psychology (ICSPP), publish newsletters.

Specialized Magazines. Specialized groups and organizations publish hundreds of magazines.[60] MedWorks Media published *Mental Fitness, Psychopharmacology Bulletin, Trends in Evidence-Base Neuropsychiatry, CS-Chronic Comorbidity in CNS Medicine and Mental Fitness DDP* (Doctor Directed Publication). On a copy of *Mental Fitness* in my doctor's office (April 2003, Vol. 2, No. 3), the subtitle on the front cover was "The Science of Mental Illness." This issue promoted a biomedical view of mood disorders. The role of serotonin was vigorously asserted as true with no mention of critiques of its role (e.g., Burns, 1999). This issue contained ads for Abilify with subtitles such as "a different path to success in your continuing treatment of schizophrenia" (first unnumbered page after 26). Ads for Seroquel were also included. As with other kinds of publications, including professional journals, we should ask: How good is the evidence for claims made? Are alternatives clearly and accurately described? Who funds the publication? Do we find the "trappings" of science (e.g., scientific sounding words) without the substance (e.g., description of critical tests of claims)?

Related Middlemen

Pharmacy benefit manager companies distribute drugs. Here too millions of dollars are involved. Related companies include Express Scripts, Medco Health, and CVS. Instead of saving money, such companies may increase costs.[61] Annual cost of therapy per person for drugs distributed by such companies range up to $500,000 per year (for Adagen) distributed by Medco (Freudenheim, 2008).

Laboratories

Thousands of laboratories conduct various tests including blood and urine tests. Here too, bogus claims may be made about accuracy to maintain and expand economic interests. Sparrow (2000) describes some of the many egregious billing frauds conducted by some laboratories:

> During the 1980s, in one quite famous New York scam, Surinder Singh Panshi, a physician, earned the media nickname "Dracula, Inc.: Bloodsucker of the

Decade." On August 4, 1988, Panshi was convicted of stealing over $3.6 million from the Medicaid program between January 1986 and July 1988. His scam involved purchasing blood from addicts and Medicaid mills and then falsely charging the state for thousands of blood tests that had never been ordered, referred, or authorized by physicians and were in no way medically necessary. Panshi had previously been prosecuted in 1986 for false billings and lost his license to practice medicine. He went into the lab business instead and purchased two labs in Queens and one on Long Island. (Sparrow, 2000, p. 13)

THE PUBLIC RELATIONS INDUSTRY

Public relations firms and the strategies they use and the customers for whom they work play a vital role in distributing propaganda and influencing beliefs and behavior. (See website of the Center for Media and Democracy.) The influence of the public relations industry and the creativeness and savvy of individuals key in creating related strategies to influence our behaviors are truly awesome. Many public relations firms have large, lucrative, separate divisions to handle pharmaceutical marketing and some specialize in this area. For example, GSK hired Cohn & Wolfe (owned by a much larger company) to promote "social anxiety disorder," as an alleged "mental illness," claiming this was at epidemic levels, in preparation for release of their drug Paxil, to favorably compete with Zoloft, produced by a rival.

> **Cohn & Wolfe** is a strategic marketing public relations firm dedicated to creating, building and protecting the world's most prolific brands. Areas of expertise include consumer marketing, healthcare, information technology and business-to-business communications. Its mission is to support clients in achieving their goals by helping them create, build and defend brands. This is done through a mix of both traditional and unconventional marketing and public relations techniques designed to build media visibility, develop customer relationships and drive brand favorability and sales. The company has 11 offices worldwide and several affiliates around the globe. (Retrieved March 6, 2007, from Wikipedia)

Edward Bernays, Sigmund Freud's nephew, is considered to be the creator of the public relations industry. He appealed to the claimed scientific status of Freud's theories to sell his services to corporate executives.[62] Bernays promoted the view that public relations experts are in a position to evaluate "the maladjustments and adjustments between his clients and the publics upon whom the client is dependent for his socially sound activity" (pp. 41–42). He argued that the scientific manipulation of public opinion was needed to overcome societal chaos and conflict.

> The conscious and intelligent manipulation of the organized habits and opinions of the masses is an important element in democratic society. Those who manipulate this unseen mechanism of society constitute an invisible government which is the true ruling power of our country.

> We are governed, our minds molded, our tastes formed, our ideas suggested, largely by men we have never heard of. This is a logical result of the way in which our democratic society is organized. Vast numbers of human beings

must cooperate in this manner if they are to live together "as a smoothly functioning society.... In almost every act of our lives, whether in the sphere of politics or business, in our social conduct or our ethical thinking, we are dominated by the relatively small number of persons . . . who understand the mental processes and social patterns of the masses. It is they who pull the wires which control the public mind. (Bernays, 1928, p. 42)

subject to the passions of the pack in [their] mob violence and passions of the herd in [their] panics . . . the average citizen is the world's most efficient censor. His own mind is the greatest barrier between him and the facts. His own "logic-proof compartments," his own absolutism, are the obstacles which prevent him from seeing in terms of experience and thought rather than in terms of group reaction. (p. 43)

Rampton and Stauber (2001) emphasized the paradox in Bernay's use of Freudian methods (talking) to identify unconscious drives and hidden motives in the belief that their conscious recognition would help people lead healthier lives. He used psychological techniques to hide his clients' motives as part of a strategy to keep the public unaware of planned actions designed to influence their beliefs and actions. Bernays was also influenced by Gustav Lebon, critic of democracy and author of *The Crowd* (1909). (See also Ewen, 1976.) For Lebon the crowd responds solely to emotional appeals and is incapable of thought or reason. His social psychology encouraged the creation of organizations that constantly probe public feelings and beliefs using survey research, opinion polls, and focus groups. Bernays believed that people are not merely unconscious but herdlike in their thinking. He believed that it was fortunate that this herdlike quality made people very susceptible to "leadership" (p. 43).[63]

The scope of public relations endeavors is so large that it is difficult to appreciate. This is mainly because it is in the background. One of Bernay's rules was that the influence of public relations should be invisible. He used the term "invisible wire pullers." He, as well as others who developed this industry, took advantage of a variety of techniques including those described in the social/psychological literature. The philosophy of many who work in public relations firms is postmodern: the view that truth is illusive, and since some truths are as good as others, there is nothing wrong in promoting "truths" that favor their clients. The Public Relations Association has a code of ethics, but this does not seem to have a great impact.[64] The Code of Ethics of the Council on Public Relations Firms states that "in communicating with the public and media, member firms will maintain total accuracy and truthfulness. To preserve both the reality and perception of professional integrity, information that is found to be misleading or erroneous will be promptly corrected and the sources of communications and sponsors of activities will not be concealed" (<http://www.prfirms.org>). Research regarding bias in advertising and public relations shows that this code is often violated as described in chapter 9.

THE ADVERTISING INDUSTRY

Advertising companies are sought out by the various players described in this chapter to promote products; this often involves hiding harmful effects, for example, side effects of drugs. We are inundated with advertisements on a daily basis in multiple sources: TV, magazines, the Internet, infomercials (advertisements disguised as articles). Television is a ubiquitous presence, even in schools. Like other technologies, it may change our habits, even how we think and process information as suggested by McLuhan and Fiore (1967).[65] Direct-to-consumer advertisements for drugs are a daily presence, encouraging self-diagnosis and self-referral for medications. (See Figure 2.1.) A study investigating the effects of requesting a specific drug for depression showed that this request had a profound influence on the physician's behavior, that is, he or she prescribed the drug requested (Kravitz, Epstein, Feldman, Franz, Azari, Wilker, et al., 2005). (Trained actresses made 300 office visits to 152 physicians posing as patients with depression.) Ellul (1965) emphasized the key role of advertising in advanced technological societies. Many publications in the professional literature are more advertisement than scientific descriptions as illustrated in chapter 9.

THE COMMUNICATIONS INDUSTRY: THE MEDIA

The communications industry is a multi-billion dollar industry with billions spent on mass communications. Ownership has been increasing concentrated in fewer giant conglomerates (Bagdikian, 2004). Such control permits ever more influence regarding what is good and what is bad, what is wrong and what remedies are best. The mass media shapes our views of social and personal problems, especially in ways that forward profit (e.g., Altheide, 2002). Fortunately, technological advances such as the Internet offer access to divergent views including sources such as Wikileaks. Marshall McLuhan (1964) coined the term "the medium is the message." He argued that it is the medium (not the content) that influences our lives, noting, for example, the decrease in oral transmission of information following the invention of printing and the mass distribution of TV, radio, and now the Internet, blogs, and Twitter. He used the word "medium" very broadly, including even "light bulbs" and suggested that each one engages us in different ways. Recurrent images are easy to remember (impossible to forget?), such as the videotaped destruction of the Twin Towers on September 11, 2001 (Ewen, 1999). The media play a role in spreading misinformation concerning risks, diseases, practices, and policies related to the helping profession.[66] Even though a science writer may want to be honest and keep up with new developments, this may not be possible because of time pressures. Editors may be reluctant to offend advertisers and so censor adverse material (not publish it). Links between major newspapers such as the *New York Times* and corporations in the helping industry are illustrated by the quarter page ad with the headline: "The New York Times Newspaper in Education Program Thanks the Pfizer Foundation" (March 16, 2004, p. D6).

> Thanks to the support of the Pfizer Foundation, participating schools in cities where the traveling science exhibit "BRAIN: The World Inside Your Head" is visiting in 2004—St. Louis, MO, Kansas City, MO., and Chicago, IL—are receiving classroom copies of the New York Times including Science Times, together with a curriculum guide to enhance literacy in all scientific topics, among them the latest in brain research.

Notice the emphasis on the BRAIN. Newspapers, radio, magazines, TV, and the Internet are prime sources of advertisements for products and related lifestyles and services claimed to help (now often with "pop-ups" on our monitors). Newspapers must find "news"; bad news sells more papers than good news. News includes reports of "new" medical discoveries and new "risks." We are told that if you are Asian and drink alcohol and turn red you are at risk of esophageal cancer (*News Report on TV* of December 2010). Pictures are shown before and after consuming a drink. What is the risk? Creating fears and worries encourages viewers and readers to seek remedies to avoid or minimize alleged risks. The mass media provides a key source of pre-propaganda that lays the groundwork for agitation-focused propaganda (Ellul, 1965). An example of its success is the fact that many people believe that "death panels" are part of the new U.S. Health Act—the belief that panels will have the authority to decide which people live or die, even though this is not (and never was) a part of the Health Act.

The Internet

Control of major media in fewer hands is accompanied by a huge diversity in websites and blogs. Many are designed to market a product, for example, a drug (e.g., see <http://www.concerta.net>). Many sites encourage critical appraisal of material such as the Center for Media and Democracy (<http://www.sourcewatch.org>). Here too, viewers must exercise skepticism. For example Quackwatch uncritically promotes the AIDS/HIV link, as well as the mental illness model. Some have bogus names, hiding their true intent and source of funding as discussed earlier. Consider the term "junk science" (< http://junkscience.com>). Rampton and Stauber (2001) note that this "is the term that corporate defenders apply to any research, no matter now rigorous, that justifies regulations for protecting the environment and public health. The opposing term 'sound science,' is used in reference to any research, no matter how flawed, that can be used to challenge, defeat or reverse environmental and public health protections" (p. 223). This term was used to refer to hired expert witnesses who testified in court.[67] Some websites claim an educational purpose. The pharmaceutical company Lilly sponsors the Schizophrenia Resource Center on Medscape. We are told that his center "contains a collection of the latest psychiatric and medical news and information on schizophrenia." A review of material from the website shows that the uninformed reader would never be aware of controversies concerning the concept of schizophrenia (e.g., Boyle, 2002). At the top we see the slogan "Making reintegration into society the goal," and, to the right we find Lilly, and the slogan: "answers that matter." Internet surfing is accompanied by thousands of ads. Individual physicians may be bombarded by communications regarding a particular "disorder" such as ADHD.

Hundreds of thousands work in the information technology industry. So much money was spent by U.K. government consultants on information technology including "schemes" related to medical care, that Craig (2006) entitled his book *Plundering the Public Sector*. Scholars who draw on Foucault's work, such as Orr (2006), highlight the role of information technology in "routinizing" health care and use of surveillance to keep track of both patients and helpers (for example, computer-simulated diagnosis of mental disorders) what she argues is "a key element of U.S. biopsychiatry and the biomedicalization of psychic distress" (p. 356).

Other Industries

A variety of other industries are involved in the helping professions. There is a huge self-help industry. Millions of self-help books, CDs, DVDs, and videos are sold each year, many authored by professionals. Thousands of self-help programs and tens of thousands of self-help products are available including books.[68] Self-help is especially popular in the United States with its emphasis on individualism (Starker, 1989). Hospitals pay millions of dollars to financial, risk management, and other consultants. There is a large industry that markets therapy aids for use by therapists such as therapeutic games, dolls, sand trays, play therapy kits, dollhouses, bop bags (AND MORE). Multi-page catalogs describe scores of products including books for use with special populations, such as children with developmental disabilities. Do these products do more good than harm? Does anyone know?

The psychological assessment industry is another multimillion dollar one. It includes residential assessment centers for children and adolescents, thousands of self-report measures designed to describe psychological characteristics distributed by scores of companies.[69] Most psychological tests advertised are considered confidential in order to "protect the public." Of course, such a policy also protects profits of companies with exclusive rights to sell material. Consider the following:

> To provide clients with test items, scoring criteria, and other test protocols would be to reveal trade secret information on which the scores are based and would render the Test Materials useless. Studies confirm that if test items and test protocols were readily available, the integrity of the test and scoring model could be compromised and would harm the public. There are a limited number of tests for particular purposes that cannot be easily replaced or substituted if made available upon request.
>
> The test publishing industry considers Test Materials to be confidential information and trade secrets and protects these accordingly. (MHS (Multi-Health Systems, Inc.), 2007, Catalogue, p. 135)

The ever expanding *Diagnostic and Statistical Manual* of the American Psychiatric Association (DSM) and related products is an industry unto itself. And, there is also a huge educational testing industry. Advertisements from the past and present illustrate promotion of assessment methods. (See Figure 2.2.) In addition to those advertising professional services, thousands of others claim to help us enrich our lives by understanding ourselves.

QUACKS AND FRAUDSTERS

The terms "quack" and "fraud" were introduced in chapter 1. (For a history of quackery, see "The Literature on Quackery: Amusement and Understanding" <http://http://www.ohsu.edu/xd/education/library/about/collections/historical-collections-archives/exhibits/hom-exhibit-quackery.cfm>. Some professionals become quacks and some provide fraudulent service. A noteworthy example is the dentist Dolly Rosen who billed the state Medicaid program for more than $7 million since she

NASW NEWS

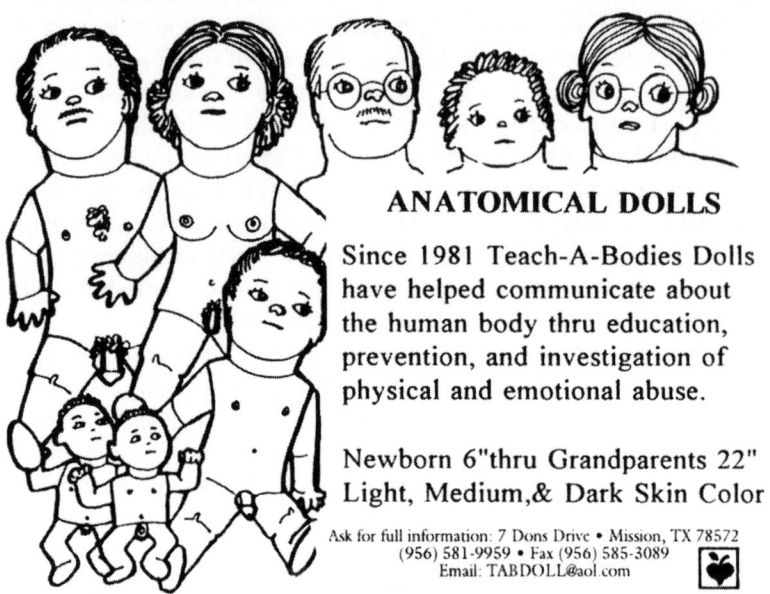

Figure 2.2. Example of ad for a psychological assessment device.
SOURCE: *NASW News* (1998) 43 (a) p. 21.

began to participate in 2002. She claimed to have performed 991 procedures a day in 2003. A criminal complaint alleged that 80% of the services for which she billed the program "were not performed, were unnecessary or were improper."[70] Concerns have been raised about unscrupulous fertility clinics.[71] Exposures of cover-ups concerning negative or harmful findings regarding drugs produced by pharmaceutical companies and other producers are daily fare in our newspapers.[72] Here are two examples from *License to Steal* (2000) by Sparrow:

> *Diapers for everyone*: William Harris, of Toledo, Ohio, owned a firm that between 1993 and 1996 sold incontinence kits to nursing homes. His firm purchased adult diapers for between $.25 to $.45, which he then billed to Medicare as more complex devices (such as 'female urinary collection devices') at between $8.35 and $22.57. After his firm was suspended from Medicare for billing fraud, he set up three more companies and kept on billing. He eventually pleaded guilty to a count of conspiring to submit $42 million in false claims to Medicare, and of laundering $9 million. He also consented to seizure of his real estate assets, which included more than 1,000 rental units in Toledo, and eleven properties in the Cayman Islands. (p. 24)

> *Lock them up*: In 1994, National Medical Enterprises (NME), owners of one of the nation's largest psychiatric hospital chains, pleaded guilty to paying kickbacks

and bribes for patient referrals. Many of the allegations involved the recruitment of community workers and church workers to refer patients for psychiatric care, and many patients complained of being held against their will. NME agreed to pay $362.7 million in what was, at the time, the largest settlement between the government and a health care provider. In addition, NME paid over $230 million in settlement of suits brought by sixteen private insurers and more than 130 patients. (p. 25)

The Office of the Inspector General has a hotline for taking reports of fraud. Since 1996 it has sought to involve Medicare beneficiaries and other members of the public in the control of fraud including training Medicare beneficiaries to examine their statements and report suspicious billings such as billing for procedures never conducted (Sparrow, 2000).

In 1997, the Administration on Aging awarded $2 million in grants to twelve states for the recruitment and training of thousands of retired professionals to serve as health care "fraud busters." These trained volunteers work with older people in their communities to review benefit statements and report potential cases of waste, fraud, and abuse. In 1999, this 'fraud buster' program budget was expanded to $7 million. A separate program, sponsored under HIPPA, has spent $1.4 million to train existing aging network staff and volunteers to educate Medicare beneficiaries about fraud, waste, and abuse as a part of their ongoing activities. (Sparrow, 2000, p. 88)

We should also consider those who make counterfeit drugs, a billion dollar industry.[73] Fake drugs may be sold in pharmacies (unknowingly) and marketed on the Internet.

On three occasions during recent months, the FDA received information that counterfeit versions of Xenical 120 mg capsules, a drug manufactured by Hoffman-La Roche Inc. (Roche), were obtained by three consumers from two different Web sites. Xenical is an FDA-approved drug used to help obese individuals who meet certain weight and height requirements lose weight and maintain weight loss. (*FDA News*, May 1, 2007)

FDA warns consumers about counterfeit drugs from multiple Internet sellers.[74] Many pharmaceutical companies have been found guilty of fraud.

WASHINGTON, June 11—The drug maker **Bristol-Myers Squibb** pleaded guilty on Monday to making false statements to a federal agency, ending an unusual criminal case involving its blockbuster blood-thinner drug Plavix.

The case involved accusations that the company had entered a secret deal to head off a generic competitor to Plavix, its biggest-selling product. (Saul, 2007a).

Illegal marketing has resulted in multi-million dollar fines against pharmaceutical companies (e.g., Feeley & Fisk, 2010; Kmietowitz, 2009). Manufacturers of medical products have also been charged for making false claims. For example, Lonza, Inc., the largest U.S. manufacturer of hospital disinfectants, was charged by the Environmental Protect Agency (EPA) with making false claims about the effectiveness of its products. Claims on labels that products killed Pseudomona, aeruginosa, and staphylococcus aureus were found to be untrue.[75] Overbilling of Medicare and Medicaid is a recurrent revelation.

> "Some patients at a Queens substance abuse clinic who had only minor alcohol problems were given intensive treatments, four or five days a week, for up to two years, with Medicaid picking up the bill, investigators said. Other patients needed more serious psychiatric care but were instead kept in unnecessary treatments for chemical dependency, again at taxpayer expense.
>
> The clinic, Community Related Services Inc., which investigators say specialized in treating elderly Russian patients, was fined $16.5 million for overbilling the state's Medicaid system, Gov. George E. Pataki's office said yesterday.
>
> It was the largest fine levied by the state's new Medicaid inspector general's office, created last year to combat rampant abuse in the joint federal-state health care program for the poor. (Rivera, 2006)[76]

The titles of many articles offer other concerning examples.[77] Quackery and fraud are so common that Internet resources designed to help us avoid them have flowered. (See Table 2.4.)

WHISTLEBLOWERS

Only through whistleblowers have many frauds, scams, and related propaganda ploys been revealed. For example Jaydeen Vicente, a former Eli Lilly sales representative "described years of what she said were illegal Zyprexa [an antipsychotic] marketing efforts" (e.g., to sedate unruly nursing home patients, to save nursing time and effort, and to treat disruptive children).[78] Whistleblowers play a key role in exposing plagiarism and data fabrication.[79] Whistleblower Protection Acts have been passed to protect people from negative consequences as a result of their exposure. Columbia/HCA, a large health care provider in the Untied States, has been the subject of many whistleblower lawsuits and federal and state investigations (Sparrow, 2000, p. 7). Whistleblowers risk their jobs by exposing fraud and harm[80] as illustrated by Alison and Bass (2007) in *Side Effects: A Prosecutor, a Whistleblower, and a Best Selling Antidepressant on Trial*. Calls to create standard procedures to note poor services and safety violations are increasing.

SUMMARY

Many different players contribute to propaganda in the helping professions in many venues. They cooperate with each other to pull the wool over our eyes in terms of promoting bogus claims about what behaviors or conditions are a problem that can

Table 2.4 INTERNET RESOURCES REGARDING FRAUD & QUACKERY

- *American Council on Science and Health* "founded in 1978 by scientists who became concerned that many important public policies related to health and the environment did not have a sound scientific basis. . . ." <http://acsh.org/>
- *Chirobase*: A Skeptical Guide to Chiropractic History, Theories, and Current Practices. <http://www.chirobase.org/>
- Commission for Scientific Medicine and Mental Health <http://hermanohme.com/>
- *Scientific Review of Alternative Medicine and Aberrant Medical Practices* "is the only peer-reviewed journal devoted exclusively to objectively analyzing the claims of 'alternative medicine.'"
- *The Scientific Review of Mental Health Practice* "is the only peer-reviewed journal devoted exclusively to distinguishing scientifically-supported claims from scientifically-unsupported claims in clinical psychology, psychiatry, social work, and allied disciplines."
- *Dietfraud.com* DietFraud HQ: Home of the diet and weight loss scams and dubious treatments.
- Federal Trade Commission for the Consumer
- *Health Watcher:* Canada's Consumer Health Watchdog
- *Internet Healthcare Coalition*: mission is quality healthcare resources on the Internet
- National Association of Attorneys General
- *National Council Against Health Fraud*: "enhancing freedom of choice through reliable information."
- *National Fraud Information Center:* The National Consumers League tracks complaints of inappropriate healthcare practices works in conjunction with the Federal Trade Commission, National Association of Attorneys General
- National Library of Medicine, Medlineplus Health Fraud
- National Patient Safety Foundation, American Medical Association
- *QuackWatch*: Guide to Health Fraud, Quackery, and Intelligent Decisions. www.quackwatch.com
- Skeptic's Dictionary: Alternative Medicine, by Robert T. Carroll
- *State Attorney General Offices:* addresses and phone numbers of every State Attorney's office in the United States from the National Association of Attorneys General
- Taxpayers Against Fraud
- healthyskepticism.org
- United States Food and Drug Administration, Center for Food Safety and Applied Nutrition, *Protecting Yourself Against Health Fraud*: collection of links to government agency resources.

be solved by taking a pill and what will help us to avoid or minimize concerns to encourage us to part with our money, time, and/or gratitude. The influence of some players is now well known, such as the creation of bogus "diseases" by the pharmaceutical companies. Other players, such as the involvement of staff in public relations agencies hired by pharmaceutical companies may not be well known—especially regarding the vast sums of money involved. And, you may be surprised to learn that professionals can take courses in just about anything to satisfy continuing education requirements even though there is little, no, or counter evidence that content will be of value to clients. Pharmaceutical companies often pay for continuing education programs. The next chapter describes more incestuous relationships among the players.

3

Interactions Among the Players

Illustrations of interactions among the players are offered in this chapter.[1] Some incestuous relationships are described in chapter 2, such as the funding of medical education by pharmaceutical companies. Figure 3.1 illustrates chains of influence. Conflicts of interest have become so marked that past editors of medical journals wrote books describing them (Kassirer, 2005; Angell, 2005).[2] Related conflicts of interest help us to understand the prevalence of propaganda in the helping professions and the extent to which this deprives us of "the straight scoop" concerning decisions that affect our lives. As a result, we may forgo effective interventions or agree to treatment that results in adverse side effects.[3] Many drugs have been withdrawn from the market because of harmful side effects, including Vioxx (prescribed for pain relief) marketed by Merck after this was linked to heart disease and stroke.[4] Staff in public relations firms draw on social psychological research to devise strategies to sell products and related grand narratives such as biochemical causes of behaviors and emotions. Public relations firms help companies handle delicate matters such as side effects of drugs as illustrated in Table 3.1. Corporations such as Quintiles offer services to pharmaceutical companies such as carrying out research, strategic planning, data processing, and operating laboratories. It employs 23,000 people in 60 countries.[5] Conflicts of interest are illustrated by the many roles one player may fill.

Conflicts of interest are illustrated by the many roles one player may fill. Consider D. Martin Leon, a cardiologist (Eichenwald & Kolata, 1999b). He is a physician and an educator (he runs an educational forum and industry trade show for other cardiologists). He conducts research and is founder of a company that designs and oversees research for the manufacturing of devices. He is an investor (holds stock in device manufacturers), an evaluator (reviews data submitted by other researchers through laboratories associated with his foundation), a product developer, and principle and shareholder of Medivai, a company that acquires patents on devices, and a board member (of Angiosonimcs).

Academic researchers promote new diagnostic categories and their application to new groups as illustrated by Dr. Joseph Biederman's promotion of the diagnoses of pediatric bipolar disorder for children and promotion of risky expensive antipsychotic medication for these children (Harris, 2008; Harris & Carey, 2008; Healy 2006b). Such researchers often have financial ties with pharmaceutical companies:

- This summer, The New York Times reported that three prominent Harvard University researchers [Dr. Joseph Biederman, Thomas Spencer, and

Authors and presenters at a conference define evidence-based practice (EBP) as use of empirically-based practices (the EBPs approach), ignoring the process and philosophy of EBP described in original sources (Straus et al., 2005).
↓
People assume evidence-based practice means use of EBPs.
↓
People criticize the EBPs approach, assuming (incorrectly) that they have been informed about the process and philosophy of EBP (Gambrill, 2006).

Bogus claims regarding the causal role of self-esteem in professional newsletters and journals (e.g., NASW California News).
↓
False beliefs acquired by professionals who read bogus claims
↓
Incorrect assumptions about the causes of client concerns as due to low self-esteem (e.g., ignoring social inequalities).
↓
Use of ineffective intervention methods (focusing on individuals as the locus of problems).
↓
Forgoing effective interventions such as increasing social and academic skills of children that result in more positive consequences.

Pharmaceutical companies transform problem-in-living into mental illness with help of in-house product strategy teams, public relations firms and the continuing expansion of the DSM.
↓
Offer medication as a solution.
↓
Psychiatrists hired to conduct drug trials
↓
Pressure to promote the funder's interest
↓
Slanted presentations of results
↓
Media diffusion of slanted results.
↓
Increased sales of products promoted.

Figure 3.1. Examples of Chains of Influence Regarding Propaganda in the Helping Professions.

Timothy E. Wilens] responsible for discovering bipolar disorder in children—and for treating it with psychiatric drugs—were found to have failed to report a combined $3.2 million in income from drug companies to their university. Between 1994 and 2003, the number of children diagnosed with bipolar depression increased 40-fold, and the sales of the drugs used to treat it doubled.

Table 3.1 CASE STUDIES ON ETHICAL STRATEGIES WEBSITE

Tackling Issues Head-on: Side Effects in Context

- **Challenge**: To announce the PBS listing of a treatment for Parkinson's disease while ensuring the therapy's unique—and highly newsworthy—side-effect profile did not become the focus of media attention.
- **Strategy**: Positively engage sufferers and third-party opinion leaders to tell their individual Parkinson's stories while proactively communicating and putting into perspective the side effects of this class of medication within context of the condition.
- **Result**: Limited media interest in the treatment's side-effect profile and, where reported, reported within context of the condition. Extensive print, radio, online, and television coverage raised awareness of the condition, as well as the availability of treatment options for sufferers.

Launching a Landmark Medical Study

- **Challenge**: To communicate, on behalf of a leading pharmaceutical company, the results of a landmark cardiovascular medical study in a credible and authoritative manner in accordance with the industry's code of conduct.
- **Strategy:** The "investigator-led study" required "investigator-led communication" to ensure its significance was fully recognized and regulatory restrictions were satisfied. Through an educational grant, Ethical Strategies formed a truly independent and autonomous group of leading medical specialists and acted as Secretariat to the Group—developing and implementing an integrated communications program on its behalf.
- **Results:** The program strengthened the company's relationships with some of its key stakeholders—members of the Group—and provided a forum though which to communicate the study's results directly to medical specialists. The national media campaign, which generated more than 150 brand mentions, was deemed the most successful of all of the company's 136 subsidiaries following an analysis by its international headquarters.

SOURCE: Retrieved June 2, 2009, from <http://www.ethicalstrategies.com>.

- An El Paso psychiatrist who prescribed psychiatric drugs to nearly 300 foster kids between 2002 and 2005 won nearly $150,000 in research funding from Pfizer and Eli Lilly, according to the Web site of the university he is affiliated with. He was also a guest lecturer for an AstraZeneca-sponsored conference at a California beach resort, according to the conference's brochure.
- A Houston psychiatrist who prescribed psychiatric drugs to 490 foster children since 2002 has helped run ADHD, depression and schizophrenia clinical trials. His research facility has received funding from Eli Lilly, GlaxoSmithKline and Janssen, according to the facility's Web site. (Retrieved November 26, 2008, from Parents Against Teen Screen, p. 3)

The history of each helping profession reflects the use of a variety of ways to enhance its status and to expand and protect its turf, including deception (e.g., hiding lack of effectiveness of remedies promoted). Professors of psychiatry promote governmental initiatives such as mental health screening even when there may be no evidence that such programs do more good than harm.[6] Professions take advantage of emerging technologies, such as the typewriter and case record and now the Internet, to forward particular approaches. Less well known than psychiatry's history is the use of publicity methods in social work to win support, including theater productions and traveling exhibits such as "Mrs. Docare and Mrs. Don'tcare," contrasting kitchens or bathrooms of the bad housekeeper with the good one (e.g., Routzahn & Routzahn, 1918). Less well known is social work's acceptance of money from Big Pharma, such as $100,000 from the Amgen Foundation to help fund a consumer website (*NASW News*, 50(3), 2005, p. 1).

CREATION AND CONTROL OF MARKETING CHANNELS

Brody (2007) describes the complex interactions among the many players in the promotion and sales of pharmaceutical products. One of the central arguments in his book is that: "We won't understand the problem, and we won't be able to propose helpful solutions, unless we see how all these levels of activity are interconnected" (p. 6). Applbaum (2009b), an anthropologist, describes the interactions required to shape marketing channels in order to transform a drug such as Zyprexa into a blockbuster bringing in billions a year. He drew on records obtained by subpoena from Eli Lilly & Co in a lawsuit in Alaska in 2006. Related records included 358 documents consisting of marketing plans, sales training manuals, scientific reports, and internal correspondence. Players include providers (e.g., physicians), hospitals, manufacturers (e.g., pharmaceutical companies), distributors (e.g., pharmacies), payers (insurance companies), regulatory groups (e.g., state agencies), patients, and case managers.

Physicians must be converted into middlemen who "push" (prescribe a drug). He argues that the key interaction in marketing drugs is the patient-provider-payer interaction. General practitioners must acquire the confidence, for example, by virtue of their interactions with drug sales reps, industry-sponsored symposiums, and ghostwritten articles, to prescribe drugs for psychiatric problems. The boundaries of related diseases must be stretched and new uses promoted including off label uses. And, all this must be accomplished without the appearance of manipulation using popular technology such as the DSM, which is a pharmaceutical company's dream aid for marketing drugs for an ever-expanding diagnostic base (Lakoff, 2005). Prevalence figures regarding comorbidities are manipulated in order to fit sales requirements. All this must be accomplished by use of masterful persuasion strategies designed to channel conflicts of interest among different parties into one direction of flow—the selling of the drug.

Nothing impresses the reader more concerning the complexity of the process than the strategic plans revealed in the internal documents described by Applbaum (2009b). Detailed scripts are written so drug reps can handle different kinds of concerns physicians may have, for example, about side effects. Market research is drawn on to prepare these scripts. Scripts are written for different kinds of physicians: "certainty seeker," "independent skeptic," "referrer," "cautious practitioner." Applbaum's research revealed a patterns of collaborative competition among drug companies, not a free market economy as claimed, in which a key aim is to convert partial truths into whole ones, for example, about side effects of drugs and their effectiveness.

A CASE EXAMPLE: PLAYERS INVOLVED IN THE CREATION OF SOCIAL ANXIETY DISORDER

The role of pharmaceutical companies in medicalizing everyday concerns is described by Moynihan and Cassels (2005). They note that the CEO of Merck informed *Fortune Magazine* over 30 years ago that "the companies' potential markets [have] been limited to sick people" and he hoped "to make drugs for healthy people" (p. ix). Direct to consumer marketing, initiated in 1997, allows pharmaceutical companies to suggest new risks and illnesses needing remedies. A key role of public relations firms was to create a need for remedies offered by drug companies. Marketing time-lines may be in terms of years. The public relations firm is called "Ethical Strategies."

- The brochure said the marketing of a drug should begin years before it was approved, even before it was tested in human subjects. During this time, known as the preclinical stage, the company should identify and recruit doctors who would be paid to speak on the drug's behalf, the consultants said. The drug company should also begin looking for non-profit health groups, like the American Heart Association, that it could partner with to promote the product. It was also a good idea, the firm said, to start at this early stage to identify the "key journalists" who could be counted on to get out the drug's story.
- When the experimental drug moved from being tested in animals to its first trials in humans, which are known as Phase I studies, the company should start paying for meetings at which the experimental drug can be promoted to certain physicians. At this time, even though the drug is still years away from approval, the company should begin paying as well to have articles written and published in medical journals that supported the drug's use. Ethical Strategies also suggested the company prepare its media strategy during this period to "seed market with preclinical information."
- As the months and years passed and the drug continued to move through human studies, the company should train and ready its recruited doctors for their "lecture tours," the brochure said. It should also develop written "therapeutic guidelines" that doctors would use to diagnose and treat patients with the company's product once it was on the market. As the drug got closer to approval, the company should "launch key messages and story platforms" by providing information to journalists. And "where gaps exist," the company should "establish" new patient groups to help promote the new drug. Representatives of Ethical Strategies said that these steps were "a look at a typical program." (Petersen, 2008, p. 158)

Moynihan and Cassels (2005) describe the interaction of many players and settings in the creation of social anxiety as a disorder and the marketing of Paxil as a remedy. For example, advocacy groups earn money from drug companies by providing suffering patients to talk to journalists. Public relations firms organized teleconferences with sufferers. The pharmaceutical company GSK hired Cohn & Wolfe to lay the groundwork for the introduction of Paxil, which they hoped would replace Zoloft for the treatment of "social anxiety disorder." Cohn & Wolfe specializes in unconventional ways to market pharmaceuticals. Their task was to create social anxiety disorder as a "severe condition." This occurred before Paxil was approved for the treatment of social anxiety in order to "cultivate the market place" (p. 121). "To put it bluntly, the public was to be educated about a new condition by a campaign whose primary goal was to maximize sales of a drug" (p. 121).

Cohen & Wolfe arranged "the distribution of video news releases, press kits, and the setting up of a network of spokespeople" to increase attention to "social anxiety disorders." This resulted in articles in sources such as the *New York Times* and *Vogue,* and spots on the Howard Stern show and "Good Morning America."

> In the space of a little more than a year Paxil's manufacturer GSK took a little-known and once-considered rare-psychiatric condition and helped transform it into a major epidemic called social anxiety disorder—claimed at one point by the company to affect 1 in 8 Americans. The transformation would ultimately help rack up sales of Paxil worth $3 billion dollars a year, and make it the world's top-selling antidepressant. (Moynihan & Cassels, 2005, p. 120)
>
> In keeping with modern public relations techniques the PR firm [Cohn and Wolfe] helped orchestrate what looked like a grassroots movement to raise public awareness about a neglected disorder. The awareness raising campaign was based on the slogan "Imagine being allergic to people." Posters that featured a sad-looking man and listed commonly experienced symptoms were distributed across America. "You blush, sweat, shake—even find it hard to breathe. That's what social anxiety disorder feels like." The posters appeared to come from several medical and advocacy groups under the umbrella of a Social Anxiety Disorder Coalition: all three members of the "coalition" rely heavily on sponsorship from drug companies. Calls from the media to the "coalition" were handled by Cohn and Wolfe. (pp. 121–22)

Moynihan and Cassels (2005) point out that marketing guru Vince Perry described this PR program as a good example of "branding a condition." "I'd say that the area that has been most ripe for condition branding has been anxiety and mood disorders," said Perry, explaining that for these disorders there is no blood test a person could take—so the diagnosis is made with a checklist of symptoms (p. 127). Description of symptoms are vague—"experienced by vast swathes of the entire population reinforce[ing] the arguments of critics who suggest we are witnessing a blurring of the boundaries between normal life and treatable illness" (p. 127). Selective omission (hiding the negatives—telling half-truths) was a key propaganda ploy in the selling of social anxiety as a disorder of epidemic proportions and Paxil as a remedy. Carefully hidden were withdrawal problems. Subjects in trials who become suicidal when taking Paxil were mislabeled as noncompliant (Bass, 2008). And, taking Paxil is expensive. As all critics of pharmaceutical hype note, no doubt for some people, antidepressants (including Paxil) can be beneficial, even life saving. But for others the experience was quite different.

Aggressive marketing encourages and indeed, in part creates, the biomedicalization of common problems-in-living: the increasing number of people labeled "mentally ill." "As with other conditions like ADD [attention deficit disorder], recent revisions of the DSM have widened the definition [of social anxiety disorder]—expanding the number of social situations a person can fear to qualify for the disorder, and removing the need for *avoidance* of those situations as a strict criterion"

(Moynihan & Cassells, 2005, p. 129). Kessler, a Harvard professor "estimated that 13.3 percent of people suffered this disorder at some point in their life—the source of the one-in-eight claim by the Paxil manufacturer" (p. 130). Is this estimate accurate? William Narrow and his colleagues (2002) believe it is wildly inflated. They suggest a figure of fewer than 4%, and possibly lower (p. 130). Has shyness been converted into a "mental illness"? (See also Lane, 2004.)

> GSK's social anxiety disorder campaign appears to be another case where those with mild illness, or sometimes none at all, are being told they may have a serious psychiatric disorder. As we saw with the attempts to paint menopause as a condition of hormone deficiency requiring treatment, part of the selling strategy here has involved the calculated use of celebrities, including in this case the U.S. football phenomena, running back Rickey Williams. (Moynihan & Cassels, 2005, pp. 130–31)

Williams, a well-known football player, was paid by GSK to raise public awareness about this disorder. Like many others "he only realized that he had a mental illness after watching a TV commercial" (p. 131)—diagnosis of mental illness by TV.[6] We have aggressive propagandistic marketing of drugs—claims do not match the science. Harms such as increased risk of suicide as a result of taking drugs such as Paxil are hidden (Bass, 2008; Breggin, 2008). This adverse effect was hidden until forced into public awareness by investigators such as David Healy.[7]

There is a masquerading of marketing as education, awareness, training, and research to alter our views about what constitutes a treatable illness to encourage us to buy the latest pill (Angell, 2005).

> Parry assigns much of the credit for the fact that psychiatry's DSM, the *Diagnostic and Statistical Manual of Mental Disorders*, has grown to its "current phonebook dimensions" to the fact that "newly coined conditions were brought to light through direct funding by pharmaceutical companies, in research, in publicity, or both." As a "legendary example" of condition branding, Parry offers the example of panic disorder. Upjohn, through its strategic funding, managed to disentangle panic disorder from the broader category of anxiety neurosis and at the same time install its drug alprazolam (Xanax) as the first choice drug to treat the new disease. (Brody, 2007, p. 240)

As with depression, "part of the 'awareness-raising' about social anxiety disorder was designed to narrowly portray the condition as being caused by a 'chemical imbalance in the brain,' to be fixed with chemical solutions like Paxil" (Moynihan & Cassels, 2005, p. 136).[8] This "distracts all of us from a broader understanding of the complex sources of social anxiety—whether it is defined as a mental disorder or not" (p. 137). As critics document, even when marketed most enthusiastically, there was no good evidence that antidepressants were better than placebo (p. 134). The situation got so bad that Elliott Spitzer, then New York Attorney General, launched a legal action against GSK, publicly accusing the company of fraud.

> Spitzer alleged that Glaxo-SmithKline had deliberately concealed the results of four research studies of the antidepressant drug Paxil when used in children

and adolescents. These four studies all showed that the drug either did not work well or that it caused harm. By contrast, a fifth study was interpreted as showing that Paxil was helpful in treating childhood depression. The firm rapidly published and then gave considerable publicity to the fifth study while doing its best to conceal from the medical community the contrary results of the other four studies. (Brody, 2007, p. 2)

He accused the drug company of concealing data about the dangers of Paxil and the lack of evidence of benefit in depressed children and of misleading both doctors and the public. An internal GSK memo sent to its drug detailers in 2003 advised sales representatives not to discuss the potential association with suicidal behavior. GlaxoSmithKline agreed to pay $2.5 million to avoid the cost of further legal action.

Drug companies have spent millions promoting other kinds of alleged disorders such as attention deficit disorder, menopause as a mental illness, irritable bladder, irritable bowel syndrome, and female sexual dysfunction, as medical conditions requiring medical treatment—medication. The higher the number of bogus problems that can be created, especially for the "healthy," the more drugs can be sold.

We now have drugs proven, to varying degrees of efficacy, to treat baldness, shyness, childhood hyperactivity, adolescent adjustment problems, lackluster sex, premenstrual moodiness, incontinence and ugly toenails. All these conditions, once the normal burdens of living inside an aging or imperfect human body, have been transformed into pathologies, because they can now be treated with medications. The drug companies did not create these clinical realities; they uncovered them in their desperate search for the next drug they could make, test, and sell. In the process they have done a brilliant job of medicalizing human unhappiness. An insured American suffering from one of these problems is grateful to have a medical remedy—purchased with the tax-advantaged status of a health care transaction—that did not exist 10 years ago. (Kleinke, 2004, p. 41)

The more "the healthy" can be lured into concerns about bogus risks, the greater the pool of potential buyers. Such medicalization can have harmful effects, including adverse withdrawal reactions and distraction from the enjoyment of life. Most members of groups involved with creating diagnostic categories in the DSM have some financial tie to a pharmaceutical company (Cosgrove, Krimsky, Vijayaraghaven, & Schneider 2006). This "selling" of biomedical views obscures environmental causes of depression, anxiety, alienation, and boredom (e.g., Double, 2006; Luyten et al., 2006). These examples also illustrate the subversion of scientific inquiry.

It is because the scientific method actively fosters uncertainty that it must inevitably be subversive of authority. . . . If these authorities are to be effective propagandists for their diverse practices and causes then, unlike scientists, they need the self-confident certainty that they know what is good and what is bad. Searching questions about how they know are only unsettling, they threaten to complicate the simple messages which are such an important component of their work. (Chalmers, 1983, cited in Skrabanek & McCormick, p. 11)

Thus, all is not what it seems. The creation of "social anxiety disorder" was a result of marketing rather than of scientific investigation. Researchers themselves are caught up by this marketing in using it for their own purposes as "experts" in treating clients and as researchers in investigating presumed disorders. We in turn are reeled in by our awe of researchers and experts, and by the constant assault from ads alleging risks and offering presumed remedies. It is an old game played in increasingly sophisticated ways as new technologies allow ever more novel approaches, including individual targeting of different groups based on social and psychological research. How much do such research findings benefit corporations compared to clients?

CORPORATE FUNDING OF NOT-FOR-PROFIT ORGANIZATIONS

The Integrity in Science website describes sources of corporate funding for nonprofit organizations. For example, sponsors of the Academy of General Dentistry include 3M Corporation, ESPE, OraPharma, and Oral-B (<http://www.agd.org/corporate.sponsors/corporate.alliances.htm>). Among sponsors giving $100,000 or more annually to the Arthritis Foundation are Abbott Immunology, Amgen, Bayer Consumer Care, Bristol-Myers Squibb, Cenboca, Genentech, Pfizer Animal Health, and Wyeth Pharmaceuticals. Contributors to the Gerontological Society of American include Merck Institute of Aging & Health and Pfizer, Inc. (See Table 3.2.) Consider also the close alliance between an Alzheimer's Society and drug manufacturers, which Chalmers (2007) argues, encouraged members of this group to promote harmful products. This charity is subsidized by the government in the United Kingdom. It fails to report on its website sources and amounts of revenue it receives from drug companies.

Ties between academic researchers, advocacy groups, and pharmaceutical companies is illustrated by funding sources and activities of the American Obesity Association (AOA) founded by Dr. Richard L. Atkinson, an obesity researcher.

- The AOA was intended to be an advocacy organization for the millions of persons in this country with obesity. Unfortunately, a major aspect of its advocacy appears to be for the diet-pill-producing pharmaceutical industry. In a 1994 *Chicago Sun Times* article, Dr. Atkinson was quoted as saying that it was time to stop thinking of obesity as a problem of willpower, and start thinking of it as a chronic disease that required long-term treatment.
- ... AOA publicly admitted that it received most of its funding from major pharmaceutical companies that market diet pills including Roche Laboratories (makers of Xenical), Knoll Pharmaceutical (makers of Meridia), Wyeth Laboratories (makers of Redux and Pondimin), and Medeva Pharmaceuticals (makers of Phentermine). A widely distributed book of recommended treatments for obesity, published jointly by AOA and Shape UP America! was supported by American Home Products, the parent company of Wyeth-Ayerst. Atkinson's work has also been supported by Weight Watchers International. (Kassirer, 2005, p. 34)

Not-for-profit organizations such as research and treatment centers have concerning ties with pharmaceutical companies. A congressional investigation revealed that Dr. Joseph Biederman, a well-known child psychiatrist earned far more money from

Table 3.2 EXAMPLES OF CORPORATE FUNDING OF NONPROFIT ORGANIZATIONS

UNITED SENIORS ASSOCIATION/USA NEXT
"USA Next (United Seniors Association) considers itself to be the conservative alternative to the American Association of Retired Persons (AARP) which it regards as too liberal. USA Next is part of the Uniting the Generations for America's Future Network, which claims more than 1.5 million members across the nation. Its motto is: 'Building a Legacy of Freedom for America's Families.'" (Retrieved March 28, 2005, from <http://rightweb.irc-online.org/org/usanext.php>)

According to the Akron Beacon Journal, the group accepted donations of $1.5 million from Pharmaceutical Research and Manufacturers Association, $664,000 from an industry group called Citizens for Better Medicare, and $50,000 from Pfizer. (Steven Thomma, "AARP opposed in bid for members, money," *Akron Beacon Journal*, March 27, 2005, p. 5)

NATIONAL ALLIANCE FOR THE MENTALLY ILL
According to its website, "NAMI is a nonprofit, grassroots, self-help, support and advocacy organization of consumers, families, and friends of people with severe mental illnesses, such as schizophrenia, schizoaffective disorder, bipolar disorder, major depressive disorder, obsessive-compulsive disorder, panic and other severe anxiety disorders, autism and pervasive developmental disorders, attention deficit/hyperactivity disorder, and other severe and persistent mental illnesses that affect the brain." (Retrieved August 26, 2003, from <http://www.nami.org/template.cfm?section=About_NAMI>)

   NAMI corporate sponsors include:

- Abbott Laboratories
- AstraZeneca Pharmaceuticals
- Bristol-Myers Squibb Company
- Eli Lilly & Company
- Forest Laboratories Inc.
- GlaxoSmithKline
- Janssen Pharmaceutica inc.
- Magellan Health Services
- McNeil Consumer Healthcare
- Novartis Pharmaceuticals Corporation
- Organon Inc.
- PacificCare Behavioral Health Inc.
- Pfizer Foundation
- Pfizer Inc
- PhRMA
- WellPoint Health Networks
- Wyeth Pharmaceuticals

(NAMI 2002 Annual Report, retrieved August 26, 2003, from <http://www.nami.org/Content/NavigationMenu/Inform_Yourself/About_NAMI/AnnualReports02-proof.pdf>).

SOURCE: Integrity in Science. <http://www.cspinet.org/integrity/nonprofits>.

pharmaceutical companies than he reported to his university. He earned about $1.6 million in consulting fees from pharmaceutical companies from 2000 to 2007 but reported only 200,000 of this income to university officials for years (Harris & Carey, 2008). He said that "his interests were 'solely in the advancement of medical treatment through rigorous and objective study'" (Harris & Carey, 2008).[9] However, e-mail messages and internal documents from Johnson & Johnson made public in a court filing showed that he encouraged this company to finance a research center at Massachusetts General Hospital with a goal to "move forward the commercial goals of J.& J." Related documents showed that Johnson & Johnson prepared a draft summary of a study that Dr. Biederman was said to have written.

FINANCIAL TIES BETWEEN DRUG COMPANIES, PROFESSIONAL ORGANIZATIONS, RESEARCHERS, AND PHYSICIANS

Examples of the incestuous relationships between physicians and drug companies were given in chapter 2. Bekelman et al.'s (2003) systematic review describing the scope and impact of financial conflicts of interest in biomedical research reveals alarming interactions. Brody (2007) suggests the following kinds of interaction between helping professionals and related industries:

- the individual physician receiving gifts, information, and free samples from drug reps;
- physicians attending formal continuing medical education courses funded in part by the industry;
- industry support of medical professional organizations;
- industry support of "grassroots," patient advocacy groups;
- industry advertising aimed at consumers;
- industry support of medical journals;
- industry support of research, and consulting and speakers' fees paid to individual investigators and "opinion leaders";
- industry's role in lobbying government for favorable laws and regulations; the role of the FDA in regulating the industry (pp. 39–40).[10]

Brody (2007) quotes Harry Lloyd, past president of Park Davis and Company: "If we put horse manure in a capsule, we could sell it to 95% of these doctors." A review of Minnesota records illustrate financial ties between drug companies and physicians raising concerns about undue influence on prescribing practices.[11]

Sales representatives market drugs to professionals and distribute gifts and other perks such as dinners. Today there are about 90,000 sales representatives (Angell, 2005). Drug representatives are trained to maximize their influences on doctors. Brody (2007) draws on Oldani's (2004) description. Oldani was a drug rep for nine years.

- Training focuses heavily on spin. For example, one goal is to find a way to turn every objection the physician offers against the drug into a point in the drug's favor.

- Reps were trained to take full advantage of any indebtedness the physicians felt toward them.
- The actual everyday pharmaceutical economy is based on social relationships that are forged and strengthened through repetitive and calculated acts of giving.
- The everyday function of the pharmaceutical gift economy . . . works by limiting and disguising economic interests. The industry works very hard to maintain a feel-good economy for doctors and reps to co-exist.
- The reps themselves must learn the importance of giving first hand.
- Food is the reps weapon of choice.
- Reps depend on computer-generated data on physicians prescribing practices gained from independent companies. (p. 177)

Brody (2007) describes the collaboration with psychologists to promote pharmaceutical profits. For example, the Pharmaceutical Advertising Club collaborated with the Institute for Motivational Research, headed by Ernest Dichter, to produce *A Research Study on Pharmaceutical Advertising* (1955).

The Dichter study broke new ground by identifying how important the process of *rationalization* was in successful pharmaceutical marketing. The company had to treat the physician in one way yet be perceived as if they were treating him in a very different way. The ideal contact with the company fed message and rationalization simultaneously. For example, a visit from the rep might *really* be a break in a busy afternoon of seeing patients, a chance to talk with an old buddy about a hobby, or an exchange of gossip about other physicians in town. But just enough scientific information had to be exchanged—even a brochure that would never be read—so that the physician could rationalize the visit as "education." (p. 147)

He notes that companies would not now allow such a document to be circulated openly today. Drug wholesalers have been around a long time. William Osler, professor of medicine at Johns Hopkins and the most famous American physician of his era, wrote in 1902 that "the 'drummer' of the drug house" was a dangerous enemy to the mental virility of the general practitioner (p. 141). Brody describes the shift from small ethical firms into huge corporations. Giving gifts, even a pen, creates feelings of reciprocal obligations (Cialdini, 2001).[12] A review of gifts from drug companies to doctors in Vermont (for example, for lectures and other services) showed that psychiatrists topped the list.[13] Jerome Kassirer (2005), former editor of *The New England Journal of Medicine* describes troubling practices in "*On the Take*." The environment within medical education that promotes acceptance of reps and their gifts is a culture of entitlement.

Most medical students begin their education with a sense of duty and commitment, which slowly fades and is replaced by cynicism. By the time the student has become a resident, idealism has often been replaced by self-pity: we work so hard, we are underpaid, we are unappreciated, lawyers are the enemy, even patients are the enemy (by making more work for us to do at all hours of the day and night). In exchange for having to put up with all this, we deserve some love and we deserve some rewards. Perhaps even more important the average medical graduate today may be in debt for as much as $120,000 or more after completing medical school. (Brody, 2007: p. 192)

Other conflicts of interest are seen in speaker's bureaus and promotion of "off label" drugs by physicians.[14] Physicians are recruited to be members of company-supported speakers' panels. Speakers may be reluctant to criticize companies' products. Or, some physicians may knowingly become spokespersons for marketing efforts of a company. Medical schools have become alarmed about the influence of propaganda and gifts from pharmaceutical companies on physicians and students. Some schools now include courses on propaganda (Wilkes & Hoffman, 2001). (See also educational material on <http://www.pharmedout.org>.)

Marketing Masquerading as Education

Until recently, pharmaceutical companies funded most continuing medical education programs.[15] They controlled much of what physicians learned about drugs. The intrusion of commercial interests into professional organizations, including continuing education and conferences, is suggested by the following:

> The Web Site for the 32nd meeting of the [Society of Critical Care Medicine] in San Antonio held early in 2003 contained a 20-page insert entitled "*Sponsorship Opportunities.*" The more than 50 opportunities for sponsorship add up to approximately two million dollars. They included the opening reception (can be purchased by a company for $100,000), the President's reception ($30,000), The Rustlers Rodeo Roundup ($150,000), The Chili Cook-off ($5,000 each). The Internet Pavilion ($40,000), and various educational grants ($125,000 for the President's Circle, $75,000 for Platinum Level, $50,000 for Diamond Level, etc.). For various smaller sums companies can buy tote bags, pens, highlighters, and notepads for all the participants. (Kassirer, 2005, p.120)
>
> The American Psychiatric Association is paid by industry to interweave pharmaceutical-company-sponsored lecturers with nonsponsored lectures at its annual meeting. The two major allergy societies, both of which receive funding from manufacturers of nonsedating antihistamines, sent a representative to the FDA to prevent less-sedating new antihistamines from being sold without a prescription, thus helping to preserve the profits of the pharmaceutical companies producing these drugs. These are but a few of many examples of the complex ties between professional organizations and industry. (Kassirer, 2005, p. 104)

Burton (2008) reported that in the last six months of 2007 Australia's drug industry "organized more than 14,633 'educational events' for the benefit of medical professionals."[16] The extent of the pharmaceutical industry support for continuing medical education is suggested by activity in 2003:

1. Total income, all ACCME accredited providers. $1,774,516,395.
2. Total commercial support: $971,100,096.
3. Support from pharmaceutical companies: $943,608,302.

4. Percentage of all commercial support from pharmaceutical companies: 97%.
5. Percentage of total income from pharmaceutical support: 53% (2004).

Over 50 years ago (in 1956), Dr. Charles DeMay, a professor of pediatrics at Columbia, criticized the placing of education in the hands of commercially interested parties (the pharmaceutical industry) (p. 149).

> Is the public likely to benefit if practicing physicians and medical educators must perform their duties amidst the clamor and striving of merchants seeking to increase the sales of drugs by conscripting 'education' in the service of promotion? Is it prudent for physicians to become gravely dependent upon pharmaceutical manufacturers for support of scientific journals and medical societies, for entertainment, and now also for a large part of their education? Do all concerned realize the hazard of arousing the wrath of the people by an unwholesome entanglement of doctors with the makers and sellers of drugs? (May 1961, quoted in Brody, 2008, p. 150)

He pointed out the vast differences in resources by drug companies in terms of preparing slick publications and the small staffs of legitimate journals and noted the willingness of his colleagues in academic medicine to lend their names and reputations to drug marketing, presumably for "their share of payola" (p. 152).

Brody (2007) reviews the evidence that continuing medical education programs have a biasing influence on those who attend these programs. Here is an example.

> Spingarn and colleagues compared residents who had attended a company sponsored grand rounds on Lyme Disease with residents who had not attended, assessing their knowledge of treatment with a survey three months later. They found the attendees more likely to use an expensive intravenous antibiotic sold by the company. The residents were prone to use that antibiotic both when it was appropriate and when it was not, and even when cheaper oral antibiotics would have done as well. (Quoted in Brody, 2007, p. 207)

Dubovsky and Dubovsky (2007) suggest that

> In the psychiatric setting, industry-sponsored teaching begins in medical school, intensifies during residency, and reaches it maturity in CME. It is now difficult to find practitioners who do not receive the bulk of their postgraduate exposure to new data either directly from industry representatives or in industry-sponsored programs and publications. (p. 25)

Medical education was viewed as a key venue in promoting pharmaceutical products. Studies of material provided show that presentations favored drugs produced (e.g., Ziegler, Lew, & Singer, 1995). Drug companies paid up to $50,000 to a doctor who agreed to speak about psychological diseases and possible treatment at a conference. Wyeth prepared a supplement regarding its menopausal hormone therapy Prempro and distributed 1,28,000 copies to physicians and another 1,500 copies to its sales force (Fugh-Berman, 2010). Material underplayed risks of adverse events and promoted unproven benefits. Continuing medical education credit via a test was also offered. Conferences often include presentations by a pharmaceutical representative prior to faculty lectures. Information about potential harmful side effects is played down and competitors may not be mentioned.

In July 2010, a federal medical advisory panel recommended that Avandia be withdrawn or have sales greatly restricted because of risks of heart attacks (Harris, 2010f). Jerome Kassirer (2005) reported that one of the his research assistants who attended an Aventis-sponsored seminar "perceived an erosion of objectivity" in that "speakers exaggerated the value and underplayed the risks of low molecular weight heparin and that the references provided to the attendees were heavily weighted toward the Aventis product, Lovenox." The continuing medical education market has encouraged growth of private medical education companies. The increased attention to financial ties between physicians and drug companies has resulted in policies to limit pharmaceutical payment to U.S. doctors (e.g., Kmietowticz, 2008b). The board of trustees of the American Psychiatric Association voted in March 2009 to phase out industry-supported symposia and meals at its annual meetings. Some medical schools now prohibit acceptance of any gifts/perks from pharmaceutical companies.

Academics and Researchers as "Marketeers"

There is an increasing commercialization of research (Brody, 2007; Deyo & Patrick, 2005). There are hundreds of contract-research organizations. Such research may include many layers.

> Dr. Thomas Bodenheimer, surveying the scene in 2000, noted that ultimately a large clinical drug trial might involve four layers. At the lowest notch might be a private physician who is paid to recruit patients into the trial and perhaps to gather some rudimentary data. Next up the ladder is an SMO that organizes a network of similar physicians' offices, facilitates recruitment, and delivers patient data to the CRO. The next rung up is the CRO, organizing the entire trial, obtaining human subject approvals, coordinating the trial protocol and facilitating data collection. Finally at the top is the manufacturer's scientific team, who will eventually analyze the assembled data. (Brody, 2007, p. 120)

There are even for-profit institutional review boards. Selling confidential and critical details of ongoing drug research to Wall Street firms is common (Steinbrook, 2005c). "These practices were denounced as a 'moral cesspool' by Arthur Caplan of the Center For Bioethics at the University of Pennsylvania and as 'outrageous and completely unethical' by Drummond Rennie, then Deputy Editor of the JAMA" (Brody, 2007, p. 194).

> Another way to reduce quality is to forget that one is doing scientific research and to imagine that one is doing something else instead . . . for the marketing division to imagine that the research division is merely one of its branch offices. When the goals of marketing take over from the goals of proper scientific research, the result is shoddy from a scientific point of view and shoddy from the point of view of a medical profession that relies on accurate, dispassionate data to know how best to treat patients. (Brody, 2007, p. 125)

Bero and Rennie (1996) described ways in which research can be designed to reach a certain conclusion: (1) asking too narrow a question, (2) playing tricks with randomization, (3) inappropriate dosing, (4) inappropriate comparisons, (5) lack of blinding, (6) inventing your own scale, (7) first shoot the arrow, then draw the target, (8) don't ask, don't tell, (9) protocol violations and poor recording keeping, (10) if you get good results, publish and publish again, (11) sales pitch in the articles abstract, (12) lying with statistics, (13) refuse to publish unfavorable results, (14) hide company sponsorship (pp. 125–28). Strategies used by advertisers are remarkably similar to misleading practices on the part of those who publish in professional sources. So too is there an overlap in goals as described in chapter 9.

Opinion Leaders and Pharma

The term "KOL" refers to key opinion leaders. KOLs are recruited by Pharma as lecturers and researchers in drug trials.[17]

> Some of these physician leaders, who are generally academics, are soon making more money from Pharma than from their academic day jobs and easily qualify as "physicians for sale." The lucrative Pharma advisory groups, lectures, research grants, symposia, and other payoffs for the MPO's physician officers encourage their cooperation. They begin to work for Pharma, perhaps without realizing it. Full disclosures of such payments to KOLs are rare. (Grouse, 2008, p. 8)

Revelations of undeclared income of KOLs from drug companies sparked a congressional inquiry spearheaded by Senator Charles E. Grassley.[18] As a result of investigations of individual doctors' arrangements with drug makers, Senator Grassley called for an accounting by the American Psychiatric Association of its financing. Drug companies paid for 30% of the American Psychiatric Association's $62.5 million in financing in 2006 (Carey & Harris, 2008). About half the money was spent on drug advertisements in psychiatric journals and exhibits at the annual meeting and the remaining half was used to sponsor fellowships, conferences, and industry symposiums at the annual meeting.[19]

Pharmaceutical Companies and Medical Professional Organizations (MPOs)

Specialty MPOs abound. The percentage of physicians who are general practitioners (GPs) fell from 75% prior to 1950 to 13% in 2007.[20] In "Physicians For Sale: How Medical Professional Organizations Exploit Their Members," Grouse (2008) identifies the following concerns.

1. MPOs that have become so dependent on Pharma funding that these funders exert control over MPO policies and cause them to violate precepts of medical ethics;
2. MPOs that are fundamentally trade organizations and use their resources to inappropriately increase their specialties' financial status with little regard for the welfare of patients or the public health;

3. MPOs (and their foundations) that receive advertising, grants, convention and meeting support, project support, payments . . . and other tangible benefits from Pharma in which such funding represents a substantial percentage of their earnings;
4. MPOs whose actions violate medical ethics to benefit their Pharma funders and their own members;
5. MPO leaders (key opinion leaders—KOLs) who control the policies of their MPOs for their own benefit and the benefit of their Pharma funders;
6. KOLs who profit from projects, prestige, honoraria, and connections with Pharma, and reap perquisites, prestige, and influence from the MPOs;
7. KOLs whose yearly total of Pharma funding represents a substantial percentage of their earnings as practicing physicians or physician educators; and
8. All physicians whose actions violate medical ethics to benefit their Pharma funders and to generate payments for themselves. (p. 2)

He argues that influence by "Big Pharma" limits consideration of approaches apart from expensive drug therapy such as prevention and public health measures in medical practice. Consider a review by Grouse of the program of an American College of Cardiology annual meeting.

I found a prominent listing of more than 350 Pharma and other medical companies that would be exhibiting at the convention. In the list of more than 250 scientific sessions that are enumerated, there were:
- No sessions whose title indicates any coverage of public health issues of cardiology;
- No session that appeared to cover other healthcare professionals or alternative healthcare givers' role in cardiology;
- No sessions on cost issues or socioeconomic or epidemiologic issues in delivering cardiology care;
- No sessions on lack of access or minority issues in cardiology care; and
- Only 2 sessions on prevention of cardiovascular disease. . . .

Preventing illness, providing fair and universal care, and caring about the patient do not appear in the program. . . . It seems to me that most of them follow the long tradition of the AMA in securing the welfare of their members and lining their own pockets. (p. 7)

Pharma control of the KOLs of the specialty further increases its influence on MPOs. Grouse (2008) estimates that a typical specialty MPO could receive $14 million a year from Pharma, which, as he notes, is small change for a Pharma budget, most of which have revenue of $4–18 billion. He also raises concerns about a new source of Pharma revenue created by the AMA—licensing its physician Masterfile.[21]

Pharmaceutical Advertising in Professional Journals

Brody (2007) devotes an entire chapter to professional organizations and journal advertising. This funding source is often vital to support publication of a journal.

Some professional journals include almost as many ads, often multi-page full color ads, than articles. (See past issues, *Psychiatric Services*.) Studies of these ads reveal a variety of propaganda ploys as discussed in chapter 9.

Ghost Writing

Ghost writing is a common way that pharmaceutical companies promote their products. A research or medical writing company is hired by a pharmaceutical company to prepare articles that hide or underplay adverse effects of a drug or exaggerate benefits and arrange for academics to appear as authors and to place articles in professional journals.[22] Brody (2007) notes that instances of ghost writing have been recorded as far back as the 1960s and suggests that the practice is probably much older. Sales representatives promote ghostwritten articles to physicians as "proof" that a drug is safe and effective.[23] Universities, as well as the National Institute of Health (NIH), have been reluctant, until recently, to acknowledge the extent of ghostwriting and to take steps to stop it, for example, to issue a policy prohibiting this practice. Few academic medical centers have policies prohibiting such practices (LaCasse & Leo, 2010). Litigation involving 14,000 plaintiffs concerning the menopausal hormone therapy Prempro produced by Wyeth, reveals the breadth of these practices. Related documents were made public by intervention of *PLoS Medicine* and the *New York Times*. These documents highlight the planting of ghostwritten manuscripts in professional journals which:

- Mitigate perceived risks of hormone-associated breast cancer
- Promote unproven, off-label uses, including prevention of dementia and Parkinson's disease.
- Raise questions about the safety and efficacy of competing therapies (competitive messaging)
- Defend cardiovascular benefits, despite lack of benefit in RCTs
- Position low-dose hormone therapy. (Fugh-Berman, 2010, p. 5)

Instructions were given by Wyeth to medical writing firms to play down the risk of breast cancer as a possible adverse effect (Singer, 2009d). In addition to ghostwritten articles and reviews and commentaries in medical journals used to "promote unproven benefits and downplay harms of this therapy and to cast competing therapies in a negative light" (p. 1), supplements were prepared and distributed to physicians.

> The articles were published in medical journals between 1998 and 2005—continuing even though a big federal study was suspended in 2002 after researchers found that menopausal women who took certain hormones had an increased risk of invasive breast cancer and heart disease. (Singer, 2009d)

Ross and his colleagues (2008) reviewed guest authorship and ghostwriting in publications related to rofecoxib (Vioxx). They concluded that:

> This case-study review of industry documents related to rofecoxib demonstrates that Merck used a systematic strategy to facilitate the publication of guest

authored and ghost written medical literature. Articles related to rofecoxib were frequently authored by Merck employees but attributed first authorship to external, academically affiliated investigators who did not always disclose financial support from Merck, although financial support of the study was nearly always provided. Similarly, review articles related to rofecoxib were frequently prepared by unacknowledged authors employed by medical publishing companies and attributed authorship to investigators who often did not disclose financial support from Merck. (p. 8 of 20)

This review was based on documents discovered in lawsuits concerning this pain drug. Vioxx was taken off the market in 2004 because of evidence linking it to heart attacks. The company paid $4.85 billion to settle tens of thousands of lawsuits filed by former Vioxx patients or their families (Saul, 2008). A firm called Current Medical Directions working for Pfizer arranged for 87 articles on the blockbuster antidepressant Zoloft (sertraline) (Healy, 2004). Fifty-five were published in journals including the *New England Journal of Medicine, Journal of the American Medical Association, Archives of General Psychiatry*, and the *American Journal of Psychiatry* by 2001. Healy (2004) estimated that in only five cases were the authors likely to have the raw data from studies they reported. Such drugs have a rare but serious side effect called akathisia characterized by a severe agitation and distortion of reality. "It is in a state of akathisia that a number of people taking SSRIs have committed suicide or homicide" (Brody, 2007, p. 133).

PHYSICIANS, STOCKHOLDERS, AND BIOTECHNOLOGY CORPORATIONS

The manufacturing of and marketing of medical devices is another billion-dollar industry with many players including physicians who create and/or promote devices, manufacturers, public relations and advertising firms, and regulatory agencies. (See Figure 3.2.) Here too conflicts of interest are rife. Physicians may hold stock in biotech or other kinds of commercial companies that may bias their decisions.[24] Financial ties may be hidden by promoters of a device. For example, during his talk at a convention Dr. Levin did not tell his audience that he was an investor in the company that manufactured a stent that he was promoting. He stood to share in up to $75 million in stock if the company achieved certain goals (Eichenwald & Kolata, 1999b).

In a recent 8–1 ruling, justices ruled if a device has been approved by the FDA, users cannot sue. "Makers of medical devices like implantable defibrillators or breast implants are immune from liability for personal injuries as long as the Food and Drug Administration approved the device before it was marketed and it meets the agency's specifications, the Supreme Court rules on Wednesday" (Greenhouse, 2008, p. 1). A physician may hold stock in a company that markets a product he uses such as metal hip replacement. Lack of a national database regarding outcomes of using a product prevents early discovery of harmful products. Sweden has a national registry and stopped use of a faulty hip replacement product after 30 harmful events were discovered. There is no such national registry in the United States. As a consequence, thousands of patients continued to have a faulty hip replacements inserted requiring removal and yet another replacement operation

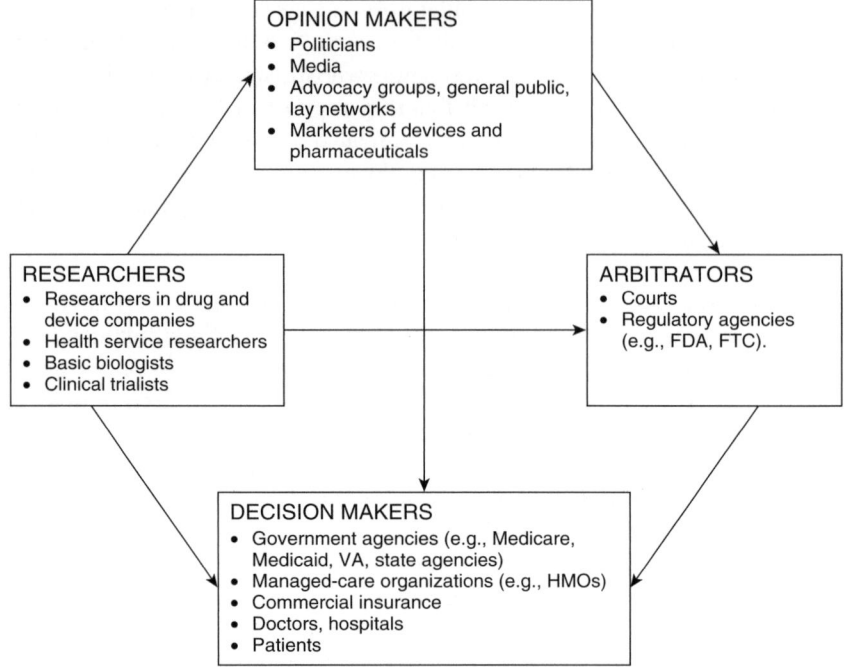

Figure 3.2. Influences on the use of new medical technology.
SOURCE: R. A. Deyo (2002). *Cascade Effects of Medical Technology Annual Review of Public Health* 23: p. 23–44.

(Meirer, 2008). Physicians promote expensive gene tests to make treatment decisions and to determine risk.[25]

PHARMACEUTICAL COMPANIES AND THE PUBLICATION OF BOOKS AND GUIDELINES

What may appear to be a book written by academic researchers with no ties to corporations with special interests may be an advertisement for a pharmaceutical or biotech company.[26] Clinical guidelines may reflect corporate influence rather than objective scientific reports. Warner and Roberts (2004) estimate that up to 90% of those who prepare clinical guidelines have some financial ties with for-profit corporations.

> Practice-guideline development is vulnerable to bias if members participating on panels have financial conflicts of interest with the companies whose products they are reviewing. Even if an organization is reviewing existing data—a seemingly straightforward, objective process—the results can be quite subjective, especially when the requirements of practice exceed the available data. (Kassirer, 2005, p. 101)

Guidelines may be based largely on industry-funded research (Healy & Thase, 2003).

> A remarkable example of drug company involvement in practice guidelines was the development of clinical guidelines for treating AIDS. A group of experts

was convened by Ortho Biotech, which funded the meeting that produced the guidelines. All six members of the panel had been paid by Ortho for consulting or lecturing. The guidelines which were published in Clinical Infectious Disease in 2004, recommended epoetin alpha, a drug marketed by Ortho Biotech, for treating anemia. According to Drummond Rennie, deputy editor of JAMA, "drug company sponsors see guideline-issuing bodies as perfect places to exert influence. The practice stinks" (Quoted from Dubovsky and Dubovsky, 2007, pp. 33–34)

Thus, in publications, as well as lectures, physicians with financial conflicts of interest provide educational material.

CONFLICTS OF INTEREST BETWEEN REGULATORY AGENCIES SUCH AS THE FDA AND THOSE WHO FUND AND PARTICIPATE IN THEM

As illustrated in some of the examples already discussed, there are troubling interconnections between staff in regulatory agencies such as the Federal Drug Administration (FDA) and pharmaceutical companies.[27] The pharmaceutical industry contributes $300 million in annual fees to the financing of the drug approval and regulation process (the FDA). A company can pay to have fast track approval of a drug. The United States is well behind European countries in removing dangerous drugs from general use such as Paxil in the treatment of depression in children and adolescents because of cases of suicide. A review of the approval process for several nonsteroidal anti-inflammatory drugs (NSAIDs) in the 1970s and 1980s revealed commercial bias and poor quality of basic research (Abraham, 1995). Consider the commonly used drug Naprosyn. Problems with a related study included some animals appearing to die many times and some reported "to have been weighed alive after their recorded date of death" (Brody, 2007, p. 118). The FDA has been accused of acting as an accomplice in allowing hiding of adverse events in clinical trials.[28]

Experts serving on panels have had significant financial ties to the pharmaceutical industry in the form of speaking fees, consultantships, and research grants. Few efforts were made to screen out people with conflicts of interest such as stock holdings in a company. In one egregious example, a panel that favored marketing the controversial painkillers Bextra and Vioxx would have made the opposite recommendation if the experts with industry ties had been excluded from voting (Harris & Berenson, 2005). New rules proposed would not allow anyone whose financial interests in a company with a product being reviewed—or its competitors—to exceed $50,000 in stock ownership, consulting fees, or research grants to serve on an advisory committee. Those with small financial interests could participate in discussions but would not be allowed to vote.[29] Concerns about the due diligence of the FDA are illustrated by Thalidomide.[30] This drug was not removed from the market in the United States until long after it was removed in Europe, resulting in continuing prescriptions being written for patients long after it was clearly shown that harm was a strong possibility. Other distressing examples include halcyon, (a sedative) fen-phen (prescribed for weight loss), and Rezulin (prescribed for diabetes) (Brody, 2007).[31] There is no regulation of "off label" uses of drugs, which is rampant. Politicians may exert pressure on the FDA. Concerns about the approval process of the FDA have resulted in many challenges, sometimes by advocacy groups working together with members of Congress.

ADVOCACY GROUPS AND DRUG COMPANIES

Ties between pharmaceutical companies and nonprofits are illustrated by the following example:

> After a study last week showed Vytorin, an expensive combination of two drugs for cholesterol, worked no better than cheap Zocor alone in reducing artery plaque that can lead to heart attacks, the American Heart Association came to the drug's defense.
> In a statement issued on Jan. 15, the day after the report's release, the heart association said the study was too limited to draw conclusions about Vytorin's ability to reduce heart attacks or deaths. The group advised patients not to abruptly stop taking it without consulting their doctors.
> What the association did not note in its statement, however, was that the group receives nearly $2 million a year from Merck Schering-Plough Pharmaceuticals, the joint venture that markets Vytorin. (Saul, 2008b, p. B1)[32]

The National Alliance for the Mentally Ill (NAMI) is funded in part by pharmaceutical companies. NAMI received $23 million in drug industry grants between October 2007 and October 2009. A list of sponsors donating more from $5,000.00 is posted on its website in reaction to Senator Grassley's investigations. Children and Adults With Attention Deficit Disorder (CHADD) also receives money from the pharmaceutical industry (e.g., see Harris, 2009b).[33] The National Resource Center on ADHD is the CDC (Center for Disease Control) funded national clearinghouse for "evidence-based" information about ADHD (Attention Deficit Hyperactivity Disorder). This center claims to serve "both professionals and the general public by providing information on the most relevant topics" including diagnosis of ADHD, treatment options, school and workplace challenges and guidelines, and tips on parenting, time-management, legal issues, social skills, coaching and more. This organization, like most others, promotes a particular view of a problem. For example, related material states that ADHD "is a neurobiological condition that affects an estimated 3–7 percent of the population. In most cases ADHD is thought to be inherited."

The report "Sucked into the Herceptin maelstrom" by Jane Keiden (2007), a physician, illustrates how easy it is to get caught up in promotion of a new drug, spurred in part by advocacy groups (Keidan, 2007). Dr. Keidan was diagnosed with HER2 positive breast cancer in August 2005. A campaign on the BreastCancerCare website <http://www.breastcancercare.org.uk/> promoted the availability of Herceptin to all HER2 positive women. Herceptin was described as a very effective agent in both medical press sources and the media. Dr. Keidan became involved in writing letters to promote the availability of this to all women with breast cancer who were HER2 positive. She noted that the "Herceptin campaign rose to fever pitch as several women took their PCTs [Primary Care Trusts] or trusts to court" (p. 18); articles appeared almost daily in the press, as well as in features on radio and television. "I began to feel that if I did not receive this drug that I would have very little chance of surviving my cancer." When she discussed taking Herceptin with her oncologist, he raised concerns about side effects of the drug, which received little attention either on the breast cancer care website or in the media. The 50% benefit widely quoted in the medical and non-medical press "actually translated into a 4–5% benefit to me, which equally balanced the cardiac risk." She summed up by saying that her story "illustrates how even a medically trained and usually rational woman becomes vulnerable when diagnosed as having a potentially life-threatening illness."[34]

FINANCIAL TIES BETWEEN CORPORATIONS AND UNIVERSITIES

Many have raised concerns about the increased corporatization of universities and related incestuous relationships.[35] Cutbacks in public funding for universities have encouraged both researchers and university administrators to pursue collaboration with businesses and industries. The push to get research grants has increased as the states have reduced funding for higher education. Universities, such as the University of California at Berkeley, have entered into multi-million dollar contracts with industries to jointly pursue research. This kind of interlinking between universities, with their historical obligation to pursue truth wherever it may lead, and corporations, whose bottom line is making money, for example, by guarding research findings from competitors, has long been of concern (Veblan, 1918) because of potential conflicts of values (Bauer, 2001). Bok (2003) suggests that "we have allowed what should have been a pillar of professionalism to deteriorate into a massive e-Bay, with the users hoping to obtain something of value without paying the full price for it; and a variety of commercial predators taking full advantage of these hopes to line their own pockets" (p. 211).

Bauer (2004) argues that conflicts of interest have resulted in research cartels and knowledge monopolies that impede the pursuit of knowledge.

> Increasingly corporate organization of science has led to *knowledge monopolies*, which, with the unwitting help of uncritical mass media, effect a kind of censorship. Since corporate scientific organizations also control the funding of research, by denying funds for unorthodox work they function as *research cartels* as well as knowledge monopolies. (p. 643)[36]

Marcia Angell (2004) points out the influence of the Bayh-Dole Act of 1980:

> Bayh-Dole enabled universities and small businesses to patent discoveries emanating from research sponsored by the National Institutes of Health, the major distributor of tax dollars for medical research, and then to grant exclusive licenses to drug companies. Until then, taxpayer-financed discoveries were in the public domain, available to any company that wanted to use them. But now universities, where most NIH-sponsored work is carried out, can patent and license their discoveries, and charge royalties. Similar legislation permitted the NIH itself to enter into deals with drug companies that would directly transfer NIH discoveries to industry. (M. Angell, 2004, p. 7)

Critics such as Sheldon Krimski argue that academic science has been far too eager to sell its integrity and to deny that integrity has been lost. He sees the major loss of scientific values in precisely the place that Bok (2003) believes values have been protected, the questions that scientists choose to study. He argues that no meaningful reform will occur until certain roles are kept strictly separate:

- those who produce knowledge in academia and those who have a financial stake in the knowledge.
- those who have fiduciary interest in protecting human research subjects and those with a financial stake in products being tested; and
- those who assess therapies versus those with a financial stake in the success or failure of the products. (Brody, 2007, pp. 80–81)

Brody (2007), as well as others, have raised alarms regarding the quality of pharmaceutical research; that is, how good is it? Consider the Celecoxib long-term arthritis safety study, known as the Class Study. The original article published in the *Journal of the American Medical Association* listed 16 authors. They reported only data from the first six months. However, they had collected a year's worth of data and the last six months showed an increasing number of adverse side effects of a very serious nature. (See also Bekelman et al., 2003.)

LAWYERS, PHARMACEUTICAL COMPANIES, AND RESEARCHERS

Large corporations can afford to hire lawyers to threaten researchers who make public research findings unfavorable to a product. Brody (2007) devotes a chapter to the suppression of research data facilitated by threats of legal action. Consider Nancy Olivieri, an internationally respected hematologist. Her research suggested that a drug manufactured by Apotex for iron overload in thalassemia, a severe form of inherited anemia, may not be superior to its competitors (Brody, 2007, pp. 98–102). She disclosed her results despite signing a contract forbidding such disclosure. Apotox aggressively defended the safety and effectiveness of the drug. This example is also infamous because of failure of the hospital in which Olivieri worked (the Hospital For Sick Children) to defend her. Nor did the University of Toronto help her.[37] In his blog (<http://brodyhooked.blogspot.com>), Brody brings up this example in the context of Dr. Claire Bomdardier being hired by the University of Toronto. "Dr. Bombardier is well known to us critics of medicine-Pharma relationships as the principal author of the VIGOR study (*New England Medical Journal*, 2000) that purported to show that rofecoxib (Vioxx) caused significantly fewer serious gastrointestinal bleeds than a standard anti-inflammatory medication for arthritis" (Aug. 30, 2008).

> VIGOR actually contained within it much of the data needed to conclude that Vioxx caused more heart attacks than GI bleeds prevented—four years before Vioxx was finally taken off the market—even though the authors, apparently with the active complicity of the *NEJM* editors, did their best to conceal this inconvenient truth. (<http://www.brodyhooked.blogspot.com/>)

This is the third case in which the University of Toronto has been implicated in scandals related to taking money from drug firms. Another case concerned Dr. David Healy, who was hired by the University of Toronto to head a psychiatric research institute, then de-hired when he raised concerns about adverse effects of Prozac, which was manufactured by Eli Lilly, a major donor to the institute.

Another well-known example involved the giant UK drugstore Boots. Betty J. Dong of the University of California at San Francisco (UCSF) and her colleagues were commissioned by Flint Laboratories to investigate the effectiveness of Synthroid compared to three other thyroid preparations. Flint was purchased by Boots Pharmaceuticals. Dong and her colleagues concluded that Synthroid was no better than other products; that is, generic drugs were as good as the expensive one. Dong's work was attacked and a smear campaign launched against her. Boots prevented publication of her work. In 1993 Boots was bought by BASF AG for $1.4 billion. An expose in the *Wall Street Journal* was an embarrassment to the new owner (see Brody, 2007, for more detail). Yet again we see the important role of journalists in exposing cover-ups and the often complicit role of universities and hospitals in participating in them.

LAWYERS, CONSUMERS, AND STATE GOVERNMENTS

Lawyers also play a key role in consumer groups and in protecting individuals who wish to share research results, who expose fraud and corruption, and who allege harm due to products used. Lawyers are involved in class action lawsuits brought against health-related industries. Consider state lawsuits brought against manufacturers of Abilify, Geodon, Risperdal, Seroquel, and Zyprexa.

> Lilly has received civil investigative demands or subpoenas from the attorneys general of a number of states. Most of these requests are now part of a multistate investigative effort being coordinated by an executive committee of attorneys general. Lilly says they are aware of 26 states participating in this joint effort and they anticipate that additional states will join the investigation. These attorneys general are seeking a broad range of Zyprexa documents, including remuneration of health care providers. (Retrieved on November 26, 2008, from <http://www.psychsearch.net/lawsuits, p. 1>)

> The State [of Florida] contends BMS [Bristol-Meyers Squibb] knowingly and willfully offered and paid illegal remuneration in the form of consulting arrangement fees to physicians to induce them to prescribe Abilify. The State contends that BMS's promotion of Abilify for pediatric use and to treat dementia-related psychosis violated the Food, Drug, and Cosmetic Act ("FDCA"), 21 U.S.C. " ~ 331 (a) & (d). Furthermore, the State contends that, during the relevant time period, these uses of Abilify were not medically accepted indications, as defined by 42 USC ' 1396r-8(k)(6) (uses approved under the FDCA or included in or approved for inclusion in specified drug compendia), and that certain State Medicaid Programs did not cover Abilify dispensed for these uses. In addition, the State contends that, during this time period, BMS knowingly

caused false and/or fraudulent claims to be submitted to its Medicaid program for Abilify for pediatric use and for dementia-related psychosis.

State of Louisiana v. Janssen

A multimillion dollar civil lawsuit against Janssen Pharmaceutical alleges unfair business practices and violations of consumer protection laws. The lawsuit seeks damages for increased medical costs due to side effects suffered and for increased Medicaid expenses due to misleading sales pitches. The suite was filed in connection with the production and marketing of the drug Risperdal.[38]

Professional organizations may join state associations in suing health insurers, for example, for alleged efforts to underpay physicians for claims.[39]

INTERACTIONS BETWEEN JOURNALISTS, JOURNALS, AND FOR-PROFIT COMPANIES

Journalists play a major role in deciding what research studies to report and which ones to ignore. Press releases describing alleged "startling" discoveries are often passed on to the public by journalists who are unskeptical of claims about risks or the effectiveness of a product or service.[40] Schwartz and her colleagues (2008) highlight the financial ties between journalists and pharmaceutical companies.

> One of the more astonishing forms of financial ties between journalists and drug companies is the sponsored award, which often involves lucrative cash prizes or opportunities for international travel. For example, Eli Lilly and Boehringer Ingelheim have cosponsored an award for "reporting on urinary incontinence," carrying a prize of international travel. Boehringer has an award for reporting on "chronic obstructive pulmonary disease," offering prizes worth €5000 each, Eli Lilly one for reporting on oncology, and Roche one for "obesity journalism," with a prize of €7500.
>
> Sometimes awards are sponsored by organizations that are themselves heavily funded by industry, such as the non-profit Mental Health America. Its 2007 annual report shows that almost half of its funds came from drug companies, including more than $1m each from Bristol Myers Squibb, Lilly, and Wyeth.
>
> Studies of similar interactions between the industry and medical professionals show that they can produce feelings of reciprocity in the beneficiary and can affect prescribing judgments. (p. 1203)

Thus, as these authors note, although journalists have an important role in revealing interconnections between physicians, researchers, and the drug industry, perks from these sources may bias what is reported.[41] Reports in the media affect our opinions about treatments (but not necessarily our decisions) (Passalacqua et al., 2004). Expensive drugs for treating cancer that have adverse side effects may be heavily promoted even though they have modest effects on prolonging life. For example, Erbitux, a drug for treating lung cancer costs $80,000 for an 18-week regime, but increases survival by only 1.2 months (Silverman, 2008).

SUMMARY

Conflicts of interest among players contribute to propaganda in the helping professions as illustrated in this chapter. The assertion by pharmaceutical companies that there is a free market is contradicted by a number of factors including the wide disparities in the price different groups pay for drugs, the suppression of generic competitors, and widespread fraud. The influence of Big Pharma in all areas of professional activity including professional organizations, research, teaching (including continuing education), funding of research, peer review, and professional practice, is so extensive and so clearly inappropriate and unethical, it is hard to believe. Reactions may be: Could this be true? How could we let this happen? Isn't she exaggerating? But the related documentation clearly shows the enormous influence, often bordering on or actually consisting of corruption and fraud, especially when looked at from the perspective of patients/clients and of students who sign up for an education, not a corporate indoctrination. Indeed, it is only because conflicts of interests among involved players has become so great ("over the top"), that a counter-reaction has ensued including related policy and law changes such as no longer taking money from pharmaceutical or device makers for continuing education. These nefarious relationships are often hidden. As always, censorship (partiality in the use of evidence) is a key propaganda tactic. It is often difficult to discover what is hidden. We must seek it out.

4

Propaganda Analysis: Different Levels

We can approach propaganda on different levels ranging from philosophical and sociological analyses to strategy (device) focused approaches such as use of particular persuasion ploys and informal fallacies. Some of our best-known writers including Machiavelli, Orwell, and Huxley, are among the many contributors to this area. Analyses that focus on propaganda ploys, such as appeal to fear, provide an incomplete view. They omit sociological analyses, as well as ethical and epistemic issues of truth, falsity, and rationality; they ignore philosophical issues, such as the criteria used to investigate claims (Cunningham, 2002).[1] Propaganda seeks to "induce action, adherence and participation with as little thought as possible" (Ellul, 1965, p. 180). There is an indifference to truth to attain certain goals. (See Table 4.1.)

> propaganda, . . . at its very core, is an epistemically structured phenomenon: It exploits information; it poses as knowledge; it generates belief systems and tenacious convictions; it skews perceptions; it systematically disregards superior epistemic values such as truth and understanding; it corrupts reasoning and the respect for evidence, rigor, and procedural safeguards; it supplies ersatz certainties. . . . because of these inversions, [propaganda] is inherently a profoundly unethical social state of affairs. All this means that what needs to be acknowledged and hasn't yet is that what we have been calling 'propaganda' for most of the last century is originally, primarily, and unavoidably a philosophically significant idea. (Cunningham, 2002, p. 4)

Many programs emphasizing critical thinking focus on a semantic approach to propaganda—identifying tactics of manipulation (fallacies) such as card-stacking. A focus on individual statements and claims increased the chances that political preferences will obscure propaganda of favored groups and in certain venues such as education (Sproule, 1994).[2]

JACQUE ELLUL'S SOCIOLOGICAL ANALYSIS

Ellul (1965) makes a compelling argument for approaching the study of propaganda at the highest level, which takes into consideration the kind of society in which we live. This is the technological society, dominated by the mass media in which traditional sources of grounding, such as religion and the family, have waned, leaving us

Table 4.1 THE TEN COMMANDMENTS OF PROPAGANDA

1. Divide and conquer.
Possibly the oldest political tactic known to man. As long as the people are busy fighting each other, they will never know their real enemy. Hate speech is valuable to this end.

2. Tell the people what they want.
Not to be confused with telling them what they want to hear, you are telling them what they want, and why they cannot live without it.

3. The bigger the lie, the more people will believe it.
Coined by Joseph Goebbels, this truth has been proven time and time again, especially in times of war.

4. Always appeal to the lowest common denominator.
Abraham Lincoln supposedly said, "You can't fool all of the people, all of the time." But, if you can fool enough of the people, enough of the time, you can get away with anything. The trick is to find the common hopes and fears of the largest majority.

5. Generalize as much as possible.
Specifics are not very important. Most people would prefer to think in the simplest terms possible—black and white, good and evil.

6. Use "expert" testimonial.
A degree and screen presence is pretty much all you need to be an authority on anything in the modem world. People like celebrities.

7. Always refer to the "authority" of your office.
Once your authority is established, you need to periodically remind the people of it. It will add credibility to your purpose.

8. Stack the cards with "information"
Statistics and facts work wonderfully, especially when the average person only partially understands them, and when conflicting data is censored.

9. A confused people are easily led.
When a person hears the truth, he won't know it, because it will be lumped together with disinformation, half-truths, and lies.

10. Get the "plain folks" onto the "bandwagon"
John Doe is your propaganda agent. Middle Americans will "relate" to him, and so will their friends, and their friends.

And remember: when all else fails, use FEAR

SOURCE: Expanded and updated from the original *Seven Rules of Propaganda* identified by the Institute for Propaganda Analysis in 1937.

more adrift and in need of guidance. He suggests that propaganda fulfills this vital need. Propaganda both creates needs and offers solutions for them (Ellul, 1965). This is precisely the method of "disease mongering" promoted by the biomedical industry and involved players in which common risks and behaviors are transformed into medical illnesses (disorders). Ellul's (1965) analysis of propaganda is sociological, psychological, and philosophical. For anyone who wishes to think deeply about propaganda, *Propaganda: The Formation of Men's Attitudes* (Ellul, 1965) is must reading. The most insightful analyses of propaganda draw on his work.

Ellul distinguishes between political and sociological propaganda. He refers to propaganda as it is traditionally known, as *political propaganda* in which techniques are used to alter behavior of the public. Here, the choice of methods is deliberate and the desired goals are precise (p. 62). He defined sociological propaganda as methods used in a society "to integrate the maximum number of individuals into itself, to unify its members' behavior according to a pattern, to spread its style of life abroad, and thus to impose itself on other groups" (p. 62). Ellul (1965) views *sociological propaganda* as the cement that holds a technological society together. Not all propaganda is intentional. Much is not. Propaganda seeks to reach the individual through psychological channels.[3] A variety of methods are used to encourage emotional responses rather than critical appraisal of competing views.

Propaganda works partly through suggestions (associative learning) and other psychological processes, such as desires to be one of the "in group." Misleading language such as euphemisms is used. It appeals to myths, stereotypes, and dispositions common to many people; it requires mass communication that appeals to accepted myths reflecting popular beliefs. It would take too much time to individually target the unique concerns, hopes, values, and goals of each individual. Popular personalities embody these myths. Propaganda must be used in a democracy to "manipulate the masses" because the masses have come to participate in political affairs (Ellul, 1965, p. 121). Yet to be effective, it must give the impression of being personal; applying to the individual; little distinction is made between the group and the self. Government must make timely decisions, it cannot wait for popular opinion for guidance; so it acts and then manipulates opinion. A variety of strategies are used to create an illusion of openness, as well as to direct attention away from lack of openness and consideration of divergent views.

Propaganda as Integral to a Technological Society

Ellul links the prevalence of propaganda in modern society to the creation of the technological society. We live in a technological society, one pervaded by technicians of all sorts, including millions in the helping professions. Technique refers to all methods rationally arrived at and having absolute efficiency in all areas of human activity (Ellul, 1964). It refers to standardized means for achieving a given outcome. Stivers (2001) argues that our belief in technology has become a belief in magic—a belief that technology can solve all problems. Ellul (1964) approaches technology in a broad sense, far beyond the invention of machines. We live in a technological milieu. The mass media, advertising, public relations, and bureaucracies are techniques. Case records and surveillance systems are technologies. The psychiatric classification system (the DSM) is a technique. Human relations and psychotherapy are techniques. Technology presses toward efficiency, standardization, systematization, and the elimination of variability, which requires inattention to individual differences. We spend our time looking at, listening to, and talking to machines, now including Twitter, Facebook, and YouTube (Richtel, 2010). Thus, today's propaganda is a "new propaganda" as it permeates all areas of our lives.

> It is a matter of reaching and encircling the whole man and all men. Propaganda tries to surround man by all possible routes, in the realm of feelings as well as

ideas, by playing on his will or on his needs, through his conscious and his unconscious, assailing him in both his private and his public life. It furnishes him with a complete system for explaining the world, and provides immediate incentives to action. . . . Through the myth it creates, propaganda imposes a complete range of intuitive knowledge, susceptible of only one interpretation, unique and one-sided and precluding any divergence. (Ellul, 1965, p. 11)

In this kind of society, all forms of information are dominated by the imperative of *la technique* (Ellul, 1973). Individual thoughts, feelings, and behaviors are reduced to abstractions; they are objectified (stripped of individual variations and meaning) requiring technological fixes, such as therapy and pills, to attempt to regain meaning.[4] Cognitive therapy reduces us to our thoughts. Biological views reduce us to our brain chemistry. Both ignore cultural contexts and individual subjectivities and complex interactions among them. There is a preoccupation with productivity and cost-effective results even in areas such as birth and death. Pragmatic concerns, such as broadcast ratings, shape information and message exchange; values other than truth and honest instruction predominate (Cunningham, 2002, pp. 103–4). Different economic systems such as capitalism are techniques as are different kinds of military systems. Technologies in different areas are more and more closely integrated in a system of technologies so that, if a change occurs in one area, change occurs in others. Ellul's sociological analysis of the role of propaganda in a technological society requires consideration of the "big picture" (the total context) in understanding propaganda in the helping professions and possible remedies including the consumer-oriented society in which we live, defining ourselves by the commodities we possess, promoted by endless advertisements for goods. Propaganda is an indispensable condition for technical progress and creation of a technological civilization; it integrates us into this world.

Ellul (1965) views propaganda as inevitable in a technological society to solve problems created by technology, to play on maladjustments, and to integrate us into such a world. Propaganda is the means used to prevent increasing mechanization and technological organization from being felt as too oppressive and to persuade us to submit with grace (p. vxiii).[5] "The aim of modern propaganda is no longer to modify ideas, but to provoke action. It is no longer to change adherence to a doctrine, but to make an individual cling irrationally to a process of action." Although much propaganda is planned by organized groups, Ellul (1965) suggests that even more results from the increasing development and integration of technique (Ellul, 1965, p. 25). It is propaganda that encourages consumers to buy the goods that fuel the economy and maintains the myth of work needed to encourage people to work long hours.[6] He distinguishes between vertical propaganda made by a political or religious head who acts from a superior position of his authority and horizontal propaganda, which he views as a more recent development. Here propaganda is made inside the group. In vertical propaganda, the apparatus of the mass media of communication is needed whereas in horizontal propaganda, an organization of people is required.

Ellul (1965) argues that we need propaganda because we exist in a mass society deprived of traditional groups and must draw on our own resources, which are inadequate to handle the complexities of life in a mass society and the resultant anxieties caused, for example, by the hostile impulses of others. Such an individualistic society is fertile ground for modern propaganda. "What man thinks either is totally without effect or must remain unsaid ... propaganda is the instrument to attain this effect ... [There is] a radical devaluation of thought" (p. 180). Indeed, Ellul (1965) argues that in a technological society such as our own, there is a separation between thought and action (because no real action is possible that would have an effect on the corporations and bureaucracies that influence our lives), as well as a separation between public and personal opinion. "He does not need to think in order to act; his action is determined by the techniques he uses and by the sociological conditions" (p. 179). Such splits between thought and action create an "attitude of surrender"; of resignation combined with occasional defensive reflexes of "flight into involvement" (p. 182). Propaganda prevents confusion created by contradictory facts; it provides group belonging. One can be an "insider." Propaganda offers "ready-made opinions for the unthinking."[7] Not to have an opinion is to be "out-of-touch." It provides us with ready-made justifications for prejudices and valued ideologies. It decreases anxiety and prevents confusion about "what to think," which occurs when contradictory facts and messages are considered. We can feel superior to the excluded or allegedly deluded (e.g., those who question the assumptions that "mental illness" is a brain disease).

> But one of man's greatest inner needs is to feel that he is right. This need takes several forms. First, man needs to be right in his own eyes. He must be able to assert that he is right, that he does what he should, that he is worthy of his own respect. Then, man needs to be right in the eyes of those around him, his family, his milieu, his co-workers, his friends, his country. Finally, he feels the need to belong to a group, which he considers right and which he can proclaim as just, noble, and good. (Ellul, 1965, p. 155)
>
> ...
>
> Man, eager for self-justification, throws himself in the direction of a propaganda that justifies him and thus eliminates one of the sources of his anxiety. Propaganda dissolves contradictions and restores to man a unitary world in which the demands are in accord with the facts. . . . It permits him to participate in the world around him without being in conflict with it. (p. 159)

The technological society in which we live creates negative psychological and social consequences including fragmentation and splits such as that between beliefs and actions. It is often impossible to act on our beliefs and our actions have little effect on the large interrelated bureaucracies that influence our lives. These organizations have a life of their own—pressing toward greater efficiency, which requires ignoring the qualitative—unique individual differences (Perez-Alvarez et al., 2008). More and more the subjectivity—the uniqueness of individuals including their unique desires—is squeezed out and individuals are treated as code numbers, perhaps by a computer, which tells them "We value your e-mail." Diagnostic Related Groups (DRGs) are required for hospital admission.[8] The press for standardization and efficiency inherent in a technological society can be seen in the use of code numbers and labels for an ever-increasing number and variety of behaviors viewed as "mental illness" in the popular *Diagnostic and Statistical Manual of Mental Disorders, DSM-IV-TR* (American Psychiatric Association), now numbering in the hundreds. DSM 5 is on track to be even more inclusive with even more codes to refer to even more behaviors. This classification system must be used for third party payment in the mental health system, as well as by researchers who seek funding for projects concerning related behaviors, thoughts, and feelings (e.g., anxiety, depression). Increased standardization and efficiency can also be seen in the many examples of goal displacement in agencies and organizations in the health care system, for example, focusing on easily measurable outcomes that may not reflect those valued by clients (or promoted as valuable by the organization), because they are easy to measure on check-boxes. This press for standardization and efficiency combines with the emphasis on productivity.

Pervasive propaganda (the systemic technology in such a society) creates distrust of others since, more than ever in such a society, we are "on our own," yet are approached as a mass of individuals, as when watching TV or listening to the radio, or using the Internet (even when we are alone in our living room). We now learn life skills in schools rather than from our parents. Children learn how to play during structured games rather than with other children who learn on their own to negotiate the complex interactions in play and have fun in the process. Parents read books about how to raise their children. As Stivers (2001) emphasizes, the growth of "how-to-books" reflects our technological society in which standardized means are used to attain certain ends. In the society Ellul describes, there are constant alternating themes of terror, for example, fears of crime and of impersonal forces that may affect our lives (e.g., economic depressions), and of self-assertion (calls to take action when no real action is possible), which results in "continuous emotional contrast" (p. 179). This contrast is very wearing, psychologically and emotionally.[9]

Integrative Propaganda

Ellul (1965) distinguishes between *agitation* propaganda and *integration* propaganda. The purpose of agitation propaganda is to encourage resentment as a route to rebellion. In integrative propaganda, we become "adjusted" to accepted patterns of behavior. Indeed people who do not follow accepted patterns of behavior are often labeled as deviant, mentally ill, or criminal. Integrative propaganda is the most insidious kind because we do not rebel against it. Ellul challenges the belief that the purpose of propaganda is to change opinions; he argued that the major function is to maintain the status quo and encourage action or inaction that maintain this or takes it in a similar direction. The purpose of psychological methods, such as group integration and group unanimity, is to neutralize or eliminate aberrant individuals. The concepts of adjustment and adaptation are popular in the United States. Much of this kind of propaganda occurs under the guise of education.[10] Education is central to the effectiveness of propaganda; it is a pre-condition. Ellul refers to this as *pre-propaganda*—the conditioning of minds with vast amounts of incoherent information, already dispensed for ulterior purposes and posing as "facts" and as "education." This creates automatic reactions to particular words and symbols. This background helps to structure/frame issues in certain ways making further stratagems more likely to be successful. Political, social, and economic aims are pursued in the guise of educating professionals and helping clients. Indicators of indoctrination versus education include censoring alternative views and evidence against preferred views (Gambrill, 1997). Ellul suggests that intellectuals are the most vulnerable to propaganda because: (1) they are exposed to the largest amount of second-hand unverifiable information;

(2) they feel a need to have an opinion on important questions; and (3) they view themselves as capable of "judging for themselves." The broad-ranging integrative effects of propaganda (of which we are often unaware) and its presence even in educational institutions renders critical thinking an uphill battle.

> No contrast can be tolerated between teaching and propaganda, between the critical spirit formed by higher education and the exclusion of independent thought. One must utilize the education of the young to condition them to what comes later. (p. 13)
>
> ...
>
> To be effective, propaganda must constantly short-circuit all thought and decision. It must operate on the individual at the level of the unconscious. He must not know that he is being shaped by outside forces . . . but some central core in him must be reached in order to release the mechanism in the unconscious which will provide the appropriate— and expected— action. (p. 27)

Information and Propaganda

Cunningham (2002) suggests that the relationship between information and propaganda has been described "most chillingly" by Ellul.

> It is a commonplace that propaganda involves the modification of perceptions and the manipulation of beliefs, but as it stands that sort of standard definitional portrayal is simplistic and inadequate. So too is the popular assumption that propaganda is largely a skein of lies. According to Ellul (1973), it is precisely this latter kind of simplistic assumption that facilitates the propagandist's role in lulling the public into insouciance by concealing its real nature as "an enterprise for perverting the significance of events and of insinuating intentions" (p. 58). (Cunningham, 2002, p. 97)

Propaganda methods are often "rational." "The problem is to create an irrational response on the basis of rational and factual elements" (Ellul, 1965, p. 86). Information is used to forward (often hidden) agendas.

> propaganda uses facts and poses as truthful information; it instrumentalizes truth; it does falsify, but in ways that involve the use of truths and facts as much as possible; it exploits expectations and confusion; it overloads audiences with information; it relies upon murkier epistemic moves such as suggestion, innuendo, implication, and truncated modes of reasoning; it accords priority to credibility and being believed; it discourages higher epistemic values such as reflection, understanding and reasoning, and the accumulation of evidence and its procedural safeguards. (Cunningham, 2002, p. 98)

But, because this creates an irrational situation, it remains propaganda, inner control over the individual by an outside interest that deprives him of himself (p. 87).

Ellul's portrait of the symbiotic linkage between information and propaganda is predicated on a vision of the moral and psychological emptiness within modern men and women. He speaks of the individual's laziness, the need for simple explanations and coherence, and an affirmation of his own worth; the loneliness for which propaganda is the remedy; the need to belong, to believe, and to obey; our intellectual sloth and desire for security, the state of collective passivity; the need to be right and to belong to a group viewed as right, the need "not to be just . . . but to *seem* just, to find reasons for asserting that one is just. He suggests that this corresponds to our refusal to see our own reality. As Ellul argues, we typically have little time or opportunity to become informed about vital issues that affect our lives. Propaganda fills this need and prevents troubling confusion." Thus, as he points out, we are complicit in the process of being influenced. We open the Internet, go to the movies, and turn on the radio or TV. Cunningham (2002) suggests that the weaknesses of many isolated individuals add up to a social pathology that both enables and invites the seductive effects of propaganda (pp. 105–6).

Propaganda Methods

Methods and mediums include education, publicity, public relations, and psychotherapy. Channels include radio, television, magazines, the Internet, and newspapers.[11] Huxley (1958) suggests that

> the early advocates of universal literacy and a free press envisaged only two possibilities: the propaganda might be true, or it might be false. They did not foresee what in fact has happened, above all in our Western capitalist democracies—the development of a vast mass communication industry, concerned in the main neither with the true nor the false, but with the unreal, the more or less totally irrelevant. (p. 267)

Ellul (1964) emphasizes uses of two quite different categories of techniques:

> the first is a complex of mechanical techniques (principally radio, press, and motion pictures) which permit direct communication with a very large number of persons collectively, while simultaneously addressing each individual in the group. These techniques possess an extraordinary power of persuasion and a remarkable capacity to bring psychic and intellectual pressure to bear. The second category consists of a complex of psychological (and even psychoanalytical) techniques which give access to exact knowledge of the human psyche. It can thus be motivated with considerable confidence in the results. (Ellul, 1964, pp. 363–64)

Indeed, Bernay's creation of the public relations industry made stunning use of psychoanalytic techniques (Ewen, 1976). Propaganda methods are used to create reality. Reality is distorted. Images are used "to form rather than inform" (Ellul, 1964, p. 371). "The essence of propaganda is to act upon the human subconscious but to leave men the illusion of complete freedom" (p. 372). Discussions and debate are anathema to propaganda. Ellul argues that propaganda ceases where simple dialogue begins. Indicators of propaganda include a blind confidence in beliefs, a lack of tolerance for criticism, and a lack of responsiveness to well-argued alternative views. He suggests that if we practice a profession, in addition to financial rewards, we must adorn it with idealistic or moral justification. "It becomes our calling, and we will not tolerate its being questioned" (Ellul, 1965, p. 157). Ellul considers the view of propaganda as the defense of an idea as a dangerously elementary view of propaganda given its "manipulation of the mob's subconscious" (Ellul, 1964, p. 373). He argues that propaganda requires mass communication that appeals to accepted myths reflecting popular beliefs.

> Each medium is particularly suited to a certain type of propaganda. The movies and human contacts are the best media for sociological propaganda in terms of social climate, slow infiltration, progressive inroads, and over-all integration. Public meetings and posters are more suitable tools for providing shock propaganda, intense but temporary, leading to immediate action. The press tends more to shape general views; radio is likely to be an instrument of international action and psychological warfare, whereas the press is used domestically. In any case, it is understood that because of this specialization not one of these instruments may be left out; they must *all* be used in combination. The propagandist uses a keyboard and composes a symphony. (Ellul, 1965, p. 10)
> . . .
> Finally, the propagandist must use not only all of the instruments, but also different forms of propaganda. . . . Direct propaganda, aimed at modifying opinions and attitudes, must be preceded by propaganda that is sociological in character, slow, general, seeking to create a climate, an atmosphere of favorable preliminary attitudes. No direct propaganda can be effective without pre-propaganda, which, without direct or noticeable aggression, is limited to creating ambiguities, reducing prejudices, and spreading images, apparently without purpose. . . . Oral or written propaganda, which plays on opinions or sentiments, must be reinforced by propaganda of action, which produces new attitudes and thus joins the individual firmly to a certain movement. Here again, you cannot have one without the other. (p. 15)

Ellul's (1965) broad, integrative analysis carries us far beyond persuasion strategies, communication methods, and critical thinking focused on fallacies. So too do Cunningham's (2002) and Marlin's (2002) discussions at the ethical and epistemic levels of analysis. Cunningham (2002) argues that in academic research regarding propaganda there has been a willingness to accept the neutrality thesis concerning the consequences of propaganda. As he and others point out (e.g., Combs & Nimmo, 1993), propaganda is a form of pseudo-communication (p. 164), contrary to how it is presented in communication studies. Epistemic standards are valued only as a useful strategy—attention, credibility, and mere belief is the aim (Cunningham, 2002, p. 165). (See also later discussion of palaver.)

> Because it inverts principal epistemic values such as truth and truthfulness, reasoning and knowledge, and because of its wholesale negative impact upon voluntariness and human agency, and because it also exploits and reinforces a society's moral weaknesses, propaganda is not ethically neutral. Rather, it is an

inherently unethical social phenomenon. To describe propaganda without references to its unethical complexion is to fractionalize it and to minimize it. (Cunningham, 1976, p. 176)

Propaganda is concerned with illusions of reality.

PROPAGANDA ANALYSIS

Ellul's (1965) broad integrative view of propaganda alerts us that we must consider the "big picture" to understand propaganda and its effects and to discover ways to minimize its influence on our lives. Marlin's (2002) discussion of propaganda reflects this larger context. Questions he proposes include the following:

(1) What is the source?
(2) What is the message?
(3) Who stands to gain?
(4) What techniques are used?
(5) What are the contexts and truth-reliability?
(6) Have we been fair in our assessment?

Other questions include "What is the target audience?" "What are the effects?" and "What counterpropaganda methods are used?" (Jowett & O'Donnell, 2006). We can use these questions to review efforts to "engineer our consent" (Bernays, 1928).

What is the Source?

All discussions of propaganda emphasize the importance of knowing the source. Who is the real author of a given message? Articles in professional journals may have been prepared by staff in a public relations firm (see discussion of ghostwriting in chapter 2). Discovering the source can be difficult. It may require requesting documents via the Freedom of Information Act. Consider the history of lies distributed by governmental sources regarding the alleged harms of marijuana (Herer, 2000) and by the tobacco industry about lack of harm (e.g., Combs & Nimmo, 1992). We may not know who sent a letter or editorial to a newspaper. A letter purported to be written by an individual may have been created by a public relations team. Fear mongering regarding alleged "dangerous protest groups" may be disseminated by the people the groups are protesting against. Corporations and governmental sources hire public relations firms to create organizations and names for them that promote the opposite of what the name suggests as described in chapter 3.

Who Stands to Gain?

Follow the money. Who is profiting? Information regarding this question may reveal hidden sources of messages promoted. There may be hidden alliances between a source and the beneficiaries of a message (Marlin, 2002).

Is There an Organization?

Jowell and O'Donnell (2006) encourage an analysis of the structure of the propaganda organization. Is there a strong central organization? Who is the leader? Is he or she a figurehead only? What goals are pursued and how are they pursued? What media are used to distribute propaganda? Does the organization own them? Who belongs to the organization? One can be a follower or a member of an organization. In *Mein Kampf* (1939), Hitler wrote, "The task of propaganda is to attract followers; the task of the party organization is to win members. A follower of a movement is one who declares himself in agreement with its aims; a member is one who fights for it" (pp. 474–75, cited in Jowett & O'Donnell, 2006, p. 150). Are "conversion" rituals used with symbols (stickers, flags, uniforms)? What slogans are used? What communication networks are favored in the dissemination of messages such as websites and conferences?

What is the Target Audience?

Some organizations prefer a "buckshot" approach to all groups with a consistent message. Others use a more tailor-made approach, for example, seeking out opinion leaders and journalists. Here the message is aimed at those individuals or groups most likely to be useful to the propagandist. Results of marketing research using computer technology are drawn on in targeting specific audiences.

What is the Message?

What message is promoted? What "grand narratives" are appealed to? Examples include progress or health. What actions are encouraged by the message? For example, "buy X."

What Methods and Media are Used?

A wide variety of media may be used including music, images, illustrations, and graphs. This may be distributed via films, radio, television, or the Internet. (See Table 4.2.)

> If we keep in mind the notion of propaganda as a systematic, motivated attempt to influence the thinking and behavior of others through means that impede or circumvent a propagandee's ability to appreciate the nature of this influence, then we have a basis for analyzing different techniques of propaganda. These can be separated in various categories. We can distinguish verbal from non-verbal forms of propaganda. We can focus on those techniques that appeal in some way to *ethos* roughly translatable as good character and credibility; others that are designed to affect *pathos*, or feeling; and still others devoted to persuasion by *logos*, or argument. We can also take note of large-scale strategies, which combine a whole range of techniques. Or we can choose to look at individual devices or facilitators, not enough by themselves to produce successful propaganda, but contributing to the larger end. Logic books often contain a selection of "informal fallacies." (Marlin, 2002, p. 95)

Table 4.2 MEDIA FOR PROPAGANDA

Movies	Badges
Internet	Awards
Newspapers (press)	Comic strips
Magazines	Meetings/conferences
Radio	Speeches
Television	Street names
Posters/billboards	Monuments
Phone calls	Books
Direct mail	Plays
Flags	Company reports
Music	Brochures
Coins	Slogans
Stamps	

Propaganda methods emphasized by the Institute for Propaganda Analysis are favorite ploys as illustrated in Table 4.3. Vague language and slogans may be used, as well as repetition and emotional language. "Today's dictators rely for the most part on repetition, suppression and rationalization—the repetition of catchwords which they wish to be accepted as true, the suppression of facts which they wish to be ignored, the arousal and rationalization of passions which may be used in the interests of the Party or the State" (Huxley, 1958, p. 268). Strategies for maximizing the effects of propaganda suggested by Jowett and O'Donnell (2006) include: (1) creating material that is compatible with audience predispositions, (2) providing credible sources, (3) involving opinion leaders, (4) arranging face-to-face contact, (5) appealing to group norms, (6) using rewards and punishments, (7) monopolizing communication sources, (8) using visual symbols of power, (9) using certain language, and (10) arousing emotions. Controlling the flow of information is another strategy used to create bogus associations. Certain information may be released in sequence or together with other information. Information flow is completely controlled in totalitarian societies (Arendt, 1966).

What are the Contexts?

Propaganda will only be successful if it appeals to accepted beliefs and views—what is already in our hearts.

> It has been said that propaganda is like a packet of seeds dropped on fertile soil. To understand how the seeds can grow and spread, analysis of the soil—that is, the times and events—is necessary.
>
> It is also important to know and understand the historical background. What has happened to lead up to this point in time? What deeply held beliefs and values

Table 4.3 EXAMPLES OF PROPAGANDA DEVICES AND SYMBOLS FOR THESE

____ *Name Calling*—giving an idea a bad label—is used to make us reject and condemn the idea without examining the evidence.

____ *Glittering Generality*—associating something with a <blank> word—is used to make us accept and approve the <blank> without examining the evidence.

____ *Transfer* carries the authority, sanction, and prestige of something respected and revered over to something else in order to make the latter acceptable; or it carries authority, sanction, and disapproval to cause us to reject and disapprove something the propagandist would have us reject and disapprove.

____ *Testimonial* consists in having some respected or hated person say that a given idea or program or product or person is good or bad.

____ *Plain Folks* is the method by which a speaker attempts to convince his audience that he and his ideas are good because they are "of the people," the "plain folks."

____*Card-Stacking* involves the selection and use of facts or falsehoods, illustrations or distractions, and logical or illogical statements in order to give the best or the worse possible case for an idea, program, person, or product.

____ *Bandwagon* has as its theme, "Everybody—at least all of *us*—is doing it"; with it, the propagandist attempts to convince us that all members of a group to which we belong are accepting this program and that we must therefore follow the crowd and "jump on the band wagon."

* A thumb turned down is used to symbolize name calling, a glittering gem for glittering generality, a mask is used to symbolize transfer, a seal and ribbon for testimonials, an old shoe for plain folks appeals, a card for card-stacking, and a bandmaster's hat and baton to symbolize bandwagon appeals.
SOURCE: A. M. Lee & E. B. Lee (1939). *The Fine Art of Propaganda* (p. 24). New York: Harcourt, Brace & Co. With permission of Houghton Mifflin Harcourt.

> have been important for a long time? What myths are related to the present propaganda? What is the source of these myths? (Jowett & O'Donnell, 2006, p. 156)

Have there been opportunities to challenge a claim and its premise? Or, do governments or corporations limit access to competing views and counterevidence? As Marlin (2002) notes, a one-sided presentation may be a legitimate response to a biased presentation in the opposite direction.[12] Discussions have different goals. If critical inquiry is the goal, efforts to block critical appraisal of claims are never appropriate.

What are the Effects?

What was hoped for? How have different audiences reacted to different propaganda methods? Was counterpropaganda offered? If so, how? Counterpropaganda is propaganda directed against other propaganda. Sociologists and social psychologists have long explored related issues (e.g., Katz, 1954).

Have We Been Fair?

Marlin (2002) suggests that we should be charitable in our appraisal of the motives of others in view of our tendencies to view material with which we disagree as propaganda (see also Paul & Elder, 2004). This may avoid offering "counter-propaganda" rather than critically appraising views.

BUREAUCRATIC PROPAGANDA

Altheide and Johnson (1980) define bureaucratic propaganda as "any report produced by an organization for evaluation and other practical purposes that is targeted for individuals, committees, or publics who are unaware of its promotive character and the editing processes that shaped the report" (p. 5). They argue that the major form of propaganda consists of reports of organizations designed to ensure future funding. They note that most analyses of propaganda have focused on government's efforts to manipulate people through the mass media and argue that today, official information from other spheres such as corporations and social welfare agencies claiming to be "efficient," "rational," and "scientific," have been overlooked. Such reports must appear fair and objective to maintain legitimacy. They often contain the trappings of science rather than the substance to create such appearances. [13] (See discussion of pseudoscience in chapter 7.)

Target

In traditional propaganda, the target is a mass audience. In bureaucratic propaganda, the target is often an individual, group, or specific segment of the population. Its targets are influential people and interest groups who have a role in decision making.

> It is the strategy of the organizational propagandist wittingly or unwittingly to cultivate the assumptions and 'knowledge' of these targets for personal gain. In this sense, these propagandists understand the essential and strategic use of information in the context of our rational and bureaucratically based society. Most decisions helpful to an organization's survival, continued public and governmental support, and general legitimacy involve selected people. This fact, plus the array of conflicting ethnic groups and subsocieties within our nation's borders, actually make it unwise to appeal to the mass audience; Americans will agree on very little. This pluralism makes it essential to pick and choose the correct target for each situation and purpose. (p. 15)

Medium

Traditional propaganda relies on mass media. Consider Hitler's control of press, theater, film, and radio in which themes of German invincibility, Jewish inferiority, and the eternal rightness of the Third Reich were promoted (Baird, 1974, p. 16, cited in Altheide and Johnson, 1980). Altheide and Johnson (1980) view the influence of public relations specialists, advertisements, and bribes as minor in comparison to how official reports are constructed and used. As they note, the public may not see these reports.

Purpose

Altheide and Johnson (1980) suggest that the purpose of modern propaganda is to maintain the legitimacy of an organization and its activities. The key purpose is to convince influential individuals. But, because these reports claim to be "objective" assessments and are disseminated to the public, via the mass media, their purpose changes.

> What was once only part of culture is now shaping culture. For example police crime statistics are no longer merely one way of organizationally accounting for the kind and amount of certain types of work done by individuals as a way of justifying expenditures and salaries; crime statistics are now regarded as "objective" indicators of the amount of crime in our society and the threat it poses to all our safety unless the tide is turned. (p. 18)

This kind of propaganda is part of what Ellul (1965) means by "sociological propaganda." "Without intending the cumulative effects on what amounts to an ongoing structuring of culture, people as workers in organizations can promote myths and incorrect assessments of social situations just by doing their jobs" (p. 19). Official reports give the impression that "something is being done" about a problem.

Truth

Altheide and Johnson (1980) suggest that the practical use of information by organizations is the essential aspect of propaganda (p. 23). Facts and their interpretation are promoted as the truth, taking care not to distort facts too much to avoid detection of distortions. The values of science and objectivity are appealed to in presenting the organization and its members in favorable terms. "It is massive public relations (PR) gone wild. . . . The idea is to make the reports appear to be scientific, when in fact they are not" (p. 23). They give the example of police and FBI statistics. "What matters is the appearance of legitimacy" (p. 31). Activities or inactivities that may adversely affect legitimacy are concealed. Information is deliberately distributed to certain groups/individuals. Editing is a key concern in this process of concealment. Indeed total fabrications may occur (Manning, 1977). Organizational reports are thus self-serving messages. Altheide and Johnson (1980), as do others, draw on Goffman's "dramaturgical" framing of information management. This refers to viewing social interactions in terms of theater, for example, backstage and on stage. The organization's goals determine the nature of the reports. These reports thus are ritualistic (p. 43). This approach is at the opposite pole of information management standards and values promoted in evidence-informed practice and policy with its emphasis on transparency of what is done to what effect (Gambrill, 2006).

PALAVER: COMBS AND NIMMO'S CONCEPT OF THE NEW PROPAGANDA

Combs and Nimmo (1993) suggest that the new propaganda consists of "palaver"—extended, often confusing, messages designed to create desires in our consumer society and to establish credibility rather than to explore what is true and what is false. They describe palaver as a kind of discourse in which truth and falsity are irrelevant—in which a variety of nonrational methods are used as criteria including slogans, jingles, myths, intuitions, images, and symbols, which are self-serving. It includes rambling speech and digressive claims presented in appealing ways. They note the similarity of palaver to Frankfurt's (1986) notion of "bullshit." In the following quote Combs and Nimmo (1993) substitute their term "palaver" for Frankfurt's term, "bullshit."

> What [palaver] essentially misrepresents is neither the state of affairs to which it refers nor the beliefs of the speaker concerning that state of affairs. Those are what lies misrepresent, by virtue of being false. Since [palaver] need not be false, it differs from lies in its misrepresentational intent. The [palaverer] need not deceive us, *or even intend to do so*, either about the facts or what he takes the facts to be. What he does necessarily attempt to deceive us about is his enterprise. His only indispensably distinctive characteristic is that in a certain way he misrepresents what he is up to." (Frankfurt, 1986)

In palaver, truth is irrelevant. There is no concern for truth, only to create credibility and for guile and charm. As Frankfurt (1986) suggests, "he does not reject the authority of truth, as the liar does, and oppose himself to it. He pays no attention to it at all" (cited in Combs & Nimmo, 1993, p. 340). Frankfurt (1986) suggests that faking is inevitable whenever circumstances require that we speak without knowing what we are talking about.

Palaver provides endless distractions, also emphasized by Neil Postman (1985) in *Amusing Ourselves to Death* and by Huxley ([1932], 1969) in *Brave New World*. In this *Brave New World* "controllers" encourage participation in approved pleasures (sexual play, vacations, and tranquilizing narcotics) and in return citizens are grateful and loyal to the regime. "Everyone's disposition is so tranquil in fact that no one entertains a critical thought, antisocial impulse, or independent action" (p. 233). In advertising, palaver is used to make small or no difference between products look substantial to encourage us to purchase one product rather than another. This is also the case with alleged differences among the hundreds of psychotherapies available. We are complicit in perpetrating this reign of palaver in our failure to be skeptical. Problems are viewed as solvable via discourse—expressions of concern and description of efforts. The problem actually remains but is "solved" for the politician because propaganda produces the desired effect on the public (Combs & Nimmo, 1993, p. 236). Thus, problems are viewed as "a problem of propaganda. Propaganda is the solution to political or other organizational problems because it creates a 'semblance of reality,' or what Barnum called 'great realities' that offer a postmodern solution" (p. 236).

OTHER KEY FIGURES

Other key figures in propaganda analysis include Noam Chomsky, Michael Parenti, and Carl Sagan (e.g., see Carl Sagan's *Baloney Detection Kit* available on the Internet). Parenti (1992) argues that the media's job is not to inform but to disinform, not to advance democratic discourse but to mute it, telling us what to think before we have a chance to think about it for ourselves. Rank (1984) suggests that the essence of propaganda is fourfold: (1) to overemphasize the positive aspects of what I am offering, (2) to hide and minimize the negative ones, (3) to hide and minimize the positive aspects of my opponent's views, and (4) to highlight and exaggerate their negative aspects. (See Table 4.4.) He describes the "pep talk" as a process designed to encourage certain actions: (1) create a threat (look out), (2) encourage bonding (loyalty, pride), (3) emphasize doing good (duty to defend or gain a benefit), which may contribute to our sense of moral superiority, and (4) encourage a response (specific actions to be taken). The pitch includes: (1) getting your attention ("Hi"), (2) building confidence ("Trust me"), (3) creating desire ("You need . . ."), (4) urgency stressing ("Hurry!"), and (5) response seeking ("Buy"). We can draw on this to analyze advertisements:

1. What attention-getting techniques are used (e.g., appeal to emotions, senses, thoughts)?
2. What confidence-building techniques are used (e.g., repetition, appeal to authority figures)?
3. What desire-stimulating techniques are used (e.g., audience centered associations, belonging, protection, relief, prevention, acquisition)?
4. What urgency/stress techniques are used (ticking clock, fast music)?
5. What response-seeking techniques are used (trigger words such as "buy," image-building)? (See Rank's (1984a) 30-second spot quiz for analyzing ads.)

Table 4.4 Mental Illness Model and Rank's (1984) Fourfold Classification of Propaganda

Overemphasize the positive aspects of preferred model
- Inflated claims of success in removing complaints (puffery)
- Inflated claims of success in preventing problems (puffery)

Hide and minimize negative aspects of preferred model
- Harmful effects of neuroleptic drugs
- Questionable reliability and validity of the psychiatric classification system

Overemphasize negative aspects of opposing views
- Associate alternative approaches with negative terms (mechanistic, dehumanizing).
- Allege that positive effects of alternative approaches are only temporary

Hide and minimize positive aspects of opposing views
- Ignore research showing that nonprofessionals are as effective as professionals with many problems.
- Ignore positive results achieved by alternative approaches

Tactics Michael Parenti (1992) suggests as key to propaganda promoted by the government, military, and media include suppression by omission (omitted an entire story). He gives the example of industrial brown-lung poisoning of thousands of factory workers by manufacturing companies, which was suppressed for decades. Other methods he highlights include slighting of content (the real issues are given little attention) and false balancing (favoring one side in a controversy). If these fail, we can attack the target.[14]

DEVICE-BASED APPROACHES

Many approaches to propaganda analysis focus on specific techniques such as informal fallacies. (See Table 4.5.) The study of propaganda changed from a focus on exploring the interests that lay behind information sources related to controversies to an emphasis on examining how premises relate to conclusions in nonpolitical and/or hypothetical situations.

However, fallacies and their role in arguments are only one part of the overarching epistemic feature of falsity and deception that define the essence of propaganda.

> The issue of context is central to the limitations of a device based propaganda analysis. . . . If by 'propaganda analysis' we mean the uncovering of propagandists, the exposing of self-serving efforts, and the discovery of infiltration in propaganda channels, then propaganda analysis requires the scrutiny of the discursive context more than of individual texts. In an era of pressure groups, inter-group struggle, and mass media, propaganda analysis implies getting information about the environment of discourse rather than merely knowing how to dissect the rational relationship of statement and proof in an isolated explicit message. (Sproule, 1994, pp. 335–36)

Pratkanis and Aronson (2001) use the term "propaganda" to refer to the techniques of mass persuasion that have come to characterize our postindustrial society. Critical thinking is emphasized in many educational programs as a remedy to influence by manipulative ploys. Approaches to critical thinking range from the broad integrative views in which attention to context is vital (e.g., Paul, 1993; Paul & Elder, 2004) to narrow views in which argument analysis and identification of fallacies is emphasized. Thus, whether critical thinking is enough to spot and counter propaganda depends on the breadth of the critical thinking perspective.

White (1971) approaches the question "How does propaganda differ from persuasion?" by describing morally questionable and unquestionable techniques. Morally unquestionable methods include: (1) getting and keeping attention, (2) getting and keeping rapport, (3) building credibility, (4) appealing to strong motives—including "emotions" (given that the evidence is examined), and (5) action involvement. Morally questionable techniques include: (1) lying (deliberately saying what you believe to be untrue), (2) innuendo (defined as implying an accusation without risking refutation by clearly stating it), (3) presenting opinion as fact, (4) deliberate omission (e.g., not discussing opposing points of view in a conflict situation), and (5) implied obviousness (begging the question)—speaking as if the accuracy of a claim has been established and not in need of further argument or evidence

Table 4.5 EXAMPLES OF PROPAGANDA PLOYS

Shaky foundations: starting off wrong
Bold assertions
Untrustworthy authorities
Reasoning with the wrong facts
Rationalization
Downright lying
Faulty premise for an argument

Faulty construction: illogical or unsound ways of arguing
Hasty generalization
Mistaking the cause
False analogy
Ignoring the question
Begging the question
Attacking the person, not the argument
Pointing to an enemy
Misusing statistics
Meshing fact with opinion

Tricks of the trade: intentional distortions
Twisting and distortion
Selective omission
Incomplete quotation
Quoting out of context
Innuendo and baseless speculation

Cheap gadgetry: more persuasive devices
Testimonial
Bandwagon appeal
Plain folks
Snob appeal
Glittering generalities
Name-calling
Using stereotypes
Transfer
Scientific slant
Repetition
Co-optation

Abuse of language
Carelessness
Hackneyed phrases

SOURCE: E. MacLean (1981). *Between the lines: How to detect bias and propaganda in the news and everyday life*. Montreal: Black Rose Books. With permission of Black Rose Books.

(pp. 28–34). White (1971) suggests that presenting opinion as fact, deliberate omission, and implied obviousness, are paralleled by various forms of self-deception that may occur unintentionally; we may really believe that our opinions are true facts and assume that what seems obvious to us is obvious to everyone. We are often persuaded by our own propaganda. The question "Under what circumstances is self-deception ethically questionable?" has special significance for professionals who claim to help others and avoid harming them.

PROPAGANDA PLOYS EMPHASIZED BY THE INSTITUTE OF PROPAGANDA ANALYSIS

The Institute of Propaganda Analysis was founded in New York City in 1937 and lasted until the beginning of World War II.[15]

> The IPA's seven propaganda devices appeared at a time when the nation's opinion leaders shared a concern that Depression-era charges and counter-charges were placing democracy itself in peril. Alarm about the public's seeming vulnerability to extremist propagandists was what motivated Edward A. Filene, the department-store magnate and liberal philanthropist, to guarantee three-year's funding for an anti-propaganda institute proposed by journalist/educator Clyde R. Miller. (Sproule, 1994, p. 334)

Related publications emphasized the importance of recognizing the seven propaganda ploys shown in Table 4.3.[16] A special symbol was used to represent each device.

> Thus, if Americanism 🌟 and Christianity 🌟 are opposed to both Nazism and Communism, the time has come for true Americans 🌟 and true Christians 🌟 to organize against both, to act against both, and this active organization should be characterized not so much by negative opposition 👎 as by a positive program 🌟. Let us be honest with ourselves 👤. In the first instance, Communists and their supporters have real grievances 🌟. So have the Nazis 🌟. Communism, which antedates Nazism, complains about forced unemployment. It cries out against the huge profits 👎 for the rich. It condemns the modern system of capitalism, with its legalized usury 👎, its burdens and taxes 👎, its monopolies 👎 of industry, and its commercial 👎 wars. (Lee & Lee, 1939, p. 115)

Name Calling

Here, the propagandist creates hate or fear by using negative labels (such as heretic) to describe disliked individuals, groups, nations, races, policies, or practices. Both Name Calling and Glittering Generalities make use of "*Omnibus words*," which mean different things and have different emotional tones for different people (Lee & Lee, 1939).

Glittering Generalities

A favored view is associated with virtue words such as truth, freedom, liberty, social justice, or progress. As with name calling, the idea is to appeal to the emotions—to encourage a thoughtless judgment. While name-calling encourages a judgment to reject and condemn without examining the evidence, glittering generalities encourage approval and acceptance without examining the evidence (Propaganda Analysis, 1937). To avoid influence by such ploys we should suspend judgment and ask: (1) What does the word used really mean? (2) Does the idea have a legitimate connection with the real meaning of the name? (3) What are the merits of the idea itself, leaving the key word out? (Lee & Lee, 1939, pp. 48–49).

Transfer

Relying on transfer and association is a key propaganda strategy. We associate our message with some favored cause or celebrity for example. Techniques include buying lunches for and giving gifts to professionals to encourage use of certain products such as medications (Brody, 2007). The authority, sanction, and prestige of something favored and respected is associated with something the propagandist wishes to make acceptable to us. An example is associating a political project with national or religious symbols. Here too, suspending judgment is vital to distinguish fair from unfair use. We should ask, "Is there really is an association? Is an association made to encourage a false appearance of connection?"

Testimonial

An idea or program is associated with the experience of a person or institution to convince us of an idea. Questions here include: (1) Who or what is quoted? (2) Why should we view this individual (or organization or publication) as having expert knowledge, trustworthy information or reliable opinion on the subject? and (3) What does the idea amount to on its own merits, without the testimonial (Lee & Lee, 1939, p. 75). (Case examples are also commonly used to convince us that a claim is true.)

Plain Folk

Here, "persuaders present themselves as 'just plain folks' to create an identity with ordinary people and convey a favorable impression about their ideas and proposals." Below is an example from a radio broadcast from Father Coughlin.

> As you know, this hour is in no sense a donated hour. It is paid for at all commercial rates. This is your hour. This is your presentation. As long as you desire to have Father Coughlin a guest in your home each Sunday afternoon over these same stations, and at this same hour, he will be glad to speak fearlessly and courageously to you, as he presents a message of

Christianity and Americanism to Catholics and Protestants and Religious Jews. (Lee & Lee, 1939, p. 93)

Card-Stacking

Over and underemphasis are used to put a calculated spin on ideas or proposals. These distortions and omissions encourage ignoring of inconvenient information. Here too, suspension of judgment is vital to reel us in. Questions include: (1) What are alternative proposals? (2) What is the evidence for and against alternatives? (Lee & Lee, 1939, p. 97).

Bandwagon

In bandwagon, we are encouraged to follow the crowd, to embrace an idea or plan because everybody is doing it. Ties of nation, religion, race, region, sex, or occupation may be appealed to.

THE BAND WAGON is a means for making us follow the crowd and accept a propagandist's program as a whole and without examining the evidence for and against it. His theme is: 'Everybody's doing it. Why not you?' His techniques range from those of the street-corner medicine show to those of the vast pageant ... He appeals to the desire, common to most of us, to 'follow the crowd.' Because he wants us to follow the crowd in masses, he directs his appeal to groups held together already by common ties. (Lee & Lee, 1939, p. 105).
...
With the aid of all the other Propaganda Devices, all of the artifices of flattery are used to harness the fears and hatreds, prejudices and biases, convictions and ideals common to a group.[17]

Questions here include: (1) What exactly is this program? (2) What is the evidence for and against it? and (3) Does the program serve or undermine interests I favor?

PROPAGANDA AS SELECTIVE USE OF EVIDENCE

Propaganda, defined here as encouraging beliefs and actions with the least thought possible (Ellul, 1965), is characterized by partiality in the use of evidence, for example, hiding adverse effects of prescribed drugs, and hiding lack of evidence for claims that normal variations in behavior are signs of a brain disease remedied by prescribed medication. All scholars of propaganda emphasize the selective use of evidence—just facts (if facts are given) and views that suit the propagandist's aim. Other facts and views, especially those contradictory to the view promoted, are ignored or distorted. Sources are often hidden. Propagandists aim to encourage a certain reaction (belief or action), based not on evidentiary grounds such as well-argued reasons and a balanced description of alternative views, but on a distorted (incomplete) view appealing to our emotions and prejudices. That is, they do not merely wish to communicate facts and their context and have you make up your own mind, they wish to sell (pitch), a certain view. Skillful propagandists are creative illusionists in this way. In *The Propaganda Menace* (1939), Lumley defined propaganda as: "promotion which is *veiled* in one way or another as to (1) its origin or sources, (2) the interests involved, (3) the methods employed, (4) the content spread, and (5) the results accruing to the victims—any one, any two, any three, any four, or all five" (p. 44). There is deception regarding aims, methods used, and hoped-for results. Related rules include the following:

Rule 1. Do not address real issues.
Rule 2. Attack the person or his or her associates (try to spoil their credibility).
Rule 3. Distort disliked positions and attack the distorted versions.
Rule 4. Cozy up to friends.
Rule 5. Scare the hell out of them (e.g., if they don't do X, they will lose their jobs).

Methods used include informal fallacies such as ad hominem appeals, begging the question, and appeal to authority as described in chapter 13. Thomas Szasz has been labeled a "schizophrenic," among other negative terms, for questioning the concept of "mental illness."[17] Mary Boyle (2002) describes appeals to "common sense" to promote what she argues are flawed psychiatric views and to obscure problematic methodology and conceptual analyses on which they are based. The professional literature abounds, with exaggerated claims of knowledge (what we "know") and ignorance (what we do not "know"). A common script for introduction of a fad is shown in Table 4.6.

Censorship/Omission

Propagandists offer to the major channels of communication (e.g., TV, the Internet, magazines, newspapers, books) only that content that advances their purposes. Information that does not favor a preferred point of view may be suppressed, especially if is hard to discover. For example, Assembly Bill (No. 949) introduced in the California Legislation that calls for limits on who can call themselves a social worker, does not describe controversies regarding claims of special competence (see also Dawes, 1994). Suppression is one of the most insidious propaganda methods. If material is readily discoverable, suppression would not be used by a seasoned propagandist. Adverse consequences of medications such as Zyprexa and Vioxx (Brody, 2007) were hidden by their manufacturers. Secrecy policies of the FDA are now being challenged to avoid past cover-ups of known harmful effects of drugs approved. For example, the FDA knew about the risks of heart attacks from use of Avandia, a popular diabetes medicine made by GlaxoSmithkline, but kept it secret (Harris, 2009). Clinical trials not favorable to a pharmaceutical company are hidden.[18] Other censored information includes candid description of the lack of empirical evidence for many (most?) service methods used by professionals including the results of critical tests falsifying claims (e.g., Jacobson, Mulick, & Schwartz, 1995; Lilienfeld, Lynn, & Lohr, 2003).

Table 4.6 A Common Script For Introduction of a Fad

1. A grand narrative or myth compatible with the framework of the fad. This is coupled with grandiose claims on the part of "true believers." For example, the appeal to infection as the cause of mental illness had a long prior history; it did not appear out of the blue. (See Scull's (2005) description of the harmful consequences of Joseph Cotton's focal sepsis theory of mental illness.) Thus, there is a readiness to accept claims compatible with popular myths and grand narratives—Ellul's view that pre-propaganda is ubiquitous and sets the stage for the success of later propaganda.

2. Energetic advocates who promote the fad including industries with money to spend on advertising and public relations agencies as well as to entice opinion leaders.

3. Others with stature, who support the view and suppress negative consequences, such as "opinion leaders" in medicine and hired public relations firms. Adolph Meyer, perhaps the most famous psychiatrist of his time, participated in suppressing an outcome study revealing harms of the surgeries carried out by Joseph Cotton and his collaborators (Scull, 2005). This report was kept hidden for years as harmful surgeries continued. The recovered memory movement included hundreds of therapists sympathetic to related beliefs.

4. Often, but by no means always, poor people with little resources to complain (e.g., hire lawyers). (This was not the case with clients involved in the recovered memory movement who were mainly middle class.)

5. Recruitment of fellow believers perhaps via a website and continued suppression of harming in the name of helping.

6. Consistent ignoring of criticism and defamation of critics coupled with a confident manner and bold assertions of effectiveness.

7. Refusal to publish critiques of popular views in professional journals as in the case of critics of the radical mastectomy (Katz, 2002).

8. Dissemination of ineffective or harmful practices to other countries as with facilitated communication (Jacobson, Foxx, & Mulick, 2005).

NOTE: This common sequence involves a variety of propaganda methods including Hugh Rank's (1984) fourfold strategy illustrated in Table 4.4.

Flaws in methodology are often hidden in published reports. In discussing the origins of EBP, Gray (2001) notes the increasing lack of confidence in data of potential use to clinicians: peer review, which he subtitled feet of clay, and flaws in books, editorials, and journal articles. Examples of biases include submission bias, publication bias, methodological bias, abstract bias, and framing bias. Many practice guidelines promoted as "evidence-based" are of questionable reliability (e.g., Gorman, 2003; Grilli, 2000) and the majority of those who take part in the preparation of guidelines have ties to pharmaceutical companies (Choudhry, Stelfox, & Detsh, 2002; Cosgrove, Bursztajn, Krimsky, Anaya, & Walker, 2009). In place of critical, systematic reviews of research we often find haphazard reviews that do not inform readers how authors searched, where they searched, or what criteria they used to review studies and do not include a search for unpublished, as well as published reports. Conclusions drawn based on uncritical reviews are often misleading. Rigorous critiques of research regarding programs touted as effective such as Multi-Systemic Family Therapy, suggest that such programs are no more effective than are others (e.g., Littell, 2006; Littell, Popa, & Forsythe, 2005).

Psychiatry, psychology, and clinical social work have embraced a biomedical approach to understanding troubled and troubling behavior as illustrated by the hundreds of diagnostic categories in the *Diagnostic and Statistical Manual of Mental Disorders* (DSM-IV, 2000). A review of course outlines in psychopathology in social work showed a psychiatric framing is favored (Lacasse, & Gomory, 2003). Some argue that schizophrenia is a scientific delusion (Boyle, 2002). Typically, these arguments are ignored or misrepresented by those who promote a mental illness framing of deviant behavior.[19] Pharmaceutical funding of consumer organizations such as NAMI (National Association of Mentally Ill) is hidden or downplayed. Too seldom are professionals educated about the *sociology* of the helping professions and the play of cognitive illusions and biases among both professionals and scientists (Gambrill, 2005; MacCoun, 1998). In the late 1960s at the University of Michigan School of Social Work, all students were required to take courses on social deviance and basic behavioral principles. Neither course is offered today, let alone required. Behavioral principles highlight the extent to which we are influenced by our environments, influences that we may resist if we were aware of them. Contextual frameworks reveal (rather than hide) environmental contingencies related to personal and social problems. Literature concerning deviance highlights the social judgments involved in viewing certain behaviors as bad or good, healthy or sick (Conrad & Schneider, 1992; Gusfield, 1996). It highlights historical changes in how behaviors have been labeled, first as sins, then as crimes, and now as mental illnesses as described in chapter 8. It keeps the medicalization of deviance clearly in view including its harmful consequences such as coercion in the name of helping (Conrad, 2007; Szasz, 1994).

Distortion, Diversion, and Fabrication

All propaganda methods distort reality, often by omitting relevant content such as competing well-argued views and counter evidence to claims made. Disliked views may be misrepresented. Data may be fabricated or our attention diverted from important realities.

Distortion. Distorting positions and then attacking the distorted view is a common reaction to new ideas or disliked arguments. Consider misrepresentations of behavior analysis (Thyer, 2005) and evidence-based practice (Gibbs & Gambrill, 2002). Fielding a stereotype of a position (straw person) and attacking this, misinforms rather than informs. The incidence, prevalence, or danger value of "problems" is often exaggerated to maintain or expand resources. We find propagandistic advocacy rather than a careful weighing of evidence and accurate reporting of related facts and figures (Best, 2001). Or, the incidence, prevalence, and danger value may be minimized. Distortion is often combined with the suppression of contradictory views and related evidence. Inflated claims of knowledge and ignorance are common in professional discourse including texts and journals; that is, critical appraisal of related research reveals these to be bogus (Altman, 2002; Ionnides, 2005).

Diversion. Here attention is drawn away from key issues. This may be done by focusing on trivial issues, nit-picking, ad hominem attacks and appeals and busy work such as legal harassment (Rank, 1984, p. 51). If we are preoccupied with other matters, we will be diverted from matters that a propagandist would like ignored. Diversions may be serious or humorous. Ellul (1965) suggests that "Life has become a racecourse . . . a succession of objective events which drag us along and lead us astray without anything affording us the possibility of standing apart, taking stock, and ceasing to act" (p. 330). Exaggerating the consequences of a disliked position may encourage laughter and thus undermine a position, as well as divert attention from real issues at hand. Cultivation of fear creates a diversion. Consider the Nazi's encouragement of fear that Jews were plotting to take over the world. Many diversionary tactics appeal to our prejudices and preferred ideologies, divert attention from key issues and link ideas and actions promoted with good things we want or bad things we want to minimize. Slogans are used in this way: "Fight depression"; "Empower clients"; "Seek social justice." Notice their vagueness. People can continue to do whatever they want to under the protective umbrella of fuzzy sound-bytes. Associations are made but not critically examined.

Fabrication. Fabrication is the opposite of suppression or minimization. In fabrication, what does not exist is made to exist. For example Boyle (2002) argues that there is no evidence that an entity called "schizophrenia" exists or that biochemical markers have been discovered. Szasz (2001) views the very concept of "mental disorder" to be a fabrication. False claims mislead. Consider this announcement for a workshop "Diagnosis in Depth" sponsored by the National Association of Social Workers in collaboration with the University of California, Berkeley, School of Social Welfare given by Stan Taubman, DSW, LCSW, Director of Berkeley Training Associates:

This workshop provides a systematic, comprehensive and thorough overview of the full range of mental disorders. Special attention is given to accurate, thorough and well validated differential diagnosis of mood, anxiety, psychotic, personality and substance related disorders. (12 ceus - UC Berkeley). (Feb. 14, 1997)

In fact, not only is the reliability of such diagnoses in question, the validity is event more problematic.[20] Pratkanis and Aronson (1991) define "factoid" as "an assertion of fact that is not backed up by evidence, usually because the fact is false or because supporting evidence cannot be obtained" (p. 71). They suggest that when carried far enough, minimization merges into suppression, whereas exaggeration tends toward fabrication (p. 127). Propagandists take advantage of our gullibility concerning the seeming soundness of numbers to mislead and befuddle.[21]

Confusion

Confusion is another propaganda method. Vague terms, being overloaded with data and a focus on side issues blur clarity and interfere with critical appraisal of claims and issues. Jargon may be used and not defined. Skrabanek and McCormick (1998) refer to this as the fallacy of obfuscation. Weasel words are common as described in chapter 9. Ellul (1965) suggests that academics are particularly liable to this propaganda method, since they read reams of secondary sources.

Other Propaganda Methods

Appeals to popularity ("Everyone is doing it"), consensus ("Everyone agrees"), tradition ("That's what we've always done"), and authority ("The experts say") are common ploys. Repetition and oversimplification are other strategies. The trappings of science are often used without the substance as in pseudoscience. For example, Boyle (2002) argues that promoters of biochemical views of troubled behavior use the rhetoric of science to forward their beliefs, as well as the rhetoric of medicine, including the special, indeterminate (unknowable) knowledge professionals are assumed to possess. They appeal to a (misleading) belief in progress. Advertisers, both past and present, in the media as well as in professional publications, use the trappings of science to encourage consumers to buy products.[22]

AN EXAMPLE OF PROPAGANDA IN THE GUISE OF EDUCATIONAL BROCHURES

During a workshop I attended at Langley Porter Hospital in San Francisco, California I picked up some brochures that were available in the entrance way. These addressed topics such as schizophrenia, anxiety disorders, phobias, Alzheimer's disease, and eating disorders. What claims are made in these sources? Are controversial issues described? Are research findings presented accurate and up-to-date? Are well-argued alternative views and evidence against views promoted presented? Are important uncertainties identified? Are inflated claims made about what is "known" and what treatments are effective? Consider the 15-page brochure on schizophrenia entitled "Let's Talk Facts About Schizophrenia' (revised 1997, American Psychiatric Association). On the bottom, we find 'Let's Talk about Mental Illnesses,' a phrasing using *plain folks appeal*. We read that "Schizophrenia is a severe medical illness of the brain."

At no point do we learn that rates of schizophrenia vary greatly in developed and underdeveloped countries. We read that "Research also points to structural difference in the brains of some people with schizophrenia and differences in level of chemicals in specific areas of the brain" (p. 5). At no point are we informed about dissenting views including controversies regarding whether differences found in the brains of people labeled schizophrenic compared to those without this label are due to use of neuroleptics. That is, most people diagnosed as "schizophrenic" have been on some medication (Leo & Cohen, 2003). We read that "There is some heredity basis or predisposition for schizophrenia because it runs in families. Studies show that when one identical twin has schizophrenia, there is a 40–60% chance that the second twin will develop illness" (p. 5). Again, there is no critique of these twin studies.

In the discussion of treatment, medications (anti-psychotics/neuroleptics) are discussed first, taking advantage of the recency effect. We read that "These affect the brain's chemical processes, blocking brain chemicals believed to be overactive in schizophrenic patients" (p. 6). Chemicals in our brain are always being affected. The brochure does describe side effects and we are told that the more serious side effects caused by anti-psychotics such as Tardive Dyskinesia (a movement disorder that includes tongue rolling and smacking of the lips and grimacing) "are often reversible if identified early" (p. 7). What is "often"? What is early? Are all reversible? Notice the vague language. We are not told that 73% of people stop taking these drugs because of adverse side effects. We read on page 7 that "compared with conventional antipsychotics, atypical medications usually cause fewer serious side effects and less muscular rigidity, tremors, shuffling gait, restlessness, and odd and involuntary movements, however, they are not free of side effects" and mention sedation and weight gain. What does "usually" mean? What is "fewer"? Is there evidence that these newer medications are more effective or have fewer adverse side effects? The bibliography on pages 10–11 omits sources describing well-argued counter arguments. When we examine Internet sources cited, we find no mention of cites which provide dissenting views such as the International Association for the Scientific Study of Psychiatry and Psychology, or Mindfreedom.

In a brochure titled "Psychotherapy" (1997, American Psychiatric Association), the first sentence is: "Mental disorders, like many other illnesses, are not uncommon." Note the question begging—assuming what should be argued. Here too we see vague language—"not uncommon." And, note the assumption that problems-in-living, such as anxiety, are "mental disorders." We read that "In any given year, one out of five adult Americans experience a mental illness or emotional problem severe enough to require treatment." Is this true? And, do they require treatment? In what percentage is there spontaneous remission? On page 1, we read that "Once a mental disorder is properly diagnosed, psychotherapy can enable patients to function more effectively and comfortably." What kinds of psychotherapy? What percentage improves over what time and how long are gains maintained? What indicators are used to evaluate "improvement"? For example, Burns (1999) notes that the Hamilton Depression Scale is often used to evaluate outcome. Success is claimed on the basis of a 2-point difference on this scale. This may be statistically significant, but is it clinically significant? That is, are people still depressed? He argues that they are.

We read that "psychotherapy is a process of discovery whose medical role is to eliminate or control troubling and painful symptoms so that the patient can return to normal functioning." Note the appeal to a "medical role." Is this because psychiatrists have an M.D.? "As is done with all illnesses, the psychiatrist will interview the patient, ask for details about symptoms—their severity and duration—and obtain a personal and family history. After all this information has been collected and analyzed, a diagnosis is made" (p. 3). Notice the medical language, terms such as "symptoms" and "illness." It is assumed, with no counter arguments presented, that such problems-in-living are "illnesses." There is an equation of problems-in-living and physical illness. What must be argued is assumed. These brochures contain many examples of such bold assertions (begging the question). We read that "Only psychiatrists, as physicians, are medically trained to perform and analyze medical diagnostic tests, to evaluate the physical symptoms of mental illness, and to take into account any other medical illness occurring concurrently with the medical disorder" (p. 6). But are they trained to accurately detect psychological and environmental contributors? References included represented only an illness model.

What do we find when we examine the brochure: "Let's Talk Facts about Anxiety Disorders"? Here too these are presented as illnesses: "Unfortunately many people with anxiety disorders don't seek help. They don't realize they have an illness that has known causes and effective treatments." Is this an illness? Or, is this a learned reaction on a continuum of intensities? (See discussion of the creation of social anxiety as a mental disorder in chapter 2.)

In the brochure entitled "Substance Abuse and Addiction," also published by the American Psychiatric Association (1999), we find the claim: "Addiction is a serious illness." We are told that "years of marijuana use can lead to loss of ambition and an inability to carry out long-term plans or to function effectively." For what percentage of people? What is "marijuana use"? How many years? How often? Notice the vagueness of this statement and the fear mongering. Again, there is no discussion of well-argued alternative views. In not one of these brochures distributed to the public in a major San Francisco hospital do we find any mention of evidentiary concerns about claims made or well-argued alternative views or any references to them. Examination of brochures and websites promoting mammography screening for breast cancer show that here too, we are not accurately informed (Jorgenson & Gotzsche, 2004). Typically, absolute risk reduction in mortality from screening for different forms of cancer, including breast cancer, is not described (Gotzsche, 2006).

SUMMARY

Propaganda analysis has been approached at varying degrees of complexity. A broad propaganda analysis emphasizes the importance of understanding the "big picture" and related seductive personal appeals and distortion of realities and our own complicity in this. Ellul's (1965) sociological analysis describes the central role of propaganda in advanced technological societies. He argues that this is needed to salve the psychological wounds inflicted by such a technological society—loneliness, impotence of political action, lack of meaning, insignificance. Propaganda entails selective use of "evidence" and encourages actions and beliefs based on questionable grounds. Efforts to block questions and criticism are key indicators. Ellul (1965) suggests that when discussion starts, propaganda ends. Strategies used are related to its key functions, for example, to hide counter-evidence to views promoted and well-argued alternative views. Propaganda discards epistemic values of truth, critical appraisal, as well as ethical values of avoidance of manipulation. It is a philosophical issue, both on ethical and epistemic grounds (e.g., truth claims). The aim of propaganda is to encourage action with as little thought as possible. Thus, propaganda is much more than use of fallacies and persuasion strategies. Propaganda erodes both our ethical and our epistemic understanding and obligations. We are less likely to "do the right thing" and less likely to discover what is true and what is not (epistemic issues). Ellul (1965) emphasized the vital role of pre-propaganda in educational settings for laying the groundwork for influence by propaganda.

Propaganda methods differ in how easy they are to spot. They often create an illusion of openness, while at the same time, obscuring competing views and questionable grounds for claims. Negative consequences of proposed actions are hidden so we may make a choice we otherwise would not make. It is always a challenge to see what is hidden, especially when what is said or presented appeals to our most cherished hopes, such as being healthy, avoiding pain, and finding love. Oversimplifications hinder understanding of complex issues. We lose rather than gain in our ability to understand ourselves and our world and to make up our own minds. Pitches are carefully tailored to appeal to our self-interests and deepest motives (to be right, to be a member of an in-group) and to discourage critical appraisal. This highlights both the importance of recognizing how we are affected, as well as how difficult it will be to exert counter control. Propaganda analysts suggest questions we can use to spot related ploys and avoid unwanted influences that may result in decisions that result in more harm than good.

PART THREE

Consequences of Propaganda

5

A Rogue's Gallery of Harms Related to Propaganda in the Helping Professions

Avoidable harm is a key result of propaganda in the helping professions. Certainly not all harm is caused by propaganda. But many harms are, including cover-ups of adverse effects of practices and policies and promoting harmful procedures because professionals themselves have been propagandized. Harms created by propaganda flow from its essence: encouraging beliefs and actions with the least thought possible. Critical appraisal of claims is avoided or actively discouraged. Possible consequences include: (1) failing to gain help that is available and is desired; (2) forcing people to accept "help" they do not want; (3) offering and accepting help that is not needed; and (4) using services that diminish rather than enhance the quality of life, that is interventions result in iatrogenic (harmful) effects.[1] Professionals are not necessarily responsible for harm resulting from recommended interventions (including doing nothing).

Harmful consequences can (and do) result from well-reasoned and informed decisions. No one is perfect and uncertainty abounds.[2] Propaganda contributes to harm in a number of ways. Key to propaganda is distortion (the misrepresentation of reality) created by partiality in the use of evidence, thereby telling only part of the story. An example is promoting a drug as effective while hiding adverse side effects of the drug in pharmaceutical ads. Physicians and clients may then use the drug without being fully informed. Bogus claims presented in professional education programs such as appeal to serotonin levels as a cause of "mental illness" are repeated in pharmaceutical ads directed toward doctors in professional journals and to consumers via direct marketing. Influence from these sources is passed on to clients and patients. Emphasis in psychiatry programs on a biochemical view of problems and medication as a remedy may result in ignoring well-argued alternative views and interventions that can help clients. For example, a child may be labeled as having Attention Deficit Hyperactivity Disorder because of his (mis)behavior, ignoring environmental circumstances related to this (mis)behavior (e.g., boring class activities, poor teacher behavior change skills). Many harms result from gullibility on the part of those involved in perpetuating the harm.

Greed, sloth, and negligence on the part of professionals and allied staff are often enabled and maintained by propaganda in the form of bogus claims of effectiveness and safety on the part of staff in oversight organizations such as accrediting bodies, hospitals, and agencies that employ them who neglect their accountability obligations while boldly asserting claims of "excellent service" and effective treatment. The greater the lapses on the part of such oversight institutions, which fail to review services provided and/or promote bogus claims (e.g., of surgery needed), the more likely are avoidable harms caused by professionals to continue. Consider unnecessary insertion of cardiac implants produced by Abbott Laboratories (stents) by Dr. Mides at St. Joseph Hospital in Towsan, Maryland. This hospital "agreed to pay out a $22 million fine to settle charges that it paid illegal kickbacks to Dr. Mides' medical practice in exchange for patient referrals" ((Harris, 2010c). This again illustrates the systemic nature of propaganda in the helping professions. Revelations of attempts on the part of pharmaceutical companies to block information regarding harms and ineffectiveness of drugs promoted have become common.[3] Conflicts of interests described in chapter 3 contribute to avoidable harms.[4] Recommendations may be based on unfounded authority or because they enrich bank accounts or status.

Here again, epistemic and ethical concerns, so central to both understanding and countering propaganda and its effects, point the way. The effects of propaganda depend in part on the balance of knowledge and ignorance, for example, about how to achieve an outcome, such as decreasing depression, avoiding cancer, or increasing friends and social support. The greater the knowledge, the more harm may result from not considering this. Ethical obligations of professionals and administrators to involve clients as informed participants and to offer competent services require them to exercise due diligence, to reason clearly about their decisions, to decrease avoidable ignorance by keeping up with theory and research regarding client concerns, and to minimize avoidable errors. Yet we know that many do not do so. Do clients have a responsibility to think carefully about what they agree to or request? Failing to raise vital results is a kind of self-propaganda. The rogue's gallery of harms described in this chapter should be a wake-up call for both consumers and professionals to develop propaganda-spotting skills.

VIOLATION OF OUR RIGHT TO MAKE INFORMED DECISIONS

Most examples described in this chapter share the harm of lack of informed consent. Bogus claims regarding the accuracy of theories and diagnostic methods, effectiveness of interventions, alleged "risks," and consequences of public health interventions, such as screening all people for mental health problems as suggested in the New Freedom Commission on Mental Health, limit our opportunities to make informed decisions. Most medical devices have never been tested to determine if they are safe and effective (Harris, 2009f). Are clients so informed? Inflating claims about "what works" and hiding potential harmful effects of recommended interventions deprives us of our right to make informed decisions: to decide for ourselves. Information we would consider in making decisions about whether to get a mammogram or full body scan or to take a medication, such as adverse effects, is hidden. Incomplete realities are presented as complete. Common adverse consequences of medication are often not shared with clients (Tarn et al., 2006). In a study of 520 psychiatrists from 94 state/county mental hospitals in 35 states, Kennedy and Sanborn (1992) found that only 54% of psychiatrists disclosed tardive dyskinesia as an effect of antipsychotic medication.

Consider Ellen Liversidge's 39-year-old son who died from the side effects of Zyprexa. Her son had done well on lithium. He was switched to Zyprexa and gained 100 pounds over a two-year period. When he fell into a coma and died, the ICU staff who treated him were unaware of the side effects of Zyprexa. He was tested for HIV, West Nile Virus, and other illnesses. The primary cause of death was hyperglycemia, a side effect of Zyprexa. Ellen said that the only thing her son had been told about Zyprexa was that it was safe. He had not been given any information regarding the risks and benefits of Zyprexa. (See Pringle, 2007a.)

Bogus claims of knowledge and ignorance influence policy decisions, such as whether to allow people to use marijuana to decrease pain and nausea, and whether to make effective parenting programs available to parents involved with the child welfare system. Professionals, propagandized by advertisements and articles in the professional literature containing bogus claims, daily recommend related interventions to unsuspecting clients and patients. "True believers" may not mention to clients that there is no evidence that remedies recommended do more good than harm (e.g., Bausell, 2007).

SOME EXAMPLES FROM THE PAST

Many sources illustrate the sad fate of those unfortunates who sought or who were coerced to undergo treatments based on inflated claims of effectiveness. Bleeding, purging, and blistering were treatments of choice for centuries even though there was no evidence that these procedures did more good than harm.[5] Even today, treatments for cancer are cutting, poisoning, and burning. Some argue that institutionalized psychiatry reflects a history of torture in the name of helping (Szasz, 1987, 1994; Valenstein, 1986). (See Figure 5.1.)

The Harmful Effects of Joseph Cotton's Focal Sepsis Theory of Mental Illness

One of the most amazing examples of harming in the name of helping and related propaganda methods can be seen in Andrew Scull's gripping description of Joseph Cotton and the methods he used to cure "mental illness" at Trenton State Hospital in New Jersey in the early twentieth century. He was a "true believer" in "focal sepsis"—the belief that infection was the cause of mental illness. Based on this flawed theory, hundreds of people had body parts removed. He removed especially teeth, uteruses (historically, always a suspicious organ), and also colons. There was a 30% mortality rate with the removal of colons. The unfortunates who fell into his hands were often poor women from Philadelphia who returned to their homes with no teeth because they could not afford dentures. Cotton even removed all the teeth of both of his sons, both of whom committed suicide in young adulthood. This story illustrates energetic uses of propaganda, first to prevent close scrutiny of his methods, and then to cover up a careful report that showed the harmful effects of his practices. Two social workers who worked in the hospital and who were fans of Dr. Cotton had earlier prepared a "white-wash" report, asserting that his methods were effective. However, Greenacre's follow-up of people operated on by actually going to their homes in surrounding

Figure 5.1. An example from the past: The Utica crib. Patients who refused to stay in bed might be placed in a crib-bed. The first so-called protection bed was reportedly devised by a French physician named Aubanel in 1845. In the United States, the bed was known as the Utica crib because the New York State Lunatic Asylum at Utica used a version built with rungs, making it look like a child's crib. In the early 1880s, when the Utica asylum employed more than fifty such beds, superintendent John Gray was criticized by other asylum doctors for excessive restraint.
SOURCE: L. Gamwell & N. Tomes (1995). *Madness in America: Cultural and medical perceptions of mental illness before 1914* (p. 48). Birmingham, NY: Cornell University Press. Archives of the Western Lunatic Asylum of Virginia, Staunton, courtesy Western State Hospital.

Philadelphia and New Jersey, revealed a very different picture, one of death, disfigurement, and no relief of original symptoms (often of depression). The cover-up of this report was facilitated by the most prominent psychiatrist of the time, Adolph Meyer, mentor of Joseph Cotton. Cotton was totally uninterested in the report and continued blithely along. He became famous, even traveling to Europe to promote "focal sepsis theory" and related operations for "mental illness." Here too we see bold assertions (claims with no evidence), a confident manner, censorship of adverse effects, and ignoring of criticism.

Lobotomies

Elliot Valenstein (1986) describes the hideous nature of lobotomies in *Great and Desperate Cures*: "After drilling two or more holes in a patient's skull, a surgeon inserted into the brain any of various instruments—some resembling an apple corer, a butter spreader, or an ice pick and, often without being able to see what he was cutting, destroyed part of the brain." The lobotomy was part of mainstream psychiatry for decades (see also Whitaker, 2002). Thousands of mutilating brain surgeries were performed at the treatment's height. The man who invented this, Dr. Egas Moniz, was awarded the Nobel Prize for medicine in 1949. Those opposed to the procedure published little criticism during the first ten years of its use, partly, as Valenstein notes, because of long established tradition that considered it bordering on the unethical to criticize in public another physician's treatment. "The people on whom this barbarous procedure was visited were typically in state mental hospitals and therefore limited in their ability for redress" (p. 301). Ofshe and Watters (1994) suggest that "the use of lobotomies in the 1940s and 1950s is the best recent historical example of the unwillingness or inability of professional peers to regulate and restrain an unjustified and dangerous practice" (p. 300).

Blinding of 10,000 Babies

Consider the blinding of 10,000 babies by giving premature infants excess oxygen at birth, which resulted in Retrolental fibroplasia (Silverman, 1980). It was assumed that this procedure was effective and it continued for years. No critical test had been made of this procedure. Those who raised questions about whether it did more good than harm were ignored. Groupthink reigned. Not questioning popular policies and practices is a classic example of encouraging beliefs and actions with the least thought possible. Even today, students and interns may be punished rather than encouraged to question the judgments of their superiors.[6] An emphasis on evidence-informed practice and policy in which staff are encouraged to critically appraise claims should decrease avoidable premature closure.

HARMS CAUSED BY INFLATED CLAIMS OF KNOWLEDGE (OR IGNORANCE) ABOUT THE PREVALENCE, NATURE, AND CAUSES OF PROBLEMS

The social and personal problem industry and related groups tirelessly field new problems and risks (perhaps minor variations of others made to look different), often using "advocacy statistics" (inflated claims of prevalence and seriousness) and appealing to the discourse of fear (Altheide, 2002). Different views of our troubles are related to what we believe it is to be human—what is *The Human Condition* (Arendt, 1958)? The human condition is not an easy one as illustrated by literature throughout the centuries, as well as by reports of journalists and social scientists. Alienation is a recurrent topic of discussion and concern as are the many forms of anxiety and depression. A given product such as Prozac rests on a certain view of life (Elliott & Chambers, 2004). Many argue that dubbing moral conflicts "mental illnesses," biologizes our human condition (e.g., Double, 2006; Horowitz & Wakefield, 2007; Szasz, 1987). Defining problems as due to individual psychological or biochemical deficiencies in need of remedy overlooks related moral dilemmas (conflicts) and environmental factors including discriminatory practices and policies.

> Although inequalities in health are brought about by social, economic and political factors over which the medical profession has little influence, the

dominant ideology of the medical profession, the importance it attaches to an individual biomedical model, means that the consequences of inequality are systematically played down. Nowhere can we see this more clearly than in psychiatry, and in particular in the way in which the biomedical model has been set to work in the *Defeat Depression* campaign.

. . .

For example, it assumes that 'depression' as defined by the biomedical model is the correct way of interpreting human emotional distress. It also assumes that such distress has no intrinsic value and must be got rid of through the use of antidepressants, or other technical interventions, such as therapy . . . (Bracken & Thomas, 2008). (Retrieved November 30, 2008, from <http://www.critpsynet.freeuk.com>).[7]

This individual focus is encouraged by the *fundamental attribution error* (our tendency to attribute the cause of behavior to personality characteristics and to overlook environmental variables). Environmental circumstances related to suicide may be ignored.[8]

Excessive certainty regarding claims made about what or who is responsible for an outcome, such as the death of a baby, may later be shown to be in question, as in shaken baby allegations (Tuerkheimer, 2010) and sudden infant death syndrome (Rabin, 2010). The history of public health, medicine, psychiatry, and psychology is strewn with examples of skilled (and not so skilled) detective work in the identification of causes as illustrated by the focal sepsis theory of mental illness discussed earlier. Consider also the assumption that dyslexia was a medical problem. Stanovich (1986) argues that "in all likelihood, nothing has done more to hinder the scientific study of reading disability than unwarranted popularization of medical explanations for the condition. It has taken this field decades to rid itself of the many incorrect physiological explanations that sprouted from the few uncontrolled case studies that were at one time introduced into the medical literature" (p. 169).[9]

The time lag between accurate identification of a causative factor and acceptance of this information is often prolonged because of censorship by those who favor a popular but wrong view. Maestri (2008) argues that exaggerated claims regarding the effects of osteoporosis on falls among the elderly transformed postmenopausal women into sick people and promoted magic bullets rather than taking steps to avoid falls by environmental planning, correct vision prescriptions, and adopting healthy lifestyles to minimize bone loss. Oversimplifications prevent discovery of needed information. Examples are: (1) "It's in the genes"; (2) "It's in the brain"; (3) "It's due to low self-esteem"; (4) "She had a past trauma"; (5) "She is bipolar." For example, the assertion that depression is a "brain disease" is an oversimplification on both conceptual and empirical grounds. Related research shows that environmental factors play a key role and that there are many kinds of depression and sadness (Luyten et al., 2006). (The term "disease" is discussed in chapter 6.) Controversies about whether any specific discoveries related to alleged brain diseases have been found are often hidden (e.g., Vul et al., 2009).

Who has the power to name and frame (e.g., X is a disease or C is a social problem) has the power to affect how what is framed and named is treated. Drug abusers are viewed as a threat to the well-being of others; thus, they have to be cured (or imprisoned).

In a brief article in the *Journal of the American Medical Association* (*JAMA*), Leshner repeats this theme three times: 'There are now extensive data showing that addiction is eminently treatable'; 'addiction is a treatable disease'; 'overall, treatment of addiction is as successful as treatment of other chronic diseases, such as diabetes, hypertension, and asthma' (1999, 1314–16). Leshner studiously refrains from acknowledging that 'treatment' for 'addiction' is typically imposed on the subject by force. (Szasz, 2001, pp. 141–42)

Dubbing scores of (mis)behaviors as "mental illnesses" in need of treatment allows professionals to step in, with the legitimacy of the state, to coerce treatment that may include institutionalization. Once institutionalized, more coercion often waits (e.g., forced drugging). As Szasz notes, the term *treatment* is often used in lieu of the term *coercion*. There is no doubt that institutionalizing some depressed, suicidal individuals against their will saves some lives (Halpern, 2001). Maximizing informed consent, as well as effective intervention, seems the road to take in making such difficult decisions. And, as always, the question "Who will benefit?" is key.

HARM CAUSED BY INFLATED CLAIMS REGARDING THE SCIENTIFIC BASE OF CLASSIFICATION SYSTEMS

Classification is of great interest in the helping professions and in science. Correct classification can suggest effective remedies or reveal related uncertainty. Incorrect classification can result in decisions that do more harm than good. Classification is often based on political, economic, and social grounds rather than on scientific ones. Hiding this fact is a key propaganda ploy. Distinctions between "us" and "them" are as old as recorded history and are reflected in terms such as the "deserving poor" and the "undeserving poor." Such terms highlight their moral basis (e.g., Morone, 1997; Katz, 1989). Classification often results in a label. Consider terms such as "obese," "prehypertensive," "developmentally disabled," "alcoholic." The press of technology for efficiency encourages standardization and routinization of practices including measures used such as BMI (body mass index) propelled by the use of computers to track, classify, and prescribe. Classification is integral to this standardization, including the penal system in which professionals are involved as risk estimators, therapists, and surveillance personnel. Labels reflect successful claims-making regarding a concern and how it is viewed. An incorrect label may result in offering ineffective or harmful interventions, withholding of needed services, or imposition of unwanted "services" for the "good of the client." Consider the consequences of false positives resulting from overzealous marketing of diagnostic tests. Labels can suffer from all the ways in which classifications are in error, such as over or under inclusion.

Clinical labels may give an *illusion of knowledge* encouraged by their prescriptive (in addition to descriptive) effects (Perez-Alvarez et al., 2008). That is, once a person is given a certain label, this label may shape the beliefs and behaviors of those labeled, as well as others who interact with "the labeled." (See discussions of the secondary effects of labeling.). Confirmatory biases encourage such shaping; we tend to look for indicators to support the label. This illusion of knowledge may interfere with the discovery of knowledge; equating naming with explaining is a common confusion, often encouraged by promoters of the naming. Labels are not helpful if they offer excuses for harmful behaviors ("I ate too many Twinkies"), transform us into helpless victims of alleged chemical imbalances overlooking the effects of bad choices we make that we can learn how to avoid in the future, or are used to oppress others. Consider labels such as *drapetomania* (an irresistible propensity to run away). This "disease" was alleged to be rampant among slaves in the South in the last century. Hobbs (1975) suggests that:

> Categories and labels are powerful instruments for social regulation and control, and they are often employed for obscure, covert, or hurtful purposes: to degrade people, to deny them access to opportunity, to exclude 'undesirables' whose presence in some way offends, disturbs familiar custom, or demands extraordinary effort. (p. 11)

Labels are not helpful if they mislead and obscure understanding of individual differences and discovery of potential remedies, such as environmental circumstances related to problems-in-living, or if they rob us of our liberty to make decisions that cause no harm to others and stigmatize in the bargain. They are not helpful if they offer excuses for failure to address inequities such as the harsh realities of ghettoes, which offer few opportunities for employment and high-quality education. Lack of opportunities to pursue approved means of employment and rejection of "slave labor" jobs—low pay, no future—may result in pursuit of illegal means and subsequent entry into the penal system with the label "criminal" (Wacquant, 2009). Illich (1976) suggests that negative labels can be "a surreptitious and amoral way of blaming the victim" (Illich, 1976, p. 169). Labels encourage either or thinking—either he is alcoholic or he is not. A focus on psychological and medical explanations distracts attention from "sick making" environments.

What about Psychiatric Labels?

Psychiatric labels have been applied to an ever-increasing number of behaviors viewed as mental disorders. The latest edition of the *Diagnostic and Statistical Manual of Mental Disorders (DSM-IV-R)* (2000) of the American Psychiatric Association contains hundreds of labels alleged to reflect "mental illnesses." A key propaganda strategy is to equate signs (a temperature of 102) and symptoms (feeling hot). In medicine, there are signs (temperature measured by a thermometer), as well as symptoms (feeling hot). Not so in psychiatry although we are told that we will find them someday (Boyle, 2002). Szasz (1994), as well as others (Boyle, 2002), argue that psychiatric labels are used for social control purposes and often result in harming rather than helping people, for example via coerced treatment. Psychiatric labels are based on a list of symptoms. (See Table 5.1.) In an effort to be objective, lists of behaviors assumed to reflect a disorder are removed from unique individual contexts—the qualitative. Even biopsychiatrists such as Nancy Adresseson raise this critique. Indeed, the DSM is being subjected to sharper critiques by "insiders," as well as "outsiders" (e.g., Frances, 2010). The introduction to the DSM (2000) states that classifications in this source neither suggest etiology nor offer guidelines for selection of services. Thus, they are really not "diagnoses" in terms of detecting causes; they are labels. The American Psychiatric Association claims that its classification system

Table 5.1 EXAMPLES OF DIAGNOSTIC CRITERIA FOR
ATTENTION-DEFICIT/HYPERACTIVITY DISORDER

A. Either (1) or (2):

(1) six (or more) of the following symptoms of **inattention** have persisted for at least 6 months to a degree that is maladaptive and inconsistent with developmental level:

Inattention

(a) often fails to give close attention to details or makes careless mistakes in schoolwork, work, or other activities

(b) often has difficulty sustaining attention in tasks or play activities

(c) often does not seem to listen when spoken to directly

(d) often does not follow through on instructions and fails to finish schoolwork, chores, or duties in the workplace (not due to oppositional behavior or failure to understand instructions)

(e) often has difficulty organizing tasks and activities

(f) often avoids, dislikes, or is reluctant to engage in tasks that require sustained mental effort (such as schoolwork or homework)

(g) often loses things necessary for tasks or activities (e.g., toys, school assignments, pencils, books, or tools)

(h) is often easily distracted by extraneous stimuli

(i) is often forgetful in daily activities

SOURCE: DSM (2000), pp. 92–93. Reproduced with permission.

is based on scientific evidence. Critics argue otherwise. The individual variability of behavior and related unique environmental circumstances are overlooked, resulting in lost opportunities to understand clients and their troubles.

> There is ample evidence to suggest that in the psychiatric diagnosis of children, misdiagnoses frequently occur because the *DSM* criteria sets are of inconsistent reliability and are prone to overdiagnosis. The *DSM* criteria, however, have a seductive usability tinged with a scientific patina, providing the illusion of establishing the presence of specific disorders without the need for a comprehensive understanding of clients or their social environments. Children's diagnoses are convenient but frequently incorrect. (Kirk, 2004, p. 266)

The enormous success of the DSM is remarkable, given the questionable reliability and validity of psychiatric labels. DSM labels are required for access to care, prescription medications, and research funding. This is perhaps the most successful propaganda campaign in the history of the helping professions. In *The Mismeasure of Women* (1992), Tavris contends that labels included in the DSM-IV (1994) continue to misdirect attention away from political, social, and economic conditions related to expected gender roles and toward alleged individual deficiencies. In *The Selling of DSM* (1992), Kirk and Kutchins discuss the role of political and economic considerations in the creation and marketing of the DSM and document reliability and validity problems with this system (see also Kirk, 2010). These include the consensual nature of what is included (agreement among individuals is relied on rather than empirical criteria), lack of agreement about what label to assign clients (poor reliability), boundary problems (overlap in symptoms in different diagnoses), and lack of association between a label and indications of what plans will be effective. Panels of experts, many of whom have ties to the pharmaceutical industry, decide on behavior to be labeled (Cosgrove et al., 2009; Cosgrove, 2010). Conspicuously absent are (mis)behaviors such as "Conflict-of-Interest Disorder" and "Rapacious Hedge Fund Obsession." Diagnostic labeling implies the need for specialists to help people with their problems. As more behaviors are assigned a psychiatric label, the mental health industry can grow ever greater. Key questions such as: "What is mental illness?" "What is a disease?" "What is a disorder?" are glossed over.[10] Psychiatric classification systems medicalize problems-in-living and encourage a focus on internal phenomenon such as brain diseases. Controversies are hidden. John Knight argues that human service advocates persuade us that vulnerable people should be surrounded by professional services and are therefore removed from community life to receive these special service programs. "The result of this professional pedagogy is a disabled citizenry and impotent community associations, unable to remember or understand how labeled people were or can be included in community life" (p. 6).

Psychiatric labels are stigmatizing (Verhaeghe, Bracke, & Christiaens, 2010); they result in "spoiled identities" (Goffman, 1990). They say too little about positive attributes, potential for change, and change that does occur and too much about presumed negative characteristics and limits to change. There is no sign that the stigma of labels is decreasing. Pharmaceutical companies are now pursuing de-stigmatization efforts realizing that stigmatizing mental patients may decrease sales of medication (Applbaum, 2009). Examples of personal stories of harm related to psychiatric labeling follow:

Ava C
I was adopted from the Asian country where I was born and raised by a white family in a small American town. No one I saw while I was growing up looked anything like me, and neither my family—wonderful though they were in many respects—nor anyone else ever mentioned my being Asian. Certainly no one ever talked with me about my culture or country or religion of origin or about what it felt like to be the only Asian person in town. I felt so weird and alienated that I became very depressed. I was given a psychiatric diagnosis. This did not help. In fact, it only added to my conviction that something was wrong with me. Added to feeling strange and different in the first place was the "knowledge" that I was also "mentally ill." Then one day I came to a large city and by chance ended up in Chinatown. All around me were people who looked like me, and some were buying groceries, and some were riding bicycles, and some were talking with friends . . . just living ordinary lives, not looking different and apparently not feeling alienated and "sick." That is when my depression lifted. (p. 2)

Story of Johnny
When I began working with him, Johnny was a 15-year-old Native American boy who had been diagnosed with "Attention Deficit Hyperactivity Disorder."

After 6 years on Ritalin, we discovered he had a hearing deficit in his left ear, a fact that was known but ignored in his original ADHD diagnosis. Because of hearing loss, he would try to sit close to the front of the class, but because his head was cocked when listening, it looked like he was staring out the window. With this long-ignored hearing problem, Johnny had many academic failures and was anxious about class tests and assignments. I sent him to an audiologist, then taught him to meditate in order to cope with his performance anxiety. He began to excel at school. He was the first among his siblings to successfully graduate from high school. Because of his ADHD diagnosis, Johnny had spent 6 years in special education classrooms, with his hearing problem ignored. (p. 9)

Story of Stevie
Native American Stevie was 10 years old when he was diagnosed with "Bipolar Disorder, Childhood Onset," an "unapproved" DSM [psychiatric diagnostic manual] category increasingly utilized around here. He had been placed on heavy dosages of several psychiatric medications, rather than being taken out of the place where he lived with periodic physical and sexual abuse, violence, and abandonment. After several weeks on twice the recommended adult daily dose of Zoloft, he hung himself from a cherry tree behind his grandfather's house. More recent revelations linking SSRI antidepressants, "akathisia" and suicide in children and youth might have saved his life. His psychiatric label of "Bipolar Disorder"—though not even officially approved for the diagnostic manual— was carte blanche for providers to experiment on him. (p. 10)

Ted Chabasinski J.D. (see full story on <http://www.mindfreedom.org>)
[was in a foster home as a child.] When [I wanted to] stay in the back yard and make mud pies with my sister, [I was labeled] passive and withdrawn, and my mommy and daddy were supposed to encourage me to explore the neighborhood more. When I started to wander around the neighborhood, I went to a neighbor's garden and picked some flowers. As a result, [I was labeled] "hostile." [I] was admitted to Bellevue Hospital's psychiatric ward, where [I was] one of the first children to be 'treated' with electric shock. I was six years old. (pp. 10–11)

Anonymous 6
My friend was diagnosed with Major Depressive Disorder when she was thirteen. Despite the fact that Wellbutrin was specifically not supposed to be prescribed for people under eighteen, her psychiatrist gave it to her.

She began to hallucinate. She could no longer see her reflection in the mirror and began to think that she did not have any blood in her veins, and became scared that she was going to die. She began to cut herself on a regular basis in order to check that she had blood. Her parents hospitalized her. While at the hospital, the doctors told her that she was showing signs of Schizophrenia (due to the hallucinations).

No one bothered to connect her hallucinations to a possible effect of a drug that she should have never been taking, and her medical records now say that she was once considered to be Schizophrenic. (p. 25) (<http://www.PsychDiagnosis.net> a web site established by Paula Kaplan)

Giving psychiatric labels to clients, encouraged by Big Pharma,[11] often results in intrusive interventions such as prescribing psychotropic medication, which may have harmful effects resulting in the creation of abnormal brain states (Breggin, 2008; Whitaker, 2010; Moncrieff, 2008) and even death. A number of medications have been linked to increased violence (Moore, Glenmullen, & Furberg, 2010). And what happens when the anxious or depressed stop taking medication? Will they experience adverse withdrawal effects?[12] Have they solved their problems? There is no doubt that some are helped. But what about others? Increasing calls for surveillance of all children and screening programs for "mental illnesses" are concerning given their dubious evidentiary status.[13] Psychiatrists, social workers, and psychologists are typically trained in the use of the DSM. Related conceptual and methodological concerns regarding the DSM and alternative views may not be reviewed during professional education (LaCasse & Gomory, 2003). Once labeled "mentally ill," those so named may be subjected to experimental procedures that result in harm. Consider the example at Columbia University in which mental patients were injected with drugs that contained dangerous impurities. Researchers continued to violate FDA safety regulations over a four-year period (Carey, 2010). Another example concerns injection of mental patients in Guatemala with syphilis in the 1940s to test the effects of penicillin (McNeil, 2010). The controversies concerning the empirical status of psychiatric labels are so sharp and so important to understand to avoid related propaganda, that you should read relevant material for yourself.[14]

Race and Ethnicity as Classifications

We live in a racialized society in which ethnic and color difference are constantly emphasized. Yehudi Webster argues that racial and ethnic descriptions of events are "forms of propaganda, an indoctrination into a conviction that U.S. society has different racial and ethnic groups that are locked in a relationship of domination/oppression" (1992, p. 13). He argues that the view that certain physical differences imply a racial identity is propagated by social scientists, governmental institutions, and the media and suggests that racial classification was initiated as a justification for certain political and economic arrangements. Once persons are racially classified, there is no escaping the implications of racial motives (e.g., racism). Webster views racial classification itself as racism. He notes that racism refers to many things, including "a belief system or ideology, discriminatory policies and behavior, theories of genetic inferiority, and socioeconomic inequality" (1992, p. 241). The government, social scientists, and the media daily use the categories of race and ethnicity, which he considers bogus categories that do more harm than good (e.g., they underplay our shared humanness and, in so doing, make it easier for us to dehumanize others). They obscure class differences in economic resources. Some of our most inspiring leaders such as Martin Luther King also emphasized our shared humanness. One in 50 Americans describe themselves as multiracial (Roberts, 2010). And, one's color may not reflect one's DNA. Thus, depending on a person's color to make medical decisions may result in serious errors, such as assuming that symptoms of a white person could not be due to sickle cell anemia (e.g., Hoffman, 2006; Braun, Fausto-Sterling, Fullwiley, Hammonds, Nelsen, Quivers et al., 2007).

CONTINUING TO OFFER AND PROMOTE INTERVENTIONS FOUND TO BE HARMFUL

Interventions that have been critically tested and found to do more harm than good continue to be promoted and used.[15] Children have been pushed to the point of death in wilderness programs. Such programs continue to operate encouraged by bogus claims of effectiveness in brochures and other sources such as the Internet.[16] Some examples of harmful programs follow.

Boot Camps and Prison Style Juvenile Facilities

A variety of interventions claimed to redirect behavior of youth in a positive direction, including "boot camps," have been and are widely promoted.[17] Altheide (2002) argues that such facilities are a direct result of media hyping of fear of youth. Inflated claims of effectiveness can be seen on web sites and in brochures and advertisements. Desperation to deal with difficult behavior and hope for a remedy when others have failed may combine to make parents and others blind to promotion of dubious methods. Scandals in relation to children dying in such facilities have been reported in the media.

Consider the example of Martin Lee Anderson who died in January 2006 after being beaten at a boot camp in Panama City Florida (Sexton, 2007). The seven guards and a nurse who were charged with aggravated manslaughter in the death of this 14 year old boy were acquitted in October 2007.

When this boy's death was initially announced there was a cover-up attempt. He was said to have choked and to have died of natural causes. Further investigation revealed that he had been beaten to death by the guards who were supposed to protect him. (See also Fanta, 2006.) A federal report prepared by the Government Accountability Office which investigated the cases of 10 teenagers who died at youth boot camps reported "significant evidence of ineffective management" and "reckless or negligent operating practices." "The report detailed evidence that teenagers were starved, forced to eat their own vomit and to wallow for hours in their own excrement. In one instance, a boy was so hydrated that he ate dirt to survive, according to witnesses and an autopsy" (Schemo, 2007). The contingency systems in these residential centers (the relationships between behaviors and environmental antecedents and consequences) are often the opposite of what research suggests should be arranged (Miltenberger, 2008); they are very punitive. Youth are shouted at and pushed around.[18] Boot camps model aggressive behaviors such as shoving, yelling, and pushing. It is assumed that treating them in this negative manner will alter their behavior. The most effective way to decrease undesired behavior is to identify and reinforce positive alternatives to disliked behavior. And, change efforts are most effective when carried out in real-life circumstances.[19] Boot camps provide a very unnatural environment. Scared Straight programs remain in use despite research showing that not only are they not effective, they are harmful (Petrosino, Turpin-Petrosino, & Buehler, 2003). Here too, we see bogus claims of effectiveness in advertisements and other material together with ignoring counterevidence to such claims.

Brushing and Joint Compression

A variety of interventions have and are being used to address concerns associated with autism (Metz, Mulick, & Butler, 2005). Some do more harm than good (Thyer & Pignotti, 2010). Consider this example promoted as beneficial.

> This case involved a nonverbal 8-year-old boy with autism.... His problem behaviors included self-induced vomiting, other self-injurious behaviors, feces smearing, aggressive behaviors (hitting), and food selectivity issues.
>
> The occupational therapist at the child's school strongly recommended to his parents that he would benefit from sensory integration therapy.... She argued that sensory integration deficits and 'sensory overload' probably caused the child's aggressive behavior and recommending brushing and joint compression therapy....
>
> The agreed-on target was episodes of hitting behavior per hour. As defined for this study, hitting included blows directed at himself, staff members, or his table....
>
> Brushing and joint compression were delivered by the occupational therapist and a trained assistant. During brushing, the child's skin was firmly stroked by a specialized flexible plastic brush. After the child's limbs and torso were brushed, the occupational therapist firmly pushed specific body parts so that the joints were compressed....
>
> Instruction in completing a shape sorter was chosen as a neutral treatment to be compared with sensory integration.... A coin flip was used to determine whether the boy received the brushing and joint compression therapy or shape sorter instruction, and observers were blind to what treatment had been given. The child received two interventions a day.
>
> The results of the experiment are shown in [Figure 5.2]. In every instance except one, the child's rate of hitting episodes was higher after receiving brushing and joint compression therapy, and in that case hitting occurred at the same rate for both treatments. The study showed clear evidence that an unproven treatment—even one that appears benign—can have significant detrimental effects. (Kay & Vyse, 2005, pp. 270-71)

If this test had not been conducted, the parents would have had difficulty recognizing the negative effects of sensory integration therapy and may have continued it much longer than they did. However, after seeing the data, they asked for the brushing and joint compression therapy to be discontinued.[20]

The Recovered Memory Movement

Recovered memory therapy became popular in the late 1980s. Problems such as depression were claimed to be due to a past history of sexual abuse, often by a parent. It was assumed that only if this abuse was recalled and there was an abreaction would problems diminish. (Abreaction refers to use of exposure to rid adverse experiences of their "emotional charge.") After prolonged counseling, many clients would recall that their father had sexually molested them. Some came to believe that they had

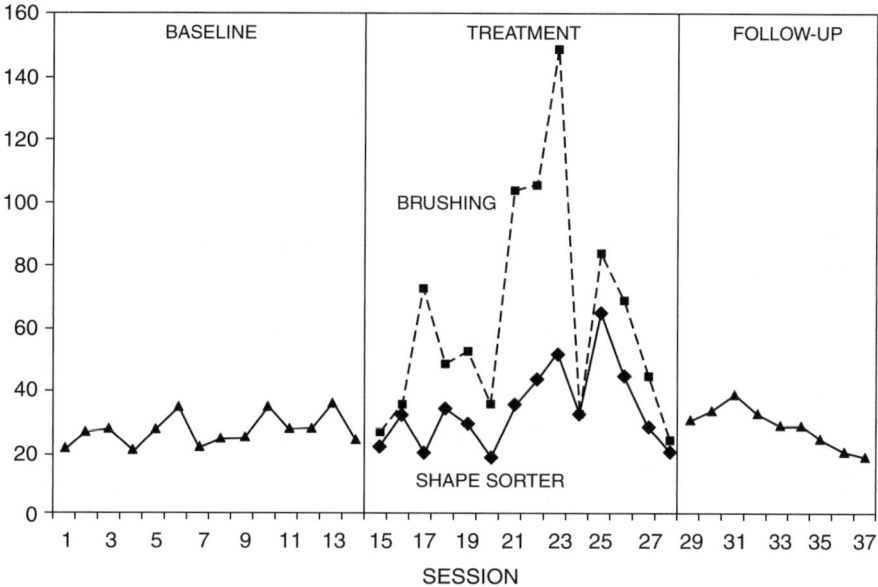

Figure 5.2. Hitting episodes per hour during discrete trial training sessions. During the intervention phase, the child received sensory integration therapy (brushing and joint compression; broken line) or instruction in using a shape sorter (solid line) just prior to his discrete trial session. The follow-up phase was a return to the baseline condition in which neither sensory integration theory nor shape sorter instruction was given prior to the daily session.
SOURCE: S. Kay & S. Vyse (2005). Helping parents separate the wheat from the chaff: Putting autism treatment to the test. In J. W. Jacobson, R. M. Foxx, & J. A. Mulick (Eds.) (2005), *Controversial treatments in developmental disabilities: Fad, fashion and science in professional practice* (p. 272). Mahwah, NJ: Erlbaum.

been involved in Satanic rituals, including cannibalism. Ofshe and Watters (1994) note that the assumptions and ideas involved in recovered memory therapy reflected ideas in psychotherapy throughout the century. Freud "pressured clients to confirm his preexisting belief that all hysterics suffered abuse as small children" (p. 291). (He later repudiated this theory.)

> Indeed, Freud compared his methods to the pressure required to elicit confessions from suspected witches. Freud's techniques were brutal and unyielding. Simply put, he bullied his patients in order that they may confirm his theories and interpretations. This conclusion is inescapable, for Freud himself admits as much: 'Having diagnosed a case . . . with certainty and having classified symptoms correctly, we are in a position to translate the symptomatology in the etiology: and we may then boldly demand confirmation of our suspicion from the patient. We must not be led astray by initial denials. If we keep firmly to what we have inferred, we shall in the end conquer every resistance by emphasizing the unshakeable nature of our convictions.' (Ofshe & Watters, 1994, p. 292)
>
> In the end, Freud made two unforgivable mistakes: coercing false memories from his clients and then blaming the client for the creation of those beliefs.

It is perhaps the latter mistake—the conclusion that almost all accounts of sexual abuse, whether produced in therapy or simply remembered, were the fantasies of his clients—that was his most damaging. By lumping all accounts of sexual abuse together and labeling them fantasy, Freud gave those portions of Western society impressed with psychoanalysis an excuse to ignore the reality of childhood sexual assault for much of the twentieth century. (p. 293)

These authors argue that "Freud created a pseudoscientific paradigm in the mental health profession. That is, unconstrained by any substantiated or agreed upon body of data, close observations, or demonstrated effects, Freud proposed what appeared to be an impressive intellectual structure for the understanding of behavior" (p. 294). This is a good example of creating an illusion of understanding. "His theories were accepted by consensus—not by anything resembling empirical proof but because of his magnetism and the seductively broad nature of the idea" (p. 298). "His patients became a means to an end"—the confirmation of his theories. Ofshe and Watters (1994) argue that a similarly grandiose conceit was adopted by many recovered memory therapists.

The role of the therapist established by Freud permits therapists to dismiss a patient's pretherapy sense of self as hopelessly flawed, inauthentic, or clouded by the mind's own defenses. Patients often allow this to happen because they believe their healer possesses unique knowledge of all facets of human nature, including memory and symptomatology, and has a near-magical ability to know their true past. (Ofshe & Watters, 1994, p. 297)[21]

Many people have been falsely accused and some have confessed to crimes they never committed. Those who critique the recovered memory movement have been viciously attacked, even threatened. For example, Elizabeth Loftus had to travel with bodyguards when she attended a national conference at which she received an award for her work.[22]

The recovered memory movement contributed to false charges against day care staff regarding abuse of children in their care.

In his 400 page judgment, (available online in three parts [1], [2], & [3]) the judge highlights the intellectual dishonesty of the review team in compiling their report, Abuse in Early Years. The report, published in 1998, had branded the two innocent former nursery workers as bizarre and dangerous pedophiles who were abusing young children both in the nursery and in the local area in concert with others in an unknown 'pedophile ring.'

The full judgment is a model critique of the flawed investigative techniques and theories that arose in the 1980s in tandem with the 'recovered memory' methodology which affected so many families in the 1990s. (Ofshe & Watters, 1994)[24]

Members of the British False Memory Society (BFMS) sent a copy of this amicus brief as well as the Ceci and Bruck (1995) research showing how false memories can be implanted in children to the two staff members, but this was ignored.[23]

Other Examples

Holding therapy "involves physical and psychologically enforced restraint of the child and physically intrusive practices such as grabbing, poking and lying on top of the child with the full weight of the adult's body" (Pignotti & Mercer, 2007, p. 515). Attachment theory is drawn on in use of this practice. The purpose of holding therapy is to regress children who had experienced trauma. Holding is claimed to reduce rage and create attachment with a new parent figure. Harms of holding therapy have been described by Pignotti and Mercer (2007) who note that such effects are not mentioned by Craven and Lee (2006) in a discussion of this therapy. This oversight will misinform rather than inform readers about the consequences of holding therapy.[24] Deaths have also occurred as a result of rebirthing therapy (Janofsky, 2001). Here too we can ask: What sources and methods of propaganda came into play such as inflated claims of effectiveness and hiding adverse effects? Is the underling theory compatible with empirical data?

AVOIDABLE HARMS RELATED TO MEDICATION

Promotion of claims regarding the biomedical cause of human distress encourages use of medication as a remedy (e.g., see Jacobs, 1995). There is no evidence that serotonin level is a cause of depression (LaCasse & Leo, 2005). Related harms include unnecessary medication that results in adverse consequences, as well as medication prescribed in a high one-size-fits-all manner (Cohen, 2001) or in contradiction to other medications or physical conditions. Harms from drugs are especially concerning, given that the drugs prescribed may not even be effective.[25] A drug may create the very problems it is promoted as preventing such as bisphosphonates prescribed to prevent fractures (e.g., see Kolata, 2010b). Misleading reports of drug research—those that exaggerate claims of effectiveness—encourage unnecessary medication.[26] The FDA has approved drugs with a history of failure.[27] Whitaker (2010) and Moncrieff (2008) argue that neuroleptic medications actually create brain dysfunctions. Abilify, an atypical antipsychotic, is now being heavily advertised as a treatment for depression.

Adverse consequences of medication have received great attention over the last decade as scandal after scandal has revealed harm, often hidden by pharmaceutical companies until forced onto the stage of public awareness (Brody, 2007; Kassirer, 2005).[28] Journalists have taken a leading role in reporting harmful effects.[29] So too, have web sites such as PharmedOut (<http://www.pharmedout.org>) and the Alliance for Human Research Protection (<http://www.ahrp.org>). (See also <http://www.criticalthinkrx.org>.) Eli Lilly agreed to pay $500 million to settle 18,000 lawsuits from plaintiffs who claimed they had developed diabetes and other illnesses as a result of taking Zyprexa, a drug for schizophrenia and bipolar disorder.

> Documents provided to the *New York Times* last month by a lawyer who represents mentally ill patients show that Lilly played down the risks of Zyprexa to doctors as the drug's sales soared after its introduction in 1996. The internal documents show that in Lilly's clinical trails, 16 percent of people taking Zyprexa

gained more than 66 pounds after a year on the drug, a far higher figure than the company disclosed to doctors.

The documents also show that Lilly marketed the drug as appropriate for patients who did not meet accepted diagnoses of schizophrenia or bipolar disorder, Zyprexa's only approved uses. (Berenson, 2007a)

Consider also harm caused by the diet pill fen-phen (Brody, 2007) and from Vioxx, an anti-inflammatory found to increase thrombus formation. Avandia, a pill for diabetes, was recently removed from the market in European countries.[30] A lawsuit was filed against Merck by 1,400 patients who claimed that their jawbones deteriorated as a result of taking Fosamax to address osteoporosis (Singer, 2010). (See also Van Voris, 2010.) Drugs that result in harm are often promoted based not on increased years of high quality life, but on surrogate indicators that are not associated with such a happy outcome. For example, Lipitor reduces plaque but not mortality (Eisenberg & Wells, 2008).

Many players are involved in the promotion of bogus claims regarding the effectiveness of prescribed medication including drug companies, which distribute hundreds of thousands of advertisements, and academic researchers in their pay, as described in chapter 3. Big Pharma is a global enterprise including the conduct of thousands of clinical trials in third world countries (e.g., Barlett & Steele, 2011; Petryna, Lakoff, & Kleinman, 2006; Wilson, 2010g). Some players, such as ghostwriters, are hidden in the wings until forced to emerge on stage such as staff in a writing company hired by SmithKline Beecham to write "Recognition and Treatment of Psychiatric Disorders: A Psychopharmacology Handbook for Primary Care" published under the names of the psychiatrists Charles Nemeroff and Alan Schatzberg (Wilson, 2010, Nov. 30, 2010 B3).

Unveiled court documents showed that ghostwriters paid by Wyeth Pharmaceutical Company produced scores of scientific papers supporting use of hormone replacement therapy in women (Singer, 2009d). These documents were made public by efforts of *PLoS Medicine*, a medical journal and the *New York Times*. They showed that Wyeth routinely hired medical-writing firms to ghostwrite articles that appeared in medical journals under the authorship of an academic researcher.

> The lawsuits [about 8,400] focus on whether Wyeth hormone therapy drugs Prempro and Premarin, used to treat symptoms of menopause, have caused breast cancer in some women.
>
> . . .
>
> On June 11, a biomedical journal, PLoS, published by the Public Library of Science, filed a motion to intervene in the Prempro litigation. PLoS, represented by a public-interest law firm, Public Justice, wanted to set aside the confidential designation that had been placed on the documents before a series of trials began in 2006. The documents were shown to jurors at trial but were otherwise unavailable publicly.
>
> Plaintiffs say ghostwriting is when a drug company conjures up the concept for an article that will counteract criticism of a drug or embellish its benefits, hires a professional writing company to draft a manuscript conveying the company's message, retains a physician to sign off as the author and finds a publisher to unwittingly publish the work.

Drug companies disseminate their ghostwritten articles to their sales representatives, who present the articles to physicians as independent proof that the companies' drugs are safe and effective. (Associated Press, Judge orders Wyeth papers unsealed, July 25, 2009)

Investigations document use of excessive antipsychotic medication for adults (Diaz & De Leon, 2002). Given the adverse side effects drugs may have, such as tardive dyskinesia (an irreversible condition including uncontrollable trembling, tics, and jerky movements), this is alarming. High percentages of adults receiving antipsychotics such as Risperdal, Zyprexa, and Seroquel suffered severe adverse effects (64%–82%) and dropped out of studies (e.g., Lieberman, Stroup, McEvoy, Swartz, Rosenheck, Perkins, Keefe et al., 2005). Antidepressants increase the likelihood of falls among the elderly (Darowski, 2009). Hip fractures are common among the elderly and often result in death. Thus, they are vital to minimize. Use of antipsychotics with older adults with dementia increases mortality (Gill, Bronskill, Normand, Anderson, Sykora, Lam et al., 2007; Schneeweiss, Setogushi, Brookhart, Dormuth, & Wang, 2007). Federal drug regulators reported that older patients with dementia who are given antipsychotic medication are far more likely to die prematurely compared to those given dummy pills.[31] Antipsychotic medications are prescribed to over 25% of U.S. Medicare users in nursing homes (e.g., see Briesacher et al., 2005).

Drugs promoted as having fewer side effects compared to older drugs such as Haldol for psychosis, which causes tardive dyskinesia, including Zyprexa, Symbyax, Risperdal, Seroquel, Abilify, Clozaril, and Geodon, are now required to contain a black-box warning, the agency's most severe, warning users about increased risk of diabetes. These second generation antipsychotics have not been found to be any more effective than older generation antipsychotics (e.g., Leucht, Kissling, & Davis, 2009; Rummel-Kluge, Komossa, Schwartz, Huner, & Schmid, Lobos et al., 2010). Harms of medication such as serious damage to heart valves have been found with drugs for Parkinson's Disease, pergolide (Permax), and cabernoline (Dostinex).[32] As a licensed psychologist in the State of California I received an FDA Public Health Advisory (April 11, 2005) from the U.S. Food & Drug Administration concerning "Deaths with Antipsychotics in Elderly Patients with Behavioral Disturbances regarding Use of Atypical (Second Generation) Antipsychotic Medications Because of Increased Mortality." Included here were Zyprexa, Abilify, Risperdal, and Seroquel. This warns that: "All of the atypical antipsychotics are approved for the treatment of schizophrenia. None, however, is approved for the treatment of behavioral disorders in patients with dementia."[33]

The Food and Drug Administration has determined that the treatment of behavioral disorders in elderly patients with dementia with atypical (second generation) antipsychotic medications is associated with increased mortality. Of a total of seventeen placebo controlled trials performed with olanzapine (Zyprexa), aripiprazole (Abilify), risperidone (Risperdal), or quetiapine (Seroquel) in elderly demented patients with behavioral disorders, fifteen showed numerical increases in mortality in the drug-treated group compared to the placebo-treated patients. These studies enrolled a total of 5106 patients, and several analyses have demonstrated an approximately 1.6–1.7 fold increase in mortality in these studies. Examination of the specific causes of these deaths revealed that most were either due to heart related events (e.g., heart failure, sudden death) or infections (mostly pneumonia).

There has been an enormous rise, starting in 1994, in the rate of psychotropic drugs prescribed for American children. A larger proportion of Medicaid-insured children compared to privately insured children are prescribed psychotropic drugs (Martin, Sherwin, Stubbe, Van Hoof, Scahill, & Leslie, 2002). (See also Wilson, 2009c.) Hazards of taking these drugs, including creating abnormal brain states, are typically hidden from parents.[34] Millions of children are on medication in the United States as a result of being diagnosed with Attention Deficit Hyperactivity Disorder (ADHD) (Baughman, 2006), (Carey, 2011). Research showing increased risk of suicide from some prescribed medications for youth has forced drug companies to include related warnings on labels (e.g., see Healy, 2004). Concerns about overmedication of children with Ritalin have been raised for over a decade. Here is what one study showed (Hansen, 2007).

> During a 10-month period from January 2006 to October 2006, Michigan Medicaid statistics show:
> 100% increase in children under age 18 on 3 or more mood stabilizers.
> 100% increase in children age 6–17 on 4 or more psychiatric drugs.
> 79% increase in adults on 5 or more psychiatric drugs.
> 67% increase in adults on 3 or more psychiatric drugs.
> 49% increase in adults on 2 or more insomnia agents.
> 45% increase in children under age 18 on a benzodiazepine for at least 60 days.
> 45% increase in children under age 18 on 2 or more antipsychotics.
> According to Michigan Medicaid records from 2005, the top 5 psychiatric drug classes prescribed to children under 5 years old were:
> 1. Anxiolytics/Sedative Hypnotics (1,265 patients under age 5).
> 2. Antidyskinetics (972 patients under age 5).
> 3. Anticonvulsants/Mood Stabilizers (933 patient under age 5).
> 4. Sympathomimetics/Stimulants (408 patients under age 5).
> 5. Atypical antipsychotics (322 patients under age 5).

Drugs are often tested in less developed countries (see Petryna et al., 2006). Desperate people may agree to participate in experiments that cause harm to participants especially if possible harms are hidden from them. Companies with staff in countries such as Nigeria, China, and India provide the infrastructure to pharmaceutical companies to conduct trials. Concern over procedures was illustrated by a 49 million pound settlement by Pfizer regarding a controversial trial for a meningitis drug in Nigeria. A Pan-African clinical trial registry was created to increase transparency. (See Wilson, 2010g)

HARMS CAUSED BY USE OF UNNECESSARILY INTRUSIVE OR UNNEEDED INTERVENTIONS

Intrusive interventions promoted as useful but that are unnecessary cause harm to thousands each year. Availability of effective but less intrusive methods may be hidden because they are less expensive or require more training. A variety of propaganda methods including bold assertions are used to promote dubious methods.

Medical sociologists bring to our attention variations in rates of medical procedures such as hysterectomies in different locations. Still as of 2007, more are performed in the United States compared to other countries, controlling for population differences. Are they all needed?[35] Similar questions have been raised regarding Caesarean births.[36] Certain heart surgeries for the elderly have also been questioned.[37] Deyo and Patrick (2005) include the following examples in a chapter titled "Ineffective and Needlessly Extensive Surgery": radial mastectomy for breast cancer, boosting the blood supply to the heart, arthroscopic surgery for arthritis of the knee, bypassing clogged arteries in the brain, fetal-cell therapy for Parkinson's disease, and episiotomy during childbirth.[38] Unneeded medical devices may be used such as pedicle screws in back operations and andrografts for aortic aneurysms.[39]

Unnecessarily Intrusive Diagnostic Tests

Vacuum assisted core needle biopsy may be recommended to diagnose breast lumps rather than the much less invasive fine needle aspiration, which, in the hands of a trained user, is just as accurate (e.g., Ljung, 2007). However, such training requires considerable time and some physicians have not taken the time to learn to use this procedure with high accuracy. Informed consent requires that patients be told about options, for example, that a less invasive but equally accurate alternative is available. But they may not be so informed.[40] This illustrates one of the most pernicious forms of propaganda on the part of professionals—hiding alternative options.

Avoidable Harms in Group Homes and Institutional Settings

Hundreds of thousands of people, old and young, live in group homes and other residential facilities. Related industries are huge, including the nursing home industry, the group home industry for youth and psychiatric patients, residential centers for substance use. These money-making enterprises advertise widely. When profit is of concern, residents may suffer, especially when regulating agencies neglect their obligations, allowing harmful practices to continue. Programs provided may not reflect claims made in propagandistic promotion of services nor reflect required oversight responsibilities of state agencies. Facilities are promoted as successful in brochures, advertisements, and on the Internet.[41] The focus in many psychiatric settings on biomedical causes and remedies results in ignoring life circumstances associated with problems. Patient advocates filed a lawsuit against the State of New Jersey alleging that patients are routinely medicated against their will without any review by an external arbiter (Perez-Pena, 2010). Such a review may reveal that less intrusive methods should first be used. To those with little power, often comes even less.

Investigations reveal children, adolescents, and adults unnecessarily hospitalized in psychiatric hospitals, particularly in the for profit sector (Payer, 1992). Abuse of children and adolescents in institutional care has a long and alarming history (e.g., Bessant, Hill & Watts, 2005). Status offenders have been labeled as "mentally ill" and confined, without due process, to inpatient psychiatric and chemical dependency units of private hospitals (Schwartz, 1989). (The term "status offender" refers to youths who fall under juvenile court jurisdiction because of conduct prohibited only because of their juvenile status, e.g., disobedience, curfew violations, running away, and truancy.) Schwartz (1989) refers to this relabeling of typical teenage behavior as mental illness as *"the medicalization of defiance."*

Reasons related to unneeded hospitalization include insurance policies favoring inpatient care, advertising of residential treatment centers, and lack of community-based services for youth (Schwartz, 1989). Contingency systems in settings promoted as helpful in group homes and residential settings may be counter habilitative, that is promote undesired behaviors and discourage desired ones (Meinhold & Mulick, 1990). (See also earlier discussion of "boot camps" in this chapter.) Residential staff are often not trained in use of positive methods for altering behavior and use punishment and tranquilizing medications instead. The history of institutional care reveals a continuing saga of avoidable harm and neglect including coerced drugging, physical abuse, sexual abuse, and neglect, as well as harmful use of restraints, in a context of promotional advertising.[42]

An investigation of group homes for adult mental patients in the state of New York revealed scores of violations of patients' rights and ineffective or harmful treatment. Harmful conditions often continue because state and/or federal regulation agencies do not carry out their monitoring obligations.

> Summing up the *Times* survey of the 26 homes [for adult mental patients] series author Clifford J. Levy noted that from 1995 to 2001, 946 of the 5,000 patients living in these facilities had died. 'The analysis shows that some residents died roasting in their rooms during heat waves,' he wrote. 'Others threw themselves from rooftops, making up some of at least 14 suicides in that seven year period. Still more, lacking the most basic care, succumbed to routinely treatable ailments, from burst appendixes to seizures.
>
> The state agencies charged with oversight of the adult home industry have done little or no investigation of these deaths. Indeed, the state and federal governments have been lax in conducting any probes into the abysmal conditions in which helpless mentally ill residents are forced to live. Penalties for operators are few and far between, and even those charged with stealing patients' money and other abuses are allowed to remain in business. State inspectors who have proved too vigorous in pursuing complaints have faced reprimands and transfers. (Severin, 2002, pp. 4–5)

HARMS CAUSED BY CONTINUING TO PROMOTE PRACTICES AND POLICIES FOUND TO BE INEFFECTIVE

Continuing promotion of programs found to be ineffective wastes valuable resources, encourages false hopes, and violates ethical obligations of professionals. Consider promotion of ineffective weight loss technologies, as well as alternative therapies that have been found to be ineffective (Bausell, 2007).

Facilitated Communication

This procedure was introduced in the early 1970s by a teacher in Australia. It is designed to assist people with severe developmental disabilities to communicate.

The technique involves providing physical support to people with disabilities as they type out messages on a keyboard or letterboard. It was widely promoted as effective.

> Before its adoption as a teaching-treatment technique, the only research evidence in support of its validity consisted of a small number of descriptive reports in the professional literature and anecdotal reports in the popular press and disability media. . . . Controlled research using single and double blind procedures in laboratory and natural settings with a range of clinical populations with which FC is used have determined that, not only are the people with disabilities unable to respond accurately to label or describe stimuli unseen by their assistants, but that the responses are controlled by the assistants. (Jacobson, Mulick, & Schwartz, 1995, p. 75)

Content typed (guided by facilitations) sometimes implicated significant others in sexual abuse, creating yet more unnecessary harm.

Sex Education Program for Teenagers

Concerns about the frequency of teenage pregnancy and sexually transmitted disease encouraged the creation and dissemination of sex education curriculums in schools including promotion of abstinence. In a review of programs it was concluded that "strong evidence is lacking that abstinence based programs significantly delay the initiation of sex, maintain abstinence until marriage, reduce the number of sexual partners or hasten return to abstinence" (Underhill, Operario, & Montgomery, 2007). Consider also the ineffectiveness of virginity pledges as a method to decrease teen sex (Tanne, 2008c).

The War on Drugs in the United States

Billions of dollars have been and are being spent on "the drug war" in the United States. Fallouts from the "drug war" include discriminatory patterns of arrest and incarceration of thousands of African American youth as described in *The New Jim Crow Laws* by Alexander (2010). The "drug war" has been so unsuccessful in achieving its goals that the Cato Institute, a conservative think tank, issued a report calling for the decriminalization of all drugs as done in Portugal in 2001. (See Wood, Werb, Fisher, Hart, Wodak, Bastos, et al., 2010).[43] In the United States, "drug Czars" continue to promote drug war policies and hide their negative consequences. The hundreds of thousands of drug counselors and substance addition programs and residential centers all benefit from the criminalization of drugs. Here too, we can use Hugh Rank's analysis to identify the kinds of propaganda ploys used, for example, hiding the benefit of medical marijuana and exaggerating the harms of recreational use (alleging that it leads to violence and will turn your brain into a scrambled egg) and hiding the success of Portugal's decriminalization policy. Obsessive interest in policing drugs creates avoidable cruelties for those in pain and discomfort including lack of effective, timely pain control (Leland, 2010) and avoidable exposure to crime (stealing prescription drugs from the elderly) (Goodnough, 2010).

PROPAGANDA AS A CONTRIBUTOR TO AVOIDABLE ERRORS

There will always be errors, however there are two types: avoidable and unavoidable. And, not all errors cause harm. Certainly not all errors, even avoidable ones, are due to propaganda. Yet just as certainly, many are. Although there has been considerable attention given to identifying and decreasing avoidable errors in medicine,[44] this has not been true of other professions such as social work, psychology, and psychiatry. Research concerning error in medicine, aviation, and nuclear power shows that errors are typically due to systemic causes including the technology used, training provided to those who use the technology, adequacy of warning systems, and arrangement for redundancy so that if one part fails other arrangements designed to prevent catastrophic breakdowns are engaged. Other causes include regulatory and oversight agencies and organizations that promote false claims about the safety of practices used in a hospital or other service. Propaganda in the helping professions contributes to avoidable errors; errors are hidden rather than sought out and used as an opportunity to take timely, corrective action.

Many avoidable errors are due to self-propaganda, including inflated views of our own knowledge, skills, and entitlements as described in chapter 10. It is estimated that 98,000 people die each year in the United States due to preventable medical errors and 99,000 die from hospital-acquired infections (e.g., Kohn, Corrigan, & Donaldson, 2000). Recent reports show that little has changed (Grady, 2010). This makes this cause of death among the 10 leading killers. Over one and a half million people a year are harmed by taking medication as prescribed by a physician. One in four people are prescribed the wrong drug (Goulding, 2004).[45] Both unfortunate results are directly related to aggressive marketing of pharmaceutical products. One in three hundred patients who are admitted to a hospital die as a result of a medical error and one in ten are harmed (Hawkes, 2009). Half of all identified adverse events are related to errors in reasoning or decision quality (Scott, 2009), which may be encouraged by bogus claims. These errors resulted in "death or permanent disability in at least 25% of cases and at least three quarters were deemed highly preventable."

Inflated claims of accuracy may result in avoidable errors such as using an inaccurate test—a test that does not measure what it claims to measure or has a high false positive rate (it identifies many people who do not have a certain condition as having it) or high false negative rate (it misses many people who do have a condition). Or, it encourages us to get unneeded (or controversial) tests by hiding inaccuracies such as false positives and adverse effects such as harmful radiation. Just as we can be harmed by unneeded tests and misdiagnoses, we can be harmed by delay in accurate diagnosis and timely intervention. Treatment may be expensive and so early detection may be discouraged by managed care companies. Here too, propaganda contributes by hiding the negative consequences of tardy diagnosis. Mayor (2009) argues that many cases of rheumatoid arthritis are not diagnosed or treated quickly enough to stop preventable damage to joints in a report published by the National Audit Office (NAO). Symptoms of ovarian cancer are often neglected (Hamilton, 2009).

Mission statements of professional organizations and social service agencies often claim that services "ensure" effective care for clients. Constant repetition of such bold assertions—impossible even in the best of circumstances—and belied by continued revelations of harming in the name of helping, discourages an active search for and candid recognition of avoidable errors. Many child welfare agencies have been placed in receivership because of concerns about children being unnecessarily harmed as a result of avoidable errors. Only after a judicial order may case records be opened to examination, even in agencies funded by the government.[46] Inflated claims regarding the validity of "benchmark" indicators on the part of researchers, legislators, and policy makers involved in child welfare distract staff from quality work with children by bureaucratic paperwork. Children are returned to homes deemed safe who are then killed. Certainly, some or even many of these tragedies could not be avoided; however, it is clear that some could be avoided, for example, by attention to errors rather than hiding them.[47]

Avoidable harms are directly related to misleading marketing pitches on the part of parent organizations.

> But some experts argue that responsibility for the accident may lie with the kidney center and its parent, National Medical Care Inc. The New Mexico clinic used older dialysis machines that distribute solution to many patients at once, rather than through individual stations as in newer versions. Worse, the system did not sound an alarm when the wrong solution was being used, as newer machines would. (Eichenwald, 1995, p. A1)

Horror stories concerning excessive radiation have been reported at many hospitals (Bogdanich, 2010). Consider Dr. Kao, a radiation oncologist accused of mishandling radioactive seed implants at the Veteran's Hospital in Philadelphia. He carried out ninety-two substandard implants of radioactive seeds out of 116 cases over six years (Bogdanich, 2009).[48] Some were found in the bladder. Incorrect placement resulted in elevated dosage of radiation to the rectum, bladder, or perineum of many patients. Staff in the program knew, but failed to report errors. Staff continued to carry out radioactive seed implants for a year in spite of the fact that the equipment that measured whether patients were given the proper radiation dose was not working. Propaganda contributed to these avoidable errors in at least two ways: (1) bogus claims that all was well on the part of the American College of Radiation Oncology, which accredited this program; (2) failure of the outside contractor, the University of Pennsylvania, to review this program while advertising itself as one of the best medical centers. This is a striking example of continuation of a harmful, error-ridden program due to hiding negative information and promoting bogus positive reports.

AVOIDABLE HARMS CAUSED BY PROMOTING UNTESTED METHODS

Most interventions have not been tested. We do not know if they do more good than harm or harm than good. Failure to test popular procedures is common. Continuing to offer untested methods is encouraged by propaganda ploys such as bold assertions regarding effectiveness—"We know it works." Harms that may result are illustrated in the earlier description of the blinding of 10,000 babies. Dr. Spock advised parents to lay children on their stomachs. This advice resulted in the death of many children.

> Iain Chalmers: I bought a copy of Dr. Benjamin Spock's book Baby and Child Care and I actually marked the passage saying that babies should be put to sleep

on their fronts. Now I promulgated that advice—we now know that had people looked at the evidence by 1970 it would have been clear that this was actually lethally bad advice and it's been estimated that in the UK, had we taken notice of the evidence, it might have prevented about 10,000 deaths from cot death. And the estimates for US, Australia and Europe is over 50,000 unnecessary deaths and that's a tragic consequence of not paying attention to the need for evidence. (Transcript of Health Report on Facing the Evidence—part one. September 11, 2006, p. 2. <http://www.abc.net.au/rn/healthreport/stories/2006/1735075.htm>)

Consider also the operation for a condition called nonarteritic ischemic optic neuropathy in which one or two incisions are made in the sheath surrounding the optic nerve to reduce pressure on it. This common surgical procedure to save vision was found to be ineffective and possibly harmful (Altman, 1995). Premature promotion of thalidomide is one of the most unfortunate examples of harming in the name of helping.

> DES (diethylstilbestrol) was hailed as a great achievement offering enormous practical value in preventing miscarriages, facilitating growth in cattle, treating problems of menopause, acne, gonorrhea in children, and certain types of cancer. Early on, research raised concerns about carcinogenic effects of DES. Early results showed "the first known human occurrences of transplacental carcinogenesis—the development of cancer in offspring due to exposure in utero to a substance that crossed the mother's placenta." (Dutton, 1988, p. 339)

Over 3,000 patients with emphysema have had part of their lungs removed to improve lung function. This is a very expensive operation. Findings from a 2001 study suggest that it is not effective. Still, it is being used by surgeons who believe that "it works" (Kolata, 2001a).

HARMS DUE TO INFLATED CLAIMS REGARDING THE NEED FOR AND ACCURACY OF TESTS

We can be harmed by diagnostic tests. Results of a genetic test may be used to fire someone (Greenhouse, 2010). These too are interventions and can affect our well-being. Harms include injuries from the tests themselves and harm by providing misleading data such as false positives and false negatives. And, they may waste money better spent elsewhere. Gene tests may create needless worry.[49] Consider also controversies about an automated device made by Neurometrix that checks patients for nerve damage (Abelson, 2006a). Critics protest that serious illnesses such as brain tumors have been missed by use of this test. Unnecessary heart X-rays may result in harm.[50] In Britain, Hobbs and Wynne (1989) (two pediatricians) suggested that a simple medical test could be used to demonstrate that buggery or other forms of anal penetration had occurred. Here is their description:

> Reflex dilation well described in forensic texts . . . usually occurs within about 30 seconds of separating the buttocks. Recent controversy has helped our

understanding of what is now seen as an important sign of traumatic penetration of the anus as occurs in abuse, but also following medical and surgical manipulation.... The diameter of the symmetrical relaxation of the anal sphincter is variable and should be estimated. This is a dramatic sign which once seen is easily recognized.... The sign is not always easily reproducible on second and third examinations and there appear to be factors, at present, which may modify the eliciting of this physical sign. The sign in most cases gradually disappears when abuse stops. (Hanks, Hobbs, & Wynne, 1988, p. 153)

News of this test spread quickly, and because of this test, many children were removed from their homes on the grounds that they were being sexually abused—when this was not true. Questions that should have been asked were not raised, such as what is the rate of false positives (children alleged to be abused who were not) and rate of false negatives.

HARMS DUE TO EXAGGERATED CLAIMS OF BENEFIT FROM POPULATION-BASED SCREENING

Do calls to screen entire populations do more good than harm? Here too, the costs and benefits of screening must be considered. However, costs are typically hidden by promoters of such screening.

Full Body CT (Computed Tomography) and MRI Scans

Advertisements for full body CT scans arrive in our mail and can be seen in magazines and newspapers. These promise to detect hidden (occult) disease. But do they? And what about harm from radiation? Brenner and Elliston (2004) compared the amount of radiation exposure during each CT scan to occurrence of cancer due to exposure to the atomic bomb. They suggest that a single CT scan results in a 0.08 percent lifetime risk of developing cancer due to that radiation or one of every 1,250 persons who get a body scan may suffer from cancer as a result of the test.[51] Even if their estimate is an exaggeration, there is no doubt that harm from radiation is a possibility. Other harms include false negatives (overlooking real concerns) and false positives (identifying abnormalities that would never result in harm if ignored). Mobile vans now offer MRIs allowing users to stand up rather than lie in an enclosed space. Will these do more good than harm?

Screening Entire Populations for Mental Illness

Is it a good idea to screen the entire U.S. population, including preschool children, for mental illness as promoted in former President Bush's "New Freedom Initiative" (Lenzer, 2004a)?[52] Will this do more harm than good? Who profits from such programs? Will those labeled "mentally ill" benefit from such a program? Are "diagnoses" given accurate? How many false positives and false negatives will occur? What is "mental illness?" (See prior discussion regarding this term.) Are conflicts of interest involved? The Texas Medication Algorithm Project (TMAP) is noted in the New Freedom Initiative as a model medication treatment plan "illustrating an evidence-based practice that results in better consumer outcomes." Is this so? Lenzer (2004) describes concerning conflicts of interests in this screening proposal and related endorsements. What about the Mother's Act, which advocates screening all new mothers for mental illness?[53] Will memory clinics to screen for dementia do more good than harm?[54]

Routine Mammography Screening

Promotional materials designed to encourage women to get mammograms typically hide potential harms in overdiagnosis (the high rate of false positives and subsequent pain and infections due to biopsies, anxiety, and worry) (Gotzsche, 2009; Jorgensen & Gotzsche, 2009). They usually hide the fact that two-thirds of women diagnosed with breast cancer are 60 years of age or older. Thus, should all women be routinely screened? Also, the small effect of screening on mortality is typically hidden. (See Figure 5.3.) Welch (2004) asks: "In the next 10 years, out of 1,000 American women, how many will die of breast cancer? And how many will avoid death because of screening?" (p. 25):

Age	Die from breast cancer *without* mammography	Die from breast cancer *with* mammography	Avoid death *because of* mammography
50	6	4	2
60	9	6	3
70	13	8.5	4.5

Welch (2004) argues that microscopic "cancers" detected by increasingly sophisticated technology may *never* develop into a harmful stage, which he suggests, raises the question: "What is cancer?" Should all suspicious cells be an indication for further intrusive intervention? And, as Welch notes, reliability among pathologists is not as good as you may think: "whether or not you are told you have cancer depends in part on who your pathologist is" (p. 104). (See Figure 5.4.)

In some specimens almost all the pathologists agreed that cancer was present (specimen 7, for example), while in others almost all agreed that there was no cancer (specimen 15, for example). But in many cases the disagreement is more widespread, with some pathologists saying cancer, others saying no cancer, and some saying they're not sure (the lighter gray squares).

Figure 5 also provides some insight into *why* pathologists disagree. Look at the checkerboard again, but this time focus on the rows. Note that pathologist G made a melanoma diagnosis in only 5 specimens, while pathologist F did so in 16 specimens. Among these questionable specimens, pathologist F was more than three times as likely to diagnose melanoma as pathologist G. This suggests that the reason for disagreement is not simply that pathologists make random mistakes, but that different pathologists have different standards for calling an abnormality cancer. In other words, one reason pathologists

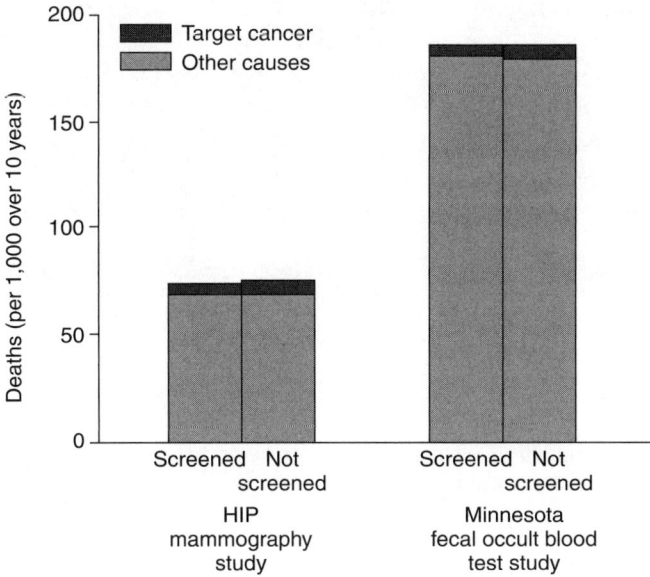

Figure 5.3. Death rate for all causes in the two U.S. randomized trials of screening. SOURCE: H. G. Welch (2004). *Should I be tested for cancer? Maybe not and here's why* (p. 29). Berkeley, CA: University of California Press.

disagree is that some have a greater tendency to diagnose cancer than others. (Welch, 2004, p. 1200)

As technology becomes more sophisticated (able to detect microscopic abnormalities), more suspicious findings will occur. Given the high percentage of people who have abnormal cells upon autopsy, in the absence of any symptoms, Welch asks the question, "If someone is found to have abnormal cells at death and no one knew about it during their life, did the person have cancer?" (p. 88). "The harder we look the more we find" (p. 68).[55] The more "slices" are taken the more cancer is found. For example in a study of thyroid tissue at autopsy (in non-symptomatic people) almost all of the 281 people had some evidence of thyroid cancer (p. 81). Cancer cells differ in their growth rates meaning that some detected grow so slowly we never have any symptoms and die of other causes. Only recently (in 2009) did the National Health Services pull "its leaflets inviting women to undergo mammography in response to criticism that it failed to mention major harm of screening—overdiagnosis" (Welch, 2009). This was in response to a systematic review by Jorgensen and Gotzsche (2009) suggesting that screening resulted in overdiagnosis of breast cancer in Canada, Australia, Sweden, Norway, and the United Kingdom. They suggested that about one in three of all breast cancers detected represent overdiagnosis.[56]

Newspaper reports may not fully inform readers. Welch (2010) argues that the recent analysis of the impact of screening in Norway between 1986 and 2005 (Kalager, Zelen, Langmark, & Adami, 2010) translates into the following: "If you screen 2500 women over age 50 for 10 years, one breast cancer death might be avoided at the cost of 1000 false alarms and between five and fifteen women being overdiagnosed and treated needlessly with surgery, radiotherapy and chemotherapy."

Figure 5.4. Grid of 24 skin specimens in which pathologists *disagreed* whether melanoma was present.
SOURCE: H. G. Welch (2004). *Should I be tested for cancer? May not and here's why* (p. 100). Berkeley, CA: University of California Press.

Controversy continues about potential benefits and harms of mammography screening (e.g., Beral & Peto, 2010). As Fiona Godlee, editor of the *British Medical Journal*, suggested, what is being asked "is simply that women should be made aware of the potential harm of overdiagnosis so they can make an informed decision."[57]

Screening for Alzheimer's Disease

Brown and his colleagues (2009) recommend use of a self-administered cognitive screening test to detect Alzheimer's disease. Stephen Black (2009) argues that use of this test will create too many false positives. "For every individual correctly declared to have Alzheimer's disease, about 11, on average will be falsely declared to have this dread disease." He argues that dissemination of this test would be unfortunate due to the potential for misunderstanding of results. Screening via spinal tap has also been recommended. Will this do more good than harm?[58] Frances (2010) considers guidelines proposed by the National Institute of Cancer and the Alzheimer's Association for diagnosing Alzheimer's as an example of narrowly focused experts getting far ahead of the available technology. False positives and negatives will abound. And, as he notes, there is no effective treatment. Does it make sense to test in this situation? Some argue that it does and that clients should be informed of the results.

HARMS CAUSED BY PREMATURE USE OF INTRUSIVE INTERVENTIONS

Interventions differ in their intrusiveness—how much pain, suffering, and life-affecting consequences they entail. Professionals are ethically obligated to use the least intrusive, effective methods. This obligation is often ignored. Altering lifestyle and taking medication may be just as effective as implanting cardiac stents in preventing clots (Ozner, 2008). Intrusive interventions, those which cause harms avoidable by use of less intrusive interventions may be promoted by managed care companies because they cost less. For example, children are often placed on medication as a first (rather than last) resort. (See earlier section describing medication of children.) This saves time and money needed to carry out an individualized contextual assessment of circumstances related to behaviors of concern and to rearrange them as needed.

Forced Electroshock Therapy (ECT) on Children and Involuntary Adults

In Italy in the 1930s two Italian psychiatrists learned about use of electric shock across the animal's brain in a slaughterhouse and the resultant effect on hogs. They tried this out on an involuntary mental patient (described in Breggin, 2008). When the man awoke, he was cooperative (no longer resistant). ECT became widely used. Guidelines call for use of less intrusive methods as a first option because of possible adverse effects of ECT such as memory loss (Sackheim, Prudic, Fuller, Keilp, Lavori, & Olfson, 2007). Is this guideline followed? Baldwin and Oxlad (1996) reviewed literature describing ECT administered to 217 minors. The authors note that ECT was used extensively only with adults until 1947 when a study published by Bender (1947) reported administration of ECT to 98 children and adolescents. Examination of the behaviors of concern showed that ECT was viewed as appropriate for a wide range of conditions that many clinicians would view to be in the "normal developmental" range and as appropriate forms of behavioral expression (pp. 457–58).

> ECT became a 'cure all' treatment for some psychiatrists who worked with children/adolescents with mental health problems. As the list of index behaviors was expanded during the 1950s and 1960s, other minors were given ECT. According to the medical judgment of psychiatrists, indications for ECT included (but were not limited to): schizophrenia; mania; catatonia; eating disorder; mood disorder; thought disorder; Alzheimer's disease, intellectual disability and Gilles de la Tourettes Syndrome.

Oxlad and Baldwin (1996) argue that informed consent requirements are often violated in using ECT with children and adolescents who explicitly refuse such treatment. Parental objections may also be ignored.

> A 17-year-old girl suffering from post-traumatic stress disorder, which resulted from multiple rapes at the age of 12, was admitted to an adult psychiatric hospital, where a course of ECT was prescribed. The parents strongly objected to this form of treatment and made their views known to the health care team. Despite the parental opposition, the psychiatrist obtained a mental health order, which required ECT to be given, which appeared to produce deterioration in the girl's condition. The next treatment proposed was psychosurgery. As with the administration of ECT, this did not have parental consent. Only with the help of the advocacy group, MIND (www.mind.org.uk), were the parents able to withdraw their daughter from the psychiatric hospital to prevent the psychosurgery. (p. 324)[59]

ECT remains a controversial treatment, one some argue is effective (Shorter & Healy, 2007). Others argue that it is both ineffective and harmful and encouraged by special interests including companies that produce electric shock devices (Andre, 2009). Here, as always, we should examine the evidence related to claims of effectiveness and of harm and consider ethical concerns such as informed consent.

INFLATED CLAIMS OF KNOWLEDGE HINDER KNOWLEDGE DEVELOPMENT

Bogus claims about what is true and what is not stifles innovation. Promotion of harmful and ineffective treatments and censorship of promising new methods hinders the discovery of better ways to help people. Harmful bloodletting, purges, and use of emetics continued unchanged for centuries. New ideas are often met with indifference, if not hostility, as in the case of Ignas Semmelweiss (e.g., see Best & Neuhauser, 2004). (See also discussion of research cartels in chapter 7.) Premature claims of knowledge as "the truth," for example the genetic theory of cancer, impede funding for exploration of alternative views such as the chromosomal theory of cancer (Duesberg, Mandrioli, McCormack, & Nicholson, 2011).

The Radical Mastectomy

Radical surgery as the treatment for breast cancer became popular in the late 1860s. William Halsted claimed that he had found a cure for breast cancer. He published a paper in 1894 entitled "The Results of Operations for the Cure of Cancer of the Breast Performed at the Johns Hopkins Hospital from June 1889 to January 1894." The Halsted procedure includes "the en bloc removal of the entire breast, the underlying chest muscles, and the lymph nodes in the armpit" (Katz, 2002, p. 177). This procedure was adopted by most practicing surgeons. Halstead proclaimed that "Now we can state *positively* that cancer of the breast is a curable disease if operated properly and in time. I cannot emphasize too strongly the fact that internal metastases occur very early in cancer of the breast, and this is an additional reason for not losing a day in discussing the propriety of an operation" (cited in Katz, 2002, p. 178). This operation became routine with only mild reservations raised. Katz (2002) notes that Halsted's paper "electrified the medical community and quickly transformed the prevailing pessimism about treatment into optimism" (p. 177). But on what was this claim based? The paper states that "in 50 cases operated upon by what we call the complete method we have been able to trace only 3 recurrences" (cited in Katz, 2002, pp. 177–78). This achievement was never replicated. Bold assertions and a confident manner were used to promote this method, which is still used today. In fact, even today as Welch (2004) notes, radical mastectomies are almost at the level of lumpectomies, even though the former are no longer recommended as needed.

Although some expressed concern that this kind of radical surgery was not needed, Halstead's authority

> was so great that a number of surgeons experienced difficulties in getting papers published that disputed his claims. Others did not even dare to submit their

contrary results. Fifty years had to elapse before serious reservations about Halstead's operation were with increasing insistence raised by distinguished members of the medical profession. . . . On the basis of the most limited data, Halstead's sweeping claims about the defeat of an ancient foe were accepted by the medical community. (p. 179)

Katz concludes by saying that "Halstead should serve as a reminder that orthodoxy and authority are powerful forces that tend to obliterate awareness of uncertainty; they do not easily bow to the contrary claims of science: that in the search for truth, professionals must constantly scrutinize their certainties against the uncertainties of existing medical knowledge" (p. 181). This example illustrates that once something is accepted as routine, it is very difficult to challenge it. In fact, as illustrated here, papers critical of popular procedures and views may not be accepted for publication. Some of the popularity of radical mastectomy is driven by women themselves who are fearful of developing cancer and eager to take preventive action, even if invasive. But is such fear warranted? Certainly not by results comparing radical mastectomies with lumpectomy. Aren't women influenced by the relentless media attention to cancer, as well as by advocacy groups that promise that a cure will be found? (See also Moran, 1998.)

Misleading Lists of Alleged "Best Practices" and "Evidence-Based Practices"

It is popular today for entities such as the Department of Health and Human Services to create lists that they pronounce as "evidence-based". Have programs included on such lists been demonstrated to be effective? Are they best? Although the answer may be "yes" regarding some, this is not necessarily so. For example, critical appraisal of research reports cited as "evidence" for drug prevention programs for youth showed use of questionable data analysis techniques, including data dredging (Gandhi et al., 2007). Indeed, Gorman and Huber (2009) noted that if similar data analysis methods were used, DARE (Drug Abuse Resistance Education) assumed to be ineffective, would be proclaimed effective.

> A research culture based on hypothesis verification, rather than falsification, permits evaluators to conduct multiple analyses of their data sets, to selectively report out their findings, and to emphasize positive results over null or negative results. Consequently, more and more preventive interventions are socially constructed as "effective." Our reanalysis indicates that with a suitably sympathetic set of analyses, the DARE program might also be considered an 'effective' prevention practice. (p. 410)

Mistakenly anointing programs as "evidence-based" is a particularly pernicious form of propaganda, given our tendency to go along with "what the experts say" and given pressure on agencies to use such methods.

Other Examples

Hundreds of other examples could be given of inflated claims regarding effectiveness. Tip-off weasel words and phrases include "proven," "well established," and "empirically validated." What do these vague terms mean? What percentage of people who undergo the intervention are helped? Although some remedies such as Ibuprofen have a very low number needed to treat (NNT = 2), this level of effectiveness is rare. Number Needed to Treat (NNT) refers to how many people have to be treated to help one person. We should also ask about Number Needed to Harm (NNH): How many people have to receive a treatment for one to be harmed? A treatment in which one person is harmed for every two treated would not be very enticing. How long do positive effects last? Is this information shared with clients? The history of science shows that most claims of "what we know" have been found to be false.

CREATION AND PROMOTION OF NONDISEASES AND BOGUS RISKS

Creation of pseudo-diseases and inflation of risks are key harms of propaganda in the helping professions. These bogus risks and diseases sap our lives of joy as they occupy our minds with unnecessary worry and related self-surveillance of our thoughts, feelings, behaviors, and interiors of our bodies in an attempt to avoid the risks and alleged diseases, including other people who may "have them" (e.g., dangerous criminals). In *Follies and Fallacies in Medicine*, Skrabanek and McCormick (1998) suggest that "because there is no need to confirm diagnosis by strict, objective criteria, psychiatry is at a particular risk of creating diseases" and that the use of "Latin and Greek helps to reify dubious entities" (p. 79), such as kynophobia, common in postmen, fear of dogs and phobophobia, fear of fear (p. 84). They suggest that new terms for diseases may serve as camouflage for a lack of understanding. "As doctors are generally uncomfortable about exposing their ignorance, there is a temptation to 'diagnose,' to label inappropriately, to create non-diseases" (p. 86). (See chapter 6 for further discussion of medicalization and biomedicalization.)

HARMS CAUSED BY NEGLECT OF COMMON CONCERNS

Although diarrhea kills 1.5 million children a year in developing countries, the oral rehydration solution that cost pennies is not promoted as millions are spent on AIDS (e.g., Dugger, 2009).[60] Parasitic infections are rampant in some parts of the world due to contaminated water supplies; too little attention is given to this cause of cognitive and health problems (Holez, 2008). Lack of attention to illnesses and diseases that kill millions each year because there is no profit to be made in addressing these is highlighted in the open access peer reviewed journal *PloS Neglected Tropical Diseases*. Death due to hypothermia in the winter may occur, as well as death due to lack of air conditioners and fans in the homes of poor elderly people during heat waves. Loeske (1999) emphasized our tendency to focus on extreme problems, ignoring less vivid concerns such as poor quality schools and lack of health care. The marginalized are confined in ghettoes offering sparse opportunities for escape, except to the penal system (Wacquant, 2009). Economic inequities are related to premature mortality (e.g., Thomas, Dorling, & Smith, 2010). Ofshe and Watters (1994) make a compelling argument for the damage that the recovered memory movement has done. "Pursuing imaginary monsters requires that one ignores garden-variety evils. Who has time to make incremental improvements in our society when he or she believes a Satanic cult is killing and reprogramming our children at will?" (p. 202). They suggest that hundreds of millions of dollars were wasted including the founding of dissociative disorder units in hospitals.

> Unlike useless treatments that merely do patients no good, the practitioners of this therapy harm patients and cause them to suffer. This need not happen. Tolerating recovered memory therapy harms us all because it diverts attention from problems that are real and may be solvable, and squanders funds dedicated to the care of people in need. (p. 303)

HARMS CAUSED BY NOT OFFERING EFFECTIVE METHODS

Perhaps the greatest harm of propaganda in the helping professions and related venues is failure to use effective interventions.[61] Although our ignorance is great about what can help and what cannot, effective methods are available for many concerns. Many are low cost including interventions for those who have attempted suicide in poor countries (Mayor, 2008). Other examples are clean burning cookstoves, which decrease illnesses caused by smoke (Broder, 2010), low-cost bed nets treated with insecticide, which help to protect people from malarial mosquitoes,[62] and low-cost ($19.00) self-adjustable glasses for the millions of people with poor eyesight (Harmon, 2009).[63] Consider also distortion and ignoring of applied behavior analysis in many (most?) programs in social work and psychology (Thyer, 2005). Such censorship and misrepresentation affects what is offered to clients. You can look in vain in the indexes of popular social work practice texts and not find the terms "behavior analysis" or "applied behavior analysis" even though this approach is state-of-the-art in successful pursuit of a range of outcomes in areas such as behavioral medicine, children and adults with developmental disabilities, parent training, school-based social work, and work with elderly clients and their families. Students in most professional education programs in social work, psychology, and counseling graduate with little if any working knowledge of basic behavior principles and how to apply them.

The Dilution Effect. Propaganda in the helping professions discourages use of services found to be effective with high fidelity, that is, in a form most likely to maximize positive effects and minimize negative ones. The *dilution effect* is a key source of low-quality service in the helping professions. This term refers to claiming that an intervention found to be effective when provided at a certain level (dosage, number of sessions), is equally effective in a diluted form, for example, offering a 12-session social skills program found to help clients for only six sessions.

SUMMARY

The essence of propaganda is partially in the use of evidence resulting for example in bogus claims of knowledge and ignorance. Such bogus claims may and often do, result in harm, for example, promoting harmful practices and hiding effective interventions and not involving clients and patients as informed participants. Harms include hospitalizing people against their will, stigmatizing them by means of negative diagnostic labels, and not fully informing clients, with the result that they make decisions they otherwise would not make. Faulty technology is used based on aggressive, misleading marketing. We are often propagandized without being aware of this. Professionals are typically not well educated concerning harms and their sources, both past and present, that may affect clients who are so unfortunate to experience them due to promotion of exaggerated claims of knowledge and ignorance. Fraudsters and quacks employ propaganda methods for their own benefit with little or no regard for the consequences for clients. Quacks say they care about clients and may think they do. But as this chapter illustrates, good intentions do not protect clients from harm. Many of the harms described in this chapter resulted (or continue to result) from gullibility on the part of those involved in perpetuating the harm. They result from a failure to critically appraise assertions (claims), which have life-affecting consequences. If propaganda in the helping profession contributes to decisions that result in more harm than good, including avoidable errors, it is important to be skilled in propaganda spotting and to use this knowledge. Keeping in mind the harmful consequences of propaganda should help us all to be motivated.

6

The Medicalization of Life

Exaggerating dangers and creating diseases and risks are key marketing tactics used by promoters of propaganda in the helping professions.[1] The term *medicalization* describes "a process by which non-medical problems become defined and treated as medical problems, usually in terms of illness and disorders" (Conrad, 2007, p. 4). The terms "healthy" and "unhealthy" have been applied to an ever wider range of behaviors, thoughts, and feelings.[2] Ivan Illich (1975) argued that physicians have medicalized many aspects of everyday life such as aging, pain, death, healing, and prevention; private areas of life were being expropriated by governmental institutions and by what he referred to as the "disabling professions." He called this "medicalization" and argued that it impaired rather than benefited health and decreased our freedom. Lynn Payer (1992) introduced the term "disease mongering" to refer to the selling of sickness and increasing the markets for those who sell and deliver treatments. The boundaries of illness that are treatable are widened.[3] Varieties of disease mongering suggested by Lynn Payer (1992) are shown in Table 6.1.

Pharmaceutical companies (or others with financial interests) expand the market for selling their products by persuading people that they are sick and in need of medical intervention such as medication (Moynihan & Cassels, 2005). Terms such as adjustment and health suggest their opposites, dysfunction and illness. The health of the body as good has replaced the goodness of the soul. Conrad (2010) estimates that medicalization cost $77 billion in the United States in 2005—3.9% of total health care expenditures. Included were anxiety disorders, normal pregnancy and delivery, normal sadness, obesity, sleeping disorders, and substance related disorders. It is important to identify pathology, especially if treatment implications follow. Creating "bogus" risks and transforming common variations in behavior, feelings, or physiological reactions into diseases that create anxiety and distract us from the pursuit of valued goals is another matter. We are more vulnerable to this kind of propaganda if we are unaware of the history of the helping professions and related industries. For example in medieval times, melancholy was often viewed as a sign of spiritual struggle, not as a mental illness. Medicalization has become so rampant that there now is a vigorous counter-reaction. The first international conference on selling sickness was held in October 2010 in Amsterdam, sponsored by http://healthyskepticism.org.

Table 6.1 Disease Mongering Tactics

1. Taking a normal function and implying that there is something wrong with it and it should be treated ("medicalization"). Implying that physicians have a solution.
2. Imputing suffering that is not there.
3. Defining as large a proportion of the population as possible as suffering from the "disease"; exaggerate the prevalence of disease.
4. Hiding side effects. Promoting technology as risk-free magic.
5. Creating confusion; for example, failing to distinguish between treatments aimed at eliminating symptoms and those aimed at preventing long-term consequences.
6. Drawing an analogy between a problem promoted and one of unquestioned severity (e.g., comparing menopause with diabetes).
7. Defining a disease as a deficiency disease or one of hormonal imbalance, which sets the stage for drug treatment.
8. Gaining the cooperation of the right spin doctors, for example, to proselytize at conferences.
9. Framing the issues in a certain way (e.g., as a brain disease rather than environmentally caused).
10. Crying malpractice.
11. Using case examples and testimonials about a particularly pathetic patient who supposedly has the disease (but may not) that is easily remedied. If you object to disease mongering, you may be viewed as unsympathetic.
12. Using statistics selectively to exaggerate the benefits of treatment. Consider the following: "Jonathan Cole, writing in Columbia magazine shows how use of one statistic will tend to show a great benefit of treatment, whereas use of another will not. In a large study where 1,906 men received the cholesterol-lowering drug cholestyramine, 30 died of heart attacks over a period of ten years. In the control group of 1,900 men who didn't receive the drug, 38 died. This was a difference of 8 deaths, and one could say that this was a 24-percent reduction but the absolute death rate was 2.0 in the control group and 1.6 in the group that received the drug, a difference that was of some statistical significance perhaps, but not of much practical importance."
13. Using misleading surrogate end points. For example, the Breast Detection and Follow-up Study was designed not to measure whether mammography worked in preventing deaths from breast cancer, but whether women could be persuaded to get mammograms.
14. Making treatment sound more urgent than it really is. A purported survey about whether women would be interested in taking hormones for the prevention of osteoporosis was worded like this: "OSTEOPOROSIS is caused by thinning of the bones. Bones that become thinned by OSTEOPOROSIS are more likely to break—the HIP and the WRIST are common places for breaks. OSTEOPOROSIS may also cause back pain. These problems become more common as women get older."
15. Not correcting death rates for age.
16. Taking a common symptom that could mean anything and making it sound as if it is a sign of a serious disease.
17. Suggesting that all diseases should be treated.

SOURCE: Adapted from L. Payer (1992). *Disease mongers: How doctors, drug companies, and insurers are making you feel sick*. New York: John Wiley & Sons.

A key tactic of pharmaceutical advertisements is to "raise awareness" of alleged problems (some of which we never knew we had) and to promote remedies for conditions for which there may be none.

Pharmaceutical companies are actively involved in sponsoring the *definition* of diseases and promoting them to both prescribers and consumers. The social construction of illness is being replaced by the corporate construction of disease. Although some sponsored professionals or consumers may act independently and all concerned may have honorable motives, in many cases the formula is the same: groups and/or campaigns are orchestrated, funded, and facilitated by corporate interests, often via their public relations and marketing infrastructure.

A key strategy of the alliances is to target the news media with stories designed to create fears about the condition or disease and draw attention to the latest treatment. Company sponsored advisory boards supply the "independent experts" for these stories, consumer groups provide the "victims" and public relations companies provide the media outlets with the positive spin about the latest "breakthrough" medications. (Moynihan, Heath, & Henry, 2002, p. 886)

Examples include the medicalization of aging such as andropause (claimed to be the result of low testosterone), baldness, erectile dysfunction, the expansion of the diagnosis of ADHD in children to adult ADHD, promotion of growth hormone products, and use of biomedical enhancements in sports and athletics (Conrad, 2007, p. 75). Gagnon and Lexchin (2008) estimate that $57.5 billion was spent in 2004 in the United States by pharmaceutical companies on marketing. The term "biomedicalization" refers to an expansion of the term "medicalization" to incorporate not only the vast increase in what is focused on as health issues including risks and related surveillance systems but also the biopolitical economy that supports it, the expanding technology that accompanies it, changes in knowledge production, management, and dissemination, and as a result of all the above, the alteration of bodies and identities. (See Clarke, Mamo, Fosket, Fishman, & Shim, 2010).[4]

Science (as ideology not as critical appraisal) is a key grand narrative appealed to in the creation of bogus diseases and risks both in professional sources and the media. Scientific sounding terms are used including jargon in the *DSM* that sounds impressive such as "factitious disorder by proxy," "dyspareunia," and "social anxiety disorder." More and more "interiors" (thoughts and feelings) - even vaginas - are promoted as "not normal." Consider the ad in Figure 6.1.

Doctors, and society as a whole, need to stop confusing health with happiness. This confusion is at the root of much of the medicalization of normal human variation that we are witnessing. Male pattern baldness and shyness, to take just two examples, are not diseases but normal parts of the range of human experience. We are witnessing diagnostic drift in a whole range of conditions, from depression to hypertension, with pressure for more and more people to be included within the range of abnormal and offered treatment. The justification for these treatments is often based on short-term studies, which are then extrapolated over much longer time periods. There is insufficient recognition of the fact that the less the need for treatment, the higher the number needed to treat

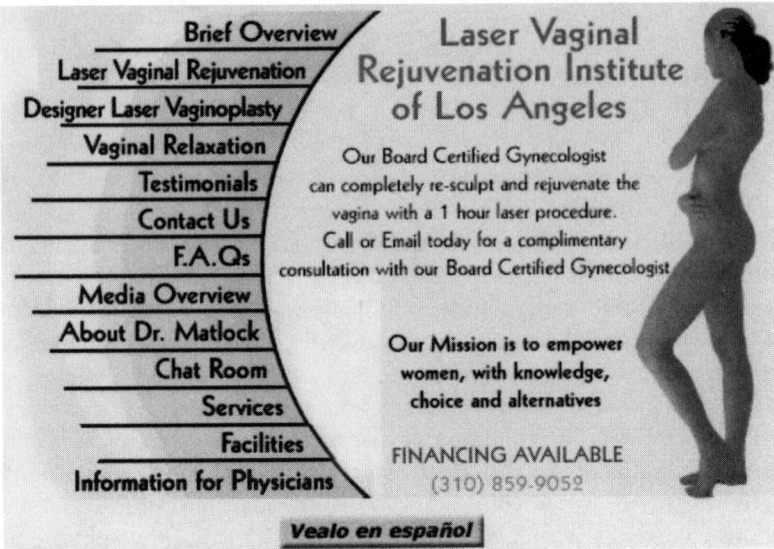

Figure 6.1. Advertisement for Laser Vaginal Rejuvenation.
SOURCE: The Laser Vaginal Rejuvenation Institute of Los Angeles (www.drmatlock.com) (2000).

for given outcomes and the higher the risk to patients, since the rate of adverse effects remains constant. (Heath, 2006)

More and more behaviors and risk factors are referred to as "sicknesses" requiring the help of experts, including normal body processes such as menopause (Foxcraft, 2009) and common blood pressure levels (Moynihan, 2010b). The more I medicalize everyday behaviors (conflate them with physical diseases), the more services I can sell or enforce.

As emphasized by Moynihan, Heath, and Henry (2002), "There's a lot of money to be made from telling healthy people they're sick" (p. 862). Intrusion into ever more areas of life via surveillance and control is disguised as "care" or protection of the public health. Thomas Szasz (1961, 2002) has long been a critic of the "therapeutic state," which thrives on the "medicalization of good" (p. 160). The more diseases, the more research funds can be sought to study them, the more drugs and other interventions can be promoted to remedy them, the more screening measures can be created to detect them and the more professionals can be employed in the helping profession industry. The more fear that can be created the more money can be made promoting products alleged to decrease feared consequences, such as child abduction. The belief that remedies are always possible (when they are not) or are, but only with harmful side effects, is encouraged by related propaganda pitches. This creates pseudo pathology and pseudo risks that result in unnecessary worry and treatment and direct attention away from real problems that affect the quality of our lives. The Johns Hopkins website offers daily "Health Alerts." Everyday problems are transformed into alleged mental illnesses with the help of public relations firms hired by pharmaceutical companies with the complicity of academics and their host universities as described in chapter 3.

This medicalization has been achieved only through the active collaboration of many different players.

Conrad argued that when disorders previously viewed as non-medical are redefined as sicknesses, non-medical people often perform the "everyday routine work" of disseminating understanding of the new sickness [7]. A temperance society worker, for example, might have disseminated the concept of alcoholism as a disease through everyday contacts with alcoholics and their families. With ADHD, the teacher's work extends beyond simply ensuring the disorder is understood by parents. Instead, the teacher participates in the diagnosis, and may broker different forms of treatment, or rejection of treatment. Brokerage is not a disinterested activity: teachers may have a vested interest in detecting and managing disruptive children, or they may adhere to beliefs about learning disorders which lead them to dissuade parents of the need for treatment. (Phillips, 2006)

School social workers identify and frame children's (mis)behaviors as mental illnesses and offer "special" services, often medication. Szasz argues that as in past time "people embraced totalitarian states, now they embrace the therapeutic state." By the time they discover the therapeutic state is about tyranny, not therapy, it will be too late" (p. 168). Consumer organizations, as well as individual patients and entire social movements, have been in the vanguard of advocating for medicalization (Broom & Woodward, 1996; Conrad, 2007).

SOME EXAMPLES OF BOGUS SICKNESS

Irritable Bladder. Perhaps next to the old ad for Zoloft, showing an isolated blob looking longingly into a happy blob group, the ad for Enablex (darifenacin) to "cure" irritable bladder in which large, very full pear-shaped balloons waddle awkwardly about depicting discomfort is the most entertaining. But does entertainment come at a cost such as worry that you have an illness? What is "irritable bladder"? An ad for Enablex was included on both the first and last page of a report entitled "Blood Pressure Trouble(s) Leave Eyes at Risk for Glaucoma" in Health News (retrieved July 20, 2007, from <http://www.everydayhealth.com>). The ad on the last page urges us to "Ask your doctor about Enablex" and notes that I can "get a free trial." But is it really "free"? What if taking this drug has harmful effects? What's missing here? How good is the evidence that taking Enablex will result in more good than harm? How many times do people in different groups urinate in a 24-hour-period? That is, what are the norms? What is optimal? Many people do not drink enough water, so they urinate less often. But what if you are well-hydrated? What if you do drink enough water? How many times a day do you urinate then? My doctor's advice is to drink, drink, drink water and to urinate as often as you have to to be well-hydrated. Does promoting the malady of "irritable bladder" have a harmful effect on decreasing fluid intake? And, what other treatments are available? Is a pill the best solution? Are there side effects of taking Enablex? To determine this I would have to read the small print in "safety information"? How long has this drug been on the market? Public Citizen advises readers to avoid any drug that has not been used for at least five years to avoid possible long-term adverse side effects. The ads for irritable bladder address none of these questions except to include the required "important safety information." As usual, silence is the rule (mums the word) for probing questions that may compromise sales.

Social Phobia. The promotion of social phobia as a "mental illness" is described in chapter 2.

> Marketing diseases, and then selling drugs to treat those diseases, is now common in the "post-Prozac" era. Since the FDA approved the use of Paxil for SAD [social anxiety disorder] in 1999 and GAD [general anxiety disorder] in 2001, GlaxoSmithKline has spent millions to raise the public visibility of SAD and GAD through sophisticated marketing campaigns. The advertisements mixed expert and patient voices, providing professional viability to the diagnoses and creating a perception that it could happen to anyone (Koerner, 2002). The tag lien was, "Imagine Being Allergic to People." A later series of advertisements featured the ability of Paxil to help SAD sufferers brave dinner parties and public speaking occasions (Koerner, 2002). Paxil Internet sites offer consumers self-tests to assess the likelihood they have SAD and GAD (wwwpaxil.com). The campaign successfully defined these diagnostic categories as both common and abnormal, thus needing treatment. (Conrad, 2005, p. 6)

Both Moynihan and Cassells (2005) and Brody (2007) provide detailed descriptions of the promotion of this pseudo disease.[5]

Depression. Feelings, thoughts, and behaviors related to depression are real. But are they indicators of a disease? Are related behaviors and feelings caused by thoughts (e.g., Jacobson & Gortner, 2000)?[6] Should related complaints be treated with medication? If so, under what circumstances? The claim that depression is related to serotonin level is not supported by research, even though pharmaceutical ads make such claims (LaCasse & Leo, 2005). This claim is repeatedly made in the professional literature including reports of trials concerning "social anxiety disorder" (Gambrill and Reiman 2011). Views that "We have a right to be happy and free of worry" encourage promotion of low moods as pathology in need of treatment (Elliot and Chambers, 2004; Herzberg, 2009). A wide variety of states and feelings are labeled as "depression," some of which may require medication. But what about others?[7] Horwitz and Wakefield (2007) raised concerns about labeling low moods, sadness, and loss, as a mental illness. Jacobson and Gortner (2000) argue that there is no evidence for the discontinuous nature of different intensities of depression regarding vastly different causes (e.g., physical and/or environmental). Survey data from more than 8,000 Americans suggest that one in four people who appear depressed, are in fact struggling with the normal reactions from a recent emotional challenge such as a ruptured relationship, loss of a job, or loss of an investment (Wakefield, Schmitz, Horwitz, & First, 2007). This suggests that prior estimates of the number of people who suffer from depression at least once during their lives are 25% too high (Carey, 2007). In *Psychopathology of Everyday Life* (1901), Freud converted conflict, which is an integral part of life, into a manifestation of psychopathology.

Panic Disorder. New categories included in the *Diagnostic and Statistical Manual of Mental Disorders* combined with pharmaceutical marketing propel new kinds of discomfort into major concerns such as panic disorder (e.g., Healy, 2006c).

Parry [2003] assigns much of the credit for the fact that psychiatry's DSM, the *Diagnostic and Statistical Manual of Mental Disorders*, has grown to its 'current phonebook dimensions' to the fact that 'newly coined conditions were brought to light through direct funding by pharmaceutical companies, in research, in publicity, or both.' As a 'legendary example' of condition branding, Parry offers the example of panic disorder. Upjohn, through its strategic funding managed to disentangle panic disorder from the broader category of anxiety neurosis and at the same time install its drug alprazolam (Xanax) as the first-choice drug to treat the new disease. (Brody, 2007, p. 240)

Pseudobulbar Affect. Conrad draws our attention to "A recent, little-known example illustrating the promotion of new disorders. Avanir, a pharmaceutical company, is attempting to obtain FDA approval for its drug Neurodex, for a disorder the company is calling 'pseudobulbar affect,' or PBA. According to Avenar, Pseudobulbar affect is a condition characterized by episodes of uncontrollable laughing and/or crying that may be inappropriate or unrelated to the situation at hand which can be caused by a variety of neurological diseases or injuries (e.g., muscular sclerosis, and amyotropic lateral sclerosis, stroke) (<http://www.pseudobulbar.com>)" (p. 153).

Consider also creation of the alleged "disease" of female sexual dysfunction (Moynihan, 2010) and promotion of drugs for pre-osteoporosis (Alonso-Coello, Garcia-Franco, Guyatt, & Moynihan, 2008). Glassner (1999) uses the term "Fear Industrial Complex" to highlight the creation and promotion of fear in our society and the many players involved. Journalists contribute to disease mongering. (See Figure 6.2.)

STRETCHING THE BOUNDARIES

"Much disease mongering relies on the pathologizing of normal biological or social variation and on the portrayal of the presence of risk factors for disease as a disease state in itself" (Heath, 2006, e146)—in effect medicalization. Natural processes such as baldness or common changes in mood are now regarded as pathological and as treatable "illnesses."[7] Many risk factors have been converted into diseases. Obesity is now viewed as a disease. Is it?

> All human misery exists along a spectra, or better, along two spectrums. One ranges from mild to severe; the other ranges from resistant to management with medications to very accessible to management with medications. If we look only at cases at the severe end of the first spectrum, and also toward the treatment end of the second spectrum, it will seem cruel and callous to talk about the industry 'selling disease.' Instead, we will be struck by the extreme misery that the individual suffered from before drug therapy was available, and the significant improvement in individual's life that occurred after drug therapy was administered. (Brody, 2007, p. 241)

Variations in behavior, anatomy, and physiological reactions are common and may not reflect any disease at all, but be mislabeled as a "disease." Most human characteristics are normally distributed; only small percentages of people have very low or very high levels. In this view what are called diseases are simply extremes of a normal distribution of characteristics (p. 32).[8] Different labels are given to these extremes at different times, rendering definitions of "normal" often arbitrary

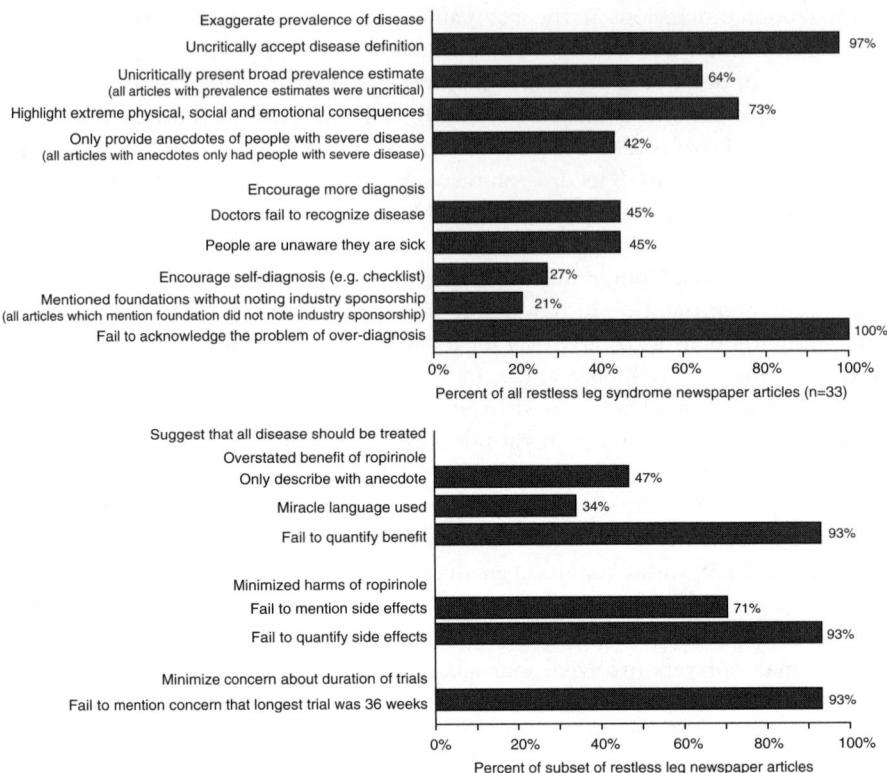

Figure 6.2. Frequency of key elements of disease mongering in newspaper articles. Top bar graph analyzes all articles about restless legs syndrome. Bottom bar graph analyzes the subset that mentions ropinirole.
SOURCE: S. Woloshin & L. M. Schwartz (2006). Giving legs to restless legs: A case study of how the media helps make people sick. *PLoS Med*, 3(4), e 170.

(culturally determined). Cutpoints in this normal distribution are dropped at different places at different times to suggest unusually low or high levels, for example, of anxiety or blood pressure. Drug companies have had an increasing role in setting the boundaries of the normal and the pathological; they have become active agents of social control. Conrad refers to these involved parties as *corporate medicalizers* (p. 144).

> Companies choose never to sell only a few drugs; whenever possible their goal is to sell a lot of drugs. No company can succeed by sending the message that only the most severe cases merit medical attention and drug therapy. The industry hopes that use of the medication will be extended as far as possible toward the other end of each spectrum – the milder-suffering end and the less-responsive-to-medication end. Due to the shape of the typical disease bell curve, lowering the severity threshold at which people think they have a 'real' disease and need drug treatment typically expands the potential market by a factor of ten or more. It is only with a low severity threshold that a PR firm can whip up a

proper scare campaign about a hidden epidemic of disease that affects ten, twenty, or fifty million people (Brody, 2007, p. 241).

Empirical information describing individual differences and base rates of concerns such as shyness are ignored or distorted and the boundaries of what is considered an illness are expanded resulting in labeling normative reactions as pathological. Promoting "off label" uses of a drug is a common strategy. Pharmaceutical companies seek approval of a new product for a population with a rare disease hoping to involve a larger market later. Once a drug has been approved, it can be used for other concerns even though such use has never been evaluated regarding benefits and harms. Physicians then prescribe drugs for ailments other than for those they were tested and developed. Consider AndroGel, which is approved for the rare condition of hypogonadism. On AndroGel's website (http://www.andogel.com) viewers are invited to

"Take the Low T Quiz." The questionnaire is derived from a 1997 AndroGel 'Deficiency and Aging Questionnaire'; the questions are vague and mirror many life changes that occur as men age. Question such as 'Have you noticed a recent deterioration in your ability to play sports?' or 'Are you falling asleep after dinner?' hardly seem like clear medical symptoms, yet the implicit promotion of AndroGel turns these common life events into symptoms of a medical problem and suggests that a physician review the checklist" (Conrad, 2007, p. 32).

Pfizer, the manufacturer of Viagra took steps to make sure that its use would not be confined only to men who had erectile dysfunction (ED) due to organic difficulties.

To make Viagra into a lifestyle drug, Pfizer needs to convince men that it is the first choice for therapy for any degree of ED, whatever the genesis of the problem. However drug therapy may not always be the most appropriate treatment option. The National Health and Social Life Survey data indicate that emotional and stress-related problems such as a deteriorating social and economic position generate elevated risk of experiencing sexual difficulties. In these cases, Viagra may be less important than counseling or help in finding a new job. These possibilities are never mentioned on the Viagra web site. (Lexchin, 2006, p. e132)

This stretching of boundaries makes us less tolerant of mild symptoms and more demanding of relief from them (Barsky & Boros, 1995). Now being uncomfortable may be viewed as a disease. Although promoters of disease mongering suggest that this enhances health, the effects are the opposite. We worry more (McCormick, 1996). New "risks" are news. Typical ways of presenting risk, such as relative risk, are highly misleading as discussed later in this chapter. Statistical illiteracy on the part of both laypeople and professionals contribute to the promotion of pathology.

The *Diagnostic and Statistical Manual of Mental Disorders* published by the American Psychiatric Association has become ever longer, increasing to almost 1,000 pages in 2000. This includes hundreds of (mis)behaviors (named diagnoses) claimed to be due to brain diseases.[9] This focus on individual deficiencies encourages a biomedical view of behavior treatable with pills. Third-party payment requires use of this system and researchers must use these labels when applying for research grants from federal agencies.

> Since 1979, for example, some of the new disorders and categories that have been added include panic disorder, generalized anxiety disorder, post-traumatic stress disorder, social phobia, borderline personality disorder, gender identity disorder, tobacco dependency disorder, eating disorders, conduct disorder, oppositional defiant disorder, identity disorder, acute distress disorder, sleep disorders, nightmare disorders, ruminations disorders, inhibited sexual desire disorders, premature ejaculation disorders, male erectile disorder and female sexual arousal disorder. (Kirk quoted in Conrad, 2005, p. 5)

It is claimed that "nearly half the population will have a diagnosis of mental disorder (based on the diagnoses in the DSM-IV) in their lifetime." It is claimed that "a large segment of the population at some time in their lives have anxiety disorders, 28.8%, impulse disorders such as attention deficit disorders, 24.8%, and mood disorders, 20.8%" (Kessler et al., 2005a, p. 130). Critiques of such estimates are usually ignored.[10] Narrow et al. (2002) argue that such studies "pathologize difficulties as symptoms and create punitive diagnoses. A hugely wide range of behaviors must be included in this paradigm so that roughly half of the population has a lifetime probability of mental disorder" (p. 130). The research interview used excludes discussion of context and individual history.

> Community studies like the NCS-R inevitably overestimate the prevalence of mental disorders. They include problems that don't require professional treatment and pathologize normal life difficulties. This encourages the medicalization of everyday troubles and suggest psychiatric treatment as their solution. This approach aligns with, and perhaps encourages the enormous rise over the past decade in the use of psychotropic medications for an increasing range of problems. (Conrad, 2007, p. 132)

Here again we see partiality in the use of evidence that is so key to propaganda. Drafts of DSM5 (http://www.dsm5.org) suggest that a new category of mental disorder of behavioral addictions (e.g., hypersexuality and binge eating) be added (Frances, 2010a, c, e, & f). Frances (July 6, 2010) argues that "false epidemics" of alleged mental diseases occur such as autism, attention deficit, and childhood bipolar disorder. Endless adding of alleged mental disorders encourages overdiagnosis. As Frances suggests, "Normality is an endangered species."

CONSEQUENCES OF ENLARGING THE TERRITORIES OF HEALTH AND RISK

Moynihan and his colleagues (2002) have been eloquent critics of medicalization.

> Inappropriate medicalization carries the dangers of unnecessary labeling, poor treatment decisions, iatrogenic illness, and economic waste, as well as the opportunity costs that result when resources are diverted away from treating or preventing more serious disease. At a deeper level it may help to feed unhealthy

obsessions with health, obscure or mystify sociological or political explanations for health problems, and focus undue attention on pharmacological, individualized, or privatized solutions. More tangibly and immediately, the costs of new drugs targeted at essentially healthy people are threatening the viability of publicly funded universal health insurance systems. (Moynihan, Heath, & Henry, 2002, p. 886)

Corporate sponsorship is often hidden as are the enormous profits of involved corporations, which claim, "We are doing it for you."

Creating Fear

Iona Heath (2006) suggests that disease mongering "exploits the deepest atavistic fears of suffering and death." Promoting pathologies and risks opens us to influence by propaganda ploys appealing to fear. Historically, appeal to fear is a key propaganda strategy as illustrated by cultivation of the fear of Jewish people in National Socialist Germany. It takes advantage of the fact that we are risk adverse; we weigh risks of negative events more heavily than risks of lost opportunities (e.g., for enjoyment and fun).[11]

Encouraging Intrusive Interventions

More women die of heart disease than of cancer. Yet the risk of breast cancer receives far more attention in the media and in related groups that sponsor activities such as marathons to raise money and bring attention to this disease. Such fear mongering encourages the likelihood that women will choose the most intrusive intervention (the radical mastectomy) over the less invasive but equally effective lumpectomy. It increases the likelihood that woman will seek out related diagnostic tests, which may lead to a diagnosis of "ductal carcinoma in situ" which, although this may never progress in a harmful way in a woman's lifetime, may result in a request for or recommendation of surgery. (See discussion in chapter 5.) Here again, we see the involvement of many players including pharmaceutical companies, which promote breast cancer awareness events and which make billions selling chemotherapies for breast cancer. Radiologists and radiation departments profit as do hospital surgery departments. This again illustrates the close relationship between self-propaganda and propaganda from corporate sources.

Ignoring Real Risks

Focusing on alleged medical causes of hundreds of (mis)behaviors and common moods directs attention away from stresses caused by the technological society in which we live and related social, economic, and political arrangements such as increased bureaucratization (Charlton, 2010). The more I can convince you to attend to bogus risks and pseudodiseases, the more you will be distracted from conditions that really are risks to your health, autonomy, and well-being such as meaningless work and poor quality education. "Attention to smaller waistlines, quieter children, and better erections, occurs in the context of 47 million Americans who go without health insurance" (Brody, 2007, p. 241). A focus on the individual as the locus of health problems provides an excuse to ignore social causes, as well as excuses for behaviors that harm others, as Szasz notes. I can escape responsibility for my actions by claiming that "voices made me do it"—I have a brain disease. Although there is a great deal of talk and writing about empowering clients and focusing on client strengths in the helping professions, in everyday practice, clients are often not involved as informed participants and individual deficiencies are often focused on. A focus on pathology encourages attention to what is wrong with people. Lack of participation on the part of clients and patients is often attributed to their deficiencies, such as lack of insight or motivation.

The search for personal causes of "resistance" deflects attention from the role of ineffective clinical skills such as excess negativity (Lampert, 2004) and environmental obstacles such as lack of transportation or day care for children. Brody (2007) points out that "as one starts to offer drug treatment to people with progressively less severe conditions, bad things usually happen. The chance of suffering a serious drug side effect starts to become greater than the chance of substantial benefit. He gives the example of chloramphenicol, a new claimed 'miracle' antibiotic which resulted in aplastic anemia in some patients. (See Brody, 2007 for more detail.) This medicalization of problems is a huge burden to the health insurance industry and whoever else funds the diagnosis and treatment of "problems." It provides a huge source of patients and clients for the helping professions.

Encouraging Self-Medicalization and Anxious Self-Surveillance

As highlighted by Conrad (2005), a decreased tolerance for mild symptoms and benign problems encourages "self-medicalization" (p. 9). The more we "internalize" beliefs in bogus risks and psychopathologies, the more we may worry about these and the more time we may spend attempting to control our behavior to avoid them (e.g., high cholesterol). We are increasingly encouraged to determine if we have a malady—to diagnose ourselves.[12] Self-medicalization encourages self-surveillance. This saves the state money and effort needed to exert external control. We "police" (discipline) ourselves (Foucault, 1965). Views promoted in our educational systems (for example, to be healthy) encourage internalization of related values and self-surveillance. Promotion of fears and risks of mental illness encourage worry about abnormality in others, as well as in ourselves.

Vas and Bruno (2003) argue that the daily focus on risks and diseases propel self-control to the center of both social and individual attention experienced as anxiety about our capacity to manage pleasurable activities" (p. 281). But in reality, options for self-control and choices are eroded in the therapeutic state. For example, the state describes what drugs you can take and which you cannot and even how you can die. Creation of pseudopathologies and risks saps our daily lives of enjoyment and distracts us from real concerns. We may experience behaviors, feelings, and thoughts related to the pseudodiseases and risks promoted and these may be troubling—or may not until targeted by Big Pharma and other involved players. However, there may be no remedy, distress may be self-limiting (many depressions lift in a few weeks), conflict in life is normative (not pathological and deviant) and may require struggling with related moral issues.

Increased Surveillance by Others: Decreased Privacy

More and more of our behaviors, moods, and thoughts (e.g., on e-mail) are subject to surveillance in therapy and on the Internet (through our own actions). More and more of our bodies, inside and out, are subject to surveillance by MRI, CAT scans, and genetic analyses. The surveillance arranged in the panopticon (a prison designed for complete surveillance) grows ever more inclusive (Foucault, 1980). Public health continues to expand its surveillance into ever more categories of behavior. Some suggest that sexual dysfunction should be recognized as a public health problem. The term "surveillance society" is now used to describe contemporary Western society.[13] Concerns about increased surveillance are reflected in titles such as "Snooper squad: New guidelines obliging professions to pry into the sex lives of teenagers would do more harm than good" (Munro, 2005). A plan to create a giant database of all children in the United Kingdom to identify children at risk was dropped following critiques (high cost, false positives, helping sexual predators to locate potential victims). Critics also noted that the children in 50,000 families (of the rich and famous) would be exempt (at their request).

Hart and Wellings (2002) suggest that research serves a key function in promoting surveillance. They highlight studies of sexual behavior such as Master and Johnson's accounts of the male and female orgasm (Masters & Johnson, 1966) and British surveys of sexual attitudes and lifestyles. Such studies create norms and standards people can use to assess themselves. Sexual satisfaction is now presented as integral to a happy life and pharmaceutical companies pursue a potential enormous number of eager buyers of products to correct female sexual dysfunction (Moynihan & Mintzes, 2010). Other examples of the use of research data to establish norms, which then create "dysfunction," include grade point average, blood pressure, and weight. One concern here is the poor quality of some of the research on which alleged norms are based.

Decreased Agency

A medical framing of common variations in behaviors, thoughts, feelings, and physical bodies permits intrusion by representatives of the state (armies of social workers, psychiatrists, psychologists, and counselors) into ever more aspects of our lives, compromising our autonomy to make our own decisions about our own bodies and time. If I can declare you a danger to yourself or to others, I can harness the power of the state to intrude into your life. In our culture of therapy, we are encouraged to manage our thoughts and emotions in accord with clinical prescriptions (Illouz, 2008). In an early paper raising concerns about the medicalization of hyperactive behavior, Conrad (1975) suggested the following trends: "1. the problem of expert control, relinquishing authority over problems to experts like physicians; 2. the uses of medical social control, especially drug and surgical treatments; 3. the individualization of social problems; and 4. the depoliticization of deviant behavior, where behavior is seen only in terms of its clinical, rather than social meaning" (quoted in Conrad, 2007, pp. 63–64). He later added "the dislocation of responsibility from the individual to the nether world of biophysiological functioning" (Conrad & Snyder, 1992). He argues that all of these points pertain to adult, as well as to child, ADHD. Diagnoses such as ADHD bestow a "disability" status on those labeled resulting in entitlement to benefits and/or accommodations (Conrad, 2007, p. 65). The medicalization of ADHD provides a medical explanation for underperformance. "For adults, the issue surrounding ADHD is performance, not behavior" (Conrad 2007, p. 64). "The simple fact of hyperactivity or impulsivity is not the chief concern for teens and adults: rather, it's their disorganization, irresponsibility, procrastination, and inability to complete tasks" (Diller, 1997, p. 277).

RHETORICAL USES OF THE WORD "DISEASE" AS A KEY PROPAGANDA PLOY

The term "disease," as in brain disease and "heart disease," permeates our health conscious society. It is used in ways that mislead and confuse rather than clarify and enlighten and is thus vital to think about critically. The word "disease" is used to describe physical illnesses such as tuberculosis, as well as hundreds of (mis)behaviors, thoughts, and feelings labeled as "mental illnesses" asserted to be brain diseases. Szasz (1994) distinguishes among the terms "disease," "discomfort," and "deviance." Disease refers to a demonstrable alteration in the structure or function of the body considered harmful to the organism such as a cancerous lesion. Virchow (1821– 1902) suggested three key characteristics of a disease: (1) a specific causal agent, (2) the agent always induces the disease, (3) the disease becomes worse without treatment. Discomfort refers to person's complaint, for example, pain or depression. Deviance refers to the complaint of individuals about the behaviors of other people or groups such as the use of illegal drugs or behavior causing injury or death to others or the self. Szasz argues that deliberate confusions are created among these three terms in the service of political, social, and economic interests.

> If we count discomforts and deviances as diseases, we change the criterion for what counts as a disease and set the ground for steadily expanding the category called 'disease.' Patients suffering from discomforts can classify their feelings of malaise as diseases and can try to convince others to accept their claims. Many prominent persons now engage in this kind of disease promotion: some advertise their depression as a brain disease, others their impotence as ED (erectile dysfunction), still others their former drug use from which they are 'in recovery.' Physicians and politicians can do the same with other people's deviance. Because physicians and politicians regularly function as agents of the therapeutic state, this is an ominous development: acting in concert, they possess the power needed to convince, co-opt, or corrupt the public to accept the *illness inflation* they promote. (Szasz, 1994, p. 7)

The fact that a professional organization decides what is and what is not a mental illness, such as homosexuality, illustrates the consensual basis of psychiatric labels.[14] Szasz (1994) has long critiqued the obscuring of differences between physical illness and what is labeled as "mental illness." He, as well as others, argue that there is a failure to distinguish between literal and metaphorical uses of this term. Mind is reduced to brain as in the statement "What we call 'mind' is the expression of the activity of the brain" (Andreasen, 1997). Szasz argues that the category error of treating the mind as an object (using terms such as "diseased mind") was a deliberate, not an innocent error, to benefit its promoters. This view has certainly benefited the pharmaceutical industry, which sells billions of dollars of pills prescribed for "mental illnesses." He suggests that the belief that troubled and troubling behavior is due to mental illness is ingrained in Western culture, which decreases the likelihood that critiques receive the attention they deserve.

Yet another type of non-disease consists in the creation of a disorder because it is claimed that a treatment exists to treat it. Fatness, menopause, unhappiness, reduced sex drive, and male baldness illustrate the medicalization of new "diseases" for which drugs are promoted as effective in treating (Conrad, 2007).[15] Skrabanek and McCormick argue that new terms for diseases may serve as a camouflage for a lack of understanding. "By pronouncing Greek or Latin, the doctor pretends to be in charge of the daemon of disease" (p. 85). "As doctors are generally uncomfortable about exposing their ignorance, there is a temptation to 'diagnose,' to label inappropriately, to create non-diseases. Although attaching dubious labels may be rationalized as response to patient need, too often the label becomes firmly attached" (p. 86).

More Non-diseases: Labeling Risks as Diseases

A common ploy is to label a risk as a disease. Examples include obesity, osteoporoses, and hypertension. These may be risks, but they are not diseases. Both weight and blood pressure are continuous. Cut points are claimed to delineate who has a disease and who does not.

> The reality is that the evidence that being a bit fat is bad for you is poor and for minor degrees of fatness non-existent. In fact the plump may live longer than the thin.
>
> . . .
>
> The designation of fatness as a disease has a number of consequences, few of which are desirable. It leads to a belief that telling a person that they are 10 pounds overweight is beneficial, because that will make them weight-conscious. It leads to a belief that taking off 10 pounds will prevent disease and lengthen life. It leads to a belief that it is good for the 'patient' to start looking at food as a source of calories rather than as a source of comfort and enjoyment. This is certainly good for the pockets of those who write about diet and those who operate food-fad stores. Finally it leads to a belief, that by analogy with smoking, overweight people should, even more than at present, be viewed as ugly and irresponsible. . . . Some cases of anorexia in adolescents may be related to the present obsession with slimness. (Skrabanek & McCormick, 1998, pp. 72–73)

Skrabanek and McCormick (1998) argue that hypertension (high blood pressure) "is perhaps the most widespread and damaging of present day non-diseases" (p. 73).

Blood pressure and cholesterol levels have been lowered still further as falling in the range of "to be treated" (e.g., Moynihan, 2010). It is impossible to predict which individual out of the hundreds who take medication will benefit. But, as they note, we do know that many will be harmed by the side effects of the pill.

> The likelihood of diagnosing non-hypertension increases with age. Messerli and others found that half of 24 'hypertensive' patients over the age of 65, had 'pseudo-hypertension.' Pseudo-hypertension is an artifact caused by increased resistance to compression of the artery by the sphygmomanometer cuff because of hardening of the arterial wall. The degree of pseudo-hypertension, that is the difference between cuff pressure and true pressure (as measured by direct intra-arterial measurement), ranged from 10 to 54 mm. Hg with a mean of 16 mm. Hg for both systolic and diastolic pressures. This would suggest that about half the patients over 65 whose mean cuff blood pressure was 180/100, had a true blood pressure of less than 165/85, which is normal for their age and would not justify treatment. If these patients' blood pressure were to be lowered by drugs it would not only be inappropriate and wasteful of resources but would also place these people at the risk of side effects and even of death. (Skrabanek, & McCormick, 1998, p. 75)

Given potential harms of treatment this is a questionable direction. Eisenberg and Wells (2008) note that although Lipitor for women is ineffective in decreasing cholesterol levels there is an indication that it increases risk for heart problems. This information is hidden in advertisements for this drug.[16]

Thus, "disease" is a complex concept with many different meanings. Creating confusion among different meanings is a key propaganda ploy used to medicalize problems-in-living and to create diseases out of risks to encourage us to seek and pay for remedies. Normal variations are labeled as diseases. Arbitrary cutpoints in continuous distributions are promoted as scientific estimates.

> Most variables are distributed across a continuum, but despite this, the medical tradition has been to dichotomize the continuum into normal and abnormal. Within a continuum, there can never be a clear boundary, so the definition of disease is inevitably both arbitrary and fluid. It is in the interests of pharmaceutical companies to extend the range of the abnormal so that the market for treatments is proportionately enlarged. We have seen this process operating, for example, in the continual lowering of thresholds for treatment of blood pressure and lipids—the most recent guidelines from the European Society of Cardiology can be used to identify 76% of the total adult population of the county of Norway as being at "increased risk." (Heath, 2006)

Questions of value in clarifying related claims include: (1) What is the base rate? (2) What is the natural course? (3) Is there a remedy? and (4) Does decreasing risk affect mortality? For example, does lowering cholesterol result in decreased mortality? Diagnosis is rendered more difficult by changes in a disease over time. And, the natural course of an illness or complaint or the course modified by treatments may be unknown. Failure to recognize this may result in avoidable errors such as overtreatment. Many complaints spontaneously go away or come and go.

Additional Factors That Encourage an Overemphasis on Pathology

Professionals tend to emphasize pathology (e.g., Ganzach, 2000). A variety of factors encourage this in addition to making money selling remedies. One is our dispositional bias—the tendency to attribute the cause and locus of problems to individuals rather than to environmental events or to the interaction of personal and environmental factors. (See also discussion of the fundamental attribution error in chapter 11.) People rather than their environments are examined and considered the locus of deficiencies.[17] Meehl (1973) referred to the focus on pathology as the "sick-sick" fallacy. Without effective skills for minimizing and handling the inevitable uncertainty in making life-affecting decisions and lack of success involved in professional practice, it is easy for professionals to fall into a pathological focus as a protection against failure both on the part of clients, as well as professionals (Houts, 2002). Lack of success can be blamed on the client's "mental disorder." An interest in appearing erudite by use of obscure jargon describing pathology is another contributor. Vague metaphorical descriptions of exotic pathology that appear profound offer an *illusion of knowledge*. Then it can be used to befuddle the gullible. Clear descriptions of complaints and related causes may appear simpleminded and uninteresting. And, mistaking a well person for an ill person is considered not as bad as judging a sick person as well.

Required use of the psychiatric classification system (DSM) directs attention to pathology. Many clinicians have not been exposed to political, economic, and social perspectives on deviance—to the fact that what is considered a problem is consensual and relative (ascribed), rather than inherent (fixed). Rarely are they well versed in the medicalization of everyday behaviors as "mental illnesses." Lack of knowledge about historical differences in how a certain pattern of behavior is viewed encourages pathologizing clients. In *Shrinking Violets and Casper Milquetoasts,* McDaniel (2003) describes the changing views of reticent, shy behavior (see also Lane, 2007; Orr, 2006). That is, what is considered *pathological* changes with the times and differs in different cultures and may even be decided by a vote of members of a professional association. The history of psychiatry illustrates the imposition of expected gender roles, especially on women, in view of their claimed special vulnerability to "disorders." (See chapter 8.) Many biases are implicit and reflect accepted views of our therapeutic culture and it is thus easy to impose beliefs about what is normal and what is not, and what is "healthy" and what is not on clients. Since professionals' beliefs usually mirror commonly accepted norms of proper and improper behavior, little in the way of contradiction may challenge personal beliefs. How many practitioners carefully review personal biases that may affect their work with clients? Thus, professionals, as well as clients, are easy prey for related propaganda ploys appealing to popular grand narratives. In his classic article, "Why I Never Attend Case Conferences," Meehl (1973) suggested that "Many family psychiatrists have a stereotype of what the healthy family ought to be; and if anybody's family life does not meet this criteria, this is taken as a sign of pathology" (p. 237). This tendency is increased by the fact that practitioners tend to be from the middle class and many of their clients are poor or "working class."

The common occurrence of negative experiences in the history of both people who do not seek help and those who do, make it easy to discover pathogenic experiences that are assumed to be responsible for complaints and render the causative character of these experiences questionable.[18] Ignoring information about individual differences in the base rates of different reactions and environmental challenges increases the likelihood of pathologizing clients and making inaccurate judgments. Clinical case studies reported in the professional literature focus on pathology and often neglect positive attributes of individuals and families and their environments (the allure of pathology). Lack of knowledge about ethnic and cultural differences may result in the imposition of negative labels that do more harm than good (see Garb, 1998). Yet another reason clinicians may overemphasize pathology is the biased sample of people they encounter, for example, those with rare patterns of behavior such as severe depression are overrepresented in the clinical population.

ARE YOU REALLY AT RISK? IF SO, HOW MUCH?

Risks are an inescapable part of life. The risk of "sin" haunted the religious in past times and still does today for some. What has changed is the promotion of solutions for risks for which there are no solutions and creating bogus risks, while at the same time, underplaying real risks to health and well-being for which companies do not make money. A review of advertisements, both past and present, show that risks have always been used to try to sell products such as risk of lost opportunities for love, friendship, health, wealth, and beauty (because of bad breath, dirty houses, corns, pimples, coughing, body odor). If you do not use my product, you risk losing opportunities for wealth and happiness. This era has been described as the risk society (Beck, 1992; Giddens, 1990). Risk connotes danger, chance, and suffering. Douglas (1992) argues that risk plays a role equivalent to taboo or sin (p. 28). Now, even though we feel well, we are encouraged to restrict our behavior in ever more ways to stay well. This broadens the extent to which each individual must engage in self-monitoring of related behaviors.

There has been great interest (some argue excessive) in identifying "alleged" risk factors for certain problems and conditions viewed as "unhealthy" or troubling. Instead of distributing "goods," risks are distributed (Beck, 1992). There has been "a substitution of norm by risk" (Vas & Bruno, 2003). Slovic (2000) points out that risks are socially constructed. Many scholars have commented on what they describe as a "culture of fear" (e.g., Glassner, 1999; Furedi, 2002). David Altheide (2002) argues that the media play a key role in transforming risks into dangers, an inherent and not necessarily scary part of everyday life, into fears, an uncomfortable emotional reaction. Since we are risk adverse; it is easy to encourage false fears about risks. Indeed, propagandists take advantage of this emotion (Ellul, 1965). A large portion of public health endeavors is occupied with identification of risks of certain diseases and providing and promoting strategies to minimize them, for example via screening programs. "Surveillance" to track public health "risks" is an industry unto itself. (See discussion of surveillance as a social control device.)

The Fallacy that Prevention is Always Better than Cure

This fallacy is highlighted by Skrabanek and McCormick in *Follies and Fallacies in Medicine* (1998). They point out that prevention has a price and that this price may be more costly than any problems (p. 87). Do screening programs do more good than harm? Will the government plan to screen all residents of the United States for "mental illness" do more good than harm? (see Lenzer, 2004d). Is screening all children for mental health problems a good idea as assumed in recent legislation in Massachusetts? Each measure carries a possibility for error during screening for prevention and subsequent (and unneeded) early treatment. This applies to medical as well as psychological tests. An incorrect sample may be included on a smear that misses cancer cells, resulting in false negatives. Variations and abnormalities are common, much more common than the disease. (See earlier discussion of varieties of non-diseases.) In general practice, medically unexplained physical symptoms are common. Calling something a public health problem allows coercive "prevention" policies that intrude on our freedom.

> The advocates of pharmacratic politics threaten liberty because they obscure or even deny the differences between the kinds of risks posed by a public water supply contaminated with cholera bacilli and the risks posed by a private lifestyle that includes the recreational use of a prohibited psychoactive drug. Individuals cannot *by an act of will* provide themselves with a safe public water supply, but they can *by an act of will* protect themselves from the hazards of smoking marijuana. What makes coercive health measures justified is not so much that they protect everyone equally, but that they do so by means not available to the individual. By the same token, what makes coercive health measures unjustified is not only that they do not protect everyone equally, but that they replace personally assumed self-protection by self-control with legal sanctions difficult or impossible to enforce. (Szasz, 2001, p. 138)

In his article *The Arrogance of Preventive Medicine*, Sackett (2002) notes the (1) aggressive assertiveness (e.g., pursuing healthy asymptomatic individuals for intervention), (2) presumption (confidence that the preventive interventions will, on average, do more good than harm), and (3) attacks on those who question the value of prevention. (See also Gorman, 1998.) We are encouraged to avoid certain behaviors, such as smoking and eating fat. Prevention efforts in public health make use of screening measures to detect disease at an early point. The importance of some screening programs is suggested by the fact that you could have a risk factor for illness without feeling ill (such as hypertension), or could feel ill without having an illness (Gray, 2001). However, do they do more harm than good (e.g., avoid overdiagnosis)? A disease should be both common and serious and an effective treatment should be available for screening to be of value (Wilson & Jungner, 1968). Even good tests will result in many false positives if a disease is rare in the population screened; each of which may be further investigated resulting in intrusive tests such as biopsies. Many others note that efforts to detect rare conditions result in overdiagnosis and overtreatment.

The Medicalization of Risk Factors

We are daily warned about alleged new risks. There has been a medicalization of risk factors accompanied by hiding data showing limited or no decrease in mortality from population-based screening programs and negative consequences such as false positives and further intrusive tests (see Gøtzsche, 2004; Jorgensen & Gøtzsche, 2009).

> A middle-aged man with pneumonia may wonder why the attending doctor is inserting a finger into his rectum. This is a screening test—it has nothing to do with the patient's disease. The physician may find a localized prostate cancer, and the patient may subsequently undergo radical prostatectomy, although no evidence from randomized trials shows that this operation is effective. The patient with pneumonia cannot be sure that the prostatectomy will increase his chance of living longer, but his life will probably feel longer, because the operation renders most men impotent. This disastrous consequence has received too little attention, but when properly informed, many men will decide not to have a screening test.
> The man's risk factor for prostate cancer was his age. Increased age leads to other unanticipated interventions. In some countries, women are invited for mammography in a letter in which the date and time of the appointment have already been fixed. This puts pressure on these women, who must actively decline the invitation if they don't want to be screened.
> ... The main outcome of cancer screening trials—disease specific mortality—is unreliable and biased in favor of screening.... The biggest risk for the population right now may be the uncritical adoption of screening tests for cancer—for example, for cervical, breast, prostate, colon, and lung cancer, despite lack of evidence of an effect on total mortality. Precursors to cancer can be seen in most healthy people above middle age, and the potential for screening to cause harm and lead to a diagnosis of 'pseudo-disease' is frightening. Whether risk factors should be turned into diseases also needs careful reflection for other screening tests—for example, detection of mild hypertension or mild hypercholesterolaemia. (Gøtzsche, 2002)

Gøtzsche (2002) considers the belief that debates about the relative risks and harms of screening should not be carried on in public as "misguided paternalism." (See also Welch, 2004; Gøtzsche et al., 2009; Jorgensen & Gøtzsche, 2009.)

CHALLENGES IN ASSESSING RISKS

Risks differ in the degree of certainty that they will occur, knowledge about how to reduce them, severity, timing, and type (Martinic & Leigh, 2004). Selection of interventions is influenced by the perceived risk associated with different options. People differ in how they weigh risks (Slovic, 2000). Individual risk may differ from population-derived risks. We fall into the *ecological fallacy* when we assume that what is a risk factor to most people is a risk factor for an individual. Most people are risk-adverse; that is, they make decisions in a way that minimizes risk of negative consequences such as losses. At the other end of the pole are those who seek risks such as sky divers, mountain climbers, and high stake gamblers. Our perceptions of risk do not match their actual probability.

1. Voluntary risks are viewed as less risky than those that are not voluntary.
2. Natural risks are assumed to be less hazardous than artificial risks (p. 298).

3. We tend to overestimate the risks of events that kill or injure a great number of people and underestimate the risks associated with less vivid conditions or events that affect many more people, such as asthma.
4. We tend to think that risks are less if we think we have control over them.
5. We tend to think that things that we cannot see and that are associated with very dreaded outcomes such as radioactive waste and AIDS are riskier than events that involve known risks but have less dreaded outcomes, such as auto accidents. (Halpern, 2003, p. 299)

Thus, public opinion is influenced by the following factors:

- *Control*—People are more willing to accept self-imposed risks or those they consider to be "natural," than to have risks imposed on them.
- *Dread and scale of impact*—Fear is greatest where the consequences of a risk are likely to be catastrophic rather than spread over time.
- *Familiarity*—People are more willing to accept familiar risks than new risks.
- *Timing*—Risks seem to be more acceptable if the consequences are delayed rather than immediate.
- *Social amplification and attenuation*—Concern can be increased because of media coverage or graphic depiction of events, or reduced by economic hardship.
- *Trust*—A key factor is how far the public trusts regulators, policy-makers or industry. If these bodies are open and accountable—being honest, admitting mistakes and limitations and taking account of differing views without disregarding them as emotive or irrational—then the public is more likely to place credibility in them. (Parliamentary Office of Science and Technology, 1996; see also Allan, Anderson, & Petersen, 2005)

The media play a key role in shaping perceptions about risk by what they emphasize and whether they accurately report related data (e.g., see Altheide, 2002.)

Innumeracies Contribute to Inaccurate Estimates of Risk

Most people, including physicians, do not understand probabilities (Gigerenzer, 2002). One (of the many) consequences of statistical illiteracy is the susceptibility to manipulation of anxieties and hopes (Gigerenzer et al., 2008). Consider these answers given by 20 AIDS counselors to the question "If one is not infected with HIV, is it possible to have a positive test result?" (Gigerenzer et al., 2008, p. 68).

- "No, certainly not"
- "Absolutely impossible"
- "Never"
- "The test is absolutely certain"
- "False positives never happen"
- "Definitely not" . . . "extremely rare"

- "Absolutely not" ... "99.7% specificity"
- "More than 99% specificity"
- "Don't worry, trust me"

These answers reflect the *illusion of certainty,* a key source of innumeracy. Inaccurate understanding of risks and related tests is illustrated in Table 6.2. Such misunderstanding is a result of statistical illiteracy including the assumption that certainty is possible. All tests have an error rate. Framing effects influence decisions. For example different decisions are made if potential outcome is described in positive terms (75% chance of success) than if they are described in negative terms

Table 6.2 Dialogue between a Client and a Social Worker Regarding an AIDS Test

Session 1: The Counselor Was a Female Social Worker

Sensitivity?

- False negatives really never occur. Although, if I think about the literature, there were reports of such cases.
- I don't know exactly how many.
- It happened only once or twice.

False positives?

- No, because the test is repeated; it is absolutely certain.
- If there are antibodies, the test identifies them unambiguously and with absolute certainty.
- No, it is absolutely impossible that there are false positives; because it is repeated, the test is absolutely certain.

Prevalence?

- I can't tell you this exactly.
- Between about 1 in 500 and 1 in 1,000.

Positive predictive value?

- As I have no told you repeatedly, the test is absolutely certain.

The counselor was aware that HIV tests can lead to a few false negatives but incorrectly informed Ebert that there are not false positives. Ebert asks for clarification twice, in order to make sure that he correctly understood that a false positive is impossible. The counselor asserted that a positive test result means, with absolute certainty, that the client has the virus; this conclusion follows logically from her (incorrect) assertion that false positives cannot occur. In this counseling session, Ebert was told exactly what Susan had been told by her Virginia physicians: If you test positive, it is absolutely certain that you have the virus. Period.

SOURCE: G. Gigerenzer (2002a). *Calculated risks: How to know when numbers deceive you* (pp. 129–30). New York: Simon & Schuster.

(25% chance of failure). The words used by professionals to describe risks are typically vague such as "high risk," "some risk," "low risk," creating many opportunities for miscommunication.

Paulos (1988) describes sources and consequences of innumeracy (mathematical illiteracy) to which we are prone, such as the illusion of certainty. Statistical illiteracy on the part of professionals hinders conversion of information regarding risk into language that helps clients understand "what is likely to happen to me." Different ways to present benefits/risks include the following:

> *Absolute risk reduction*: The proportion of patients who die without treatment (placebo) minus those who die with treatment. Pravastatin reduces the number of people who die from 41 to 32 in 1,000. That is, the absolute risk reduction is 9 in 1,000, which is 0.9 percent.
>
> *Relative risk reduction*: The absolute risk reduction divided by the proportion of patients who die without treatment. For the present data, the relative risk reduction is 9 divided by 41, which is 22 percent. Thus, Pravastatin reduces the risk of dying by 22 percent.
>
> *Number needed to treat*: The number of people who must participate in the treatment to save one life. This number is derived from the absolute risk reduction. The number of people who need to be treated to save one life is 111, because 9 in 1,000 deaths (which is about 1 in 111) are prevented by the drug. (See Figure 6.3.) (Gigerenzer, 2002, p. 35)

The relative risk reduction looks much more impressive than absolute risk reduction. Relative risks are larger numbers than absolute risks and therefore suggest higher risks (and/or benefits) than really exist. Statistical illiteracy increases the likelihood that you will fall for propaganda appeals that take advantage of this lack of knowledge (for example, giving only relative risk). Consider the example of the contraceptive pill scare given in Gigerenzer et al. (2008):

> In October 1995, the U.K. Committee on Safety of Medicines issued a warning that third-generation oral contraceptive pills increased the risk of potentially life-threatening blood clots in the legs or lungs twofold—that is, by 100%. This information was passed on in 'Dear Doctor' letters to 190,000 general practitioners, pharmacists, and directors of public health and was presented in an emergency announcement to the media. The news caused great anxiety, and distressed women stopped taking the pill, which led to unwanted pregnancies and abortions (Furedi, 2002).
>
> How big is 100%? The studies on which the warning was based had shown that of every 7,000 women who took the earlier, second-generation oral contraceptive pills, about 1 had a thrombosis; this number increased to 2 among women who took third-generation pills. That is, the *absolute risk* increase was only 1 in 7,000, whereas the *relative* increase was indeed 100%. Absolute risks are typically small numbers while the corresponding relative changes tend to look big—particularly when the base rate is low. Had the committee and the media reported the absolute risks, few women would have panicked and stopped taking the pill.

	Outcome	
	Yes	No
Exposed	a	b
Not exposed	c	d

Relative risk (RR) $\dfrac{a/(a+b)}{c/(c+d)}$

Relative risk reduction (RRR) is $\dfrac{c/(c+d) - a/(a+b)}{c/(c+d)}$

Absolute risk reduction (ARR) $\dfrac{c}{c+d} - \dfrac{a}{a+b}$

Number needed to treat (NNT) $\dfrac{1}{ARR}$

Odds ratio (OR) $\dfrac{a/b}{c/d} = \dfrac{ad}{cb}$

Figure 6.3. The 2 x 2 table.
SOURCE: Adapted from G. Guyatt and D. Rennie (2002). *Users' guides to the medical literature: A manual for evidence-based clinical practice* (p. 88). Chicago: American Medical Association. With permission of The McGraw Hill Companies.

The pill scare led to an estimated 13,000 additional abortions (!) in the following year in England and Wales.

. . .

Ironically, abortions and pregnancies are associated with an increased number of thrombosis that exceeds that of the third-generation pill. The pill scare hurt women, hurt the National Health Service, and even hurt the pharmaceutical industry. Among the few to profit were the journalists who got the story on the front page. (p. 54)

Here is another example given by Gigerenzer and his colleagues (2008) of a telephone survey in New Zealand.

respondents were given information on three different screening tests for unspecified cancers (Sarfati, Howden-Chapman, Woodward, & Salmond, 1998). In fact, the benefits were identical, except that they were expressed either as a *relative risk reduction*, as an *absolute risk reduction*, or as the *number of people needed to be treated* (screened) to prevent one death from cancer (which is 1/absolute risk reduction):
- Relative risk reduction: If you have this test every 2 years, it will reduce your chance of dying from this cancer by around one third over the next 10 years
- Absolute risk reduction: If you have this test every 2 years, it will reduce your chance of dying from this cancer from around 3 in 1,000 to around 2 in 1,000 over the next 10 years

- Number needed to treat: If around 1,000 people have this test every 2 years, 1 person will be saved from dying from this cancer every 10 years.

When the benefit of the test was presented in the form of relative risk reduction, 80% of 306 people said they would likely accept the test. When the same information was presented in the form of absolute risk reduction and number needed to treat, only 53% and 43% responded identically. (Gigerenzer et al., 2008, p. 65)

Consider also hormone replacement therapy and risk of breast cancer. The first oncologist I consulted said that my breast cancer was definitely caused by taking HRT for many years. Was she correct? What do the data show?

In the large epidemiological studies that generally include tens of thousands of people, it is very easy to find a small relationship that may be considered "significant" by statistical convention but that, in practical terms, means little or nothing. For example, in July 2002, the Women's Health Initiative reported a 26% increase in breast cancer risk for women on hormone replacement therapy, which sounded worrisome. Even if that number were statistically significant—and it was not, by the way—this is what it translates into: The risk of breast cancer would increase within the studied population from five in 100 women to six in 100 women.

We now have a fat file folder of all the studies we could find that have reported an association between some purported risk factor and breast cancer. Of these, the ones that got the most attention were three Women's Health Initiative reports. In 2002, investigators found an increased relative risk of 25% from using combined estrogen and progesterone; in 2003, it was 24%; and in 2004, the relative risk from using estrogen alone was minus 23% (suggesting it was protective against breast cancer).

In 2006, the Women's Health Initiative investigators reanalyzed their data and found that the risk of breast cancer among women who had been randomly assigned to take hormone replacement therapy was no longer significant. Women assigned to take a placebo but who had used hormone replacement therapy in the past actually had a lower rate of breast cancer than women who had never taken hormones.

This reassuring but non-scary news did not make headlines. Neither did the real findings from the March 2008 Women's Health Initiative report, which followed women in the sample who had stopped taking hormones for the previous three years. The researchers reported that the risk of cardiovascular events, malignancies, breast cancers and deaths from all causes was higher in the hormone-replacement-therapy group than in the placebo group even three years after stopping the therapy—pretty alarming. But when we read the article closely, we saw that not one of the associations between hormone replacement therapy and breast cancer, or between the therapy and mortality rates from any cause, was statically significant. Unfortunately, this did not stop the investigators from highlighting their negative findings as meaningful and troubling, and that is what most of the media picked up. (Tavris & Bluming, 2008)

Using Test Results

Tests are used to assess risk and to predict future behavior. They may be used to estimate the likelihood that a person has a certain problem such as depression or tuberculosis. Will taking a test decrease uncertainty about a particular assessment or diagnostic picture? Tests should be used to revise subjective estimates, that is, to change a decision about what should be done. If a psychiatrist suspects that an elderly client has Alzheimer's disease based on an interview (base rate probability) and obtains results from a test as well, results should be used to choose among different options in light of the new estimate based on the results of the test. That is, estimates of the probability that the client has Alzheimer's disease will be revised.

Common Misinterpretations: Professionals tend to make certain kinds of misinterpretations of test results. *Test sensitivity* (the test's accuracy in correctly identifying people who have a disorder) may be confused with *test specificity* (accuracy of a test in correctly identifying people who do *not* have a disorder), resulting in incorrect predictions. Test sensitivity is often incorrectly equated with the predictive value of a positive test result and test specificity is often incorrectly equated with the predictive value of a negative test result. Steurer and his colleagues (2002) found that a sample of Swiss general practitioners (n = 263) were unable to interpret correctly numerical information on the diagnostic accuracy of a screening test. Only 22% selected the correct answer for the post-test probability of a positive screening test when given only test results. They grossly overestimated the value of a positive result alone. They overestimated information derived from screening tests and underestimated information from a client's clinical history.

ACCURATELY ESTIMATING RISK

There are easy ways to determine your risk (e.g., see Gigerenzer & Edwards, 2003). However, many professionals are not aware of them. They may have been propagandized by misleading pharmaceutical ads and marketing promotions disguised as education.

Pay Attention to Base Rate

It is vital to consider base-rate information in evaluating test accuracy. Ignoring base-rate data is a key cause of overestimating the predictive accuracy of test results. The predictive accuracy of a test depends on the initial risk of a condition in the person receiving the test. Two kinds of odds should be considered (Arkes, 1981). One kind consists of prior odds—odds before additional information about a client is available. Obtaining more information (data that are useful in decreasing uncertainty) should change these prior odds. The probability that a client with a positive (or negative) test result for dementia actually has dementia, depends on the prevalence of dementia in the population from which the patient was selected—that is, on the pretest probability that a client has dementia. Because there is little appreciation of this point, predictive accuracy often is overestimated. What percentage of applicants would succeed on the job anyway—without any testing procedure? If 90%

would, then testing does not add much information. As highlighted in this book, the availability of information (data that decrease uncertainty), is no guarantee that it will be used (and used accurately). Such gaps were a key reason for the development of evidence-based practice (Gray, 2001). Clinicians may either fail to revise or incorrectly revise their probability estimates when considering additional data. Bayes's Theorem can help us to improve the accuracy of judgments in situations in which base rate data (that is, prior odds) tend to be ignored. It can help us to consider the effect of case-related data, such as the results of a diagnostic test in determining posterior odds. But using natural frequencies is easier, as described in the next section.

Errors concerning the predictive accuracy of tests are also a result of confusion between two different conditional probabilities. We tend to confuse *retrospective accuracy* (the probability of a positive test given that the person has a condition) and *predictive accuracy* (the probability of a condition given a positive test result). Retrospective accuracy is determined by reviewing test results after the true condition is known. Predictive accuracy refers to the probability of having a condition given a positive test result and the probability of not having a condition given a negative test. It is predictive accuracy that is important when considering a test result for an individual. Another source of error in making predictions is the assumption that the accuracy of a test can be represented by one number. In fact, test accuracy will vary, depending on whether a test is used as a screening device in which there are large numbers of people who do not have some condition of interest or whether it is used for clients with known signs or symptoms. In the latter case, the true positive and true negative rates are much higher than in the broad screening situation, and so there will be fewer false-positives and false-negatives. Overlooking this difference results in overestimations of test accuracy in screening situations resulting in a high percentage of false-positives.

Use Natural Frequencies Rather Than Probabilities

Gigerenzer (2002a) and others have demonstrated that using natural frequencies rather than probabilities can help us to estimate risk. (Table 6.3.) Let's say information is available about asymptomatic women aged 40 to 50 in a given region who participate in mammography screening:

> The probability that one of these women has breast cancer is 0.8 percent. If a woman has breast cancer, the probability is 90 percent that she will have a positive mammogram. If a woman does not have breast cancer, the probability is 7 percent that she will still have a positive mammogram. Imagine a woman who has a positive mammogram. What is the probability that she actually has breast cancer?

Here is the problem in natural frequencies:

> Eight out of every 1,000 women have breast cancer. Of these 8 women with breast cancer, 7 will have a positive mammogram. Of the remaining 992 women who don't have breast cancer, some 70 will still have a positive mammogram.

Table 6.3 SOME CONFUSING AND TRANSPARENT REPRESENTATIONS OF HEALTH STATISTICS

Confusing representations	Transparent representation
Single-event probabilities Definition: A probability that refers to an individual event or person, as opposed to a class of events or people, is called a single-event probability. In practice, single-event probabilities are often expressed in percentages, and occasionally as "X chances out of 100," rather than as a probability ranging between 0 and 1. Example: "If you take Prozac, the probability that you will experience sexual problems is 30% to 50% (or: 30 to 50 chances out of 100)."	*Frequency statements* Definition: A frequency states the risk in relation to a specified reference class. Example: "Out of every 10 of my patients who take Prozac, 3 to 5 experience a sexual problem."
Relative risks Definition: A relative risk is a ratio of the probabilities of the event occurring in one group (usually the treatment group) versus another group (usually the control group). The relative risk reduction of the treatment is calculated as 1 minus the relative risk: Relative risk reduction = $1 - \frac{P_{treatment}}{P_{control}}$ Example: "Mammography screening reduces the risk of dying from breast cancer by about 20%."	*Absolute risks* Definition: The absolute risk in both the treatment and the control group is simply the corresponding baseline risk. The absolute risk reduction is calculated by subtracting the absolute risk in the treatment group from the absolute risk in the control group: Absolute risk reduction = $P_{control} - P_{treatement}$ Example: "Mammography screening reduces the risk of dying from breast cancer by about 1 in 1,000, from about 5 in 1,000 to about 4 in 1,000."
Survival rates Definition: The survival rate is the number of patients alive at a specified time *following diagnosis* (such as after 5 years) divided by the number of patients diagnosed. Example: "The 5-year survival rate for people diagnosed with prostrate cancer is 98% in the USA vs. 71% in Britain."	*Mortality rates* Definition: The mortality rate is the number of people in a group who die annually from a disease, divided by the total number of people in the group Example: "There are 26 prostate cancer deaths per 100,000 American men vs. 27 per 1000,000 men in Britain."
Conditional probabilities Definition: A conditional probability $p(A|B)$ is the probability of an event A given an event B.	*Natural frequencies* Definition: A class of N events (persons) is subdivided into groups by two binary variables. The four resulting joint frequencies are called natural frequencies. Note that these are "raw counts" that sum up to N, unlike relative frequencies or conditional probabilities that are normalized with respect to the base rates of the event in question. Generalization to more than two variables and variable values are straightforward.

SOURCE: G. Gigerenzer, W. Gaissmaier, E. Kurz-Milcke, L. M. Schwartz, & S. Woloshin, S. (2008). Helping doctors and patients make sense of health statistics. *Psychological Science in the Public Interest*, 8, 89. With permission of Association for Psychological Science.

The Medicalization of Life

Imagine a sample of women who have positive mammograms in screening. How many of these women actually have breast cancer? (p. 42).

Here is the depiction of both natural frequencies and probabilities (p. 45):

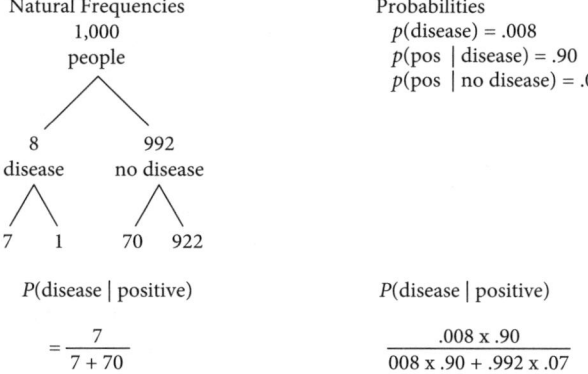

Another example from Gigerenzer:

> To diagnose colorectal cancer, the hemoccult test—among others—is conducted to detect occult blood in the stool. This test is used from a particular age on, but also in routine screening for early detection of colorectal cancer. Imagine you conduct a screening using the hemoccult test in a certain region. For symptom-free people over 50 years old who participate in screening using the hemoccult test, the following information is available for this region (p. 104).

Conditional Probabilities Format—First 24 Participants

> The probability that one of these people has colorectal cancer is 0.3 percent. If a person has colorectal cancer, the probability is 50 percent that he will have a positive hemoccult test. If a person does not have colorectal cancer, the probability is 3 percent that he will still have a positive hemoccult test. Imagine a person (over age 50, no symptoms) who has a positive hemoccult test in your screening. What is the probability that this person actually has colorectal cancer? ___ percent.

Natural Frequencies Format—Remaining 24 Participants

> Thirty out of every 10,000 people have colorectal cancer. Of these 30 people with colorectal cancer, 15 will have a positive hemoccult test. Of the remaining 9,970 people without colorectal cancer, 300 will still have a positive hemoccult test. Imagine a sample of people (over age 50, no symptoms) who have positive hemoccult tests in your screening. How many of these people actually have colorectal cancer? ___ out of ___ (pp. 104–5).

Here we have the natural frequency depicted (p. 107).

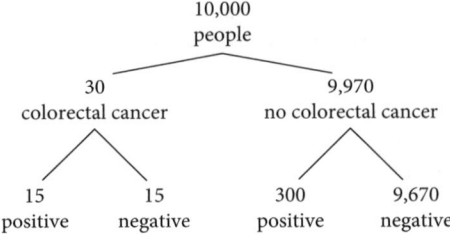

The results of different forms of presentation are illustrated in a study by Hoffrage and Gigerenzer (1998) in which 48 physicians were given four problems, one of which involved screening with the fecal occult blood test (FOBT).

Half of the physicians were given the relevant information in conditional probabilities (a sensitivity of 50%, a false-positive rate of 3%, and a prevalence of 0.3%), which is the form in which medical studies tend to report health statistics. The physicians were then asked to estimate the probability of colorectal cancer given a positive test . . .

Estimates ranged between 1% and of 99% chances of cancer.

Yet when the information was provided in natural frequencies rather than conditional probabilities, those who believed themselves to be innumerate could reason just as well as the others. The information was presented as follows: 30 out of every 10,000 people have colorectal cancer. Of these 30, 15 will have a positive FOBT result. Of the remaining people without cancer, 300 will nonetheless test positive. . . . Most physicians estimated the positive predictive value precisely, and the rest were close. . . . Thus, the problem is not so much in physicians' minds but in an inadequate external representation of information, which is commonly used in medicine. (pp. 68–69)

Here is an example from the field of child protection (Munro, 2004).

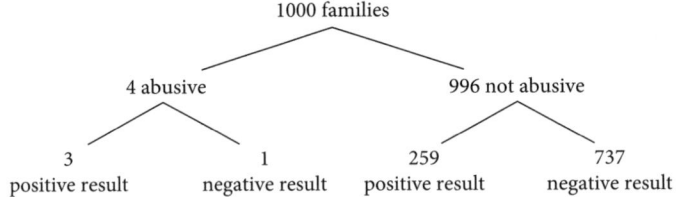

The probability of a positive result being accurate is

$$\frac{3}{3 + 259} = 0.12$$

Paling (2006) notes that over 40% of patients confuse which of the two following probabilities is more likely to happen: 1 in 250 or 1 in 25.

Clearly Describe Both Risks and Benefits

We should be given all relevant information in clear terms regarding benefits and side effects. (See Table 6.4.) Often, the benefits of taking a test (or drug) are emphasized and the possible risks are hidden. For example, Goetzse (2009) found that benefits of getting a mammogram were described in terms of relative risk and harms in terms of absolute risk. This gives a false impression of great benefits and little harm.

For example, over a 5-year period, 15 out of 1000 post menopausal women are predicted to get breast cancer—even if they don't take hormone therapy. If they

Table 6.4 RISK CHART SUMMARIZING BENEFITS AND SIDE EFFECTS OF A DRUG SO THAT COMPARISON IS MADE EASY (FROM SCHWARTZ, WOLOSHIN, & WELCH, 2007)

Prescription drug facts: NOLVADEX (Tamoxifen)

What is this drug for:	Reducing the chance of getting breast cancer
Who might consider taking it:	Women at high risk of getting breast cancer (1.7% of higher risk over 5 year). You can calculate your breast cancer risk at http://bcra.nci.nih.gov/btc.
Who should *not* take it?	Women who are pregnant or breastfeeding.
Recommended testing	Have a yearly checkup that includes a gynecological examination and blood tests.
Other things to consider doing	No other medicines are approved to reduce breast cancer risk for women who have not had breast cancer.

NOLVADEX Study Findings

13,000 women at high risk of getting breast cancer were given either NOLVADEX or a sugar pill for 5 years. Here's what happened:

What difference did NOLVADEX make?	Women giving a sugar pill	Women given NOLVADEX (20 mg. a day)
Did NOLVADEX help?		
Fewer women got invasive breast cancer	3.3%	1.7%
(16 in 1,000 fewer due to drug)	33 in 1,000	17 in 1,000
No difference in dying from breast cancer	About 0.09% in both	
	groups of 0.9 in 1,000	

Did NOLVADEX have side effects:		
Life threatening side effects		
More women had a blood clot in their leg	0.5%	1.0%
or lungs (additional 5 in 10,000 due to drug)	5 in 1,000	10 in 1,000
	0.5%	1.1%
	5 in 1,000	11 in 1,000
More women got invasive uterine cancer	0.5%	1.1%
(additional 6 in 1,000 due to drug)	5 in 1,000	11 in 1,000
No difference in having a stroke	About 0.4% in both	
	groups or 4 in 1,000	
Symptom side effects		
More women had hot flashes (additional	68%	80%
120 in 1,000 due to drug)	680 in 1,000	800 in 1,000
More women had vaginal discharge		
(additional 200 in 1,000 due to drug)	35%	55%
	350 in 1,000	550 in 1,000
More women had cataracts needing		
surgery (additional 8 in 1,000 due to drug)	1.5%	2.3%
	15 in 1,000	23 in 1,000
Bottom Line		
No difference in deaths from all causes combined	About 1.2% in both groups	
	or 12 in 1,000	

How long has the drug been in use?
Nolvadex was first approved by the FDA in 1982. Studies show that most serious side effects or recalls of new drugs happen during their first 5 years of approval.

SOURCE: G. Gigerenzer, W. Gaissmaier, E. Kurz-Milcke, L. M. Schwartz, & S. Woloshin, S. (2008). Helping doctors and patients make sense of health statistics. *Psychological Science in the Public Interest*, 8, 87. With permission of Association for Psychological Science.

do take hormone therapy over that period, 19 out of 1000 can be expected to get the disease. It is immediately evident that this strategy for communicating likelihoods is far easier for patients to understand than comparing odds of 1 in 67 with the odds of 1 in 53. Frequencies immediately show we are dealing with a difference of 4 extra people out of 1000 over a 5-year period. (Paling, 2006, p. 13)

Thus, the motto is: use frequencies not odds.[19]

Ask for Absolute Risk

Relative risk is often presented without giving information on absolute risk. Some consider this so misleading as to be unethical. Relative risk sounds much more alarming than absolute risk. My oncologist recommended a first-generation chemotherapy to decrease my chances of recurrence of breast cancer within 10 years because of my very high OncogeneDx score of 41. I asked her about the benefits. She said there was a 50% decrease in the likelihood of a recurrence in 10 years. (She gave me relative risk.) I asked her about the absolute risk. She said that out of 100 women, rather than 6 having a recurrence in 10 years, 3 would have a recurrence. I declined. Other women may decide to take the recommended chemotherapy. The key ethical issue here is to be given the opportunity to make an informed decision.

> For over a decade, experts in risk communication have been pointing out that statements of relative risks totally fail to provide 'information' to patients because they have no context to know what, say a '50% increased risk' is measured in relation to. In view of this universal condemnation of the practice, it is shameful when health care agencies, pharmaceutical companies and the media persist in making public pronouncements about risks or benefits solely in this manner. It is well known that if patients only hear data expressed as relative risks, they take away deceptively exaggerated impressions of the differences. (Paling, 2006, p. 14).

Here again, we see partiality in the use of evidence—context is hidden. Professionals (and researchers) should provide absolute risk and use easy-to-understand visual aids as illustrated in Figure 6.4.

> Say that the records show that for a defined population of people, about 2 out of 100 are at risk of having a heart attack over the next year. Then imagine that a new study comes out reporting that if such patients take an aspirin daily, their risks of a heart attack will be lowered. Instead of 2 out of 100 suffering a heart attack, only 1 person out of 100 would be expected to do so....
> one doctor might tell the patient, 'Aspirin reduces your risk of heart attack by 1%' while another doctor (using the same data) might say, 'Aspirin reduces your risk by 50%.'...
> 50% feels far more dramatic than 1% which is why the media and sometimes drug companies encourage it. (Paling, 2006, p. 15)

Be Aware of Challenges in Understanding Risk

We tend to assess risks based largely on our emotions rather than facts and overreact to description of relative risks, which provide misleading views of risk and effectiveness of a treatment. This makes us unduly influenced by the media, professionals, and pharmaceutical companies. The professionals you consult may be statistically

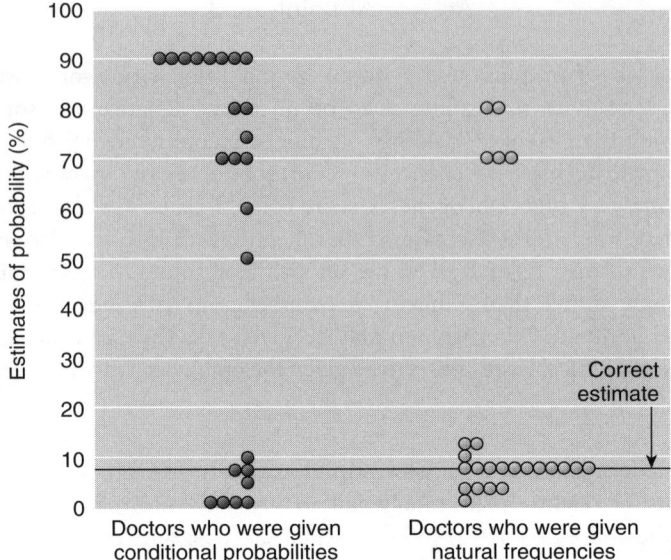

Figure 6.4. Different representations of the same benefits of treatment: the reduction after treatment in the number of people who have a stroke or major bleeding looks much larger on the left, where the reference class of 100 patients who have not had a stroke or bleeding is not shown.
SOURCE: G. Gigerenzer and A. Edwards (2003). Simple tools to understand risks: From innumeracy to insight. *British Medical Journal*, 327, 741–44. With permission of BMJ Publishing Group Ltd.

illiterate as illustrated earlier. Other challenges Paling suggests include confusions created by professionals because of their lack of awareness that they can alter patients' perceptions and decisions by how they frame risks (emphasizing negative versus positive outcomes), failure to use visual aids to clearly describe risks in a meaningful context, and concerns that fully informing patients may not be in their (the patients') best interests. (See Gigerenzer et al.'s (2008) discussion of paternalism as a cause for not accurately informing clients.)

Accept What Cannot Be Changed

Paling (2006) notes that doctors often view patients' emotions as an obstacle to sound decision making (p. 24). However, "A patients' emotions are fundamental to how choices are made. . . . This explains why in every generation, large sections of the public embrace unproven medical solutions based purely on their feelings of trust for the product, the practitioners, or an unqualified but convincing friend" (p. 10). This will require abandoning the *illusion of certainty* hoped for by clients and promoted by professionals.

Use Words That Clearly Communicate

Words such as "most," "often," "few" have different meanings for different people. They are vague. It is thus important to clarify exactly what they mean.

> Physicians should not expect that the common descriptive words they use to describe risks mean the same thing to patients. . . . 'Low risk' may mean a likelihood of 1 in 5 to some listeners and 1 in 10,000 to others. All the other descriptive words (rate, remote, high, moderate, possible, and qualifiers like 'very,' 'rather,' 'quite,' etc.) only have a clear meaning from the perspective of the person doing the communication—typically the doctor. Problems arise because patients use the same words themselves but often intending different levels of likelihood.
> . . .
> For effective risk communication, then, doctors must communicate in language that takes into account how it will be 'received' by the patient. For instance, doctors are surprised to learn that over 40% of patients will confuse which probability is more likely to happen: 1 in 250 or 1 in 25.
> By changing all the statements of odds into frequencies, it is unmistakable which option represents the bigger probability. (The above numbers would then transpose to 4 out of 1000 people as compared to 40 out of 1000 people.) (Paling, 2006, p. 12).

The more skilled a professional is in recognizing and minimizing (or revealing) uncertainty, and communicating this accurately to clients, the less likely he or she is to propagandize their clients with false estimates of risk.

Highlight the Positive (Avoid Negative Framing Effects)

Paling (2006) recommends framing decisions in positive (chance of success) rather than in negative terms (chance of failure) to avoid errors due to our tendency to be risk adverse.

Use Visual Aids to Explain Risk Numbers

Visual aids such as Paling's palettes can help us to understand risks, for example, of having a heart attack. Such aids can describe the risk of a given outcome in relation to risks of other negative events. (See Figure 6.5.)

SUMMARY

The helping professions have expanded greatly. This expansion has been facilitated by propaganda creating bogus fears and risks and transforming normal variations in bodies, thoughts, behaviors, feelings, and existential struggles into medical illnesses

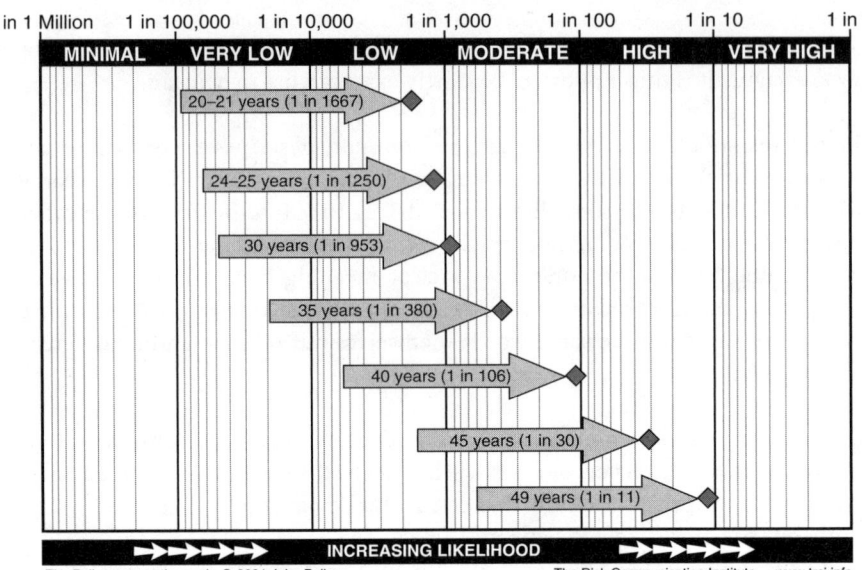

Figure 6.5. Risk of Down's syndrome in a term infant for mothers of different age, using the one thousand woman palette.
SOURCE: Bandolier on Risk. Retrieved July 16, 2006, from <http://www.medicine.ox.ac.uk/bandolier/band144/b144-3.html>. With permission of Bandolier.

requiring medical remedies. Non-medical concerns are viewed as medical ones requiring medical remedies. Pharmaceutical companies sell sickness to promote sales of medication as seen in disease mongering. Normal variations in behaviors, bodies, and psychological functioning are transformed into risks that we must spend time and money to guard against (fear mongering). We are daily warned of dangers from criminals. Struggles common to the human condition are transformed into "mental illnesses" in need of treatment by medication. Individuals rather than their environments are investigated and blamed. A narrow searchlight is used. This view stigmatizes clients and often results in unneeded interventions. It obscures environmental causes of avoidable miseries. Factors that contribute to this tendency include practice theories and classification systems that focus on alleged pathologies of individuals and ignore the role of "sick making" environments including hyping of drugs by the pharmaceutical industry and fellow travelers. Clients are often complicit in this process by not thinking critically about claims.

Potential losses include worry about bogus risks and alleged diseases, overdiagnosis and overtreatment, drawing attention away from real risks and avoidable miseries, erosion of self-reliance and a loss of freedom due to buying into the latest bold assertions regarding what is normal and what is not. Potential losses to professionals include blurring the distinctions between outcomes that can be attained and those that cannot (at least with current resources), obscuring the causes of problems, and focusing on areas offering little if any leverage. Managed care companies pay less for pills than would be required to alter environmental circumstances or to provide long-term counseling. Although more critical attention is being paid to the medicalization of everyday behaviors, normative conditions, and risks, this remains a trickle compared to the juggernaut of the worry creation industry. Classification systems such as the DSM have received more critical attention from a wider array of sources, but still, a dribble compared to the promotion of this system which transforms (mis) behaviors into "mental illnesses."

PART FOUR

How They Reel Us In

7

Obscure Different Views of Knowledge and How to Get It

Propaganda promotes misleading beliefs about what is true and what is false; there is an emphasis on conclusions (claims) and a "deemphasis on developed reasons" (Sproule, 1994, p. 6, chapter 1). Related claims may involve false assertions about risks, accuracy of tests, alleged causes, and effectiveness of interventions. Propagandists take advantage of lack of education regarding different "ways of knowing" and their likelihood of yielding accurate information. Criteria on which claims of knowledge are based include folklore, practice wisdom, scripture, common sense, supernatural causes, and empirical tests. People differ in the standards of evidence they use to make and critically appraise claims as reflected in the following examples:

- "Experts have found that . . ." It must be true.
- "Cognitive behavioral therapy for depression was found to be effective in two well-designed randomized controlled trials. It is a proven method." Can two trials "prove" something is true (or false)? Proof implies certainty.
- In 1968 Nathan Kline, a psychiatrist, wrote that tardive dyskinesia (uncontrollable movements and other typically irreversible adverse effects from neuroleptic medication) is a "rare side effect" that is "not of great clinical significance" (p. 204 in Whitaker, 2002). Is this true? Is it of little clinical significance, especially to clients?
- "We know that depression is caused by a biochemical imbalance in the brain because people get better after they take an antidepressant."
- "If 87 people say that ADHD (Attention Deficit Hyperactivity Disorder) is a brain disease, it must be" (see Barkley et al., 2002).
- "We know that PMDD (premenstrual dysphoric disorder) is a mental disorder because it is included in the DSM."
- "Maintaining chemotherapy for cancer patients helps people live longer." How much longer?
- In *Psychosurgery* Freeman and Watts (1950) claimed that lobotomy "helped more than 80 percent of the 623 patients they had operated on" (Whittaker, 2002, p. 121)." Did this surgery do more good than harm?

We use different standards of evidence in different situations in our every day lives. Does this mean that all criteria are equally sound?[1] Can I find out whether a treatment works by reading testimonials from satisfied customers?

Surveys show that many people do not understand what science is (National Science Foundation, 2006). Quacks, fraudsters, and propagandists take advantage of our lack of understanding of what science is and what it is not to bamboozle us into using their products. Inflated claims of knowledge are common in the professional literature, as well as in the media as shown in Table 7.1. Indeed many professional publications are more advertisements for a particular view promoted rather than an accurate account of the topic discussed as seen in hiding well-argued alternative views and "glittering generalizations" about what the authors "found" in place of measured reports."[2]

Researchers themselves often appeal to consensus to argue that X is true (or false). Science does not rely on consensus. Propagandists use the trappings of science (Latin names, testimonials by alleged 'scientists,' claims of 'Has been tested') without the substance, as in pseudoscience described later in this chapter. Whittaker (2002) points out that "Mad doctors . . . have always constructed 'scientific' explanations for

Table 7.1 EXAMPLES OF PROBLEMATIC PHRASES IN CONCLUSIONS OF PUBLISHED STUDIES OF EFFECTIVENESS

Type of Design	Phrase
Quasi-experiment with vulnerability to selection bias	"The intervention had a significant effect on the treatment group's knowledge about . . . attitudes towards prevention, and coping with . . . high-risk situations" (p. 71).
Quasi-experiment with vulnerability to selection bias	"the findings suggest that the program was effective in increasing . . ." (p. 98).
Correlational	"The study found that these programs would greatly increase the . . ." (p. 163).
Correlational	". . . significantly reduced placement rates or delayed placements . . . is shown to be effective in reducing out-of-home placements" (p. 5).
Case study	"evidence of program engagement and short term behavioral change such as that reported here is promising" (p. 155).
Correlational	"the results of the education and collaboration showed increased . . . and greater success in early referrals for intervention and treatment" (p. 593).
Case study	"the . . . appears to enhance the child's ability to attend to the difficult circumstances" (p. 203).

SOURCE: A Rubin & D. Parrish. (2007). Problematic phrases in conclusions of published outcome studies: Implications for evidence-based practice. *Research on Social Work Practice*, 17(3), 334–47. With permission of Sage.

why their treatments worked" (p. 196). Figures 7.1 and 7.2 illustrate advertisements using the discourse of science and related images to forward dubious claims.

Criteria used to evaluate claims about what is true and what is false range from emotional appeals and repetition of bold assertions to critical tests of claims. But what is a critical test? (See Figure 7.3.) At a workshop on evidence-based practice a professor of social work claimed that pre-post tests are just as sound as rigorous, blinded, controlled trials with random distribution of participants in evaluating the effectiveness of a treatment and said he was happy to recommend services to clients based on pre-post tests.[3] Can pre-post tests critically test whether a treatment is effective? Isn't one person's truth another person's propaganda; isn't everything relative? What is evidence? When do we have enough? What criteria should we use to review the accuracy of a claim such as: "Attention deficit hyperactive disorder is due to a biochemical disorder." How much evidence is needed to claim that a treatment is "appropriate," should be used, and should be paid for? (Eddy, 1993, p. 521). Professional codes of ethics call on professionals to draw on practice-related research and to accurately inform clients about the risks and benefits of recommended services and alternatives. But do they? Do they rely on case examples and testimonials to decide what is effective and what is not? These questions highlight the importance of thinking about how (or if) we can acquire knowledge—information that decreases

Figure 7.1. Advertisement illustrating appeal to "science" to sell products.
SOURCE: B. McCoy (2000). *Quack! Tales of medical fraud from the museum of questionable medical devices* (p. 113). Santa Monica, CA: Santa Monica Press.

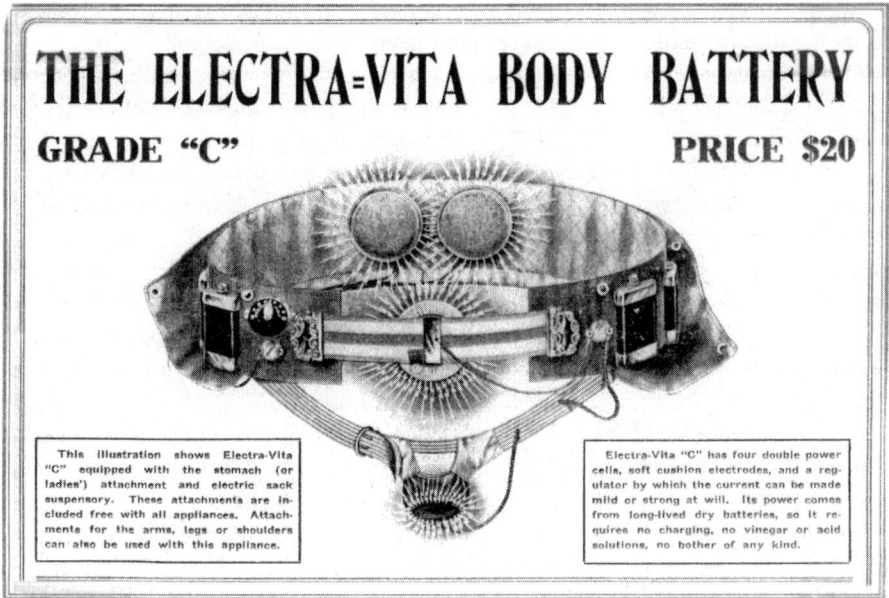

Figure 7.2. Appeal to scientific discoveries.
SOURCE: B. McCoy (2000). *Quack! Tales of medical fraud from the museum of questionable medical devices* (p. 63). Santa Monica, CA: Santa Monica Press.

(or reveals) uncertainty about how to attain a certain outcome. As Popper (1994) points out, if we do not critically evaluate assumptions, they function as prisons that limit our vision rather than as tools to discover what is false. Others can bamboozle us for their benefit, to our detriment. If we rely on false claims and theories, we may be harmed rather than helped; we may miss opportunities to use effective methods. Inflated claims of knowledge (or ignorance) by researchers and academics employed in prestigious institutes, universities, and governmental agencies may be wrong and stifle exploration of well-argued alternatives.

THE IMPORTANCE OF A HISTORICAL PERSPECTIVE

History shows that there is a tendency to travel with the herd in misleading directions encouraged by herd leaders, often members of the establishment, such as academics and professionals (e.g., Bikhchandani, Hirshleifer, & Welch, 1998). Descriptions of this herd mentality and its consequences, such as hindering use of effective procedures, are alarming, as the history of harming in the name of helping reveals (see chapter 5). False theories about what helped people and what harmed them were believed for centuries such as bleeding, purging, and blistering. It also shows that what was proclaimed as impossible (e.g., flying in airplanes) was possible. Major discoveries are often disregarded, such as the discovery that eating citrus fruit can prevent scurvy (Carpenter, 1986).[4] History shows the prevalence of deception and "disinformation" disseminated in order to make money to our detriment and/or

Figure 7.3. What to believe?: Perceptions of disarray and lack of credibility can result from conflicting study results in medical research.
SOURCE: F. M. Wolf (2000). Summarizing evidence for clinical use. In J. P. Geyman, R. Deyo, & S. D. Ramsey (Eds.), *Evidence-based clinical practice: Concepts and approaches* (p. 136). Boston: Butterworth Heineman. Reprinted with permission from Copley News Service.

to promote certain political agendas. Consider selective reporting of antidepressant trials (Turner, Matthews, Linardatos, Tell, & Rosenthal, 2008). Political, social, and economic concerns in the helping professions and related venues including pharmaceutical companies, research centers, and governmental organizations often discourage "telling the truth," pursuit of accurate answers wherever this may lead. Consider censorship of negative findings so often revealed regarding drugs promoted (Brody, 2007). A job offer from the University of Toronto to Dr. David Healy was withdrawn after he presented a lecture suggesting that Prozac and other SSRIs can lead to suicide. This was found to be true and the label now contains a warning. (The clinic received 50% of its funding from the manufacturers of Prozac, Eli Lilly.) Healy sued for 9.5 million dollars. The suit was settled out of court. This is but one of scores of examples of the ostracism of those who raise questions because of concerns regarding economic losses.

Some argue that the increased collaboration between industry and universities impedes transparency of what is done and censors dissenting views.[5] Bauer (2001) contends that science is dominated today by research cartels and knowledge monopolies. (See also Greenberg, 2007; Ziman, 2000.)

While the changes in the circumstances of scientific activity were quite gradual for 2 or 3 centuries, they have now cumulated into a *change in kind*. Corporate science, Big Science, is a different kind of thing than academic science, and society needs to deal with it differently. Large institutional bureaucracies now dominate the public face of science. Long-standing patrons—private foundations like Rockefeller and Ford, charitable organizations like the American Heart Association and the American Cancer Society—have been joined and dwarfed by government bureaucracies like the Centers for Disease Control and Prevention, the NIH, and the National Science Foundation, which, in turn, are being overshadowed by international bodies like the World Bank and various agencies of the United Nations—the World Health Organization, the Food and Agricultural Organization, UNAIDS, and more. Statements, press releases, and formal reports from these bodies often purport to convey scientific information, but in reality these releases are best viewed as propaganda designed to serve the corporate interests of the bureaucracies that issue them. Of course there are exceptions; but as a general rule one should nowadays no more trust a press release from the World Bank or from UNAIDS than one issued by, say, the Central Committee of the Communist Party of the former Soviet Union.

The fine print in some of the reports from these organizations actually concedes that they should not be trusted, a disclaimer not found in traditional scientific publications: 'UNAIDS does not warrant that the information contained in this publication is complete and correct and shall not be liable for any damages incurred as a result of its use.' (UNAIDS, 2004) (Bauer, 2004, pp. 649–50)

As Bauer (2004) notes, recommendations are often accepted uncritically by the media—"passed on as factual and reliable" (p. 650) when they are not.

What 'everyone knows' about the science related to major public issues, then, often fails to reflect the actual state of scientific knowledge. In effect, there exist *knowledge monopolies* composed of international and national bureaucracies. Since those same organizations play a large role in the funding of research as well as in the promulgation of findings, these monopolies are at the same time, *research cartels*. Minority views are not published in widely read periodicals, and unorthodox work is not supported by the main funding organizations. Instead of *disinterested* peer review, mainstream insiders insist on their point of view in order to perpetuate their prestige and privileged positions. This is the case even on so academic a matter as the Big-Bang theory of the universe's origin. When it comes to an issue of such public prominence as HIV/AIDS, any dissent from the official view has dire consequences. (Bauer, 2004, p. 651)

The upshot is that policy makers and the public generally do not realize that there is doubt about, indeed evidence against, some theories almost universally viewed as true, about issues of enormous public import: global warming; healthy diet, heart-disease risk-factors, and appropriate medication; HIV/AIDS; gene therapy; stem cells; and more. (Bauer, 2004, p. 650)

This does not mean the earth is flat, but that political and economic factors influence what is claimed to be true (or false) in the name of science—the ideology of science rather than the open critical inquiry that is the essence of science.

WHAT IS KNOWLEDGE? WHAT IS EVIDENCE

The question "what is knowledge?" has been of concern to philosophers throughout the ages. Different "ways of knowing" differ in the extent to which they highlight uncertainty and are designed to weed out biases and distortions that may influence assumptions. Knowledge serves different functions, only one of which is to encourage the growth of knowledge. Munz (1985) suggests that the function of *false knowledge* (beliefs that are not true and that are not questioned) is to maintain social bonds among people by protecting shared beliefs from criticism (the growth of knowledge). This may be necessary to encourage cooperation in a group. Cultures often thrive because of false knowledge. Such cultures "are doubly effective in promoting social behavior because, not being exposed to rational criticism, they enshrine emotionally comforting and solidarity-producing attitudes" (pp. 283–84). This view suggests that the growth of knowledge can only take place in certain circumstances (cultures)—those in which alternative views are entertained and all views are subject to criticism, that is, in environments in which rationality is valued and practiced.

Raymond Nickerson (1986) defines knowledge as information that decreases uncertainty about how to achieve a certain outcome (I would add or reveals). We can ask: "What information will help us to solve a problem?" Policy makers must consider many kinds of evidence including: (1) experience and expertise; (2) judgments; (3) resources; (4) values; (5) habits and traditions; (6) lobbyists and pressure groups, and (7) pragmatics and contingencies (Davies, 2004). Professionals are ethically obligated to consider the values and expectations of clients, for example, regarding preferred outcomes. Professionals are assumed to have unique knowledge as a result of special education, experience, and training.[6] Research related to assumptions about knowledge (what can be known and what cannot, how we can acquire knowledge, and how certain we can be) suggest a scale ranging from the belief that we can know reality with certainty by direct observation to the view that there is never certainty and that we must critically appraise and synthesize information from multiple sources (King & Kitchener, 2002). Domains of ignorance suggested by Kerwin and Witte (1983) include known unknowns (all the things you know you do not know), unknown unknowns (all the things you do not know you do not know), and unknown knowns (all the things you do not know you know).[7] Can there ever be certainty? Popper (1992) defines knowledge as problematic and tentative guesses about what may be true resulting from selective pressures from the real world in which our guesses come into contact with the environment through a process of trial and error.[8]

Certain "ways of knowing" compared to others are designed to rigorously test claims. The purpose of experimental studies is to avoid biases that result in unwarranted assumptions about effects as described in chapter 9.[9] Some people believe that nothing can be known "for sure." This is assumed in science. Others argue that because we know nothing for sure, we really know nothing. The success of critical testing in hundreds of areas shows that all methods are not equally effective in evaluating claims. If we know nothing, then what is the rationale for professional education? Evidence-informed practice arose in part because of flaws in published reports of research findings such as hiding methodological limitations and inflated claims of effectiveness (Gray, 2001). But what is a flaw? (See Figure 7.3) When is it so significant that we should dismiss a claim? Criteria include what is "standard or accepted" or what a professional believes to be a client's "best interests." However, as Eddy notes, "the credibility of clinical judgment, whether examined individually or collectively, has been severely challenged by observations of wide variations in practices, inappropriate care, and practitioner uncertainty" (p. 521). A concern for helping and not harming obligates professionals to be informed about knowledge, ignorance, and uncertainty associated with decisions they make that affect our wellbeing. But are they so informed? How can you find out? (See chapter 14.)

QUESTIONABLE CRITERIA

Propagandists appeal to questionable criteria for accepting claims about what is true and what is false such as popularity, testimonials, newness, and tradition, that do not provide sound grounds on which to accept claims, typically because they consider only part of the picture, for example, only examples that support a belief. Depth of belief, manner of presentation, and anecdotal experience are other misleading guides. (See Table 7.2.)

Appeal to Authority

As emphasized throughout this book, propaganda ploys take advantage of common human tendencies. For example, we grow up learning to respect authority and those who appeal to authority take advantage of this tendency. (See Figure 7.4.) Administrative authority (e.g., via a position of legal or administrative authority) should be distinguished from cognitive authority "a relationship between two individuals where what one says carries weight or plausibility, within a certain domain or field of expertise, for the other individual" (Walton, 2008, p. 211). Appeals to authority are used to present favored views with an aura of credibility. They can be recognized by bold assertions such as "Play therapy is the best method to use with acting-out children" based solely on someone's status or position, with no description of the reasons as to why it is best, such as data from related empirical studies (Gibbs, 1991). There are many forms of appeal to authority.[10] Appeal to the authority of celebrities is a common persuasion strategy. The authority of the psychiatric profession is often appealed to bolster claims as in "Most psychiatrists believe that psychotropic medication is of benefit for clients." Pharmaceutical companies hire celebrities to offer testimonials for their drugs in ads or on TV programs (the authority of the celebrity). Such appeals also take advantage of the principle of social proof, our tendency to be influenced by what other people think is as in appeals to traditional wisdom and to consensus. Some informal fallacies involving propagandistic uses of language such as pseudotechnical jargon could be included here.

As Walton (2008) notes, "appeal to authority is an inherently weak type of plausible argumentation that can go badly wrong. It can be [and often is] weak and undocumented" (p. 244). Appeals to unfounded authority are common in the professional literature, such as citing a famous person to support a claim when in fact he or she has not conducted any critical tests of the claim and including citations that do not provide empirical support for related claims. Lists of programs distributed by

Table 7.2 QUESTIONABLE CRITERIA FOR EVALUATING KNOWLEDGE CLAIMS

Criteria	Example
Authority (what the "experts" say)	"If Freud said it, it must be true."
Uncritical documentation	Accepting a claim based on citations with no explanation of alleged related evidence.
Characteristics of the person (ad hominem)	"She presents a good argument, but look at the school she graduated from."
Popularity (consensus)	"Eighty percent of people use _____, I'm going to use it too."
Tradition	"That's the way we have always done it. We should continue to use these methods."
What is new	"It's the latest thing. We should try it, too?"
Manner of presentation	"She gave a convincing talk. I'm going to use her methods."
Good intentions	In response to a question about the effectiveness of a procedure, a doctor says, "We care about our patients."
What makes sense	I think bioenergetics works. It makes sense.
Entertainment value	This is a fascinating account of depression. I think it is correct.
Emotional appeals	I trust my feelings when making decisions.
Case examples	"You present a vivid case example to support a claim. I used narrative therapy with my client, and she improved dramatically."
Testimonials	"I tried it and it helped."
Experience	"I've seen five clients and used facilitated communication successfully with all of them."
Intuition	I just know that support groups will be best.

governmental agencies alleged to be "evidence-based" have been found to be based on research that has significant methodological flaws (Gorman & Huber, 2009). And, just because a claim is accompanied by a reference, is not a good reason for assuming it is accurate. We would have to know what is in the reference cited. For all we know, the reference refers to someone's uninformed opinion. Misleading citations are a key form of propaganda in the professional literature. They give an illusion of credibility.[11]

The fallacy adverecundiam (appeal to respect or reverence) refers to fallacious appeals to authority in argument—that is, to the abuse of appeals to alleged authority or expert opinion in order to prevent a respondent in argument from asking critical questions in further dialogue on an issue (Walton, 1995, pp. 278–79). These fallacious instances should be "distinguished from instances of critically weak, faulty or

Figure 7.4. Appeal to authority.
SOURCE: B. McCoy (2000). *Quack! Tales of medical fraud from the museum of questionable medical devices* (p. 210). Santa Monica, CA: Santa Monica Press.

incomplete appeals to authority in argument where the proponent has failed to back up one or more of the required steps of documentation" (p. 279). Those who use unfounded authority try to prevail unfairly. There is an effort to suppress critical questions. (See also discussion of authority in chapter 12.) Evidence-based practice arose as an alternative to authority-based practice (Gambrill, 1999; Straus et al., 2005). Any appeal to authority, such as "expertise," is a kind of plausible argument and should be "treated as fallible' (Walton, 2008, p. 211). Experts may be influenced by a variety of biases and prejudice. They may misunderstand material. They may be paid for their testimony and thus have something to gain. People contacted for "expert opinion" by journalists may not be those most knowledgeable in a subject. Thus, questioning their "cognitive authority" is wise.

What about credentials? Do they reflect special knowledge?[12] The possession of a credential or degree in an area may indicate some level of knowledge in a subject. But is the appeal to a credential a substitute for offering cogent reasons for a claim? Appeals to expert status are often buttressed by use of pseudotechnical jargon geared to impress unwary listeners. In some cases ("Doctors report that," "Studies show that"), we may not even be informed about who is responsible for the statement (Michalos, 1971).

Characteristics of the Person or Their Circumstances (Ad Hominem Appeals)

Rather than address a person's question regarding a claim, the claim maker may attack or praise (appeal to flattery) the questioner in an attempt to close off argument. When I first arrived at the School of Social Welfare at Berkeley and offered a curricular suggestion at a meeting of faculty in the Human Behavior sequence, a faculty member responded: "What do you know about this? You're just a nurse." (Actually I am not.) Rather than addressing my argument she attacked what she (erroneously) thought was my background. Consider the ad hominem attack by the editor-in-chief of *JAMA* (*Journal of the American Medical Association*) on the author of a letter to the *British Medical Journal* (Leo & Lacasse, 2009) criticizing a study published in *JAMA* rather than addressing concerns raised. She referred to Leo as a "Nobody and a nothing."[13] Bauer (2007) suggests that when we feel a rise of temperature when asked a question about a claim, it is a sign that we may be unsure of our grounds because we do not get hot under the collar when someone raises a question about a belief that we can easily support, for example, that the earth is not flat.

Popularity/Consensus

This refers to the acceptance of a claim simply because many people believe it (appeal to the authority of the many). Researchers may adopt a popular (but flawed) view and try to impose it on others on the ground that most people accept it as "proven" (see prior discussion of research cartels) (e.g., Spence, Greenberg, Hodge, & Vieland, 2003). An agency may adopt psychoanalytic methods because other agencies use them. What is the evidence? Are programs included on lists of "best practices" really "best" (Gorman & Huber, 2009)? Reliance on popularity is similar to a reliance on consensus (what most people believe). But what most people believe may not be correct. In today's world of "corporate science" consensus may reflect a successful struggle based on political rather than evidentiary grounds. Resort to voting on an issue as with the American Psychiatric Association referendum to remove or keep homosexuality in the *Diagnostic and Statistical manual of Mental Disorders* reflects appeal to consensus. The vote was 5,854 (58%) in favor of removing this category and 3,810 (37%) opposing removal.

Abstentions were 367 (3%) (Bayer, 1987. P. 395, in *Scientific Controversies*). Appeals to consensus are reflected in terms such as "Researchers agree," "Experts agree," "Everybody knows." Indeed, there may be counter evidence to such claims. Consider the following:

> "Everyone knows" that diets low in cholesterol and saturated fats are heart-healthy. The actual evidence does not support this claim (McCully, 1998; Ravsnkov, 2000).
> "Everyone knows" that it is desirable to lessen or remove 'risk factors.' In actual fact, most so-called risk factors are mere statistical correlations that have not been shown to be causes, necessary or sufficient or even partial.
> "Everyone knows" that a bit of aspirin each day keeps heart attacks away. What everyone does *not* know is that there are better ways, with fewer side-effects, of doing that (Kauffman, 2000).
> "Everyone knows" that AZT was the first medication that could prolong the lives of AIDS patients. What everyone does *not* know is that AZT is a deadly poison (Lauritsen, 1990) avoided by long-term survivors of HIV or AIDS diagnoses" (see Maggiore, 2000). (Bauer, 2004, p. 651)

Tradition

Tradition (what has been done in the past) may be appealed to support claims (the authority of the past). For example, when asked why she was using genograms, a social worker answered, "That's what our agency has used for the past five years." Advertisers often note how long their product has been sold, suggesting that this establishes its effectiveness. *Provincialism* is a variety of the use of traditional wisdom and popular sentiment. It appeals to the tendency to identify with an in-group and to assume that the familiar is better or more important. Imposition of Western views of psychological problems and proposed remedies on non-Western clients is a form of provincialism in clinical practice.[14] Provincialism is carried to an extreme when professionals base their beliefs on loyalty to a position favored by a group rather than on evidence. Because a method has been used for many years does not mean it is effective. In fact, it may be harmful as illustrated in chapter 5. Testing as well as guessing is needed (systematic exploration) to determine the accuracy of claims. One antidote to persuasion by appeals to traditional wisdom is being informed about the history of science or medicine. This offers countless examples of times when the majority view or traditional wisdom was incorrect, often resulting in harming in the name of helping.

Newness

Newness (the latest method) is often appealed to as in "We use the new co-addiction model with all our clients" (the authority of the new). Simply because something is new or innovative does not mean it is effective. After all, everything was new at some time.

Manner of Presentation

We are often persuaded that a claim is correct by the confident manner with which it is presented, such as bold assertions—simply claiming that X is true, no argument or evidence is given.[15] This fallacy occurs when (1) a speaker or writer claims that something is true of people or that a method is effective; (2) persuasive interpersonal skills are used such as building the self-esteem of audience members, joking; and (3) data describing the effectiveness of the method is not given (Gibbs, 1991). Being swayed by the style of presentation underlies persuasion by entertainment value. How interesting is a view? Does it sound profound? Does it claim to empower clients? Here, too, the question is whether there is any evidence for claims.

Good Intentions

We may accept claims of effectiveness because we believe that those who make them have good intentions, that is, they want to help us. The history of the helping professions shows that good intentions and use of services that help clients and avoid harm do not necessarily go together. Programs that have been critically tested and found to be ineffective or harmful continue to be used as illustrated in chapter 5. Consider brief (one hour) psychological debriefing to prevent post-traumatic stress disorder. A systematic review of related controlled studies found this to be ineffective and, one study reported a negative outcome: those experiencing it were more likely, compared to those in a control group, to develop post traumatic stress disorder a year later (Rose, Bisson, & Wessley, 2002).

> Of all tyrannies a tyranny sincerely exercised
> for the good
> of its victims may be the most oppressive.
>
> It may be better to live under robber barons
> than under the omnipotent moral busybodies.
>
> The robber baron's cruelty may sometimes
> sleep,
> his cupidity may at some point be satiated;
>
> but those who torment us for our own good
> will torment us without end, for they do so
> with the approval of their own conscience. (C. S. Lewis)

What Makes Sense

You may have read that expressing anger in frustrating situations is helpful in getting rid of your anger. This may make sense to you. But is it true? Research suggests that it does not have this happy effect (Averill, 1982; Bushman, 2002). Explanations always "make sense" to those who accept them. "People's thinking is logical if seen on its own premises" (Renstrom, Andersson, & Marton, 1990, p. 556). Whether these premises are accurate is another question. What about common sense? This may refer to cultural maxims and shared beliefs or shared fundamental assumptions about the world (Furnham, 1988). One problem here is that different maxims often give contradictory advice. History shows that scientific discoveries are often (if not typically), counter-intuitive—they do not make immediate sense.

Entertainment Value

Distraction by entertainment is a key propaganda strategy. An interest in being entertained may win over a desire to be informed as illustrated in the following situation:

Situation: Classroom
Me: What is the major service offered at your agency?
Student: We use play therapy.
Me: Why was this selected?
Student: My supervisor said that she and the other staff really enjoy doing play therapy.
Me: Do you know if it helps clients?
Student: My supervisor said that she is not interested in research. She enjoys using play therapy.

If this preference is at the expense of clients, this is a problematic. Entertainment offers a much needed escape from the burdens of life in our technological society (Ellul, 1965). Claims may be accepted because they sound interesting, even though interest value does not indicate accuracy. A focus on entertainment pervades our society propelled by scores of different technologies (Postman, 1985a). A number of scholars highlight the close relationship between fear and entertainment. We use the latter to escape the former and in the latter find repeated reasons to be fearful, as in the hundreds of detective stories about crime. This suggests Ellul's (1965) concern with the constant contrasting of emotions characteristic of our technological society. Altheide (2002) argues that "fear is a manufactured response that has been produced by a mass-mediated symbol machine" (p. 23). We become preoccupied with fear and the search for relief, for example, via medication or movies on the Internet or spectator sports.

Emotional Appeals

When evaluating claims, we are easily swayed by our emotions, and politicians and advertisers take advantage of this. They may appeal to our pity, fear, or self-interest with no accompanying argument. Successful propaganda appeals to our deepest goals and hopes, for example, to be healthy and happy as discussed in chapter 8. Vivid testimonials and case examples play on our emotions. A TV commercial for an alcohol treatment center may show an unkempt, depressed man with a drinking problem and describe the downward spiral allegedly caused by drinking, including loss of job and family. We may then see him in the Detox Now Treatment Center, which is clean and whose staff seem caring and concerned. Next we see our client shaved, well dressed, employed, and looking happy and healthy. Words, music, and pictures may contribute to the emotive effect. Because of the commercial's emotional appeal, we may overlook the absence of evidence for the effectiveness of the Center. However, we should not dismiss an argument simply because it is presented emotionally. It may be a sound argument.

Case Examples

In the case example fallacy, conclusions about many clients are made based on a few unrepresentative examples (e.g., see Loftus & Guyer, 2002). The case example fallacy involves faulty generalization. What may be true in a few cases may not be at all true of many other cases. Here again we have partiality in the use of evidence. Gibbs (1991) suggests three reasons why case examples snare the unwary: (1) detailed description of case examples has considerable emotional appeal, especially in comparison to dull data from large representative samples that may be reported in the literature; (2) professionals become immersed in the details of a particular case and forget that what may be true of this case may be untrue of others; and (3) cases that "prove the point" can always be found. Case examples are easy to remember because they have a story-like quality. They are vivid. Extreme examples are often selected, making them easy to remember even though they are unrepresentative of other cases. We tend to overestimate the probability of characteristics described in detailed examples.

Testimonials

Testimonials are reports by people who have used a product or service and report that the product or service is effective. Someone who has attended Alcoholics Anonymous may say, "I tried it and it works." The testimonial is a variant of the case example fallacy and is subject to the same limitations; neither case examples or testimonials provide comparative information needed to evaluate the accuracy of a claim. Here again, there is partiality in the use of evidence. We see only part of the picture. Testimonials may include vivid descriptions of distress prior to use of a remedy followed by equally vivid depiction of relief after use of a method. Testimonials are widely used in human service and pharmaceutical ads. The problem with testimonials is not that the report of an individual's personal experience is not accurate, but the further step of making a claim that this experience means that a method is effective.

Experience

Professionals often appeal to their anecdotal experience to support claims. A psychologist may say: "I know cognitive behavioral methods are most effective with depressed clients because they are effective with my clients." Relying on a carefully documented track record of success with many clients is quite different, as this offers a systematic record but still, there may be no comparative data—what might have happened in the absence of these methods. Experience in everyday practice and beliefs based on this, are the source of what is known as *practice wisdom*.[16] Although anecdotal experience (practice wisdom) provides an important source of "guesses" about what may be effective, it is not a sound basis for evaluating claims of effectiveness (see earlier discussion of testimonials and case examples). The key problem with relying on experience as a guide to what is accurate is the *lack of comparison* (Dawes, 1988). Comparison is a hallmark of scientific thinking. Our experience is not a sound guide because it is often restricted and biased. For example, a social worker may assume that few child abusers stop abusing their children because she sees those who do not stop abusing their children more than those who do stop. Her experience with this biased sample results in incorrect inferences about recurrence of abuse—an overestimate).

When relying on experience professionals may not recognize that conditions have changed; that what worked in the past may no longer work in the present. Western-style mental health services may not be appropriate for many clients. In addition, we tend to recall our successes and forget our failures. That is, we tend to selectively focus on "hits." Unless we have kept track of both hits and our misses, we may arrive at incorrect conclusions. Our tendency to be *overconfident* of our beliefs and the *illusion of control* (overestimation of how much control we have) magnify misleading views. And, as Dawes (1988) points out, we create our own experiences. If we are friendly, others are likely to be friendly in return. If we are hostile, others are likely to be hostile. He refers to this as "self-imposed bias in our own experience" (p. 106). We create our own self-propaganda. Another problem with relying on experience concerns the biased nature of our memory of what happened. We tend to remember what is vivid, which often results in biased samples. Again we see partiality in the use of evidence—attending to only part of the picture. We often alter views about the past to conform to current moods or views. And, we do not know what might have happened if another sequence of events had occurred. Overlooking this, we may unfairly praise or blame ourselves (or someone else). Relying on experience opens us. Our tendency to look for causes encourages premature assumptions that may lead us astray. We may assume that mental illness results in homelessness because many homeless people are labeled "mentally ill." But does it?

So experience, while honing skills in many ways, may also have negative effects including a reluctance to consider new ideas and overconfidence in certain views. We may learn "the wrong things." With all these concerns about learning from experience, what can be done? As Dawes suggests, we can be cautious about generalizing from the past and present to the future. "In fact, what we often would do is to learn how to avoid learning from experiences" (1988, p. 120). Hogarth (2001) suggests that becoming aware of the limitations of experiential (intuitive) learning is a two-step process: (1) we discover that it is to our benefit to take greater control of our processes, and, (2) we "must understand at an intellectual level why learning from experience has limitations" (p. 224). He emphasizes the importance of becoming informed about different kinds of learning environments. He describes these along a continuum ranging from kind to wicked. Whether an environment is kind or wicked depends both on whether feedback gained is relevant or irrelevant and on whether the involved task is lenient or exacting (Hogarth, 2001). Professionals often work in environments that do not provide timely feedback concerning the outcomes of their decisions—they work in 'wicked' environments.

What Is An Expert and How Is Expertise Developed? Experts differ from novices both in quality of outcomes achieved (experts are superior) and in processes used.[17] Experts pay more attention to problem definition and structure problems at a deeper (more abstract) level compared to novices, who tend to accept problems as given. They possess domain-specific knowledge and can more rapidly identify what information is needed to solve a problem in this area. They seem to use a different reasoning process compared to novices, based on many experiences providing corrective feedback. They develop skill at *meta-reasoning* such as asking questions that prime the use of helpful data and reviewing assumptions in terms of their consistency with the evidence at hand. They are more aware compared to novices of what they know and what they do not (their ignorance). They are better at critiquing themselves when things are "slipping away." Experts do not necessarily perform better than novices in unstructured problem areas such as psychology and psychiatry. For example, Goldberg (1959) compared the ability of psychiatrists with that of their secretaries in diagnosing brain damage by using the Bender-Gestalt test. There was no difference between these two groups. And no relationship was found between individual diagnostic accuracy and degree of confidence. (See also Hinds, 1999.) Experts, as well as novices, are prey to a variety of illusions, such as the illusion that one can have control over an outcome when this is not possible and, they make a variety of errors even in their own area of expertise (see Hammond, 1996). Being an expert in no way removes the obligation to answer questions. (See previous discussion of authority.)

Skill in solving unstructured problems seems to require a great deal of experience with the domain. Based on interviews with experienced firefighters, nurses, and paramedics, Klein (1998) argues that expert decision-makers quickly size up a situation based on *informed* intuition created by multiple experiences providing corrective feedback. They draw on this to identify important cues, relying on the similarity of the new situation to others previously experienced. Thus, expertise is closely related to *"pattern recognition,"* based on extensive experience offering corrective feedback. "Pattern matching" refers to the ability of the expert to detect typicality and to notice events that did not happen and other anomalies that violate the pattern. (See also the discussion of fast and frugal decision trees in Gigerenzer 2007.) Mental simulation refers to quickly running things through one's mind as to what could happen in real time, in real-life. By recognizing "typicality" (a certain kind of pattern), experts identify when this pattern is violated—when there is an anomaly that should be attended to. Indeed, failure to recognize anomalies is related to escalation toward a major mistake. This view highlights the close connection between methods used by scientists and methods used in developing expertise, such as trying out "hunches," and seeing what happens.

Appeal to expertise, as if this is sufficient to make an argument when it is not, is inappropriate in a context of critical inquiry—it is a kind of "suppression of argument that deceptively aims to close off the process of legitimate dialogue prematurely, and to defeat the respondent by a short cut to persuasion" (p. 244).

The fallacious aspect of *ad verecundiam* relates to the use of expert opinion by one party to unfairly put pressure on the other party by saying, in effect, 'Well look, you're not an expert, so nothing you can say about the matter is anything less than presumptuous.' The implication is that the second party does not have sufficient respect for the opinion of an expert. What is exploited is the proponent's commitment to expert opinion as something that should command respect in argumentation. The fallacy tries to prevent the respondent from asking critical questions. It is an attempt to fix commitment. The tactic is to awe the opposition into silence. So the fallacy is the abuse of appeal to expert opinion by pressing ahead too aggressively and not leaving the other party enough room to challenge or critically question the expert opinion that has been used against him in a dispute. (Walton, 2008, pp. 244–45)

What about Intuition?

Intuitions (inferences) may refer to looking back in time (interpreting experience) or forward in time (predictions). For example a psychiatrist may "diagnose" by gaining information about a clients' past or predict that a client will act in a certain manner in the future. Intuition ("gut reaction") is a quick judgment. It comes quickly into a person's consciousness. The person does not know why they have this feeling. Yet, this is strong enough to make an individual act on it. You do not fully know where it comes from (Gigerenzer, 2007). You make a judgment based on your first feeling and ignore all else. These quick judgments are based on heuristics (simple rules-of-thumb) such as the recognition heuristic; if one alternative is recognized faster than another, infer that it has the highest value on the criterion (Gigerenzer & Brighton, 2011). Another heuristic suggested by Gigerenzer is imitate the successful; look for the most successful person and imitate her or his behavior. We make what Gigerenzer calls a fast and frugal decision. It is rapid (fast) and relies only on key cues (it is frugal). We ignore irrelevant data. We do not engage in calculation such as balancing pros and cons. He emphasizes the importance of ecological rationality—correspondence to a certain environment. When "our gut reaction" is based on vital cues, it serves us well. When it is not (when in Hogarth's term, it is not "informed" intuition), it is best to use a more analytic approach to making decisions. Thus, we use two systems when making judgments—a rapid intuitive one and a more analytical one. Kahneman (2003) encourages us to use our analytic skills to make best use of intuition.

The view that intuition involves responsiveness to information that although not consciously represented, yields productive insights, is compatible with the research regarding expertise (Klein, 1998). No longer remembering where we learned something encourages attributing solutions to "intuition." When a professional is asked what made her think a particular method would be effective in increasing motivation of a client, his answer may be, my "intuition." When asked to elaborate, he may offer sound reasons based on past experiences offered corrective feedback. That is, his "hunch" was an informed one. Intuition will not be a sound guide for making decisions when misleading cues are focused on. Research comparing clinical and actuarial judgment consistently shows the superior accuracy of the latter (e.g., Grove & Meehl, 1996; Quinsey, Harris, Rice, Cormier, 2006). Actuarial judgments are based on empirical relationships between variables and an outcome, such as future abuse. Attributing judgments to "intuition" decreases opportunities to teach others. One has "it" but does not know how or why "it" works. If you ask your supervisor "How did you know to do that at that time," and he says, "My intuition," this will not help you to learn what to do. And, intuition cannot show which method is most effective in helping clients; a different kind of evidence is required for this—one that provides critical comparisons controlling for biases.

SCIENCE AND SCIENTIFIC CRITERIA

Propagandists use the discourse of science (e.g., jargon) to promote an illusion of objectivity and scientific rigor. It is important to understand what science is so you can spot look-a-likes that may fool you into embarking on a course of action that does more harm than good and that hides a good option. Science is a way of thinking about and investigating the accuracy of assumptions about the world. The essence of science is guessing and testing—identifying problems or questions and trying to solve (answer) them in a way that offers accurate information about whether a conjecture (a guess or theory) is correct (Asimov, 1989). Popper (1972) suggests that it is a process for solving problems in which we learn from our mistakes. Science rejects a reliance on authority, for example, pronouncements by officials or professors, as a route to knowledge. Authority and science are clashing views of how knowledge can be gained (Popper, 1994). The history of science and medicine shows that the results of systematic investigation often frees us from false beliefs that harm rather than help and decreases our susceptibility to fraudulent claims.

Some claims are testable but untested. If tested, they may be found to be true, or uncertain (Bunge, 2003). Discovering what is true and what is false often requires ingenious experiments and the invention of new technologies such as the microscope and the long-range telescope. Consider the creative experiment designed by Emily Rosa, age 11, a 4th grader, to test the effectiveness of therapeutic touch.[18]

> Emily designed an experiment in which the healer and Emily were separated by a screen. Then Emily decided, by flipping a coin, whether to put her hand over the healer's left hand or the right hand. The healer was asked to decide where Emily's hand was hovering. If the healer could detect Emily's human energy field he or she should be able to discern where Emily's hand was.
>
> In 280 tests involving the 21 practitioners, the healers did no better than chance. They identified the correct location of Emily's hand just 44 percent of the time; if they guessed at random, they would have been right about half the time. (Kolata, 1998, p. A1)

There are many ways to do science and many philosophies of science. The terms *science* and *scientific* are sometimes used to refer to any systematic effort—including case studies, correlational studies, and naturalistic studies—to acquire information about a subject. All methods are vulnerable to error, which must be considered when evaluating data they generate. Nonexperimental approaches include natural observation, as in ethology (the study of animal behavior in real-life settings), and correlational methods that use statistical analysis to investigate the degree to which events are associated. These methods are of value in suggesting promising experiments, as well as when events of interest cannot be experimentally altered, or if doing so would destroy what is under investigation.[19]

The view of science presented here, critical rationalism, is one in which the theory-laden nature of observation is assumed (i.e., our assumptions influence what we observe) and rational criticism is viewed as the essence of science (Phillips, 2000; Popper, [1963] 1972). "There is no pure, disinterested, theory-free observation" (Popper, 1994, p. 8). Concepts are assumed to have meaning and value even though they are unobservable. By testing our guesses, we eliminate false theories and may learn more about our problems; corrective feedback from the physical world allows us to test our guesses about what is true or false. For example, the cause of ulcers was found to be *Helicobacter pylori* not stress (Marshall & Warren, 1983; Van der Weyden, Armstrong, & Gregory, 2005). Stress may exacerbate the results, but is not the cause. It is assumed that nothing is ever "proven" (Miller, 1994; Popper, 1972).

Criticism (Self-Correction) is the Essence of Science

The essence of science is creative, bold guessing and rigorous testing in a way that offers accurate information about whether a guess (conjecture or theory) is accurate (Asimov, 1989). Popper argues that "the growth of knowledge, and especially of scientific knowledge, consists of learning from our mistakes" (1994, p. 93).[20] The scientific tradition is the tradition of criticism (Popper, 1994, p. 42). "I hold that orthodoxy is the death of knowledge, since the growth of knowledge depends entirely on the existence of disagreement" (Popper, 1994, p. 34). There are hundreds of different theories. They cannot all be correct. Paradoxically, in the social sciences theories are often claimed to be true with excessive confidence, ignoring the fact that they cannot all be accurate. Although the complexity of questions regarding human behavior make it difficult to acquire the kind of knowledge that is available in the physical sciences, careful evaluation of claims about what may help and what may harm is vital when making life-affecting decisions (e.g., see Jacobson, Schwartz, & Mulick, 2005). Popper considers the critical method to be one of the great Greek inventions.

The interplay between theories and their testing is central to science. For example, an assumption that verbal instructions can help people to decrease their smoking could be tested by randomly assigning smokers to an experimental group (receiving such instructions) and a control group (not receiving instructions) and observing their behavior to see what happens. There is a comparison. Let's say that you think you will learn some specific skills in a class you are taking. You could assess your skills before and after the class and see if skills have increased. Testing your belief will offer more information than simply thinking about it. What if you find that your skills have increased? Does this show that the class was responsible for your new skills? It does not. There was no comparison (for example, with students who did not take the class). There are other possible causes, or *rival hypotheses*. For example, maybe you learned these skills in some other context. Scientists are often wrong and find out that they are wrong by testing their predictions.

Scientific statements are those that can be tested (they can be refuted). Consider the question, "How many teeth are in a horse's mouth?" You could speculate about this, or you could open a horse's mouth and look inside. If an agency for the homeless claims that it succeeds in finding homes for applicants within 10 days, you could accept this claim at face value or systematically gather data to see whether this claim is true. A theory should describe what cannot occur as well as what can occur. If you can make contradictory predictions based on a theory, it cannot be tested.

Testing may involve examining the past as in Darwin's theory of evolution. Some theories are not testable (falsifiable). There is no way to test them to find out if they are correct. Psychoanalytic theory is often criticized on the grounds that contradictory hypotheses can be drawn from the theory. As Karl Popper points out, irrefutability is not a virtue of a theory, but a vice. Theories can be tested only if specific predictions are made about what can happen and also about what cannot happen.[21] In evidence-informed practice and policy, it is assumed that the evidentiary status of a claim is related to the rigor with which it has been critically tested, for example, does a measure of suicide risk accurately predict future behavior?

Many people focus on gathering support for (justifying, confirming) claims and theories. Let's say that you see 3,000 swans, all of which are white. Does this mean that all swans are white? Can we generalize from the particular (seeing 3,000 swans, all of which are white) to the general, that all swans are white? Karl Popper (and others) contend that we cannot discover what is true by means of induction (making generalizations based on particular instances) because we may later discover exceptions (swans that are not white). (In fact, black swans are found in New Zealand.) (One of my favorite reactions to this discussion is a well-known academic who said "Who cares about swans?") Explanations that are untestable are problematic. A theory should describe what can happen, as well as what cannot happen. Can you make accurate predictions based on a belief? Falsifiability is emphasized as more critical than confirmation because the latter is easier to obtain. If, as Popper argues, nothing can ever be proven, the least we can do is to construct falsifiable theories: theories that generate specific hypotheses that can be tested.

Popper maintains that attempts to falsify, to discover the errors in our beliefs by means of critical discussion and testing is the only sound way to develop knowledge (Popper, 1992, 1994; see Table 7.3).[22] Confirmations of a theory can readily be found if one looks for them. Popper uses the criterion of falsifiability to demark what is or could be scientific knowledge from what is not or could not be. For example, there is no way to refute the claim that "there is a God," but there is a way to refute the claim that "assertive community outreach services for the severely mentally ill reduces substance abuse." We could, for example, randomly distribute clients to a group providing such services and compare those outcomes with those of clients receiving no services or other services. Although we can justify the selection of a theory by its having survived more risky tests concerning a wider variety of hypotheses, compared with other theories that have not been tested or that have been falsified, we can never accurately claim that this theory is "the truth." Further tests may show otherwise. The term "proof" implies certainty about a claim as in the statement "The effectiveness of case management services to the frail elderly has been proven in this study." Since future tests may show a claim to be incorrect, even one that is strongly corroborated, no assertion can be "proven" (Popper, 1972) and the word should be avoided. It encourages an illusion of knowledge.

Some Tests Are More Rigorous Than Others

Some tests are more rigorous than others in controlling for sources of bias and so offer more information about what may be true or false. Many "hierarchies" of

Table 7.3 CONTRASTS BETWEEN TWO PHILOSOPHIES OF SCIENCE: THE VERIFICATIONIST PHILOSOPHY AND THE REFUTATIONIST APPROACH PROPOUNDED BY POPPER

Verificationist	Refutationist
Certainty is possible.	Certainty is impossible.
Science is based on proof.	Science is based on disproof.
Observation reveals truth.	Observation involves interpretation.
Recognition of facts precedes formulation of theories.	Formulation of theories precedes recognition of facts.
A good theory predicts many things.	A good theory forbids many things.
A good theory is probable: it has been repeatedly confirmed.	A good theory is improbable yet it has repeatedly failed to be refuted.
A prediction is more informative the more it conforms to experience.	A prediction is more informative the more it is risky or deviant from expectations.
Induction is the logical foundation of science.	Deduction is the logical foundation of science.
Inductive inference is logical.	Induction is illogical.
A theory can be validated independently, and absolutely.	A theory can be corroborated only relative to other theories.
Among competing theories, the preferable is the one that has been more often verified.	Among competing theories of equal refutability, the preferable is the one that has withstood more diverse tests.
Theories become more scientific the more they have been proven true by objective observations.	Theories become more scientific as they are made more refutable both through reformulations and technological advances in methods.

SOURCE: M. Maclure (1985). Popperian refutation in epidemiology. *American Journal of Epidemiology*, 12(3), 343–50.

evidence have been suggested. (See chapter 14.) Compared with anecdotal reports, experimental tests are more severe tests of claims. Unlike anecdotal reports, they are carefully designed to rule out alternative hypotheses about what may be true and so provide more opportunities to discover that a theory is not correct. Making accurate predictions (e.g., about what service methods will help a client) is more difficult than offering after-the-fact accounts that may sound plausible (even profound). Every research method is limited in the kinds of questions it can address successfully. The question raised will suggest the research method required to explore it. Thus, if our purpose is to communicate the emotional complexity of a certain kind of experience (e.g., the death of an infant), then qualitative methods are needed (e.g., detailed case examples, thematic analyses of journal entries, open-ended interviews at different times).

A Search for Patterns and Regularities

It is assumed that the universe has some degree of order and consistency. This does not mean that unexplained phenomena or chance variations do not occur or are not considered. For example, chance variations contribute to evolutionary changes (Lewontin, 1991, 1994; Strohman, 2003). Uncertainty is assumed. Since a future test may show an assumption to be incorrect, even one that is strongly corroborated (has survived many critical tests), no assertion can ever be "proved." This does not mean that all beliefs are equally sound; some have survived more rigorous tests than have others (Asimov, 1989).[23]

Parsimony

An explanation is parsimonious if all or most of its components are necessary to explain most of its related phenomena. Concepts may be unfalsifiable. Unnecessarily complex explanations may get in the way of detecting relationships between behaviors and related events.[24]

Scientists Strive for Objectivity

Popper (1992) argues that "the so-called objectivity of science lies in the objectivity of the critical method; that is, above all, in the fact that no theory is exempt from criticism, and further, in the fact that the logical instrument of criticism—the logical contradiction—is objective" (p. 67). Two different proposed theories for an event cannot both be true. "What we call scientific objectivity is nothing else than the fact that no scientific theory is accepted as dogma, and that all theories are tentative and are open all the time to severe criticism—to a rational, critical discussion aiming at the elimination of errors" (Popper, 1994, p. 160). Basic to objectivity is the critical discussion of theories (eliminating errors through criticism). Observation is always selective (influenced by our theories/concepts). Scientists are often wrong and find out that they are wrong by testing their predictions. In this way, better theories (those that can account for more findings) replace earlier ones.

Science is conservative in insisting that a new theory account for previous findings. It is revolutionary in calling for the overthrow of previous theories shown to be false, but this does not mean that the new theory has been "established" as true.

> It most important to see that a critical discussion always deal with more than one theory at a time. For in trying to assess the merits or demerits even of *one* theory, it always must try to judge whether the theory in question is an *advance*: whether it explains things which we have been unable to explain so far—that is to say, with the help of older theories. (Popper, 1994, p. 160)

Although the purpose of science is to seek true answers to problems (statements that correspond to facts), this does not mean that we can have certain knowledge. Rather, we may say that certain beliefs (theories) have (so far) survived critical tests or have not yet been exposed to them. And, some theories have been found to be false. An error "consists essentially of our regarding as true a theory that is not true" (Popper, 1992, p. 4). Objectivity implies that the results of science are independent of any one scientist so that different people exploring the same problem will reach the same conclusions. It is assumed that perception is theory-laden (influenced by our expectations). This assumption has been accepted in science for some time (Phillips, 1987, 2000). People often confuse values external to science (e.g., what should be) with values internal to science (e.g., critical testing) (Phillips, 1987).

A Skeptical Attitude

Scientists are skeptics. They question what others view as fact or "common sense." They ask for arguments and evidence. They do not have sacred cows.

> Science ... is a way of thinking. ... [It] invites us to let the facts in, even when they don't conform to our preconceptions. It counsels us to consider hypotheses in our heads and see which ones best match the facts. It urges on us a fine balance between no-holds-barred openness to new ideas, however heretical, and the most rigorous skeptical scrutiny of everything-new ideas and established wisdom. (Sagan, 1990, p. 265)

Scientists and skeptics seek criticism of their views and change their beliefs when they have good reason to do so. Skeptics are more interested in arriving at accurate answers than in not ruffling the feathers of supervisors or administrators.[25] They value critical discussion because it can reveal flaws in their own thinking, which should enable better guesses about what is true, and these in turn can be tested. Knowledge is viewed as tentative. Scientists question what others view as facts or "common sense." They ask:" "What does this mean? How good is the evidence?" Skepticism does not imply cynicism (being negative about everything). Scientists change their beliefs if additional evidence demands it. If they do not, they appeal to science as a religion—as a matter of authority and faith—rather than as a way to critically test theories. For example, can a theory lead to guidelines for resolving a problem? Openness to criticism is a hallmark of scientific thinking. Karl Popper considers it the mark of rationality. This skeptical attitude is not valued by all who appeal to science or who call themselves scientists:

> Skepticism toward research claims is absolutely necessary to safeguard reliability. In corporate settings, where results are expected to meet corporate goals, criticism may be brushed off as disloyalty, and skepticism is thereby suppressed. As Ziman (1994) pointed out, the Mertonian norms of "academic" science have been replaced by norms suited to a proprietary, patent- and profit-seeking environment in which researchers feel answerable not to a universally valid standard of trustworthy knowledge but to local managers. A similar effect, the suppression of skepticism, results from the funding of science and the dissemination of results by or through non-profit bureaucracies such as the NIH or agencies of the United Nations. (Bauer, 2004, p. 649)

Other Characteristics

Science deals with specific problems that can be solved (that can be answered with the available methods of empirical inquiry). For example, is intensive in-home care for parents of abused children more effective than the usual social work services? Is the use of medication to decrease depression in elderly people more (or less) effective than cognitive-behavioral methods? Saying that science deals with problems that can be solved does not mean, however, that other kinds of questions are unimportant or that a problem will remain unsolvable. New methods may be developed that yield answers to questions previously unapproachable in a systematic way. Scientific knowledge is publicly reviewed by a community. Science is collective. Scientists communicate with one another, and the results of one study inform the efforts of other scientists.

MISUNDERSTANDINGS AND MISREPRESENTATIONS OF SCIENCE

Surveys show that most people do not understand the basic characteristics of science (National Science Foundation, 2006).[26] Even academics confuse logical positivism (discarded by scientists long ago) and science as we know it today. Logical positivism emphasizes direct observation by the senses. It is assumed that observation can be theory free. It is justification focused, assuming that greater verification yields closer approximations to the truth. This approach to knowledge was discarded decades ago because of the induction problem (piling up confirmations does not necessarily bring you closer to the truth (see earlier discussion), the theory-laden nature of observation, and the utility of unobservable constructs. Science is often misrepresented as a collection of facts or as referring only to controlled experimental studies. Misunderstandings about science leave us vulnerable to pseudoscientific appeals. Misconceptions include the following:

- There is an absence of controversy.
- Theories are quickly abandoned if anomalies are found.
- Intuitive thinking has no role.
- There is no censorship and blocking of innovative ideas.
- It is assumed that science knows, or will soon know, all the answers.
- Objectivity is assumed.
- Chance occurrences are not considered.
- Scientific knowledge is equivalent to scientific thinking.
- The accumulation of facts is the primary goal.
- Linear thinking is required.
- Passion and caring have no role.
- There is one kind of scientific method.
- Unobservable events are not considered

Dispute and controversy is the norm rather than the exception in science. Consider differences of opinion in the study of nutrition and health:

Some researchers argued that in the area of nutrition, epidemiology should be regarded primarily as a source of hypotheses rather than a means of testing them. In their view, experimental studies in laboratory animals—or, better yet, clinical trials in humans—were needed to resolve the scientific issues. Other researchers placed much more confidence in epidemiology, arguing that its critics displayed an unscientific bias against a valid research method. Still another axis of debate concerned the standards of proof that should apply when incomplete evidence bears on public health. In particular, the question of whether public health agencies should aim dietary recommendations intended to reduce chronic disease at the general public was controversial, with some health professionals arguing that physicians should assess risks and offer advice on an individual basis. Disputes also broke out about what types of nutrition information should appear on food labels, and about whether fast food restaurants should be required to disclose the nutritional content of their burgers, shakes, and fries. (Hilgartner, 2000, p. 31)

Discovery of accurate answers is usually preceded by false starts and disappointing turns. This history of uncertainty is typically hidden because of page limits enforced by journal editors. The "messiness" of inquiry is obscured by the organized format of texts and journals.

The differences between formal scientific texts and the activities required to produce them are well known in science studies: scientists tinker in the privacy of the laboratory until they are ready to "go public" with neatly packaged results; their published work systematically excludes the contingencies of actual research; and at times, they even stage spectacular public demonstrations, displaying results dramatically and visually in a carefully arranged theater of proof. (Hilgartner, 2000, p. 19)

Bell and Linn (2002) note that "when textbooks attempt to synthesize historical accounts of discovery, they often omit controversy and personality. These accounts may overemphasize and give an incorrect illusion of a logical progression of uncomplex discovery when indeed the history is quite different: 'serendipitous, personality-filled, conjectural and controversial'" (p. 324).[27] New ideas and related empirical evidence often show that currently accepted theories are not correct, however, as Kuhn (1970) argued, old paradigms may continue to be uncritically accepted until sufficient contradictions (anomalies) force recognition of the new theory.[28] Manuscripts submitted to journals regarding every major discovery over the past 50 years were rejected by prestigious journals such as *Nature* and *Lancet*.[29]

As "big science" becomes more common (research institutes jockeying for limited research funds) and collaboration between industry and universities increases, resistance to new ideas becomes more likely. Political correctness (censorship of certain topics and the castigation of those who raise questions) is not confined to any one area. Researchers with certain kinds of laboratories have a big stake in maintaining certain views of reality, those that call for the kind of methods used in their laboratories. For example, virologists with laboratories set up to pursue the viral theory of cancer (to no avail), used these to pursue the viral theory of HIV/AIDS (Duesberg,

1996; Lang, 1998).[30] Many people confuse science with pseudoscience and scientism (see Glossary). Some protest that science is misused; saying that a method is bad because it has been or may be misused is not a cogent argument; anything can be misused. Some people believe that critical reflection is incompatible with caring. Reading the writings of any number of scientists, including Loren Eiseley, Carl Sagan, Karl Popper, and Albert Einstein, should quickly put this false belief to rest.[31] Far from reinforcing myths about reality, as some claim, science is likely to question them. All sorts of questions that people may not want raised may be raised such as: "Does this residential center really help residents? Would another method be more effective? Am I really at risk for _____? Will taking Paxil really help me? How accurate is this diagnosis?"

Many scientific discoveries, such as Charles Darwin's theory of evolution, clashed with (and still does) some religious views of the world. Consider the church's reactions to the discovery that the earth was not the center of the universe. Only after 350 years did the Catholic Church agree that Galileo was correct in stating that the earth revolves around the sun. Objections to teaching evolutionary theory remain common (see *Reports* published by the National Center for Science Education). Others object that controlled testing violates ethical obligations. Chalmers (2003) draws our attention to Donald Campbell's (1969) statement years ago that "selectively designating some interventions as 'experiments'—a term loaded with negative associations—ignores the reality that policy makers and practitioners are experimenting on other people most of the time. The problem is that their experiments are usually poorly controlled. Dr. Spock's ill-founded advice to parents to let babies sleep on their stomachs would probably not be viewed by many people as a poorly controlled experiment, yet this is what it was" (p. 30). As a result, many babies died.

THE DIFFERENCE BETWEEN SCIENCE AND PSEUDOSCIENCE

The term "pseudoscience" refers to material that makes science-like claims but provides no evidence for them. Pseudoscience is characterized by a casual approach to evidence (weak evidence is accepted as readily as strong evidence). Pseudoscientists make use of the trappings of science without the substance.[32] The terms "science" and "scientific" are often used to increase the credibility of a view or approach, even though no evidence is provided to support it as illustrated in the figures in this chapter. The term *science* has been applied to many activities that in reality have nothing to do with science. Examples are "scientific charity" and "scientific philanthropy." Proselytizers of many sorts cast their advice as based on science. They use the ideology and "trappings" of science to pull the wool over our eyes in suggesting critical tests of claims that do not exist—cures that elude even the rich. The misuse of appeals to the grand narrative of science to sell products and encourage beliefs is a key form of propaganda, even in the professional literature as illustrated in chapter 9. Examples of pseudoscience in published journals include vague scientific-sounding jargon and precision of figures not warranted by data (e.g., "There is a correlation of 1.23"). Classification of clients into categories included in *The Diagnostic and Statistical Manual of Mental* Disorders lends a misleading aura of scientific credibility to this system in view of questionable reliability and validity of this technology (Boyle, 2002;

Houts, 2002; Kutchins & Kirk, 1997). Hallmarks of pseudoscience include the following (Bunge, 1984; Coker, 2001; Gray, 1991):

- Uses the trappings of science without the substance (such as scientific sounding language: "proven," "clinically tested").
- Relies on testimonials and anecdotal evidence.
- Is not skeptical; is not self-correcting.
- Equates an open mind with an uncritical one.
- Overuse of ad hoc hypothesis to avoid refutation; ignores or explains away falsifying data. Indifferent to facts.
- Absence of connection with scientific findings.
- Relies on vague, exaggerated, or untestable claims (vague language).
- Produces beliefs and faith but not knowledge.
- Is often not testable.
- Seeks confirming data rather than seeking to critically test assumptions.
- Often contradicts itself.
- Reverses burden of proof.
- Makes little progress.
- Creates mystery where none exists by omitting information; uses obscure language.
- Relies on the wisdom of the ancients, the older the idea, the better.
- Appeals to unfounded authority (or authority without evidence), emotion, sentiment.
- Personalizes issues.
- Argues from alleged exceptions, errors, anomalies, and strange events.

A critical attitude, which Karl Popper ([1963] 1972, 1963) defines as a willingness and commitment to open up favored views to severe scrutiny, is basic to science, distinguishing it from pseudoscience. Indicators of pseudoscience include irrefutable hypotheses and a continuing reluctance to revise beliefs even when confronted with relevant criticism. It makes excessive (untested) claims of contributions to knowledge. Results of a study may be referred to in many different sources until they achieve the status of a law without any additional data being gathered. Richard Gelles calls this the "Woozle Effect" (1982, p. 13). Pseudoscience is a billion-dollar industry. Products include self-help books, "subliminal" tapes, and call-in advice from "authentic psychics" who have no evidence that they accomplish what they promise (Beyerstein, 1990; Druckman & Bjork, 1991). Pseudoscience can be found in all fields.

SCIENTICISM

The term "scienticism" refers to the assumption that science should have authority over all other views of life—the tendency to "ape the methods in the natural sciences" (Hayek, 1980). "Scienticism dogmatically asserts the authority of scientific knowledge" (Popper, 1992, p. 6). It reflects a "dogmatic belief in the authority of the method of the natural sciences and its results" (1992, p. 41). Serge Lang (1998) critiqued favoring quantitative methods simply because they are quantitative and gives examples.[33]

Because of our tendency to be impressed with authority (e.g., of science and scientists) scientific material can easily fool us.

QUACKERY

Quack reasoning reflects pseudoscience. Examples of characteristics of quackery include the following:

- Promises quick, dramatic, miraculous cures of a wide variety of maladies ("Lose weight while you sleep"; grow hair in the process).
- Uses vague terms ("Purify the blood").
- Claims that physicians are trying to silence them, claims of being persecuted.
- Uses words such as "amazing," "revolutionary," "miracle drug."
- Relies on anecdotes and testimonials to support claims.
- Does not incorporate new ideas or evidence; relies on ideology and dogma.
- Objects to testing claims.
- Forwards methods and theories that are not consistent with empirical data.
- Relies on influences by a charismatic promoter.
- Claims that effects cannot be tested by the usual methods such as clinical trials.
- Appeals to secret cures discovered in remote locations not yet available here.
- Mixes bona fide and bogus evidence to support a favored conclusion (see e.g., Herbert, 1983; Jarvis, 1990).
- Appeal to questionable credentials.
- Attacks those who raise questions about claims.
- Uses scare tactics; Tries to convince you that you have some deficiency (e.g., vitamin).
- Appeals to alleged "evidence" that is not available.
- Appeals to unfounded authority.
- Appeals to freedom of choice.

Billions of dollars are spent by consumers on worthless products.[34]

Consider money spent on use of magnetic devices to treat pain (e.g., Winemiller, Robert, Edward, & Scott Harmsen, 2003).

> How much is spent in the USA every year on magnetic devices to treat pain? $500 million, with a total worldwide market to date above $4 billion. To put that into some sort of perspective, that $500 million is just half the annual sales that the pharmaceutical industry defines as a 'blockbuster.' And what do you think is the evidence for magnets affecting pain? You guessed it. None. There is a trial in a Cochrane review of interventions for plantar heel pain, and that was negative, and poor. A new, well-conducted, randomised trial provides a powerful negative, and a great example of trial design. (Magnetic insoles for foot pain. <http://www.jr2.ox.ac.uk/bandolier/band116/b116-5.html> Jan. 2003).

Fads are often advanced on the basis of quackery (Jacobson et al., 2005). Fraud takes advantage of pseudoscience and quackery. Fraud is so extensive in some areas that special organizations have been formed and newsletters are written to help consumers evaluate claims.[35] For every claim that has survived critical tests, there are thousands of bogus claims in advertisements, newscasts, films, TV, newspapers, and professional sources whose lures are difficult to resist. Rules for becoming a quack include the following (see Porter, 2000; Young, 1992):

1. Choose a disease that has a natural history of variability.
2. Wait until a period when the patient's condition is getting progressively worse.
3. Apply the treatment.
4. If the patient's condition improves or stabilizes, take credit for the improvement, then stop the treatment or decrease the dosage.
5. If the patient's condition worsens, report that the dosage must be increased, that the treatment was stopped too soon and must be restarted, or that the patient did not receive treatment long enough.
6. If the patient dies, report that the treatment was applied too late—a good quack takes credit for any improvement but blames deterioration in the patient's condition on something else.

DANGERS OF SCIENTIFIC ILLITERACY INCLUDING THE HISTORY OF SCIENCE

An accurate understanding of science can help us to distinguish between science and pseudoscience. Bogus uses, as seen in pseudoscience, quackery, and fraud may create and maintain views that decrease the quality of our lives. If we do not understand what science is and are not informed about the history of science, we will fall into the following errors:

1. Assume science can discover final answers and so accept inflated claims of knowledge that may result in avoidable harms.
2. Assume that there is no way to discover what may be true or false because scientists make errors and have biases and so make inflated claims about what is possible (or not) to discover.
3. Assume that those who question accepted views, for example, about mental illness, cause of cancer, or the HIV/AIDS connection, are crackpots when indeed they may raise well-argued concerns (e.g., see Bauer 2007; Boyle, 2002; Lang, 1998).

The history of science highlights that what was thought to be true, such as the cause of ulcers, was often found to be false. It also shows that new ideas are censored and that those proposing them have difficulty getting a hearing for their views in scientific journals and in the media. (See Lang, 1998.) Thus, there is science as open criticism, and science as ideology in which competing well-argued views are censored.[36] Appeals to consensus and traditional wisdom may block the acceptance of new methods for decades or centuries. Consider the neglect of Semmelweiss's discovery that puerperal fever could be eliminated "by having doctors wash their hands in a chlorine solution before examining the mother" (Broad & Wade, 1982, p. 137).

His work was ignored for years, resulting in thousands of unnecessary deaths. Prestigious journals often rejected the work of scientists who overturned prevailing beliefs (e.g., Nickerson, 2009). Conflicts of interest created by financial incentives and status concerns often prevent open critical inquiry as shown by the systematic efforts of the tobacco companies to undermine scientific findings (e.g., Oreskes & Conway, 2010). As the groups involved become larger and more powerful (as research cartels replace individual scientists working alone), such conflicts have become ever more pervasive (Lo & Field, 2009). An understanding of what science is and what it is not is one valuable anecdote to influence by propaganda. Promoters of pseudoscience depend on your ignorance of what science is and what it is not to reel you in.

ANTISCIENCE

Antiscience refers to rejection of scientific methods as valid. For example, some people believe that there is no such thing as "privileged knowledge"—that some is sounder than others. (See discussion of relativism that follows.) Typically, such views are not related to real-life problems such as building safe airplanes and to a candid appraisal of the results of different ways of solving a problem. That is, they are not problem focused, allowing a critical appraisal of competing views in relation to real world effects. Antiscience is common in academic settings (Gross & Levitt, 1994; Patai & Koertege, 2003), as well as in popular culture (e.g., Burnham, 1987). Many people confuse science, scienticism, and pseudoscience, resulting in an antiscience stance (see Glossary).

RELATIVISM

Relativists argue that all methods are equally valid in testing claims (e.g., anecdotal reports and experimental studies). Postmodernism is a current form of relativism. It is assumed "that knowledge and morality are inherently bounded by or rooted in culture" (Gellner, 1992, p. 68). "Knowledge or morality outside of culture is, it claims, a chimera." "Meanings are incommensurate, meanings are culturally constructed, and so all cultures are equal" (p. 73). Gellner (1982) argues that in the void created, some voices predominate, throwing us back on authority, not a criterion that will protect our rights and allow professionals to be faithful to their code of ethics. If there is no means by which to tell what is accurate and what is not, if all methods are equally effective, the vacuum is filled by an "elite" who are powerful enough to say what is and what is not (Gellner, 1992). He argues that the sole focus on cognitive meaning in postmodernism ignores political and economic influences and "denies or obscures tremendous differences in cognition and technical power" (pp. 71–72). Gellner emphasizes the real constraints in society that are obscured within this recent form of relativism (postmodernism) and suggests that such cognitive nihilism constitutes a "travesty of the real role of serious knowledge in our lives" (p. 95). He argues that this view undervalues coercive and economic constraints in society and overvalues conceptual ones. "If we live in a world of meanings, and meanings exhaust the world, where is there any room for coercion through the whip, gun, or hunger?" (p. 63).

Gellner (1992) suggests that postmodernism is an affectation: "Those who propound it or defend it against its critics, continue, whenever facing any serous issue in which their real interests are engaged, to act on the non-relativistic assumption that one particular vision is cognitively much more effective than others" (p. 70).[37] If all ways of knowing are of equal value, what is the purpose of professional education? Appeal to "practice wisdom" still requires some way to determine whether reliance on practice wisdom does more harm than good—some way to evaluate the effects on clients of relying on practice wisdom.

WHEN ACCURACY IS NOT OF CONCERN

Yet another possibility is that presenters do not care about truth or falsity. (See discussion of Palaver in chapter 4.) Frankfurt (2005) views "bullshit" as a kind of bluff. Thus the production of bullshit is stimulated whenever a person's obligations or opportunities to speak about some topic exceed his knowledge of the facts that are relevant to that topic" (p. 63). "For the essence of bullshit is not that it is *false* but that it is *phony*." "Although it is produced without concern with the truth, it need not be false. The bullshitter is faking things. But this does not mean that he necessarily gets them wrong" (pp. 47–48).

> Since bullshit need not be false, it differs from lies in its misrepresentational intent. The bullshitter may not deceive us, or even intend to do so, either about the facts or about what he takes the facts to be. What he does necessarily attempt to deceive us about is his enterprise. His only indispensably distinctive characteristic is that in a certain way he misrepresents what he is up to.
>
> This is the crux of the distinction between him and the liar. Both he and the liar represent themselves falsely as endeavoring to communicate the truth. The success of each depends upon deceiving us about that. But the fact about himself that the liar hides is that he is attempting to lead us away from a correct apprehension of reality; we are not to know that he wants us to believe something he supposes to be false. The fact about himself that the bullshitter hides, on the other hand, is that the truth-values of his statements are of no central interest to him; what we are not to understand is that his intention is neither to report the truth nor to conceal it.
>
> It is impossible for someone to lie unless he thinks he knows the truth. Producing bullshit requires no such conviction. (Frankfurt, 2005, pp. 54–55)
>
> . . .
>
> The contemporary proliferation of bullshit also has deeper sources, in various forms of skepticism which deny that we can have any reliable access to an objective reality, and which therefore reject the possibility of knowing how things truly are. These 'antirealist' doctrines undermine confidence in the value of disinterested efforts to determine what is true and what it false, and even in the intelligibility of the notion of objective inquiry. One response to this loss of confidence has been a retreat from the discipline required by dedication to the ideal of *correctness* to a quite different sort of discipline, which is imposed by pursuit of an alternative ideal of *sincerity*. Rather than seeking

primarily to arrive at accurate representations of a common world, the individual turns toward trying to provide honest representations of himself. Convinced that reality has no inherent nature, which he might hope to identify as the truth about things, he devotes himself to being true to his own nature. (pp. 64–65)

And, as Hilgartner (2000) points out "the poles of sincerity and cynicism are not the only possibilities."

Performers vary in the extent to which they are, as Goffman puts it, 'taken in by their own act.' In a reciprocal way, audiences express a range of responses to the possibility of being 'taken in'—sometimes tactfully suspending disbelief in the identity the performer projects and sometimes warily searching for signs that they are being intentionally or unintentionally misled. (Hilgartner, 2000, p. 14)

Accuracy is not a concern to those who want to cover up scientific findings that draw attention to harm of a product. For example, creating doubt about research related to smoking and health was a key public relations strategy used by the tobacco companies.[38] This illustrates how characteristics of science such as recognition of uncertainty, can be used in deceptive ways. Thus, there is criticism that contributes to an accurate appraisal of scientific findings and criticism designed to discourage such appraisal. Similarly, although it is true that "experts" in an area may be knowledgeable, their ties to corporations with vested interests may create troubling conflicts-of-interests if they serve on "expert panels." As always, it is wise to inquire about potential conflicts of interest (e.g., Who set up the panel? Who is funding it?) Keep in mind that public relations agencies are expert in mounting deceptive campaigns to forward the interests of those who hire them. They are masters of persuasion and often of deceit. That is what they get paid for.

SUMMARY

There are many views of knowledge—what it is and how to get it. Some, compared to others, are more likely to offer a sound guide as to what is false and what is true. Propagandists obscure differences between sound guides (critical inquiry) and bogus ones. Thus, thinking about knowledge and how to get it is integral to avoiding influence by propaganda ploys that contribute to ill-informed decisions. The history of the helping professions shows that professionals can harm as well as help, often because they have fallen for propaganda ploys. This also shows that discoveries are often stifled, sometimes for hundreds of years by dogmatic belief in a popular view. This illustrates that indeed the study of the history of ignorance (for example, deliberate efforts to encourage it) is as important to be familiar with as the history of knowledge. If professionals rely on questionable criteria for evaluating claims, false hope may be created, harmful effects experienced, and effective methods forgone. Some professionals rely on authority as a guide, for example, what high-status people say. Others rely on popularity (how many people use a method) or tradition (what is usually done). These criteria do not provide sound guides about the accuracy of claims. They all suffer from partiality in the use of evidence, seeing just part of the picture. Indeed they are classic propaganda appeals. Quackery and fraud take advantage of propaganda ploys.

Understanding science—what it is and what it is not—can help us to avoid deceptive use of the discourse of science (pseudoscience). It is valuable in spotting pseudoscience so integral to propaganda in the helping professions—use of the trappings of science without the substance. Lack of understanding of what science is is common, allowing propagandists to snare us by illusions of objectivity. Scientific sounding terms may lure us to accept bogus claims as in pseudoscience. We may be taken in by the alleged "objective" findings of an "expert panel" that, in reality, was created by a drug company to push its remedies and hide harms. Avoiding confirmation biases (searching only for data that confirm our views and ignoring data that do not) requires us to seek evidence against, as well as in support of, favored views. It requires considering well-argued alternative views. It requires looking at *all* the evidence. Sound criteria for evaluating knowledge claims include well-reasoned arguments and critical tests that systematically explore what option is more likely than another to result in valued outcomes.

GLOSSARY

Alchemy: "An occult art whose practitioners' main goals have been to turn base metals such as lead or copper into precious metals such as gold or silver (the transmutation motif); to create an elixir, potion, or metal that could cure all ills (the panacea motif); and to discover an elixir that would lead to immortality (the transcendence motif).... Alchemy is based on the belief that there are four basic elements—fire, air, earth, and water—and three essentials: salt, sulphur, and mercury" (<http://www.skepdic.com>).

Antiscience: Rejection of scientific methods as valid.

Critical discussion: "Essentially a comparison of the merits and demerits of two or more theories (usually more than two). The merits discussed are, mainly, the *explanatory power* of the theories . . . the way in which they are able to solve our problems of explaining things, the way in which the theories cohere with certain other heavily valued theories, their power to shed new light on old problems and to suggest new problems. The chief demerit is inconsistency, including inconsistency with the results of experiments that a competing theory can explain" (Popper, 1994, pp. 160–61).

Cynicism: A negative view of the world and what can be learned about it.

Eclecticism: The view that we should adopt whatever theories of methodologies are useful in inquiry, no matter what their source and without undue worry about their consistency.

Empiricism: The position that all knowledge (usually excluding that which is logical or mathematical) is in some way based on experience. Adherents of empiricism differ markedly over what the 'based on' amounts to—'starts from' and 'warranted in terms of' are, roughly, at the two ends of the spectrum of opinion (Phillips, 1987, p. 203).

Evidence: Ground for belief, testimony or facts tending to support or falsify a conclusion.

False knowledge: Beliefs that are not true and that are not questioned (Munz, 1985).

Falsification approach to knowledge: The view that we can discover only what is false, not what is true.

Hermeneutics: "The discipline of interpretation of textual or literary material, or of meaningful human actions" (Phillips, 1987, p. 203).

Justification approach to knowledge: The view that we can discover the truth by seeking support for our theories.

Knowledge: Problematic and tentative guesses about what may be true (Popper, 1992, 1994); "guess work disciplined by rational criticism" (1992, p. 40). Criticism is "the crucial quality of knowledge" (Munz, 1985, p. 49).

Logical positivism: The main tenet of logical positivism is the verifiability principle of meaning: "Something is meaningful only if it is verifiable empirically (i.e., directly, or indirectly, via sense experiences) or if it is a truth of logic or mathematics" (Phillips, 1987, p. 204). The reality of theoretical entities is denied.

Nonjustificationist epistemology: The view that knowledge is not certain. It is assumed that although some claims of knowledge may be warranted, no warrant is so firm that it is not open to question (see Karl Popper's writings).

Paradigm: A theoretical framework that influences the problems "that are regarded as crucial, the ways these problems are conceptualized, the appropriate methods of inquiry, the relevant standards of judgment, etc." (Phillips, 1987, p. 205).

Phenomenology: "The study, in depth, of how things appear in human experience" (Phillips, 1987, p. 205).

Postmodernism: Disputes assumptions of science and its products. All grounds for knowledge claims are considered equally questionable (see, for example, Rosenau, 1992; Munz, 1992).

Postpositivism: The approach to science that replaced logical positivism decades ago (see, for example, Phillips, 1987, 1992).

Pseudoscience: Material that makes science-like claims but provides no evidence for them.

Quackery: The promotion of products and procedures known to be false, or which are untested, for a profit (Pepper, 1984).

Rationality: An openness to criticism. "A limitless invitation to criticism is the essence of rationality" (Munz, 1985, p. 50). Rationality consists of making mistakes and eliminating error by natural selection (p. 16).

Relativism: Relativists "insist that judgments of truth are always relative to a particular framework or point of view" (Phillips, 1987, p. 206). This point of view prevents criticism from outside a closed circle of believers.

Science: A process designed to develop knowledge by critically discussing and testing theories.

Scientific objectivity: Scientific objectivity is solely the critical approach (Popper, 1994, p. 93). It is based on mutual rational criticism in which high standards of clarity and rational criticism are valued (Popper, 1994, p. 70). See also Critical discussion.

Scientism: A term used "to indicate slavish adherence to the methods of science even in a context where they are inappropriate" and "to indicate a false or mistaken claim to be scientific" (Phillips, 1987, p. 206). Scientism refers to the view that "authority should be conferred upon knowledge and the knower, upon science and the scientists, upon wisdom and the wise man, and upon learning and the learned" (Popper, 1992, p. 33).

Skepticism: A provisional approach to claims; the careful examination of all claims.

Theory: Myths, expectations, guesses, and conjectures about what may be true. A theory always remains hypothetical or conjectural. "It always remains guesswork. And there is no theory that is not beset with problems" (Popper, 1994, p. 157).

Theory ladenness (of perception): "The thesis that the process of perception is theory-laden in that the observer's background knowledge (including theories, factual information, hypotheses, and so forth) acts as a 'lens' helping to 'shape' the nature of what is observed" (Phillips, 1987, p. 206).

Truth: "An assertion is true if it corresponds to or agrees with, the facts" (Popper, 1994, p. 174). We can never be sure that our guesses are true. "Though we can never justify the claim to have reached truth, we can often give some very good reasons, or justifications, why one theory should be judged as nearer to it than another" (Popper, 1994, p. 161).

8

Appeal to Popular Grand Narratives and Metaphors

Propaganda in the helping professions takes advantage of and promotes myths, fears, and grand narratives that saturate a society such as the belief that deviant behaviors are caused by "mental illness" created by brain diseases and that unregulated capitalism is the best economic system. It appeals to grand narratives such as progress, health, happiness, and material prosperity that we take for granted as important, in part because they are so often repeated; since they are omnipresent, they seem natural and true (Ellul, 1965).[1] Popular narratives influence what we view as a problem, what outcomes are sought, and what methods are used to pursue them. What problems do we focus on? What problems do we ignore? Should related behaviors (or their lack) be controlled? If so, how and in what ways? There are spirited controversies about the prevalence of many problems, for instance, stranger abduction of children and the dangers of smoking marijuana.[2] Best (2001) suggests that a social problem claim consists of an argument with four parts: (a) that some condition exists; (b) that it is troubling and ought to be addressed; (c) that it has certain characteristics such as being common with known causes or serious consequences, or is a particular type of problem; and (d) that some action should be taken to deal with it (p. 8). Different views result in different beliefs about personal responsibility, change possible, and recommendations for intervention. They guide selection of public policies and related legislation and thus they have real-life consequences.[3] Consider these examples that reflect varied views about problems, causes, responsibility, and hoped-for outcomes:

- Demons are responsible for bad behavior. (See Figure 8.1.)
- We have a right to be happy.
- We can attain happiness by taking a pill (prescribed medication).
- Anxiety and depression are mental illnesses caused by chemical imbalances in the brain.
- The person who murdered Mayor Moscone of San Francisco and City Council Member Harvey Milk did so because he ate "too many Twinkies" and so was not responsible for his behavior.
- Children's misbehaviors are signs of mental disorder (e.g., Attention Deficit Hyperactivity Disorder-ADHD) caused by a brain disease.

Figure 8.1. (A) Demon causing women to gossip during Mass. (B) Demons keeping score on the babbling of women during Mass.
SOURCE: From Geoffroy de Latour Landry's Ritter vom Turn, printed by Michael Furter, Basle, 1493.

Figure 8.2. Appeals to science. Advertisement for a potion.
SOURCE: An advertisement for Kennedy's Medical Discovery circa 1890. Collection of Business Americana, Smithsonian Institution.

- Science and technology can solve our problems. (See Figure 8.2.)
- We can expect progress; knowledge in the helping professions will advance.
- We have an inner true self.
- Problems can be solved by increasing self-esteem.
- It is good to be free of anxiety and sadness.

We see the same strategies used to promote grand narratives in the helping professions, as we see in the promotion of products such as soap or beer; the ancient ploys of glittering generalizations, begging the question (asserting what should be argued), and fear mongering. (See chapter 7.) Our longings to avoid the feared and gain the revered contribute to their effectiveness. Propagandists obscure differences among three kinds of statements: (1) factual (did a father assault his child?), (2) conceptual (why did he do it?), and (3) evaluative (was it right or wrong?) creating confusion between what is and what should be. They disguise value judgments as scientific findings, forward bogus claims, and attack critics. Both the media and popular culture play a key role in shaping views of problems and remedies, for example, by the plethora of negative, problem-oriented content; crime is transformed into a major form of entertainment in endless detective stories (Altheide, 2002). The fast pace of news items confine individual experiences to quick sound bytes: "Deranged homeless man kills tourist." In our technological society, appeal to popular narratives, including fear, is ever more present by virtue of the increasing array of devices through which messages are distributed.[4] The promotion of fear in the mass media, in popular culture, and in the helping professions, has been so great that in addition to fears of particular objects, people, or events, there is also an amorphous negative emotion most accurately referred to as anxiety. No wonder so much Prozac is sold. Indeed, Altheide (2002) suggests that fear, and I would argue anxiety, is the common factor that connects us.[5]

Awareness of "grand narratives" that influence life-affecting decisions and related propaganda can help us to detect questionable claims about what is a problem, how common it is, what causes it, and how (or if) it can (or should) be prevented or minimized. It can help us to avoid being bamboozled by related propaganda ploys. Certain behaviors and views of problems are forwarded by "claims makers" who try to influence others to accept their views. Language is a potent weapon in such influence attempts. Consider the widespread use of medical language: healthy/unhealthy, wellness/sickness, health/disease. Problem "crusaders" exaggerate the prevalence of problems of concern to them and "problem deniers" do the opposite using, via a variety of propaganda methods such as use of bogus statistics. The words we use influence how we think about problems and behaviors.

Lakoff and Johnson (1980) have described how metaphors affect our beliefs and behaviors. (See also Nerlich, Elliott, & Larson, 2009.) The metaphor of war, as in the "war against drugs," makes it easier to use violent means against "them"—those who use drugs (e.g., arresting people, seizing property). Moral, social, economic, and political factors related to use of drugs are obscured. Prevalence estimates are exaggerated, gripping stories described, and the problem personalized—it will (or does) affect you. Related complexities are oversimplified as reflected in slogans such as "It's in the genes." The image must be kept simple to direct us to simple solutions such as taking a pill. A key way to keep it simple is to focus on individuals (Jane has a "mental illness") rather than on the complex social structures and their interactions that may affect Jane as suggested by Ellul (1965) in his description of the psychological effects of living in a technological society. The discourse of science is used to offer credibility.

Neither professionals nor clients may be aware of how their beliefs are shaped by related slogans and images repeated by many players in many venues. The promoters of claims may be taken in by their own propaganda. Slick marketing guided by the latest psychological research cuts through otherwise skeptical reactions. We may not know that public relations firms were hired by pharmaceutical companies to convert common behaviors and feelings into "mental illnesses" to forward prescribed medication as a remedy.[6] Professionals taken in by propaganda inflict their views on unsuspecting others. As always we must have our antennae up for "what's missing." As always, partiality in the use of information is key in propaganda. A key aim of this chapter is to offer an overview of grand narratives so you will know what may be missing in a given description. Past, as well as current, examples are given to highlight the importance of a historical perspective in understanding current practices and policies and related pitches.

Grand narratives influence what we expect and what we feel entitled to. In current times we are urged to stay healthy, look young, be popular, be happy, find your "true self." "Be you." Learning to recognize them and to understand their uses and abuses and related propaganda ploys will help you to select options you value and to avoid those that are irrelevant, misleading, or harmful. Related pitches rarely acknowledge possible downsides to pursuit of these outcomes such as creating a nation of "Charlie Chuckles"—happy-go-lucky, superficial, uncaring people (Percy, 1991); people so anxious and worried about "staying healthy," that they do not enjoy life (Hadler, 2004), and people so indoctrinated into the therapeutic culture that they lack spontaneity (Illouz, 2008). They do not mention what may be lost by the "tyranny of happiness' (Elliot & Chambers, 2004) or endless efforts to fill "the empty self" (Cushman, 1995).

Certain disciplines and professions favor certain grand narratives. (See Table 8.1) Each profession and discipline claims a special domain of knowledge that overlaps with (or contradicts) the domains of other disciplines and professions to different degrees. The search for explanations reflects a shifting balance between a focus on individual characteristics (e.g., biological or psychological) and environmental causes (e.g., political, social, and economic influences). Theories differ in what they include in "environment," ranging from political, social, and economic influences to a narrow focus on family relationships. Related assumptions are based on different

Table 8.1 PROPOSED CAUSES FOR PROBLEMS

Moral: They are due to moral deficiencies of individuals.

Psychiatric/medical: It is assumed that problems result from a disease (mental illness) that has a biochemical and/or constitutional base.

Psychological: Problems result from individual characteristics, such as differences in personality. Examples include psychodynamic, developmental, and cognitive models.

Social interactional: Problems result from the interaction between personal characteristics and social experiences.

Sociological/cultural/critical theory: Problems are related to social/cultural characteristics (e.g., disorganization, contingency patterns, socioeconomic status, discrimination). Problem categories are created and remedies proposed in accord with political, social, and economic interests.

Ecological/contextual: Both personal and environmental factors are considered.

Philosophical/moral (humanistic, hermeneutic linguistic, phenomenological/existential, and moral/legal). An example of a moral/legal argument is that mental illness is rare and that many behaviors (e.g., assault) labeled as indicators of mental illness, should be criminalized or considered to be one's own business and decriminalized and demedicalized.

beliefs about human nature, why we behave in certain ways, how we change, if we can change.[7] Professionals address client concerns in ways that reflect their assumptions about problems, causes, and remedies. Consider varying views of depression:

- A result of low social ranking (Sloman & Gilbert, 2000)
- Due to negative thoughts (Beck, 1976)
- Due to a decrease in pleasant events
- Caused by brain differences such as low serotonin
- A result of persistent discrimination (Mirowsky & Ross, 2003)
- A result of lack of community and public spaces for dialogue
- Due to an interaction among all of the above.

Currently, psychology, clinical social work, and psychiatry are united in promoting a culture of therapy (see later discussion).

Since we live in and have been raised in a particular society in which certain myths and narratives are forwarded, it will be a challenge to see them as ideas that are in question, especially when they are not questioned within a group to which we belong, such as the National Association for Social Workers or the American Psychiatric Association. Many grand narratives are "big ideas" in the sense that it takes effort to understand them. The more complex and controversial the idea, the more distorted views may be presented and believed because people do not take the time to understand them before they describe and critique them. Consider, for example, distorted views of evidence-based practice (Gibbs & Gambrill, 2002) and radical behaviorism (Thyer, 2005). Here, everyone loses, except the person who publishes the distorted material who can chalk up another publication, especially if no one blows the whistle on the distorted version.

DIFFERENT VIEWS HAVE DIFFERENT CONSEQUENCES

There are great stakes in how problems are framed, and organizations and individuals with vested interests devote considerable time, money, and effort to influence what others believe as illustrated by the billions spent on advertisements and public relations. Is anxiety in social situations a "mental illness"? Is it a learned reaction that provides valuable clues about stresses in life shared by many people but transformed into a "medical" problem (medicalized) by a public relations firm hired by a pharmaceutical company (Moynihan & Cassels, 2005)?[8] Are parents who mistreat their children bad people who should be imprisoned or overburdened people who should be helped? Are they themselves victims of the inequitable distribution of employment, housing, and education opportunities? Are the hundreds of thousands of African American men in our jails in the United States dangerous "others" who violated our laws or are they themselves victims of discriminatory policies that create few options for gainful employment viewed as acceptable? Who is hurt by certain views? Who gains? Is gambling a learned behavior maintained by a complex reinforcement schedule? Is it a "moral failing"? Is "pathological gambling" (Code 312.31) a mental disorder as presented in the DSM (the classification system created by the American Psychiatric Association (2002)? Is this a disease? Is there a (1) known etiology, (2) predictable course, and (3) a worsening without treatment?[9]

Different beliefs about problems and their causes have different consequences in how people view themselves, for example, as responsible or not, and how they are treated. The state gives psychiatrists power to label people as "mentally ill" and to place them against their will into institutional settings and force them to take prescribed medication "for their own good" (Szasz, 1994; Morrissey & Monahan, 1999). Outpatient commitment is increasingly popular. Costs of a particular view may not be apparent until many years later as illustrated by follow-up studies of antisocial children (Scott, Knap, Henderson, & Maughan, 2001) as well as exposure of harmful treatments in the guise of helping (see chapter 5). Szasz (1987, 1994) argues that many people who injure others and are labeled mentally ill have committed criminal offenses and should be treated accordingly. Others believe that many criminals are mentally ill and should be excused for their crimes and receive psychiatric care. Defining behaviors as indicators of "mental illness" results in quite different consequences than defining them as criminal. Throughout history, poverty has been variously viewed as a crime, a personal limitation, or a reflection of discrimination and oppression (social injustice).

Views about problems and their causes affect who receives aid, as well as what is offered and the spirit in which it is offered (Handler & Hasenfeld, 2007). New claims about new problems may result in new responsibilities and new rights. Insurance programs pay for new services now viewed as a "right," such as sex therapy. Loeske (1999) argues that social problems reflect and perpetuate inequality and cultural worries and create public policy problems dilemmas such as competing claims for resources and validation; she argues that they reflect and perpetuate a "culture of mistrust and fear." A focus on some problems results in ignoring others. She quotes Joel Best: "A society which is mobilized to keep child molesters, kidnapper Satanists away from innocent children is not necessarily prepared to protect children from ignorance, poverty, and ill health (Best, 1990:188)" (Loeske, 1999, p. 187).

THE HOOK: FEAR, SUFFERING, AND THE PROMISE OF RELIEF

Throughout history claims of knowledge have met hopes for relief from fear and suffering.[10] (See Figure 8.3.) Consider this sent to a professor of medicine by Francis Petrach in 1370: "Doctors promote themselves shamelessly, making exorbitant claims about their competence. Yet when faced with an emergency like plague, they can only inveigle the trustful out of their money and watch them die" (see Trone, 1997; Petrarca, 2003). Hoped-for cures and redress from suffering meet seductive claims couched in popular narratives by those who profit, often at others' expense. What has changed over time is how suffering is viewed, the source of fear appealed to (e.g., purgatory or mental illness), and what is offered as a remedy. What are legitimate causes? How should suffering be expressed? What remedies are best? What intensities warrant help? Since the beginning of time myths have been created and rituals used to relieve suffering. The shaman and medicine man have been abandoned by many in favor of the technologically sophisticated hospital, even when cure is not possible—even when a medicalized approach may push aside valuable forms of healing and relief such as spiritual growth (Illich, 1976).

Just as the meaning of "healing" has changed over time, so too has the meaning of suffering. In earlier times, some kinds of suffering were viewed as positive. Christianity

Figure 8.3. A doctor wearing a bird beaked mask stuffed with a herbal preventative substance to protect against plague.
SOURCE: P. Fürst (1656). Plague Doctor in Rome, Medicinsk-Historisk Museum, Copenhagen.

promised relief in the afterlife from the afflictions of this life, whether physical pain or psychological distress such as melancholy. The history of healing is the history of our search for remedies to avoid or relieve suffering or provide rationalizations for it, for example, as a route to bliss in the afterlife. Our sufferings are shaped by our social milieus. Ellul (1965) suggests that "Propaganda's artificial and unreal answers for modern man's psychological suffering . . . allow him to continue living abnormally under the conditions in which society places him [e.g., dissociated from the end products of his work]. Propaganda suppresses the warning signals that his anxieties, maladjustments, rebellions, and demands once supplied" (p. 175). But in our highly propagandized environment these signals are muted or misdirected as to their causes, creating emotional confusion. Illich (1976) argues that the medicalization of our lives has removed suffering from being a natural part of life to be confronted with courage and support of loved ones and used as an opportunity for growth.

Exaggerated claims of healing (cure) and prevention are a key form of propaganda in the helping professions. Advertisements and content in professional sources forward diagnoses and remedies to sooth the anxious (the nervous), brighten the depressed (the melancholic), and energize the bored (those suffering from anomie). Propagandists take advantage of the usual arsenal of propaganda ploys to delude us, including censorship of lack of evidence for views promoted, use of scientific sounding terms ("panels of experts," "clinically proven"), and bold assertions ("well-established"). A new chemotherapy for cancer may be promoted as more effective than any other. Hidden may be the fact that "effective" means living an average of two months more and feeling sick during one's last days because of the side effects of the drug.

THE IMPORTANCE OF A HISTORICAL PERSPECTIVE

A historical perspective is vital for minimizing influence by propaganda in the helping professions about social and personal problems and their claimed causes and proposed remedies. This shows the changing nature of beliefs about causes, the incorrectness of most of these beliefs, and the role of economic, political, and social interests in shaping grand narratives and views of behavior that often nudge out scientific findings in bold assertions (often inaccurate) about what is a problem and what is not, what kind it is, and how prevalent it is.[11] (See Figure 8.4.) It shows the continuity of interest in discipline and containing the deviant (the marginal), including strangers (immigrants) and strange groups and those who attempt to break out of prescribed roles. (See Table 8.2.) It also shows what may befall us if we are labeled by a professional as marginal (mentally ill, a criminal, a welfare recipient), including being used as uninformed research subjects and a life-path of limited opportunities (e.g., See Harriet, 2006; Wacquant, 2009). History shows the appeal to fear to achieve political and economic goals such as creating fear of immigrants and "the underclass" (e.g., Morone, 1997). Despots, benevolent and malevolent throughout history, have found fear of great service in controlling the populace. That is, they create fear, for example, of burning in the afterlife, to influence behavior in the quick life. Because we grow up in a society in which variations in behaviors are responded to in certain ways, we may assume that this is the way things have always been and should be. But history shows wide variations in the response to different behaviors. Such variations can also be seen today in different countries. Ignorance regarding the history of the helping professions and its relationships to the state (e.g., legal rights to remove our freedom) makes us easy prey for propagandists; we can more easily be mislead by bogus claims about what is "normal" and what is not; what are causes and what are not; what is for our own good and what is not.

"What is sickness in one society might be chromosomal abnormality, crime, holiness, or sin in another. Each culture creates its response to disease" (Illich, 1976, pp. 117–18). Experiences such as melancholy differ in different cultures (e.g., Galik, 1996). Mania, vague discontents, melancholy, and anxiety have been discussed both in literature and in professional venues from early times. Names for related complaints, as well as explanations, change over time. History reveals a complex interplay of gender, race, class, politics, religion, economics, and an interest in the preservation and growth of professional status, and the use of various kinds of propaganda to promote favored views. "Dixen (2004) describes how the illness of vapors once considered epidemic among the privileged, was related to melancholia (also called hypochondria) and hysteria."[12] Swinging was viewed as a remedy. Mechanistic accounts offered a different view. Here, the body was viewed as a complicated hydraulic system.

Physicians once believed that every human being has a limited supply of nerve energy and so one could become exhausted resulting in neurasthenia. At the beginning

Figure 8.4. Nostrums and children.
This late nineteenth-century poster dates back to the period when children, to be considered healthy, had to be fat. (From the Warshaw Collection of Business Americana, Archives Center, National Museum of American History, Smithsonian Institution.)
SOURCE: J. H. Young (1992). *American health quackery* (p. 143). Princeton, NJ: Princeton University Press.

of the twentieth century, in both popular sources such as magazines and advertisements, and in the professional literature, the "nerves" were singled out for blame for the stresses, strains, and discontents of life. Focus on the "nerves" is reflected in the past popularity of the tonic, Dr. Miles "Nervine." (See Figure 8.5.) Terms such as "nervous tension" were popular. Herzberg (2009) refers to this as the "nervous illness tradition" (p. 156). This tradition has a long history, now viewed as remedied by prescribed medication for anxiety, depression, and mood swings.[13] Feelings of being "out-of-sorts," the "blahs," feeling "nervous" and stressed, were given medical sounding

Table 8.2 CLASS, GENDER, ETHNICITY, AND RACE AS ARBITERS OF ONE'S FATE

"Reflecting racial attitudes found throughout nineteenth-century American society, practitioners of asylum medicine repeatedly claimed that political freedom caused insanity in primitive peoples. Many asylum doctors, who associated civilization with higher intellect, argued that savages could not become free citizens of a democratic society without becoming deranged. It followed, then, that society should guard against unleashing these irrational forces—in the case of African Americans by the institution of slavery, and for Native Americans, by confinement to reservations" (Gamwell & Tomes, 1995).

"Samuel A. Cartwright, a professor of medicine specializing in 'diseases of the Negro' at the University of Louisiana (now Tulane University), argued that slavery was justified on both anatomical and biblical authority. In 1851 the Medical Association of Louisiana commissioned Cartwright to prepare a report on African Americans, in which he stressed what he termed 'the great primary truth, that the Negro is a slave by nature, and can never be happy, industrious, moral or religious, in any other condition than the one he was intended to fill.' Cartwright claimed that 'several forms of mental illness were peculiar to blacks, including an obsessive desire for freedom—a 'flight-from-home-madness'—for which Cartwright invented the term—'drapetomania', from the Latin drapeta, meaning fugitive ('Report on the Diseases and Physical Peculiarities of the Negro,' *The New Orleans Medical and Surgical Journal*, 1851, vol. 7, pp. 707–708)" (Gamwell & Tomes, 1995, pp. 101–3).

"Uncontrolled passion as a cause of insanity had a supposedly higher incidence in female patients. Its diagnosis mirrored prevailing gender roles in several ways. Victorian women were often portrayed as the passive objects of aggressive male sexual desire; many medical authorities described excessive passion in a woman as both physiologically and psychologically dangerous. An illustration in mid-nineteenth-century medical text labels a woman's reproductive organs as her 'region of insanity' (Joseph R. Buchanan, *Outlines of Lectures on the Neurological System of Anthropology*, Cincinnati, 1854, fig. 2.76)" (Gamwell & Tomes, 1995, pp. 105–9).

"With rare exceptions, both northern and southern asylum doctors regarded racial segregation as a mark of superior management. According to Thomas Kirkbride, superintendent of the Pennsylvania Hospital for the Insane, 'The idea of mixing up all color and classes, as seen in one or two institutions in the United States, is not what is wanted in our hospitals for the insane' (AJI, 1855, vol. 12, p. 43)." (Gamwell & Tomes, 1995, p. 56).

"Protestant asylum physicians and staff found the practice of moral treatment to be complicated by their religious and cultural differences from the Irish, whom they often characterized as particularly depraved and offensive. Echoing their sentiments about black patients, some asylum superintendents felt that the Irish should be cared for in separate wards to avoid distressing the 'better class' of patients. Merrick Bemis, superintendent of the Massachusetts State Lunatic Hospital at Worcester, wrote of the Irish in the hospitals" annual report for 1858: "Opposite in religion and all the notions of social life, it would not be well to class the two races in the same wards, where each must bear from the other what was considered troublesome and offensive while in health" (p. 57). (Gamwell & Tomes, 1995, p. 59).

Why DON'T YOU TRY DR. MILES NERVINE

MRS. Sears, who has a music store in Cottonwood, Arizona, has found Dr. Miles Nervine so effective that she recommends it whenever she has the opportunity. Recently her friend Mrs. H. A. Arnold was in a very nervous condition — couldn't sleep — couldn't sit still — felt utterly miserable. She took all kinds of treatments but nothing seemed to help her.

"Dr. Miles Nervine was recommended to me by Mrs. Sears of Cottonwood last week. I called at her store and complained of being very nervous. I had been advised by specialists that rest and relaxation was the proper treatment for me so I tried it for three months without results. Mrs. Sears said that Nervine had worked wonders for her at several times during her life when she had gone all to pieces nervously. I decided to try it. I took a dose before dinner Friday and one on retiring and then on Saturday morning another dose. It made me feel so much better that I went to see Mrs. Sears and thanked her for recommending it to me. You can't imagine what it did for me. It made me sleep like a brick, and I feel like a different person. Thanks to your Nervine and Mrs. Sears' faith in it."

When you are Nervous, Restless, Wakeful, when you have Nervous Headache or Nervous Indigestion, why don't you try the same medicine that Mrs. Sears and Mrs. Arnold and thousands of others find so effective.

DR. MILES NERVINE
(Liquid or Effervescent Tablets)

Dr. Miles Nervine is not habit forming; does not depress the heart; acts to *permit* rather than to *induce* sleep.

Dr. Miles Nervine is sold under a positive guarantee, satisfaction or your money back.

Liquid Nervine — Large Package $1.00, Small Package 25¢.

Effervescent Nervine Tablets — Large Package 25 tablets $1.00— after January 1, 1938 75¢. Small Package, 4 tablets 25¢ — after January 1, 1938, 8 tablets 35¢.

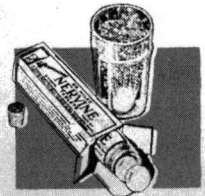

DR. MILES NERVINE
LIQUID OR EFFERVESCENT TABLETS

Figure 8.5. Ad for Nervine.
SOURCE: *Dr. Miles New Weather Almanac and Handbook of Valuable Information* (1938), p. 32. Published by Miles Laboratories, Inc. Elkhart, Indiana.

names such as depression and anxiety. Anxiety was key in Freud's theory of the unconscious and remains a key focus of psychotherapy today.[14]

The more lacking your knowledge about environmental influences on behavior and the less you have read of literature describing the effects of historical events on individuals, such as economic depressions and wars throughout the ages, the more easily you will buy into a view of the cause of troubles as inside yourself. Situational influences on drug addiction are highlighted by the rat park experiment that compared addictive behavior of rats placed in small cages with rats in a large "park like" environment (Alexander, Beyerstein, Hadaway, & Coambs, 1981). Rats in the latter, even those addicted, preferred water to heroin. Those in small cages preferred heroin. Poor education, starting in elementary school, create students, who, even if they graduate, may not be able to critically appraise claims, including their sources and strategies used to forward them.

An Interest in the Social Control of Deviance

From a purely descriptive point of view, deviance refers to the variability of signs, symptoms, or behavior (their range, form, variety, and timing). Deviance becomes defined as actions or conditions regarded as inappropriate to or in violation of powerful groups or conventions. Both the penal system and the social welfare system reflect a concern with "behavioral control of marginalized populations" (Wacquant, 2009). As Szasz (1961) notes, societies have always had to deal with troubled, troubling, and very dependent behavior. Illich (1976) argues that "any society to be stable, needs certified deviance."

> People who look strange or who behave oddly are subversive until their common traits have been formally named and their startling behavior slotted into a recognized pigeonhole. By being assigned a name and a role, eerie, upsetting freaks are tamed, becoming predictable exceptions who can be pampered, avoided, repressed, or expelled. In most societies there are some people who assign roles to the uncommon ones; according to the prevalent social prescription, they are usually those who hold special knowledge about the nature of deviance. (Illich, 1976, p. 117)

Pfohl (1994) argues that deviants exist only in opposition to those whom they threaten and who have sufficient power to contain such threats. Winners of the battle of deviance and social control organize social life according to their preferences. "Losers are trapped within the vision of others. They are labeled deviant and subjected to an array of current social control practices" (pp. 3–4).

> The story of deviance and social control is a battle story. It is a story of the battle to control the ways people think, feel, and behave. It is a story of winners and losers and of the strategies people use in struggles with one another. Winners in the battle to control 'deviant acts' are crowned with a halo of goodness, acceptability, normality. Losers are viewed as living outside the boundaries of social life as it ought to be, outside the 'common sense' of society itself. They may be seen by others as evil, sleazy, dirty, dangerous, sick, immoral, crazy, or just plain

deviant. They may even come to see themselves in such negative imagery, to see themselves as *deviants*.

...

Depending upon the controlling wisdom at a particular moment in history, deviants may be executed, brutally beaten, fined, shamed, incarcerated, drugged, hospitalized, or even treated to heavy doses of tender loving care. But first and foremost they are prohibited from passing as normal women or men. They are branded with the image of being deviant. (Pfohl, 1994, pp. 3–4)

Sociologists emphasize the reframing of political concerns, such as equality of rights or freedom from unwanted control, into personal ones over which the state has power. Those who have more power are usually more successful in creating and imposing views about deviance and related rules and sanctions on those who are less powerful. The biomedical industry promotes diseases and risks requiring surveillance and treatment, especially of the poor and lower middle class and people of color. Crime is framed as due to individual criminals, ignoring structural causes such as impoverished opportunities in poor neighborhoods. Creative options are used for exerting control such as declaring that the poor, unwanted or dishonorable are "mentally ill" and require or need "treatment." Many scholars argue that professionals are involved not so much in problem-solving as in problem-setting (e.g., Schon, 1990). Labeling behaviors as "healthy" or "unhealthy" depoliticizes issues.

> By locating the source and the treatment of problems in an individual, other levels of intervention are effectively closed. By the very acceptance of specific behavior as an "illness" and the definition of illness as an undesirable state, the issue becomes not whether to deal with a particular problem, but *how* and *when*. Thus the debate over homosexuality, drugs, or abortion becomes focused on the degree of sickness attached to the phenomena in question or the extent of the health risk involved. And the more principled, more perplexing, or even moral issue, of *what* freedom should an individual have over his or her own body is shunted aside. (Zola, p. 477) (Reprinted in Conrad, 2009)

The aggressive demands of women for voting rights were put down to excessive masculinity. According to physician Herbert J. Claiborne: "Now while I do not mean to state that all suffragettes are inverts [homosexuals] . . . I believe that exaggerated masculine traits in their structural and psychic being is the original cause" ("Hypertrichosis in Women," *New York Medical Journal*, 1914, vol. 99, p. 1183).

According to British physician John Russell Reynolds, men with symptoms of hysteria, the disease of the passive sex, must be "either mentally or morally of feminine constitution" ("Hysteria," *A System of Medicine*, ed. J. Russell Reynolds, London, 1866–79, vol. 2, p. 207) (Gamwell & Tomes, 1995, p. 162).

What is a political issue (such as rights of gay/lesbian/transgender people) is transformed into a "social problem." "Framing concerns as an illness or deficiency enables creation of a technology (knowledge and skill) that can be acquired by professionals licensed to handle this problem" (Gusfield, 2003). This framing serves two goals: (1) containing the deviant, and (2) creating jobs for professionals. However, some groups successfully resist an illness framing view.

> The gay rights movement is perhaps the most salient example of how the ability to mobilize has enabled a subject group to transform its status. During this century, homosexuals have been thought of as sinful and as sick, objects of condemnation or of medical benevolence. What the gay rights movement did was to resist the public designation of deviance, of abnormality, by attacking the presumed norms and denying that homosexuality constituted a social problem. In the process the phenomena of homosexuality lost its status as a 'social problem' and became a matter of political and cultural conflict over the recognition of alternative sexual styles. What had been an uncontested meaning has been transformed into a political contest. (Gusfield, 2003, p. 15)

Changing Views

Approaches to disliked behaviors, discontents, and suffering change with changing times as shown by the history of psychiatry and psychology. In medieval times demons were considered to be responsible for (mis)behavior (sins) including gossiping during Mass. (See Figure 8.1.) Demons carrying condemned souls to purgatory are illustrated in the fourteenth-century woodcut in Figure 8.6. People viewed as "mad" were believed to be possessed by the devil. Behaviors once viewed

Figure 8.6. Condemned souls of sinners are carried by Demons to their place of punishment. After a miniature in a Milanese manuscript, fourteenth century.
SOURCE: Milan, 14th Century. Drawing based on a miniature in a manuscript.

as sins were later considered crimes and are now viewed as "mental illnesses" (Szasz, 1961, 1994).

> Many in the general public, however, continued to believe that madness was symptomatic of possession by the devil. Most Christians, especially evangelical Protestants, took biblical accounts of Christ casting out demons as literal statements of fact. Also popular were fictional accounts of demoniac possession, such as Washington Irving's 1824 tale of the miser who sold his soul to the devil, "The Devil and Tom Walker". Thus when citizens became deranged and were admitted to an asylum, it is not surprising that some believed they were possessed by a devil or were being punished for their sins. (Gamwell & Tomes, 1995, p. 50)

The view of "heretical actions" as sinful is alive and well today as illustrated by Bishop Michael J. Sheridan of Colorado Springs "who said in a pastoral letter that Catholics who vote for candidates who support gay marriage, euthanasia or abortion rights must confess their sin before receiving communion" (Woodward, 2004, p. A21).

Problems have careers. We could plot the changing ways a given behavior or complaint has been viewed over time, and to what effect. Consider masturbation, previously named onanism (Szasz, 1970).[15] At one time it was thought to be responsible for a vast array of problems including mental retardation (Szasz, 1970).

> Benjamin Rush's dire pronouncement on the topic, published in 1812, was typical of views held by American asylum physicians throughout the century: "When indulged in an undue or a promiscuous intercourse with the female sex, or in onanism, [the sexual appetite] produces seminal weakness, impotence, dysury [difficulty in urination], tabes dorsalis [uncoordinated movement], pulmonary consumption, dyspepsia, dimness of sight, vertigo, epilepsy, hypochondriasis, loss of memory, manalgia [dementia], fatuity, and death" (Medical Inquiries and Observations upon the Diseases of the Mind, Philadelphia, 1812, p. 347). (Gamwell & Tomes, 1995, p. 111)

Now, masturbation is viewed as "normal," even "healthy," but not by all people as illustrated by the firing of Joycelyn Elders, past U.S. Surgeon General, for suggesting that masturbation was a good substitute for unprotected sex among teens.

In the past, housewives who wanted to work were often regarded as pathological (Oakley, 1976).

> In 1873 physician Edward Clarke published an influential book entitled Sex and Education in which he blamed the overeducation of adolescent girls for women's physical and nervous debility, including insanity. Clarke cautioned that the mental weaknesses of educated women would be compounded in what few children their puny reproductive systems could produce.... the idea that overtaxing the female brain resulted in both insanity and degeneration of the human species remained very common in medical circles at the turn of the century. (Gamwell & Tomes, 1995, p. 126)

Co-education was thought to be one of the situations responsible for neurasthenia (stress caused by an effort to compete with men). In the early twentieth century, middle-class women in the United States were first blamed for wanting to explore life outside of the home and then blamed for not being able to both have a family and work outside as in depictions of the "super-mom."[16] Homosexuals were considered mentally ill until political activism forced removal of this from the psychiatric classification system in 1974.[17] Still, thousands of psychiatrists in 1974 voted to keep homosexuality as a mental illness. Advances in knowledge change how people view a problem. It had been assumed that tuberculosis was inherited because people who lived together tended to "get it." When the bacillus responsible for tuberculosis was isolated, people were no longer blamed for developing it. Ulcers originally believed to be due to psychological stress were found to be caused by bacteria (Marshall & Warren, 1983).[18]

THE GRAND NARRATIVES OF CAPITALISM AND CONSUMERISM

The grand narrative of consumerism has been spectacularly successful, propelled by corporate monopolization of key channels of communication (e.g., newspapers and TV) and sophisticated promotional pitches and ingenious and pervasive use of technologies. In the grand narrative of capitalism it is assumed that competition maximizes free choice—free choice to consume. America is often criticized for creating an atomized society in which individualism and consumerism run rampant. Consumerism equates personal happiness with consumption and the purchase of material possessions. Now, we can purchase happiness with a pill. Cushman (1995) views psychotherapy as perfect for our consumer culture; we can fill up empty selves by products, whether soap or psychotherapy.[19]

> A great variety of social and institutional actors compete with one another to define self-realization, health, or pathology, thus making emotional health a new commodity produced, circulated, and recycled in social and economic sites that take the form of a field. The constitution of this "emotional field" explains the emergence of new forms of capital and new schemas to understand the self in terms of disease, health, suffering and self-realization. (Illouz, 2008, p. 171)

Illouz (2007) suggests that there is a synergistic connection between the rise of the self-help culture and the spread of claims of suffering—the enshrinement of disease, suffering, and pain as public goods. This contributes to healthism, as well as consumerism—"individual salvation through the consuming of commodities and the liberation of the enchanted interior"—the self (Cushman, 1995, p. 274).

Consumerism fuels the success of direct to consumer advertising of drugs and healthism. It focuses attention on the individual and the purchase of commodities in the satisfaction of desires and pursuit of status. What we own affects our "social ranking," which influences how others respond to us and our feelings and behavior as Gilbert (1989) describes in his discussion of depression and anxiety. It offers a path to identity and to a "good life." It lends meaning in a society stripped of traditional sources of meaning. You are what you own. Achieving a more perfect body, emotional tranquility, and health are emphasized in advertisements. The seemingly endless choice of products, often with little real differences among competing ones, creates a need for guidance by experts and advertisers (Marchand, 1987) and distracts us from other pursuits, such as the creation and use of public spaces for political dialogue (Arendt, 1958). Many people now shape their identity (now often a lifestyle) via the prescribed drugs they consume—mood brighteners.[20] Both Cushman (1995) and Illouz (2008) describe the symbiotic ties between therapy and corporate culture in manipulating people and controlling the workforce.

> By *exercising* power while *disguising* power, psychotherapy is an unintentional but major player in sociohistorical processes, including the maintenance of a modern era, Panopticon-like self-surveillance, the concept of intrapsychic interiority, and the emphasis on internal emptiness—processes that reproduce the current configuration of the self and the political arrangements and moral agreements in which the self is embedded. In other words, the claim that psychotherapy is an apolitical, amoral practice is itself a political act. (Cushman, 1995, p. 285)

New technologies allow ever more vivid and omnipresent advertisements and public relations ploys. These constantly repeated pitches make it difficult to see "outside" the fishbowl. The public life of active individuals is devalued in favor of a leisure world of private experience (p. 68). Expert advice is offered to attain every goal.

SCIENCE AND TECHNOLOGY AS GRAND NARRATIVES

With the Enlightenment came greater attention to reason and technological solutions to problems and distress. Progress and solving problems via science and technology were emphasized. Many advances in science and technology offer invaluable help. But how many? The clear advances of the former, including simple checklists that can contribute to avoiding errors (Gawande, 2010), may hide the harmful effects of pseudoscience and unneeded or harmful technologies including squandered resources. Consider the past popularity of phrenology. (See Figure 8.7.) The eclipse of traditional forms of authority set the stage for the ascendance of experts as secular guides and the use of an ever-expanding collection of technologies to be used. Measurement technologies describing the "normal" render ever more individual variations as abnormal. The self as independent of the church and communal identity became a possibility, now to be managed by experts (Cushman, 1995, p. 345). Bracken and Thomas (2005) suggest that this set the stage for the increasing medicalization of distress as seen in psychiatry, psychology, and clinical social work, and the increased development of technologies, allegedly scientific, to relieve suffering. The greatest struggles were now located in the psychological—not spiritual self—as in Freud's vision, and in the body in ever more minute forms, such as differences in genetic profiles. Cushman describes the turn of the century self as "lonely, undervalued, unreal, fragmented, diffused, obsessed with gaining personal recognition and lacking in guidance" (p. 67). The authority of science and medicine provided answers

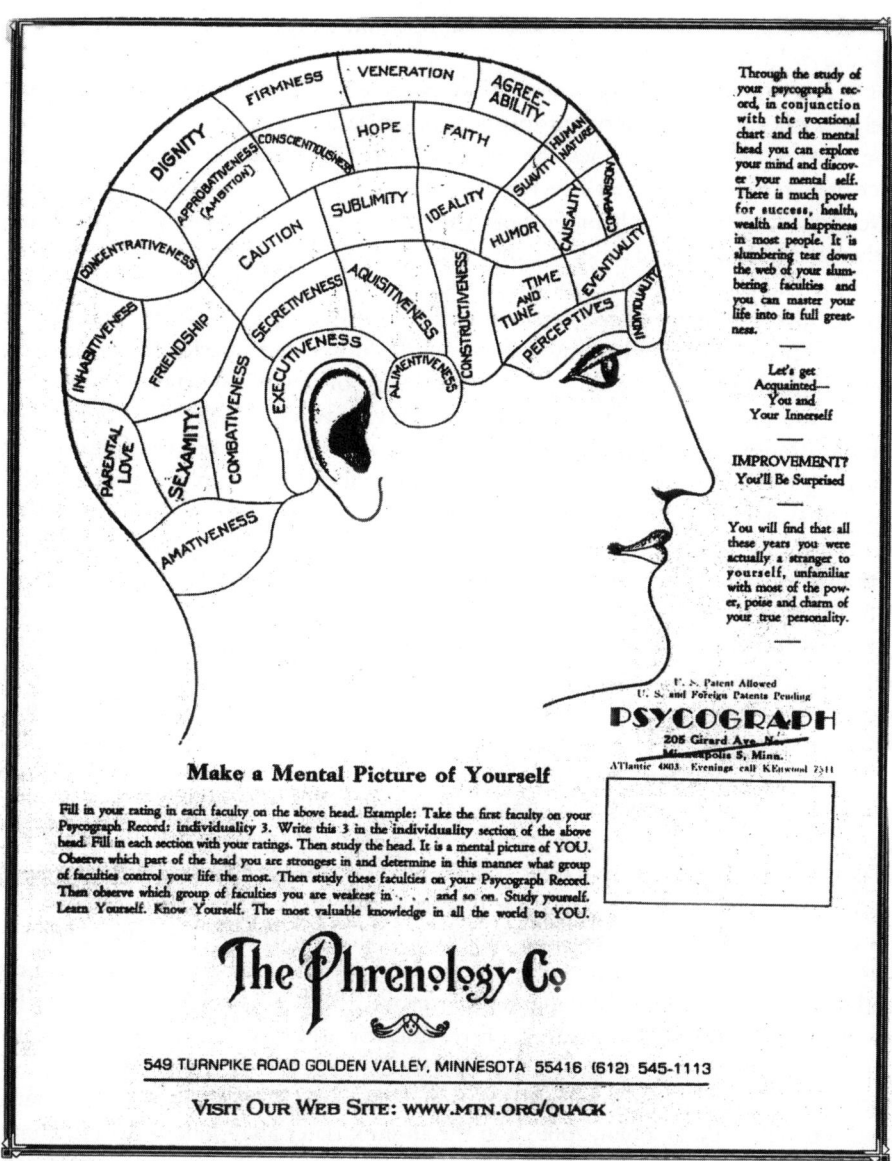

Figure 8.7. Character traits associated with each part of the head.
SOURCE: McCoy, B. (2000). *Quack: Tales of Medical Fraud From The Museum of Questionable Medical Devices*. Santa Monica, CA: Santa Monica Press (p. 148).

facilitated by advances in information technology including computerized diagnostic systems (Orr, 2010); psychiatric, psychological, and medical therapies offered cures through science (p. 67). When suffering or fearful of death, sickness, or loss, we are especially vulnerable to propaganda that appeals to the grand narratives of technology and science—progress, cure, magic bullets, simple solutions, the latest chemotherapy, and technological fixes. We turn to professionals who we assume have special knowledge, technology, and skills that will help us to avoid risks, relieve suffering and prevent our worst fears from being realized (Marris, 1996). Without an understanding of what science is and what it is not, we are patsies for pseudoscientific ploys.[21]

Ellul (1965) viewed modern man as obsessed with technology. Technology includes not only machinery but forms of organization, assessment, and classification systems, clinical guidelines, the "medical gaze" (Foucault, 1973) and other gazes, such as the "social work gaze." Technology profoundly affects us as illustrated by the invention of the clock (changing how we view and spend time—now clock time rather than psychological time) and the weighing scale (forwarding views of "normal" weight). The invention and proliferation of the "survey" (opinion polls) and their reports in the media, replace personal opinion with mass opinion. Products of all sorts are popular in the helping professions including self-quizzes for diagnosing yourself (e.g., Do you have adult ADHD? Are you "bi-polar"?), portable blood pressure measures and pedometers to determine how far we run. Technology presses for standardization and efficiency (Ellul, 1965) as illustrated by the routinization of practices overlooking important individual differences, for example, ignoring differences that should be considered in dosage levels of medication (Cohen, 2001). Central to therapeutic culture is having a method (a technique) "to talk, explain, verbalize emotions and negotiate or compromise over one's needs" (Illouz, 2008, p. 135). Managed care systems need easily billable hours, based on clearly defined "needs"—coded by number. Pains and symptoms are "objectified" and classified so administrative forms can be easily completed. Latin names and code numbers lend an aura of objectivity. Advertisers promote use of brief scientific looking questionnaires to see if we are "bi-polar" (and need medication).

Measures of emotion used in our therapeutic culture strip them of their context and variations; what is ever changing is transformed into something frozen, as in a science museum where we gaze upon dead objects under glass plates (Illouz, 2008). Classification systems (technologies) such as the DSM, purport to tell us what is normal and what is not—how to live our lives. Scientific experts have become the modern day "priests" in conveying "the word" regarding what is normal and what is not (Reiff, 1965). Today, their guise is often in the form of expert consensus panels with ties to pharmaceutical companies (Cosgrove, 2010). This assumption of priestly status, sometimes only self-assumed, is revealed by arguments for secrecy. Only the experts can (or should) "know," illustrated by the negative reactions on the part of representatives of professional organizations concerning the posting of Rorschach cards on Wikipedia (Cohen, 2009) and the attempt (later abandoned) to hold secret discussions regarding creation of the next edition of the DSM. Before the invention of the printing press, there were vigorous efforts to make sure that the written word was available only to priests who read Latin. This elite could then function as the sole interpreter of "the word."[22] A mediator role is advocated today by many academics, researchers, and center directors; they will decide which practices and policies have been established as "evidence-based" and should be used by professionals.[23] Indeed, I have heard prominent academics protest that masters' students in social work should not be expected to acquire critical appraisal skills because this is too difficult for them. This position gives alleged experts (the annointed) free reign to propagandize clients, students, and professionals. A heavy hand in such recommendations is not sensitive to vital individual differences in client characteristics and circumstances or available resources. It also ignores the important role of common factors in influencing outcomes (e.g., Wampold, Imel, & Miller, 2009).

Technology as magic: Ellul (1964) argued that technology replaced nature as a supernatural force in our technologically society. Technology tends to perpetuate itself, often as part of organizations with vested interests in survival and growth, such as hospitals, professional organizations, and social service agencies, both not-for-profit and for-profit (Charlton, 2010). Stivers (2001) suggests that administrative and psychological technology has assumed a magical status: our expectations for their effectiveness are magical. The essence of magic is an attempt to influence something, such as rain by a certain action (dancing) or inaction (not stepping on cracks). There is an effort to predict and influence the future. Stivers (2001) views the ever-changing variety of management practices as a form of magic—an endless series of "new" practices claimed to be able to solve problems previous ones could not. Professionals attend workshops to hear about the latest advances. Because the problems addressed are not solvable by these (or perhaps any) means, these management practices are a form of magic in our modern world. "Magic established an indirect or symbolic relationship between a set of practices and a desired outcome so that the magical practices [such as a different therapy or management practice] become, as it were, operational indicators of the outcome" (p. 11). The practice itself becomes the magical action. If I wear a certain perfume, my romantic hopes will be realized. If I eat a certain kind of seaweed, I will remain healthy. If I identify and change my distorted thoughts, I will be happy. Stivers suggests that such indicators are believed to contain the "sacred power of technology," but really do not. The effects are placebo effects that contribute to belief in the magical activities; there is a self-fulfilling prophesy.

The symbolic nature of magic lends this a spiritual caste—"magical ritualizations that spiritualize every consumer good" (p. 13). As with dancing to draw rain, we believe in the power of psychological practices, managerial systems, and medical technology to fulfill our desires. These psychological techniques "include advertising and the media, therapy, self-help, positive thinking, sales, human relations management techniques, and the plethora of how-to books about childrearing, marriage, friendship, relating to one's boss, and the like. In each case the technique entails what is perceived as an objective process or set of steps to produce the desired outcome" (p. 9). Many scholars highlight the use of psychological techniques to control the workforce (e.g., Ellul, 1965; Illouz, 2008). Stivers (2001) suggests that the psychological techniques of scientific and humanistic management are in reality "a means of manipulating employees into being servants to their managers" (p. 10).

THE GRAND NARRATIVES OF HEALTH AND DISEASE

The grand narrative of health rules the day. Currently we are obsessed with health and well-being as illustrated by the enormous growth of the "health industry" propelled by the ever-increasing variety of behaviors, conditions, thoughts, and feelings encompassed under the banner of health. Engaging in a growing list of activities too much or too little is now viewed as unhealthy. In his classic article, Zola (1972) argues that medical control has increased, not only by finding new diseases, but by creating new ones and claiming jurisdiction over new problems. "The most powerful empirical stimulus for this belief is the realization of how much everyone has or believes he has something organically wrong with him, or put more positively, how much can be done to make one feel, look or function better" (p. 475). Indeed, the rates of clinical entities reported on surveys or by periodic health examinations range from 50% to 80% of the population. One out of five people are supposed to have a diagnosable mental disorder. Zola (1972) suggests that this medicalization of society "is as much a result of medicine's potential as it is of society's wish for medicine to use that potential" (p. 477). Here again we see a symbiotic relationship. Moral dilemmas reflected in social and personal problems are transformed into medical concerns. More and more everyday problems are viewed as "health" problems, remediable by experts (Conrad, 2007; Zola, 1972). (See discussion of medicalization in chapter 6.)

> With the development of the therapeutic service sector of the economy, an increasing proportion of all people come to be perceived as deviating from some desirable norm, and therefore as clients who can now either be submitted to therapy to bring them closer to the established standard of health or concentrated into some special environment built to cater to their deviance. (Illich, 1976, p. 123)

> Medicine is becoming a major institution of social control, nudging aside, if not incorporating, the more traditional institutions of religion and law. It is becoming the new repository of truth, the place where absolute and often final judgments are made by supposedly morally neutral and objective experts. And these judgments are made, not in the name of virtue or legitimacy, but in the name of health. Moreover, this is not occurring through the political power physicians hold or can influence, but is largely an insidious and often undramatic phenomena accomplished by "medicalizing" much of daily living, by making medicine and the labels "healthy" and "ill" *relevant* to an ever increasing part of human existence. (Zola, in Conrad, 2007, p. 470)

In her chapter on the "Triumph of Suffering," Illouz (2008) points out how more and more people are considered to be victims requiring the help of professionals.

> Feminists, psychologists, the state and its armies of social workers, academics working in the field of mental health, insurance companies, and pharmaceutical companies have "translated" the therapeutic narrative because all these actors, for different reasons, have had a strong interest in promoting and expanding a narrative of the self defined by pathology, thereby de facto promoting a narrative of disease. (p. 170)
>
> . . .
>
> These various actors have all converged in creating a realm of action in which mental and emotional health is the primary commodity circulated, a realm in turn marking the boundaries of an "emotional field," namely a sphere of social life in which the state, academia, different segments of cultural industries, groups of professionals accredited by the state and universities, and the large market of medications and popular culture have intersected and created a domain of action with its own language, rules, objects, and boundaries. The rivalry between various schools of psychology, or even the rivalry between psychiatry and psychology, should not overshadow their ultimate agreement on

defining emotional life as something in need of management and control and on regulating it under the incessantly expanding idea of health channeled by the state and the market. (Illouz, 2008, p. 170–171)

The Grand Narrative of Mental Health and Biological Psychiatry

It is widely believed that "mental illness" is the cause of troubled, troubling, and very dependent behaviors. (Mis)behaviors, troubled or troubling feelings and thoughts, are translated into illness such as bi-polar disorder, schizophrenia, attention deficit hyperactivity disorder, and hundreds of others including gambling and female sexual dysfunction (Moynihan, & Mintzes, 2010). Biomedical psychiatry is the main instigator and promoter of this view. This category error, assuming that behavior—what people do—equals illnesses, is widely ignored by players in the mental health industry and their audiences. Indeed, to question it, is often viewed as heretical and deluded. This reaction shows the spectacular success of propaganda equating (mis) behavior and illness. Psychiatrists and pharmaceutical companies have been very successful in forwarding medical views of problems including transforming everyday behaviors, thoughts and feelings into illnesses requiring medical solutions (medication), as illustrated by the ever lengthening list of behaviors viewed as signs of mental illness and promotion of medical remedies (prescribed medication).[24] Medical views of problems sell pills. Herzberg (2009) describes the multiple pathways that contributed to the increasing focus on prescribed medication as the answer to life's ills and increasingly, to lifestyles—how to be happy. The number of listings in the *Diagnostic and Statistical Manual* of the American Psychiatric Association continues to increase (from 80 in 1980 to almost 400 in 2000). Version V of the DSM will include a number of "risk" additions such as "at risk of autism," which critics argue will generate high false positive rates (Frances, 2010). The slogan, "And more," truly characterizes this enterprise.

The boundaries around categories of alleged disorders such as anxiety in social situations continue to expand. The client is viewed as having an illness (mental) in need of a diagnosis and treatment. Now mental health is considered to be a public health problem warranting screening of the entire population for "mental health" problems (e.g., O'Connell, Boat, and Warner, 2009). The promotion of the belief that deviant or troubling behaviors are caused by an illness (a brain disease) has spawned scores of industries and thousands of agencies, hundreds of research centers, and thousands of advocacy groups which forward this view, none more successful than the industry of the Diagnostic and Statistical Manual of Mental Disorders (2000) published by the American Psychiatric Association, soon to appear in a 5th edition in 2013. A disease model of alcohol abuse rules the day. This model has fostered the development of a thriving industry of specialized counselors and treatment centers for "addiction." Treatment of mental health and substance abuse disorders now has parity with treatment of physical illnesses. Psychologists, social workers, and counselors have jumped on the biomedical bandwagon as reflected in the professional literature, as well as in professional education programs. Special interest groups, the pharmaceutical and health industry, the advertising and public relations industries, and patients themselves have all contributed to this.

Attribution of distress or disturbing behaviors, feelings, and thoughts to something amiss in the brain is quite ancient.

> In portraying the brain as the master organ of the mind, nineteenth-century medical authorities betrayed their social prejudices. The comparative study of brain anatomy was widely used in the era as a "scientific" proof of the superiority of white Euro-American culture. Anatomists routinely misinterpreted, and even falsified, data on brain size and capacity to justify the subordination of certain ethnic groups, nonwhites, and women. This distasteful tradition of "mismeasuring" the brain only ended in the present century, when researchers conclusively showed that brain size is determined by overall body size, not gender or race, and has no direct relationship to intelligence. (Gamwell & Tomes, 1995, p. 70)

Biomedical explanations are used to account for an ever-increasing range of behaviors, thoughts, feelings, and body conditions, even human agency (Lavassa & DeCaro, 2010). Anxiety, depression, and (mis)behaviors of children are claimed to be due to a brain disease. Factors focused on include biochemical changes, brain damage, and genetic differences. Pharmaceutical ads promote claims that concerns such as anxiety and depression are related to too much or too little of certain biochemical substances such as serotonin. Physical characteristics (abnormalities) in the brain are assumed to be responsible for "mental illness" including depression and (mis)behaviors of children. Promotion of medication as a remedy encourages a biochemical view of behavior and emotions. The finding of biochemical abnormalities related to certain behaviors only establishes that abnormalities in biochemistry are present, not that they cause the behavior. In 1999 the U.S. Surgeon General concluded that there was no anatomical, biochemical, or functional sign that reliably distinguishes between the brains of mental patients and those of others. Yet still, at that time, anxiety, depression, and other common concerns were asserted to be "mental illnesses."

Even today, there are no agreed on independent signs of "mental illness." Biochemical changes may result from stress caused by limited opportunities due to discrimination; indeed our experiences create brain changes. Another kind of biomedical explanation assumes that brain damage is responsible for "disorders." Here, too, even when brain damage can be detected, it does not necessarily indicate that it causes any particular behavior changes. Additional problems with these kinds of explanations include limited intervention knowledge and predictive validity. Alberto and Troutman (1990) argue that biophysical explanations give teachers excuses not to teach. Such explanations are at best incomplete; environmental factors also play a role.

> To say that Rachel can't walk, talk, or feed herself because she is retarded tells us nothing about the conditions under which Rachel might learn to perform these behaviors. For [some one] to explain Ralph's failure to sit down on the basis of hyperactivity caused by brain damage does not provide any useful information about what might help Ralph learn to stay in his seat. Even apparently constitutional differences in temperament are so vulnerable to environmental influences as to provide only limited information about how a child is apt to behave under given conditions. (Alberto & Troutman, 1990, p. 9)

Fancher (2007) argues that the assumption that physical causes are responsible for distress reflects a confusion that "gives biological psychiatry a specious credibility and drugs a specious aura of significance" (p. 283). He notes that "psychology (and other sciences) have as much claim to explain material states as biology has to explain psychological ones. We are all talking about the same thing, though we are saying very different things about it" (p. 283).

> By failing to think through what it means to say that the brain is the mind, [a category error] biological psychiatry also makes many nonsensical claims about its own status and its relationship to other fields of study. Once we abandon dualism, the distinction between different disciplines becomes a distinction between types of discourse and levels by which reality is organized. All the structures and systems composing reality are made of the same stuff. Thus, to speak of physics versus chemistry is to speak of different modes of discourse addressing different levels of how reality is organized. (Fancher, 2007, p. 283)[25]

Premature acceptance of biophysical explanations and related assessment methods such as neuroimaging techniques interferes with exploration of alternative views such as Heyman's (2009) view that biological factors do not make addict's behavior compulsive. He argues that although drug use alters the brain and genetic factors render some people more susceptible to addiction, research demonstrates that such individuals can assess the consequences of their actions.

Although some troubled or troublesome behaviors, thoughts and feelings may indeed be due to brain dysfunction, if they are so caused, they would become a subject for neurology (not psychiatry) as Szasz suggests. Appeal to the trapping of science (picture of brains) is one of the many strategies used to forward this belief.[26] Other strategies used in the service of perpetuating this claim include its sheer repetition in thousands of journal articles, books, and workshops—and now webinars, direct to consumer advertisements, and in the halls of academia in which professional schools of social work, psychology, and psychiatry are located. Thomas Szasz (1961, 2007) has been the most consistent critic of the assumption that mental illness is a cause of distressed and distressing behavior.[27] He considers the very notion of "mental illness" as a rhetorical device designed to obscure the differences between physical illness and problems in living such as anxiety in social situations and depression. He argues that a false analogy with physical illness is made in order to impose control on those labeled or to allow the labeled to escape responsibility for their behavior.

Szasz has been the most consistent in highlighting ethical travesties resulting from this framing of problems-in living as brain diseases, including coercion in the name of helping, drugging people, and interfering with our right to make our own decisions when our behavior does not harm others (e.g., Szasz, 2002). He has been a consistent witness to the incestuous relationships between self-interests of helping professionals such as psychiatrists for status and money, and goals of the state (to control and contain deviance) in his description of the therapeutic state—now a pharmacracy.

> The institution of psychiatry, like the institution of slavery, consists of a socially sanctioned relationship between a class of superiors coercively controlling a class of inferiors. The system rests on the idea of mental illness, its semantic clones, and their legal implications; it is destined to engender disdain on the

one side, and defiance on the other. The juxtaposition of persuasion and coercion lies at the heart of mankind's great moral conflicts—relations between men and women, leaders and followers, capital and labor, expert and lay person. The true healer of the soul is a 'doctor' of persuasion, not coercion. Psychiatric peace and tolerance are contingent on the recognition that 'mental illness' is a misleading metaphor and on the rejection of psychiatric coercion as a crime against humanity. (Szasz, 2002, p. 227)

Szasz (1994) argues that we now live in a therapeutic state (a pharmacracy) characterized by psychiatric control of (mis)behaviors, primarily via prescribed medications. Psychiatrists have the power to coerce people to participate in interventions "for their own good."[28] He suggests that suffering is no longer permitted, we must be happy and healthy. Coercion is now defined as "treatment." Common variations in behavior are transformed into potential risk factors dubbed "unhealthy" and in need of treatment. Ellul (1965) argued that propaganda creates artificial needs (p. 176); the propagandist "is master of both excitation [you are mentally sick] and satisfaction" [taking medication]—master of creating worries and offering remedies; but what are excited are artificial and deeply misleading "needs."

It's in the Genes: Genetic Explanations

There is a great interest in searching for genetic markers for concerns. Premature claims abound in this area.[29] Causes of behavior may be attributed to inherited traits or temperamental variations. There are genetic differences in personality and intelligence.[30] Views that emphasize the interaction among genes, behavior (our actions), and our environments differ in how reciprocal these relationships are assumed to be and in the range of events considered (e.g., family, neighborhood, governmental health policies, economic opportunities). Some argue that genotype (genetic makeup) can never be separated from phenotype (visible characteristics that result from the interaction between genotype and the environment), because the environment, as well as random developmental factors (developmental "noise"), affects how genotype is expressed (Lewontin, 1994; 2009; Strohman, 2003). They contend that the biological and the social are neither separable, nor antithetical, nor alternatives, but complementary (e.g., see Schneider, 2007). This epigenetic view in which environmental influences are considered to be a key contributor to gene expression is not promoted by those who benefit from a simplistic genetic view.

> Certainly genes are essential for defining any phenotype, but by themselves they remain just inert materials. In order for genetic information to be replicated or "decoded" and used to assemble phenotypes, the DNA must first be manipulated by systems of enzymes and small molecules that constitute the efficient cause for constructing phenotypes. Nearly all biologists now acknowledge this reality. . . . this second informational system: an epigenetic system, [is] so named because of its ability to activate and silence elements of DNA and thereby to produce specific patterns of gene expression and proteins in a context-dependent (time and place) manner. (Strohman, 2003, p. 190)

Thus, with rare exceptions, attributing behavior to genes is a false claim. Questions here include "What percentage of the variance do genes account for?" Even, when a genetic influence is found, it usually accounts for only a small portion of the variance in understanding behavior. Although many people accept the findings of twin studies purporting to show a strong hereditary component to developing schizophrenia, others do not, pointing out methodological flaws (Boyle, 2002). From a helping point of view, a key question is: What variables provide the greatest leverage for achieving valued outcomes? (See Hall, Mathews, & Morley, 2010.) Genetic tests regarding cancer have been disappointing (Kolata, 2011).

PSYCHOLOGICAL GRAND NARRATIVES

Psychology is a huge field with many different areas. Psychoanalytic views emphasize helping patients to grow through understanding themselves and their conflicts better. Edward Bernays, the founder of the field of public relations and a double nephew of Freud, based his successful strategies on appeal to unconscious desires in areas ranging from promoting Russian ballet, encouraging women to smoke, and bringing down the government of Guatemala. In cognitive explanations, a causal role is attributed to thoughts. (See Figure 8.8.) There is an interest in identifying and altering beliefs, expectations, schemas (views of the self and world), and attributions (e.g., Beck, 2005; Ellis, & McLaren, 2005). Promotion of "mind cures" has a long history, attesting to the enduring appeal of the belief that "thinking makes it so." Albert Ellis drew on the writings of Epictetus: "It is not he who reviles or strikes you, who insults you but your opinion that these things are insulting." In behavioral views, actions, thoughts, and feelings are considered to be largely a function of our learning histories, both past and present. Varied social histories result in a wide range of behavior as illustrated in anthropological research. Behaviorists argue that environmental contingencies associated with feelings and thoughts (e.g., expectations and "states of mind") remain unknown in cognitive accounts of behavior. Developmental accounts describe differences and related factors at different ages (e.g., infancy, childhood, adolescence, adulthood, old age) and/or speculate about such differences as in literature on life-span development.[31] Words and phrases such as (1) She is not "ready" yet, (2) He is getting older, so acting that way suggest developmental explanations. Belief in a stage theory of development may get in the way of identifying environmental factors that can be altered. We may incorrectly assume that a person is "stuck" in a given stage and that there is nothing to do but wait for time to pass.

THE THERAPEUTIC GRAND NARRATIVE OF CLINICAL PSYCHOLOGY

Illouz (2008) draws on multiple areas of inquiry, including popular culture, as well as her own experience in attending workshops describing therapeutic methods, in her description of the therapeutic grand narrative of clinical psychology.[32] She, as does Ellul and other contextual thinkers, attends to the "big picture," and, like Ellul,

Figure 8.8. The Man with the "Grasshopper Mind".
SOURCE: Popular Mechanics, June 1930.

emphasizes the splits created by our technological society and its alienating effects, for example, between beliefs and actions.

> On the face of it, therapeutic culture is a reaction against a stultifying technical and bureaucratic disenchantment. Because of its stress on individual uniqueness, pleasure, and introspection, therapeutic culture is, at face value, a vast cultural effort to recapture meaning and feeling in an otherwise barren and technical world of meanings . . . at the same time that it has made available a rich and elaborate lexicon of inwardness and emotions, therapy has also

heralded a standardization and rationalization of emotional life. . . . As was the case in the corporation, making relationships more "emotional" went hand in hand with making them more rational . . . [there is] the intertwining and intensification of emotional and economic cultural models to address social relations [emotional capitalism]. (Illouz, 2008, pp. 149–50)

Illouz argues that therapy in advanced capitalist economies "provides the cognitive and emotional 'toolkit' [technology] for disorganized selves to manage the conduct of their lives" (p. 241) and that such a toolkit is needed to orient "the self within the intricate terrain of social relationships which are in turn transformed by the social practices they themselves have helped orient and organize" (p. 241).[33] She notes the persuasiveness of the language of psychology in intimate relationships, as well as in work environments, and attributes the initiation of this language to the rise of psychoanalysis. Psychoanalysis offered "plans of action, metaphors, and narrative templates [technologies] that helped modern men and women cope with the increasing complexity and normative uncertainty of modern lives" (p. 241). These could be used to solve practical everyday problems.

> The self has become the prime site for the management of the contradictions of modernity, and psychology has offered techniques to manage those contradictions. . . . the self had to perform many more, contradictory tasks to monitor social relationships: become self reliant, yet attuned to others' needs; conduct relationships in a highly rational way, yet be highly focused on its own and others' emotions; be a unique individual, yet constantly cooperate with others. Psychology played a crucial role in providing dialogical models of interaction that could presumably manage these tensions, inside the workplace and the family. (Illouz, 2008, pp. 243–44)

She notes that therapeutic prescriptions (psychological knowledge) became prevalent in the corporation, family, mass media, and state in the context of the growing authority of experts (p. 161). Psychology was made a key feature of modern identity. Corporations used related language to manage the workforce. The media codified, legitimized, and disseminated psychology's worldview and provided a venue for "performance of the therapeutic self" (p. 242). An ideal of social communication was created, incorporating the view that we gain self-knowledge by introspection, which can provide guidance in understanding, controlling, and dealing with both our social and emotional environment. Verbal disclosure was viewed as central in social relations. She, as do many others (e.g., Ellul, 1965; Sennett, 1970), emphasizes the breakdown between the private and the public. What used to be private is now public, such as confessions on Oprah Winfrey's show and the sharing of individual narratives in support groups. The therapeutic culture of psychology encourages a "reflexive monitoring of the self," particularly for the middle class.[34] "Middle-class emotional culture has been characterized by an intense introspectiveness and reflexivity . . .[in which] men are joining in the rationalization of intimacy" (p. 150). Central to the therapeutic culture is having a technique—a methodology to talk, explain emotions, and negotiate one's needs. Emotions are separated from their immediate contexts. They become objects to be exchanged but in a language that is both neutral and subjective. The language is neutral because one is supposed to focus on the objective content of a sentence and try to avoid misinterpretations and related emotions. It is subjective "because the justification for making a request or experiencing a need is ultimately based on ones' own subjective needs and feelings, which never require any higher justification than the fact that they are felt by the subject" (p. 135).

Illouz suggests that the language of therapy has been responsible for a cognitive and cultural process of "verbal overshadowing" that makes self-introspection a substitute for nonverbal ways of acting in social exchanges. She suggests that this verbal overshadowing encourages a "cementifying of personality" and ignoring of situational factors that influence behavior. Yet another splitting is between emotions and actions. "In taking a reflexive posture toward emotions essential to selfhood and, in positing a model of disengaged mastery over one's emotions, therapeutic culture has paradoxically contributed to a splitting of emotions and actions" (Illouz, 2008, p. 150). As Ellul (1965) argues, we act without thinking [or feeling?] and think without acting [or feeling]?

> The therapeutic discourse offers endless possibilities for coherently narrativizing the life story through its "diseases" . . . if failure can always be corrected, then it has to be somehow the result of "a disease of the will", that is, to be self-made, and if it is self-made, it can also be unmade, which in turn legitimizes and perpetuates the very existence of the therapeutic institution. (Illouz, 2008, p. 196)

She suggests that the narratives about the self used to enhance understanding of the self, including one's problems, make "too much sense of one's life"—bind too tightly the present, past, and the future in a "seamless narrative of psychic wounding and self change" (p. 196).

Self-observation, self-knowledge, and the responsibility to work on and alter our relationships are emphasized. New ways were introduced of attending to emotions, as well as labeling, explaining, and transforming them. She suggests that feminism and therapy contributed to a vast process of disciplining the emotions inside the private sphere (p. 136). Rather than being sensitive to changing emotions, emotions become like flies pinned to a paper by endless tests produced by the psychological assessment industry and by pharmaceutical companies, which promote a "recoding and disciplining of the psyche" (p. 136).[35] There has been an "objectification of emotion" (p. 138); "numerical metaphors [scores on tests] are used to characterize personalities and relationships" (p. 138). Balance is emphasized, for example, in assertiveness and shyness and warmth and coldness. Illouz argues that this interest in balance enabled therapists to view a wide variety of forms of intimacy and personalities as problematic; if balance is the ideal, all departures—too much or too little—become problems. This view both enlarges the client pool and creates uncertainty "about the nature of a 'healthy' emotional makeup" (p. 139). Our private life and feelings are converted into measurable objects, to be captured in quantitative terms. It is presumed that "to know that I score a ten in the statement "I become anxious when you seem interested [in] other women" will presumably lead to a different self-understanding and corrective strategy than if I had scored a "two" (p. 139).[36] This illustrates the press for ever-greater efficiency and standardization in a technological society emphasized by Ellul (1965).

Illouz (2008) suggests that Freud's fatalistic determinism was countered by Erickson's view that every crisis provided an opportunity to grow and to develop mastery. Thus, "those who did not conform to these psychological ideals of self-fulfillment were now sick" (p. 160). She considers the DSM to be one of the main instruments (technology) forwarding expansion of psychological modes of explanation (p. 165). Indeed, the category of illness has been applied to an ever-widening pool of individuals. She, like Szasz, argues that therapeutic discourse has resulted in a mass "cultural recoding" of what was previously defined as immoral behavior "into a disease in which the self's capacity to monitor its actions and to change them has lapsed." Indeed, mainstream clinical psychology and clinical social work have embraced this psychiatric classification system, in many cases ignoring research supporting a social learning view of problems-in-living.

> The creation of a classification system in which symptoms signified and thus qualified as markers of a mental or emotional disorder now pathologized a wide range of behaviors. For example, "oppositional disorder" (coded 313.81) is defined "as a pattern of disobedient, negativistic and provocative opposition to authority figures," "histrionic personality disorder" (coded 301.50) occurs when individuals are "lively and dramatic and always drawing attention to themselves," and "avoidant personality disorder" (coded 301.82), is characterized by "hypersensitivity to potential rejection, humiliation, or shame and unwillingness to enter into relationships unless given unusually strong guarantees of uncritical acceptance." With the attempt to carefully codify and classify pathologies, the category of mental disorder became very loose and very wide, including behaviors or personality traits that merely fell outside the range of what psychologists postulated was "average." Behaviors or personality features that might have been previously categorized as "having a bad temper" were now in need of care and management and were henceforth pathologized. (p. 165)

> Thus the DSM, willfully or not, helps label and chart new mental health consumer territories, which in turn help expand pharmaceutical companies. Hence the expansion of the category of mental illness, dysfunction, or emotional pathology is related to the professional and financial interests of mental health professionals and drug companies (p. 166).

Does this focus on interiors have a beneficial outcome? Her answer is "No." She contends that questions about "Why do the innocent suffer and the wicked prosper? . . . that [have] haunted world religions and modern social utopias, [have] been reduced to an unprecedented banality by a discourse that views suffering as the effect of mismanaged emotions or a dysfunctional psyche or even as an inevitable stage in one's emotional development" (Illouz, 2008, p. 246).

> Clinical psychology is the first cultural system to dispose of the problem altogether by making misfortune a result of a wounded or mismanaged psyche. It brings to perfect completion one of religion's aims: to explain, rationalize, and ultimately always justify suffering. [She draws on Max Weber to note the regressive nature of this kind of explanation.]; the most powerful form of

preservation of the status quo, namely the retrospective explaining and therefore legitimizing of good or bad fortune by hidden virtue or vice. Psychology resuscitates such forms of theodicy with a vengeance. In the therapeutic ethos there is no such thing as senseless suffering and chaos, and this is why, in the final analysis, its cultural impact should worry us. (pp. 246–47)

As many have argued before her, but Illouz (2008) does this most systematically in terms of recognizing multiple cultural pathways, "suffering has become a problem to be managed by experts of the psyche" in the contemporary therapeutic worldview (p. 246).

The more the causes for suffering are situated in the self, the more the self is understood in terms of its predicaments, and the more 'real' diseases of the self will be produced. Because the therapeutic narrative discusses, labels, and explains predicaments of the self, the self in turn is invited to conceive of itself as ridden with emotional and psychological problems. Far from actually helping manage the contradictions and predicaments of modern identity, the psychological discourse may only deepen them. (Illouz, 2008, p. 246)

The cueing functions of our emotions have been dismissed.

MORAL, EXISTENTIAL VIEWS

Competing with practices and policies in the therapeutic state (the joining of government and institutionalized psychiatry in deciding what is good and what is not) are philosophical moral views. Moral views emphasize our responsibility for our decisions, no matter what the circumstances.[37] Szasz (1987) views psychoanalysis as a dialogue, voluntarily sought, in which the professional functions as a catalyst in helping clients explore moral alternatives. Taking responsibility can be a burden as suggested by the many ways in which we try to *Escape from Freedom* (Fromm, 1941), for example, by being constantly busy. Ellul (1965) suggests that this is a prime reason why propaganda is successful; it removes the burden of making one's own choices. A moralistic view of problems encourages the belief that people with these problems deserve whatever fate awaits them, including "justified" punishment or enforced "treatment." Zola (1973) suggests that although we have (for the most part) stopped torturing people we have not stopped making their lives miserable in many ways. For example, we blame people for eating unhealthy foods or watching too much TV. Zola (1972) suggests that although an "immoral character is not demonstrated in his having a disease, it becomes evident in what he does about it. . . . if one listed the traits of people who break appointments, fail to follow treatment regimes, or even delay in seeking medical aid, one finds a long list of 'personal flaws. . .' In short, they appear to be a sorely troubled if not disreputable group of people" (Conrad, 2009, p. 472). Competing with the view that discrimination and oppression are the principal causes of many problems—containment of the marginal—is the view that lack of individual initiative and responsibility contribute to or create problems. Sykes (1993) argues that we have become a nation of victims, using past difficult experiences as excuses to continue to wallow in self-pity. But who encourages this victim status? Isn't there a victim industry? Here, as always, we should consider the context, including political and economic incentives.

SOCIOLOGICAL PERSPECTIVES: THE BIG PICTURE

Sociological perspectives emphasize political, economic, and social influences on our behavior, thoughts, feelings, and bodies, including what and who we view as a problem, as well as related cause(s) and remedies. They highlight the importance of context including who has the power to decide what is acceptable and what is not and what should be done about it. A sociological grand narrative encourages us to keep in mind that what are defined as problems, using scientific and technical discourse, may disguise social and political conflicts and competing efforts to control resources (power). Values are often disguised as "scientific findings." Contemporary states have three strategies to control offensive or threatening behavior: socialization (Ellul's propaganda), medicalization, and penalization (Wacquant, 2009).

> Social definitions of social problems have this in common with other processes in society: those occupying strategic positions of authority and power of course carry more weight than others in deciding social policy and therefore, among other things, in identifying for the rest what are to be taken as significant departures from social standards. (Merton & Nisbet, 1976, p. 52)

Certain behaviors and/or conditions are transformed into social problems, each of which has an entire industry associated with it, including specialized agencies and specialized professionals such as substance abuse counselors (Loeske, 1999). Gusfield (2003) suggests that "the idea of 'social problems' is unique to modern societies."

> I do not mean that modern societies generate conditions which are problem-laden and cry for reform and alleviation while primitive and pre-industrial ones do not. I do mean that modern societies, including the United States, display a culture of public problems. It is a part of how we think and how we interpret the world around us, that we perceive many conditions as not only deplorable but as capable of being relieved by and as requiring public action, most often by the state. The concept of 'social problem' is a category of thought, a way of seeing certain conditions as providing a claim to change through public actions. (p. 7)

We assume such conditions are scientifically determined, ignoring their social construction—the indicator (e.g., label) becomes proof of the accuracy of such framing—a kind of "bold assertion" or form of magic. This highlights the threat that accurate facts and figures may pose to those who promote particular constructions. Certain concerns/conditions are selected out and labeled as a personal or social problem and acquire related accoutrements such as psychiatric labels and cadres of helping professionals and technological fixes. "While we live in a world that creates endless amounts of want and pain, constructivists study how humans define this want and pain" (Loseke, 1999, p. 175).

> To give a name to a problem is to recognize or suggest a structure developed to deal with it. Child abuse, juvenile delinquency, mental illness, alcoholism all have developed occupations and facilities that specialize in treatment, prevention and reform; for instance: shelters for runaway adolescents and battered women; alcohol and drug counselors and recovery centers; community services for the aged; legal aid for the indigent; community mental health counseling, and centers for the homeless. There is even a national organization called the Society for the Study of Social Problems. (Gusfield, 2003, p. 8)

People act in different ways at different times. Some variations in behavior are labeled as personal or social problems, such as child and elder abuse. An apolitical view of deviance dominates many helping efforts: It is assumed that deviance (e.g., psychopathology) is definable by "objective" criteria. Those who embrace this view pursue answers to questions such as "Who are they?" and "Why do they do it?" Those who argue that problems are socially constructed note that although certain needs have been recognized throughout the centuries, such as those of the sick, poor, elderly, and very young, they have been defined differently at different times and receive more or less attention at different times. They argue that social problems are "constructed" in accord with cultural, political, and economic influences. That is, they are social judgments often cloaked in the guise of science, not empirically determined illnesses. "Values as well as economic and power differences are intimately related to carving out a social problem, such as 'inequality.'

A social problem is a putative condition or situation (at least some) people label a 'problem' in the arenas of policy discourse and define it as harmful and frame its definition in particular ways" (Hilgartner & Bosk, 1988, p. 70). Loeske (1999) suggests that a social problem is some condition that is viewed as "wrong, widespread and changeable" (p. 7). Personal problems are similarly viewed by the helping industry. The game of constructing problems is won by convincing audiences that a problem is at hand and that something must be done (p. 19). In this view, moral or right behavior is considered to be socially constructed (not given), relative to actors, context, and time. It is assumed that:

- Deviance is universal but there are no universal forms of deviance. Deviance is contextual; what is labeled as deviant varies in different social situations.
- Deviance is a social definition, not a property inherent in any particular behavior.
- Views of deviance are integrally related to morality (beliefs about what is right or wrong).
- Defining and sanctioning deviance involves power. Social groups create roles and enforce their definitions through judgments and social sanctions.

Ellul (1965) emphasized the pervasiveness of sociological propaganda (integrative propaganda) designed to socialize us into a certain way of acting and thinking—"to integrate people into the 'normal' patterns" (p. 107)—"conformance with a certain way of life" (p. 107). Conflict is contained by shaping motivation and perception—by encouraging people to be satisfied, even happy with their life. Feminist scholars and advocates have been in the vanguard in emphasizing the relationship between the personal (including bodies) and the social. As Mills (1959) long ago suggested, "the personal is political."[38]

Loeseke (1999) argues that "each social problem must be constructed as a particular kind of problem with a particular kind of cause" (p. 81). This construction must be compatible with "larger cultural biases," or popular grand narratives and metaphors (such as "The war on drugs"). A common tactic is framing a problem as a variation of one already accepted and expanding the domain as in the medicalization of behaviors described in chapter 6. For example, misuse of alcohol is now viewed as a disease and as a disability. (For an alternative view, see Heyman, 2009.)[39] The way a problem is constructed shapes the image of what kind of people have it, what should be done, and who should do it. The changing ways in which certain behaviors have been viewed reflects the social construction of deviance. For instance, only when women gained more political and economic independence was greater attention given to battered women. Changing ideas about what is and what is not a "mental illness" illustrate the consensual nature of psychiatric diagnoses.

Class, Gender, Culture, and Race

In the *Mismeasure of Women*, Carol Tavris (1992) suggests that labels such as *dependent personality disorder* which are most often given to women, punish women for fulfilling expected roles. She contends that we should examine the conditions in society that result in so many women showing these characteristics such as expected gender roles and unequal educational and job opportunities and alter them. Women often accept a psychiatric view of problems and related labels that obscure environmental causes and related options. Indeed, women are the primary consumers of psychotropic medication and are labeled more often than are men (see Herzberg, 2009). Illouz (2008) argues that the therapeutic culture of psychology affects mainly middle class people. Working class people are excluded, and from her point of view, to their benefit (see earlier discussion). A woman may view her low-paid job as a result of a personal flaw, overlooking gender discrimination. Betty Friedan argued that "women's anxiety came from stymied dreams rather than too much ambition" (1963, p. 79).

> women's psychic suffering was not a medical phenomenon to be soothed by tranquilizers but a political problem to be cured through social change. Women were not sick because they had abandoned the home and domesticity; rather, they were sick because they were being restricted to unfulfilling family life. In fact, one of their biggest problems was that they had listened to "experts" telling them that their nameless problems were medical illnesses. The result? They visited a physician and "blotted out the feeling with a tranquilizer." Friedan reported with alarm that "many suburban housewives were taking tranquilizers like cough drops."
> . . .
> Like the Miltown-swallowing men who lost ambition at work or passion in politics, tranquilized women were merely dulling themselves into accepting

circumstances that needed changing. The root issue, Friedan argued, was self-fulfillment. Women, like all humans, needed lives that "permitted the realization of one's entire being." A suffering housewife's "anxiety can be soothed by therapy, or tranquilized by pills or evaded temporarily by busywork. But her unease, her desperation, is nonetheless a warning that her human existence is in danger.... If she is barred from realizing her true nature, she will be sick." (Herzberg, 2009, p. 79)

Natural biological changes such as menopause are viewed as needing the help of experts to negotiate. The influence of cultural differences is often overlooked. For example, Lock (1993) found that Japanese women were apt to complain of stiff shoulders during menopause, whereas Western women complained of hot flashes.

Gender, class, culture, and race influence how certain behaviors and the rights to engage in them are viewed.[40] White middle- and upper-class people can buy prescribed medications to alter their moods; use of street drugs by poor African American youth results in arrest and imprisonment (Alexander, 2010). White middle-class people have access to high-quality educational opportunities. African Americans living in ghettos may refuse a life of "slave labor" (low paid jobs with no future) and pursue illegal routes to obtain money such as selling drugs (Wacquant, 2009). Zola (1972) singles out psychiatry and public health in terms of their commitment to changing social aspects of life. He notes that medicine has been involved from its very origin in reporting diseases and making decisions about what diseases to focus on, the diseases of the rich or the diseases of the poor such as malnutrition and high infant mortality. Both in the past and present, medicine attends more to diseases of the rich. Mirowsky and Ross (1989, 2003) explored the relationship between psychological distress (depression and anxiety) and social factors and concluded that half of all symptoms of depression can be attributed to social factors. They suggest that lack of control over negative events may result in biochemical changes.

> The realities of socio-economic status—amount of education, type of employment or lack of it, family income—have a profound influence on a person's sense of control. Minority status is associated with a reduced sense of control partly because of lower levels of education, income, and employment, and partly because for members of minority groups, any given level of achievement requires greater effort and provides fewer opportunities. (Mirowsky & Ross, 1989, p. 16)

Ellul (1965) emphasized the close relationship between sociological propaganda and psychological needs.[41]

In the nineteenth century, doctors often cited the pressure of civilization, specifically the stress of life in growing American cities, as a social cause of madness. City life was thought to interfere with the individual's bond with nature and "to overtax a nervous system bombarded by jarring stimuli" (Gamwell & Tomes, 1995, p. 90). A quickened pace and stress in life was viewed as a key cause of distress. Related complaints and causes were viewed as primarily of concern to the middle and upper classes. Women were viewed as especially susceptible because of weak physiogamy and emotional nature. Both Illouz (2008) and Herzberg (2009) highlight the role of gender and class in influencing what is promoted as therapeutic, to whom (mostly women), and for what. Dealing with the discontents created by modern life in the white middle classes was a key theme as illustrated in ads for tranquilizers (Herzberg, 2009). Discontents such as being confined in the home could be muted by taking a pill. Herzberg (2009) illustrates how outcomes offered by taking a pill broadened to taking a pill as a way to achieve happiness itself.

Hiding Agency in the Creation and Definition of Problems

Creating categories viewed as problems is the result of human activity. It is a form of claim-making. Different people benefit and lose from particular problem creations and alleged causes; interested players are actively involved in this process, for example, by planting stories and hiding competing alternative views.[42] This activity is often hidden. Consider the construction of the use of marijuana as a social problem. Becker (1973) showed that the Federal Marijuana Tax Act of 1937, which was passed to eradicate use of this substance, was the product of a campaign carried out by the Treasury Department's Bureau of Narcotics. Anti-marijuana material in magazines and newspapers 1932–1937 was prepared by the Bureau of Narcotics. However, these activities were carefully hidden. There is an "obliteration of human agency in the construction of the social problem" (Aronson, 1984). The source of the stories was hidden. Methods used to create facts are not described. Problem definition is influenced by professionals' interest in maintaining and gaining power, status, and economic resources, as well as by differences of opinion about what makes one explanation better than another. Thus, what is viewed as right or wrong (mental illness or not)—judgments about how people should live their lives—is the product of certain people and groups making claims based on their particular interests, values, and views. Consider examples Maddux and Winstead (2005) give in their book on *Psychopathology:*

> If you drink large quantities of coffee, you may develop Caffeine Intoxication or Caffeine-Induced Sleep Disorder. If you have "a preoccupation with a defect in appearance" that causes "significant distress or impairment in ... functioning" (p. 466), you have Body Dysmorphic Disorder. A child whose academic achievement is "substantially below that expected for age, schooling, and level of intelligence" (p. 46) has a Learning Disorder. Toddlers who throw tantrums have Oppositional Defiant Disorder. Not wanting sex often enough is Hypoactive Sexual Desire Disorder. Not wanting sex at all is Sexual Aversion Disorder. Having sex but not having orgasms or having them too late or too soon is Orgasmic Disorder. Failure (for men) to maintain "an adequate erection ... that causes marked distress or interpersonal difficulty" (p. 504) is Male Erectile Disorder. Failure (for women) to attain or maintain "an adequate lubrication or swelling response of sexual excitement" (p. 502) accompanied by distress is Female Sexual Arousal Disorder.
>
> The past few years have witnessed media reports of epidemics of Internet addiction, road rage, and "shopaholics." (p. 15)

Unsubstantiated claims constantly repeated acquire the status of immutable truths. Ilouz (2008) highlights the disappearance of human agency in the objectification of emotion (measuring emotion on a checklist), ignoring context and changes in our emotions.

THE ECLIPSE OF THE BIG PICTURE IN THE TRIUMPH OF THE FOCUS ON INTERIORS

Views emphasizing the social have lost out to views focused on certain characteristics of the individual, particularly easily measured interiors of thoughts and interiors of bodies, such as alleged serotonin imbalances. Well-being has become the end rather than a byproduct of seeking some communal goal (Reiff, 1965, p. 67). Rather than being viewed as individuals whose behaviors are evaluated based on an external moral standard, we are viewed as patients whose behavior is an uncontrollable indicator of medical illness (p. 67). Social-political and moral issues related to human suffering are eclipsed in this focus on interiors.[43] As Moncrieff (2008) and many others point out "The transcription of deviant behavior into medical conditions [mental illnesses] serves many important functions. It authorizes coercive actions such as the incarceration and restraint of disturbed individuals. It conceals the moral and political judgments that are imbedded in their actions." As Szasz (1987) has long argued, it encourages a disguised form of social control.

Problems of the state such as anti-social behavior are transformed into problems of the medical profession (psychiatry) and psychiatrists are given power to "treat" alleged mental disturbances. This has been a huge propaganda success. There has been a turning away from environmental influences such as being poor, African American, and living in a ghetto (Wacquant, 2009) in the focus on individual characteristics, such as low self-esteem.[44] The effects of living in a technological society permeated by propaganda, such as anxiety and loneliness, are cast as remediable by self-help or thinking positive thoughts. Environmental sources of troubling emotions and unhappiness are hidden; they are off stage. Individual differences created by different environmental realities are ignored, including the subjective ones. Again we see the press for standardization and the neglect of the qualitative.

Grand narratives in Western societies encourage a focus on individuals and what is inside them such as brain differences, personality dispositions, and "the self" and its thoughts. Such narratives foster growth in industries focused on individual deficiencies such as psychiatry, psychology, clinical social work, pharmaceutical and biotech companies, and armies of educators in professional schools and researchers. The grand narratives of consumerism, healthism, and self-help, which focus on the individual, have triumphed over views emphasizing the role of social, political, cultural, and economic factors on our lives. Victimization, suffering, and triumph by individual efforts (with the help of experts) over suffering are emphasized in the therapeutic culture. Positive psychology is a modern-day version of positive thinking promoted by Norman Vincent Peele. We are encouraged to think positive thoughts. We are urged to be content with the way things are. Ehrenreich (2009) describes this movement as conservative in its preservation of the status quo "with all its inequalities and abuses of power" (p. 171). Research concerning self-psychology is appealed to to justify this view. Viewing our problems as the result of our personal deficiencies is one of four factors Goldenberg (1978) suggests that make up and encourage oppression defined as "a state of continual marginality and premature obsolescence." Others include: (1) containment (restricting and narrowing the scope of possibilities); (2) expendability (assuming that specific groups are expendable and replaceable without loss to society); and (3) compartmentalization, which prevents people from living an integrated life (e.g., there is little relationship between life interests and work) (1978, p. 3). Policies that focus on changing individuals or families and ignore related political, economic, and social factors, in effect, "blame the victim" (Ryan, 1976). Labeling behaviors as healthy or illness depoliticizes related issues.

> By locating the source and treatment of problems in an individual, other levels of intervention are effectively closed. By the very acceptance of a specific behavior as an "illness" and the definition of illness as an undesirable state, the issue becomes not whether to deal with a particular problem, but *how* and *when*. Thus the debate over homosexuality, drugs, or abortion becomes focused on the degree of sickness attached to the phenomena in question or the extent of the health risk involved. And the more principled, more perplexing, or even moral issue, of *what* freedom should an individual have over his or her own body is shunted aside. (Zola 1972, reprinted in Conrad, 2009, p. 477)

Hiding the Politics of Problem Creation

Propaganda in the helping professions hides the role of political and economic interests in the construction of social and personal problems and proposed remedies. I do not mean to say that people do not have real problems. They do; people are lonely, are caught in difficult moral conflicts, are physically ill, have no money or housing. But are these the problems we find highlighted in sources such as the *Diagnostic and Statistical Manual of Mental Disorders* (2000) of the American Psychiatry Association? Do we find the words "loneliness," "sadness," or "moral conflicts" in the index of this manual? We do not. Those in the helping professions and related enterprises focus on certain social and personal problems and frame them in certain ways. Parts of the puzzle are missing. Such partiality in the use of evidence is key in propaganda.

Where are the diagnoses of "Conflict-of-Interest Disorder" (Cosgrove, 2010) or "Rapacious Hedge Fund Obsession"? There is an objective reality (e.g., a certain percentage of people smoke), and, there are claims about the problem (e.g., prevalence, causes), which may not reflect reality, such as inflated claims of prevalence that may actually shape reality. The play of politics in creating this reality gap is hidden. The political nature of problem definition is hidden and the grand narratives of technology and science are used in the service of this form of politics. This, together with an educational system which falls short in helping us learn how to critically appraise claims of knowledge and ignorance and is also lacking in educating us about the play of politics and special interests, lays the ground for vulnerability to propaganda in the helping professions, especially when we are miserable or in pain and searching for hope and cure. These influences help to account for the triumph of a standardization in which the realities of individual circumstances and characteristics are hidden as in use of a psychiatric classification system. Hiding political, social, and economic influences on problem creation and definition, such as making billions from sale of a medication—hiding context—is a key strategy. The politics of problems is hidden. We see inflated claims of accuracy and evidentiary status regarding a favored view and hiding and/or distorting of alternative views and related evidence.[45] Hiding well-argued alternative views may result in misdirections and oversimplifications that mislead rather than inform us about what is a problem, what kind it may be, what causes it, and what should be done (if anything) about it. This kind of deception goes hand-in-hand with seductive appeals to our self-interests in being healthy, popular, right-living, achieving the good life and avoiding the bad.

CONTEXTUAL VIEWS: ANECDOTE TO PROPAGANDA

Propaganda in the helping professions often appeals to oversimplified views of life experiences; "It's in the brain"; "It's in the genes"; "It's caused by our thoughts."[46] Asking "What's missing?" can help to protect us from misleading oversimplifications. Behavior is influenced by a range of variables and can be analyzed at different levels including physiological, psychological, and sociological. Individual variations may occur in response to different life experiences that in turn, result in different kinds and degrees of vulnerability and resilience. This should caution us to be wary of simplistic causal accounts (e.g., "It's in the genes"). A contextual view emphasizes the mutual influence of people and their environments. It highlights the importance of understanding a person's "environment" and related risks, problems, and opportunities. A contextual perspective encourages us to view our environments as multiple interlinked levels, each of which holds certain risks and provides certain opportunities. It encourages us to use a sociological imagination, which allows us to shift from one level of explanation to another (Mills, 1959). The knowledge, skills, and values we develop and the environments we create are related to the risks and opportunities we confront which are influenced by environmental contingencies. Our experiences create changes in the brain that in turn influence our moods and behavior. Change on one level may create opportunities or risks on another. If it is not possible to create changes on one level, it may be possible on another. Recognizing the connections between the social and the personal can help us to avoid simplistic views that focus on interiors—psychological or biological characteristics of individuals—ignoring environmental influences. It can protect us from influence by the distorted realities propagandists promote.

In everyday life we often attribute behavior to feelings. A counselor may write in her record, "Mrs. Jones tried to kill herself because she felt lonely and believed no one cared about her." But, why did she feel lonely? What is going on in her life that may be related to feelings, related thoughts, and the suicide attempt? Such accounts stop too soon. They are incomplete. Feelings and thoughts are vivid, thus readily available to assume as causes of behavior. Propagandists take advantage of this vividness to encourage confusion between feeling free and being free. They may pronounce: "You are free to choose," when, because key information is hidden and alternatives offered have been shaped by others, you are not free. As Skinner (1971) suggests, just because you feel free does not mean you are uninfluenced by your environments. Environmental circumstances are often less vivid, and so easily overlooked, especially by professionals who rely on clients' self-report in interviews (the office bound professional). So too is our past history (biographies that shape our behavior) typically less vivid, unless focused on, as in certain kinds of therapy. Lewontin (1994) suggests that we must rid ourselves of the metaphor of adaptation, the view that organisms are adapting to a fixed world and either they adapt or they do not (p. 32). He views metaphors of stability, harmony, and balance of nature as ideological inventions characteristic of a particularly insecure time in the history of the Western world (p. 47). Lewontin suggests that based on what little we know about genes, organisms, and environment, a more accurate metaphor is that of *construction*. He contends that only through careful observation of organisms in their environment can we discover their environments. What is the "environment" to one differs from what it is for others. "There is an external world but there is no single environment out there" (p. 38). Contexts remain unknown in a focus on the individual. This constructive view of our lives encourages action to alter our environments.

A Contextual View is Inherently Political

A contextual view emphasizes the role of value judgments and clashing political, social, and economic interests in the selection of problems to focus on and their definitions and proposed remedies. It emphasizes the importance of understanding who the players are and how they create and maintain practices and policies. It reveals rather than hides context. It encourages us to dig beneath the surface of slogans such as "empowerment," "social justice," and "well-being" to explore what they mean—do hoped-for outcomes occur? If so, at what cost? Focusing on interiors such as thoughts, personality traits, and chemical imbalances allows the creators of influential contingencies such as governments and corporations to remain unknown, while blaming and containing the less powerful and undesirables, all the while, claiming that "We are doing it for the good—safety—of society."

Those who create and maintain policies, and the laws to enforce them, benefit from obscuring their influence and its harmful effects. If I can convince you that your problems are due to a brain disease or to your thoughts, you are not likely to look around and examine your environments to explore related factors. As Szasz (2007) argued, "Although a person may behave abnormally because of having a brain disease, the typical madman behaves the way he does because of his particular adaptation to the events that comprise his life" (p. 66). Consider who benefits and who loses from focusing on altering self-esteem of children in classrooms when change is needed in the behavior of local school boards, school principles, parents, and school teachers (e.g., Sugai & Horner, 2005). Over a quarter of a century ago, Illich (1976) suggested that labeling children as ADHD excuses bad teaching. Far more children are so labeled today (Baughman, 2006). A contextual view threatens vested interests and reveals harming in the name of helping. Contextual views are the enemy of propagandists. Understanding the role of social, political, and economic factors in creating and maintaining concerns such as high blood pressure, depression, and anxiety decreases the likelihood of being misled by incomplete accounts.

AWARENESS OF CONTROVERSIES AS AN ANTIDOTE FOR PROPAGANDA

Hiding controversy and creating bogus controversies are key propaganda strategies. Thus, one antidote to influence by propaganda is to be aware of controversies in an area. Controversies include the relative importance attributed to biological, psychological, and environmental factors and how the "environment" is defined. Psychological theories focus on the individual. Sociological perspectives focus broadly on political, economic, and social influences including what becomes a "problem" and what kind it is assumed to be. Contextual views consider multiple levels of causality. Consider different views about ADHD (attention deficit hyperactivity disorder). Some view related (mis)behaviors as created by dysfunctional schools and family environments and a decreased tolerance for individual variations in children's behaviors (e.g., Baughman, 2006; Diller, 2006; Timini, 2008). Others argue that related behaviors are caused by a "brain disease." Different views have different implications, for example, medicating children compared to altering dysfunctional environments. Medication is often in a "one-dose-fits-all" manner and is often a first, rather than a last, option used as described in chapter 5. Here again, we see the press toward standardization and ignoring of the subjective and qualitative—the unique characteristics and circumstances of different individuals including their preferences and values. The less attention to individual differences, the greater the efficiency of manuals and tick boxes.

SUMMARY

Professionals, as well as a variety of other players, including those in the media, are integrally involved in problem creation and definition, often by promoting health scares based on inaccurate descriptions of prevalence and risk. Professionals taken in by propaganda inflict their views on unsuspecting others. Propaganda in the helping professions promotes the grand narratives of "health," the authority of science, and hope in technology. Profit is the key goal of related industries including the media, which pours out messages and images that shape our beliefs about "problems," risks, and their causes. Grand narratives are hard to spot because they are taken for granted. They are the sea in which we swim. They are part of the basic social fabric and related belief systems in which we live, unquestioned and even unrecognized, such as the premise that hundreds of (mis)behaviors are signs of "mental illness" and that up to one third of the population suffers from a mental illness. Without a historical understanding of the changing views of personal and social problems and their social construction, for example, by a vote among a group of "experts" with ties to Big Parma as with behaviors dubbed as "mental illnesses," we may miss the relationship between the personal and the political. We may miss the political nature of problem definition, often cloaked in the guise of science. Behaviors once viewed as sins were later viewed as crimes and are now viewed as symptoms of "mental illness" (a brain disease).

A sociological grand narrative encourages us to keep in mind, that what are defined as problems using scientific and technical discourse, may disguise social, economic, and political goals and competing efforts to control resources (power). Propaganda hides context. It appeals to personal desires to promote profit-making technologies (such as medication) that may harm you but profit others. Related strategies have been very successful in focusing us on interiors and creating a therapeutic state. Hiding or minimizing environmental influences result in overestimating what can be accomplished at the individual level to the benefit of those who offer products at this level. Although different helping professions emphasize their uniqueness, all forward a culture of therapy focused on the individual as the locus of problems and proposed remedies. Without a historical and contextual understanding, it is easy to focus on "changing individuals" and to ignore related environmental conditions including the biomedical-industrial complex that promotes a focus on interiors. It is easy to lose sight of the changing nature of what is defined as a problem and how it is viewed and addressed. The only way out of the fishbowl is to question popular views—to seek out well-argued alternative views and critiques of views promoted. *Historical* literacy is vital. The history of institutionalized psychiatry shows the ad hoc nature of theories behind treatments that did more harm than good. Women were put in mental hospitals because they wanted to work. Remember this. A historically informed contextual perspective leaves us less vulnerable to embracing views that limit options for pleasure, as well as freedom from unwanted influence, freedom to make informed decisions.

9

Disguise Advertisements as Professional Literature

Many publications in professional sources are of high quality; authors are honest brokers of knowledge and ignorance. They accurately describe what they hoped to find and what they did find, as well as conceptual and methodological limitations. But many do not share these characteristics. These publications are more advertisements than material designed to forward understanding of what is true, what is false, and what is uncertain. Common propaganda ploys include bold assertions regarding "what we know" (or "do not know"); hiding or distorting well-argued alternative views, appeal to unfounded authority such as consensus (authority of "the many"), bogus citations (citations that do not provide support for claims), and vague descriptions. Weasel words and phrases are common such as "It is well known that," "It is widely accepted that" (when there is controversy). Increasing attention has been given to the quality of publications in professional sources spurred in part because of misleading claims and related conflicts of interests (Lo & Field, 2009). Articles and reports that purport to "tell the truth" may, in reality, function as advertisements for the profession, the university, the agency, or the individual publishing the report. Like illusionists in theaters, misleading professional discourse provides an illusion of knowledge. It hides ignorance (Proctor & Schiebinger, 2008), as well as knowledge. As a result of reading an article you may think you are more informed, but you may have acquired or strengthened beliefs that are untrue.

Similar purposes and strategies are evident in propagandistic professional literature and advertisements. Certainly they are not depicted equally in any given product (article, text, or advertisement) but, overall, there are striking similarities. In both, technologies are perfected to suggest consumer benefits (e.g., learn new therapies). In both, images and discourse are used to encourage us to buy products and to adopt related lifestyles such as medication. In both, realities are promoted that do not exist by exaggerating the accuracy of some content and hiding other content such as counterevidence to views promoted and alternative well-argued views. In both, the trappings of science are used to create credibility. As in advertisements, so too in propagandistic professional discourse, it is hoped that we will suspend critical appraisal and trust "the experts" and are lured by hopes of solving problems and satisfying our deepest longings. If sucked in, we are deprived of opportunities to make informed decisions. In both, there is distortion of reality in favor of interests of those who promote dubious claims in organizations such as professional associations and professional degree programs. This is also true of reports by organizations and governmental agencies as described by Altheide and Johnson (1980) in *Bureaucratic Propaganda*. There is partiality in the use of evidence, a hallmark of propaganda. Evidence may be fabricated to sell a product such as a particular view of gambling and a related alleged remedy.

THE PLETHORA OF ADVERTISEMENTS

We are deluged with advertisements on the Internet, TV, radio, magazines, and newspapers. Human-service advertisements include claims made by managed care companies, hospitals, professional organizations, agencies, schools, or individuals concerning a problem and related interventions in the media, including the Internet, videotapes, films, audiotapes, DVDs, and professional journals, to encourage us to accept a view, for example, of depression, and/or to use a particular service. Evidence needed to make an informed decision is often hidden such as the effectiveness of (and/or lower cost of) alternative interventions. Consider the ad for Concerta in Figure 9.1. Contextual variables that affect children's behavior such as overcrowded classrooms, poor curriculum design skills on the part of teachers, and other environmental factors are not mentioned. Hallmarks of human service advertisements include the following:

1. Claims that some assessment method is accurate, some treatment works, some causal relationship exists, or some problem exists (personal or social).
2. Describes no related data involving valid outcome measures.
3. Offers testimonials as evidence (statements by those who claim to have been helped by a program).
4. Appeals to our emotions (e.g., sympathy, fear, anger) as a persuasive tactic. Such appeals may include music or strikingly attractive or unattractive people and/or locations.
5. Presents case examples as evidence: a professional describes or shows in detail what went on in the treatment and how the client responded.
6. Does not mention the possibility of harmful (iatrogenic) effects of the claim promoted.
7. Does not describe counter-evidence or well-argued competing views.
8. Presented by a speaker whose presentation and manner were rehearsed, smooth, polished, and attractive.
9. Presented by a well-known or high-status person, implying that the claim is true because this person says it is.
10. Does not encourage critical appraisal of claims promoted (Gambrill & Gibbs, 2009).

Advertisements often promote causes for which there is no evidence, such as the serotonin hypotheses—even pictorially illustrating them as in ads for Pristiq, an antidepressant. LaCasse and Leo (2005) described bogus claims and faulty reasoning

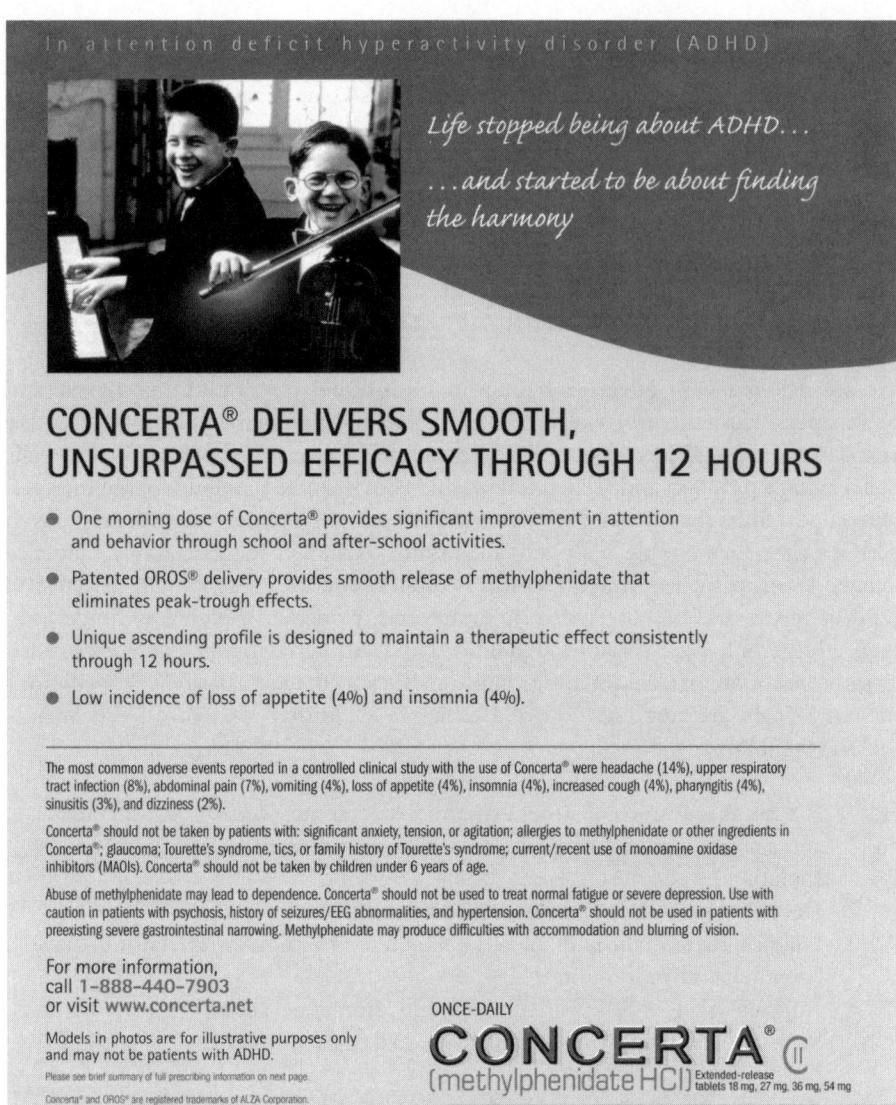

Figure 9.1. Ad for Concerta.
SOURCE: Monitor on Psychology, Jan., 2003, 34 (1) rt after p. 32.

regarding the role of serotonin in depression in pharmaceutical ads. (See also Moncrieff, 2008.) Professional conferences include presentations that meet the criteria of human service advertisements. For example, a "credible" person (an "opinion leader") describes a treatment method, ties it to an oversimplified view of causal factors related to a concern (such as anxiety in social situations), presents it in an enticing way, does not present evidence concerning effectiveness or alleged accuracy of causal accounts favored, and discourages and gives vague answers to probing questions. Until recently, most continuing education programs in medicine were paid for by pharmaceutical companies that promote certain drugs (Brody, 2007).

The Ubiquitous Pharmaceutical Ad

The ban on direct to consumer advertising (DCA) for drugs was removed by the FDA (Food and Drug Administration) in 1997 resulting in an explosion of pharmaceutical ads in multiple sources. Direct to consumer advertising increased prescriptions. DCA has increased requests from patients for advertised drugs from physicians. Sales of Zoloft were $3 billion in the United States in 2004. Professional journals contain scores of advertisements. Total revenue of Pfizer in 2008 was $49.5 billion, of which only $7.9 billion was spent on R & D (research and development) illustrating money spent on advertisements. The pharmaceutical industry purchases advertising space in medical journals, funds special journal supplements favorable to its products, and purchases reprints of articles or of entire journal issues (see Brody, 2007).

Are claims accurate? Reviews of pharmaceutical advertisements in medical journals have consistently raised concerns about claims made. These reviews show the prevalence of disease mongering in ads. (See chapter 6.) Wilkes, Doblin, and Shapiro (1992) carried out one of the earliest studies of advertisements in professional sources. They found numerous instances of unbalanced and misleading ads, and ads with no clear educational value (p. 222). Loke, Koh, and Ward (2002) reviewed claims made in a consecutive three-month sample of advertisements that appeared in six popular Australian medical publications. The authors classified every claim into one of the following four categories:

A: *Unambiguous clinical outcome*: When compared with DRUG X, DRUG Y delivers faster symptom relief.
B: *Vague clinical outcome*: DRUG X is the new, effective, 20 Ng pill with a low incidence of discontinuation of skin problems.
C: *Emotive or immeasurable outcomes*: DRUG X—one of a kind or DRUG X—a source of healing power.
D: *Non-clinical outcome* (e.g., drug plasma half-lives or biochemical markers): Using DRUG X resulted in a 30% increase in arterial luminal diameter in post-mortem dissections.

They found a total number of 1,504 claims in the 1,000 advertisement appearances. Of these, 640 made one claim; 227 made two, 122 made three, and 11 made four. Claims were classified as follows: D: 23%; C: 20%; B: 29%, and A: 28%. They concluded that we "found the quality of claims unsatisfactory, with only 28% of claims being unambiguous." While nearly half (46%) of the clinical claims were supported by evidence from at least one randomized control trial or more, (level 1 or 2), a similar proportion (45%) could not be substantiated at all (unretrievable evidence). Examples of how to cheat on statistical tests when writing up results suggested by Greenhalgh (2010) include ignoring withdrawals (dropouts and non-responders) and ignoring outliers if they interfere with good results.

SHARED GOALS OF ADVERTISEMENTS AND PROPAGANDA-LIKE CONTENT IN THE PROFESSIONAL LITERATURE

The professional literature includes publications in journals, textbooks, the Internet, monographs on special topics, and newsletters. Typically, all those who belong to a professional organization receive a journal published by that organization as part of their membership fees. The manifest reason for this material is to help professionals keep up-to-date. But there are other goals as well; publishers want to make money as do professional organizations whose greatest source of profit may be from publications, including advertisements in these sources. (See Table 9.1.) Any article can be approached as an argument (Jenicek & Hitchcock, 2005). We can examine the claims made and their warrants. (Claims may be so vague or ambiguous that we cannot critically appraise them without clarification.) We can use the term *marticles* to refer to material published in professional journals and newsletters that are marketed to readers as scholarly publications designed to enhance readers' knowledge, but which in fact, share characteristics of advertisements and function as an advertisement for the author(s), publisher, university, and/or profession. A key indicator of a "marticle" is a discrepancy between claims made and evidence presented as found in research reports reviewed by Rubin and Parrish (2007). All is not what it seems to be. Weak standards of evidence such as popularity or consensus may be relied on. The journal *Social Work* is distributed to all members of the National Association of Social Workers. Scores of different topics are contained in this journal. There is no way readers can be informed about all of these topics. It is my experience that the better informed I am about an area, the less accurate is the content in an article—the more inflated claims, the more exclusion of well-argued alternatives and counter-evidence to views promoted. We had to abandon efforts to rate the quality of literature reviews when examining claims made in professional articles because, unless we were well read in an area, there was no way to tell if relevant research and alternative well-argued views were included (Gambrill, Shaw, & Reiman, 2006).

In advertising, illusions are created that using a certain product such as a deodorant or an antidepressant, or exercise program, can remove our miseries and make our dreams come true to encourage us to purchase the product. (See Figure 9.2.) These often emphasize loss of control and regaining control, as well as social appeal,

Table 9.1 SIMILARITY IN GOALS BETWEEN ADVERTISEMENTS AND PROPAGANDA-LIKE MATERIAL IN THE PROFESSIONAL LITERATURE

1. Encourage consumption of a product
    the author
    the therapy described
    the organization in which the author is employed
    the journal, publisher
2. Fulfill desires for fantasy—solves (or give the illusion of solving) a problem
3. Hide troubling realities (concentrate on people's thoughts and forget about the lack of jobs)
4. Provide entertainment—an opportunity to escape (see also 3 above)
5. Integrative in effect (into our technological society)

Figure 9.2. Charles Atlas with friends.
SOURCE: © Bettmann/Corbis. Reprinted in D. Armstrong & E. M. Armstrong (1991). *The great American medicine show* (p. 212). New York: Prentice Hall.

via use of medication (Frosch et al., 2007). What are the purposes of advertisement-like material in professional venues? Manifest goals include knowledge development and dissemination, for example, helping professionals to keep up-to-date with new developments. But, if much of this material is more propaganda than well-reasoned clear discourse and critical appraisal of claims, there must be latent functions. The purpose of propaganda is not to inform by reasoned argument, but to manipulate—to encourage beliefs and actions with the least thought possible (Ellul, 1965). The key purpose may be to maintain and strengthen social bonds within a profession (Munz, 1985) and to integrate us into society by appealing to shared grand narratives such as progress, "wellness," and "adjustment." Latent functions include giving the illusion of knowledge development (of progress) and keeping up-to-date, and giving the illusion of credibility to a profession, university, or author. Only if progress is made are the millions of dollars consumed by research and related publications well spent. Consumers of the professional literature include clinicians, as well as researchers and academics. What are readers' fantasies and wishes? Certainly they include being effective, competent clinicians and successful, well-regarded researchers. Clinical manuals are a product. They are a commodity. They have to be marketed. They have to be brought to people's attention, which they are in articles, books, and governmental publications. If we examine the various ways in which this is carried out we find use of similar strategies such as testimonials and appeal to authority ("panels of experts"). Typically hidden, is the fact that many authors of clinical guidelines have ties with the drug industry (Bekelman et al., 2003; Cosgrove et al., 2009) and that citations given provide a distorted view of the evidentiary status of claims.

SHARED STRATEGIES OF ADVERTISEMENTS AND PROPAGANDA-LIKE CONTENT IN THE HELPING PROFESSIONS

Similar methods are used in both human service advertisements and propaganda—like material in professional sources to encourage readers to accept certain points of view, products, and interventions, and to ignore others such as inflated claims of ignorance, hiding negative effects of what is recommended, and scare tactics. A variety of strategies are used to create the illusion that claims are true, progress is being made, and rigorous standards of critical appraisal are being honored. (See Table 9.2.) In both, reality is distorted by selective use of evidence. Key details are missing or offered in distorted form. In both, bold assertions substitute for a candid, clear description of related evidence that allows readers to decide for themselves in a context of transparency. Related reasons include those discussed in the previous section.

Use of Persuasive Parables

Advertisements use short simple stories from which a moral can be drawn (parables) to sell products. These stories emphasize the relation of the product to the needs and desires of consumers. Parables used in advertisement included "first impressions," essential in a "culture of personality" emphasizing one's ability to please other people (Marchand, 1985). (See Figure 9.3.) Another parable concerned "the democracy of goods" emphasizing consumption as a way of life. The parables of professional discourse include appeals to science, technology, and progress and the importance of experts in transmitting this knowledge. Parables reflected in the professional literature are suggested by the grand narratives discussed in chapter 8: (1) the broken brain fixed by medication; (2) the faulty thoughts fixed by cognitive restructuring; (3) the disturbed social relationships fixed by interpersonal therapy; (4) the traumatized fixed by trauma therapy. There are also the grand parables of the clinical guideline and evidence-based practices anointed by consensus groups. Today, the parable of "best practices" is popular as seen in the numbers of books published claiming to describe them and the number of organizations claiming to know how to detect them.

Appeal to Authority

Advertisements both past and present appeal to authority including revered figures and alleged experts. The trappings of science, including uninformative statistical terms (e.g., 99% better) are used to market rather than to inform in both advertisements and professional discourse. (See Figure 9.4.) Professional publications appeal to the "authority of the text" (the authority of the word) and especially, "the authority of the citation." But how many citations actually contain evidence in support of the claim? Examination of this question reveals a high rate of bogus citations—those that provide no support for the claim made, or, which do only in some people's eyes. In a detailed citation analysis of 242 papers concerning the belief that βamyloid, a

Table 9.2 SIMILARITIES BETWEEN ADVERTISEMENTS AND PROPAGANDA-LIKE MATERIAL IN THE PROFESSIONAL LITERATURE

1. Card-stacking (cherry-picking):
   counter-evidence to claims made is not described
   well-argued alternatives views (e.g., framing of issues) are not described
   negative effects are hidden or downplayed
2. Bold assertions:
   claims with weak (or no) evidence provided
   excessive certainty is claimed: "X is well established"; this is a "best practice"
3. Appeal to authority:
   of the empty citation (it does not provide evidence for the claim)
   to the consensus panel in the pockets of BigPharma
   to the vague "We as in 'we know that...'"
4. Vagueness: (e.g., more, fewer, most common, associated with, disabling)
5. Repetition: popular framing of concerns is repeated in hundreds of sources (e.g., claiming anxiety in social situations is a psychiatric disorder)
6. Oversimplifications; "Depression is caused by a chemical imbalance"
7. Misleading statistics and figures
8. Appeal to popular grand narratives (mental illness)
9. Bogus claims of uniqueness
10. Emphasize the new
11. Use case examples and testimonials
12. Use scientific sounding language: jargon
13. Use persuasive parables
14. Appeal to a particular audience
15. Appeal to emotions
16. Create desires and needs

protein accumulated in the brain in Alzheimer's disease, is produced by an injured skeletal muscle in patients with inclusion body myositis, Greenberg (2009) found distortions that included bias (systematic ignoring of papers that contain content conflicting with the claim), amplification (expansion of belief without any data), and invention (conversion of hypotheses into fact through the act of citation alone). He argued that these "information cascades" result in unfounded authority for claims. The printed word, in this sense, serves a ceremonial/ritualistic function similar to the laying on of hands, as well as being an example of palaver; that is, truth or falsity is not at issue.

Appeal to Emotions Such as Pity, Joy, Fear, and Guilt

The use of heart-wrenching case examples evoking pity may lull our critical appraisal skills into abeyance in articles in the professional literature, as well as in advertisements for charities. Advertisers, politicians, pharmaceutical companies, and professionals take advantage of our interest in avoiding adverse events, for example, the latest risk. Both advertisers and professionals appeal to fear of adverse consequences if we do not follow their recommendations.

Figure 9.3. An advertisement illustrating appeal to fear and the importance of first impressions.
SOURCE: R. Marchand (1985). *Advertising the American dream: Making way for modernity 1920–1940* (p. 211). Berkeley: University of California Press.

Scare copy (negative appeals) enacting dramatic episodes of social failures and accusing judgments became increasingly popular in advertisements in the 1920s and remains popular. (See Figure 9.3)

Jobs were lost, romances cut short and marriages threatened. Germs attacked . . . and neighbors cast disapproving glances. In each instance, the product stepped forward—not to argue with the reader, but to offer friendly help.

Disguise Advertisements as Professional Literature

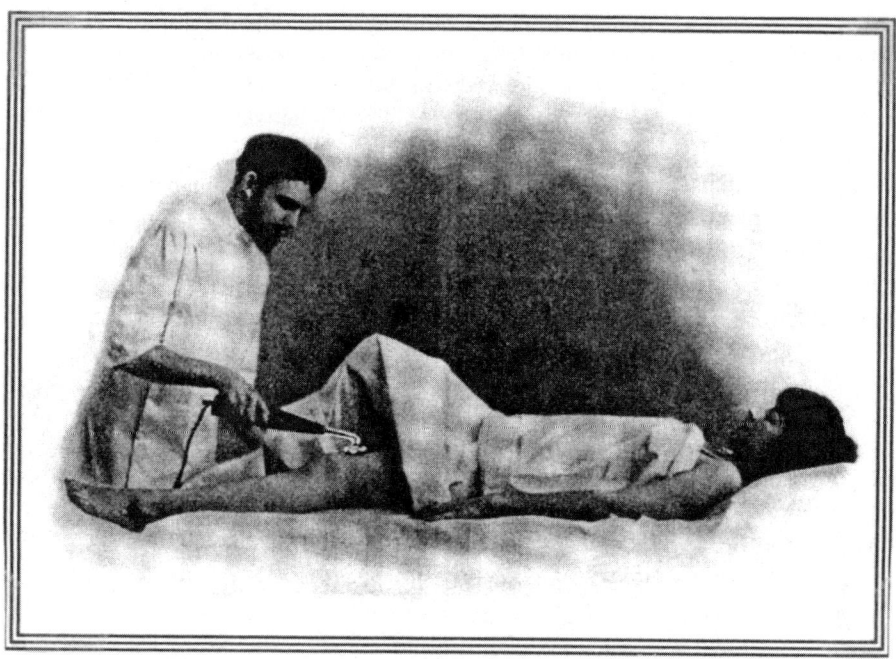

Figure 9.4. Healer treating a patient with a high-frequency violet ray device.
SOURCE: B. McCoy (2000). *Quack ! Tales of medical fraud from the museum of questionable medical devices* (p. 128). Santa Monica, CA: Santa Monica Press.

Scare copy posited a universe in which the fate of each consumer lay in the hands of external disinterested forces and unsympathetic, judgmental observers, a world of normative expectations applied with unmerciful severity. By contrast, the advertiser was solicitous and caring, a friend in need. (Marchand, 1985, p. 14)

Researchers warn clients of dire consequences if their recommendations are not followed (e.g., another suicide attempt). And, as Pratkanis and Aronson (2001) emphasize, "Guilt sells." If I can make you feel guilty, for example, by not taking steps to stay healthy, you are more likely to do so.

Use of Lax Standards of Evidence

Scholars of advertising suggest that a "standard of proof" is adhered to only insofar as total disregard for this may result in people not buying a product (Marchand, 1985). Prolific use of vague words (e.g., "most") and claims ("We're the best") illustrate lax standards. Ioannidir (2005) argues that most published research findings are false. Thornley and Adams (1998) reviewed data in 2,000 trials on the Cochrane Schizophrenia Group's register and found consistently poor quality of reporting, which they suggest "is likely to have resulted in an overly optimistic estimation of the effects of treatment" (p. 1181). Less rigorous studies report more positive findings compared to research that controls for biases (e.g., Schultz, Chalmers, Hayes, & Altman, 1995). The more journals accept material with bogus claims, the more readers are exposed to such material. Those who protest that they want a candid appraisal of claims and clear descriptions may be referred to as "positivists" and other ad hominem appellations. Biased research questions and designs tilt outcome in favor of a remedy promoted (e.g., see Andre, 2009). Glaring flaws in research studies may be easily detected, but not deceptive problem framing (Gambrill & Reiman, 2011). The questionable quality of material, including articles in peer-reviewed journals, was a key reason for the creation of the process and philosophy of evidence-based practice and problem-based learning in professional education (Gray, 2001).

Overwhelm with Material

We are bombarded by ads—now on the Internet. The sea of advertisements in which we exist is ever present, seeping into all facets of our lives. The number of professional journals has vastly increased, complemented by hundreds of blogs and websites. This plethora of information creates an illusion of knowledge.

Use of Vagueness

Advertising is filled with words and phrases such as "revolutionary," "new," "best seller," "lowest price." Similar kinds of vagueness abound in the professional literature. Consider this, which appears often in reports of research regarding social anxiety: "Social phobia is a common and disabling anxiety disorder associated with considerable social and occupational handicaps that is unlikely to remit without treatment" (Mortberg, Clark, Sundin, & Wistedt, 2006, p. 142). What is common? What is disabling? What is considerable? What does "unlikely to remit" mean? What is a disorder? Do citations used provide evidence for claims made? Are well-argued alternative views described? Often they are not. Vague terms such as "high," "low," "least likely," "more likely" are classic weasel words. The professional literature is filled with vague claims of association between variables as in, "most people . . ."; "X is associated with Y"; "We found a high association." What is the correlation? Such terms have different meanings for different people. Acceptance of vague phrases and words gives an illusion of shared understanding. Asking what 'high,' 'low,' etc. mean is key to avoiding acceptance of misleading beliefs that, if acted on, may result in actions that harm rather than help.

Use Misleading Figures, Tables, and Charts

Advertisements are notorious for using misleading tables and charts. Tufte's (1990, 2006) books on graphics illustrate the many ways these can be deceptive. He describes a "lie chart" for use to review graphics and describes guidelines for reviewing the integration of text and graphics. Prevalence of problems/(mis)behaviors are exaggerated (e.g., see Sheldon, 2008). The text may not match data described in tables or figures in articles published in the professional literature. Areas in figures may not match percentages claimed. (See also the classic book, *How to Lie With Statistics*, Huff, 1954.)

Card-Stacking: Partiality in the Use of Evidence

Censorship is a key propaganda strategy—only information favorable to a view or product is shown. "The most widespread and serious obstacle to learning the truth from an evidence-based report is *cherry-picking*, as presenters pick and choose, select and reveal only the evidence that advances their point of view" (Tufte, 2006, p. 144). Such partiality in the use of evidence occurs in both advertisements, as well as in propaganda-like profession discourse. Consider the ad for Boniva (a drug claiming to "be proven" to prevent and even reverse bone loss). "It's clinically proven not only to maintain bone density but to actually help to reverse bone loss in 9 out of 10 women in one year" (retrieved on July 16, 2009, from Boniva website, <http://www.bloniva.com>). Sally Fields gives a testimonial. This ad does not inform viewers that Boniva is 10 times more expensive that other equally effective drugs (*Consumer Reports*, June 2009). Advertisements claiming that a drug works may not include information that it is effective for only a certain percentage of users or a certain percentage of time for an individual. Biased selection in the use of evidence (cherry-picking) is common in the professional literature.

Exaggerated Claims of Knowledge

"Card-stacking," described in the previous section, results in exaggerated claims of knowledge and effectiveness. Advertisements hold out promises of removing our problems and gaining our desires. For example, by using products developed via science, such as Listerine, we could outwit problems of civilization such as a hurried pace, competition, and nervous tension (Marchand, 1985). The product was the antidote, just as interventions described in professional sources are promoted as "proven" remedies for depression, anxiety, and other concerns when indeed related literature may show a high (but hidden) relapse rate and a high percentage of people who are not helped. "The ideology of advertising is an ideology of efficacious answers. No problem lacks an adequate solution. Unsolvable problems may exist in the society, but they are nonexistent in the world glimpsed through advertisements" (Marchand, 1985, p. 227).

Repeated use of vague weasel terms and phrases such as "well-established" and "validated" illustrates exaggerated claims of effectiveness in the professional literature. Books with titles such as *What Works in Child Welfare* (Kluger, Alexander, & Curtis, 2002) and *Treatments that Work* (Nathan & Gorman, 2007) convey exaggerated claims of remedies in their very titles given that interventions described work only for some people, some of the time, positive effects may not last, and claims are in dispute.

Oversimplify: Avoid Complexity and Hide Controversies

Oversimplification is a key characteristic of advertisement, especially regarding alleged causation and proposed remedies. "Despite the improvements over the years, much advertising is still characterized by oversimplification, superficiality, and shoddy standards of proof. Heavy exposure to such logic may dull critical thinking in all areas of life" (Jacobson & Mazur, 1995).

Failure to cleanse the bowels used to be (and still is) promoted as a cause of many troubles, just as masturbation was claimed to be the cause of myriad problems (Allen, 2000; Szasz, 1970). (See Figure 9.5.) Our yearning for a remedy contributes to our belief in simple remedies; it contributes to the "triumph of the superficial" (Ewen, 1999)—skating on the surface. Oversimplification is a kind of partiality in

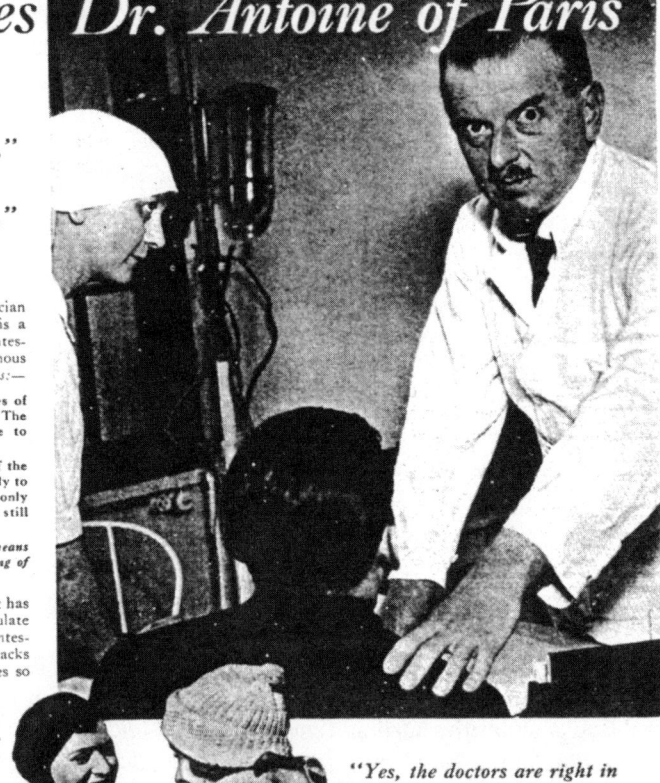

Figure 9.5 Constipation: A perennial concern.
SOURCE: Rowsome, Jr., F. (MCMLIX). *They laughed when I sat down: An informal history of advertising in words and pictures.* New York: Bonanza Books. Ad is circa 1929.

the use of evidence: the complexity of causation and ignorance about causes and remedies is hidden. Examples of oversimplifications in the helping professions include unfounded claims that changes in serotonin levels cause depression and "It's in the genes." Behavior is complex. The brain is the most complex organ in the body.

> The reason simplistic explanations like the serotonin depletion theory of depression survived, Healy and others argue, is not because they were proven true but because they were so useful for virtually everyone involved: the pharmaceutical industry, which used them to prove efficacy to the FDA and to advertise its wares; professional psychiatry, which used them to claim true understanding of mental illness while highlighting the importance of their prescribing power in comparison with other kinds of therapists; insurance companies, which benefited from cheaper therapy; and patients, who often preferred a physical to a mental illness and were grateful for a simple cure. With such institutional power behind them, it is not surprising that simple models of mood and molecules drowned out more complex arguments that did not promise such easy payoffs. (Herzberg, 2009, p. 168)

Textbooks that offer an overview of theories often do not provide the in-depth description needed for accurate understanding. If it is true that merely hearing a concept creates an illusion of knowledge that interferes with learning, (we think we know more than we do), such overviews are harmful rather than helpful. (See discussion of the validity effect in chapter 11.) Brief overviews that present caricatures do more harm than good by spreading false information. Superficial coverage encourages an illusion of understanding and competence in the reader that may result in ritualistic actions—those unlikely to help clients.

Promote Distorted Realities

In advertising, some realities are distorted and others hidden. I can sell more of my products if I ignore or offer a distorted view of my "competition." Just as an advertisement may hold up a distorting mirror of reality to use Marchand's metaphor, so too may material in the professional literature. Examples include distortions of applied behavior analysis and its accomplishments (Jensen & Burgess, 1997; Thyer, 2005), as well as distorted presentations of evidence-based practice (Gambrill, 2011). Well-argued critiques of views promoted are often ignored, even though they are readily available. For example, typically, no mention is made of Mary Boyle's (2002) critique of the validity of the diagnosis of schizophrenia in related discussions. Propaganda-like material in the professional literature hides controversy by bold assertions such as "Social anxiety is a mental disorder," ignoring well-argued alternative views. Authors who promote use of Motivational Interviewing based on Prochraska and DiClemente's Stages of Change model, rarely note the critique of this model by Littell and Girvin (2002), arguing that there is no evidence for the validity of this model. Articles describing multisystemic family therapy rarely cite Littell, Popa, and Forsythe's (2005) systematic review illustrating that MST is no more effective than other interventions. Ignoring or promoting distorted views of well-argued alternatives and related evidence saves the time needed to understand other views and to critically appraise related evidence. Ignoring or misrepresenting the views of disliked perspectives and hiding evidence of their effectiveness and overemphasizing negative evidence are classic propaganda ploys.

Assumption of Uncritical, Incompetent, Lazy Consumers

Like many propagandists, Hitler among them, advertisers often had (and have) a jaded view of the average person's competence. "Just as actors had to create illusions and employ deceptions in order to give the audience the enjoyment it expected, so advertising agents had to excel in strategies of manipulation in order to carry out their social function" (Marchand, 1985, p. 48). Reviews of the professional literature show alarming gaps between what is claimed and research methods used. Such a plethora of false claims could not be possible if readers (and editors and reviewers) were well trained in critical appraisal and were motivated to use these skills. Lapses in evidentiary quality of content in professional sources shows that just as advertisers judge their audiences as incompetent, lazy, and gullible, so too do many authors of material forwarding bogus claims. Or, they may assume that reviewers, readers and editors are mainly interested in palaver—material that appears credible. Readers, unless well educated in critical thinking skills, are easily hoodwinked by vague, pseudoscientific discourse in the professional literature, professional education programs, and the media. Concerns about the poor quality of professional training programs in psychology, has led to calls for creating new venues offering a more rigorous professional education (e.g., McFall, 1991).

Exaggerate Miniscule Differences

Much advertising exaggerates differences between their product, for example, an underarm deodorant, and others in order to sell a particular product. Advertisements must give the impression that one product is better than all its competitors. Otherwise people may not buy that brand. In reality, there may be no difference except in name and claims and propaganda appeals used. What is minor or nonexistent is presented as major and vital. This tendency can also be seen in the professional literature. By hiding (not mentioning) previous published work describing content emphasized in an article, I can make my idea seem new. Endless new variations of hundreds of psychotherapeutic and medical remedies are promoted as new discoveries that "work."

Rely on Fallacies and Flawed Arguments

Advertisements make use of informal fallacies such as glittering generalizations, begging the question, and bandwagon appeals. This can also be seen in the professional literature as illustrated by reviews of research revealing little relationship between conclusions and methods used to reach them (e.g., Ionnides, 2005a & b). We are encouraged to hop on the bandwagon of what is promoted as good, desirable, effective, to join the latest fad, to follow the crowd. Perhaps the most egregious example is the International Consensus Statement regarding ADHD signed by 186 people (Barkley et al., 2002), as if consensus is equivalent to accuracy. Instead of encouraging critical inquiry, methods are used that discourage probing questions such as bold assertions (simply asserting what must be argued) and appeal to consensus.

Take Advantage of Transfer Effects

Transfer effects are one of seven propaganda methods emphasized by the Institute of Propaganda Analysis as described in chapter 4. Slogans, illustrations, and photographs are used to create associations between views promoted and positive images (transfer effects). Using images and slogans that attach emotional reactions to a product or view promoted is key to successful advertising. Scott et al. (2004) consider imagery used in drug advertisements to be one of the most powerful weapons of drug promotion. Vague images, often of an erotic nature, are used in pharmaceutical advertisements. There is a creative use of shadow to suggest certain effects. (See Figure 9.3.) Uninformative brain images in professional articles encourage unwarranted belief in content in the accompanying text as demonstrated by McCabe and Castel (2008). Posed photographs were used to lend credibility to the diagnosis of hysteria as illustrated by Didi-Huberman's (2003) description of photographic images of women of the Salpetriere in Paris.

Repetition

In both advertising and the professional literature, certain themes, topics, and values are repeated. Repetition is a key propaganda strategy. Marchand (1985) suggests that frequently repeated media images and ideas "establish broad frames of reference, define the boundaries of public discussion, and determine relevant factors in a situation" (p. xx). So too in the professional literature, certain themes are emphasized and claims made repeatedly, some over a long period.

> There is monumental literature that takes as a given that ADHD is a neurobiological condition and starts from there to talk about different forms of treatment. Once you have many thousands of articles published about something how can it possibly make sense for someone to stand up and say 'this is not an entity'? I want to emphasize that I quite clearly acknowledge that there are children who are very compromised because of difficulties with impulsiveness, attention and activity. I am not saying that these children are not suffering or are not worthy of attention. I am saying that, as a disorder, ADHD is a spurious entity (Jureidini, 2001, p. 119). (Quoted in Wadham, undated, p. 139)

Consider repetition that social anxiety is a psychiatric disorder in reports of randomized controlled trials. Well-argued alternative views are typically ignored (Gambrill & Reiman, 2009). Consider also repetition in the professional literature of the view that our troubles are caused by chemical imbalances in the brain that can be cured by drugs with no critiques of this view (Moncrieff, 2008).

Emphasize the New

Marchand (1985) suggested that advertisements have a bias toward the new and against the old and old fashioned. A key purpose of the professional literature, especially for clinicians, is to give readers a sense of keeping up-to-date and being informed. Boyle (2002) argues that empirical discourse in professional sources "represents research and practice as objective, and thus reasonable" (p. 209) and that an illusion of progress is created by appeals to new technology (neuroscience).

Create an Illusion of Credibility and Sincerity

Creating an illusion of credibility is vital to successful ads, as well as successful professional discourse. Authors must use the "good" words and phrases such as "progress," "empowerment," and "culturally competent" and avoid the bad words such as "modest correlation" and "not significant" (Rank, 1984). They must use the good images (of brains) and avoid the bad images (charts showing flaws in assumed correlations, e.g., Vul et al., 2009). Graphs and tables may be used to distort rather than to accurately describe as so well described by Tufte (2006). Sincerity and credibility are equated with use of "proper" language and protestations of good intentions ("we care") in place of evidence. Advertisements in the guise of professional discourse can only flourish under certain circumstances, those in which credibility (palaver) is valued over discovering what is true and what is false—circumstances in which critical appraisal is not valued. As Phillips (1992) has noted, credibility is not a valuable guide as to what is true or false. In exploring this issue, we must consider all players and the symbiotic relationships among them—publishers, authors, reviewers, editors, journalists, clients, patients, and readers.

Appeal to Popular Grand Narratives/Values/Myths

Similarities between advertising strategies and aims and those of the professional literature include appealing to and promoting popular views such as the culture of therapy in which we live (Illouz, 2008) and use of medication to create happiness and diminish distress. Parables used appeal to these grand narratives.

BUT CAN A STORY EVER BE COMPLETE?

Can a professional publication ever tell the whole truth and nothing but the truth? And, who is to say? Given the complexity of life including the many different realities and views of different players and the challenges of accurate communication, perhaps a story can never be complete. The story will typically be incomplete in terms of the many twists and turns made on the way to a question and the method used to investigate this, mainly as a result of journal requirements of brevity. As many have pointed out, this gives those who do not engage in the messy business of research the false idea of a lock step march to the final product, leaving out all the uncertainties and related decisions. But are some accounts more "truthful" (transparent) and complete than others? Consider an author's description of their methodology. From the reader's, reviewer's, and editor's perspectives, a truthful description is vital to identify biases that may limit conclusions that can be drawn. This information allows us to make up our minds for ourselves, a hallmark of critical thinking—thinking things out for ourselves. The same applies to data analysis. Researchers are obligated to tell the truth, for example, to clearly and accurately describe the statistical tests they used and to use these appropriately (e.g., see Vul et al., 2009). They are obligated to accurately describe limitations in their research. They are not supposed to hide these. They are not supposed to engage in fraud, that is to "fake" what they did and what they found (e.g., see Rosenthal, 1994).

If authors accurately describe what they did, reviewers and readers may catch problems that researchers overlooked, which is how science works—self-correction. The questions in chapter 14 can be used to review different kinds of research. Readers of professional journals should be given sufficient information so they can make up their own minds. (See DUETS website <http://www.library.nhs.uk/duets>.)

> "Few presenters are saintly enough to provide their audience with competing explanations, contrary evidence, or an accounting of the full pool of evidence tapped to construct the presentation. But thoughtful presenters might at least privately test their analysis: *Has evidence been filtered or culled in a biased manner? Do the findings grow from evidence or from evidence selection? Would the findings survive the scrutiny of a skeptic or investigator of research fraud? What would Richard Feynman think?* Such questions may help presenters get it right before enthusiasm for their own work takes over. To avoid being fooled, consumers of presentations must ask these questions as well.
>
> It is idle, however, for skeptics to claim that the evidence presented in a report has been selected. Of course there is more evidence than that published. The key issue is whether evidence selection has compromised the true account—if we only knew what it was—of the underlying data. (Tufte, 2006, p. 144)

EBP emphasizes transparency—revealing uncertainties about what is done to what effect, rather than distorting or hiding the results of practice and policies. Getting as close to the truth as possible (about what was done and what was found), is an obligation of authors (and editors and reviewers) to readers, especially in professional journals in which what is read and acted on may have life affecting consequences. It is not ethical to hide lack of evidence for claims. Omitting descriptions of limitations of research methodology and making inflated claims of knowledge or of ignorance, are deceptions. It is not ethical to misrepresent the evidentiary status of a claim and to hide well-argued alternative views. To do so represents propaganda rather than science. The phrase "it's not for me to say," as in the song, should guide authors to include material that allows readers to accurately appraise the accuracy of claims made. They should honor Grices's maxims described in chapter 12.

SUMMARY

There is a troubling overlap in the characteristics of advertisements and discourse in professional venues. Both are designed to integrate us into our society (or profession) and a certain role within it. Both advertisements and content in the professional literature distort reality by selective presentation of data to forward a certain view and related product and use similar techniques to do so. Similar goals and strategies are evident in both. Certainly they are not reflected equally in any given product but overall, there are striking similarities. Both create an illusion of knowledge and satisfaction of valued goals. We see our usual propaganda ploys—bold assertions including inflated claims about "what we know," and "what works" or what is done, hiding context such as well-argued alternative views, distorting facts and figures, and appeals to authority such as uncritical documentation (attaching citations to a claim without any description of what these citations contain). Weasel terms such as "it is well known that..." "It is widely accepted that..." (when indeed there is controversy) are used in lieu of arguments. The ad-like character of much material in the professional literature (articles, chapters and texts), in tandem with common biases to which we are subject such as overconfidence and confirmation biases, increase the likelihood that we will be bamboozled. For example, our belief in a view may result in missing or dismissing methodological limitations in studies favorable to this view, especially when they are minimized or ignored by authors. This contributes to an *illusion of learning*—an illusion of knowledge acquisition and dissemination. If material includes well-reasoned arguments, including related counter-evidence, as well as accurate description of well-argued alternative views and related evidence, this would not be so. However, all too often, content in the professional literature does not reflect these characteristics.

Illusionists of professional discourse inhabit our colleges, research centers (including those owned by large advertising companies) and universities. They include those who prepare articles for journals and books for publishers, including ghostwriters hired by pharmaceutical companies to prepare articles published under the names of well-known academics. They are skilled in use of propaganda strategies such as distracting our attention from the lack of evidence for claims by name dropping (e.g., "as Freud said"), bogus citations (they contain no support for the related claim), and censorship of well-argued competing views. These skills may be polished in graduate school. Being on the lookout for propaganda in the professional literature is especially important since our guard may be down, perhaps because a journal uses peer review; readers may not be aware of problems with peer review. But, isn't being truthful what academics and researchers get paid for—to be honest brokers of knowledge and ignorance? Can't we trust the "experts"? The answer is no. There seems to be a negative correlation between the status of a profession and the tendency to publish advertisements disguised as research articles (marticles). That is, the lower the status, the more marticles appear as in social work and psychiatry compared to medicine. The old adage "Buyer beware" can be generalized to be critical of what you read, even in professional texts and journals.

10

Propagandistic Use of Language and Social Psychological Persuasion Strategies

Language provides the propagandist playpen. Language may mislead us because of carelessness, lack of/skill in writing and thinking, or deliberate intent to mislead on the part of a speaker or writer. Unless we are skilled in avoiding the misleading influence of words, our lives may be shaped by the words we use, see, and hear in ways that harm rather than help. Just as thought may corrupt language, language may corrupt thought (Orwell, 1958). Examples of ways in which language may influence our decisions can be seen in Table 10.1. "Weasel words" provide an illusion of argument or clarity. Examples include:

- "Many people say . . ." How many? Who says so? On what basis?
- "Some people argue that . . ." Who? On what basis?
- "Studies show . . ." What studies? How sound are they?
- "Expert suggests . . ." What experts? On what basis?
- "It is notable that . . ." On what basis is it notable?
- "Obviously . . ." How is it obvious? What is the evidence?

Weasel words give an illusion that something sound is being said when it is not or at least no supporting evidence is offered. Perverse uses of language are the subject of the famous essay by Orwell (1958), "Politics and the English Language." Complexities created by language have been discussed by philosophers such as Wittgenstein (1958) and are of concern in conversations between clients and professionals (Heritage & Olayman, 2010; Katz, 2002).[1] Language plays a vital role in the helping professions, for example, in interviews and in the professional literature, offering abundant opportunities for the play of propaganda. Decisions are influenced by the manner in which clients and professionals talk to each other and there is much room for misunderstandings that may not be recognized, as well as for censorship, such as hiding alternatives. There are many sources of mis-communication, some intentional, some not, especially when the stakes are high and emotions intense as in life-threatening physical illness, scary feelings of detachment from reality, and loss of social support. Use of language is integral to decisions made during case conferences and in court presentations, as well as in interpretations of case records. Without an understanding of the use of language as a propaganda ploy, we may be influenced in many ways that have negative consequences.

Table 10.1 SOURCES OF ERRORS RELATED TO USE OF LANGUAGE

1. Assumption of one word, one meaning
2. The fallacy of composition
3. The fallacy of division
4. Use of vague terms
5. Shifting definitions of terms
6. Reification (acting as if an abstract concept actually exists)
7. Influence by semantic linkages and cuing effects
8. Predigested thinking
9. Confusing verbal and factual propositions
10. Use of pseudotechnical jargon (bafflegarb)
11. Misuse of speculation (assuming that what is can be discovered by merely thinking about a topic)
12. Conviction through repetition
13. Insistence on a specific definition that oversimplifies a situation
14. Influence through emotional words
15. Use of a confident manner and bold assertions
16. Judgments based on primacy effects
17. Newsspeak
18. Excessive verbiage
19. Misuse of labels
20. Confusion of different levels of abstraction
21. Confusion between descriptive and emotive uses of words
22. Careless use of language
23. Eloquence without clarity
24. Misleading or harmful metaphors

Lourenco (2001) argues that ignoring the misleading effects of words is responsible for fallacies such as illusions of explanations, reifications, and hasty generalizations. The *fallacy of the alchemist* refers to using vague terms and thinking that you have gained some knowledge about a topic. Drury (1976) refers to the vocabulary of psychiatry and the DSM as a "repository of 'fallacies of the alchemist'; simple presumptions are converted into fundamental truth" (cited in Lourenco, 2001, p. 90). The fallacy of Molière's doctor refers to pseudo-explanations, for example, saying a child has anti-social behavior and, when asked why, saying that he has an "anti-social personality." Misuses of citations (uncritical documentation) is another example (Gambrill & Gibbs, 2009)—references that provide little or no evidence for related claims. In such instances an *illusion of evidentiary status* is created (e.g., see Greenberg, 2009). Terms may be used in a deceptive way, for example, to convey choice when there is a lack of choice. One of the eleven unethical managed care practices every patient should know about (with an emphasis on mental health care) described by the National Coalition of Mental Health Professionals and Consumers (retrieved on December 18, 2008, from <http://www.thenationalcoalition.org>) is "using deceptive language."

Professional ethics emphasize giving patients accurate and straightforward information. Managed care, on the other hand, uses misleading language at every level. Companies which intentionally restrict choice call themselves names like "Choice Health" or "Options Health." . . . Cost cutting programs are called "quality improvement programs." Gatekeepers, hired to divert patients from treatment, are called "patient advocates."

The Role of Language in Constructing Reality

Many scholars have argued that language constructs our reality (e.g., Wittgenstein,1953). Borchers (2005) suggests that we "constantly use words to manage reality and the reality of others. Politicians, advertisers, and activists all seek to create reality for their audience members, maintain current beliefs, or transform cultural beliefs to better serve their interests" (p. 193).[2] When repeated scores or hundreds of times and promoted by "experts," both those seeking help and those hoping to offer it, many come to believe that the words they use reflect reality, when they do not. Think how many times a day do you hear bold assertions that various behaviors such as drinking alcohol are mental illnesses, just like physical illnesses such as diabetes. Metaphors (assuming mental illness is like a physical illness) are converted into received 'truths' after constant repetition. The term *dramatism* refers to the theory that we are motivated by language to act in certain ways. Kenneth Burke (1972) developed a critical technique called dramatism as a way of explaining motivation. He viewed language as a mode of symbolic action. He argued that language shapes behavior and is used strategically. For example, names influence our relationships with others. Language shapes who we are for or against. "The symbols persuaders use and how they use those symbols are important determinants in how successful they will be" (Borchers, 2005, p. 194).

Many authors suggested that the rise of language created fragmentation in our lives, a separation from everyday realities so that less and less, are we fully in the present. The present now may be staring into our Ipods and Twittering distant people. Such technologies remove us even more from "the present." Describing someone or some event decreases accuracy of subsequent efforts to identify an event (or face) (Meissner, Sporer, & Schooler, 2006). For example, people who were asked to describe a face after seeing it were worse at recognizing the same face later. People asked to describe a wine after drinking it were worse at recognizing the same wine later. This effect is called *verbal overshadowing*. Illouz (2008) suggests that the language of therapy has been responsible for a process of "verbal overshadowing."

> I would argue that culturally the therapeutic persuasion may have been responsible for a vast process of verbal overshadowing that makes linguistic self-introspection a substitute for nonverbal ways of functioning in social interactions. What I call a cultural process of verbal overshadowing is the broad process by which increasing verbality comes to interfere with decisions that require us to use our "intuition," "insight, or snap judgment." (p. 245)

She argues that we often do better without verbalizing what we are doing and why we are doing it. She suggests that this verbal overshadowing encourages a "cementifying of personality" and ignoring of situational factors that influence behavior. Perhaps this explains in part the ignoring of applied behavior analysis that attends to environmental contingencies (e.g. Thyer, 2005).

Functions of Language

Words are used to describe people and events, to persuade people, and to express evaluations. These many functions provide opportunities for influence by propaganda ploys. Understanding the different functions of language can help us to avoid such ploys. One function is description. Descriptions of clients, procedures used, and progress achieved is an integral part of clinical records. The aim of descriptive statements is to inform (for example, "Mr. Larkin has been hospitalized three times."). We can find out whether they are true or false. Vagueness may limit shared understandings of terms such as schizophrenia, bi-polar, co-dependent, glucose intolerant as discussed later in this chapter. A second function is persuading others to believe or act differently. Clients and patients seek to persuade professionals to provide certain services. Professionals attempt to persuade clients to act, think, or feel differently. They may do so in propagandistic ways such as hiding or misrepresenting options and hiding adverse effects of recommended procedures, or in a participatory way in which options are described, as well as their evidentiary status (Coulter, 2002). Freeman and Sweeney (2001) conducted a qualitative study investigating why general practitioners do not implement evidence. Participants included 19 physicians. They reported that:

> Doctors realized that the words they chose to present the evidence could have a strong influence on the patient's decision. They effectively limited the options while seeming to invite the patient to make the decision. The contributors framed these themes with phrases such as "It's how you put it over," and "It depends on how you feed information to people." The semantics then affect the way in which evidence is implemented by swaying the patient in a particular direction. . . . Some talked of 'selling' a particular view on clinical evidence . . . .
>
> The choice of words or the use of metaphors like "slanting" or "selling" were mechanisms the doctors used to influence patients to make a decision about their treatment that was consistent with what the doctor had decided was appropriate. Doctors would refer to "rat poison" when describing warfarin if they felt its use would be difficult or inappropriate, or describe pills as "having been shown to keep the heart young" when they wanted a patient to agree to treatment. (pp. 3–4)

A third function of language is purely expressive—to express some emotion or feeling or to create such a feeling without trying to influence future behavior. Other statements direct or guide us, as in "Call the parental stress hotline." Any one statement may serve several functions; not only may a speaker or writer have more than one purpose in mind, but the listener or reader may have more than one in mind which may or may not match those of the speaker. We use the context to interpret a speaker's or writer's purpose.[3] Language also has presymbolic functions, such as affirming social cohesion, as in "Isn't it a nice day?" Lack of understanding of this function may result in naive assumptions about the triviality of conversation as Hayakawa (1978) notes in his "Advice to the Literal-Minded" (p. 85). Only if we understand the motive behind a sentence may we translate it correctly. Misunderstanding motives also plays into the propagandist's hands. That is, we may assume a person's true intent is to help us to make an informed decision when, in reality, it is to sell a product that is not in our best interests to use.

Different Levels of Abstraction

Words differ in their level of abstraction as illustrated in Hayakawa's (1978) abstraction ladder (p. 155). At the lowest level are definitions in extensional terms. The *extensional meaning* of a word refers to what it points to in the physical world. It is what the word stands for. A psychiatrist could point to the disheveled clothes of an elderly man admitted to an emergency psychiatry unit or to the behavior of "pushing" by a nurse. Many words have no extensional meaning; there is nothing we can point to. Technologies such as MRIs, CAT scans, and microscopies allow us to "see" things that are not observable to the naked eye. However, often there are differences of opinions about what is seen and we may not even see what occurred. (See Chabris & Simons, 2009.) In *operational definitions,* a rigorous attempt is made to exclude nonextensional meaning, as in the definition of length in terms of the operations by which it is measured. The *intentional meaning* of a word refers to what is connoted or suggested. Labels and concepts such as "schizophrenia," "mental disorder," "bi-polar," and "personality disorder" are abstract terms used in varied ways including description and explanation. Reactions to terms such as "sociopath" or "welfare recipient" may go far beyond the extensional meaning of these terms without our recognizing that this is happening. We may act toward people in accord with the affective (emotional) reactions associated with labels such as "elderly client" or "psychotic." *Definitions* describe our linguistic habits. They are statements about how language is used. The higher the level of abstraction, the less the utility of referring to a dictionary definition to capture meaning, especially intentional meaning. Not recognizing that words differ in level of abstraction increases our vulnerability to propaganda and may create confusion and needless arguments.

Propaganda Ploys Related to Language

Understanding the different functions of language and different levels of abstraction can be of value in avoiding influence by propaganda ploys using language. For example, propaganda may take advantage of our lack of attention to different levels of abstraction and failure to recognize emotive use of language. The list of propaganda ploys related to use of language described in this chapter together with suggested remedies is by no means exhaustive, and readers are referred to other sources for greater detail (e.g., Halpern, 2003; Hayakawa, 1978; Thouless, 1974). Carelessness may be responsible for foggy writing and speaking—not taking the time and thought to clearly state inferences and reasons for them. On the other hand, lack of clarity may be deliberately used to mislead us, as so well described by George Orwell (1958).

Predigested Thinking: Oversimplifications

This term refers to the tendency to oversimplify complex topics, issues, or views into simple trivializing statements that distort content, such as describing Freudian theory as reducing everything to sex, or describing behaviorists as believing in mechanistic stimulus-response connections. Simplistic accounts misrepresent or ignore important discoverable interactions among variables and create an illusion of explanation and understanding that may result in inaccurate accounts of client/patient distress. Predigested thinking obscures complexities and so may result in unsound decisions. This kind of thinking is encouraged by work pressures, as well as individual characteristics such as indifference, lack of information, and idleness, and the fact that it often offers a practical guide. It is a popular propaganda ploy facilitated by cognitive biases (see chapter 11). The tendency to simplify complex matters may help to account for ignoring the undistributed middle (substituting all for some) and the readiness to accept an unwarranted extension of a position. Stereotyping is a form of predigested (oversimplified) thinking.

A popular oversimplification promoted by Big Pharma is the assertion that a wide variety of behaviors, thoughts, and/or feelings are caused by "chemical imbalances in the brain" and that medication can solve related concerns (Moncrieff, 2008). The brain is very complex. Compared with what there is "to know"; we know little, contrary to inflated claims of knowledge regarding what "We have found" (e.g., Vul et al., 2009). What is a "chemical imbalance"? How do different chemicals interact? Has the influence of medications on the brain been considered (Moncrieff & Cohen, 2006)? Referring to hundreds of different behaviors, feelings, and thoughts as "mental disorders" (diseases) ignores the continuous nature of related behaviors and feelings such as drinking alcohol or anxiety. Bold assertions often reflect oversimplifications, which if acted on, may result in avoidable errors and impede further inquiry. Varieties of oversimplification include the following:

- Seeing different entities as more similar than they actually are
- Treating dynamic phenomena as static
- Assuming that some general principle accounts for all of a phenomenon
- Treating multidimensional phenomena as unidimensional or according to a subset of the dimensions.
- Treating continuous variables as categorical.
- Treating highly interconnected concepts as separable
- Treating the whole as merely the sum of its parts (Woods & Cook, 1999, p. 152, based on Feltovich, Spiro, & Coulson, 1993)

Analogies used to simplify complex phenomena may result in ignoring the complexity of concerns such as hallucinations or depression. Describing depression as a "mental disorder" and assuming that related complaints are caused by a brain disease and prescribing medication, ignores the role of environmental causes that if changed, would decrease related distressing reactions (and indeed, alter related brain characteristics) (Luyten et al., 2006) (See also discussion of metaphors.)

Another example of an oversimplification is reflected in the answer of a doctoral student in a discussion of twin studies: "We know the environment was the same because the twins were raised in the same home." Is it the same home for each individual? Research suggests that it is not, that even twins have different environments. We are often guilty of reducing an answer to a simple (uninformative) formula, such as "rapists will rape again." A practitioner who does not believe that evaluation of client progress can be done in a meaningful way may say, "Evaluation is mechanistic," "It trivializes concerns"; or "It does not represent the true complexity of human problems." This view overlooks the fact that evaluation can be carried out in an irrelevant or relevant manner. Another example is the statement "a scientific approach to clinical questions offers trivial answers." What is the meaning of "a scientific approach" here? What is a "trivial answer"?

The emotional appeal of predigested thinking (it often has a slogan quality) and the fact that it may provide a practical guide for daily life, make it difficult to detect or challenge. For example, you may object to the oversimplistic presentation of Freudian theory that "Everything is related to sex." The other person may protest that the objections raised are too "learned," that "nothing will convince him that art, romantic love, and religion are just sex, which is generally agreed by everybody to be the teaching of Freud" (Thouless, 1974, p. 161). Note the reaffirmation of the original position (begging the question) and the appeal to consensus. As Thouless notes, if this is a discussion with other people, the user of predigested thinking can usually rely on "having their sympathy, for his opponent will seem to be a person trying to make himself out to be too clever and who makes serious argument impossible by throwing doubt on what everyone knows to be true" (pp. 161–62). The only recourse here may be to state an argument so clearly that the inadequacies of a position are quite obvious. Negative reactions may be avoided by posing questions in a tactful manner (e.g., "Could it be . . .?") and by emphasizing common interests, such as discovering accurate answers. Thouless (1974) suggests that we can guard against predigested thinking by avoiding mental idleness, which encourages us "to accept mental food well below the limits of our digestion" (p. 164). The remedy is to consider the actual complexity of the issue at hand *as needed*, to arrive at well-reasoned decisions. Recognizing complexities may increase tolerance for other positions.

Missing Language (Censorship)

We are less likely to make sound decisions if we do not have access to relevant information. Propagandists hide information that sheds a negative light on views and products they promote (e.g., beliefs, deodorant, lobotomy, medication). Missing language is the most deceptive language ruse. Hundreds of terms for alleged negative states ("disorders") are in use compared to few terms for positive states of being. This is a prime example of missing language. Political and economic aims increase the likelihood that stratagems will be used such as hiding the questionable effectiveness of services. The goal of protecting and expanding professional turf encourages presenting one's own profession in a uniquely favorable light in comparison with other professions. Readers may not be informed about negative findings and well-argued alternative views.[4] Too seldom are controversial issues discussed.

Misleading Use of Scientific Discourse

Boyle (2002) gives many examples of how the discourse of science is used to create a false impression of objectivity and rigor, for example, by using specialized terminology that is often unfamiliar to lay readers, as well as to many in the mental health profession. She notes that terms are often misused (e.g., "base rate") in a manner that favors the assumption that schizophrenia exists as a unique entity, that it is a "mental disorder," and that it is biochemical in origin. Questionable appeals to the language of neuroscience are rife. She, as well as Houts (2002), suggests that narratives of scientific progress are used to imply that advances are being made when they are not. For example, even though biochemical correlates have not yet been discovered, claims are made that they soon will be. She points out that the language of medicine is also appealed to and that this combines with the language of science in a potent rhetorical mix to give illusions of objectivity, knowledge, and progress. Our tendency to rely on "experts," and to believe that if there is a word, it refers to something in the real world (reification), combines with other factors, such as lack of time or interest in digging deeper, a desire to understand ourselves and others with little effort, ridding ourselves of troubling significant others via psychiatric intervention, and an interest in avoiding responsibility for our behavior or troubles by attributing them to a mental disorder. This is a powerful mix. (See also critiques of other psychiatric labels such as ADHD, e.g., Diller, 2006.)

Pseudotechnical Jargon/Bafflegarb

Jargon can be useful in communicating in an efficient manner if listeners (or readers) share the same meaning of technical terms and if the jargon used is informative (contributes to making an informed decision). However, jargon may be used to conceal ignorance and "impress the innocent" (Rycroft, 1973, p. xi; Tavris, 2000). Excessive wordiness may make it impossible to ferret out the nature of an argument. Consider the earlier discussion of misleading oversimplifications such as claims that problems are due to "chemical imbalances in the brain." An economic incentive may encourage obscure writing. Highly specialized jargon in the legal profession increases the need to hire lawyers who can understand it. Physicians use the word "nulliparious" to refer to women who have never had a child. Technical jargon can be used to squelch critical questions. Jargon in psychiatry often hides conceptual problems with scientific sounding words such as "schizophrenia," "parasomnia," and "schizotypal personality disorder" (Boyle, 2002; Houts, 2002). We tend to be impressed with things we cannot understand. Professors rated journals that were hard to read as more prestigious than journals that were easier to read (Armstrong, 1980). It is possible that more prestigious journals discuss more complex subjects that require more difficult language. This possibility was tested in a classic study by Armstrong (1980). Portions of management journals were rewritten to increase readability; unnecessary words were eliminated, easy words were substituted for difficult ones and sentences were broken into shorter ones. A sample of 32 management professors were asked to rate as easy or difficult versions of four such passages and also rate them on a scale of "competence" ranging from 1 to 7. They knew neither the name of the journal nor the name of the author. Versions that were easier to read were considered to reflect less competent research than were the more difficult passages.

Obscurity may be desirable in some circumstances, as when exploring possibilities. However, it is often used as a propaganda ploy to forward special interests (inflated claims of knowledge) and to hide conceptual and methodological deficiencies. Examples of pseudotechnical jargon include *psychic deficiencies, structural frame of reference,* and *generational dysfunctions.* The proliferation of terms adds to pseudojargon in psychotherapy.[5] Who has not suffered from "bureaucratese"—turgid unnecessarily complex descriptions that yield only to the most persistent. (See discussion of palaver in chapter 4.) Examples include "mumblistic" (planned mumbling) and "profundicating" (translating simple concepts into obscure jargon) (Boren, 1972). The remedy is to simplify and clarify.[6] The potential for obscure terms to become clear can be explored by asking questions such as "What do you mean by that?" "Can you give me an example?" Asking such questions when reading case records and practice-related literature is a valuable rule of thumb.

Obscure terms often remain unquestioned because of worries that the questioner will look ignorant, stupid, "difficult," or as having a psychiatric disorder (e.g., borderline personality). Indeed, numerous studies of client–professional interaction show that this is a real possibility (see Katz, 2002). Research regarding raising questions that influence the quality of care clients receive shows that silence often reigns because of fear of negative consequences (e.g., Henriksen & Dayton, 2006; Tangirala & Ramanujam, 2008). You should consider the risks of lack of clarification (a poor decision), as well as the risks of revealing a lack of knowledge or of offending someone. Codes of ethics obligate professionals to raise vital questions and can be appealed to.

Writers and speakers should clarify their terms, bearing in mind appropriate levels of abstraction, especially when life-affecting decisions are involved. If they do not, it may be because they cannot or because doing so would reveal intent to persuade via propaganda ploys such as glittering generalizations (e.g., "Empowerment is good") or hiding alternatives (less invasive but equally accurate diagnostic options). They may have a different goal in a dialogue than your goal. (See chapter 12.) If arriving at well-reasoned decisions is the goal, participants should be thankful that someone cares enough to want to understand options and that lack of clarity is discovered. However, many professionals are not open to questions. "The great enemy of clear language is insincerity. When there is a gap between one's real and one's declared aims, one turns as it were instinctively to long words and exhausted idioms like a cuttlefish squirting out ink" (Orwell, 1958, p. 142). Professionals may become defensive and try to put you down for asking questions, using their prestige (MD) and related jargon to do so. They may share Humpty Dumpty's attitude: "When I use a word Humpty Dumpty said in a rather scornful tone, it means just what I choose it to mean neither more nor less. The question is, said Alice, whether you *can* make words mean so many different things. The question is, said Humpty Dumpty, who is to be master, that's all" (Carroll, [1871] 1946, p. 229). A question could be asked in such a straightforward manner that if the person still cannot understand it, his own lack of astuteness is revealed (Thouless, 1974).

Use of Emotional or Buzz Words or Images

Persuading people to act is a common aim in many kinds of discourse, including content in professional venues. This is often accomplished through use of emotive language. Aristotle's emotional appeals can be seen in Table 10.2. Professionals, as

Table 10.2 ARISTOTLE'S EMOTIONAL APPEALS

Emotion	Definition	Appeal
Anger	Desire for retaliation because of a slight directed, without justification, against oneself or others.	"We cannot let terrorists inflict their will upon innocent victims around the world."
Calmness	A settling down and quieting of anger.	"Now is not the time to harbor feelings of anger against each other; now is the time to come together as a united party to win the general election."
Fear	A sort of agitation derived from the imagination of a future destructive or painful evil.	"Purchasing a cellular telephone is good insurance against being stranded in your car in a winter snowstorm."
Shame	A class of evils that brings a person into disrespect.	"Your children deserve the best. Don't settle for anything less than the nutrition of Gerber goods."
Pity	A pain that happens to one who does not deserve it.	"Help the less fortunate in our city by donating to the local food bank."
Envy	Distress at apparent success on the part of one's peers.	"Nothing says style and success like a Lincoln Navigator."

SOURCE: T. A. Borchers (2005). *Persuasion in the media age* (2nd Ed.) (p. 309). New York: McGraw Hill. With permission of The McGraw Hill Companies.

well as advertisers and politicians, make use of emotional words and images to forward their goals as illustrated in the letter to the editor, *NASW News*:

Example	Comments
The conspiracy of silence continues to state implicitly that social workers because of their training and clinical expertise, cannot possibly be impaired by alcohol and drug abuse. As long as this conspiracy exists, impaired social workers will be afraid to seek help and to come out into the open about their addiction, just as I am ("Letter to the Editor," 1986, p. 15).	The term "conspiracy" is pejorative, as is "impaired." No evidence is offered that there is a "conspiracy of silence," or for the assumption that the "conspiracy" stops social workers from disclosing their "addiction." No evidence is offered for the claim that people assume that social workers "cannot have a substance abuse problem because of their training and expertise." And it is assumed that substance abuse is "an addiction."

We use positive terms for views we favor and negative ones to views we dislike (Rank, 1984). Emotional terms are rife in the turf battles between psychologists and psychiatrists. Consider the opening sentence in an article in the *Psychiatric Times*: "Clinical psychology is in a war for survival against American psychiatry" (Buie, 1987, p. 25). Our emotions offer rapid, often automatic, information linked to fight or flight reactions. Related reactions influence our decisions and how we respond to new material or if we seek out certain material (Slovic, Finucane, Peters, & MacGregor, 2002). Both our emotions and perceptions may precede our thoughts. Thus, cues may occur without our awareness that affect behavior (Gilovich & Griffin, 2002). These automatic perceptions and associative responses comprise two of the three processes for making judgments and contribute to the effectiveness of propaganda ploys as described in chapter 4. Confusing factual and emotional use of words makes us easy prey for propagandists. Distinguishing between the emotive and informative uses of language is important in avoiding misleading influences. The use of emotionally toned words is not always dysfunctional; however, in the context of trying to make correct inferences, such words may interfere with making well-reasoned decisions. Emotional reactions that may influence decisions can be coaxed out by exploring reactions to terms such *developmentally disabled youth*.

Metaphors

Proverbs, similes, analogies, or metaphors are used to persuade via emotional effects and related associations. (Table 10.3.) Metaphors work by transferring associations from one idea to another. Sarbin (1967) suggests that the first recorded use of the metaphor of "mental illness" for physical illness was by a mother superior who described a sister to an official of the inquisition at the door to arrest the nun, as if "she were mentally sick." Use of a metaphor increases a persuader's credibility (Sopory & Dillard, 2002). Although they may be of value in discovering how to solve a problem, metaphors such as the "war on drugs" may obscure rather than clarify an

Table 10.3 METAPHORS FOR CHANGE

Physical/Chemical Metaphors (Fix and Rebuild)

Machine	Fix the problem, Re-engineer
Travel	Move to a new place, Turnaround
Construction	Build something new, Restructure
Chemical	Catalyze, Mix, Compound, Crystallize

Biological/Medical Metaphors (Care and Growth)

Agricultural	Grow, Regenerate, Bear fruit, Harvest
Medical	Care, Inoculate, Cut, Exercise

Psychological/Spiritual Metaphors (Rebirth, Revitalization)

Psychological	Provide insight, Change mental models
Spiritual	Convert, Liberate, Create, Transform

Sociological Metaphors (Regroup, Reorganize)

Change roles and norms, Change culture

SOURCE: In E. H. Schein (1998). *Process consultation revisited: Building the helping relationship* (p. 57). Reading, MA: Addison Wesley. With permission of Pearson Education.

issue and potential solutions (MacCoun & Reuter, 2001). They may lead to faulty attributions and harmful practices and policies. Metaphors may create a feeling of understanding without an accompanying increase in real understanding. Consider the misleading metaphor used to promote AndroGel. (See also Figure 10.1.)

An advertisement for AndroGel from a recent issue of *Clinical Endocrinology* represents another way in which testosterone is framed to physicians and their male patients. The advertisement depicts a gas gauge with the arrow pointing to Empty. The text states, 'Low sex drive? Fatigued? Depressed mood. These could be indicators that your testosterone is running on empty.' Here, testosterone is

Figure 10.1. Ad for AndroGel.
SOURCE: Web MD Magazine: May 2009, after p. 29.

depicted as fuel that can be used up; the male body does not naturally replace the material essential to sustaining its gender. Playing on the body-as-machine metaphor, with the brightly covered dial illustrating two poles, Empty and Full, the advertisement suggests that men can simply "fill up" with testosterone supplementation to regain sex drive, energy, and optimism—essentially masculine qualities. Testosterone supplementation is promoted as something that many men will need as part of the regular maintenance of their bodies. Instead of being depicted as a rare condition, andropause emerges as a mundane, kind of typical, and predictable aspect of the daily life (and bodies) of men. (Conrad, 2007, p. 33)

Professionals who do not believe that policies and practices can be evaluated may refer to such efforts as "mechanistic" and argue that evaluation entails treating people like machines.[7]

Euphemisms

This term refers to use of words that are supposed to be less distasteful or offensive than others, often in order to hide what is actually going on. Consider this example from the National Coalition of Mental Health Professionals and Consumers (retrieved on December 20, 2008, from <http://www.thenational coalition.org>, p. 2).

> Professional ethics emphasize giving patients accurate and straightforward information. Managed care on the other hand uses misleading language at every level. Companies which intentionally restrict choice call themselves names like "Choice Health" or "Options Health." Companies who are hired to restrict access to treatment call themselves a name like "Access Health." Cost cutting programs are called "quality improvement programs." Gatekeepers, hired to divert patients from treatment, are called "patient advocates." Such misleading language does not belong in health care.

Perhaps the most common euphemism in the helping profession is calling enforced incarceration "treatment" for the benefit of the client.

Naming

Who has the power to name often wins the propaganda game. Many writers have discussed the magical quality of words. Burke (1966) suggests that words reflect attitudes and accompanying emotional reactions toward events, objects, and people, attitudes and emotions that we may not even be aware that we have. Whoever has the power to name often controls attitudes and actions. Stigmatizing labels are often applied to clients, which have few if any implications for selection of treatment methods (see discussion of labeling in chapter 5). Naming hundreds of everyday behaviors and/or feelings (or their lack) as "mental illnesses" in need of treatment influences our feelings and attitudes toward the people so labeled. (See, e.g., Verhaeghe, Bracke, & Christians, 2010.) Calling these "mental illnesses" transfers our associations with physical illness onto what are now labeled "mental illnesses" as Szasz (1961, 1994) has long argued in his discussion of the rhetorical nature of such assumptions. Labels are often used in ad hominem arguments—attacking or praising the person rather than addressing his or her argument. Labels are one kind of good/bad words we use to persuade others via emotional reasoning. Consider words such as "prostitute," "racist." Reactions to such terms may stray far beyond the extensional meaning of these terms without our awareness that this is happening. Such extensions may have stigmatizing effects on those labeled and result in unwanted consequences such as coerced intervention.

Labels may be deliberately misused to forward a view, hiding the fact that a term is misused. The term "evidence-based practice" is often used to describe practices that do not reflect the process and philosophy of evidence-informed decision making as described in original sources (Gambrill, 2006). Practices described as "best" may not be "best" (e.g., Gandhi et al., 2007; Gorman & Huber, 2009). A label such as *behavior modification* may be used inaccurately to describe a program that is just the opposite of what a behavioral program would be like.

The Assumption of One Word, One Meaning

Words have different meanings in different contexts. As Hayakawa (1978) has bluntly put it, "Ignoring of contexts in any act of interpretation is at best a stupid practice. At its worst, it can be a vicious practice" (p. 56) as when a sentence is taken out of context. Differences that exist in the world may not be reflected in different use of words, or differences in language may not correspond to variations in the world. Here too, propagandists take advantage of related confusions. Misunderstandings arise when different uses of a word are mistaken for different opinions about a topic of discussion. "Unless people mean the same thing when they talk to each other, accurate communication is impossible" (Feinstein, 1967, p. 313). Two people discussing "addiction" may not have the same definition of this term and a muddled discussion may result. One way to avoid this is to define key terms. Vague terms such as *probable* and *unlikely* are often used which have a wide range of meaning to different people as discussed in the next section. Definition of terms such as *panic reaction* or *dementia* may be shared initially but change over time or diverge as a discussion proceeds. To avoid confusion it is important to check how key concepts are being used. Such questions are never inappropriate in a dialogue in which inquiry is the goal. (See chapter 12.)

Use of Vague Terms

The vagueness of words and phrases such as "often," "high risk," "usually" and our different histories with given words provide much room for confusion. The study of vague quantitative terms such as "many," "few," "often" shows that such terms have very different meanings for different people (Pepper, 1981; Timmermans, 1996). Linguists have explored the frequency distributions of different meanings for vague terms (see Channell, 1994). Related studies of vague numerators show that they are all vague except terms such as "all" or "never." Different images may be associated with the same word for different people. Consider terms such as "alcohol abuse," "depression," and "anxiety." What do they mean? The topic of vagueness has been of interest in many areas including philosophy, psychology, linguistics, and literary criticism. It has even been explored in describing wine (Lehrer, 1975) cited in Channell, 1994, p. 14). There are many ways to be vague and many reasons to be vague. Some argue that vagueness serves an important function. Popper (1994) suggests that we should never be more precise than we need to be. Indeed, a precision that is not accurate can be used to deceive us that more knowledge is available than is the case as in pseudoscientific ploys making use of the discourse of science. Insisting on a specific definition of a term is inappropriate if this obscures the complexity of a situation. Vagueness of terms may be an advantage in the early stages of thinking about a topic to discover approaches that otherwise may not be considered.[8] Conversational uses of vague language include: (1) giving the right amount of information, (2) deliberately withholding information, (3) using language persuasively, (4) hiding a lack of specific information, (5) self-protection, (6) increasing power and being polite, and (7) creating informality and atmosphere. We may have information but not wish to share it. Vague terms are often used when no one knows the cause of events of interest.[9]

A key reason for vagueness is to increase the likelihood that people will be persuaded to act in ways favorable or of interest to the persuader. (See Table 10.4.) Vagueness is a favorite ploy in propaganda. Vagueness abounds in the helping professions and it serves many functions such as obscuring lack of sound argument for a position. Examples of vague terms include *uncommunicative, aggressive, immature, high risk, low risk, effective, harmful, drug dependency, dysfunction,* and *psychic deficiencies*. Weasel words such as those shown in the beginning of this chapter are remarkably effective and, if related content is repeated often enough, claims may come to be accepted as true even though there is no evidence that they are accurate.[10] Vague terms such as "most," "less," "more likely," "less likely," and "is associated with" are routinely used in articles in professional journals and in interactions between clients and professionals and require clarification. These are weasel words that serve questionable purposes such as obscuring ignorance, inflating or underestimating associations (correlations), and saving time (for the author) of finding out the actual correlation. Fashionable phrases or terms often become vague phrases over time such as *supportive therapy* and *case management*. If such terms are not clarified, different meanings may be used, none of which may reflect the real world. Two individuals with different meanings of "evidence-based practice" may make little progress in discussing related advantages and disadvantages because of different meanings of this term. Hackneyed phrases and clichés are often used by propagandists to create emotional reactions or to give an illusion of clarity. Clichés and unoriginal remarks highlight similarities (bonds) between people; that those present are on the 'right-side' (Hayakawa, 1978; Rank 1984a).

Words such as "likely" and "seldom" are used to express degrees of uncertainty. Channell (1994) suggests that "speakers use vague expressions when there is uncertainty about what they want to say" and "as a safeguard against being later shown to be wrong" (p. 188). Fuzzy descriptions of quantity may be used to present data in a way that favors a preferred argument but still meets academic norms of clarity in presenting data.

Table 10.4 Examples of Problematic Descriptions in the Methods Section of Papers

What the authors said	What they should have said (or should have done)	An example of
"We measured how often GPs ask patients whether they smoke"	"We looked at patients' medical records and counted how many had their smoking status recorded"	Assumption that medical records are 100% accurate.
"We measured how doctors treat low back pain"	"We measured what doctors say they do when faced with a patient with low back pain"	Assumption that what doctors say they do reflects what they actually do
"We compared a nicotine replacement patch with placebo"	"Subjects in the intervention group were asked to apply a patch containing 15 mg nicotine twice daily; those in the control group received identical looking patches"	Failure to state dose of drug or nature of placebo
"We asked 100 teenagers to participate in our survey of sexual attitudes"	"We approaches 147 white American teenagers aged 12–18 (85 male) at a summer camp; 100 of them (31 males) agreed to participate"	Failure to give sufficient information about subjects (note in this example the figures indicate a recruitment bias toward females).
"We randomized patients to either 'individual care plan' or 'usual care'"	"The intervention group were offered an individual care plan consisting of . . .; control patients were offered . . ."	Failure to give sufficient information about intervention (enough information should be given to allow the study to be repeated by other workers)
"To assess the value of an educational leaflet, we gave the intervention group a leaflet and a telephone helpline number. Controls received neither."	If the study is purely to assess the value of the leaflet, both groups should have got the helpline number.	Failure to treat groups equally apart from the specific intervention.
"We measured the use of vitamin C in the prevention of the common cold"	A systematic literature search would have found numerous previous studies on this subject.	Unoriginal study.

SOURCE: T. Greenhalgh (2006). *How to read a paper* (3rd Ed.) (p. 63). New York: Churchill-Livingstone. With permission of Elsevier.

Reification, Word Magic

Yet another propaganda ploy is to act as if a word corresponds to something real when it does (or may) not. (See also earlier discussion of different levels of abstraction and views of Kenneth Burke.) In reification, it is mistakenly assumed that a word corresponds to something real. But "the existence of a word does not guarantee the existence of any corresponding entity" (Fearnside & Holther, 1959, p. 68). Both the *one word–one meaning fallacy* and *reification* (the incorrect assumption that a term refers to a real world entity), reflect a confusion among or ignorance of, different levels of abstraction. The term *aggressive* used as a summary term for specific behaviors may also be used to refer to a related disposition believed to be responsible for these actions—an aggressive personality. This disposition then comes to be thought of as an attribute of the person (Bromley, 1977). Staats and Staats (1963) refer to such circular accounts as *pseudo-explanations*. Such accounts give an illusion of explanation, and, if delivered in a confident manner, may win the day. Noting the circularity of such terms reveals that no new information is offered. This will reveal that no evidence other than the behaviors noted support the inference of the abstraction of an aggressive personality. Such slight of hand may not matter if we are just passing time in causal conversation. But, if such a conversation takes place between a teacher and a child's parent (about the child), premature assumptions may be made such as assuming that the cause of the behaviors lies in the child (his alleged aggressive personality), cutting off a search for alternative possibilities, for example, that actions on the part of the teacher and his peers maintain related disliked behaviors.

The most common example of reification in clinical psychology, psychiatry, and social work is the metaphorical use of the term "mental illness" as akin to physical illness. In the uncritical use of the word "mental illness," we assume that an associated entity exists when no such evidence is provided. Related behaviors, thoughts, or feelings are real. However, the presumed cause ("mental illness") may not. In propagandistic use of language, the propagandist tries to create an illusion that behaviors or events of interest have been accounted for when they remain a mystery. In *Schizophrenia: A Scientific Delusion?* (2002), Mary Boyle describes how language used (such as repeated use of the word "clinical"), kinds of arguments presented, and benefits—both touted and actual—intersect to maintain an illusion that a coherent entity called schizophrenia exists and that the methods used to identify it are unproblematic. As Boyle (2002) notes, it is easy to believe that what is referred to by a word actually exists, particularly if authority figures such as psychiatrists and prestigious professional organizations repeatedly use the term and act as if it is unproblematic. Scores of books contain the word "schizophrenia" in the title. Thousands of articles contain this word, and we see it daily in the press. Surely "it" (as a construct) must exist. Boyle (2002) illustrates the problematic nature of terms such as "mental illness" and "mental disorder" on both methodological and conceptual grounds.

Questions (such as "What is a borderline personality?") often involve disputes about use of words as if they were questions of facts. Questions of fact cannot be settled by arguments over the use of words. The problem of how to use a word is different from the problem of what is a fact. Discussions of the meaning of "mental illness" are often conducted as if an independent objective cause has been discovered ("mental illness") when this assumption is in dispute. That is, the premise of "mental illness" is accepted as given, when it is questionable. What must be established by critical inquiry is presuming as fact, as in the fallacy of begging the question (see chapter 13). Noting the lack of objective criteria is helpful when there is confusion between verbal and factual propositions.

Influence of Semantic Linkages and Cuing Effects (Association/Transfer)

Influence by association (transfer of effects) is one of the seven propaganda strategies highlighted by the Institute of Propaganda Analysis described in chapter 4. If we think of one word, similar words may come to mind. (See <http://www.visualthesaurus.com>). Manufacturers of drugs select names for drugs, such as chemotherapies, to encourage sales. Abel and Glinert (2007) conducted an analysis of the sound symbolism of 60 frequently used cancer-related medications. Their results showed that the names of chemotherapy medications contained a high frequency of sounds associated with lightness, smallness, and fastness. The authors suggest that such associations may influence decisions made by patients regarding use of chemotherapy. They suggest that given that "recent research has shown that physicians often fail to communicate vital information about new medications to patients (Tarn et al., 2006), we suggest that, imbued with symbolic power, the names themselves—partly created by marketers (in designing trade names) and partly by providers (in adopting common usage names)—may be filling this gap" (p. 1867).

Associative links with "grand narratives" are an example of transfer effects. (See chapter 8.) Certain metaphors increase certain semantic cues. This is one reason they are so powerful. (See previous discussion of metaphors.) Association effects range from the subtle to the obvious. A familiar example is the tendency to think in terms of opposites such as good/bad or addicted/nonaddicted. Such thinking obscures the situational variability of behavior, as well as individual differences in behavior, feelings, or thoughts in a given context. Consider the term "addiction." Patterns of substance abuse vary widely. The description of a client as addicted is not very informative. This does not indicate what substances are used with what frequency, in what situations, nor offer any information about the functions served by ingestion of related substances (although within some practice perspectives all clients who are "addicted" are assumed to have similar personality dynamics, which purport to account for the addiction, and a description of the exact nature of the addiction may not be considered important). Decisions concerning degree of responsibility for an action differ depending on whether a person is the subject of the sentence as in: "Ellen's car hit the fireplug" compared to "The fireplug was hit by Ellen's car" (Loftus, 1979, 1980). (See also Loftus, 1997, 2004). Familiarity with the influence of semantic linkages and cuing effects may help you to avoid misleading effects. Statements can be rearranged to see if this yields different causal assumptions.

Use of Slogans/Synecdoches

Synecdoches refer to the representation of large amounts of information in a short representational bit. A part is selected to represent the whole. Predigested thinking in the form of slogans, such as "Support community care," are used to encourage actions. The history of the community mental health movement reveals that such slogans were common, despite minimal available community care for patients (Sedgwick, 1982). Slogans are easy to remember and so are readily available to influence us on an emotional level. Consider the following examples: "Be well," "Stay healthy," "Maximize your potential," "Proven effective," "Be the person you always wanted to be," "Find your true self." In *Why Superstition Won and Science Lost*, Burnham (1987) illustrates journalists' increasing use of fragmented facts presented out of context regarding scientific developments. These have been called "factoids." Short statements are increasingly valued and used in the media. Borchers (2005) suggests that "synoptic phrases *reinforce the communal bond between audience members and the persuader*. Consider the phrase 'life, liberty, and the pursuit of happiness' making certain guarantees about equality of opportunity in the United States" (p. 204). He suggests that we store persuasive events by these "capsule" bits. He reminds us that "a rhetorical vision can be built upon a few carefully crafted, memorable, fantasy themes" (p. 204). These may be connected to popular grand narratives such as "cure" and progress.

Misuse of Verbal Speculation

This refers to the use of "speculative thinking to solve problems which can only be solved by the observation and interpretation of facts" (Thouless, 1974, p. 78). Speculation is valuable in discovering new possibilities, but it does not offer information about whether these insights are correct. What is cannot be deduced from what ought to be nor can vague terms referring to behaviors or situations of interest be clarified simply by thinking about them. For example, if a client is described as a drug abuser and no information is provided about what this means, speculation will not be helpful. Facts gathered from some reliable and valid source are needed. Propagandists use a variety of ploys to block critical appraisal of speculations, including ad hominem arguments as described in chapter 13. They use pseudo-technical jargon to impress us with their erudition and our lack of it. Misuse of speculation is not without its effects, since what we think about influences what we attend to. Thus, a little unchecked speculation can be a dangerous thing. The philosophy and process of evidence-based practice encourages critical appraisal of claims that influence the quality of our lives.

Conviction Through Repetition

Repetition is a key propaganda strategy. Consider the title "Treatments that Work: The Gold Standard in Behavioral Intervention" (Nathan & Gorman, 2007). (Note that there is no question mark after "work.") The phrase "treatments that work" is repeated countless times in published sources including the professional literature. Readers think—surely this must be true, especially when prestigious publishing firms, such as Oxford University Press, touts the term. But do all these treatments "work"? And what does "work" mean? (See chapter 14.) Propagandists are aware that simply hearing, seeing, or thinking about a statement many times may increase belief in the statement. As Thouless (1974) notes, we tend to think that what goes through our mind must be important. Simply repeating a position increases the likelihood of its acceptance, especially if the statement is offered in a confident manner by a person of prestige and has a slogan quality that plays on our emotions. Results of a weak study may be repeated so many times in different sources (e.g., professional journals) that they (undeservedly) achieve the status of a law. Gelles (1982) calls this the *Woozle Effect* (p. 13). A willingness to challenge even cherished beliefs helps to combat this source of error. "If our examination of the facts leads to a conclusion which we find to be inconceivable, this need not be regarded as telling us anything about the facts, but only about the limits of our powers of conceiving" (Thouless, 1974, p. 80). Repeated affirmation, conviction, or the manner in which something is said do not provide evidence for claims. Conviction through repetition may be attempted in case conferences to influence group members. For example, a client may be continually referred to as mentally incompetent, when in fact no evidence has been offered. Pointing out the danger of repeating unsupported assertions may discourage such descriptions.

Repetitions of a statement are more effective if they are varied; we are less likely to discover that no reasons are provided as to why we should believe or act in a certain manner (Thouless, 1974). Consider the repetition in the media, professional journals, books, conferences, human service advertisements, and websites of the term "mental illness" and biomedical accounts of related behaviors. This biomedical view of problems dominates these many venues. Only the motivated and the skeptical will raise questions and seek out well-argued alternative views. The economic support of the American Psychiatric Association and billions spent on promotion of biomedical accounts of problems by "Big Pharma," daily primes exposure of the public to this medical view of behavior (Angell, 2005; Kassirer, 2005). Environmental factors are ignored. Indeed our experiences change our brains.[11] And, as Szasz (1994) suggests, if it is discovered that certain symptoms are caused by biochemical factors, related disorders pass into the field of neurology as in certain kinds of dementia.

Bold Assertions

People often simply assert a position as true, with no attempt to provide evidence for it; they act as if a conclusive argument has been made when it has not. A clinician may say, "Mr. Greenwood is obviously a psychopath who is untreatable." Bold assertions are the propagandist's favorite ploy. A confident manner and bold assertions often accomplish what should be achieved only by offering sound reasons for a position. Words that are cues for this tactic include: *unquestionable, indisputably, the fact is, the truth is, well-established, validated.* Consider the following bold assertion: "We know that social work is effective. More than any other single profession, we see the youth in the settings where we work. We know what is needed and what works" ("From the President," National Association of Social Workers, 1986, p. 2). In fact, there is considerable debate about this, and some research suggests the opposite (harming in the name of helping, e.g., McCord, 2003). Concerns about the gap between practice and policy-related research and what practitioners draw on was a key reason for the development of evidence-informed practice and health care. Bold assertions are a form of *begging the question;* the truth or falsity of the point is assumed. This informal fallacy, like many others, takes advantage of our tendency to be lulled into accepting a position because of the confidence with which it is described. Evidence should be requested for the position asserted.

Newsspeak

Newsspeak refers to "language that distorts, confuses, or hides reality" (MacLean, 1981, p. 43). Examples include *neutralized* (meaning, killed), *misspoke* (meaning, lied), and *air support* (meaning, bombing and strafing). Newsspeak refers to the intentional abuse of language to obscure the truth. Misleading titles or headlines may be used. Editors and publishers are aware that many more people read the headlines than read the material under the headlines. Thus, even if the small print presents an accurate view, the title may be misleading. Orwell (1958) wrote, "In our time, political speech and writing are largely in defense of the indefensible. . . . political language has to consist of euphemisms, question begging, and sheer cloudy vagueness" (p. 136). Newsspeak is popular in the helping professions as illustrated in the following examples:

Statement or Term	Translation
Fiscal constraints call for retrenchment.	Some people are going to be fired; clinics will be closed.
New policies have been put in place to ensure better services.	All services will be provided by psychiatrists.
Improve your practice tenfold.	Attend Dr. X's workshop.
Pregnancy crisis center	Pro-life anti-abortion centers
Community care in place of warehousing	Patients will be discharged from mental hospitals even though no adequate community care is available.

Here are some more examples based on the funnies by Andy Chap:

- "It has long been known" . . . I didn't look up the original reference.
- "Currently it is not possible to give definite answers." Even though my experiment was unsuccessful, I want to get it published.
- "I selected three of the samples for detailed study" . . . The other results didn't make any sense.
- "It is generally believed that" . . . A couple of others think so, too.

Manner of Presentation

The *eloquence* with which material is presented, whether in writing or in speech, is not necessarily related to its cogency. Words that move and charm may not inform.

To the contrary, eloquence may short-circuit critical appraisal as illustrated by the famous Dr. Fox lecture described in Chapter 11. A focus on the eloquence of a presentation may decrease motivation to carefully examine arguments. Given the scarcity of eloquence, it is hard to resist a desire for more. Best of all, is the combination of eloquence, as well as clarity and soundness of argument.

MAKING EFFECTIVE USE OF LANGUAGE

The term "rhetoric" has varied definitions: (1) "the art of using words effectively in speaking or writing; now, the art of prose composition"; (2) "artificial eloquence; language that is showy and elaborate but largely empty of clear ideas or sincere emotion" (*Webster's New World Dictionary*, 1988). It is in the latter sense that the term is in ill-repute. In its broader sense, as in the first definition, it is an important area of study and skill, especially in the helping professions, which rely so heavily on the spoken and written word with real life consequences. Many critical thinking skills involve recognizing ways in which language affects decisions (Halpern, 2003; Walton, 2008). All writing in the professions and the social sciences can be viewed as rhetorical in that a position is advanced and a point of view is presented that is then reviewed for its soundness (Edmondson, 1984). Claims are made and arguments for them presented. Ethical limits on how far a writer or speaker may go in being persuasive are suggested by Grice's maxims of conversation such as: "Do not say what you believe to be false." "Do not say that for which you lack sufficient evidence" (Grice, 1975, p. 46). The latter rule is routinely broken in professional discourse. That is, claims are made for which there is little or no evidence. Tips for making effective use of language include the following:

- Be alert for special interests. Is someone trying to sell you something?
- Recognize use of emotional language and vagueness.
- Clearly describe arguments.
- Be on the look out for reification and palaver.
- Be wary of analogies and metaphors; examine their similarity and claimed relationships to conclusions.
- Keep the context of a dialogue in mind (e.g., Is the goal to discover what is true or false?)
- Use different examples when thinking about members of a category to avoid stereotypes. (Halpern, 2003, p. 133)

SOCIAL PSYCHOLOGICAL PERSUASION STRATEGIES USED BY PROPAGANDISTS

The essence of persuasion is influencing someone to think or act in a certain manner. Professionals try to persuade clients to carry out agreed-on tasks and try to convince other professionals to offer needed resources. Conversely, they are the target of persuasive attempts by clients, drug detailers, colleagues, and the mass media (e.g., see

<http://www.proveneffective.org>). There is an extensive literature on persuasion in diverse contexts including political advertising (Kaid & Holtz-Bacha, 2006; Dillard & Pfau, 2002; Pratkanis, 2007). Persuasion attempts may or may not be conscious and recipients may or may not be aware that a persuasive attempt is being made. Consider examples of tactics used by drug reps to manipulate doctors shown in Table 10.5.

One route to persuasion is via thoughtful consideration of different arguments related to a topic. (This review could be distorted because of cognitive biases such as wishful thinking.) Another route to persuasion is through emotional appeals including associations or inferences based on peripheral cues such as our mood or the status of the person offering a "pitch"—is she an "opinion leader"? Such cues may influence our beliefs by affecting how much we think about a view or may bias us in one direction (Fabrigar, Smith, & Brannon, 1999). In the first route, we consider arguments for and against a position. In the second we do not. Becoming familiar with social psychological persuasion strategies and decreasing "automatic" reactions to such tactics, will help you to avoid influence by related propaganda ploys. (See Table 10.6.) In everyday life, the principles on which these strategies are based often provide convenient shortcuts. We do not have time to fully consider the merits of each action we take or "pitch" we hear. Compliance-induction strategies take advantage of our natural tendencies; other people can exploit them for their own purposes; our automatic reactions work in their favor. "All the exploiters need do is to trigger the great stores of influence that exist in a situation and direct them toward the intended target. . . . Even the victims themselves tend to see their compliance as due to the actions of natural forces rather than to the designs of the person who profits from that compliance" (Cialdini, 1984, p. 24). These strategies offer others opportunities for manipulation without the appearance of manipulation.

Persuasion by Affect

Persuasion by affect, including fear and guilt, comes into play when we are influenced not so much by what people say (their arguments), but by extraneous variables such as how attractive they are, who they are (their status), and how confidently they present their views (Slovic, Finucane, Peters, & MacGregor, 2002). Figure 10.2 shows an appeal to the fear of urinary leakage. Successful propagandists are skilled in encouraging such effects. Persuasion strategies based on liking and authority attain their impact largely because of affective associations. The unconscious nature of related effects highlight that we must be both motivated as well as able to critically appraise claims. Here we have yet another example of different ways to evaluate claims—quickly based on emotions, or in a deliberative, thoughtful manner. Advertisers encourage the former style.

Principle of Liking

We like to please people we know and like. Concerns about disapproval discourage raising questions about popular views. The liking rule is often used by people we do

Table 10.5 Examples of Tactics for Manipulating Physicians

Physician Category	Technique	How It Sells Drugs	Comments
Friendly and outgoing	I frame everything as a gesture of friendship. I give them free samples not because it's my job, but because I like them so much. I provide office lunches because visiting them is such a pleasant relief from all the other docs. My drugs rarely get mentioned by me during our dinners.	Just being friends with most of my docs seemed to have some natural basic effect on their prescribing habits. When the time is ripe, I lean on my "friendship" to leverage more patients to my drugs...say, because it'll help me meet quota or it will impress my manager, or it's crucial for my career.	Outgoing, friendly physicians are every rep's favorite because cultivating friendship is a mutual aim. While this may be genuine behavior on the doctor's side, it is usually calculated on the part of the rep
Aloof and skeptical	I visit the office with journal articles that specifically counter the doctor's perceptions of the shortcoming of my drug. Armed with the articles and having hopefully scheduled a 20-minute appointment (so the doc can't escape) I play dumb and have the doc explain to me the significance of my article.	The only thing that remains is for me to be just aggressive enough to ask the doc to try my drug in situations that wouldn't have been considered before, based on the physician's own explanation.	Humility is a common approach to physicians who pride themselves on practicing evidence-based medicine. These docs are tough to persuade but not impossible. Typically, attempts at geniality are only marginally effective.

SOURCE: Selected examples from A. Fugh-Berman & S. Ahari (2007). Following the script: How drug reps make friends and influence doctors. *PLoS Medicine, 4*, e150, Table 1.

Table 10.6 USE OF SOCIAL PSYCHOLOGICAL PERSUASION STRATEGIES TO CREATE FEAR OR ANXIETY

Social-psychological principle	Anxiety-arousing appeal
Liking	You don't like me if you don't go along with my position (and therefore I won't like you as much).
Consistency	You're inconsistent with your beliefs if you don't agree with me.
Reciprocity	I helped you out in the past, now you're not fulfilling your obligation to return the favor if you don't support my position.
Authority	Other people (namely me) know what is best to avoid ineffective remedies.
Scarcity	We won't have this opportunity long; it's now or never.
Social proof	Everyone (but you) accepts this position; what's the matter with you?

not know to gain our compliance. Physical attractiveness, similarity, compliments, familiarity, and cooperation encourage liking. "Compliance professionals are forever attempting to establish that we and they are working for the same goals, that we must 'pull together' for mutual benefit, that they are, in essence, teammates" (Cialdini, 1984, p. 182). The "good guy/bad guy" routine takes advantage of the liking rule—we like the good guy (in contrast to the bad guy), so we comply with what he wants. The rule of liking also works through conditioning and association. We are more receptive to new material if we like the person presenting it. Associating "pitches" with food as in the "luncheon technique" is a well-known strategy. Pharmaceutical companies spent millions on lunches and dinners for professionals they hoped to influence to prescribe their products. Policies that permit such practices are now being questioned.

The Grand Falloon Effect

Simply being put into a group of people you never saw before may create an identity with that group and against out groups. Pratkanis and Aronson (2001) refer to this as "the grand falloon technique." Phony grassroots organizations (astroturfs) take advantage of this effect. We are attracted to the people in our grand falloon even if those people "are disreputable and unscrupulous" (p. 218). As Pratkanis and Aronson point out, con artists take advantage of the grand falloon technique when they claim, often falsely, that they also are a member of X group after you tell them that you are a member of X, to encourage this shared groupiness.

"Sharing emotion and feeling can also create a grand falloon—a sense of oneness with others can be produced by sharing fun time, a sad situation, or a harrowing experience" (p. 222). We tend to exaggerate differences between different groups and to underestimate differences within a group. These examples illustrate the ease with which propagandists can take advantage of us for their own purposes. Related effects often occur outside of our awareness. Thus, unless we learn how to identify and to think critically about claims, we are easily lulled into being influenced without our awareness.

Figure 10.2. Advertisement appealing to fear.
SOURCE: Reprinted by permission of Waveland Press, Inc. From T. A. Borchers (2005). Persuasion in the Media Age (2nd Ed.). Waveland Press, Inc., 2005 (reissued 2011) All rights reserved.

Appeals to Consistency

Another persuasion strategy is based on a desire to be (and appear) consistent with what we have already done. Gaining commitment sets the consistency rule into effect. "Commitment strategies are . . . intended to get us to take some action or make some statement that will trap us into later compliance through consistency pressures" (p. 75). An advertisement for a workshop may urge readers to reserve a space now to ensure a place (scarcity principle) and to send a refundable deposit of $50.00 (commitment). We may then attempt to be consistent with our earlier actions (i.e., attend the event). Being consistent usually works for us. However, because it is usually in our interests to be consistent, "we easily fall into the habit of being automatically so, even in situations where it is not the sensible way to be" (Cialdini, 1984, pp. 68–69). Consistency can protect us from troubling realizations we would rather not think about. Since automatic consistency "functions as a shield against thought" (p. 72), it can be exploited by people who want us to comply with their requests. Inappropriate demands for consistency are a type of ad hominem fallacy as discussed in chapter 13.

The Reciprocity Rule: Beware of Bearers of Gifts

We feel obliged to return favors. Obtaining an initial concession or offering a favor may be used to gain compliance through the influence of the reciprocity rule. Pharmaceutical companies make use of this rule, giving small gifts (pens for example) as well as lavish dinners. Small, seemingly inconsequential gifts, contrary to pharma promoters who say "It was just a pen," create a greater tendency to reciprocate than do larger gifts.[12] Oldani (2004) who himself was a drug rep for many years, describes how drug reps ("detailers") are trained to take advantage of any indebtedness physicians feel toward them. "The actual everyday pharmaceutical economy is based on social relationships that are forged and strengthened through repetitive and *calculated* acts of giving" (p. 174). "The everyday function of the pharmaceutical gift economy . . . works by limiting and disguising the play of economic interest and calculation that exists at every level of pharmaceutical product promotion. The industry works very hard to maintain a *feel-good economy* for doctors and reps to co-exist, where decisions for prescriptions can be based on other criteria" (p. 174). Food is "the reps' weapon of choice." Studies regarding the effects of pharmaceutical marketing contacts on physicians show that these contacts affect their behavior, whether or not physicians think they do (e.g., Orlowsky & Wateska, 1992). It may be difficult to counter or neutralize the influence of reciprocation, since we often do not know whether an offer is an honest one or the first step in an exploitation attempt. The rule of reciprocity "entitles a person who has acted in a certain way to a dose of the same thing" (Cialdini, 1984, p. 65). Thus, if an action is viewed as a compliance device instead of a favor, this rule will not work. Tips for how to handle persuasion ploys by drug detailers can be found on <http://www.proveneffective.com>.

Promote False Scarcity

The scarcity principle rests on the fact that opportunities seem more valuable when their availability is limited. A nursing home intake worker may say, "If you don't decide now, space may not be available" (which may not be true). Here too, as with the impulse to use other shortcuts, it is accurate in its basic thrust; things that are scarce are usually more valuable; also, freedom is lost as opportunities become less available. Cialdini (1984) provided a good example of the influence of the scarcity principle.

> One set of customers heard a standard sales presentation before being asked for their orders. Another set of customers heard the standard sales presentation plus information that the supply of imported beef was likely to be scarce in the

upcoming months. A third group received the standard sales presentation and the information about a scarce supply of beef, too; however, they also learned that the scarce supply news was not generally available information. It had come, they were told, from certain exclusive contacts that the company had. Thus the customers who received this last sales presentation learned that not only was the availability of the product limited, so also was the news concerning it—the scarcity double whammy. . . . Compared to customers who got only the standard sales appeal, those who were told about the future scarcity of beef bought more than twice as much. But the real boost in sales occurred among the customers who heard of the impending scarcity via "exclusive" information. They purchased six times the amount that the customers who received only the standard sales pitch did. (Cialdini, 1984, p. 239; based on Knishinsky, 1982)

Principle of Social Proof

Propaganda takes advantage of our tendency to be guided by what other people think is correct. This is encouraged by weasel words and phrases such as "We know . . ." or "It is agreed that . . ." (See also discussion of appeal to consensus in chapter 7.) (Creative people are not as likely to follow this principle.) This principle provides a convenient shortcut that often works well. However, if accepted automatically, it may lead us astray. The danger in appealing to this principle is the "pluralistic ignorance phenomenon" (Cialdini, 1984, p. 129); the majority view may be (and often is) incorrect. The censorship of well-argued alternative views in science and medicine illustrates the power of "social proof" (consensus). As with other social-psychological sources of influence, this one is more effective under some conditions than others. Uncertainty increases the effect of this principle; we are more likely to go along with what other people do in ambiguous situations. Similarity also influences the impact of social proof. Imitating the majority may or may not be a successful strategy. (See discussion of fast and frugal heuristics in chapter 11.) False evidence may be fabricated to influence us through the principle of social proof, such as claiming (without evidence) that hundreds have benefited from use of a new therapy.

Contrast Effects

We are influenced by contrast effects. Consider contrasting before and after images in advertisements. Kenrick and Gutierres (1980) found that men assign more negative ratings to pictures of potential blind dates when watching "Charlie's Angels" on TV than when watching another program.

Make It Personal

Persuasive messages are more likely to be successful if they are personal—apply to those we are trying to persuade. Advertisers carefully select actors or actual consumers of a product in their ads to create the greatest feeling of intimacy with the greatest number of listeners/watchers. They select individuals who embody the ideas or products promoted. Case examples are often used in this way to create identification with the person depicted as well with the imbedded message.

Appeal to Authority

Related informal fallacies such as appeal to alleged "experts" take advantage of our tendency to go along with authorities—for our "reverence," for example, for experts. (See chapters 7 and 12.) Continuing education workshops promoted are associated with "big names," for example. (See discussion of Big Pharma's ties with opinion leaders in chapter 3.) Many appeals to authority are symbolic, such as to certain titles; they connote rather than offer content in support of the claimed expertise of the authority. (See also chapter 12.)

SUMMARY

Language is one of the propagandists' key tools. It is daily used to hide, confuse, and distort to encourage us to act in certain ways, for example, to seek certain diagnostic tests and therapy. Deliberate confusions between different functions of language and different levels of abstraction may be created to promote claims. Using descriptive terms as explanatory terms offers an illusion of understanding without providing any real understanding. Confused discussions (or thinking) may occur due to the false assumptions of one word, one meaning. On the other hand, a pseudo-scientific "precision" such as use of code numbers in the DSM may delude us that certain things (diseases) exist which do not. (Symptoms exist but do alleged mental disorders?) Technical terms may hide lack of evidentiary status as in "bafflegarb" or "psychobabble," words that sound informative but are not. Labels such as "psychotic" not only are vague but have emotional connotations that influence us. Metaphors may lead us astray. Propagandists misuse verbal speculation; they encourage us to assume that what is, can be discovered by merely thinking about it. Knowledge of propaganda ploys related to use of language and care in using language can help us to avoid being bamboozled. Awareness of social-psychological persuasion appeals, such as appealing to scarcity to influence our behavior, can also help us to avoid unwanted influences.

11

Appeal to Our Psychological Vulnerabilities

Our psychological vulnerabilities contribute to influence by propaganda. We are gullible creatures, subject to a myriad of persuasion strategies (e.g., Cialdini, 2001; Gilovich, 1993). We are even influenced by smells, which others may use to affect our beliefs and actions (e.g., Liberman & Pizarro, 2010). The balance of influences from different sources may change over our lifetime. We typically assume that we ourselves arrived at what we think is best, when, indeed, we acquired certain habits, thoughts, ideas, and ideologies in our childhood and may have never questioned them. If it is true, as Ellul (1965) suggests, that propaganda is an integral part of a technological society such as our own, it is an inescapable part of life. Many influences at many levels, psychological, as well as sociological, contribute to making us patsies for propaganda ploys, including our own self-propaganda such as our inflated estimate of our knowledge. (See Dunning, Heath, & Suls, 2004.) There is a close relationship between the propaganda we feed ourselves and that which comes from other sources, such as the media. Let us say a young child is raised in a family in which all adult relatives are members of the Ku Klux Klan. This child grows up believing that the beliefs and related actions of the Klan are good—that they serve a just purpose, that they will improve the world. What percentage of such children question these beliefs as adults and to what effect? How many, after thinking carefully about them, decide that they are not just, that they do more harm than good? Thousands of staff in thousands of agencies are busily writing reports characterized by palaver that mystifies rather than informs. (See chapter 4.) The greater our need for social approval, the more we may gallop along with others in the wrong direction. If we are "true believers" our eyes are closed to divergent views. (See Figure 11.1.) Thus, our beliefs and the rigidity with which they are held affect the potential for learning and the discovery of information that will help us to make sound decisions. There is an overlap in strategies that we fall into ourselves such as emotional reasoning (If I feel it, it must be true) and methods used by others. The advantage of this overlap is that if we become familiar with these, they should be of value in avoiding propaganda and its unwanted effects from others as well as from ourselves.

HOW COULD WE BE SUCH DUPES?

Billions of dollars are spent on "duping us." The money spent on preparing the ground for acceptance of a new drug is enormous as illustrated in chapter 3. Millions of

Figure 11.1. The preconceived notion.
SOURCE: W. H. Schneider (1965). *Danger: Men talking.* New York: Random House.

dollars are spent by Big Pharma on medical ghostwriting (Singer, 2009d). Contracts with pharmaceutical companies are so large that public relations firms have special departments to handle them. Billions of dollars from Big Pharma flow to researchers and academics to promote and test drugs. The thousands of people who work in advertising and public relations are busily creating ads, lobbying politicians, creating phony grassroots organizations, and staging events to influence our behavior (Ewen, 1976).[1] Medical writing firms such as Designwrite churn out articles for medical journals, slanting material as directed by drug companies (e.g., Singer, 2009d).[2] We are bombarded with inflated claims about problems, remedies, and presumed causes in the media, as well as in the professional literature. No one is immune to these influential strategies, although we can increase our immunity if we are motivated to do so—want to find the straight scoop—and cultivate related skills. Distractions abound.

> Even in Rome there was nothing like the non-stop distraction now provided by newspapers and magazines, by radio, television and the cinema [and now the Internet, Blackberries, Ipods]. In Brave New World non-stop distractions of the most fascinating nature (the feelings, orgy-porgy, centrifugal bumble-puppy) are deliberately used as instruments of policy, for the purpose of preventing people from paying too much attention to the realities of the social and political situation. The other world of religion is different from the other world of entertainment; but they resemble one another in being most decidedly "not of this world." Both are distractions and, if lived in too continuously, both can become, in Marx's phrase, 'the opium of the people' and so a threat to freedom. Only the

vigilant can maintain their liberties, and only those who are constantly and intelligently on the spot can hope to govern themselves effectively by democratic procedures. (Huxley, 1958, pp. 267–68)

If it is true that people who read a great deal are especially prone to influence by propaganda since they read many secondary sources, those in the helping professions, including educators, are especially prone to influence by propaganda ploys. The symbiotic relationship between the efforts of propagandists to lure us (the Pied Pipers of propaganda) and our own tendencies that encourage us to heed their siren calls (self-propaganda) is a key theme emphasized in this book.

THE APPARENT TRUTH OF VAGUE DESCRIPTIONS: THE BARNUM EFFECT

Barnum believed that you can sell anything to anybody. He documented this in *Humbugs of the World* (1865). The Barnum effect, also called the "Forer Effect," refers to our tendency to rate vague statements as highly accurate of ourselves even though the statements could apply to many people. This is also known as the subjective validation effect (searching for personal meaning in ambiguous statements). Astrologers and psychics take advantage of our tendency to believe vague descriptions about our behavior. Vagueness is a characteristic of many forms of propaganda. Forer (1949) found that we tend to accept vague personality descriptions as uniquely applicable to ourselves even though the same descriptions could be applied to almost anyone. Forer gave a personality test to his students but ignored their answers and gave each student the following evaluation.

> You have a need for other people to like and admire you, and yet you tend to be critical of yourself. While you have some personality weaknesses you are generally able to compensate for them. You have considerable unused capacity that you have not turned to your advantage. Disciplined and self-controlled on the outside, you tend to be worrisome and insecure on the inside. At times you have serious doubts as to whether you have made the right decision or done the right thing. You prefer a certain amount of change and variety and become dissatisfied when hemmed in by restrictions and limitations. You also pride yourself as an independent thinker; and do not accept others' statements without satisfactory proof. But you have found it unwise to be too frank in revealing yourself to others. At times you are extroverted, affable, and sociable, while at other times you are introverted, wary, and reserved. Some of your aspirations tend to be rather unrealistic.

Students were asked to evaluate the description from 0 to 5, with "5" meaning the recipient felt the evaluation was an "excellent" assessment and "4" meaning the assessment was "good." The average evaluation was 4.26. The test has been replicated many times.

> In short, Forer convinced people he could successfully read their character. His accuracy amazed his subjects, though his personality analysis was taken from a

newsstand astrology column and was presented to people without regard to their sun sign. The Forer effect seems to explain, in part at least, why so many people think that pseudosciences work. Astrology, astrotherapy, biorhythms, cartomancy, chiromancy, the enneagram, fortune telling, graphology, rumpology, etc. seems to work because they seem to provide accurate personality analyses. Scientific studies of these pseudosciences demonstrate that they are not valid personality assessment tools, yet each has many satisfied customers who are convinced they are accurate.

The most common explanations given to account for the Forer effect are in terms of hope, *wishful thinking*, vanity, and the tendency to try to make sense out of experience, though Forer's own explanation was in terms of human gullibility. People tend to accept claims about themselves in proportion to their desire that the claims be true rather than in proportion to the empirical accuracy of the claims as measured by some non-subjective standard. We tend to accept questionable, even false statements about ourselves, if we deem them positive or flattering enough.[3]

Replications of the Barnum effect include a study by Furnam (2004) using hair samples.

THE ALLURE OF SCIENCE AND TECHNOLOGY

The essence of pseudoscience is using the trappings of science without the substances as described in chapter 7. These "trappings" can fool us because of the allure of the "authority" of science and scientific experts. (See Figure 11.2.) They can lull our critical thinking skills into quiescence. McCabe and Castel (2008) presented university students with 300-word news stories about fictional findings that were based on flawed scientific reasoning. One story claimed that watching TV was linked to math ability because both TV viewing and math activated the temporal lobe. Students rated stories accompanied by a brain image to be more scientifically sound than the same story accompanied by equivalent data presented in a bar chart or when there is no graphical illustration at all. (See blog of the British Psychological Society.)

As the authors report in their abstract:

> Brain images are believed to have a particularly persuasive influence on the public perception of research on cognition. Three experiments are reported showing that presenting brain images with articles summarizing cognitive neuroscience research resulted in higher ratings of scientific reasoning for arguments made in those articles, as compared to articles accompanied by bar graphs, a topographical graph of brain activation, or no image. These data lend support to the notion that part of the fascination, and the credibility, of brain imaging research lies in the persuasive power of the actual brain images themselves. We argue that brain images are influential because they provide a physical base for abstract cognitive processes, appealing to people's affinity for reductionist explanations of cognitive phenomena. (p. 343)

Age Spots On Skin Signal "Brown Slime" On Brain Neurons

•

Clinical Tests Show What Causes Condition And How To Reverse It

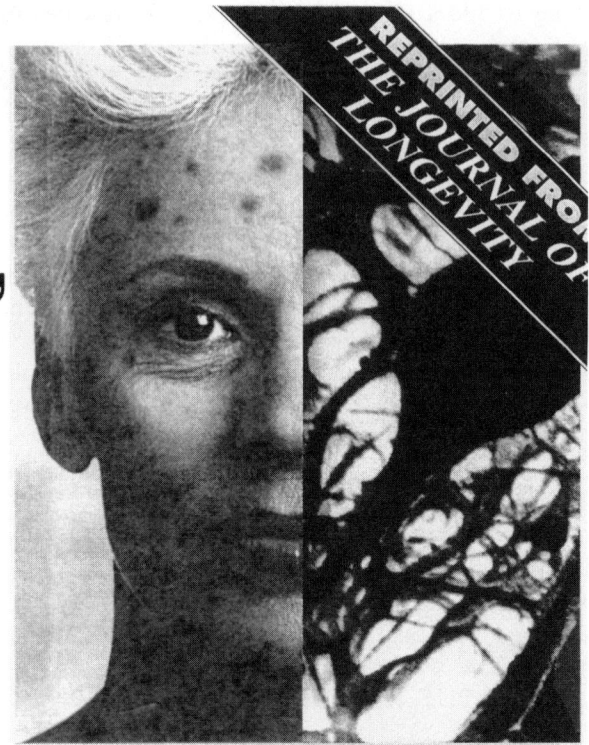

At the same time you develop age spots on your skin, a brown slime (lipofuscin) begins to form on the neurons in your brain, and short-term memory begins deteriorating. Many scientists are certain that a deficiency of some essential brain nutrients is the cause. This condition is much more common today than it was 100 years ago. According to the *Los Angeles Times:* "Today, the odds are one in five of developing some type of dementia (severe mental problems). Alzheimer's disease, first discovered in 1907, was considered rare...now, there are more than 4.1 million cases of Alzheimer's in America." (And about 8 million cases of senility and dementia.)

By Marcus Welbourne,
Senior Science Editor

Probably the scariest aspect of getting older is the possibility that we will become senile, with its attendant forgetfulness, mental confusion, inability to manage our money and vulnerability to being taken advantage of.

Worse yet, senility is the first step toward various types of age-related dementia, including the awful Alzheimer's disease.

Age spots, or lipofuscin, are well-accepted in medical science as the first warning that we are progressing in the direction of senility or dementia. As we age, lipofuscin accumulates in the brain, retinal nerves of the eyes, heart muscle, liver and other organs, with spots surfacing on the skin.

Although scientists haven't figured out how it affects the operation of the heart, liver, etc., there is considerable clinical evidence that lipofuscin dramatically alters the response of the delicate neurons of the brain and eyes.

Dr. J.H. Dowson of Cambridge University examined the brains of numerous people of comparable ages who died with and without dementia. The sane people had much less lipofuscin than the demented group.

Nerve cells communicate with each other electrochemically through microscopic gaps between them called "synapses." The brown, slimy lipofuscin apparently prevents, alters or slows the communication through those synapses.

What Causes Lipofuscin?

A deficiency of some very important nutrients has been correlated with substantial increases of lipofuscin

Figure 11.2. The Allure of Science.
SOURCE: Gero Vita Laboratories. Senility Epidemic—1 in 5 over 60 Affected. Inside: The Causes and How to Deter it.

OBEDIENCE TO AUTHORITY

The authority of the priests has been replaced by the authority of the experts in the helping professions. Blind obedience to alleged authorities eclipses skeptical appraisal of claims. This may have many roots including the wish to be identified with revered others or a wish to save the time and effort needed to think things through for yourself. It may be encouraged by anxiety around authority figures and a wish to avoid this anxiety, coupled with a lack of effective skills for posing questions and responding to efforts to squelch inquiry. Signs of defensiveness on the part of "authorities" such as a raised voice, a knowing laugh, a roll of the eyes, and a well-timed dramatic yawn may create fear rather than being accurately tagged as a "cool out" effort. We are socialized from a young age to accept the word of authorities, our parents, teachers, professors, and priests. Medical journalists, educators, physicians are often viewed as "authorities" who should not be questioned. The strength of influence by authority is shown by the results of Milgram's experiment (1963). (See also Burger, 2009.) When urged by experimenters, subjects gave what they were told were high intensity shocks to others. The Stanford Prison Study by Zimbardo (1971) also illustrates influence by authority. Here, students were assigned the role of prisoner and/or guard and in a remarkably little time fell into their roles to such an extent with such consequent abuse of "inmates," that the experiment had to be stopped. (See also Zimbardo, 2007.) Only with a sound education in critical thinking offered in our schools and/or by our parents, do we learn that authorities may be wrong and should be questioned.

In the classic experiment on conformity by Asch (1956), all but one member of a group is a stooge. Each group member is asked whether one line is longer than another or whether a light moved. Actually, the lines are of equal length and the light does not move. The stooges in the group, one after the other, claim that one line is longer than another or that the light moved. Then it is the turn of the one subject. This person usually says "Yes one line is longer," or, "Yes the light moved." The Ash experiment has been replicated many times showing the effects of pressures for conformity. It is difficult to buck the herd, not to be one of the herd, to stick our (perhaps) lone head above the parapet. Advertisements often appeal to our wish to enhance our social status and be popular.

INFLUENCE BY A CONFIDENT MANNER: THE DR. FOX STUDY

We are influenced by manner of presentation. It would be hard to find a more charismatic speaker than Adolph Hitler who was a consummate master of propagandistic oratory. Style of presentation can emerge victorious over content when students rate their instructors; presenting the same material in a more entertaining style increases positive student evaluations.[4] Naftulin and his colleagues (1973) hired a charismatic actor to present a lecture on the application of mathematical game theory to psychological phenomena. The purpose was to see if people would fall for content presented by a charismatic speaker who in fact knew nothing about the topic. Here is the abstract for this classic study:

> On the basis of publications supporting the hypothesis that student ratings of educators depend largely on personality variables and not educational content,

the authors programmed an actor to teach charismatically and nonsubstantively on a topic on which he knew nothing. The authors hypothesized that given a sufficiently impressive lecture paradigm, even experienced educators participating in a new learning experience can be seduced into feeling satisfied that they have learned despite irrelevant, conflicting, and meaningless content conveyed by the lecturer. The hypothesis was supported with 55 subjects responding favorably at the significant level to an eight-item questionnaire concerning their attitudes toward the lecture. The study serves as an example to educators that their effectiveness must be evaluated beyond the satisfaction with which students view them and raises the possibility of training actors to give 'legitimate' lectures as an innovative approach toward effective education. The authors conclude by emphasizing that student satisfaction with learning may represent little more than the illusion of having learned (Naftulin, Ware, & Donnelly, 1973, p. 630)

No one in the audience detected the ruse. Many people thought they had read some of his articles. They presented Dr. Fox to another audience of professionals and got the same results. Since then, the experiment has been replicated several times and more complex designs have controlled for content, style, and other variables.[5] Professional conferences present ideal conditions for Dr. Fox: The audience is exposed only once to a short speech, expects to be entertained, and will not be rated on its ability to master the content of the speech. Posing as a guru or esteemed expert offers great allure as Jarvis (1990) suggests.

THE VALIDITY EFFECT

We tend to believe that information is valid if we have heard it many times; if we have heard information before, we ascribe greater truth to it than if we are just hearing it for the first time (Renner, 2004). (Repetition is a key propaganda method.) This is referred to as the validity effect. Students who had taken a psychology class in high school did more poorly on examinations in psychology in college compared to students who did not. They attribute this to the "validity effect." That is, simply being exposed to a concept gives the illusion that we know more about it than we do when we hear about it later. Thus, as Renner (2004) notes "students equate repetition of information with familiarity of information that further prompts them to think they are knowledgeable about the information" (p. 211). This effect could discourage critical thinking.[6]

MOTIVATIONAL AND EMOTIONAL VULNERABILITIES

Propagandists appeal to our emotions; propaganda can only be successful when it does so. Our emotional reactions to certain people or "pitches" influence our vulnerability to propaganda ploys as illustrated by research regarding social psychological persuasion strategies. Propaganda appeals take advantage of our prejudices. Indeed, if the propaganda does not match these, it will not be effective. Propagandists are clever and insightful in identifying the biases and prejudices of different groups and then casting their messages in ways that feed on and into these. Emotional reasoning is common in our personal lives: "If I feel it, it must be true." Indeed this is identified as a key cognitive distortion in cognitive behavioral theories. Beliefs that increase our susceptibility to propaganda are often difficult to alter because they are linked to a worldview—a grand narrative for understanding reality as discussed in chapter 8. Views of behavior and how (or if) it can be changed form a basic part of our beliefs about our very nature and thus have emotional connotations. Views that differ from accepted ones in significant ways may be rejected out-of-hand. Our "reinforcer profile" (what consequences we value and how much) plays a role in our vulnerability to propaganda. Although some consequences are biologically based such as food, most are not, such as a preference for a certain kind of car or psychotherapy; our learning history in a particular culture shapes our reinforcer profile.

Fear of Social Rejection (Disapproval)

We are social creatures and most of our pleasures (and pains) are mediated by other people. There is a pressure to conform. Indeed, in some societies social ostracism, the extreme of social rejection, may lead to death. The greater the fear of social rejection the more likely we are to go along with what (valued) others think. Positive social exchanges are related to our very well-being and health. Questioning claims, especially those promoted by alleged authorities, is often met with attacks and attempts to belittle the uppity questioner. Positive perks may be withheld. Questioning claims that are accepted as proven will make you a deviant; you are raising questions about what others accept as facts. Examples include the widespread beliefs that serotonin influences depression, that ADHD is caused by a brain disorder, and that good intentions result in good outcomes. The more our well-being is tied to positive responses from others, the less likely we may be to question claims, even those that are clearly bogus. The less our curiosity about the world, the less likely this motive is to compete successfully with the motive to avoid social disapproval. The less our courage training (persistence in the face of obstacles), the less likely we are to resist pressure to conform. The more our well-being is tied to being "one of the herd," the more we open ourselves to fear of social rejection. And, the higher our anxiety about social disapproval, the more likely we will yield (even against our better judgment) to pressure to conform and the more likely we are to fear appearing ignorant.

Fear of Appearing Ignorant. Challenging accepted ideas such as the biochemical basis of problems-in-living and the labeling of deviant behaviors as mental illnesses is likely to result in other people viewing you as ignorant—ignorant of views and alleged related evidence on which they are based. No wonder most people do not do so, even if they have their doubts. They remain silent in the face of the steady repetition of questionable claims. It takes courage to raise heretical questions regarding assertions made by members of prestigious organizations such as the American Psychiatric Association and fellow travelers such as staff in the pharmaceutical industry and researchers funded by this industry. Questioning generally accepted causes such as that of "mental illness" or that HIV is the cause of AIDS, is essentially heresy. How can you tell? By the reactions. Consider different reactions to someone who claims that the earth is flat and someone who questions that HIV is the cause of AIDS.[7]

Fear of Failure

Self-handicapping strategies such as expecting to fail may be used to remove responsibility for poor performance and negative outcomes (Arkin & Oleson, 1998). Success is emphasized in our competitive society—who is the best? What is the best? Who belongs to what prestigious group? The greater the need for achievement, the greater may be the fear of failure. Raising questions and trying out new beliefs requires a willingness to discover that you have been wrong, that your favorite view is not correct. Trying something new may be scary. But we learn from our mistakes, thus it is vital to make them.

Lack of Curiosity

Attitudes many authors view as vital for sound decision making include curiosity, honesty, skepticism, open-mindedness, and a disposition to be systematic, as well as flexible. The study of curiosity, like many other phenomenon, has waxed and waned. Berlyne (1960) posited curiosity as a key drive in understanding behavior. This view resulted in a fascinating series of experiments to test the theory. Curiosity can be operationalized as exploratory behavior of a variety of kinds. It is influenced by the quality of attachment as illustrated in the experiments conducted by Harlow with monkeys; those with a real or cloth mother were more likely to explore their environment than those with only a "wire mother."[8] The less your curiosity, the less you may question claims about what is true and what is false. However, as always, this may be situational. For example, you may be curious and exploratory about a hobby or sport but show little exploratory behavior regarding claims you encounter in the professional literature. Cultivating your curiosity should decrease your susceptibility to propaganda. If you are curious about what you read and hear, you ask questions about content. Raising questions will make reading (or listening) more interesting because you "engage" with the material. You take it seriously enough to try to understand what is being claimed, what kind of claim it is, and what may be the consequences of accepting or rejecting the claim (different degrees of belief). You may read less but read it more deeply and critically. You may become more discerning about what you read, seeking high quality systematic reviews of research related to specific questions in the Cochrane and Campbell Collaboration databases.

Reluctance to Assume Responsibility for Decisions

Although most people may prefer to be involved in making life-affecting decisions as informed participants, others may be reluctant to assume responsibility. They may prefer to leave decisions up to "the professional."

Reluctance to Hold Others Responsible for Their Actions and Decisions

You may ask "Why do they do it?" This question should be kept well separate from the question "What have they done?" There seems to be a tendency to say, "Well he did some great research 20 years ago" in response to famous researchers caught in corruption. Why people do bad things is a question explored by some of our best thinkers and researchers but this should not distract us from trying to remedy practices and policies that harm rather than help, including fraud and corruption. In his classic chapter "Why I Do Not Attend Case Conferences," Meehl (1973) identifies errors and tendencies in groups that dilute the quality of decisions such as the "buddy-buddy" syndrome—reluctance to question claims because of not wanting to hurt or embarrass others.[9]

Contentment with the Illusion of Choice

The essence of consumerist culture is claimed to be freedom to choose among different products. If we do not realize that we are being fooled (really not offered a choice), we may be taken in by slick marketing that limits rather than expands our choices. The illusion of choice is in part created by framing propaganda pitches as education. For example, companies create websites allegedly for the purpose of "educating" viewers regarding problems, risks, and "choices." But do such sources propagandize or educate? When is a program for "disease awareness" actually a program to reframe normal reactions as diseases for which Big Pharma promotes remedies? Unless such sites (and other marketing venues) describe well-argued alternative views and related evidence, there is an illusion of choice. Rarely do these sites describe adverse consequences of dubbing normal reactions as diseases.

A Preference for Entertainment

We may prefer entertainment to critical appraisal. Gurus are skilled entertainers who describe detailed case histories and stories. (See previous discussion of the Dr. Fox effect.) We may prefer to linger at the level of being entertained rather than to critically appraise related claims and arguments (if any) for them.

SELF-DECEPTION AS SELF-PROPAGANDA

Self-deception can be viewed as a form of self-propaganda. Wff'N Proof includes 10 propaganda techniques under self-deception including prejudice, rationalization, wishful thinking, and causal oversimplification. Richard Paul (1993) suggests that we consistently deceive ourselves about our knowledge, freedom, and character (Paul, 1993, xiii). The self-deceived fall into two categories: (1) those whose values match their self-deception, and (2) those whose values do not. The latter, unlike the former, can be enlightened according to their own values, whereas the former, because there is a match between their self-deception and their values, cannot be changed by appealing to (revealing) the lack of correspondence between their beliefs and actions. They are caught in the fish-bowl of self-propaganda.

Self-Inflated Assessments

A robust literature shows our tendency to make inflated assessments of our own competencies (Dunning, Heath, & Suls, 2004).[10] Both extremes of self-esteem, excessive and limited, increase vulnerability to propaganda pitches, including self-propaganda. Both encourage a reluctance to critically examine claims about what is true and what is false and what is unknown; one via fear of failure and the other by overconfidence. Inflated estimates of accuracy impede learning from corrective feedback regarding our performance that is so vital in improving it (Hogarth, 2001). Only if we seek clear feedback regarding outcomes of our decisions can we critically examine their costs and benefits. Success in real-life situations is the most influential source of accurate efficacy expectations. Simply raising self-esteem is unlikely to improve skilled performance as suggested in the title: "Does self-esteem cause better performance, interpersonal success, happiness or healthier lifestyles? Answer: No, no, probably, sporadically" (Baumeisler, Campbell, Kruger, & Vohs, 2003; see also Foxx & Roland, 2005). Self-efficacy can be enhanced by acquiring additional skills. Lack of skill in detecting propaganda ploys such as bold assertions and glittering generalizations, contributes to confusion between being entertained and being informed. If we add a post-modern tilt (the belief that there is no truth and that all speculations are equally valueless in relation to what is real and what is not), we have a potent mix that contributes to being duped.

Our Readiness to Offer Rationalizations and Excuses as a Form of Self-Propaganda

Excuses can be defined as "explanations or actions that lessen the negative implications of an actor's performance, thereby maintaining a positive image for oneself and others" (Snyder, Higgins, & Stucky, 1983, p. 45). They serve many functions, including preserving self-esteem, smoothing social exchanges, and helping us to live with our limitations. They can be an obstacle to discovering self-propaganda as well as propaganda in the helping professions and in the media. Excuses given by social workers for less than optimal service include lack of resources and high caseloads. These may reflect reality; they may be "justified excuses" (McDowell, 2002).[11] We tend to attribute our successes to our own efforts and abilities and our failures to external influences such as luck or test difficulty. Excuses are especially likely to occur when we hold ourselves responsible for a negative outcome but still want to believe that we are good people. They are helpful if they relieve us from assuming undue responsibility and encourage reasonable risk taking. They are self-handicapping if they reduce our options for attaining valued goals such as locating current research findings regarding life-affecting decisions.

Rationalizations and excuses are often used to deny responsibility, for example, to create a "disconnect" between our actions and harm we create or contribute to (Bandura, 1999).[12] Popular excuses for avoiding responsibility for harming others are: (1) I didn't know, (2) I was just following orders (from my supervisor, or from an evil administrator), and (3) I was just doing what others do; using the same standards of care (even though abysmal). Professionals may reframe negative outcomes as deserved because of moral lapses on the part of the harmed—they deserve it. They may use "cleansing" language that obscures suffering and coercion. They may resort to pseudoscientific practices such as assigning uninformative but scientific sounding diagnostic labels to clients to relieve discomfort when confronted with unsolvable problems (Houts, 2002). If an incorrect decision is made, one or more of the following accounts could be offered which may or may not be true and may or may not be a "justified" excuse:

- It was not possible to get all the information.
- This was difficult; anyone would have had trouble.
- I was pressed for time.
- I didn't have the authority to make a decision.
- I was tired.
- My graduate education didn't prepare me for this situation.
- Other people make the same mistakes.

Reframing strategies may be used to mute the negative consequences of avoidable harm; harm may be underestimated ("He wasn't really harmed"), victims may be derogated ("He's incurable"), or the source of the negative feedback may be attacked ("My supervisor doesn't have experience with such clients.") (Bandura, 1999). Acts of omission may be excused by denying there was any need for action. A clinician may protest that others would have acted in the same way. He can say that he was coerced or blame negative consequences on the shortcomings of others. If criticized he may say that others have the same negative characteristic. A temporary inconsistency in performance may be appealed to as in intentionality pleas ("I didn't mean to do it") and effort-lowering statements ("I didn't try"). Excuses may save time (and face) in the short term, but cost time (and status) in the long run. For example, not critically evaluating research related to a remedy promoted saves time in the short run but may cost time and diminish quality of life in the long run, because effective methods are not used or harmful methods continue to be used.

WE ARE SUBJECT TO A VARIETY OF BIASES

Considerable attention has been paid to biases in many different venues including decision making in professional contexts (e.g., Elstein & Schwartz, 2002; Gambrill; Garb, 1998) and the conduct and reporting of research (e.g., Jadad & Enkin, 2007; MacCoun, 1998). Propagandists take advantage of these. We are subject to *wishful thinking* (i.e., our preference for an outcome increases our belief that it will occur) and the *illusion of control* (simply making a prediction may increase our certainty that it may come true). Vested interests in certain outcomes influence our decisions. We may assign exaggerated importance to some findings to protect a favored hypothesis. We tend to overlook uncertainty and offer explanations for what are, in fact, chance occurrences. Unrealistic expectations and a desire for quick success may contribute to poor decisions. Our moods and affective reactions to different people or events influence our decisions (Bless, 2001). Slovic and his colleagues (2002) refer to reliance on feelings of goodness and badness in guiding judgments as the *affect heuristic*. Propagandists take advantage of these biases to influence our behavior.

We are subject to *framing effects* and *hindsight bias* (Hastie & Dawes, 2001). Framing effects refer to how a decision is posed—in terms of gains or losses. Framing in terms of losses results in different decisions than does framing in terms of gains. We tend to be risk adverse; we overweigh risk of losses and underweigh risk of lost gains. In hindsight bias we mistakenly assume that we could have known at time 1 what we only knew at time 2. Cognitive-biases include influence by vivid material such as case examples and testimonials, as well as our tendency to believe that causes are similar to outcomes (e.g., "If I take a pill and my depression lifts, this shows that depression is a brain disease"). Advertisers make heavy use of vivid testimonials and case examples. We are prone to making and believing oversimplifications such as the following: (1) seeing different entities as more similar than they actually are (assuming temper tantrums are all caused by the same factors); (2) treating dynamic phenomena as static (assuming our moods do not change); (3) assuming that a general principle accounts for all of the phenomena (e.g., the assumption that attachment accounts for all behavior differences); (4) treating multidimensional phenomena as unidimensional or according to a subset of dimensions (e.g., "Its' in the genes"); (5) treating continuous variables as discreet ("He is an alcoholic"); (6) treating interconnected concepts as separable; (7) treating the whole as merely the sum of its parts (Feltovich, Spiro, & Coulson, 1993, cited in Woods & Cooks, 1999, p. 152).

Examples of social biases include the actor-observer bias (our tendency to attribute the behavior of others to their personality and to underplay the role of environmental variables and the tendency to do the opposite for our own behavior). The tendency of clinicians to attribute problems to the person and to overlook the role of environmental factors (*the fundamental attribution error*) has been a topic of interest for some time.[13] Other examples include *the false consensus effect* (our tendency to overestimate the extent to which others agree with our views), *the halo effect* (the tendency to generalize positive views from one area regarding an individual to others) and the *self-serving bias* (our tendency to claim greater responsibility for successes than for failures). The influence of illusory correlations on clinical observation was explored in the late 1960s (Chapman, 1967; Chapman & Chapman, 1967, 1969).

Confirmation Biases

We tend to search for evidence that agrees with our preferred view and to ignore disconfirming evidence. That is, we try to justify (confirm) our assumptions rather than to falsify them (seek counterexamples and test them as rigorously as possible). This kind of *partiality in the use of evidence* can result in avoidable errors. Tufte (2006) refers to this as cherry-picking. This bias is one of the most robust in leading us into the propagandist's hands; if a propagandist is proposing a view with which we agree, we will tend to go along with little critical appraisal. Consider a classic experiment illustrating confirmation bias by Lord and his colleagues (1979). Stanford University students who had previously indicated whether they believed in capital punishment as a deterrent to potential murders read two studies concerning the deterrent effects of capital punishment, one offering supportive evidence and the other offering negative evidence. Conditions were counterbalanced across direction and beliefs. The studies involved two different designs. Regardless of the design, students found the study supporting their own position to be more convincing and better conducted that the study opposing their position. After reading both studies, students were more certain of the accuracy of their original position than they were before they read either of the studies. Reading only material that matches our original assumptions is unlikely to violate expectations, which is one of the triggers for learning. Confirmation biases may result in failure to check initial hypotheses regarding the causes of symptoms. Consider the following.

> A young boy with an enlarging right lower eyelid mass underwent three biopsies over an 8 month interval. The biopsies each showed chronic inflammation with eosinophils and necrosis. The anatomical diagnosis was descriptive and included the comment 'consistent with eosinophilic granuloma.' Treatment with external beam radiation on three separate occasions and several courses of a cortisosteriod was unsuccessful. Usually eosinophilic granulomas are very sensitive to radiotherapy. When the pathology slides were reviewed elsewhere, the diagnosis of fungal cellulitis was made. The boy eventually lost his right eye, eyelids, facial skin and orbit.
>
> *Areas of concern*: A boy lost nearly a third of his face because three biopsies were misinterpreted as eosinophilic granuloma and cultures of the inflamed tissue were never taken. (Margo, 2003, p. 418)

Studies of medical reasoning show that *overinterpretation* is a common error. This refers to assigning new information to a favored hypothesis rather than exploring alternative accounts that more effectively explain data or remembering this information separately.

Belief Perseverance. Once we believe something, we tend to hold on to it as if our life depended on it. Intuitive beliefs are often difficult to modify. We tend to interpret data that is not consistent in ways that make it consistent with our current views; we "assimilate" or make it fit preferred views. One way to avoid inconsistencies is not to recognize them; to simply add new beliefs without altering old ones. This has been called the *add on* principle (Harmon, 1986). The principle of *negative undermining* states that we should stop believing something whenever we do not have adequate reasons to do so (p. 39). The principle of *positive undermining* states, "we should stop believing something whenever [we] believe that [our] reasons for believing it are not good" (p. 39). We tend to cling to old beliefs for reasons that seem and often are good: they have worked for us, they are familiar and they give us a sense of control over our environment.

Our beliefs can survive logical and empirical challenges. Consider the failure of debriefing found in the classic study by Ross, Lepper, and Hubbard (1975). Subjects were asked to distinguish real from fictitious suicide notes and were provided with false feedback regarding their performance. All subjects were debriefed following this phase of the study; they were informed that the feedback they had received was false and that they had been assigned to one of three conditions: success, failure, or average performance. Debriefing was not successful in altering perception of performance. Subjects assigned to the success condition continued to rate their performance and abilities more favorably than did the other two groups. Subjects assigned to the failure condition continued to rate themselves as lacking in ability and as unsuccessful. Expert diagnosticians hold initial hypotheses tentatively and are open to revising them as new information emerges (e.g., see Elstein et al., 1978). The stronger a belief, the more it is valued, and the longer it has been held, the harder it may be to change. These factors are not necessarily related to accuracy. Public commitment to a belief makes it more resistant to change. Once a belief is formed, we are likely to fall prey to confirmation biases—selective searches for confirming data.

THE SHORTCUTS WE TAKE MAY BE MISLEADING

We readily fall into a number of "intelligence traps" such as jumping to conclusions (deciding on one option too soon) and overlooking promising alternatives. Judgmental strategies are not necessarily used consciously, which is another reason it is helpful to be familiar with them. Nisbett and Ross (1980) and others such as Tversky and Kahneman (1973) suggested that we use heuristics as short cuts (rules of thumb) for making decisions. They focused on circumstances in which we violate probability rules and principles of "rational" decision making, emphasizing errors that result from use of simplifying heuristics. More recently, there has been a shift to highlighting the adaptive nature of such heuristics as they fit certain environments—their ecological validity. This is known as fast and frugal heuristics (Gigerenzer, 2005, 2007; Gigerenzer & Brighton, 2011; Kahneman, 2003; 2011; Klein, 1998). Examples include imitating the successful and the recognition heuristic. (See chapter 7.) We often *satisfice* (select the first acceptable plan) rather than search for an optimal alternative, and often this may work as well (or better) than efforts to optimize as suggested by Simon (1982) in his discussion of bounded rationality. Fast and frugal heuristics may be most effective, especially if professional education has succeeded in establishing accurate pattern recognition skills. However, in other instances they may be misleading. Many factor that are *not* correlated with the frequency of an event may influence how important it seems. Thus, a dual process model is suggested in which we make flexible use of both intuitive and analytic styles of reasoning.

We often rely on a preferred practice theory when making decisions. Preconceptions can lead to incorrect inferences when a theory is held on poor grounds (there is no adequate reason to believe that it is relevant) and when use of the theory "preempts examination of the data" (Nisbett & Ross, 1980, p. 71). (See also earlier discussion of confirmation biases.) We tend to believe in initial judgments, even when we are aware that the knowledge we have access to has been arbitrarily selected, for example, by the spin of a roulette wheel. This is known as the anchoring effect. We are also influenced by recency—what we last see or hear. We are influenced by the vividness of material in collecting, organizing, and interpreting data. Advertisements use vivid, emotion arousing testimonials images and slogans. Vivid information is more likely to be remembered than pallid information. We tend to overestimate the prevalence of illnesses that receive a great deal of media attention and underestimate the prevalence of illnesses that receive little media attention. We tend to exaggerate our own contributions to tasks—such information is more available to us.

Vivid information can be misleading, especially when duller but more informative material is ignored. One of your greatest challenges will be avoiding misleading influences created by vivid material, whether images, case histories, or words. Keep in mind that attention getting is the first step in a successful marketing. Advertisers have to get your attention. They do so by using vivid images, words, testimonials that appeal to your inner most desires (perhaps not even known to you), for fame, prestige, financial gain, and relief from stress and strain. Propagandistic material in professional sources makes use of similar tactics including transfer of associations, engrossing case histories, and scientific looking figures, and images (e.g., of brains). Factors that are important in creating and maintaining avoidable miseries such as legislation and social policies that contribute to lack of health care, poor quality schools, and the explosive incarceration rate may be ignored (not mentioned). Client's environments are typically known only through their words during interviews in offices, which convey an incomplete picture, especially given the compressed time permitted in managed care. Only through awareness and determination can you counter the effects of vivid information, for example, by reminding yourself to seek the hidden, to peek beyond the stage set offered and ask: What's missing?

Our preconceptions and theories influence what events we notice or inquire about. The more ambiguous the data, the more descriptions are influenced by our preconceptions. The influence of preconceptions is highlighted by research on illusory correlations. Clinicians tend to overestimate the degree of covariation between variables, resulting in illusions of validity and reliability. Classic studies by Chapman and Chapman (1967, 1969) illustrate that expectations based on theories and semantic associations overwhelm the influence of data that do not match or even refute these expectations. In one study, the reports of 32 practicing clinicians who analyzed the Rorschach protocols of homosexual men were reviewed (1969). These clinicians listed signs that had face validity but were empirically invalid as responses characteristic of homosexual men. That is, they selected signs based on "what seemed to go together"—on what ought to exist—rather than on empirically determined associations between signs and the criteria. Clinicians were more likely to report illusory correlations than were lay observers. Observers tend to attribute the cause of other people's behavior to characteristics of the person rather than to situational factors; the "actor's" behavior is more noticeable compared to more static situational events. Placebo effects are powerful; expecting change may create it, not the treatment per se (Benedetti, 2009). Shiv, Carmon, & Ariely (2005) found that a low cost placebo (10 cents) does not give as much relief as does a placebo costing $2.50. We expect more pain relief from a more expensive pill.

We often make judgments based on the degree to which a characteristic seems to resemble or be similar to another characteristic or theory (Tversky & Kahneman, 1974). We overestimate the variability of in-groups (groups of which we are a member) and underestimate the degree of variability in "out-groups" (groups of which we are not a member). In representative thinking, some characteristic "triggers" an associated theory, or belief. Encouraging transfer effects is a key propaganda strategy as described in chapter 4. The problem is, similarity is *not* influenced by a number of factors we should consider: (1) whether a person/object belongs in a certain group; (2) the probability that an outcome was a result of a particular cause; and (3) the probability that a process will result in a certain outcome. Reliance on representative thinking may yield incorrect beliefs about the degree to which: (1) outcomes reflect origins; (2) instances are representative of their categories; and (3) antecedents are representative of consequences.

We often assume that causes resemble their effects when this may not be so (Gilovitch & Savitsky, 2002). Consider the error of assuming that because you took a pill and depression lifts that depression is a biochemical problem. A psychiatrist may incorrectly assume that because a homeless person is similar to someone he just saw, similar causes are involved. We often ignore sample size and advertisers and researchers take advantage of this by not giving sample sizes. The *fallacy of stereotyping*

(Scriven, 1976, p. 208) consists of treating a description as if it represents all the individuals in a group of which it may (or may not) be a fairly typical sample. If we search only for evidence that supports a stereotype, we may miss more accurate accounts.[14]

OUR LEARNING AND DECISION-MAKING STYLE

Some people tend to think carefully, others are more spontaneous. Some are avoidant, that is, they try to avoid making decisions. Decision making requires choosing among different (often competing) goals and related courses of action. One of the purposes of decision making is to reveal possibilities (Baron, 2002). Our decisions tend to be more extreme when posed in terms of possible losses rather than gains. List of options (menus) differ in their "noise level" (number and vividness of irrelevant and misleading options). Propagandists deliberately include misleading cues, those that take you in directions they (and perhaps not you) value. Valuable options maybe missing.

Misplaced Trust: Naïveté about the Extent of Propaganda in the Helping Professions

The influence of Big Pharma in the helping professions, including professional organizations, continuing education, funding of research, professional practice, and conferences (e.g., special symposia), is so extensive, and so clearly inappropriate and unethical, it is hard to believe at first. Students who sign up for a professional education may instead receive a corporate indoctrination. The reaction may be: Could this be true? Isn't he or she exaggerating? But the related documentation clearly shows the enormous influence and the complicity of academic researchers including corruption and fraud. Conflicts of interests have become so great that a vigorous reaction has ensued, as revealed in articles such as "On the Take" by Jerome Kassirer, a past editor of the *New England Medical Journal*. These incestuous relationships and related conflicts of interest are often hidden. As always, censorship, partiality in the use of evidence, is a key propaganda weapon. It is hard to see what is hidden. We must seek it out. A naïve trust in professionals and related organizations to give us the "straight scoop" is misplaced. What propaganda ploys have you fallen for? What were the consequences? What questions could you have asked to avoid their effects?

LOW TOLERANCE FOR UNCERTAINTY

Making decisions in the helping professions is an uncertain activity. Physicians usually work in a state of uncertainty about the true state of the patient. They can only estimate the probability that a client has a certain illness. Uncertainty may concern: (1) the nature of the problem; (2) outcomes desired; (3) what is needed to attain valued outcomes; (4) likelihood of attaining outcomes; and (5) measures that will best reflect degree of success. Information about options may be missing, and accurate estimates of the probability that different alternatives will result in desired outcomes may be unknown. Rarely is all relevant information available and it is difficult to integrate different kinds of data. Knowledge may be available but not used. Even when a great deal is known, this knowledge is usually in the form of general principles that do not allow specific predictions about individuals (Dawes, 1994a). Problems may have a variety of causes and potential solutions. Lack of skills for managing uncertainty on the part of professionals may interact in dysfunctional ways with reluctance to acknowledge uncertainty on the part of clients and patients.

LACK OF CRITICAL THINKING VALUES, KNOWLEDGE, AND SKILLS

Propaganda is about claims making. Professionals, as well as other players in the propaganda game, are deeply involved in claims making, for example, about risks, causes, and remedies. If you have not acquired critical thinking values, skill, and knowledge, you are likely to be reeled in by propaganda. Many authors have described what they term "innumeracy," referring to difficulties in reasoning correctly about uncertainty (Paulos, 1988). Gigerenzer (2002) highlights four sources of uncertainty: (1) the illusion of certainty, (2) ignorance of risk, (3) miscommunication of risk, and (4) clouded thinking. The first point is discussed in chapter 7 in the description of a justification approach to knowledge in which it is assumed that we can arrive at certain truth by piling up examples. Ignorance of risk refers to being uninformed about the risks associated with different decisions, such as having a mammogram or attending an anxiety screening day. The third point, miscommunication of risk, refers to not knowing how to communicate risk in an understandable way. For example, a physician may know the risks associated with a certain test but not be able to clearly communicate her knowledge so that patients can make an informed decision. The fourth kind of innumeracy, clouded thinking, refers to knowing the risks but not knowing how to draw correct inferences from them. "For instance, physicians often know the error rates of a clinical test and the base rate of a disease, but do not know how to infer from this information the chances that a patient with a positive test actually has the disease" (Gigerenzer, 2002, p. 25).

This four-some illustrates the symbiotic relationship between characteristics of clients and patients and professionals who communicate with them who may misrepresent risks, for example, to encourage us to take a certain test, intentionally or not. Professionals may be as ignorant of risks and how to calculate, communicate, and draw inferences from them as clients. Thus as Gigernezer suggests, "dare to know" is the motto that applies. (See chapter 6.) He, as well as others, illustrate the negative consequences that may occur from these sources of innumeracy such as being misinformed about the diagnostic accuracy of a test (such as a mammogram) and, as a result, having invasive unnecessary interventions such as biopsies (e.g., see Woloshin, Schwartz, & Welch, 2008).

Barriers to the development of intelligence suggested by Sternberg (1986; 2002) include lack of motivation, lack of perseverance, distractibility, and fear of failure. Our educational system, which fails to teach students to be critical thinkers, contributes to our vulnerability. Often, as Ellul (1965) suggests, such education is "pre-propaganda" that primes us for more propaganda. If you have not acquired effective skills in raising questions and responding to critics, you may be loath to raise questions. Most people do not acquire critical thinking skills during their education. Indeed, some even argue that there is an interest on the part of the government for us not to acquire such skills. Although there may not be a conspiracy, we must ask why most of us do not acquire related values, skills, and knowledge during our education. Why don't we learn to raise many of the questions described in this book, starting in elementary school?

DECREASING GULLIBILITY: CAN A FISH GET OUT OF ITS BOWL?

We are complicit in being influenced by propaganda, partly because of our education and partly because of self-interests in being accepted and appearing up-to-date. If propaganda is so ubiquitous and persistent and we are so complicit in the process by virtue of our own education (perhaps the more education, the more propagandized, if Ellul is correct), what can we do? Can we get out of our fishbowl? The "What can we do?" question has different answers for different players. There is no doubt this will be difficult for all the reasons described in this book. But seeing more is possible and this book suggests ways to peek out. As a complement, I suggest reading or viewing material in five areas, all of which encourage you to consider the "big picture." One concerns the role of the biomedical industrial complex in orchestrating propaganda about alleged maladies and remedies (e.g., Petersen, 2008; Moynihan & Cassels, 2005; and Brody, 2007). Speaking for myself without reading related materials, I would not have known that most developers of practice guidelines have ties with pharmaceutical companies. I would never have suspected that a public relations company hired by a pharmaceutical company created an alleged psychiatric disorder of alleged epidemic proportions–social anxiety disorder–and that this psychiatric framing of anxiety was so readily accepted by psychiatrists, social workers and psychologists.[15] Anxiety in social situations is now viewed as a "mental illness." Lost are opportunities to understand anxiety and related behaviors as acquired by the same learning principles that apply to all behavior and as changeable by application of these principles.

A second kind of motivational reading describes corruption and fraud in the helping professions and related industries. This includes outright lying on the part of major researchers and failure to report money accepted from pharmaceutical companies (conflicts of interest) (e.g., Lo & Field, 2009). Money and prestige may not be the root of all evil, but it certainly is the root of some. A third kind of knowledge concerns the history or the public relations industry. I recommend viewing Adam Curtis's 2002 award wining documentary for the BBC *The Century of the Self*. You will discover that Bernays encouraged women to smoke by speculating about the unconscious symbolic meaning of cigarettes (penises) and drew on this for a spectacularly successful campaign to encourage women to light their "torches of freedom" (from men's power). A fourth kind concerns political, economic, and social factors including the role of the media in influencing what is viewed as a problem and what is not. A fifth kind of material highlights what you may be losing by buying into the medicalization of unhappiness (e.g., Elliot & Chambers, 2004) and the objectification of emotions (e.g., Illouz, 2008) in terms of moral and spiritual growth, connections with others, and concern for the avoidable miseries of others.

There is no escaping influence by propaganda. But we each make decisions about how vulnerable to remain to its influence. Rising out of the ooze of propaganda that surrounds us will be possible only in part, and attaining this part will have costs, for example, in time, effort, and perhaps social reinforcers. But what pleasures await—a life lived in which you exercise more choice—in which you are more likely to avoid the illusion of choice. A life in which you see past hasty generalizations that obscure the fascinating complexities and beauty of life around us—a life in which curiosity comes alive as you probe past boring glittering generalizations and quick fixes. Freedom to think for yourself—to make your own decisions—this is a key benefit of learning to detect and avoid influence by propaganda in the helping professions and other sources. Popping a pill to allay boredom, anxiety, and down moods is what the pharmaceutical companies would like you to do. They spend millions on advertisements to entice you to follow this reductionistic, narrow path that, although it may save the lives of some and makes life bearable for some, dulls rather than enlivens the lives of many.

Helpful Rules of Thumb for Decreasing Vulnerability to Propaganda

- *Search for well-argued alternative accounts.*
- *View uncertainty as an opportunity to make better decisions.* Overlooking uncertainty does not make it go away.
- *Value mistakes and errors as learning opportunities:* seek (rather than hide) corrective feedback.
- *Seek disconfirming information.* Our preconceptions and theories influence what we assume are causes, and, if incorrect, interfere with their detection. Our preferences for a view may compromise our ability to weigh evidence and sample data objectively. Thus, a problem with offering explanations is that they may influence what you see and assume, even when they are incorrect.
- *Pay attention to context—be politically savvy.* We often overlook the influence of environmental variables resulting in faulty beliefs about causes and remedies.
- *Examine all four cells of contingency tables* to combat the tendency to focus on hits (times you predicted accurately) and overlook misses (times you were wrong). We often make incorrect assumptions about causes because our attention is focused on one cell (usually the positive-positive one) of a four-cell contingency table.
- *Watch out for transfer effects (reliance on resemblance).* We have strong beliefs about what types of causes are associated with certain effects. In reality, causes and effects may be quite dissimilar. For example, the form of a behavior may not reveal its function.
- *Avoid confusions between causes and their effects.* The proximity of one event to another may lead us to believe that a causal relationship exists (when it does not). Is depression a cause of marital conflict, or is marital conflict a cause of depression? Is cognitive disorientation a result of being homeless and/or does being homeless contribute to cognitive disorientation?
- *Recognize the role of chance.* Many events happen by chance. Chance and randomness are a part of our everyday world and are much more likely to occur than we think. We often overlook randomness and offer explanations

for events that are a result of chance. Our need for control encourages a search for explanations that may offer only an illusion of control. Outcomes that are the result of chance are often attributed to personal characteristics such as skill or its lack.
- *Avoid confusions between speculation and investigation.* Propagandists encourage us to accept speculative thinking when, what is needed, is observation and critical tests of assumptions. They may encourage us to believe that we can discover causal relationships by speculation alone. Here too, propaganda plays into common myths. As Thouless (1974) points out, the belief that we can discover what is true and what is false by speculation alone "is one of the most long-lived delusions in human thought" (p. 78).
- *Watch out for vivid examples and illustrations.* Influence by the vividness of events may lead to inaccurate assumptions. Important nonoccurrences may be ignored; they are not vivid.
- *Pay attention to base rate data.* Information about how many people act a certain way or have a certain characteristic (e.g., urinate eight or more times a day) is often deliberately hidden. Also, we underuse consensus information in self-perception. For example, subjects who were informed that feelings of depression such as the "Sunday blues" were the rule not the exception were no less inclined to inaccurately attribute their mood to personal inadequacy (Nisbett, Borgida, Crandall, & Reed, 1976). Our tendency to associate with people who are similar and the greater ease of recalling our own beliefs and actions, encourage false consensus.
- *Ask: Could I be wrong?* We tend to be overconfident of our assumptions including assumptions of causal relationships; this overconfidence discourages a search for disconfirming data. As Dawes (1993) notes, predicting the future is quite different than understanding the past. Lack of appreciation of this difference is responsible in large part for overconfidence in our intuitive abilities. Retrospective memory is biased: "we interpret past events in a manner consistent with our present beliefs concerning stability and change in the human life course." This results in overestimations of the strength and consistency of "patterns" we observe retrospectively—hence, overconfidence in what we "know."
- *Be data focused.* Being data focused, as well as theory focused, will help you to avoid reliance on dubious accounts. The more tenuous a theory is, the less you should rely on it and the more attention you should pay to the data.
- *Focus on informative data.* Data related to a decision could be (1) relevant (help you to make sound decisions), (2) irrelevant, or (3) misleading. Irrelevant data may lead you astray. A few worthless items can dilute the effect of one helpful item. Ask: "Is this data relevant here?"
- *Acquire domain-specific knowledge and skills.* Specialized content knowledge and skills may be necessary to accurately assess concerns and related circumstances. You may have to search for and critically appraise related research findings to discover promising options.
- *Be aware of what you don't know, view ignorance as a kind of knowledge.* Seek (rather than hide) gaps in your knowledge related to decisions of concern. Witte, Witte, and Kerwin (1994) offered a course on medical

ignorance at the University of Arizona School of Medicine to highlight the importance of knowing what is not known as well as what is. Carroll (2001) has his students ask "ignorance" questions based on their reading of texts.
- *Ask what's missing*: propagandists try to hide or distort information.

SUMMARY

Our psychological vulnerabilities illustrate why propaganda is often successful. Self and other propaganda are closely intertwined. Cognitive illusions and biases, our tendency to be impressed with authorities, our desire to be associated with respected authorities, and our interest in being entertained, all hinder critical appraisal of claims in propaganda pitches. This is often combined with a lack of skill in raising questions about different kinds of claims. Wishful thinking and our tendency to search for information that supports our preferred views and to ignore evidence to the contrary contribute to influence by propaganda. We are subject to a variety of innumeracies that increase our gullibility such as underestimating chance occurrences. We value social approval and thus are susceptible to appeals to be one of the in-group rather than one of the out-group. Interests in entertainment may trump concerns about the accuracy of claims. Time and effort also come into play; it takes more time to critically appraise a claim than to simply accept it as true (or false). We may be unduly awed by prevailing opinion (consensus) including standards of practice and opinion leaders (authorities). Naïveté about the pervasiveness of propaganda, coupled with weak critical appraisal skills and lack of self-knowledge, increase vulnerability to propaganda. Naïveté includes inflated estimates of our knowledge. Other sources of vulnerability include little or no interest in having a carefully thought out position and fears of being criticized or rejected for "daring" to raise questions. A low tolerance for uncertainty and unrealistic expectations also contribute to falling for propaganda ploys.

PART FIVE

What You Can Do

12

Enhance Your Argument Analysis Skills

You can decrease your vulnerability to propaganda by enhancing your skills in argument analysis. What kind of claim is made? Does it concern risk, effectiveness of intervention, or accuracy of a test? What evidence is needed to evaluate the claim? Is this described? Is anything left out? Reasoning, problem-solving, and decision making are closely related and the tasks they involve overlap. We make decisions to address concerns and problems. Valuable skills include identifying assumptions and their implications (consequences), suspending judgment in the absence of sufficient evidence to support a claim/decision, understanding the difference between reasoning and rationalizing, and striping an argument of irrelevancies and phrasing it in terms of its essentials. Seeking counterevidence to preferred views and understanding the difference between the accuracy of a belief and the intensity with which it is held are also valuable. Valuable attitudes include recognizing the fallibility of our own opinions and the probability of bias in them, and valuing the discovery of ignorance as well as knowledge. Domain-specific knowledge, including both content (knowing what) and procedural knowledge (knowing how to apply content knowledge), may be needed to make sound decisions.

Partiality in the use of evidence such as hiding adverse effects of a drug is a hallmark of propaganda as illustrated in lawsuits against Eli Lilly the manufacturer of Zyprexa (an antipsychotic).[1] Unless you are familiar with an area (such as anxiety in social situations) you may not detect what is missing in a description, such as discussion of well-argued alternative views. This was found in exploring use of a Propaganda Index for reviewing problem-framing in published articles concerning social anxiety (Gambrill & Reiman, 2011). Selective publication of drug trials is common as with investigation of antidepressants (Turner Mathew, Linardaros, Tell, & Rosenthal, 2008).[2] Propagandists often give an *illusion of argument*—pieces are missing, hoped-for actions ("Fight terror") and effects ("Be safe") are vague, and critical appraisal is discouraged. Claims may be implied through visual images such as pictures of brains, as well as described verbally (McCabe & Castel, 2008). Our fears and hopes may cloud our judgment and propagandists take full advantage of this.

Some arguments are false even though they are valid. A valid argument is one whose premises if true, offers good or sufficient grounds for accepting a conclusion. The incorrectness of premises may be overlooked resulting in poor decisions. Considering clashing perspectives regarding an issue or question is vital in exploring the cogency of different views. Popper (1994) attributes the invention of criticism to

Xenophenes who traveled outside of Greece and discovered that not everyone accepted the Gods revered in his country. Grappling with differences between our beliefs and new ideas is necessary for learning—for correcting our background knowledge about an issue and discovering our ignorance. And, being reasonable "takes courage, because it seldom corresponds to being popular" (Scriven, 1976, p. 5). Not everyone values criticism. Self-interest may result in attempts to block critical appraisal of views. Consider this from Robert Birgeneau, current Chancellor the University of California at Berkeley: "Critics who say UC Berkeley shouldn't [have taken] $500 million from a British oil company to develop alternative energy espouse an 'abhorrent' attitude and threaten academic freedom" (*Berkeley Daily Planet*, 8(a6), 2007).

DIFFERENT KINDS OF REASONS

Many kinds of reasons are appealed to in arguments and different views emphasize different ones. These differences influence what information we seek. Consider the following:

1. Bill drinks because he is an alcoholic; he has a disease.
2. Mary's hallucinations are caused by a mental disorder—schizophrenia.
3. Joe's antisocial behavior at school is related to ineffective curriculum planning and ineffective classroom management skills on the part of the teacher and few recreational activities.
4. HIV risk behaviors are due to a variety of causes all of which contribute to their frequency and all of which must be addressed.

In examples one and two, we see appeals to biomedical causes. In the third example, a social learning view is emphasized and in the fourth, a multi-causal view is proposed. Tesh (1988) argues that such multi-causal views allow planners to focus on only one cause, ignoring the rest, misleading the public that a problem has been addressed when it has not. The history of science shows that many different causes are proposed prior to the discovery of the real cause of an illness. For example, before discovery of the bacillus causing tuberculosis, a wide variety of factors were proposed including genetic causes and moral contagion (influence by immoral others).

Reasoning from Analogy

We often reason from analogy; we look to what has happened before to discover what to do in new situations; we seek and draw conclusions from a comparison of experiences. Analogies may be literal or figurative. The view that common difficulties are "mental illness" identical to physical illnesses such as diabetes is the best known analogy in the helping professions and is widely accepted. Arguments based on analogy depend on the similarity of cases compared. Propagandists attempting to forward use of a given analogy, hide ways in which the analogy does not hold. Questions here are: How many respects are similar? How many are dissimilar?

Are the bases of comparison relevant to the issue? Is there agreement on the major points? For example, those who question the disease view of alcoholism argue that problematic drinking does not have the characteristic of a disease; for example, drinking does not necessarily become worse without treatment and, for some, one drink does not lead to many (Fingarette, 1988; Heyman, 2009). Advertisements make heavy use of symbols, words, and illustrations designed to transfer feelings from the material to the product promoted as described.

Reasoning From Samples

We generalize from samples to populations. A psychiatrist may interview three Vietnamese families and make assumptions about all Vietnamese families. The accuracy of a generalization depends on the size and representativeness of the sample and the degree of variability in a population. If there is no variability, a sample of one is sufficient. Questions here include: Do the examples accurately reflect characteristics of the population? What variations occur? Propagandists use vague terms to describe samples such as "many people."

Reasoning From Signs and Symptoms

Encouraging confusion between signs and symptoms is a popular propaganda ploy. Observed signs (such as slumped shoulders, down-cast eyes, and tears) are used to infer emotional states, such as depression. The signs are used as "signifiers" of a state. Signs are used as indicative of a certain history. Consider use of the invalid "reflex anal dilatation test" to evaluate whether children had been abused sexually resulting in harm to scores of children and parents.[3] A key question here concerns validity; are the signs accurate indicators of the state assumed? In medicine there are signs as well as symptoms, although here too, this distinction may be blurred or totally obscured. For example, if you feel hot (a symptom) your physician can take your temperature (a sign). Are there "signs" in other helping professions? Many argue that technology in neuroscience such as MRI imaging has revealed brain differences between those viewed as having a mental disorder and those not so labeled. Others argue that related research is flawed (Leo & Cohen, 2009; Vul, Harris, Winkielman, & Pashler, 2009). We often see multi-colored, scientific-looking pictures and illustrations of brains alleged to depict differences between the normal and the "mentally ill." These images are vivid and scientific appearing. Do they reflect what they claim to reflect? Have differences been found, and if so, what evidence is offered that they are responsible for "mental illness"? Are there alternative well-argued explanations such as a history of taking medication? (See Whitaker, 2010.)

Reasoning by Cause

Professionals also reason by cause. They have assumptions about the causes of anxiety, substance abuse, and domestic violence. They may embrace a certain theory and apply this to all situations. We attribute the behavior of others to certain causes such as their personality and/or their living situation. Fallacies related to causal reasoning and argument can be seen in Table 12.1.

Lack of evidence for a claim does not mean that it is incorrect as shown in the history of science; scores of ideas (including those about causes) were dismissed as ridiculous that were later shown to be true. Nor does lack of evidence discourage people from believing a claim and promoting it as true. Indeed if some scientists had not persisted in their explorations of claims dismissed as impossible, we would have missed out on many discoveries. Professionals often embrace theories that have no supporting evidence or which contradict empirical findings.[4] Beutler (2000) concludes that most theories used by psychotherapists are not supported by empirical evidence. Is the picture more positive in medicine? It depends on whom you ask.[5]

Most complex events are related to multiple causes including developmental factors (e.g., a birth defect in an artery). This illustrates the oversimplistic nature of claims that "X" causes antisocial behavior—the assumption that there is one cause when there are many. It seems that the less that is known in an area, the more flagrant are the claims of knowledge. Some authors have criticized descriptions of causal factors in the social sciences as an uninformative potpourri. Consider the term *biopsychosocial*. This implies that biological, psychological, and social factors all contribute to a personal or social problem, such as domestic violence. Is this helpful to the clinician who seeks to understand this phenomena and tries to prevent or decrease it? Aren't some factors more important than others? (See Tesh's (1988) critique of multi-causal accounts.) Questions Walton (2008) suggests for distinguishing between correlation and causation include the following.

1. Is there is a positive correlation between A and B?
2. Are there a significant number of instances of the positive correlation between A and B?

Table 12.1 FALLACIES RELATED TO CAUSAL REASONING

- Inferring cause from correlation
- *Post hoc ergo propter hoc* or after this, therefore because of this
- Confounding necessary and sufficient cause
- *Argumentum* ad *ignorantiam* or arguing from ignorance
- Fallacy of division (community/individual fallacy, Rose's fallacy)
- Fallacy of accident
- Fallacy of composition
- Confusion of cause and effect
- "Domino" or "slippery slope" fallacy
- Perfectionist fallacy
- Irrelevant conclusion (irrelevant thesis, fallacy of diversion, "red herring")
- False dilemma
- *Ad populum* (or appealing to the people)
- Objectionable vagueness
- Equivocation

SOURCE: Based on M. Janicek & D. L. Hitchcock (2005). *Evidence-based practice: Logic and critical thinking in medicine* (p. 54). Chicago: American Medical Association.

3. Is there good evidence that the causal relationship goes from A to B, and not from B to A?
4. Can a third factor be ruled out that accounts for the correlation between A and B (a common cause) that causes both A and B?
5. If there are intervening variables, then can it be shown that the causal relationship between A and B is indirect (mediated through other causes)?
6. If the correlation fails to hold outside a certain range of causes, then can the limits of this range be clearly indicated?
7. Can it be shown that the increase or change in B is not solely due to the way B is defined, the way entities are classified as belonging to the class of Bs, or changing standards of the way Bs are defined or classified?"(adapted slightly from Walton, 2008, pp. 277–78).

Reasoning by Exclusion

Another form of reasoning is by exclusion. Alternative accounts for a given event or behavior are identified, and the adequacy of each is examined and those found wanting are excluded. This involves a search for rival explanations.[6] Having a rule to search for alternative explanations is a key strategy you can use to avoid premature acceptance of a claim.

Hot and Cold Reasons

Hot and cold reasons correspond to two major routes to persuasion—by affective association (hot) or by reasoned argument (cold) (e.g., MacCoun, 1998). Many people try to persuade others by offering reasons that play on our emotions and appeal to accepted beliefs and values. Simon (1983) uses the example of Hitler's *Mein Kampf*:

> Hitler was an effective rhetorician for Germans precisely because his passion and incentives resonated with beliefs and values already present in many German hearts. The heat of his rhetoric rendered his readers incapable of applying the rules of reason and evidence to his arguments. Nor was it only Germans who resonated to the facts and values he proclaimed. The latent anti-Semitism and overt anti-Communism of many Western statesmen made a number of his arguments plausible to them. (pp. 98–99)

Propaganda takes advantage of emotional reasoning. Appeal to emotions such as fear of being ostracized (because of bad breath), not having a clean house, or getting a disease is a key strategy used in advertisements throughout the ages as illustrated in chapter 9.

ARGUMENTS

There are many products of reasoning: arguments are one. An argument refers to the claims and reasons offered for these. Toulmin and his colleagues (1979) use the term *argumentation* to refer to the process of "making claims, challenging these, backing them with reasons, criticizing these reasons and responding to the criticism offered" (p. 13). The term "argument" has a different meaning in everyday use in which it refers to disagreements between two people as in they had an argument about who would go to the store. Arguments involve a set of assertions, one of which is a conclusion and the rest of which are offered to support that conclusion. A psychiatrist may argue that, because a client has a history of being hospitalized for compulsive hand-washing, current complaints indicate that another episode is imminent. The purpose of arguments is often to convince someone (perhaps yourself) that something is true or to persuade someone to act in a certain way. Another purpose is to explore the accuracy of a claim, for example about the effectiveness of a medication.

Arguments consist of parts; they can be taken apart, as well as put together. They may be strong (convincing) or weak (unconvincing), simple or complex. A complex argument usually involves several assertions in support of one or more conclusions. Propagandists promote weak, flawed arguments as sound and convincing, perhaps by use of a confidant manner. In propagandistic material, little or no evidence may be offered for a claim and criticism is discouraged. Vague weasel words may be used as described in chapter 10. Claims may involve statements of fact ("a belief for which there is enough evidence to warrant a high degree of confidence," Nickerson, 1986, p. 36), assumptions, or hypotheses. For example, there may be no doubt that someone was hospitalized. The term "assumption" refers to "an assertion that we either believe to be true in spite of being unable to produce compelling evidence of its truth, or are willing to accept as true for purposes of debate or discussion" (Nickerson, 1986, pp. 36–37).

A hypothesis is an assertion that we do not know to be true but that we think is testable. Assumptions, hypotheses, or statements of fact may be used as premises in an argument—or they may serve as conclusions; that is, an assertion may be a conclusion that is drawn from what precedes it and can also be a premise with respect to what follows it. "The credibility of a conclusion can be no greater than the least credible of the premises from which it is drawn, so a conclusion cannot be considered a statement of fact unless all of the premises are statements of fact. . . . If the conclusion follows from two premises one of which is considered to be a fact and the other an assumption, the conclusion should not be considered a statement of fact" (Nickerson, 1986, p. 7). Universal assertions that contain words such as *all* or *none* are much more difficult to defend than are claims that contain qualifiers such as *some*. The statement that all children of alcoholic parents have problems as adults would be more difficult to support than the claim that some children of alcoholic parents have problems.

A key part of an argument is the claim, conclusion, or position that is put forward (see Table 12.2). In the statement "Mary Walsh is responsible for the abuse of this child; she had the greatest opportunity," the claim or conclusion is clear. Often, excessive wordiness makes the premises and/or conclusion difficult to identify; "an eloquent speaker or writer can dress up his arguments in all kinds of ways so as to conceal their deficits and make them attractive to his audience" (Toulmin et al., 1979, p. 106). Claims or conclusions are often qualified—that is, some probability is expressed as in "I think it is likely that Mary Walsh abused this child." Conclusions may be qualified by describing conditions under which they may not hold as in the statement: "She would only abuse the child if she were under extreme stress."

Table 12.2 Toulmin's Six Types of Statement in a Rational Argument

Label	Name(s)	Logical Function
C	Claim or conclusion	States a claim or a conclusion.
D	Data, evidence, or foundation	Offers data or foundations, i.e., relevant evidence, for the claim.
W	Inference warrant	Warrants or justifies the connection between data (D) and claim (C) by appealing to a rule of inference, such as an operational definition, a practical standard or an analogy.
Q	Modal qualifier	Qualifies a claim or conclusion (C) by expressing degrees of confidence and likelihood.
R	Rebuttal or reservation	Rebuts a claim or conclusion. (C) by stating the conditions under which it does not hold; or introduces reservations showing the limits within which the claim (C) is made.
B	Backing	Backs up, justifies, or otherwise supports an inferences warrant (W) by appealing to further evidence (empirical data, common knowledge, professional practice, scientific theory, and so on).
Colloquially speaking:		
C	answers the questions "What are you claiming?" "What is your conclusion?"	
D	answers the questions "Where is your evidence?" "What data do you have?"	
W	answers the questions "What is the connection?" "Why are you entitled to draw that conclusion?"	
Q	answers the questions: "How sure are you?" "What confidence do you have in your claim?" "How likely is it that what you say is correct?"	
R	answers the questions "What are you assuming?" "Under what conditions would your argument break down?" "What reservations would you make?"	
B	answers the questions "What is the justification for your line of reasoning?" "Is there any support for the connection you are making?"	

SOURCE: From D. B. Bromley (1986). *The case-study method in psychology and related disciplines* (p. 195). New York: Wiley. Copyright 1986 by John Wiley & Sons. Reprinted by permission.

The reasons or premises offered to support the claim is a second critical feature of an argument. Sound reasons consist of those for which sound arguments can be offered. Premises can be divided into two parts—grounds and warrants. The grounds (data or evidence) must be relevant to the claim, as well as sufficient to support the claim. Warrants concern the inference or justification of making the connection between the grounds and the claim. Do the grounds provide support for the claim? Warrants may involve a variety of appeals including to common knowledge, empirical evidence, or theory. Let's return to the claim that Mary Walsh is responsible for the abuse of a child. The ground is that she had the opportunity. The warrant may be that opportunity is sufficient to yield abuse. However, there is no firm backing for the warrant; opportunity does not an abuser make. Warrants purport to offer evidence for making the step from the grounds to the claim and the strength of the support should be evaluated. Does the warrant provide required evidence? Are the grounds necessary or sufficient? For example, opportunity to commit a crime is necessary but not sufficient to determine guilt. Can the premises be established independently of the conclusion? Is the argument convincing? Possible combinations of false or true premises and conclusions are shown in Figure 12.1.

An argument may be unsound for one of three reasons. There may be something wrong with its logical structure: (1) all mental patients are people; (2) John is a person; (3) therefore, John is a mental patient. It may contain false premises: (1) all battering men were abused as children; (2) Mr. Smith batters his wife; (3) therefore, Mr. Smith was abused as a child. It may be irrelevant or circular: (1) kicking other children is a sign of aggression; (2) Johnny kicks other children; (3) therefore, Johnny is aggressive. The last two arguments contain informal fallacies; they have a correct logical form but are still incorrect. Informal fallacies are related to the content of arguments rather than to their form. There are many varieties as described in chapter 13.

Arguments often contain unfounded premises. That is, they give the impression they are valid, but, because relevant facts have not been presented (they may have been omitted or distorted), they are not. Consider the logical error of *affirming the consequent*: (1) if he has measles, he should have red spots; (2) he has spots; (3) therefore, he has measles. *Denying the antecedent* also involves a logical error: (1) if we do not conserve our resources, the supply will run out; (2) we will not waste resources; (3) therefore, our supply will not run out. In neither case does the conclusion follow from the premises. These errors involve a confusion between one-way and bidirectional implication.[7] The *premise conversion error* occurs when the claim "all *X* are *Y*" (all clinicians are human) is assumed to be the same as "all *Y* are *X*" (all humans are clinicians).

		Conclusion	
		True	False
Premises	True	Necessary (Conclusion must be true if premises are true)	Impossible (Conclusion cannot be false if premises are true)
	False	Possible (Conclusion *may* be true even if premises are false)	Possible (Conclusion *may* be false if premises are false)

Figure 12.1. The Four Combinations of True or False Premises and Conclusions in a Valid Logical Argument.
SOURCE: *Reflections on reasoning* (p. 90), R. S. Nickerson, 1986, Hillsdale, NJ: Erlbaum. Copyright 1986 by Lawrence Erlbaum Associates. Reprinted by permission.

Deductive Arguments

Deductive arguments involve a sequence of premises and a conclusion; if the reasoning is logically valid, the conclusion necessarily follows (although it may not be true because one or more of the premises may be false) (see Table 12.3). Deductive arguments can produce false conclusions either when one of the premises is false or when one of the rules of deductive inference is violated, as in the logical fallacy of affirming the consequent. The conclusion may be true but it is invalid because it is arrived at by an illogical inference. Seldom are the major premises, as well as the conclusion, clearly stated in deductive arguments; more typically, at least one premise is missing.

Inductive Reasoning

Logical (deductive) arguments use deductive inferences. There are objective criteria that can be used to evaluate such arguments. With plausible (inductive) arguments,

Table 12.3 DISTINGUISHING DEDUCTIVE FROM INDUCTIVE ARGUMENTS

Deductive Example	Inductive Example
No animals are persons	Both psychiatrists and psychologists have professional training
Only persons have rights	
Therefore, no animals have rights.	Psychiatrists have hospital privileges.
	Therefore, psychologists should also have hospital privileges.
If you see one client, you've seen them all.	
I have seen one client.	
Therefore, I have seen them all.	All clients I have seen have been demoralized.
	Therefore all clients are demoralized when they first seek help.
Although the premises may or may not be true, if they are true, the conclusion is true as well, because, in a deductive argument, the information in the conclusion is implicitly present in the premises. Thus, adding information does not change the probability that the conclusion is true.	Although the premises provide evidence for the conclusion, it is possible that the conclusion is false even when the premises are true, because in an inductive argument the conclusion contains information not present in the premises.
	In an inductive argument, the probability of the conclusion may change with the addition of further information.
A good deductive argument is called valid.	A good inductive argument is called strong (or plausible).

SOURCE: Adapted from K. D. Moore (1986). *Inductive arguments: A field guide* (p. 4). Dubuque, IA: Kendall/Hunt.

there are no objective criteria; what is convincing may differ from person to person. Inductive reasoning involves generalizing from the particular to the general. It is assumed that what is true of the sample is true of all possible cases. For example, if a psychologist sees three young successful professional men who use cocaine and who complain of stress in their work life, he or she may conclude that all such men experience stress. Thus, in inductive reasoning, we go beyond the data at hand in drawing a conclusion that we cannot affirm with certainty. (See Popper's (1972) critique of induction.) Meaningless or unfounded statistics may be put forward in efforts to persuade us that something is true such as bogus estimates of stranger abduction as children. Surveys may be biased. Post-hoc reasoning may also lead us astray of when assuming that feeling better after taking a pill means that the pill caused the effect. Other possibilities include spontaneous remission (you were just about to feel better anyway) or there really was no problem. Perhaps you experienced a placebo response.

ANALYZING ARGUMENTS

Skill in analyzing arguments will help you to avoid influence by propaganda whether your own or that of others; the former is more challenging: "Playing prosecutor, judge, and jury when one is oneself the defendant requires an unusual degree of objectivity and commitment to the truth" (Nickerson, 1986, p. 88). Arguments are typically incomplete in propaganda pitches. Consider the following claims ranging from a vague slogan to specific claims: (1) our services work; (2) anxiety in social situations reflects a mental disorder; (3) inability to concentrate can be remedied by taking Ritalin; (4) full body CT scans can save your life. Key premises or conclusions may be missing. Examining an argument requires filling in these parts. You can use the steps below to analyze incomplete logical arguments.

- Identify the conclusion or key assertion.
- List all the other explicit assertions that make up the argument as given.
- Add any unstated assertions that are necessary to make the argument complete. (Put them in parentheses to distinguish them from assertions that are explicit in the argument.)
- Order the premises (or supporting assertions) and conclusion (or key assertion) to show the structure of the argument. (Nickerson, 1986, p. 87)

Questions to raise when evaluating inductive arguments include the following:

- Are the facts accurate?
- Do the examples consist of isolated or universal instances?
- Do the examples used cover a significant time period?
- Are the examples given typical or atypical?
- Is the conclusion correctly stated?
- Is the argument really of concern—the "so what" and "what harm" questions? (Huber, 1963, p. 140)

Claims based on statistical analyses may be misleading in a number of ways that relate to the size and representativeness of the samples on which they are based. There are many different meanings of the term "representative sample" (Kruskal &

Mosteller, 1981). The most common one refers to an absence of selective factors that would render the sample unrepresentative of the population from which it is drawn. Rather than reporting accurate data, those who advocate for greater attention to a problem and more funding for related services, may distort the scope of the problem; they may engage in "advocacy scholarship." Groups with a special interest in a problem may deliberately inflate the number of people affected by a problem. Joel Best (2004) argues that the prevalence of stranger abduction is greatly exaggerated. "Hot" topics such as abortion, use of drugs, gay marriage, provide fodder for fallacy spotting. The importance of asking for precise figures is illustrated by the varied meanings of words such as *sometimes, often,* or *rarely*. For example, the meaning of the term "sometimes" has been found to range from 20% to 46% (Pepper, 1981).

Only relative risk may be given rather than both relative and absolute risk as described in chapter 6. Misleading percentages may be offered. Proponents of a new suicide prevention center may claim that there has been a 200% increase in the number of suicides over the past year. The total increase may be two additional cases. The total number of occurrences of a given event may be cited when a percentage would be more informative. A drug company may claim that more people improved using drug X than any other drug. However, the best drug on the market may only be effective 5% of the time. Drug X may be effective 6% of the time, usually not much to write home about. Tables and charts may mislead rather than inform. Giving specific numbers gives an illusion of accuracy (e.g., see Seife, 2010). Our tendency to be influenced by vivid material makes us vulnerable to distortions created by photographs, charts, and graphs (Huff, 1954; Tufte, 2006). Graphic displays often lie by omission—by what is left out. They may omit data relevant to the question: "compared with what?" Only a portion of a graph may be shown, resulting in a distorted view.[9] Visual representation may not be consistent with numerical representation. Principles of graphical excellence suggested by Tufte (1983) include the following: (1) complex ideas are communicated with clarity, precision, and efficiency; (2) the viewer receives the greatest number of ideas in the shortest time with the least ink in the smallest space; and (3) the truth about the data is depicted (p. 51).

We should interpret words as they generally would be defined. And, as Scriven (1976) points out, arguments should not be dismissed simply because they are presented emotionally or because we dislike the conclusion. The emotion with which a position is presented is not necessarily related to the soundness of an argument. Since plausible (inductive) arguments do not have to fit any particular form, objective evaluation is more difficult than it is with deductive arguments. As with all arguments, the accuracy of the premises is vital to assess. (See examples of Socratic Questions in Table 12.4.) However, even if these are assumed to be true, people may disagree as to whether they provide evidence for a conclusion. Questions of value in evaluating a logical argument include: Is it complete? Is its meaning clear? Is it valid (does the conclusion follow from the premises)? Do I believe the premises? (Nickerson, 1986, p. 88). An argument may be worthy of consideration even though it has some defects.

Rebuttal

Counterarguments should be considered. Are there arguments on the same issue that point to the opposite conclusion or to a somewhat different conclusion? Could an analogy be used to support the opposite conclusion? Would other arguments

Table 12.4 A Taxonomy of Socratic Questions

Questions of Clarification

- What do you mean by _____?
- What is your main point?
- How does _____ relate to _____?
- Could you put that another way?
- Let me see if I understand you; do you mean _____ or _____?
- Could you give me an example?
- Would this be an example?
- Could you explain that further?

Questions That Probe Assumptions

- What are you assuming?
- What could we assume instead?
- You seem to be assuming _____. Do I understand you correctly?

Questions That Probe Reasons and Evidence

- What would be an example?
- Why do you think that is true?
- Do you have evidence for that?
- What would change your mind?
- What other information to we need?
- Is there reason to doubt that evidence?
- Who is in a position to know if that is so?
- How could we find out whether that is true?
- Are these reasons adequate?
- How does that apply to this case?
- What difference does that make?

Questions About Viewpoints or Perspectives

- What would someone who disagrees say?
- What is an alternative?

Questions That Probe Implications and Consequences

- What are you implying by that?
- What effect would that have?

Questions About the Question

- How can we find out?
- What does this question assume?
- How could someone settle this question?
- Can we break this question down?
- Do we all agree that this is the question?
- To answer this, what questions would have to answer first?
- Is this the same issue as _____?
- Why is this question important?

SOURCE: Adapted from R. Paul (1992). *Critical thinking: What every person needs to survive in a rapidly changing world* (Rev. 2nd Ed.) (pp. 367–68). <http://www.criticalthinking.org>

support the same conclusion? Possible counterarguments made by astrologers to support their belief in astrology are: (1) Astrology has great antiquity and durability. (2) Astrology is found in many cultures. (3) Many great scholars have believed in it. (4) Astrology is based on observation. (5) Extraterrestrial influences exist. (6) Astrology has been proved by research. (7) Nonastrologers are not qualified to judge. (8) Astrology works (Kelly et al., 1989). Principles Damer (2005) suggests for effective rational discussion include the following:

FALLIBILITY:
A willingness to admit you could be wrong.

TRUTH SEEKING:
A commitment to search for the truth or best-argued position—to examine alternative positions and to welcome objections to your view.

BURDEN OF PROOF:
This rests on the person who presents it.

CHARITY:
Arguments should be presented in their strongest version.

CLARITY:
Positions, defenses, and challenges are clearly described.

RELEVANCE:
Only reasons or questions directly related to the merit of the position at issue are offered. (See Grice's maxims in Table 12.5.)

ACCEPTABILITY:
The premises or reasons relied on meet standard criteria of acceptability.

SUFFICIENT GROUNDS:
Those who present an argument for or challenge a position should attempt to provide reasons sufficient in number, kind, and weight to support the conclusion.

REBUTTAL:
The person who presents an argument for or challenges a position should attempt to provide effective responses to all serious challenges or rebuttals.

RESOLUTION:
An issue should be considered resolved if the proponent for a position presents an argument that uses relevant and acceptable premises sufficient in number, kind, and weight to support the premises and the conclusion and provides an effective rebuttal to all serious challenges.

SUSPENSION OF JUDGMENT:
If no position can be successfully defended, or if two or more positions can be defended with equal strength, you should suspend judgment or, if practical considerations require a decision, proceed based on preferences.

RECONSIDERATION:
Parties are obligated to reconsider the issue if flaws are found in an argument.[10] These principles reflect Gricean conversational maximum. (See Table 12.5.)

Table 12.5 GRICE'S CONVERSATIONAL MAXIMS AS A GUIDE

Grice introduced the following maxims as a guide to conversation. We can draw on these to avoid self-propaganda as well as to avoid propagandizing others.

Maxim of Quantity

1. Make your contribution to the conversation as informative as necessary.

2. Do not make your contribution to the conversation more informative than necessary.

Maxim of Quality

1. Do not say what you believe to be false.

2. Do not say that for which you lack adequate evidence.

Maxim of Relevance

1. Be relevant (i.e., say things related to the current topic of the conversation).

Maxim of Manner

1. Avoid obscurity of expression.

2. Avoid ambiguity.

3. Be brief (avoid unnecessary wordiness).

4. Be orderly.

KINDS OF ARGUMENTS: THE IMPORTANCE OF CONTEXT

Walton (2008) views argument as a pragmatic notion in which reasoning is used in a context of dialogue. Arguments occur in different contexts, including articles in professional journals, courts of law, and case conferences. These different contexts influence norms, values, procedures, and requirements for and types of evidence that are acceptable or unacceptable. (See Table 12.6.)

Courts of law favor an adversarial (competitive) format in which each party tries to settle a dispute in its favor. In both professional and scientific contexts, there should be "willingness and ability to be self-critical [self-reflexive], to deal sensibly with justifiable objections and queries from others" (Bromley, 1986, p. 233). In clinical settings, a concern such as child abuse must be considered from different perspectives including medical, legal, psychological, and educational, each of which has a unique framework for viewing problems and potential remedies. Misunderstandings and bad feelings may result when participants in a discussion do not recognize that different kinds of arguments are being used. Lawyers may view clinicians as fuzzy thinkers and clinicians may view lawyers as inhumane and legalistic in questioning the accuracy of "alleged" evidence.

Aristotle distinguished three kinds of arguments: didactic, dialectical, and contentious. The hallmark of dialectical arguments is a spirit of inquiry. The aim of people involved in teaching and learning was considered to differ from the aim of those

Table 12.6 TYPES OF DIALOGUE

Type of dialogue	Initial situation	Participant's goal	Goal of dialogue
Persuasion	Conflict of opinions	Persuade other party	Resolve or clarify issue
Inquiry	Need to have proof	Find and verify evidence	Prove (disprove) hypothesis
Negotiation	Conflict of interests	Get what you most want	Reasonable settlement both can live with
Information-seeking	Need information	Acquire or give information	Exchange information
Deliberation	Dilemma or practical choice.	Co-ordinate goals and actions	Decide best available course of action
Eristic	Personal conflict	Verbally hit out at opponent	Reveal deeper basis of conflict

SOURCE: D. Walton (2008). *Informal logic: A pragmatic approach* (2nd Ed.) (p. 8). New York: Cambridge University Press.

involved in competition. "for a learner should always state what he thinks; for no one is even trying to teach him what is false; whereas in a competition the business of a questioner is to appear by all means to produce an effect upon the other, while that of the answerer is to appear unaffected by him" (Topics, 159a 25). Aims of the questioner in contentious arguments include (1) to refute the opponent—that is, to prove the point contradictory to his or her thesis; (2) to show that the opponent has committed a fallacy; (3) to lead the opponent into paradox; (4) to make the opponent use an ungrammatical expression; and (5) to reduce the opponent to babbling (Aristotle cited in Hamblin, 1970, p. 63).

Adversarial arguments are competitive in nature; each party concentrates on defending one line of reasoning and attacking other lines presented. In arbitrational arguments, the focus is on arriving at a compromise resolution satisfactory to both parties. Neither party may be fully satisfied by the conclusion reached, but agree to abide by it. Judgments in clinical contexts must often be made under time pressures and without all needed information.

1. Persuasion (Critical Discussion)

Here, the goal is to persuade the other party of a conclusion or point of view. "Facts" may be introduced. There is an obligation to "co-operate with the other participant's attempts to prove his thesis also" (p. 5). (See Table 12.7.)

> What is distinctive about persuasion dialogue is that in order to prove something successfully, we must derive it by acceptable arguments from premises that the other party is committed to. In other words, argumentation in a critical discussion is, by its nature, directed toward the other party and is based on that

Table 12.7 Negative Rules in Different Stages of Persuasion Dialogue

Opening

Unlicensed shifts from one type of dialogue to another are not allowed.

Confrontation

1. Unlicensed attempts to change the agenda are not allowed.
2. Refusal to agree to a specific agenda of dialogue prohibits moving to the argumentation stage.

Argumentation

1. Not making a serious effort to fulfill an obligation is bad strategy. Examples include failures to meet a burden of proof or to defend a commitment when challenged.
2. Trying to shift your burden of proof to the other party, or otherwise alter the burden of proof illicitly, is not allowed.
3. Purporting to carry out an internal proof by using premises that are not commitments of the other party is not allowed.
4. Appealing to external sources of proof without backing up your argument properly can be subject to objection.
5. Failures of relevance can include providing the wrong thesis, wandering away from the point of concern, or answering the wrong question.
6. Failure to ask questions that are appropriate for a given stage of dialogue should be prohibited, along with asking appropriate questions.
7. Failure to reply appropriately to questions should not be allowed, including evasive replies.
8. Failure to define, clarify, or justify the meaning or definition of an important term used in an argument, in accordance with standards of precision appropriate to the discussion, is a violation, if the use of this term is challenged.

Closing

1. A participant must not try to force closure except by mutual agreement or by meeting the goal of the dialogue (slightly adopted from Walton, 2008, pp. 16–17).

SOURCE: D. Walton (2008). *Informal logic: A pragmatic approach* (2nd Ed.). New York: Cambridge University Press.

other party's commitments. We must always ask: what will successfully persuade this particular person [or audience]? (Walton, 1995, p. 100)

2. Inquiry

"The goal of the inquiry is to prove whether a particular proposition is true [or false] or, alternatively, to show that, despite an exhaustive search uncovering all the available evidence, it cannot be determined that a proposition is true [or false]" (Walton, 1995, p. 106). The goal is an increase in knowledge (Walton, 2008, p. 6). Such discussion are *cumulative* "in the sense that the line of reasoning always moves forward from well-established premises to conclusions that are derived by very careful [ideally, deductively valid] inferences, so that the conclusions are solidly established' (Walton, 1995, p 106). The stages include collecting relevant data, discussing what conclusion can be drawn, and presenting what has been decided, perhaps in a report. *Evidential priority* (the premises are better established or are more reliable as evidence than the conclusion they were used to prove) is a key concern in inquiry (p. 108). Different types of inquiry have different standards of proof (e.g., legal, governmental). Walton (1995) notes that a debate differs from inquiry because the judges or audience can be won over using fallacious arguments in an adversarial context.

3. Negotiation
Here "the primary goal is self interest, and the method is to bargain' (Walton, 2008, p. 6). At stake here is not truth but goods or economic resources. Thus argumentation may occur, but the goal may not be to discover the truth.

4. Information-seeking
Here one party has some information that another party wants to find out about. This kind of discussion is asymmetrical. The role of the one party is to give information that he possesses and the role of the other is to receive or gain access to it. Walton (1995) notes that this kind of dialogue is different from the inquiry in which all parties are "more or less equally knowledgeable or ignorant and their collective goal is to prove something" (Walton, 1995, pp. 113–14).

5. Deliberation
In this type of discussion there is a dilemma or practical choice that must be made. Questions may be "How do I do this?" or, "Which of two possibilities are best?"

6. The Quarrel
This kind of dialogue involves personal conflict. The goal is to share, acknowledge and deal with "hidden grievances," often to facilitate continuation of a personal relationship.

> Quarrelsome dialogue is that type of dialogue where the participants try to blame the other party for some wrong allegedly committed in the past. The aim is to humiliate or cast blame on the other party through a personal attack. In sophistical dialogue, the aim is to impress an audience [or third party] by showing how clever you are in attacking your opponent in a verbal exchange and showing how foolish her views are. Both subtypes are classified as eristic dialogues because the goal is to defeat the other party at all costs. The eristic dialogue is unique as a type of dialogue, of all the types of dialogue studied here, because it is a zero-sum game, in the sense of being completely adversarial – one party wins if and only if the other party loses. All the other types of dialogues are based upon the Gricean cooperativeness principle (Grice, 1975). (Walton, 1995, p. 112)

Shifts from one type of dialogue to another may or may not reflect deception. For example, a shift from an inquiry discussion to an information-seeking one may not reflect deception. Shifts become a problem in inquiry dialogues where there is deception or misunderstanding. One participant may not be aware of a shift and the other party may conceal it "and take advantage of the first party's confusion" (Walton, 1995, p. 120). Walton gives the example of infomercials, which have the format and appearance of a talk show, but are in fact commercials.[11] He argues that infomercials "exploit the viewer's initial expectation that he is watching a news or talk show that is presenting information in a reporting or interviewing format. Not until the viewer watches the program for a while does it become clear that the program is really an advertisement for a product" (p. 121).

> There is nothing wrong per se with a sales pitch, a commercial advertisement for a product. But if the producers are trying to disguise the sales pitch by putting it in another format [such as an allegedly objective news report], this is quite a different matter. The argumentation in the sales pitch is not fallacious or open to critical condemnation per se, just because it is a sales pitch. We all know and expect that a sales pitch is taking a one-sided approach of promoting a product, making no pretense of being unbiased reporting of the assets as well as the defects or shortcomings of the product [in the way we would expect, for example, of Consumer Reports]. (pp. 121–22)

He views this as a calculated deception. There may be a mutual misunderstanding in which both participants wrongly assume that the other party is engaged in one type of dialogue.[12] One person may view the exchange as a critical discussion; the other may assume the first party is engaged in a quarrel (Walton, 1995, p. 123). Different types of dialogue may be mixed together in the same discussion.

This pragmatic, contextual view highlights that what is viewed as a fallacy in one context may not be in another. Walton (1995) suggests that reviewing an allegation of fallacy requires posing questions appropriate to the situation. Thus, fallacies are techniques used as argumentation tactics that can be employed properly or improperly in any particular situation (Walton, 1995, p. 263).[13] Glib answers to relevant questions are out-of-order.

> fallacies may be contrasted with flaws, blunders [errors or lapses that weaken or damage someone's argument] and other weaker or less dramatic failures of argumentation, because a fallacy involves the use of a characteristic pattern of strategy of argument in discussion in order to extract some advantage or win out over an opponent in a contestive discussion unfairly. (Walton, 1995, pp. 263–64)

ARGUMENTS FROM AUTHORITY

As mentioned in chapter 7, it is important to distinguish between cognitive (always subject to critical questioning), and institutional or administrative authority (Walton, 1997).

> The second form of the appeal to authority invests some sources with infallibility and finality and invokes some external force to give sanction to their decisions. On questions of politics, economics, and social conduct, as well as on

religious opinions, the method of authority has been used to root out, as heretical or disloyal, divergent opinions. Men have been frightened and punished into conformity in order to prevent alternative views from unsettling our habitual beliefs (Cohen & Nagel, 1934, p. 194; quoted in Walton, 1997, p. 251)

Treating an expert opinion that should be open to critical questioning as if it were infallible represents a shift from one type of "authority" to another (Walton, 1997, p. 251; see also Walton, 2008). As Walton highlights, authority based on intellectual or cognitive grounds is always provisional and subject to change, for example as new evidence appears. "In contrast administrative or institutional authority is often final and enforced coercively so that it is not open to challenge in the same way. Thus treating the authority backing an argument as though it were of the latter sort, when it is really supposed to be of the former sort, is a serious and systematic misuse of argument from authority. It can be a bad error or, perhaps even worse, it can be used as a sophistical tactic to unfairly get the best of a partner in argumentation" (Walton, 1997, p. 252).[14]

If someone makes a claim and is asked for evidence, he or she may describe this, admit evidence is not known, admit that no evidence was given, or engage in palaver (vague responses designed to mislead) or attack the questioner. The key marker of the *ad verecundiam* fallacy consists of efforts to close off, block or preempt appropriate critical questions. Walton suggests that evidence of this dogmatic stance can be found in "dialogical clues,"

> If the experts or their advocates who are using expert opinions to support their arguments refuse to countenance any critical questioning of a kind that would be appropriate in the case, then that is contextual evidence of the committing of an *ad verecundiam fallacy*. To gather this contextual evidence, one has to study the profile of dialogue as applied to the sequence of argumentation used by the arguers and their dialogue exchanges, showing how each reacted to the moves of the other in a given case. In particular, you need to look for repeated attempts to block off the asking of critical questions by saying that such questioning is not appropriate in the dialogue the participants are said to be engaged in. (Walton, 1997, p. 259)

Weasel words such as "well validated," "established," "firmly established," are widely used in the professional literature as illustrated in chapter 9. Bold assertions, such as "certainly," "necessarily," "beyond doubt," and "obviously," suggest that it is not appropriate to question the speaker. An authority in one area is not necessarily an authority in other areas. An "authority" may misquote or misinterpret someone. Experts often disagree or little may be known in a field. When experts disagree, we should examine related evidence, reasons, and arguments. We can review the track record of an expert (Kahane, 1995). We should consider what kind of argument is at hand, that is, consider the *context* of the discussion.

Walton (1997) suggests that fallacious appeal to an authority can occur in three ways. Common to all "is the suppression of critical questioning by making the appeal to authority seem more absolute than it really is" (p 252).

> an appeal to institutional authority can be presented in such a way that it appears to be more absolute [less open to critical questioning] than it really is; (2) the same thing can happen with an appeal to expert opinion [an appeal to cognitive

authority]; or (3) the two types of appeals can be confused. In particular, the most common type of fallacy occurring here is the kind of case where an appeal to expertise [cognitive authority] is confused with an appeal to institutional authority, particularly when the institutional authority is portrayed as having a finality or absolute authority that admits of no critical questions. (p. 252)

Only by looking at the different moves in an argument can we distinguish among the three kinds of fallacies: "the mark of the fallacious type of case is the dogmatic or 'suppressing' way of putting the argument by the proponent that interferes with the respondent's asking of appropriate critical questions at the next move or moves, appearing to lead the respondent no room to pose critical question(s)" (Walton, 1997, p. 253). Consider this example:

Respondent: Why A?

Proponent: Because E asserts that A, and E is an expert.

Respondent: Is E's assertion based on evidence?

Proponent: How could you evaluate such evidence? You are not an expert in this field of scientific knowledge.

Respondent: No, I am not an expert but surely I have the right to ask what evidence E based her opinion on.

Proponent: The assessment of this kind of clinical evidence is the solemn responsibility of the scientists. You are not even a scientist!" (p. 254).

Variations of the general *ad verecundiam* fallacy proposed by Walton (1997) include appeal to celebrity, unidentified authority, and misquoting authority. Others include concealing the dishonesty or bias of an authority, his or her lack of conscientiousness, or the deviancy of an expert opinion. Dogmatism has a key role in these fallacies. Walton (1997) suggests that both the halo effect and obedience to authority (conformity) contribute to the appeal of the *ad verecundiam* argument as a "device of deceptive persuasion."

[T]here is a powerful institutional halo effect that seems to exclude critical questioning by a non-scientist, and make the claim seem to be unchallengeable by reasoned argumentation. The setting, or way the argument is presented in context, makes it seem impolite and socially inappropriate—here the halo effect explains Locke's notions of 'respect' and 'submission'—to question the say-so of an authority. (p. 260)

Imaginary Authority: Fabrication

Reference may be made to imaginary evidence; that is, a speaker or writer may refer to evidence that does not exist. A psychologist may report that he has seen many clients with anorexia and so he can speak with authority about this disorder, when in fact he has seen one such client. Szasz views psychiatric labels as fabrications. An infamous example of the use of imaginary authority is the case of Sir Cyril Burt.

There was a failure to spot dogma masquerading as objective truth (Broad & Wade, 1982, p. 203). Burt invented data to support his views. "He used his mastery of statistics and gift of lucid exposition to bamboozle alike his bitterest detractors and those who claimed his greatness as a psychologist" (p. 204). He submitted articles in favor of his views under an assumed name and published them in the *British Journal of Statistical Psychology*, of which he was editor for sixteen years. He not only made up data, he invented coauthors "from the vasty deep of his tormented imagination and clothed them so well in the semblance of scientific argument that the illusion fooled all his fellow scientists for as much as thirty years" (p. 204). Some argue that the fabrication of data is becoming more common as pressures mount to publish and competition for funding becomes keener. Research findings may be completely misrepresented; a sentence may be taken out of context or minor parts of a sentence may be presented as major parts. Claims may be attributed to a famous person who never said or wrote such a thing, even by well-known scholars. How many readers check sources cited in support of statements made in the professional journals and books? Systematic examinations of such sources reveal biased promotion of a favored view (e.g., Greenberg, 2009). Lists of alleged "best practices" may contain programs no better than programs not included (Gandhi, Murphy-Graham, Petrosino, Chrismer, & Weiss, 2007; Gorman & Huber, 2009).

HELPFUL DISTINCTIONS

The distinctions described in the next section can help us to critically appraise arguments and spot propaganda ploys.

Widely Accepted/True:

What is widely accepted may not be true. Consider the following exchange

- *Ms. Simmons* (psychiatrist): I've referred this client to the adolescent stress service because this agency is widely used.
- *Ms. Harris* (supervisor): Do you know anything about how effective this agency is in helping adolescents like your client?
- *Ms. Simmons*: They receive more referrals than any other agency for these kinds of problems. We're lucky if they accept my client.

Many people believe in the influence of astrological signs (their causal role is widely accepted). However, to date, there is no evidence that they have a causal role in influencing behavior, that is, risky predictions based on related beliefs have not survived critical tests.

A Feeling That Something is True Versus Whether it is True

Not making this distinction helps to account for the widespread belief in many questionable causes of behavior such as astrological influences, crystals, spirit guides, and so on (e.g., Dawes, 2001; Shermer, 1997). People often use their "feeling" that something is true as a criterion to accept or reject possible causes. However a "feeling" that something is true may not (and often does not), corresponds to what is true.

Reasoning/Persuasion

We all try to persuade people to believe or act in a certain way. The question is: How to we do so? *Reasoning* involves a *critical evaluation of claims*. The major intent of propagandistic persuasion is not to inform or arrive at a sound decision, but to encourage action with little thought. Persuasive appeals include ploys such as appeals to fear, special interests and scarcity (Brock & Green, 2005; Cialdini, 2001; Pratkanis & Aronson, 2001).

Logic and Reasoning

Logic is concerned with the form or validity of deductive arguments. "It provides methods and rules for restating information so as to make what is implicit explicit. It has little to do with the determination of truth or falsity" (Nickerson, 1986, p. 7). Effective reasoning requires much more than logic; it requires skill in developing arguments and hypotheses, establishing the relevance of information to an argument, and evaluating the plausibility of assertions. It requires a willingness to change beliefs on the basis of evidence gathered. Knowledge is required to evaluate the plausibility of premises related to an argument as in the following example: (1) Depression always has a psychological cause; (2) Mr. Draper is depressed; (3) Therefore, Mr. Draper's depression is psychological in origin. The logic of this argument is sound, but the conclusion may be false because the first premise is false. The cause of Mr. Draper's depression could be physiological.

> Like most everyday problems that call for reasoning, the explicit premises [may] leave most of the relevant information unstated. Indeed, the real business of reasoning in these cases is to determine the relevant factors and possibilities, and it therefore depends on a knowledge of the specific domain. Hence, the construction of putative counter examples calls for an active exercise of memory and imagination rather than a formal derivation of one expression from others. (Johnson-Laird, 1985, p. 45)

Truth and Credibility

Karl Popper defines truthful statements as those that correspond with the facts. Credible statements are those that are possible to believe. Phillips (1992) points out that just about anything may be credible. This does not mean that it is true. Simply because it is possible to believe something does not mean that it is true. Although scientists seek true answers (statements that correspond to the facts), this does not mean that there is certain knowledge. Rather, certain beliefs (theories) have (so far) survived critical tests or have not yet been exposed to them. An error "consists essentially of our regarding as true a theory that is not true" (Popper, 1992 p. 4).

Personal and Objective Knowledge

Personal knowledge refers to what you as an individual believe you "know." Objective knowledge refers to assumptions that have survived critical tests or evaluation. It is public. It is criticizable by others. We typically overestimate what "we know"—that is our self-assessments of our "knowledge" and skills are inflated (Dunning, Heath, & Suls 2004).

Reasoning Compared to Rationalizing

Reasoning involves the review of evidence against as well as evidence in favor of a position. In reasoned persuasion, there is an openness to changing our mind when a better argument is offered. *Rationalizing* a belief (a key form of self-deception) entails a selective search for evidence in support of a belief or action that may or may not be deliberate. "[It is] easy after having made some choice that is significant in our lives to fall into the trap of convincing ourselves of the reasonableness of that choice. It is also easy to forget, with the passage of time, what the real determinants of the choice were and to substitute for them 'reasons' that make the choice seem like a good one, and perhaps a better one than it actually was" (Nickerson, 1986, p. 14). When we rationalize arguments, we are interested in building a case rather than weighing evidence for and against an argument. When we rationalize we engage in defensive thinking. (See discussion of confirmation biases and excuses in chapter 11.) Reasoning also differs from political thinking which "is motivated by a need to be accepted, or to get ahead. To think politically is to forget about what you think is true and to voice opinions that you think are likely to win approval from your friend" (Notturno, 2000, p. 13).

Propaganda, Bias, and Point of View

Propaganda refers to encouraging beliefs and actions with the least thought possible. Propagandists play on our emotions. They may present only one side of an argument, hide counterarguments to preferred views, and attack the motives of critics to deflect criticism. For example, they may say that anyone who doubts the effectiveness of services for battered women must be trying to undermine efforts to help women. *Propagandists* are often aware of their interests or may disguise these. Messages are posed in a way to encourage uncritical acceptance. *Bias* refers to an emotional leaning to one side. Biased people try to persuade others but may not be aware they are doing so. They may use propaganda tactics and faulty reasoning and offer statements in a manner designed to gain uncritical, emotional acceptance of a position. Our own biases may make if difficult to identify biases in a statement. Maclean (1981) suggests that those with a *point of view* are also aware of their interests, but they describe their sources, state their views clearly, and avoid propaganda ploys. Their statements and questions encourage critical appraisal. Views can be examined because they are clearly stated. People with a point of view are open to clarifying their statements when asked.

Reasoning and Truth

Reasoning does not necessarily yield the truth. "People who are considered by many of their peers to be reasonable people often do take, and are able to defend quite convincingly, diametrically opposing positions on controversial matters" (Nickerson, 1986, p. 12). However, effective reasoners are more likely to arrive at claims that are closer to the truth than ineffective reasoners. The accuracy of a conclusion does nor necessarily indicate that the reasoning used to reach it was sound, for example, errors in the opposite direction may have cancelled each other out. Lack of evidence for a claim does not mean that it is incorrect. Similarly, surviving critical tests does not mean that a claim is true; further tests may show that it is false.

Knowing and the Illusion of Knowing

There is a difference between accurately understanding content and the *illusion of knowing*—a belief that comprehension has been attained when in fact, it has failed (Zechmeister & Johnson 1992, p. 151). These authors suggest that the illusion of knowing is encouraged by thinking in terms of absolutes (e.g., "proven," "well established") rather than thinking conditionally (e.g., "This may be . . ." "This could be . . ."). We often think we "know" something when we do not. Familiarity with a claim or concept creates an (often incorrect) impression of knowledge. That is, simply hearing a word representing a concept creates the impression that the hearer is familiar with what the term means, when they are not (Renner, 2004). This effect is a hindrance to acquiring knowledge because we believe we already have it. Claims may appeal to "grand narratives," for example, generally accepted ideas about what causes a certain problem, such as depression. The illusion of knowing is encouraged by mindless reading habits, for example, not reading material carefully and not monitoring understanding by asking questions such as "Do I understand this?; What is this person claiming?; What are his reasons?" There is a failure to take remedial action such as rereading and a failure to detect contradictions and unsupported claims. Redundant information may be focused on, creating a false sense of accuracy (Hall, Ariss, & Todorov, 2007). The illusion of knowing gets in the way of taking remedial steps because you think "you know" when you do not. There is a lack of comprehension without the realization this has occurred.

What to Think and How to Think

Critics of the educational system argue that students are too often told *what* to think and do not learn *how* to think. Thinking critically about any subject requires us to examine our reasoning process (Paul & Elder, 2004). This is quite different from memorizing a list of alleged facts. Examining the accuracy of "facts" requires thinking critically about them.

Logical Reasoning and Creativity

Creativity and reasoning go hand-in-hand, especially in areas such as clinical decision making involving unstructured situations in which needed information is often hard to get or missing and in which there may be no one best solution. High intelligence is no guarantee of creativity; even though people may be very intelligent, they may not have acquired effective thinking strategies. Halpern (2003) suggests the following to encourage creativity: (1) define a problem in different ways; (2) brainstorm to increase the number of ideas; (3) maximize intrinsic motivation; (4) work with people from different backgrounds; (5) encourage risk taking; and (6) combine attributes in different ways (p. 426).

Consistency, Corroboration, and Critical Testing

Assigning appropriate weight to evidence for or against a claim is a key part of what it means to be reasonable. The term evidence-based practice draws attention to the kinds of evidence (reasons) relied on to make decisions. Distinguishing between *consistency, corroboration* and *proof* is important in assigning proper weight. A psychiatrist may use "consistency" in support of an assumption. He may search for consistent evidence when exploring a depressed client's history of depression. An assertion should be consistent with other beliefs held; that is, self-contradictory views should not knowingly be accepted. However, two or more assertions may be consistent with each other but yield little or no insight into the soundness of an argument. Saying that A (a history of "mental illness"), is consistent with B (alleged current "mental illness") is to say only that it is possible to believe B given A. People often use consistency or agreement among different sources of data to support their beliefs. For example they may say that Mrs. X is depressed currently because she has a prior history of depression. However saying that A (a history of "depression") is consistent with B (alleged current "depression") is to say only that it is possible to believe B given A. Two or more assertions thus may be consistent with each other but yield little or no insight into the soundness of an argument.

Facts, Beliefs, and Preferences

A belief can be defined as "confidence that a particular thing is true, as evidenced by a willingness to act as though it were" (Nickerson, 1986, p. 2). *Beliefs* are assumptions about what is true or false. They may be testable (e.g. support groups help the bereaved) or untestable (God exists). They may be held as convictions (unquestioned assumptions) or as guesses about what is true or false which we seek to critically test. Beliefs involve claims that vary widely in their accuracy. Most people would believe the statement "childhood experiences influence adult development" to be credible. There would be less agreement concerning the assertion "Childhood experiences determine adult development." Popper (1979) suggests that *facts* refer to well-tested data, intersubjectively evaluated. These can contrasted with "factoids"—claims with no related evidence, claims that although there is no evidence to support them, may be believed because they are repeated so often. (The "Woozle Effect".) What is viewed as "a fact" may differ in different cultures. In a scientific approach it is assumed that the accuracy of an assertion is related to the uniqueness and accuracy of related critical appraisals. Facts are capable of verification; beliefs may not be. Some beliefs are matters of definition (for example, 3 + 3 = 6). *Preferences* reflect values. Beliefs are statements that, in principle, can be shown to be true or false, whereas with an opinion, it does not make sense to consider it as true or false because people differ in their preferences and opinions. Many statements, written or spoken, are opinions or points of view; "they frequently don't pass the test of providing reasons for a conclusion, reasons that can be separated from a conclusion" (Scriven, 1976, p. 67).

An example of an opinion statement is "I prefer insight-oriented treatment." This statement appeals to preferences. An example of a belief is "Play therapy helps children to overcome anxiety." Here, evidence can be gathered to determine if this is the case. Additional examples are shown below. The first is an opinion and the last two are beliefs.

- I like to collect payment for each session at the end of the session.
- Insight therapy is more effective than cognitive behavioral treatment of depression.
- My pet Rotweiler helps people with their problems (quote from psychologist on morning talk show, April 6, 1988).

The woman who offered the last statement also described the value of her pet Rotweiler in offering support to her clients during interviews: the pet would sit by the wife when she spoke and move over to the husband and offer support to him when he spoke.

Intuitive and Analytic Thinking

Another common distinction is that between mindful action in which an active effort is made to understand something and automatic functioning in which we carry out tasks fairly automatically. The effectiveness of a style depends on what is needed to solve a problem as discussed in chapter 7.

DIFFERENT KINDS OF EXPLANATIONS

Many kinds of explanations are used by professionals and clients, including biological, psychological, and sociological as discussed in chapter 8. Explanations purport to offer reasons for certain behaviors or events. Different theories suggest different explanations and predictions. The question is: "How much *real* understanding, as opposed to *feeling* of understanding, do they provide? How much better are the predictions they yield than those of a thoughtful person not using these theories but using other knowledge about events of interest?" (Scriven, 1976, p. 219). Explaining is closely connected with judging whether something is good or bad. Different explanations suggest different reasons for beliefs:

- Preferred kind of explanation → reasons → evidence sought/appealed to
- Example: biochemical → brain differences → seratonin levels in people diagnosed as "mentally ill."

Explanations are often given by defining a word in terms of other words as in dictionary definitions. Other kinds of explanations by definition include classifying, offering examples, or describing operations (as in mathematics). Explanations may be emotionally compelling but weak from an evidentiary standpoint. Astrological explanations give many people the feeling of understanding; this does not mean that these explanations are accurate.

Empathic Explanations

Some people prefer empathic explanations. These may or may not assume a causal connection. Techniques of empathy building include telling a history, describing circumstances or character, presuming needs, and describing intentions and feelings (motives). (See Table 12.8.) Nettler (1970) suggests that "The heart of empathy is imagined possibility" (p. 34). The empathizer thinks, "Under these circumstances I, too, might have behaved similarly." Empathic explanations often involve appeal to concepts that are only variant definitions of the behavior to be explained as shown in these examples (Nettler, 1970, p. 71).

CASE ONE
Probation: Why, doctor, does our client continue to steal?
Psychiatry: He is suffering from antisocial reaction.
Probation: What are the marks of "antisocial reaction"
Psychiatry: Persistent thievery is one symptom.

CASE TWO
Defense: Whether one calls him insane or psychotic, he's a sick man. That's obvious.
Psychiatry: I should think that's largely a matter of terminology.
Defense: Do you mean to suggest that a man could do what that boy has done and not be sick?

A preference for empathic explanations reflects a search for explanations in terms of underlying essences—essential properties. Popper refers to this position as *essentialism*. Essentialists seek empathic explanations and argue about the meaning of words rather than exploring meaning through critical inquiry.

Scientific Explanations

In scientific explanations, critical appraisal of claims is emphasized; there is an active effort to seek out errors in assumptions as described in chapter 7. Scientific inquiry is designed to eliminate errors, not to claim final accounts. Premature claims of knowledge or ignorance stifle inquiry; they function as prisons that limit our vision (Popper, 1994). Nor do scientific explanations assume that objective accounts can be offered—accounts uninfluenced by diverse meanings associated with how events

Table 12.8 HALLMARKS OF DIFFERENT KINDS OF EXPLANATIONS

A. *Ideological Explanations*

1. Provide few answers for many questions (a few principles cover a wide territory).
2. Seek to clarify true meaning of "scriptures."
3. Contain a high proportion of nonfactual sentences included as declarations. ("nonfactual" means ambiguous and unprovable or without empirical warrant, p. 186). Values disguised as facts.
4. Contain a high ratio of hortatory-presumptive to declarative sentences.
5. Contain many failures of logic.
6. Deny the possibility of objectivity; "all explanations of social behavior are considered to be distorted (cues for distortion include describing one's motives, "locating the "social position' from which the competing thesis allegedly originates,' p. 186).
7. Favor *ad hominem* arguments, which are viewed as tools not as errors; identification of "who said it" as an important test of a statement's validity.
8. Resort to reliance on authority.
9. Seek converts; respond to criticism with emotional defenses; attack critic's motives and develop "cultus" (practices that a believing group develops as its distinctive mode of "meeting the world," p. 186); may seek to force theories on others.
10. Prescribe action: interested in persuading rather than explaining.
11. Are action oriented.

B. *Scientific Explanations*

1. Reject *ad hominem* arguments as persuasive.
2. Encourage dispute of key ideas.
3. Do not encourage unexamined commitment to one side.
4. Value criticism and observation.
5. Question everything.
6. Seek to reduce influence of moral judgments on observations and inferences.
7. Reflect an interest in improving the accuracy of judgments.

C. *Empathic Explanations*

1. Do not require proof; consider the test of empathy to be empathy (p. 49); common sense is sufficient.
2. Use vague indicators; hard "to know when one has understanding"; no independent tests of interpretations.
3. Accept *ad hominem* arguments.
4. Entangle moral judgments with understanding.
5. Have a cognitive bias; an attempt to explain behavior "as if it arose from thought alone" (p. 56); an equation of awareness with verbal reports; knowledge of others limited by excessive attention to what they say.

Table 12.8 HALLMARKS OF DIFFERENT KINDS OF EXPLANATIONS (CONTINUED)

6. Are vulnerable to tautology; infer inner states from behaviors, and explain behaviors by reference to inner states; prove motives from acts.

7. Confuse understanding and predictive capability; consider propositions to be nonpredictive.

8. Assume that understanding of individuals can offer knowledge of groups.

SOURCE: Adapted from G. Nettler (1970). *Explanations* (pp. 49, 56, 186). New York: McGraw-Hill.

are interpreted. To the contrary, in no approach is objectivity so suspect as illustrated by the variety of methods devised to attempt to avoid bias.

Ideological Explanations

Ideological explanations are distinguished from scientific ones by their rejection of objectivity, their ready acceptance of sound and unsound premises, and their reliance on ethical judgments. Ideological explanations "became operative as they are believed, rather than as they are verified" (Nettler, 1970, p. 179). Depending on who is talking and what they are talking about, ideology is a virtue or a sin. "The term 'ideology' is someone else's thought, seldom our own" (McLellan, 1986, p. I). On the other hand, "ideology tells the point of it all. Life is no longer absurd. It describes the forces of light and darkness and names the innocent to be saved" (Nettler, 1970, p. 179). Thompson (1987) distinguishes between two uses of the term "ideology." One is as a purely descriptive term. For example, we can describe the views central to an approach. In the second use, the term refers to maintaining power. It is this use of ideology that has negative connotations, and it is in this sense that language is used as a medium of influence.

> The difference between the scientific orientation and the empathetic and ideological outlooks, however, lies in the criteria of conceptual utility. In the latter explain ways, terms are maintained as they serve the explicators' purposes of building empathy or justifying ethical-political causes. In the scientific schema, any concept or construct is, in principle, dispensable regardless of these empathetic or ideological effects (Nettler, 1970, p. 187)

Ideological explanations are used to account for "collective" behavior as empathetic ones do in the clarification of individual actions—they fill the needs of curiosity left by the gaps in knowledge" (Nettler, 1970, p. 187). Propagandists create confusion among different uses of the term. Empathic and ideological explanations may not involve arguments. People tend to feel that they should be able to justify (have sound reasons for) their beliefs. An inability to explain why a certain view is held may create feelings of anger or embarrassment, as Socrates found. Most beliefs are not examined in terms of providing explanations or justifications for these.

INDIVIDUAL AND CULTURAL DIFFERENCES

People differ in their thinking styles and skills. They differ in the kinds of explanations that satisfy their curiosity. William James (1975) suggested that temperamental differences (tender versus tough-minded) account for preference for different kinds of explanations (p. 13). These differences are related to educational and socialization experiences (Stanovitch & West, 2002). The results of such differences may be attributed inaccurately to inherent style differences, for example that women are naturally more subjective and intuitive in their approach in contrast to men who are more objective. What is attributed to gender differences may be a matter of class differences in access to educational opportunities that encourage the development of critical thinking values and skills. Encouraging intuitivism and emotional reasoning helps to protect those who offer dubious services and use propaganda strategies to maintain and expand them. As many such as Freire (1973, 1993) have argued, the economically privileged benefit most from an anti-intellectual bias in protection of their privileges. Extreme subjectivism as a reaction against disliked "male styles of thinking" neglects the role of class differences (mistakenly attributing these to gender differences) and forgoes the option of reaping the benefits of both approaches. Cultural differences include norms regarding questioning authority figures (Tweed & Lehman, 2002). If this is not permitted, propaganda ploys may win the day. "Group think" may occur in which there is a "cooling out" of disagreement and premature closure on an option (Janis, 1982). A focus on arriving at sound decisions rather than protecting the esteem of authority figures should encourage a culture in which questions are valued. Still, this may be an uphill battle in contexts in which propaganda ploys are preferred.

SUMMARY

You can decrease your vulnerability to propaganda by enhancing your argument analysis skills, including recognizing attempts to block critical appraisal of claims such as deceptive shifts in a discussion. These skills are of value in examining your own arguments, as well as those of others. Different criteria are used to assess the quality of arguments in different contexts, for example, negotiations compared to inquiry and critical discussion. Recognizing different kinds of arguments, as well as important distinctions, for example, between reasoning and rationalizing, will help you to spot faulty arguments for claims. Effective reasoning requires much more than logic in developing and evaluating arguments to arrive at those that are well reasoned. Domain-specific knowledge may be needed. Reasoning does not necessarily yield the truth nor does the accuracy of a conclusion necessarily indicate that the reasoning used to reach it was sound. Reasoning requires a certain attitude toward the truth—a questioning attitude and an openness to altering beliefs in light of evidence offered—a willingness to say "I don't know." Some people prefer empathic and ideological explanations rather than critical appraisal of views to evaluate accuracy.

This preference increases susceptibility to propaganda. For example, because I "feel" that an explanation is correct, I may accept it without critically appraising its accuracy. In some cases, I may benefit from such empathic accounts. In others, I may be harmed because the account "feels right" but is not accurate. The kinds of explanations that we find satisfying depends in part, on the context. As always, we must "choose our battles"—choose which claims to critically appraise as they affect our well-being and the well-being others.

13

Increase Your Skill in Spotting Fallacies

Propagandists use a variety of fallacies that divert, confuse, hide material, or intimidate to block critical appraisal of claims and related arguments. Such tactics are never appropriate when the goal of the discussion is to arrive at the truth. Consider the examples in Table 13.1. Can you spot the fallacy? There have been many attempts to define and classify fallacies and a variety of systems have been suggested.[1] One classification system can be seen in Table 13.2. Examples from *Follies and Fallacies in Medicine* (Skrabanek & McCormick, 1998) include the *ecological fallacy* (assuming that relationships in populations occur in an individual), the *fallacy of obfuscation* (use of language to mystify rather than clarify), the *"hush hush" fallacy* (ignoring the fact that mistakes are inevitable), and the *fallacy of the golden mean* (assuming that the consensus of a group indicates the truth). Examples of faulty reasoning from the *Biomedical Bestiary* (Michael, Boyce, & Wilcox, 1984) include *The Grand Confounder* (what is claimed to be a causal relationship is due to another factor) and *Numerator Monster* (information concerning the health of someone with no reference to the population from which this individual came).[2]

The term *trick* or *stratagem* refers to informal fallacies that are used deliberately as persuasion strategies, although they may occur because of sloppy thinking or lack of critical thinking skills. Thus, fallacies may be intentional or unintentional. Intentional uses of fallacies are called deceptions; they violate Grice's maxims. (See Table 12.5.) For example a presenter at a conference may attempt to awe his audience by "name dropping," use of pseudoscientific jargon, and bold assertions alleging consensus, such as "We know _____." Responses that do not forward inquiry may or may not reflect deliberate deception. But, as many have noted, it really does not matter. Serge Lang (1998) would ask: "Why does the chicken cross the road?" If you reply "To get to the other side," you have fallen into the "intention trap," getting involved with the motivation of participants in a discussion rather than with content. (See Table 13.3 for some examples from my own experience.) Propagandists take a chance of being exposed as propagandists when using obvious ploys and prefer using vague attention-getting devices that appeal to our emotions such as slogans ("We care"), visual images, and glittering generalizations (Marlin, 2002).

Table 13.1 EXAMPLES CONTAINING A FALLACY

Client treated by a chiropractor: Mrs. Sisneros was experiencing lower-back pain. She saw her chiropractor, felt better afterward, and concluded that the chiropractor helped her back.

Child-welfare worker to students in class: Open adoption is one of the newest advances in adoptions. In open adoption, the biological parents are allowed to stay in touch with the adoptive parents, and in many cases, the biological parents contribute to rearing the child. Your agency should try this increasingly popular option.

Politician critical of welfare benefits and welfare fraud among recipients of Aid-for-Dependent-Children: One "welfare queen" illustrates the extent of the problem. She used twelve fictitious names, forged several birth certificates, claimed fifty nonexistent children as dependents, received Aid for Families with Dependent Children (AFDC) for 10 years, and defrauded the state of Michigan out of $40,000. She drove an expensive car, took vacations in Mexico, and lived in an expensive house.

Situation: Monthly meeting of agency administrators.

Administrator: I think your idea to give more money to work with the elderly is a good one but in the long run is not a good idea because we would then have to allot more money to services for all other groups.

Client speaking to potential clients: I participated in six weekly encounter-group meetings conducted by Sally Rogers, my nurse, and the group helped. My scores on the Living With Cancer Inventory have increased. I recommend that you attend the group too.

Two psychiatric nurses discussing a patient:

First nurse: His behavior on the ward is erratic and unpredictable. He warrants a diagnosis of bipolar.

Second nurse: What makes you think so?

First nurse: Because of his behavior on the unit.

Situation: An interdisciplinary case conference in a nursing home:

Psychology intern: I don't think you should use those feeding and exercise procedures for Mrs. Shore. They don't work. Since she has Parkinson's, she'll spill her food. I also don't think you should walk her up and down the hall for exercise. I have read reports that argue against everything you're doing.

Nurse: I am not sure you are in the best position to say. You have not even completed your degree yet.

SOURCE: E. Gambrill & L. Gibbs (2009). *Critical thinking for helping professionals: A skills-based workbook* (3rd Ed.). New York: Oxford University Press.

WALTON'S PRAGMATIC VIEW OF FALLACY

Dialogues are typically concerned with "a problem, difference of opinion, or question to be resolved that has two sides" (Walton, 2007, p. 9). Walton's (1995, 2008) pragmatic view of fallacies highlights their role in blocking critical appraisal. He distinguishes between reasoning ("a sequence of propositions [premises and conclusions] joined

Table 13.2 INFORMAL FALLACIES

FALLACIES THAT VIOLATE THE RELEVANCE CRITERION
Fallacies of Irrelevance
   Irrelevant or Questionable Authority
   Appeal to Common Opinion
   Genetic Fallacy
   Rationalization
   Drawing the Wrong Conclusion
   Using the Wrong Reasons
Irrelevant Emotional Appeals
   Appeal to Pity
   Appeal to Force or Threat (intimidation)
   Appeal to Tradition
   Appeal to Personal Circumstances or Motives
   Exploitation of Strong Feelings and Attitudes
   Use of Flattery
   Assigning Guilt by Association

FALLACIES THAT VIOLATE THE ACCEPTABILITY CRITERION
Fallacies of Linguistic Confusion
   Equivocation
   Ambiguity
   Improper Accent
   Illicit Contrast
   Argument by Innuendo
   Misuse of a Vague Expression
   Distinction Without a Difference
Begging-the-Question Fallacies
   Arguing in a Circle
   Question-Begging Language
   Loaded or Complex Question
Leading Question
Question-Begging Definition
Unwarranted Assumption Fallacies
   Fallacy of the Continuum
   Fallacy of Composition
   Fallacy of Division
   False Alternatives
   Is-Ought Fallacy
   Wishful Thinking
   Misuse of a General Principle
   Fallacy of the Golden Mean
   Faulty Analogy
   Fallacy of Novelty

FALLACIES THAT VIOLATE THE SUFFICIENT GROUNDS CRITERION
Fallacies of Missing Evidence
   Insufficient Sample
   Unrepresentative Data
   Arguing from Ignorance

Table 13.2 Informal Fallacies (Continued)

    Contrary-to-Fact Hypothesis
    Improper Use of a Cliché
    Inference from a Label
    Fallacy of Fake Precision
    Special Pleading
    Omission of Key Evidence

CAUSAL FALLACIES
    Confusion of a Necessary with a Sufficient Condition
    Neglect of a Common Cause
    Causal Oversimplification
    Post Hoc Fallacy
    Confusion of Cause and Effect
    Domino Fallacy
    Gambler's Fallacy

FALLACIES THAT VIOLATE REBUTTAL CRITERION
Fallacies of Counterevidence
    Denying the Counterevidence
    Ignoring the Counterevidence
    Ad Hominem Fallacies
    Abusive *Ad Hominem*
    Poisoning the Well
    "You Do It, Too" Argument
Fallacies of Diversion
    Attacking a straw man
    Trivial objections
    Red herring
    Resort to humor or ridicule

SOURCE: T. E. Damer (1994). *Attacking faulty reasoning: A practical guide to fallacy-free arguments* (3rd Ed.) (pp. 12–16). Belmont, CA: Wadsworth. With permission of Cengage.

into steps of inference by warranted inferences), and argument (use of reasoning to contribute to a talk, exchange or conversation called a dialogue") (Walton, 1995, p. 255). This pragmatic view of fallacy emphasizes the importance of context. Thus, "a fallacy is defined as an argument that not only does not contribute to the goal of a dialogue but actually blocks or impedes the realization of that purpose" (Walton, 1995, p. 255).

The new approach is pragmatic—a fallacy is an argumentation technique that is used wrongly in a context of dialogue. Fallacies are not arguments per se, according to the new theory, but uses of arguments. A fallacy doesn't have to be a deliberate error in a particular case, but it is a question of how the argumentation

Table 13.3 EXAMPLES OF EXCHANGES FROM MY EXPERIENCE THAT ILLUSTRATE INFORMAL FALLACIES

1. *Situation*: Continuing education course through The University of California Extension given by Dr. Presti on alcohol abuse.
Me: You use the term "alcohol disorder" often. Can you tell me what this means?
Dr. Presti: A lack of order.

2. *Situation*: A faculty meeting in a school of social work
Faculty member A: We have made great strides in creating a list of empirically derived competencies for child welfare staff. We are delighted with our progress and will use this list to provide training programs.
Me: Could you describe what is "empirical" about these competencies?
Faculty member A: (Looking annoyed—frowning): We asked people in focus groups of child welfare staff what they believed to be key competencies. We went to those who could provide the information. (No information was provided about how many focus groups there were, how many people were in each, how these people were selected, whether those selected provided a representative sample of all staff, let alone whether what they reported bears any relationship to skills needed to provide high-quality services to clients).

3. *Situation*: Talking to a well-known child welfare researcher in the United Kingdom who was promoting nationwide distribution of a lengthy (25 pages) family assessment form.
Me: What is the purpose of this assessment form?
Dr. X: To gather research data regarding families in care and to improve the assessment of families.
Me: Can you tell me if there is any evidence that use of this assessment form improves the quality of assessment? This would seem good to determine before it is required to be used by all child welfare workers with all families throughout the United Kingdom.
Dr. X: That's a hard question.

4. *Situation*: Conference symposium
Me: Could you please give me an example of what you mean by "working at the integration level"?
Dr. X: You know what I am talking about.
Me: No, I do not understand what you mean, but if we take a specific example related to social work practice this may help.
Dr. X: I will not give you a specific example. You know what I mean.

technique was used in that case. . . . So conceived, a fallacy is not only a violation of a rule of a critical discussion but a distinctive kind of technique of argumentation that has been used to block the goals of a dialogue, while deceptively maintaining an air of plausibility, either by using a type of argumentation that could be correct in other cases or even by shifting to a different type of dialogue illicitly and covertly.

According to the new theory, a fallacy is an underlying systematic error or deceptive tactic. Charging someone with having committed a fallacy in his argument is quite a serious charge in matters of conversational politeness. It is a serious charge, and it calls for a serious reply, if the alleged offender is to maintain credibility as a serious proponent of his side of the issue of a discussion.... A fallacy, then, is not just any error, lapse, or blunder in an argument. It is a serious error or trick tactic. to get the best of one's speech partner illicitly. (Walton, 1995, p. 15)

This view of fallacy is pragmatic because the underlying question always to be asked in a particular case is "What is the context or dialogue?" (p. 254). Thus, we must examine the *context* of a dialogue to determine whether something is indeed a fallacy.

> The one party tries to move ahead too fast by making an important move that is not yet proper in the sequence. Or, the one party tries to shut the other party up by closing off the dialogue prematurely or by shifting to a different type of dialogue.... Or, key moves are left out of a sequence that should have been properly in. The result is that the sequence is not in the right order required for that type of dialogue and at that particular stage of the dialogue. This is where a fallacy occurs, where the resulting disorder is a type of sequence that blocks the dialogue or impedes it seriously.
>
> For example, in the case of a fallacious *argumentum ad ignoratiam*, the one party may put forth an assertion he has not proved, or has even given any argumentation for at all, and may then demand that the other party either accept or disprove it. (Walton, 1995, p. 301)

Thus, the major fallacies involve weak kinds of argumentation such as argument from authority, which are successful if they shift the burden of proof in a discussion. Key properties of this view of fallacy include the following (pp. 257–58).

1. *Dialectical.* A two-person exchange of moves in a sequence of argumentation. Whether an argument is fallacious depends on the stage of a dialogue the arguer is in.
2. *Pragmatic.* The context of dialogue is vital in determining whether a fallacy has occurred. The critic must interpret and analyze the sequence of discourse in an example.
3. *Commitment-Based.* The arguer's commitment at a given stage of a dialogue is key in determining whether a fallacy has occurred. This acceptance-based approach does not, however, rule out or denigrate the role of deductive, inductive, or knowledge-based reasoning.
4. *Presumptive.* The major fallacies involve weak, fallible kinds of argumentation, like argument from authority, argument from sign, and so forth, that are successful if they shift a burden of proof in dialogue.
5. *Pluralistic.* The notion of a dialectical shift in a dialogue is key to understanding how fallacies work as arguments that seem correct.
6. *Functional.* A fallacy is more than just a rule violation of a type of dialogue— it is a technique of argumentation that is used inappropriately by one person in dialogue against another (Walton, 1995).

This pragmatic view emphasizes the use of fallacies to squelch debate and avoid critical appraisal of claims. Errors that may result include selecting ineffective or harmful practices and policies. Relevant research findings may be ignored because of biased presentation of disliked perspectives.

> The inherent nature of fallacy . . . is to be found in the Gricean principle of cooperativeness which says that you must make the kind of contribution required to move a dialogue forward at that specific stage of the dialogue.
> . . .
> Fallacies are techniques of argumentation that have been used in a counterproductive way to steer a discussion away from its proper goals or even in an aggressive attempt to close off the effective possibilities of an adversary's critical questioning in the dialogue. But identifying the pragmatic context of dialogue is the key to fixing the claim that an argument is fallacious. An aggressive personal attack that could be perfectly appropriate for an outright quarrel, as an effective tactic to hit out verbally at your opponent, could be highly destructive to the balance required for fair and constructive persuasion dialogue [critical discussion]. In that context, the use of the same technique of argumentation could be shown to be a fallacy. In a scientific inquiry, yet another context of dialogue, the same use of the technique of personal attack could be even more outrageous and clearly out of place. . . . In this context, it could even more easily be shown to be a fallacy, by showing how the tactic used is inappropriate as an acceptable method of working toward the goals of the dialogue. (Walton, 1995, p. 258)

Becoming familiar with fallacies and developing skill in spotting and avoiding them will decrease your vulnerability to propaganda pitches. (See Table 13.5.) Familiarity with their names can be helpful in identifying and pointing them out to others (or yourself).

FALSE EVEN THOUGH VALID

Some arguments are false even though they are valid. A valid argument is one whose premises, if true, offers good or sufficient grounds for accepting a conclusion.

Doubtful Evidence

In one kind of false even though valid argument, conclusions are accepted even though the premises are questionable. For example, it may be assumed that problems have a biochemical cause based on flawed studies of neuroimaging (Leo & Cohen, 2003; Vul et al., 2009). That is, someone may insist that the form of an argument is valid while ignoring the possible (or probable) inaccuracy of the premises. It may be assumed that "All psychologists are competent. Max is a psychologist. Therefore, Max is competent." If the premises are true, the conclusion is true. However, the truth of the first premise is debatable, and because one of the premises is doubtful, the argument is unsound. (An argument must be both valid and have accurate premises for it to be sound.) Those who use doubtful evidence often try to distract us from examining the premises; they may even try to use a "below the belt" technique such

Table 13.4 EXAMPLES OF FOUL WAYS TO WIN AN ARGUMENT

- Accuse your opponent of doing what he accuses you of or worse ("You also . . .")
- Assume a posture of righteousness
- Call for perfection (the impossible)
- Use vivid analogies and metaphors to support your view even when misleading
- Create misgivings (dirty the water)
- Use of double standards (for evidence for example)
- Deny or defend inconsistencies
- Focus on inconsistencies in your opponent's argument
- Attack only evidence that undermines your case
- Demonize his side and sanitize yours
- Evade questions
- Flatter your audience
- Hedge what you say
- Ignore the evidence
- Ignore the main point
- Focus on a minor point
- Say "It is a cruel world" to justify the unethical
- Use glittering generalizations
- Make an opponent look ridiculous
- Raise only objections
- Shift the ground
- Introduce distracting jokes
- Focus on a vivid case example
- Shift the burden of proof
- Use double talk
- Tell lies
- Reify concepts (treat abstract words as if they are real)
- Use red herrings
- Use bogus statistics
- Claim the point is "old hat"
- Use "faint praise"

SOURCE: See R. W. Paul & L. Elder (2004). *Critical thinking: Tools for taking charge of your professional and personal life.* Upper Saddle River, NJ: Prentice Hall. N. Kline (1962). Factifuging. *Lancet*, 1396-99. With permission of Elsevier.

as ridicule as shown in Table 13.4. Many facts are unknowable by anyone (for example, the exact number of gay/lesbian people who live in the United States). Other facts are potentially knowable or are known by someone, but are not known by the person who is using doubtful evidence.

Suppressed Views and Related Evidence

The suppression of evidence is the most widely and successfully used propaganda strategy in the helping professions. These "errors of omission" allow educators, pharmaceutical reps, researchers, and others to create false impressions and mislead us without overtly lying. (See discussion of partiality in use of evidence in chapter 4.) Presenting only facts that serve one's own purpose while ignoring other relevant data is especially insidious, because we are often unaware of information left out. There may be a conscious effort to suppress evidence, or, it may occur because of ignorance or wishful thinking. Consider a recent newspaper article in which a pharmaceutical representative claimed that their drug was responsible for decreasing surgery for stomach ulcers. No mention was made that the decreased need for surgery was mainly due to the discovery that ulcers were caused by a bacterium. A drug company may run 10 trials to examine the effectiveness of a drug, only two of which are positive, and send only these to the FDA for approval. It may test many people on a placebo and drop all placebo reactors before randomly distributing remaining subjects to a placebo and drug condition (Antonuccio, Burns, & Danton 2002) and omit this information in published reports. Data that use of an antidepressant results in a significant risk of suicide may be hidden (Healy, 2004). Many books, articles, and media reports describe examples of censorship of negative results regarding the effects of certain drugs on the part of pharmaceutical companies.[3] A researcher may not inform readers that use of a drug results only in a two point drop in the Hamilton Depression Scale and that the other eight point drop is matched by a placebo group and that people are still depressed (Burns, 1999).

Information about the evidentiary status of recommended methods in relation to other options is often not shared with clients. A clinician may suggest that "x" intervention is best without informing you that other options are available that have greater or equal empirical support concerning their effectiveness. In such situations, you are involved as an uninformed participant in violation of professional codes of ethics that call for informed consent. We are often unaware of options not offered (such as an assessment or treatment method) so are in a disadvantaged position to request alternative methods unless we seek out relevant information. Information concerning the false-positive and false-negative rates regarding a diagnostic measure may not be reported in an article describing a measure. Without such data, we may overestimate its accuracy. Reviews of websites regarding screening for breast cancer found that the negative effects of overdiagnosis and overtreatment are often not mentioned (Thornton, Edwards, & Baum, 2003). Only relative risk may be given, omitting information about absolute risk as described in chapter 6.

Published sources such as newsletters, books, and articles in professional journals contribute to influence by suppressed evidence by failing to discuss well-argued alternative views of issues and by not including corrections of inaccurate reports. Boyle (2002), for example, describes examples of suppression of contradictory data in *Schizophrenia: A Scientific Delusion*? A sophisticated campaign may be mounted to suppress data contradictory to a preferred position, as illustrated below in excerpts from an article describing court proceedings concerning the death of a smoker.

"Evidence presented by the plaintiff," Judge Sarokin said, "particularly that contained in documents of the defendants themselves, indicates the development of a public relations strategy aimed at combating the mounting adverse scientific reports regarding the dangers of smoking."

"The evidence indicates further that the industry of which these defendants were and are a part entered into a sophisticated conspiracy. The conspiracy was organized to refute, undermine and neutralize information coming from the scientific and medical community and, at the same time, to confuse and mislead the consuming public in an effort to encourage existing smokers to continue and new persons to commence smoking."

Judge Sarokin noted that evidence had been introduced showing that results of industry-sponsored research adverse to the industry's goals had been "suppressed and concealed."

"At least one scientist testified as to threats made to him if he published his findings, and there was other evidence of attempts to suppress or coerce others," he said. (Janson, 1988, p. A13)[4]

One remedy to the use of suppressed evidence to ask whether there are well-argued alternative views and, if the answer is yes, to seek information about them. Other options include (1) seeking information from alternative sources such as talking to people holding other views or reviewing information on various websites, especially those with a reputation for rigorous appraisal such as the Cochrane and Campbell Databases; (2) asking speakers if there is anything else you should know regarding a decision such as possible adverse consequences of a proposed remedy or alternative options that have not been mentioned. They may not want to be caught in a lie and so share other vital views and evidence. They may be unwilling to appear uninformed at a later date by having failed to do so under direct questioning.

IRRELEVANT APPEALS

Irrelevant appeals include fallacies in which the wrong point is supported or when a conclusion established by premises is not relevant to the issues being discussed. Many achieve their effect by taking advantage of our natural tendencies such as wanting to please others and to go along with what others think (see chapter 10). Appeals to unfounded authority may be used as described in chapter 12.

Emotional Appeals

Emotional appeals include appeal to pity, force or threat, flattery, guilt, and shame. Propaganda appeals to our deepest motivations—to avoid danger (fear), to be one of the boys/girls (acceptance and emotional support), to be free to hate our enemies (Ellul, 1965). However, the emotion with which a position is offered does not mean that the argument is poor. Good arguments can be (and often are) offered with emotion. Appeal to emotions such as pity and sympathy may be reasonable in some kinds of arguments (Walton, 2008).

Ad Hominem Arguments

Here, the background, habits, motivation, associates, or personality of an individual are attacked or appealed to (flattery) rather than his or her argument. Rather than arguing *ad rem* (to the argument), someone argues *ad hominem,* to the person proposing it. Varieties include the abusive *ad hominem* argument, the circumstantial *ad hominem* argument (allegation of inconsistency), and attack on a person's impartiality (alleged bias). *Ad hominem* replies are common in academic settings. Consider the *ad hominem* responses Dennis Gorman (2003) received to his critical appraisal of alleged "Best Practices" in primary prevention programs. "Who are you to criticize these programs and the accompanying research when experts have declared them effective?' (p. 1088). A second response was also irrelevant: "You shouldn't criticize these programs unless you have some alternative intervention to recommend."

Appeals or attacks may be subtle or obvious. A team member may suggest that an advocacy group should be made up of community residents because they have had experience with advocacy and are eager to work together. Another staff member may respond "But how can you say this? You haven't completed your training yet." Rather than addressing your argument, he comments on your education. This example illustrates use of *ad hominem* appeals to block critical appraisal of claims. The theories of Jung may be rejected because of his alleged racism and anti-Semitism. These alleged characteristics do not necessarily bear on the cogency of his theory. Improper appeals to authority to block critical appraisal are a kind of *ad hominem* argument. The effectiveness of *ad hominem* arguments depends in part on the social psychological principles of liking (or disliking) and our tendency to go along with what authorities say. As Nickerson (1986) points out, we are more likely to agree with institutions and philosophies we favor—however, it is unlikely that we will agree with every facet, and similarly, it is unlikely that we would disagree with every aspect of a disliked view. So "Credit or discredit by association becomes a fallacy when it is applied in a blind and uncritical way. Whether or not a particular view is one that is held by a specific individual, institution, or philosophy that we generally support (or oppose) is very meager evidence as to the tenability of that view" (Nickerson, 1986, p. 116).

Ad hominems are relevant in some cases. Someone could be known to offer unreliable accounts on most occasions. However, this person may be offering a correct account this time. Thus, the credibility of the person presenting an argument is important to consider. *Ad hominem* arguments are surprisingly effective for a variety of reasons, only one of which is failure to identify their fallacious nature. Others include the following

- Implicit agreement with the implications about the individual.
- Agreement with the conclusion of the argument with little concern for its correctness.
- Unwillingness to raise questions, cause a fuss, or challenge authorities who may counterattack.
- Social pressures in group settings—not wanting to embarrass others.

The remedy in relation to *ad hominem* arguments is to point out that the appeal made provides no evidence for or against a claim.

Guilt (or credit) by association is a variation of an *ad hominem* argument—judging people by the company they keep. An attempt to discredit a position may be made by associating it with a disliked institution, value, characteristic, or philosophy, as in the statement "Behavioral methods are mechanistic." "Imposter terms" or "euphemisms" may be used to make an unpopular view or method acceptable.

Long-term lockups in a prison may be referred to as "behavior modification." Dumping patients into the community from mental hospitals has been called "community care." In the bad seed fallacy (a form of the genetic fallacy), it is assumed that a person's character or habits are passed on to his descendants (Michalos, 1971, p. 54); that because a client's parents acted in a certain way, that is why the client acts in this manner. The bad seed fallacy can be seen in the claim that "It's in the genes." Genetic factors do play a role in influencing behavior, however, correlations are typically small and may not support a causal connection (Lewontin, 2009).

An argument may be made that a position is not acceptable because the person's motives for supporting the issue are questionable. For example, a proposal that a new counseling center be created may be denied on the grounds that those who propose this will profit from such a center by gaining needed jobs. The accuracy of a view cannot be determined from an examination of the motives of those who proposed it, but only from a critical appraisal of the soundness of the argument. A psychologist who recommended placing a child on Ritalin may say that his intent is to help this child. Good intentions do not necessarily result in good outcomes as illustrated in chapter 5. Appeals to good intentions are the opposite of the assumption of suspect motives. In both cases, evidence is needed related to claims asserted as true (or false). Motives, whether altruistic or otherwise, are not evidence (Lang, 1998).

Claims of inconsistencies may be made to distract us from consideration of evidentiary issues. A discrepancy between a person's behavior and his principles may be invalidly used against him. For example, an argument may be dismissed on the grounds that the person's behavior is not consistent with his argument. A clinician who is not sympathetic to behavioral methods may say to his behavioral friend, "If behaviorists knew so much about how to change behavior, why are you still smoking when you want to stop?" Another kind of false claim of inconsistency is when a charge is made that a person's behavior is not consistent with his principles when his principles have changed. Altering a position does not necessarily entail inconsistency. It depends on whether a person states that her position has changed and explains the reasons for the changes. Not recognizing that we often have rational grounds for changing our opinions results in a false charge of inconsistency. This fallacy takes advantage of our desire to be consistent and to expect others to be consistent as well.

Fallacy of Special Pleading

The *fallacy of special pleading* involves favoring our own interests by using different standards for different people as in "I am firm, thou art obstinate, he is pigheaded" (Thouless, 1974, p. 11). A clinician may claim that she does not have to evaluate her work as carefully as other clinicians because of her lengthy experience.

The Fallacy of Ignorance

This involves the assumption that if there is no evidence against a claim it must be true or if there is no evidence for a claim it must be false. Walton (1996) suggests a few subtypes. In one, the burden of proof is shifted to the other party. In the scientific reasoning type, there is a problem of verifiability of the alleged evidence, for example, concerning the existence of ghosts. "In such cases, the *ad ignorantiam* seems reasonable, when really it is not, because of the uncertainty of knowing what would count as evidence either to support or refute the conditional premise" (Walton, 1996, p. 293). Consider witch hunts of the past. The burden or proof was placed on the "alleged witch" to prove her innocence. (See also Szasz, 1970.) And what was to serve as evidence?

A clinician may argue that because there is no evidence showing that "directed aggression" (hitting objects such as pillows) does not work, that it should be used. The fact that no one can think of a course of action that is better than one proposed may be used as an argument that the proposed course is a good one. Gorman (2003) describes this to be one of three reactions people have had to his critical analysis of research related to prevention programs for youth included on lists of "evidence-based practices." "Where an *ad ignorantiam* is evaluated as being fallacious in a given case, this means that there is a serious underlying, systematic error, or that the argument is being used as a sophistical tactic to try to unfairly get the best of a speech partner in dialogue" (Walton, 1996, p. 296). There is an illicit "attempt to shift the burden of proof."[5]

The Fallacy of Appeal to Will

An example is to say that "if he really wanted to . . . he would." A psychiatrist might say, "If she was interested in getting better, she'd come in for counseling." She may know little or nothing about this client's environmental circumstances. Appeals to "will power" offer no information about how to create desired changes.

Attacking the Example

The example given of a position may be attacked rather than the position itself. Perhaps the example offered is not an apt one. A successful attack on the example does not take away from the possible soundness of a position. Is there a better example? This fallacy is the opposite of the use of a suspect particular case as proof for a generalization.

Appeal to Common Practice

It may be argued that because other people do something, it is all right to do the same. *Common practice* is a variety of this fallacy. It may be argued that because few clinicians keep up with practice-related literature, this is ok. Objections may be countered with "You'd do it too if you had an opportunity." This argument does not provide evidence for (or against) a position. Standard practice may be (and often is) of poor quality.

EVADING THE FACTS

Fallacies that evade the facts such as "begging the question" appear to address the facts but do not: "Such arguments deceive by inviting us to presume that the facts are as they have been stated in the argument, when the facts are quite otherwise" (Engel, 1982, p. 114).

Begging the Question

This refers to assuming the truth or falsity of what is at issue; that is, trying to settle a question by simply reasserting a position. Consider the statement, "The inappropriate releasing of mentally ill patients must be ended." The speaker assumes that releasing mentally ill patients is inappropriate, instead of offering evidence to show that it is. Presenting opinions as facts is a common variant of this fallacy. Question- begging can be used as a clue that relevant facts are being evaded. This tactic is surprisingly effective often because it is accompanied by appeals to authority. Such appeals take advantage of persuasive bases such as liking (we are less likely to question poor arguments of people we like), authority (we accept what experts say), and social proof (we are influenced by what other people do) (Cialdini, 2001).[6]

We are guilty of using question-begging epithets when we add evaluative terms to neutral descriptive terms to influence through emotional reactions. For example, "Fairview Hospital opened today" is a simple declarative statement. "The long-needed Fairview Hospital opened its doors today" includes an evaluative epithet. Variations of this fallacy include the use of emotive language, loaded words, and verbal suggestion. Emotional terms may be used to prejudice the facts by using evaluative language that supports what we want to demonstrate but have not shown. "By overstatement, ridicule, flattery, abuse and the like, they seek to evade the facts" (Engel, 1982, p. 120). Circular arguments are a form of question-begging as in the following example (Engel, 1982, p. 142).

- People can't help what they do.
- Why not?
- Because they always follow the strongest motive.
- But what is the strongest motive?
- It is the one that people follow.

This argument is circular in saying that A is so because of B and B is true because of A. The conclusion that a speaker or writer is trying to establish is used as a premise or presupposed as a premise. Such circular arguments may seem so transparent that they would never be a problem. However, they occur in clinical practice. Consider the following dialogue.

- Mr. Levine can't control his outbursts.
- Why is that?
- Because he is developmentally disabled.
- Why do you say that he is developmentally disabled?
- Well, because he has outbursts when he is frustrated.

Attributing the cause of outbursts to the developmental disability offers no information about how to alter the frequency of outbursts.

Another ploy consists of altering a definition rather than admit that a counterexample to a position has been identified. Believers in the disease view of alcoholism contend that drinkers who can return to limited nonproblem drinking were never "true alcoholics." "Facts cannot shake the generalization because the truth is guaranteed by definitions" (Michalos, 1971). Apriorism is a form of question-begging in which a position is claimed as true (prior to any investigation) because it is necessary according to a particular view of the world (or of clinical practice). Consider the assertion of psychiatrists that they should supervise treatment of patients (implying that psychologists and other kinds of mental health professionals such as social workers would work under their supervision) and that to arrange services otherwise (to allow other kinds of professionals to work autonomously) would lower the quality of service offered to clients. It is assumed that psychiatrists' training is superior to other kinds of professional training. This is not necessarily true. What is needed is a description of evidence for and against this claim.

Unfounded generalizations may be used to support a conclusion. A supervisor may say, "Offering positive incentives is dehumanizing because it is behavioral." The assumptions are that behavioral methods are dehumanizing and that offering positive incentives for desired behaviors is behavioral. Since the truth of the wider generalizations is questionable, the particular example is questionable. When a more general claim is assumed, the accuracy of this claim should be examined. Complex, leading, or trick questions with indirect assumptions may be used. A question may be asked in such a way that any answer will incriminate the speaker as in "Do you still advocate use of ineffective methods?" This is the interrogative form of the fallacy of begging the question; the conclusion at issue is assumed rather than supported. "Complex questions accomplish this by leading one to believe that a particular answer to a prior question has been answered in a certain way when this may not be the case" (Engel, 1982, p. 122). These questions contain assumptions that influence how they will be answered. The remedy is to question the question. Such questions are also fallacious "because they assume that one and the same answer must apply to both the unasked and the asked question as in the example of "Isn't Dr. Green an unthinking feminist" (p. 124). If the question is divided into its parts, different answers may apply: Is Dr. Green a feminist? Is she unthinking? Thus, the remedy is to divide the original question into its implied components and answer each one at a time.

Complex questions may be used to encourage us to make a certain choice. A physician may ask you which of two different medications you would prefer to take for your depression, not mentioning that you may not have to take any kind of medication. Another variation of complex questions is requesting explanations for supposed facts that have not been supported as in "How do you account for ESP (extra sensory perception)"? Since there is controversy about whether ESP exists because research exploring such phenomena has yielded negative results, there may be no extraordinary effects to explain, perhaps just fallacies or questionable experimental designs to be uncovered.

Bold Assertions Exaggerated claims of effectiveness are the key kind of propaganda in the helping professions. Alleged certainty is used to encourage us to accept a claim without any evidence that it is accurate. (See discussion of manner of presentation in chapter 7.) The claim is presented as if it were obvious, in the hope that our critical senses will be neutralized. Examples are "No one doubts the number of alcoholics in the U.S. today"; or "It is well accepted that therapy is effective." The costs in time and money of holding people responsible for vacuous claims may be amply repaid if life-affecting decisions are involved. Self-help books have long been criticized for offering unsupported, vacuous guarantees of effectiveness (Gambrill, 1992). Advertisements directed to professionals and consumers proclaim "It works" or use popular slogans such as "Proven effective." We may be told that "a program has been found to be effective in two well-designed clinical trials" and that this warrants its anointment as a "best practice" as recommended by a task force of the American Psychological Association. Many lists of programs are declared to be "evidence-based." Careful analysis of related research shows significant methodological flaws calling such claims into question (e.g., Gorman & Huber, 2009).

Ignoring Questions

One way to respond to a criticism is to ignore it—that is, to simply proceed as if the statements had never been made. This tactic can be successful if no one is present who will object, perhaps because everyone agrees with the original position. One form of ignoring the issue is to claim there is no issue. The question may be swept aside as irrelevant, trivial, or offensive. This would never be appropriate in a dialogue involving critical inquiry and is a sign that one or more participants have a goal other than critical inquiry for the dialogue.

OVERLOOKING THE FACTS

Fallacy of the Sweeping Generalization

Relevant facts are often neglected, as in the fallacy of the sweeping generalization in which a rule or assumption that is valid in general is applied to a specific example to which it is not valid (Engel, 1982, 1994). It might be argued that since expressing feelings is healthy, Susan should do it more because it will help increase her self-esteem and make her happier. However, if expressing feelings will result in negative consequences from significant others (such as work supervisors and her husband), the general rule may not apply here. This fallacy can be exposed by identifying the rule involved and showing that it cannot be applied accurately to the case at hand. Another name for this fallacy is the *fallacy of accident* (Toulmin et al., 1979, p. 161). Unfounded appeals to consensus are a kind of sweeping generalization. Consider weasel phrases such as "Everybody knows that . . ." "It is well accepted that . . ." or "No one doubts that . . ."

The Fallacy of Hasty Generalization

This is the opposite of the fallacy of the sweeping generalization. Here, an example is used as the basis for a general conclusion that is not warranted. Let's say a psychologist has an unpleasant conversation with a social worker and claims "Social workers are difficult to work with." The generalization to all social workers is inaccurate. This fallacy is also known as the *fallacy of hasty conclusion* (Kahane, 1995) and it has many variants. All have in common making unwarranted generalizations from small or biased samples. This fallacy entails a disregard for the law of large numbers. (See also discussion of suppressed evidence and either/or thinking.)

DISTORTING FACTS/POSITIONS (FABRICATION)

A number of informal fallacies distort positions. Famous people may be misquoted or views misrepresented. Distortion of a position can make it look ridiculous and so easily overthrown. If the presenter of the original more modest view is duped into defending an extreme version, he or she will likely fail.

Straw Person Arguments

In *straw person arguments,* a position different from the one presented is attacked; an argument is distorted and the distorted version is then attacked. Such appeals are always inappropriate, even in negotiations (Walton, 1997). Such arguments are often seen in discussions of disliked approaches. Consider distortions of the process and philosophy of evidence-based practice in the professional literature (Gambrill, 2006; 2011). Given the availability of accurate descriptions of the process and philosophy of EBP in original sources, such distortions illustrate sloppy scholarship or deliberate deception (Gambrill, 2010). As Popper (1994) emphasizes, we should always present alternative views accurately–in their strongest form. Otherwise we cannot accurately critique them or discover that they are better than our preferred views. Distorted presentations of Skinner's views are common such as the incorrect view that he believes in stimulus-response Watsonian behaviorism (Thyer, 2005). Inaccurate descriptions of the prevalence of a problem are common as in the statement: "There is an epidemic of crack cocaine use" when there has been a modest increase or no increase at all (MacCoun, 2001). Such advocacy in place of accurate presentation of data is common (Best, 2004). On the other hand, problems may be hidden as in the "rule of optimism" (Bartholet, 2009; Dingwall, 1983).

Forcing an Extension

Forcing an extension may be intentionally used by someone aware of the fact that it is usually impossible to defend extreme positions, since most positions have some degree of uncertainty attached to them like the statement that insight therapy is useful with many (not all) clients. The original position may be misstated in an extreme version (insight therapy is effective with all clients) and this extreme version then criticized. The original, less extreme position should be reaffirmed. The fallacy of irrelevant thesis is a version of forcing an extension.

The Fallacy of False Cause

This involves arguments that suggest that two events are causally related when no such connection has been demonstrated. It may be argued that because one event followed another, the latter caused the former. Researchers may claim that because taking a pill relieves depression, depression is due to a chemical imbalance in the brain. A client may state that, because she had a bad dream the night before, she made a mistake the next day. This is the post hoc ergo prop fallacy. Other causal fallacies include oversimplification (e.g., it's all in the genes.), confusing a necessary with a sufficient cause, and confusion of causes and their effects. [7] Various kinds of innumeracies may also be involved. (See chapter 6.)

Irrelevant Conclusion

An argument may be made for a conclusion that is not the one under discussion. While seeming to counter an argument, irrelevant statements advance a conclusion that is different from the one at issue. This fallacy can be quite deceptive because the irrelevant argument advanced often does support a conclusion and so gives an impression of credibility to the person offering it and the impression of a lack of cogency of the original argument, but the argument does not address the conclusion at issue (Engel, 1994). An example is "the advocates of reality therapy contend that if we adopt their methods, clients will be better off. They are mistaken, for it is easy to show that reality therapy will not cure the ills of the world." There are two different points here: (1) whether reality therapy is effective and (2) whether it will "cure the ills of the world." Showing that the latter is not true may persuade people that the first point has also been shown to be untrue.

Inappropriate Use of Analogies

Analogies are often used in daily life to help us to decide what to do in novel situations. We try to identify a familiar experience and use it to make decisions in new contexts. Analogies are used to clarify meanings. For instance, the Freudian theory of motivation is sometimes likened to a hydraulic system in which repressed forces are kept in check by defenses, and if these are removed, repressed content will emerge. Analogies can be helpful if they compare two phenomena that are indeed similar in significant ways. The more familiar event can be helpful in highlighting aspects of the less familiar event that should be considered. However, if the two events differ in important ways, then the analogy can interfere with understanding. Two things may bear a superficial resemblance to each other but be quite unlike in important ways. The soundness of the analogy must always be explored. It is only a guide (Thouless, 1974, p. 171). For example does "mental illness" (disease/disorder) match the characteristics of a disease? Does it have (1) a known etiology, (2) a predictable course, and (3) get worse without treatment? Peele (1999) and Finguarette (1988) argue that alcohol abuse is not a disease because it does not have these characteristics. Heyman (2009) argues that research shows that use of drugs and alcohol is a choice, not a disease. Consider also schizophrenia. Its etiology is unknown contrary to bold assertions to the contrary. It does not have a predictable course and it does not necessarily get worse without treatment; indeed about one third of people labeled as schizophrenic get better over time.[8] Szasz (1961, 1994) has consistently argued that the term "mental illness"—implying that it is like a physical illness—is a fabrication.

Argument by mere analogy refers to the use of an analogy "to create conviction of the truth of whatever it illustrates, or when it implies that truth in order to deduce some new conclusion" (Thouless, 1974, p. 169). When an argument from analogy is reduced to its bare outline, it "has the form that because some thing or event N has the properties a and b which belong to M, it must have the property c which also belongs to M" (p. 171). Arguments from analogy may sometimes be difficult to recognize. The analogy may be implied rather than clearly stated. The mind of a child may be likened to a container that must be filled with information. This analogy carries implications that may be untrue, such as that we have sharply limited capacities. So "the use of analogy becomes crooked argumentation when an analogy is used not as a guide to expectations, but as proof of a conclusion" (Thouless, 1974, p. 176). Analogies create vivid images that are then readily available. They play on our emotions. Their vividness may crowd out less vivid but more accurate analogies and discourage a review of possible limitations of the analogy. Although they may be a useful guide to what to look for, "They are never final evidence as to what the facts are" (Thouless, 1974, p. 175). They are one of many devices for creating conviction even though there are no rational grounds for the conviction. Arguments from mere analogy can be dealt with by noting at what point the analogy breaks down.

In *argument from forced analogy*, an analogy is used to advance an argument when there is so little resemblance between the things compared to ever expect that they would resemble each other in relation to the main point under discussion. One example is "delusional processes are like a machine run amok." Those who use such analogies are often aware of their influence in creating beliefs despite the absence of rational grounds for such beliefs. Forced analogies are often used in public speeches where their deficiencies cannot be pointed out readily. The remedy consists of examining just how closely the analogy really fits the matter at hand. Thouless (1974) recommends trying out other analogies and noting that these carry as much force as the original one.

DIVERSIONS

Informal fallacies may be used to divert attention from critical appraisal of an argument. Some of the informal fallacies already discussed could be so classified, such as *ad hominem* arguments in which attention is focused on the person making the argument rather than the argument itself. Trivial points or irrelevant objections may be emphasized. As Schopenhauer suggested (n.d., p. 29), "If you find that you are being worsted, you can make a diversion—that is, you can suddenly begin to talk of something else, as though it had a bearing on the matter in dispute." In any discussion, a number of points may be raised, one or more of which may not be true. Some trivial point may be shown to be incorrect and it is assumed that the main question has been disposed of. Showing the inaccuracy of a fact that is not relevant to a position can create the impression that the entire argument is incorrect when this may not be the case. Witty comments and jokes may be used to divert attention from the main point of an argument or from the fact that little evidence is provided for a position. A joke may make a valid position appear ridiculous or poorly conceived. Attempts to defend a position in the face of such a response may seem pedantic. The remedy is to point out that, although what has been said may be true (or humorous), it is irrelevant.

Answering a Question With a Question

An example of this fallacy is responding to a "why" with a "why not?" (Michalos, 1971, p. 81). In the fallacy of answering questions with questions, hypothetical questions are introduced that provide a distraction from important points. Some questions are vital to evaluation of arguments. However, in arguments, they are never an end in themselves. (See prior discussion of the fallacy of ignorance.)

Appeal to Emotion

Words may be used to create guilt, anger, anxiety, or blind adherence to a position and to distract us from noticing flaws in an argument. Anger may be created by inflammatory statements about a position or by *ad hominem* attacks. Appeals to guilt, anxiety, and fear are widely used to distract us from the main issues. In an article entitled "Marketing: A Lifeline for Private Practice," readers are told that as more social workers go into private practice, and as competition between them and other mental health professionals heats up, marketing becomes a necessary survival tool (*NASW News*, 1987, 32(9), p. 5). Notice the term *survival* appealing to fear. In an advertisement for malpractice insurance readers are encouraged to complete a "self-test" to determine if they need professional liability insurance. Items on this test include: "I don't have my own coverage if I'm sued for malpractice," "I've heard about other social workers being sued," and "I'm aware that malpractice suits against social workers have considerably increased over the past few years"—all designed to create fear of not having malpractice insurance (*NASW News*, 1987, 32(4), p. 17). The principle of social proof (appeal to consensus) is one of the bases of appeals to anxiety—"You will be out of step with 'everyone else' if you don't agree with an accepted position." Appeals to anxiety and fear may draw on any of the sources of persuasion illustrated in Table 10.6. Appeals to fear were used by psychiatrists in their battle against psychologists to retain and expand their turf, for example, predicting that the quality of services will decrease if psychologists receive hospital admission privileges (Buie, 1989). Appeals to pity or friendship direct attention away from examination of evidence related to a claim.

Red Herring

Here, someone tries to distract you from the main point of an argument by introducing irrelevant content. The point is to divert others from critical issues.

THE USE OF CONFUSION

Some fallacies work by confusion: If you cannot convince them (or if you do not know what you are talking about), confuse them. Creation of confusion and doubt (e.g., confusing wording on ballots and raising doubts regarding scientific findings) was (and is) one of the many tactics used by the tobacco industry (Sourcewatch, "Tobacco industry public relations strategies," retrieved on July 16, 2009, from

<http://www.sourcewatch.org>). People may cite a counterexample to a position saying that "the exception proves the rule." Finding an example that does not fit a rule may be informative about the boundaries within which a rule is applicable, but may say nothing about the truth or falsity of a rule. (See also discussion of the *fallacy of the sweeping generalization* earlier in this chapter.) Excessive wordiness is often used to create confusion as so well described by Orwell (1958). Irrelevancies, unstated premises, and implicit assumptions must be culled out to reveal the actual premises and conclusions. We tend to assume that if someone is talking (or writing), he or she must be making sense. That is, we tend to think that we have missed the point and that we are limited in our lack of understanding; we "tend to put the burden of comprehension on ourselves" (Michalos, 1971, p. 79). If jargon and excessive wordiness is complemented by prestige, the use of pseudo-arguments is more likely to confuse and mislead; we are misled by our tendency to go along with what authorities (the experts) say. Liking is another persuasive influence at work here. If we like someone, we are more prone to agree with what they say and to think they are saying something of value—the buddy-buddy fallacy (Meehl, 1973).

Equivocation involves playing on the double meaning of a word in a misleading or inaccurate manner (see Hamblin, 1970). "If someone informs you that Simon Butcher is independent, exactly what has he told you? Is he politically, religiously, economically, or socially independent? Is he a free thinker or a free lover? Is he a lover of free thinking or does he just think about loving freely? The fallacy of *equivocation* would be committed if someone began with a premise attributing independence in one sense to Butcher and concluded from that that Butcher possessed independence in an entirely different sense" (Michalos, 1971, p. 71).

People may claim a lack of understanding to avoid coming to grips with an issue or try to confuse issues by repeatedly asking for alternative statements of a position (Michalos, 1971, p. 75). This tactic, like some others such as arousing anger, may be used to gain time to consider a position better in terms of what to do next in order to prevail. Feigned lack of understanding is often combined with use of power, as when a superior tells a staff member that she does not understand the point being made, with the implication that the other person's point is irrelevant or silly. A possible remedy here may be to ask the person exactly what aspect of the argument is confusing.

SUMMARY

Propagandistic use of fallacies distract us from critical appraisal of dubious claims. Most fallacies are informal; they do not involve a formal mistake. Bold assertions (exaggerated claims with no evidence) are a favorite. *Ad hominem* arguments may be used in which the background, habits, associates, or personality of the person (rather than their arguments) are appealed to. Variants of *ad hominem* arguments include guilt (or credit) by association, the bad seed fallacy, appeals to faulty motives or good intentions, special pleading, and false claims of inconsistency. Vacuous guarantees may be offered, as when someone assumes that because a condition ought to be, it is the case without providing support for the position. Fallacies that evade the facts (such as begging the question) appear to address the facts, but do not. Variants of question begging include bold assertions (use of alleged certainty), circular reasoning, use of unfounded generalizations to support a conclusion, leading questions, and simply ignoring questions.

Some informal fallacies overlook the facts, as in the fallacy of the sweeping generalization, in which a rule or assumption that is valid in general is applied to a specific example for which it is not valid. Other informal fallacies distort facts or positions. In straw person arguments, a position similar to (but significantly different from) the one presented is described and attacked. The fallacies of false cause, forcing an extension and the inappropriate use of analogies also involve distortion of facts or positions. Diversions such as irrelevant objections, humor (making a joke), or emotional appeals are used to block critical appraisal of an argument. Some fallacies work by creating confusion including feigned lack of understanding and excessive talk that obscures arguments. Increasing your fallacy-spotting skills will decrease the likelihood that you will be taken in by propaganda ploys.

Table 13.5 EXAMPLES OF QUESTIONABLE APPEALS AND FAULTY INFERENCES

1. *Argumentum ad hominem.* Attacking or praising some aspects of a person's character, lifestyle, race, religion, sex, and so on, as evidence for (or against) a conclusion, even when these circumstances are irrelevant to the situation being examined.
He has a point. But look at how he is dressed.
2. *Appeal to authority.* Arguing that a claim is true based purely on an authority's status with no reference to evidence.
Dr. Monston: It is clear that social anxiety is a mental disorder.
Question: How is this clear?
Reply: It is included in the DSM.
3. *Appeal to experience.*
I've seen thirty clients and used x successfully with all of them. It works!
4. *Emotional reasoning.* Using our emotions or feelings as evidence of a truth.
This is true because I feel it is true.
5. *Argument from ignorance.* Assuming that something is true simply because it has not been shown to be false, or that it is false simply because it has not been shown to be true.
You don't have any proof that your method works. Therefore it does not.
6. *Assume hard headed therefore hard hearted.*
She can't really care about her clients if she spends that much time questioning our agency's methods.
7. *Fallacy of labeling.* Labeling yourself or others when the label is unjustified by the circumstances, or when the label it is inappropriately used as a reason for behavior or its lack (Sternberg, 1986, p. 96).
You have done everything that could be done to discover the best dentist to perform a complex root canal. He makes a mistake. You say to yourself "I'm a failure."
8. *Hasty generalization.* Generalizing from exceptional cases to a rule that fits only those cases.
Bill and a friend were discussing the director of their agency. Bill said, "He is a total failure because he has not increased funding for our agency."
9. *Inference by manner of presentation.*
She gave a convincing talk. I'm going to use her methods.

(Continued)

Table 13.5 EXAMPLES OF QUESTIONABLE APPEALS AND FAULTY INFERENCES (CONTINUED)

10. *Argumentation ad populum.* Assuming that "if everyone else thinks this way, it must be right." Appeal to popularity.
Everyone is using this new method. We should use it too.
11. *Appeal to newness.*
It's the latest thing. We should try it too.
12. *Assume that good intentions result in good services* (e.g., protect clients from harm). Supervisor in response to a question from a client about an agency's effectiveness: "We really care about our clients."
13. *Influence by testimonials.*
I believe it works because Mrs. Rivera said she tried it and it helped.
14. *Appeal to tradition.*
That's the way we have always done it. We should continue to use these methods.
15. *Fallacy of representativeness.* Incorrectly assuming that two or more things or events are related simply because they resemble each other.
Foxes have remarkable lungs. Therefore the lungs of a fox will remedy asthma.
16. *Fallacies based on preconceptions.* Accepting the first explanations for an event that occurs to you without considering other, less obvious views.
Basing clinical decisions on a readily available theory and neglecting other well-argued views.
17. *Overlooking the role of chance.* Assuming that an outcome due to chance is related to past occurrences or a skill.
My next baby must be a boy. We've had five girls.
18. *Irrelevant conclusion.* A conclusion is irrelevant to the reasoning that led to it.
I don't think Mr. Jones abused his child. He spends time on the weekend repairing his car.
19. *Fallacy of division.* Assuming that what is true of the whole is necessarily true of each individual part of the whole.
The cancer center at Mercer Hospital has a good reputation. Dr. M. who works there is a good surgeon.
20. *False cause.* Relying on temporal succession (correlation) to identify a cause.
John's depression lifted after taking medication. This shows his depression is caused by a brain dysfunction.
21. *Invalid disjunction* (either/oring). Considering only two options when more than two should be considered.
We must either hospitalize him or leave him to wander the streets.
22. *Weak documentation.*
Accepting a claim based on vague, undocumented evidence.
23. *Fallacy of composition.* Assuming that what is true of parts of a whole is true of the whole.
Jane is behaviorally oriented. Therefore all staff at her agency are behaviorally oriented.

SOURCE: Based on Robert J. Sternberg (1986). *Intelligence Applied: Understanding and Increasing Your Intellectual Skills* (pp. 94–105). San Diego: Harcourt Brace Jovanovich.

14

Increase Your Skill in Searching for Answers for Yourself

You are more likely to spot propaganda if you know what kind of data is needed to critically appraise different kinds of claims and know how to find it. You can take advantage of the process of evidence-informed practice: (1) pose a clear question related to information you want; (2) search effectively and efficiently for related evidence; (3) critically appraise what you find or rely on a high-quality review already available; (4) decide whether related research applies to you and make a decision; and (5) evaluate what happens (Straus et al., 2005). The process and philosophy of evidence-based practice highlights the play of bias and uncertainty involved in making life-affecting decisions and describes steps for handling this honestly and constructively (Gambrill, 2006). The steps involved are designed to decrease confirmation biases such as looking only for data that support a belief. Flaws in traditional methods of knowledge dissemination, including peer-reviewed journals, were one of the reasons for the origins of evidence-based practice (Altman, 2002; Sackett et al., 1997). (See also Young, Ioannidis, & Al-Ubaydli, 2008.) Developing related skills will help you to search effectively and efficiently for information for yourself and to avoid bogus claims about what is true and what is not. A brief overview of these steps is offered in this chapter, as well as a bird's eye view regarding critical appraisal of different kinds of research.

POSING WELL-STRUCTURED QUESTIONS

A first step is to translate information needs related to a decision into a well-structured question that will facilitate a search for related research. Straus et al. (2005) suggest posing four-part questions that describe: (1) the population of clients (similar to you), (2) the intervention you are interested in (it may be a diagnostic test), (3) what it may be compared to (e.g., doing nothing), and (4) hoped-for outcomes. Forming a specific question often begins with a vague general question then proceeds to a well-built one. There are different kinds of questions, which may require different methods to answer them.

Effectiveness Questions. Many questions concern the effectiveness of interventions. Consider the 9/11 disaster at the World Trade Center. A question might be: "In people recently exposed to a catastrophic event, does brief psychological debriefing, compared to no special intervention, avoid or minimize the likelihood of post-traumatic stress disorder?" A search of the Cochrane Database would reveal the Rose, Bisson, Churchill, and Wesseley (2002) review of the effectiveness of psychological debriefing for preventing post-traumatic stress disorder (PTSD). This critical appraisal of one-hour single-session debriefing concluded that there was no benefit. Thus, you would not be inclined to seek or recommend such brief counseling.

Prevention Questions. Prevention questions direct attention to the future. An example is: "In young children, does early home visitation programs, compared with no service, decrease later antisocial behavior?" As with effectiveness questions, well-designed randomized controlled trials (RCTs) control for more biases than do other kinds of studies as described later in this chapter.

Prediction (Risk/Prognosis) Questions. Questions here include: "For depressed teenagers, does the 'X' suicide risk scale accurately predict further suicide attempts? For nonsymptomatic women aged 60, does having a mammogram every year decrease mortality for cancer?" Questions that arise include the rate of false positives (people incorrectly said to have some characteristic, such as be suicidal) and the rate of false negatives (clients inaccurately said not to have some characteristic (not be suicidal).

Assessment Questions. An example of an assessment question is: "In young children does the Eyberg Child Behavior Inventory accurately identify children with high rates of misbehavior in classrooms?" Measures used differ in their reliability (for example, consistency of responses over time in the absence of events that may create such change) and validity (do they measure what they purport to measure?). Inflated claims regarding the accuracy of assessment tools are common.

Description Questions. Here, a question may be: "In relatives caring for a dying relative, what challenges arise and how are they handled?" Description questions may call for qualitative research, for example, in-depth interviews and/or focus groups. Other description questions require survey data involving large samples. Such data may provide information about divorces and related consequences including how people cope with them. Here too, we should consider the quality of related research, such as sample size and how representative it is of the population of interest.

Questions about Harm. How many people have to receive an intervention (assessment or treatment) for one to be harmed? This is known as *number needed to harm* (NNH). For example, "In people who are smokers, how many would we have to screen to identify one person who has lung cancer?" "How many would be harmed by taking the test who are not at risk, for example, by a false positive (or negative) result?" As Gray (2001a) suggests, any intervention, including assessment methods, may harm as well as help.

Questions about Costs and Benefits. Limited resources highlight the importance of cost-benefit analyses. What is the cost of offering one service compared to another and how many people benefit from each service? (For further discussion, see Guyatt et al., 2008.)

Questions about Life-Long Learning. "Is searching for websites that offer competing views of an issue, or reading a professional newsletter, more effective in avoiding biased views?"

Errors that may occur in translating information needs into clear questions that guide a search include having more than one question in a question and posing vague questions. Giving up too soon when difficulty occurs is an obstacle. Posing clear questions may be threatening. You may find the answer and not like it. There may be no high-quality research related to a life-affecting decision. There may be more questions than answers.

SEARCHING FOR RELATED RESEARCH

You can facilitate searches by selecting key search terms that refer to each part of a well-structured question: client type, proposed intervention, alternative action (including "watchful waiting"), hoped-for outcomes, and quality filters. A search requires seeking information that challenges your assumptions, as well as for information that supports them. Different kinds of questions often require different kinds of research to critically appraise them and including related terms are of value in a search. (See Table 14.1.) Such terms are referred to as *quality (methodological) filters*. Examples are shown in Table 14.2. Filters for effectiveness and prevention questions include "metaanalysis," "systematic review," "random," or "controlled trials." Let us say you are interested in the effectiveness of brief (one hour) psychological debriefing to prevent "post-traumatic stress disorder." Terms might be "stress," "psychological debriefing," and "systematic review." Systematic reviews and meta-analyses include a search for and critical appraisal of all relevant studies.

The Internet and inventions, such as the systematic review, have revolutionized the search for information, making it more speedy and effective. As search engines have become more integrated, it is easier to search by just posing a question on Google. Sometimes this is productive. At other times, a more systematic search is needed to identify key studies related to a question. Searches may be limited in a variety of ways, for example, by date. The boolean search term "and" retrieves only articles with both words (child abuse and single parents). The term "or" locates all articles with either word (alcohol abuse or cocaine abuse). The term "not" excludes material containing certain words. Synonyms and key words can be combined by placing parentheses around OR statements as in (parent training OR parent education). Truncating with asterisks (*) is often used as in (reduce*) for reduction. The better formed the question, the more likely it is that the terms used are most relevant to your information needs. If a search results in too many hits, narrow the search by using more specific terms and more quality filters. If you get too little, widen the search by using more general terms.

Relevant Databases

Sources differ in the degree of "quality-control" regarding critical appraisal. Focus on sources that contain high-quality reviews. Keep in mind that inflated claims of what "we know" and "what we do not know" based on incomplete and/or uncritical reviews of research on a topic are common, even in the professional literature. The Cochrane and Campbell Collaborations are international enterprises, which prepare, maintain, and disseminate high-quality reviews of research related to specific questions. The Cochrane Collaboration focuses on health concerns. The Campbell Collaboration, patterned after the Cochrane Collaboration, prepares reviews related

Table 14.1 TYPES OF STUDIES

The types of studies that give the best evidence are different for different types of questions. In every case, however, the best evidence comes from studies where the methods used maximize the chance of eliminating bias. The study designs that best suit different question types are as follows:

Question	Best Study Designs	Description
INTERVENTION	Randomized controlled trial	Subjects are randomly allocated to treatment or control groups and outcomes assessed.
ETIOLOGY AND RISK FACTORS	Randomized controlled trial	As etiology questions are similar to intervention questions, the ideal study type is an RCT. However, it is usually not ethical or practical to conduct such a trial to assess harmful outcomes.
	Cohort study	Outcomes are compared for matched groups with and without exposure to risk factor (prospective study).
	Case-control study	Subjects with and without outcome of interest are compared for previous exposure or risk factor (retrospective study).
FREQUENCY AND RATE	Cohort study	As above.
	Cross-sectional study	Measurement of condition in a representative (preferably random) sample of people.
DIAGNOSIS	Cross-sectional study with random or consecutive sample.	Preferable an independent, blind, comparison with "gold standard" test,
PROGNOSIS AND PREDICTION	Cohort/survival study	Long-term follow-up of a representative cohort.
PHENOMENA	Qualitative	Narrative analysis or focus group; designed to assess the range of issues (rather than their quantification).

SOURCE: P. Glasziou, C. Del Mar, and J. Salisbury (2003). *From evidence-based medicine workbook* (p. 41). London: BMJ. Reprinted with permission.

Table 14.2 EXAMPLES OF METHODOLOGICAL FILTERS

Kind of Question	Example of Filters
Effectiveness and prevention	Random or controlled or trial or systematic review or meta-anal
Risk/Prognosis	Risk assessment or predictive validity or receiver operat or ROC or sensitivity or specificity or prognosis or false positive or false negative or sys. review or meta-anal
Assessment	Inter-rater or systematic review or meta-anal (see also risk above)
Description	random selec or survey or qualitative studies or content analy or in-depth studies or observation or systematic rev. or meta-anal

to education, social intervention, and criminal justice. Entries in the Cochrane and Campbell databases include completed reviews, as well as protocols that are expressions of intent to conduct a systematic review. Abstracts of reviews are available without charge. Cochrane and Campbell Collaboration reviews are based on a search for all high-quality research, published and unpublished, concerning a particular question, and critical appraisal of what is found. Criteria used to appraise studies are rigorous and clearly described. Journals are hand-searched.[1]

Other Sources: The U.K. National Health Service Centre for Reviews and Dissemination (CRD), located at the University of York, prepares and disseminates research on the effectiveness and cost-effectiveness of specific health-care interventions (<http://www.crd.york.ac.uk>). Libraries are a key resource. Librarians should be skilled *informaticists*—skilled in searching for information related to a question. Governmental agencies provide free statistical information of potential value. SIGLE (System for Information on Grey Literature in Europe) can be used to locate hard to find and nonconventional literature. Some sites are available only by subscription, but a library near you may have a subscription. Other databases include: PsychInfo, PubMed, MEDLINE, EMBASE, CINAHL (nursing and allied health professionals). Search engines such as Google provide a valuable source for locating research findings. Other sources can be seen in Table 14.3.

Sources include web sites concerned with a unique topic (Attention-Deficit/Hyperactivity Disorder [ADHD]); those concerned with fraud and quackery; those prepared by corporations (e.g., <http://www.zoloft.com>), and web sites concerned with harm (Alliance for Human Research Protection <www.ahrp.org>). Material differs greatly in the accuracy of reports of research findings (e.g., Kunst, Groot, Latthe, Latthe, & Khan, 2002). Just because a source has a reputation for providing accurate appraisals, does not guarantee that material will be accurately presented. As always, "buyer beware" applies. Criteria that can be used to appraise the likelihood that content is accurate include the source (does it have a reputation for critical appraisal and accurate presentation of alternative views), clarity of writing, completeness of description of studies (e.g., sample size, measures used), and references that allow readers to follow-up sources. Searching widely is one way to protect yourself from influence by bogus presentations from a single source.[2]

Table 14.3 VALUABLE WEBSITES AND TOOLS

AHRQ. Provides summaries of research regarding assessment and intervention methods. <http://www.ahrq.gov>

ASSIA. (Applied Social Science Index and Abstracts) is an indexing and abstracting tool covering health, social services, economics, politics, race relations, and education. <http://www.csa.com>

Bandolier. Provides updates regarding health and medical treatments. www.medicine.ox.ac.uk\bandolier

BestBETS. A searchable database regarding clinical questions. <http:// www.bestbets.org>

BMJ Best Treatments. (United Kingdom). <http://www.besttreatments.bmj.com/btuk/home.jsp>

Campbell Database of Systematic Reviews. <http://www.campbellcollaboration.org>

Center for Evidence Based Medicine. This site includes a toolbox for practicing and teaching evidence-informed practice. <http://www.cebm.net>

Centre for Health Evidence. This site includes the User's Guides to the Medical Literature produced by JAMA. <http://www.cche.net>

Center for Reviews and Dissemination. www.crd.york.ac.uk

Child Welfare Information Gateway. <http://www.childwelfare.gov>

Cochrane Consumers Network <http://consumers.cochrane.org/>

Cochrane Database of Systematic Reviews. <http://www.cochrane.org>

Database of Abstracts of Reviews of Effects. <http://www.library.ucsf.edu>

DISCERN. Designed to help the public and professionals assess the quality of advice and information. < http://www.discern.org.uk>

DUETS. Database of uncertainties about the effectiveness of interventions. < http://www.library.nhs.uk/duets>

EPPI-Centre. <http://eppi.ioe.ac.uk/cms/>

EQUATOR. An international initiative designed to increase the value of medical research by promoting transparency and accurate reporting of studies. <http://www.equator-network.org>

ERIC. This is a database of educational literature sponsored by the U.S. Department of Education. <http://www.eric.ed.gov>

Evidence-Based Behavioral Practice. <http://www.ebbp.org>

Health Technology Assessment Program. <http://www.hta.hca.wa.gov>

James Lind Library. This offers a variety of valuable resources. <http://www.jameslindlibrary.org>

Media Doctor Australia. This site analyzes the quality of media reports concerning medical tests and treatments. <http://www.mediadoctor.org.au>

Oxford Centre for Evidence-Based Mental Health. <http://www.cebmh.com/>

Patient Decision Aids. A critically reviewed list of decision aids produced by the Ottawa Health Research Institute. <http://www.decisionaid.ohri.ca>

PubMed. An Internet Interface for Medline. You can restrict retrieval of articles to those most likely to answer your question. <http://www.ncbi.nlm.nih.gov>.

Social Care Institute for Excellence (SCIE). Established in the UK to provide reports about best practices in social care emphasizing value of services to consumers. <http://www.scie.org.uk>

TRIP. This is a clinical search tool. <http://www.tripdatabase.com>

Glossaries

Centre for Evidence-Based Medicine Glossary. <http://www.cebm.net/index.aspx?o=1116>

Centre for Evidence Based Medicine University of Toronto. <http://ktclearinghouse.ca/cebm/glossary/>

Reporting Tools

CONSORT Statement. <http://www.consort-statement.org/consort-statement>

PRISMA. <http://www.prisma-statement.org>

TREND Statement (Transparent Reporting of Evaluations with Nonrandomized Designs). <http://www.cdc.gov/trendstatement>

Tools

Evidence-Based Medicine Toolkit. <http://www.ebm.med.ualberta.ca>

BEST Training on Evidence Based Practice. <http://www.columbia.edu/cu/musher/Website/Website/EBP_OnlineTraining.htm>

Number Needed to Treat Calculator from Bandolier. <http://www.medicine.ox.ac.uk/bandolier/Extraforbando/NNTextra.pdf>

Common Errors and Obstacles

Your question may be too narrow or too broad, resulting in too few or too many "hits." You may give up too soon (e.g., see Ely, Osheroff, Maviglia, & Rosenbaum, 2007). Obstacles include: (1) poor quality of research producing biased evidence; (2) studies too small to produce clear results; (3) unpublished research is unavailable; (4) publication biases for positive findings; (5) failure of researchers to describe evidence in accurate, useful forms; (6) inaccessible databases; (7) systematic reviews hard to find, and (8) biased reviews (Gray, 2001a, p. 355). (See also Ioannidis, 2008a, b.) You may not be aware of important databases and may not have access to knowledgeable librarians. There may be no helpful research related to your question. Gray refers to this as the *relevance gap* (Gray, 2001a). Another is failure to publish research results—the *publication gap*. A third is difficulty finding published research—the *hunting gap*. Other gaps include the *quality gap* (p. 101). Misrepresentations of results are common (e.g., Gandhi et al., 2007).

CRITICALLY APPRAISING WHAT YOU FIND

As emphasized earlier, the kind of research relevant to a claim depends on the question. And, there is no perfect study. The question is, how serious are the flaws and are they acknowledged or are they hidden? (See Ciliska, Thomas, & Buffett, 2008; Guyatt, Oxman, Schunemann, Tugwell, & Knotterus, 2010.) Some questions call for qualitative research methods, such as in-depth interviews. Questions concerning intervention, prevention, harm, or testing the accuracy of a diagnostic method may most carefully be explored using randomized controlled trials. (See Table 14.1.) Often, a mix of qualitative and quantitative research is most informative.

Although professionals should acquire skill in critically appraising research related to different kinds of questions during their professional education, they may not.[3] You could share what you find with others by preparing a CAT (Critically Appraised Topic). A CAT is a brief (one page) summary of the question raised, what was found, and the implications for making decisions. (See Straus et al., 2005.)[4]

Common Errors and Obstacles

Common errors include: (1) not critically appraising what you find, (2) becoming disheartened when you find little, and (3) misinterpreting a lack of evidence that a method is effective as evidence that it is not effective. You can save time by drawing on high-quality systematic reviews related to a question when these are available, for example, in the Cochrane and Campbell Databases. (See Moher, Liberati, Tetzlaff, & Altman, 2009.) User-friendly checklists and flow-charts can help you to critically appraise different kinds of research (e.g., see <http://www.consort-statement.org>; Greenhalgh, 2010).[5] You can save time and increase your success by reading high-quality reviews (critical, exhaustive, transparent) rather than primary research; improving your search and critical appraisal skills and being more discerning about what you read by using a scanning strategy guided by key indicators of well-designed studies (Gray, 2001a).

INTEGRATING WHAT YOU FIND WITH OTHER INFORMATION AND MAKING A DECISION

A search may reveal that little or nothing is known. This will be true for many concerns. This is an important finding in terms of making decisions. You can use the following questions to take next steps.

Do Research Findings Apply to Me?

A great deal of research consists of correlational research (e.g., describing the relationship between certain characteristics of parents and child abuse) and experimental research, describing differences among different groups (e.g., experimental and control). In neither case may the findings apply to you. The focus of practice is on individuals; science deals with generalities. Samples used in studies may differ from people like you. Norms on assessment measures may be available but not for people like you. However, norms should not necessarily be used as guidelines for making decisions. For example, the outcomes you seek may differ from normative criteria and norms may not be optimal. Consider excessively high dosage levels of medications prescribed by physicians based on recommendations of pharmaceutical companies and with the approval of the FDA (Food and Drug Administration), which result in harmful side effects (Cohen, 2001). Be sure to consider the possible differences between those who participated in research studies related to a question of concern to you and yourself. These differences may influence potential costs and benefits of an intervention to you. Your unique characteristics and circumstances may suggest that a method should not be used because negative effects are likely or because such characteristics would render an intervention ineffective if applied at a certain time. Questions here include:

1. Is the relative risk reduction attributed to the intervention likely to be different because of my particular characteristics?
2. What is my absolute risk of an adverse event without the intervention?
3. Is there some other problem or a contraindication that might reduce the benefit?
4. Are there social or cultural factors that might affect the suitability or acceptability of an intervention?
5. What do I want? (Adapted from Sheldon, Guyatt, & Haines, 1998)

Are They Important? The So-What Question

If findings apply to me, are they important? Would they really make a difference in my decisions?

How Definitive Are the Research Findings?

There may be strong evidence not to use a method or strong evidence to use it. Typically, there will be uncertainty about whether a practice or policy will do more good than harm. How much uncertainty is there? (See DUETS web site in Table 14.3.)

Will Potential Benefits Outweigh Potential Risks and Costs?

Every intervention, including assessment measures, has potential risks, as well as potential benefits, for example, a false positive or negative result. People differ in how "risk adverse" they are and in the importance given to particular outcomes. We weigh gains or losses that are certain more heavily than those that are uncertain. Presentation of risks and benefits may be quite misleading as noted in chapter 6. For example, how decisions are "framed" (in terms of gains or losses) influences decisions. Different surface wordings of identical problems influence our judgments.[6] What is the absolute risk reduction (ARR). (See chapter 6.) How many people have to receive a program to help one person? Interventions differ in the Number Needed to Treat (NNT) ranging from two (fear of flying—standard exposure vs. waiting list control) to hundreds (aspirin versus placebo for hip surgery = 232 (retrieved March 10, 2004, from <http://www.cebm.utononto.ca/glossary/nntsPrint.htm>).[7] Is there information about NNH (the number of people who would have to receive a service to harm one person)?

How Do My Preferences and Values Compare to a Proposed Intervention and Its Results?

The lack of correlation between what we say we want (our preferences) and what we do (our actions), highlights the difficulties of discovering our own preferences. That is, we often do not know what we want and our preferences change in accord with a variety of factors, including the time when we are asked about them in relation to a decision that has been made and the visibility of its consequences. For example, although many people say they want to achieve a certain goal and even pay for programs to help them to do so, many do not follow instructions. Decision aids are available in many areas to help us to understand risks and benefits of different options such as getting screening for colon cancer (or not).[8] Such aids can "personalize" information by allowing us to ask questions we think are important and can highlight issues and information often overlooked. Occasions when carefully considering our preferences is especially important include those in which: (1) options have major differences in outcomes or complications; (2) decisions require making trade-offs between short- and long-term outcomes; (3) one choice can result in a small chance of a grave outcome; and (4) there are marginal differences in outcomes between options (Kassirer, 1994).

Can This Intervention Be Used Effectively?

Can an intervention be carried out in a way that maximizes success? Are those who will offer related practices competent to do so?

Are Alternatives Available?

Are other options available, perhaps another agency? Here too, familiarity with related research can facilitate decisions.

What If the Experts Disagree?

Disagreements about what is best are common, even among experts in an area. How can you check the expertise (knowledge), and ethics (honesty regarding controversies and uncertainties) of an expert? Criteria of value in discovering whether a person is an honest expert include use of language that you can understand, description of evidence both for and against a preferred position, description of well-argued alternatives and related evidence and an openness to questions.

What If I Do Not Find Any Related Research?

Most interventions used by professionals have not been critically tested; we do not know if they are effective, ineffective, or harmful. Ethical obligations require sharing uncertainty within a supportive relationship, drawing on a well-argued practice theory to guide decisions as needed (e.g., Katz, 2002).

What If Related Research Is of Poor Quality?

This will be a common finding. Instead of well-designed randomized controlled trials regarding an intervention, you may have to rely on findings from a pre-post test, which is subject to many rival explanations regarding the cause of change. The term "best evidence" could refer to a variety of different kinds of tests that differ greatly in their ability to critically test claims. Some guidelines claim that if there are two well-designed randomized controlled trials that show a positive outcome, this represents a "well-established claim." This is marketing rather than science. It is less misleading to say that a claim has been critically tested in two well-controlled trials and has passed both tests; this keeps uncertainty in view.

Making a Decision

Many sources of information may contribute to a final decision, related research findings being but one. Others include values about how different risks and benefits are weighed. The importance of the decision also matters. This will influence how much effort you devote to making an informed decision. You may prefer to leave a decision up to an "expert." Poor decisions may result from overconfidence, influence by redundant information, confirmation biases, and overlooking the inaccuracy of information. Jumping to conclusions may result in oversimplification of causes related to concerns. Belief in a faulty theory of behavior may lead you astray. Becoming informed about common sources of bias such as influence by vivid testimonials and case examples will help you to avoid errors that result in poor decisions. The time and effort devoted to making a decision should depend on the potential consequences of making a faulty or good decision.

Evaluating What Happens

Evaluating outcome has many advantages: (1) ongoing feedback about progress (or its lack); (2) plans can be changed in a timely manner depending on outcomes; (3) positive feedback increases motivation; and (4) the relationship between services and outcomes can be explored. There is a rich literature describing valid, feasible ways to evaluate different kinds of outcomes including complex ones, such as quality of life (e.g., see Rossi, Lipsey, & Freeman, 2004). Timely corrective feedback is essential to catching and correcting harmful effects of an intervention at an early point. Some methods are more likely than others to avoid biases that get in the way of accurately estimating progress and what was responsible for it. Measures used should be *relevant* (meaningful to you and your significant others), *specific* (clearly described), *sensitive* (reflect changes that occur), *feasible* (possible to obtain), *unintrusive* (not interfere with service provision), *valid* (measure what they are supposed to measure), and *reliable* (show consistency over different measurements in the absence of change). Ways to fool yourself about degree of progress include selecting measures because they are easy to use even though they are not related to your concerns and are not sensitive to change, perhaps because they are vague. Reliance on surrogate end points may be misleading (Gotzsche, Liberati, Torri, & Rossetti, 1996). For example, taking a medication may reduce plaque in your arteries but not affect mortality.

Positive outcomes may be due to the act of treatment rather than the treatment itself, a placebo effect.[9] Negative (nocebo), as well as positive (placebo), effects may occur. The former have a negative impact on outcome and/or result in negative side effects. One or more of the following reactive effects may contribute to misleading estimates of success:

- *Hello–goodbye effect*. We present ourselves as worse than we really are when we seek help and as better than we really are when service has ended. This leads to overestimating progress (Hathaway, 1948).
- *Hawthorne effect*. Improvement may result from being the focus of attention. Going to a well-known clinic or being seen by a famous therapist may result in positive outcomes.
- *Rosenthal effect*. We tend to give observers what we think they want—to please people we like or respect.
- *Observer bias*. The observer's expectations may result in biased data.
- *Social desirability effect*. We tend to offer accounts viewed as appropriate. For example, we may under report drinking.

Extreme values tend to become less extreme on repeated assessment. If you do unusually well on a test, you are likely to do less well the next time around. Conversely, if you do very poorly, you are likely to do better the next time. These are called *regression effects*. There is a regression (a return) toward the mean (your average performance level). Overlooking these effects can lead to faulty judgments. We tend to focus on our "hits" and overlook our "misses." To accurately estimate our track record (or anyone else's), we must examine both "hits" and "misses," as well as what would have happened without intervention. We tend to attribute success to our skills and failure to chance. We engage in wishful thinking. Use of vague or irrelevant feedback obscures the true relationship (or lack thereof) between our judgments and outcomes. We tend to forget that actions taken as a result of predictions influence the outcomes.[10] We tend to overlook the role of chance (coincidences) and are swayed by hindsight bias (believing that we could have predicted an outcome after we know it, when indeed we did not have related information at an earlier time).

Propagandists take advantage of these sources of bias to promote false claims. They may hide lack of evidence of effectiveness by encouraging wishful thinking and the illusion of control. They may hide the possibility that your cold was just about over anyway. They may focus on only some symptoms suggesting improvement, ignoring others of importance, which have not changed for the better (e.g., mortality). Familiarly with common biases may help you to avoid them and their negative effects such as continuing harmful or ineffective programs and forgoing effective ones. (Many of these biases also influence selection of assessment methods.) Ongoing tracking of progress provides feedback that can be used to correct inaccurate views. Experimental N of 1 trials are ideal for discovering what method works best for a given person when the external research is murky or does not apply well to an individual. (See Guyatt et al., 2008.) The vaguer the outcome measures, the more likely that bias will creep in, because there is less chance for corrective feedback.

Fears about revealing lack of progress or harmful effects may discourage careful evaluation. Evaluation is a highly political issue; it is not for the timid (Baer, 2004). Lack of time and skill in selecting relevant, feasible progress indicators interferes with evaluation that can guide decision making. Advocating for accountability and the transparency of results this requires, as well as for use of valid measures (rather than misleading surrogates), is vital to avoid propaganda regarding the effects of practices and policies. The alternatives to careful evaluation include basing decisions on "guesstimates" (uninformed guesses), wishful thinking, and use of irrelevant or even misleading measures.

CRITICALLY APPRAISING RESEARCH: A BIRD'S EYE VIEW

You are less likely to be mislead by propaganda in the helping profession if you know how to critically appraise different kinds of claims and related research reports. Consider the following claims. Are they true?

- Raising self-esteem will decrease antisocial behavior of children.
- St. John's Wort decreases depression.
- Intercessionary prayer is effective.
- Taking cholesterol lowering medication decreases mortality.
- Wearing a magnet will help you to avoid colds.

As illustrated in this book, marketing in the guise of scholarship is common. Claims may be inflated in a number of ways—claims of effectiveness or of no effectiveness, for example. And, just because an intervention has been found to be effective or ineffective in two critical tests, does not warrant claims of certainty (e.g., "well-established"). Being informed about different kinds of research, what each kind can rigorously test and what it cannot, including biases that result in misleading results, will help you to avoid marketing in the guise of scholarship, as well as to critically appraise claims made in the media. Without this kind of research savvy you will be a pushover for ploys such as scare tactics and bold assertions. Without this knowledge and the motivation to use it, you will be a patsy for bogus claims. Skill in discovering high-quality reviews of research related to life-affecting decisions will help you to make informed decisions. We should also be skeptical of the skeptics. Just because someone says a study is flawed does not mean that it is. Minimizing or trashing disliked views and related evidence is a common propaganda ploy.

There are many kinds of research studies. They differ in their purpose (questions raised) and the likelihood that a given method can provide accurate information about the question.

Analytic: Designed to make causal inferences about relationships, for example, between certain risk factors such as poverty and an outcome such as child abuse or between taking a certain medication and lowering blood pressure. Two or more groups are compared.

Descriptive: Designed to provide information about the prevalence or incidence of a concern, for example, depression or diabetes or about the distribution of certain characteristics in a group.

Prospective: We look forward. Subjects are selected and followed up. Children who have been physically abused are followed up to determine their later histories.

Retrospective: We look back. Events of interest have already occurred (children have been abused) and data is collected from case records or recall as in case-control studies.

Contemporary Comparison. Groups that experience a risk factor such as emissions from a chemical explosion at the same time are compared.

Different kinds of research control for different kinds of biases, which may result in misleading conclusions, for example, about causal relationships. Consider critiques of complementary medicine that highlight the importance of considering placebo effects (Bausell, 2007). Sackett (1979) identified 35 different kinds of bias in case-control studies.

Controversies

There are differences of opinion even within a particular research tradition regarding questions about evidence, best methods, and how to interpret results. The research method used to explore a question reflects the researchers' views about knowledge and how it can be gained and their views concerning honest brokering of knowledge and ignorance (e.g., Glasziou, Chalmers, Rawlins, & McCulloch, 2007). Inflated claims may be made because those who make them: (1) are uninformed about the limitations of the research design used, (2) are aware, but do not care, or (3) care but need a publication. Differences in the rigor of research reviews are illustrated by reviews of multi-systemic therapy. Most sources including those edited or written by well-known clinical researchers such as Kazdin and Weisz (2003) describe this as an effective treatment. A systematic review concludes that such programs are no more effective than are other programs (e.g., Littell, Popa, & Forsythe, 2005, Littell, 2005).

MYTHS THAT HINDER CRITICAL APPRAISAL

A number of myths hinder acquiring and using critical appraisal skills.

It Is Too Difficult for Me to Learn

The ease of identifying key characteristics of rigorous studies regarding the effectiveness of interventions is suggested by the fact that social workers wanted their physicians to rely on the results of randomized controlled trials (RCTs) when making recommendations about treatment but relied on criteria, such as intuition when making decisions about their clients (Gambrill & Gibbs, 2002). What was good for the goose did not seem to be good for the gander. User-friendly checklists and scales have been developed to critically appraise different kinds of research making review of research quality easier. These range from detailed ones such as the CONSORT guidelines for reviewing randomized controlled trials (RCTs) to those that are less detailed (Greenhalgh, 2010).[11] Failure to satisfy a critical feature (such as blinded assessment of outcome) suggests that overall score on a rating scale should not be used since one critical flaw may be cancelled out by many less important characteristics.

All Research Is Equally Sound

All research is not equally informative. Research designs differ in the questions that can be carefully explored and in the extent to which biases are controlled that may result in incorrect conclusions. Errors may be made both in designing a study and when interpreting results. Because of this, you may conclude that a method is effective when it is not; it may even be harmful. Or, you may conclude that a method is not effective when it is effective. Chalmers (2003) defines reliable studies as "those in which the effects of policies and practices are unlikely to be confused with the effects of biases or chance" (p. 28). Less rigorous studies report more positive results than do more rigorous studies (e.g., Schulz et al., 1995).

We Can Trust the Experts

We rely on the assertions of experts, those with presumed special knowledge, on an everyday basis. However, depending on experts is risky. They may all be biased in a certain direction; they may share a bias towards a favored view of a problem and how to remedy it. Experts in an area prepare more biased reviews than do individuals who are well trained in methodological issues but who do not work in that area (Oxman & Guyatt, 1993). Recommendations of clinical experts differ from what is suggested based on results of carefully controlled research (Antman, Lau, Kuplenick, Mostellar, & Chalmers, 1992).

Intuition Is a Better Guide

It is important to distinguish between informed intuition based on extensive experience providing corrective feedback and intuition as an uninformed hunch. History is littered with examples of harm resulting from reliance on uninformed intuition. (See chapter 5.)

Only Certain Kinds of Research Must Be Rigorous

Another myth is that only certain kinds of research must be rigorous to avoid biased results. A concern to avoid biases, which may result in misleading conclusions, is relevant to all research, including qualitative research.

One or Two Studies Can Yield Conclusive Findings

Yet another myth is that one or two well-controlled studies yield the "truth" regarding what is effective and what is not. Such an assumption reflects an approach to knowledge in which we assume that certainty is possible.

A Study Must Be Perfect to be Useful

Yet another myth is that a study must be perfect to yield valuable findings. All studies are flawed. The question is, are the flaws so great that they preclude any sound conclusions?

Quantitative Research is Best/Qualitative Research is Best

Another myth is that quantitative research is better than qualitative research, or vice-versa. It depends on the question. Pursuit of answers to many questions requires both kinds of research. Consider *Labeling the Mentally Retarded* (1973) by Jane Mercer, in which community surveys, official records, and unstructured interviews were all used.

THE QUESTION OF BIAS

Bias is a systematic "leaning to one side" that distorts the accuracy of results. Bias can be of two types: (1) systematic, in which errors are made in a certain direction;

or (2) random fluctuations. It has long been of interest. Consider Francis Bacon's (1620) four idols of the mind:

> The Idols of the Tribe have their foundation in human nature itself, and in the tribe or race of men. For it is a false assertion that the sense of man is the measure of things. . .and the human understanding is like a false mirror, which receiving rays irregularly, distorts and discolors the nature of things by mingling its own nature with it.
>
> The Idols of the Cave are the idols of the individual man. For everyone (besides the errors common to human nature in general) has a cave or den of his own, which refracts and discolors the light of nature; owing either to his own proper and peculiar nature; or to its education and conversation with others; or to the reading of books, and the authority of those whom he esteems and admires; or to the differences of impressions, accordingly as they take place in a mind preoccupied and predisposed or in a mind indifferent and settled.
>
> There are also Idols formed by the intercourse and association of men with each other, which I call Idols of the Market-place, on account of the commerce and consort of men there. And therefore the ill and unfit choice of words wonderfully obstructs the understanding. . . . But words plainly force and overrule the understanding . . . and throw all into confusion, and lead men away into numberless empty controversies and idle fancies.
>
> Lastly, there are Idols, which have immigrated into men's minds from the various dogmas of philosophies and also from wrong laws of demonstration. These I call Idols of the Theater, because in my judgment all the received systems are but so many stage-plays, representing worlds of their own creation after an unreal and scenic fashion.

Biases occur in the design of research, how it is interpreted and how it is used (Jadad & Enkin, 2007; MacCoun, 1998). Biases in published research include: "submission bias (researchers are more strongly motivated to complete, and submit for publication, positive results), publication bias (editors are more likely to publish positive studies), methodological bias (methodological errors such as flawed randomization produce positive biases), abstracting bias (abstracts emphasize positive results), framing bias (relative risk data produce a positive bias)" (Gray, 2001b, p. 24). Studies reporting negative results are less likely to be published than studies reporting positive results.

Bias and Validity

Biases may influence both internal and external validity (e.g., see Ioannides, 2008a, b). *Internal validity* refers to the extent to which a design allows us to critically test and come up with an accurate answer concerning the causal relationships between some intervention and an outcome (Shadish, Cook, & Campbell, 2002). Biases include *selection bias* (e.g., biased allocation to experimental and control groups), *performance bias* (unequal provision of care apart from the methods under evaluation), *detection bias* (biased assessment of outcome), and *attrition bias* (biased occurrence and handing of deviations from a protocol and loss to follow up). Research on *publication bias* shows that "studies that show a statistically significant effect of treatment are more likely to be published, more likely to be published in English, more likely to be cited by other authors, and more likely to produce multiple publications than other studies" (Sterne, Egger, & G. Smith, 2001, p. 198). Sources of bias are rival hypotheses to a claim, for example, that a particular method resulted in certain outcomes. *Confounders* may occur—variables that are related to a causal factor and some outcome(s) that are not represented equally in two different groups. For example, people in a prospective cohort study may be enrolled in a way that results in systematic differences between groups. Unless a study is replicated we are not sure whether there were problems (flaws) that resulted in misleading findings. History illustrates that many results based on a single study could not be replicated and were later found to be false. *External validity* refers to the extent to which we can generalize the findings in a study to other circumstances. These may include other kinds of clients (e.g., age, risk factors, severity of problem), settings, services (e.g., timing, number of sessions [dosage], other concurrent services), kinds of outcomes reviewed, length of follow-up (Juni, Altman, & Egger, 2001, p. 42). Can you generalize the causal relationship found in a study to different times, places, and people, and different interventions and outcomes?

The literature on experimenter and subject biases highlights the importance of controlling for these effects (Rosenthal, 1994). For example, we tend to give socially desirable responses, to present ourselves in a good light. Knowing a hypothesis creates a tendency to encourage the very responses under investigation. Experimenter biases influence results in a number of ways. If the experimenters know the group a subject is in, they may change their behavior—for example, subtly lead the person in a certain direction. This is why it is vital for raters of outcome to be blind (unaware of the group to which a person is assigned). Unblinded rating of outcome (raters are aware of the purpose of a study and what subjects are in what group) can result in misleading conclusions. Experimenter effects are not necessarily intentional; still they may skew results in a certain way.

QUESTIONS TO ASK ABOUT ALL RESEARCH

Certain questions are important to raise regarding all research because of the potential for flaws that may result in misleading conclusions. These include questions about the size and source of samples used, whether there is a comparison group, the accuracy and validity of measures used, and the appropriateness of data analysis. The term "validity" refers to the accuracy of assumptions in relation to causes and effects. Methodological quality criteria include statistical conclusion validity, internal validity, construct validity, and external validity (Cook & Campbell, 1979; Shadish, Cook, & Campbell, 2002). Statistical conclusion validity refers to use of appropriate statistical tests. Construct validity refers to whether a measure acts like it is assumed to act. For example, is a measure of aggression negatively correlated with a measure of friendliness. External validity refers to the extent to which findings can be generalized to other settings, people, or times. Classic criteria for assuming a causal relationship include: (1) the cause precedes the effect, (2) the cause is related to the effect, and (3) other plausible alternatives of the effect can be excluded (John Stewart Mill, 1911). "If threats to valid causal inference cannot be ruled out in the design, they should at least be measured and their importance estimated" (Farrington, 2003, pp. 51–52). Too often limitations are not mentioned or are glossed over or minimized. Hiding limitations is a marketing/propaganda strategy. However, poor reporting of a study does not necessarily mean it was poorly constructed; it may be only poorly reported (Soares et al., 2004).

Did the Authors Describe Any Special Interests and Biases?

Who sponsored the study? It is vital to be informed about conflicts of interests that may bias conclusions, including development of practice guidelines (Lo & Field, 2009). Studies funded by drug companies report more positive findings regarding drugs they promote compared to studies funded by other sources (e.g., Bhandari et al., 2004). Midanik (2006) described the influence of a biomedical view of alcohol abuse on funding patterns for research.

Is the Research Question Clear?

Do the authors clearly describe their research question, or is this vague or confusing? Examples of clear research questions are: "What factors contribute to the repeated abuse of children returned to their biological parents?" or "Do substance abuse programs to which parents are referred help them to decrease alcohol consumption compared to no intervention?" Unclear questions do not allow for clear tests at the point of data analysis, set in advance.

What Kind of Question Is It?

Does the article address the effectiveness of a method? Is it an assessment question (such as "Is the Beck Depression Inventory a valid measure of depression?")? Does it describe a risk measure (e.g., for osteoporosis)? Does it involve a descriptive question (e.g., how many people who smoke marijuana go on to become heroin users?)

Is It Relevant to Me? Is It Important?

If you knew the answer, could you make more informed decisions? Does it concern outcomes of interest to you? Have key outcomes been omitted?

Does the Research Method Used Match the Question?

Can the research method used address the question? Different questions require different research methods. (See Table 14.1.) That is why discussions of whether qualitative or quantitative research is best are misguided; it depends on the question. Critically testing certain kinds of questions requires a comparison. Random distribution of clients to two or more different conditions is a hallmark of randomized controlled trials (RCTs). An intervention group (cognitive behavioral therapy for depression) may be compared to a no-treatment group or comparison group (interpersonal therapy). Only if there is a comparison might we discover which might be better. If all we have is a pre-post test describing how depressed people feel before and after some intervention, there is no comparison with a group receiving no service or a different service. Thus, there could be a variety of reasons for any changes seen as suggested in Table 14.4. Oxman and Guyatt (1993) suggest a scale ranging from 1 (not at all) to 6 (ideal) in relation to the potential that a research method can critically test a question.

Is the Study Design Rigorous?

The general research method may be appropriate but be carried out in a sloppy, unrigorous manner that allows the play of many biases (MacLehose, Reeves, Harvey, Sheldon, Russell, & Black, 2000; Schulz, Chalmers, Haynes, & Altman, 1995). (See other questions discussed in this section.) Well-designed randomized controlled trials control for more biases compared to quasi-experimental studies. In quasi-experimental studies allocation of participants to different groups may be arranged by the researcher but there is no genuine randomization and allocation concealment (to different groups), thus selection biases are of concern as well as other biases depending on the design. Pre-post studies are one variety; they do not include a comparison group

Table 14.4 POSSIBLE CONFOUNDING CAUSES (RIVAL EXPLORATIONS)

1. *History*. Events that occur between the first and second measurement, in addition to the experimental variables, may account for changes (e.g., clients may get help elsewhere).
2. *Maturation*. Simply growing older or living longer may be responsible, especially when long periods of time are involved.
3. *Instrumentation*. The way that something is measured changes (e.g., observers may change how they record).
4. *Testing effects*. Assessment may result in change.
5. *Mortality*. There may be a differential loss of people from different groups.
6. *Regression*. Extreme scores tend to return to the mean.
7. *Self-selection bias*. Clients are often "self-selected" rather than randomly selected. They may differ in critical ways from the population they are assumed to represent and differ from clients in a comparison group.
8. *Helper selection bias*. Certain kinds of clients may be chosen to receive certain methods.
9. *Interaction effects*. Only certain clients may benefit from certain services, and others may even be harmed.

SOURCE: Based on D. T. Campbell & J. C. Stanley (1963). *Experimental and quasi-experimental designs for research*. Chicago: Rand McNally.

so we cannot determine causation. Time series designs are another kind of quasi-experimental study (see Campbell & Stanley, 1963; Cook & Campbell, 1979).

What is the Sample Size and Source?

Most research involves a sample that is assumed to be characteristic of the population from which it is drawn. Does the sample used offer an opportunity to answer the questions raised? Clear description of the source and size of samples is important in all research. Selection biases are one kind of bias related to how subjects were selected. (Some research deals with an entire population such as all graduates of the University of California at Berkeley's social work Master's degree program in the year 2009.) Can we accurately generalize from a sample to the population from which it is drawn or from one population to another or to other years? Does the sample represent the population to which generalizations will be made? Questions here include:

- How was the sample selected?
- Is the sample selection process clearly described?
- From what population was it selected?
- Is it representative of the population?
- Were subjects lost at follow-up? If so, how many?

The answers to these questions provide clues about biases that may limit the likelihood that a study can answer questions. Small samples drawn by convenience rather than by random selection in which each individual has an equal chance of selection may not provide information that reflects characteristics of the population of interest. CONSORT guidelines for reporting randomized controlled trials includes a user-friendly flowchart for clearly describing samples. We can see how many people were excluded at different points and for what reasons and thus review possible sources of sample bias. Some studies do not find effects, not because there are no effects to be found, but because the sample size is too small to critically test whether there is an association or not; "a statistically significant result could indicate a large effect in a small sample or a small effect in a large sample" (Farrington, 2003, p. 52). Use of a very large sample may yield many significant differences, which may not be illuminating.

Are Measures Used Reliable and Valid?

Measures of concepts such as self-esteem and substance abuse are used in research. Do they measure what they purport to measure? The validity of measures is a key concern in all research. Reliability refers to the consistency of ratings—for example, between different administrations of an assessment measure for an individual at different times (stability) or between two observers of an interaction at the same time (inter-rater reliability). Validity refers to the extent to which a measure reflects what it is designed to measure. Reliability places an upward boundary on validity. That is, a measure cannot be valid if it is not reliable (cannot be consistently assessed). A measure may be reliable but invalid perhaps because of shared biases among raters.

Research using only one kind of data (self-report) may offer an inaccurate account. For example observation of children's behavior on the playground to identify instances of bullying may not match a student's self report.

Is Attrition (Drop-Out Rate) Reported?

Subjects often drop out over the course of a study. This number should be reported and is reflected in an "intention-to-treat" analysis in which participants are analyzed according to the group to which they were originally allocated regardless of whether or not they dropped out, fully complied with treatment, or crossed over and received the other treatment.

Was There Follow-Up? If So, How long?

An intervention may be effective in the short term but not in the long term. How long were subjects followed up? The effects of many programs are short term. The consumer publication *Public Citizen* encourages readers to be wary of any new drug not tested for side effects over five years.

Are Procedures Clearly Described?

Are interventions used clearly described? Only if methods are clearly described can readers determine what was done, and if methods used were offered in an optimal manner.

Are the Data Analyses Sound?

Statistics are tools used to explore whether there is a relationship between two or more variables. We ask what is the probability of finding an association by chance in samples of different sizes. This is done by estimating the probability of getting a result in a sample of a certain size. The Null hypothesis is tested (the assumption that there is no difference between two variables we think are associated, or two groups that we think will differ). We could make two kinds of errors. We may assume that there is a relationship when there is not (Type I Error) or assume there is no relationship when there is (Type II Error). The term "statistical significance" refers to whether a test falls below a 5% probability. Complex statistical methods will not correct major flaws in the design or conduct of a study. Incorrect statistical methods may be used, leading to bogus claims. Reviews of research reports show that flaws in statistical testing are common.[12]

Different statistical tests make different assumptions about variables in relation to their underlying distributions. A statistical method may be used that requires interval data, data in which points are separated by equal intervals—such as weight), for ordinal data in which differences can be rank ordered but we have no idea how much difference there is between points. It is like using a rubber ruler. Many constructs are continuous. Consider drinking—one could have no drinks, one drink, or many drinks per day. However, this is often treated as a binary variable (categorically defined); either one is or is not an alcoholic; a continuous variable is transformed into a binary one. Data is lost in changing a continuous variable to a dichotomous one—individual variations are omitted. Inappropriate use of statistical tests include fishing (running scores of statistical tests to see if any are significant). You may read an article that explored many different variables using a large sample in which the authors claim to have found 15 significant differences. The question is: How many correlations were run? A certain percentage will be significant by chance. A rudimentary knowledge of statistics is valuable, so you can ask cogent questions regarding statistical analyses. Researchers often make mistakes in how they word findings. For example, rather than stating that there was "no statistically significant difference" they may say "There was no difference/change" (Weisberg, Lum, & Yang, 2003). Controversial issues regarding statistical testing may not be mentioned (see Oakes, 1986; Penston, 2010).

Are Claims Accurate?

Problems in any of the characteristics previously discussed, such as samples and measures used, may not allow clear conclusions. Inflated claims are common. That is why is it important to learn how to critically appraise research findings for yourself. Do claims made match the kind of design used? For example, a pre-post test cannot tell us whether the intervention was responsible for results because there is no comparison group. Yet the author may say, "Our results show that X was effective." This is a bogus claim.

Are Findings Clinically Important?

How many people would have to receive an intervention (be screened or receive a treatment) for one to be helped? That is, what is the Number Needed to Treat (NNT)? Just as we can ask about number needed to treat (NNT), we can ask about number needed to harm (NNH); how many people would have to receive a service for one to be harmed? People differ in their views about when there is "enough evidence" to recommend a service or to recommend that a program not be used because it is harmful. Even a modest reduction in future delinquency may be considered important (Weisberg, Lum, & Yang, 2003). What may be true of a group may not be true for a given individual. Thus, aggregate studies must be interpreted with caution in generalizing to an individual. Otherwise we may make the *ecological fallacy*—assume that what is true of a group is true for an individual.

LEVELS OF EVIDENCE

The concept of levels of evidence draws attention to the fact that different kinds of research related to a certain kind of question offer different degrees of control regarding biases that may limit conclusions that can be drawn. Many different hierarchies have been proposed. A hierarchy for studies of effectiveness is shown below:

1. Systematic review of experimental studies (e.g., randomized controlled trials (RCTs) with concealed allocation)
2. Quasi-experimental studies (e.g., experimental study without randomization).
3. Controlled observational studies.
4. 3a Cohort studies
5. 3b Case control studies
6. Observational studies without control groups.
7. Expert opinion, for example based on consensus (adapted from Center for Research Development, University of York).

A systematic review is at the top of the list for all questions, including reviews of qualitative research. However, such hierarchies should not be rigidly used. As Glasziou, Vandenbroucke, and Chalmers (2004) note, "criteria designed to guide inferences about the main effects of treatment have been uncritically applied to questions about etiology, diagnosis, prognosis, or adverse effects" (p. 39). Balanced assessments should draw on a variety of types of research and different questions require different types of evidence (Sinclair, Cook, Guyatt, Pauker, & Cook, 2001).

SUMMARY

The best way to avoid propaganda is to ask revealing questions about claims—to seek answers for yourself. As Jerome Kassirer advised when asked what can consumers do to protect themselves: "Become informed." Currently, literature in the helping professions abounds with poor matches. There is marketing rather than scholarship. All research has flaws that may compromise its value in exploring a question. Biases that may limit the value of findings are always of concern. A key concern is the match between a question and the likelihood that the method used to test it, can do so. The research method used may be appropriate and rigorous, but the findings may not apply to you because of the sample or setting involved or the measures used. Acquiring skill in using the steps in evidence-informed practice will help you to avoid influence by propaganda. A variety of user-friendly tools and entire enterprises such as the Cochrane and Campbell Databases of systematic reviews have been developed to help us to accurately appraise claims and related research. Checklists are available for critically appraising the quality of different kinds of research. Google searches are often surprisingly effective in discovering information. Perhaps the greatest challenge is a willingness to recognize gaps between your current beliefs and what information is available.

NOTES

CHAPTER 1
1. See, for example, Berenson, 2007A, 2008.
2. See Brody, 2007.
3. In his essay "Propaganda and Social Control" (1942), Talcott Parsons defined propaganda as "One kind of attempt to influence attitudes, and hence directly or indirectly the actions of people, by linguistic stimuli, by the written or spoken word. It is specifically contrasted with rational 'enlightenment,' with the imparting of information from which a person is left to 'draw his own conclusions,' and is thus a mode of influence mainly through 'non-rational' mechanisms of behavior" (1949, p. 142).
4. Goals claimed to be of interest may not reflect goals sought as Wacquant (2009) illustrates in his book *Punishing the Poor*.
5. See, for example, Hotez, 2008; Jasti, Ojha, & Singh, 2007; Zarocostas, 2007.
6. For a rebuttal, see Goodman & Greenland, 2007.
7. See, for example, Cummings and O'Donohue, 2008.
8. Routinization (standardization) can decrease variations in practices that harm clients, for example, as in use of checklists (Gawande, 2010). On the other hand, increased standardization may encourage a routinization of practices that hinders use of clinical expertise to identify unique client characteristics and circumstances that may be important.
9. The evolution of professions is influenced by their interrelationships, which together with related "boundary disputes," are affected by the way different groups control their knowledge and skills, for example, by special certifications. Abbott (1988) describes how different professions redefine problems and tasks in order to ward off "interlopers" and enlarge their "turf" to incorporate new problems. For example, in the 1920s psychiatrists tried to gain control over juvenile delinquency, alcoholism, industrial unrest, marital strife, and other areas. (See also Evetts et al., 2006.)
10. See, for example, Elstein, Shulman, Sprafka, Allal, Gordon, Jason, et al. 1978, as well as more recent work in this area, e.g., Gambrill, 2012; Janicek & Hitchcock, 2005.
11. Based on research showing that nonprofessionals are as successful as professionals in helping clients with a variety of problems, he argues that possession of a degree or "experience" does not ensure a unique domain of knowledge nor a unique degree of success in helping people. That is, credentials may not be accompanied by a track record of success in resolving certain kinds of problems.

12. See, for example, Breggin, 1991; Illich, 1976; Szasz, 2002. The penal system has also vastly increased (Alexander, 2010; Wacquant, 2009). Concerns about loss of status may compromise a professional organization's responsibility to raise questions about concerning practices or to protect members who report unpopular findings as illustrated by the Rind Controversy (e.g., Lilienfeld, 2002).
13. See also more recent reports regarding outpatient commitment.
14. See Wakefield, 1998, for a critique of his book.
15. "Propaganda is not the defense of an idea but the manipulation of the mob's subconscious" (Ellul, 1964, pp. 373–74).
16. See, for example, Double, 2006; Moynihan, Heath, & Henry, 2002; Payer, 1992; Szasz, 1961, 1994, 2001. See also n. 2.
17. See, for example, Valenstein, 1986.
18. The history of quackery is fascinating, Porter, 2002. There used to be a museum of medical quackery in Minneapolis, Minnesota.
19. They use a variety of strategies to woo people. Entertaining examples are given in *The Best Methods for the Cure of Lunaticks* (1705) by Fallowes (cited in Scull, 1989, p. 59).
20. After Medicare cracked down on the profits that doctors made on drugs administered to patients in their offices, some physicians responded by carrying out additional treatments regardless of whether the treatment helped patients. Researchers may report studies they never conducted or hide flaws in research. For example, Dr. Scott Reuben recently admitted that he never conducted the clinical trials he reported in 21 journal articles dating back to 1996 regarding treatment of pain (G. Harris, 2009e). Gould (cited in Jensen, 1989) included fraud (manufacture of evidence, presenting fiction as fact) as one of four pathologies of science. The three others were propaganda (selective presentations of evidence), prejudice, and finagle. The latter refers to minor hoaxes and intentional errors in data description or recording that result in a misrepresentation of findings. Scientific prejudice involves use of different standards of evidence for preferred and disliked views. That is, less rigorous standards are used for preferred views. Needless surgery may be performed (e.g., see Levy, 2003).
21. Most of the big drug companies have settled charges of fraud, off-label marketing, and other offenses. TAP Pharmaceuticals, for example, in 2001 pleaded guilty and agreed to pay $875 million to settle criminal and civil charges brought under the federal False Claims Act over its fraudulent marketing of Lupron a drug used for treatment of prostate cancer. In addition to GlaxoSmithKline, Pfizer, and TAP, other companies that have settled charges of fraud include Merck, Eli Lilly, and Abbott. The costs, while enormous in some cases, are still dwarfed by the profits generated by these illegal activities, and are therefore not much of a deterrent. (Angell, 2009, p. 12)

Recent years have seen higher awards. Health care fraud cases brought in 3.1 billion dollars in civil settlements and judgments in fiscal year 2010. Most of these cases were brought to the attention of the government by whistleblowers under the False Claims Act (See Silverman, 2010.). See also Harris, 2010h; Newman, 2010; Wilson, 2010f; and http://www.consumerfraudreporting.org; Taxpayers Against Fraud <www.taf.org>.

22. Critical appraisals of publications in the helping professions illustrate the prevalence of pseudoscience (e.g., Boyle, 2002; Jacobson, Foxx, Mulick, & Schwartz, 2005; Lilienfeld, Lynn, & Lohr, 2003; Thyer & Pignotti, 2012), material with the trappings of science without the substance (Bunge, 1984).
23. E.g., *Health Letter* published by the Public Citizens Research Group, Federal Trade Commission, National Council Against Health Fraud, Center for Media Education.
24. Consider the titles of exposes in the *New York Times*: "City inquiry uncovers widespread fraud in a Bronx Charity" (S. Chan, Oct. 6, 2006, A. 23); "Drug Executive is Indicted on Secret Deal" (Saul, Apr. 24, 2008, C1). A former vice president of Bristol-Myers Squibb was accused of lying to the FTC (Federal Trade Commission) about a deal with the producer of a generic Plavix. Reported exposes have been published regarding fraudulent Medicare claims. "Medicare bilked of billions in bogus claims. Private watchdogs rife with conflicts making systems an easy target for fraud" (Holding, 2003, A1).

CHAPTER 2

1. See, for example, Wilkes and Hoffman, 2001. The website <http://advertisingpharmedout.org>, contains continuing education programs designed to help us spot and resist ploys.
2. In Los Angeles as of 2007, there were 4,112 Licensed Clinical Social Workers, 6,737 Marriage and Family Counselors, 3,890 Psychologists, 2,184 ASWs, 2,900 IMFs, and 665 PSBs. (Therapist Exchange, Chico, California, Feb. 2007, p. 2).
3. See, for example, Johnson, Kavanagh, and Mattson, 2003. As Bauer (2004) suggests, "the purpose of science, to seek the truth as a public good no matter where it leads, becomes distorted by the drive to find profitable applications and technologies" (p. 648).

[W]hat 'everyone knows' about the science related to major public issues, then, often fails to reflect the actual state of scientific knowledge. In effect, there exist *knowledge monopolies* composed of international and national bureaucracies. Since those same organizations play large role in the funding of research as well as in the promulgation of findings, these monopolies are at the same time *research cartels*. Minority views are not published in widely read periodicals, and unorthodox work is not supported by the main funding organizations. Instead of *disinterested* peer review, mainstream insiders insist on their point of view in order to perpetuate their prestige and privileged positions. (Bauer, 2004, p. 651)

4. For example, the website of the International Biopharmaceutical Association states that this "brings together biopharmaceutical and clinical research institutions and organizations from different countries . . ." "IBPA membership provide corporate members with a myriad of networking, advertising and promotional opportunities." This website lists hundreds of centers.
5. For example, the American Psychological Association has actively promoted prescription privileges for psychologists. This privilege was lobbied against by the American Psychiatric Association arguing that this would harm clients. Mental health professions compete with each other for turf (e.g., see Clay, 1998). The headline on the first page of the June 1999 issue of the *NASW News*

(National Association of Social Workers) read: "Profession Dominates Mental Health: There Are More Clinically Trained Social Workers Than Members of Other Core Mental Health Professions Combined."
6. The February 1997 *Monitor* published by the American Psychological Association included an article by the director of the APA Practice Directorate (Russ Newman) entitled "Promoting the Profession is Top Priority" (p. 32).
7. The brochure for the 21st National Conference of the Anxiety Disorder Association of America (ADAA) describes this association as:

the only national, nonprofit partnership of researchers, health care professionals, and individuals with anxiety disorders and their families. ADAA is dedicated to the early identification and diagnosis, prevention and treatment of anxiety disorders. The Association aims to promote professional and public awareness and understanding of anxiety disorders. It also seeks to increase the availability of effective treatment, reduce the stigma surrounding anxiety disorders and stimulate research. (p. 2)

8. Conflicts may arise between state and local professional organizations.

On the side that appears to be wining is the New York State Dental Association, which is run by Roy E. Lasky, one of Albany's most influential lobbyists. On the other side is a Manhattan component of the association, the New York County Dental Society, which just hired its own big-name lobbyist, Patricia Lynch. At issues is a bill that could allow the state organization to eliminate the local group. At stake, potentially, is millions of dollars that the local makes from an annual trade show. (Roberts, 2008)

9. See *The Sandal of Social Work Education*. 2007. National Association of Scholars; Stoez, Karger, Carrilio, 2009; Internecine battles within a school may compromise students' education (e.g., "President of Missouri State U. Threatens to Shut Social Work School After Scathing Report," *Chronicle of Higher Education*, Apr. 20, 2007, A17).
10. Too many schools of education are sources of pernicious innovations, the carriers of Romantic-progressivist doctrine. They induct new teachers and administrators into the Romantic-progressivist thought world and thereby ensure that another generation is prepared to receive and accept progressivist innovations (Hirsch, 1966; Ravitch, 2000). For example, a number of ed school teacher training curricula rest on and are misguided by empirically weak and logically flawed progressivist (constructivist, child-centered, developmentally appropriate) shibboleths concerning how children learn and therefore how children should and should not be taught. . .

At the same time, ed schools often do not adequately teach students the logic of scientific reasoning, specifically, how to define concepts and judge the adequacy of definitions and how to assess the logical validity of an education professor's or writer's argument and the credibility of his or her conclusions. Nor do ed schools commonly have students read original works (to see if, in fact, Piaget said what he claimed for him), original research articles, meta-analyses, and other literature or views. The result is that most ed students do not have the skill to determine the validity of the progressivist propositions and curricula they are taught, but must rely on what their professors tell them to believe. (Kozloff, 2005, p. 170)

11. For example, GlaxoSmithKline footed the bill for dozens of educational courses intended to emphasize the benefits of Avandia [for treating diabetes] over other drugs. [Advandia was noted for causing heart disease.] An influential Internet-based educational program paid for by the company focused on specific studies that highlighted Avandia's advantages without discussing one of the drug's most worrisome side effects, increased levels of the lipids implicated in heart disease.

    Avandia's chief competitor, a drug from Takeda Pharmaceuticals called Actos, improves lipid levels but was hardly mentioned. When GlaxoSmiothKline's program did cite Actos, it did so tepidly. The information in the course was presented by noted diabetes academics paid by GlaxoSmithKline and other drug companies. (Kunin, 2007; see also Harris, 2010e & f.)

    Kunin (2007) argues that "Because pharmaceutical companies now set much of the agenda for what doctors learn about drugs, crucial information about potential drug dangers is played down, to the detriment of patient care."

12. Consider the following advertisement in a 48-page Continuing and Extended Education Winter/Spring 2007 Catalogue published by John F. Kennedy University:

    SANDPLAY CERTIFICATE
    Sandplay is a nonverbal form of therapy, suited to both children and adults, that facilitates the natural capacity for healing in the psyche. [Is there any evidence for this claim?] In sandplay, an individual creates a concrete manifestation of the inner imaginable world using sand, water and miniature objects.

    This Sandplay Certificate is . . . especially suited to those who wish to enhance their understanding of the psyche and want to integrate a therapeutic modality into their work that transcends language barriers and facilitates healing at the deepest levels. (Is there any evidence for this claim?] Certificate Requirements: 60 hours. (p. 33).

13. Six dollars and forty cents are spent on pay and overhead and fringe benefits for every dollar spent on direct services according to the Cancer Prevention Coalition (<http://www.preventcancer.com>). (See Epstein, 2010.) The related Foundation Board includes high-level executives from Big Pharma. The chief executive of the American Cancer Society makes 1,000,000 dollars a year (*New York Times*, July 2010). See also Breast Cancer Deception Month: Hiding the Truth Beneath a Sea of Print (retrieved Aug. 1, 2010, from <http://www.nationalnews.com>). Conflicts of interest can be seen in the mammography, pesticide, and drug industries.

14. See, for example, Arenson, 1995; Chan, 2006. Fraud concerning charity is an ancient evil.

15. Moncrieff suggests that these developments reflect an acceptance of an increasing role for state intervention often through involvement of professionals or experts. She notes that government endorsement of medical authority can be traced back to the 1776 Act for the Regulation of Private Madhouses, which introduced the process of certification, as "mad" by a medical doctor. (See Moncrieff, 2008b.)
16. Tilly (1998) argues that politicians and others hoard opportunities and related resources. For example, they accumulate money and try to protect it from loss to others or other purposes.
17. WASHINGTON, July 10–Former Surgeon General Richard H. Carmona told a Congressional panel Tuesday that top Bush administration officials repeatedly tried to weaken or suppress important public health reports because of political considerations.

    The administration, Dr. Carmona said, would not allow him to speak or issue reports about stem cells, emergency contraception, sex education, or prison, mental and global health issues. Top officials delayed for years and tried to "water down" a landmark report on secondhand smoke, he said. ... Dr. Carmona said he was ordered to mention President Bush three times on every page of his speeches. He also said he was asked to make speeches to support Republican political candidates and to attend political briefings. ... Each [Surgeon General] complained about political interference and the declining status of the office. Dr. Satcher said that the Clinton administration discouraged him from issuing a report showing that needle-exchange programs were effective in reducing disease. He released the report anyway. ... Dr. Koop, said that he was discouraged by top officials in the Regan administration from discussing the growing AIDS crisis. He did so anyway. (Harris, 2007d, pp. A1–A16)

18. Thorazine was prescribed for a wide range of purposes. I recently obtained my mother's records from the University of Pennsylvania Hospital were she died in 1961 from metastatic breast cancer. I had always wondered why she appeared so "out-of-it" during her last months. I discovered from these records that she was prescribed Thorazine.
19. Diet Pill Makers Fined Millions for False Claims, Jan. 4, 2007, retrieved July 14, 2007, from <http://www.msnbc.msn.com>. "The largest fine was levied against the marketers of Xenadrine EFX, made by New Jersey based Nutraquest, Inc." Fines were also levied against marketers of CortiSlim and CortiStress marketed by Window Rock Health Laboratories in Brea California. "The Bayer Corporation based in Morristown, NJ will pay $3.2 million civil penalty to settle claims and agreed to stop ads that say that multivitamins can increase metabolism." FTC Chairwoman Deborah Major.

    [T]he FTC investigation found that the marketers of Xenadrine had a study that said those who took a placebo actually lost more weight than those taking the pill.
    "They not only didn't have studies to support the claim, they actually had a study that went the other way," she said.

Some of the products marketed their claims through infomercials or celebrity endorsements. Anna Nicole Smith, for example, had endorsed TrimSpa.

Sales of weight loss pills peaked at $2.1 billion in 2002. The FTC also issued a report "False Claims about Fountain of Youth Oral Spray," Oct. 18, 2005:

According to the FTC complaint, the advertisements for 'HGH Revolution' and 'Natural Rejuvenator HGH-R' made incredible claims such as:
'LOSE WEIGHT WHILE YOU SLEEP without DIETING or EXERCISE'
'Experience up to an 82% IMPROVEMENT in body fat loss while erasing 10 YEARS IN 10 WEEKS!'

20. See Brody, 2007.
21. See, for example, Harris, 2006a, b; Lenzer, 2004c; Harris, 2007a & b.
22. Saul, 2007c. Increasing concerns have been raised about this drug (e.g., see Harris, 2010a).
23. See Grady, 2004; Healy, 2004.
24. Pear, 2007a & c; Perez-Pena, 2006.
25. "In other cases, improperly certified aides billed for false work. This accounted for $1.3 billion of the $35.7 billion spent on Medicaid in New York the last year. Over 140 home care agencies are overseen by both Federal and state agencies in 2004" (Confessore & Kershaw, 2007, p. 25).
26. Press Release, Department of Law, State Capitol, Albany, New York, "Spitzer calls for passage of State False Claims Act," Jan. 12, 2003. Retrieved July 14, 2007, from <http://www.org.state.ny.us>.
27. Harris, 2009a, b; Liptak, 2009f.
28. See also Sackett, 2002.
29. Harris, 2007d.
30. Jehl, 1994.
31. *Practitioner Update* 4(4), Dec. 1996, p. 3, published by the American Psychological Association.
32. "Georgia Psychologists Use Depression Campaigns to Strengthen Referral Network," *Practitioner Update*, 1(2), May 1993, p. 3.
33. See *The Berkeleyan*, July 2010.
34. Bright Apple. Their Special Education Catalogue, Grades 3–12, is 76 pages long. Some companies specialize in selling DVDs and videos to educators to show to students. These are often quite expensive. For example, a 28-minute VHS may cost $139.00.
35. The range of activities includes the following:
    - Psychiatric Industry Watch: Criticizes what is seen as pharmaceutical industry financial and political influences upon the direction of "mental health." For example, the Watch focuses on the pharmaceutical industry's indirect support and direct lobbying for laws that create civil "outpatient commitment" that enable authorities to administer forced psychiatric drugging in the community, e.g., in a patient's home without involuntary hospitalization. MFI's activities have placed it in direct opposition to the pharmaceutical industry, resulting in legal action against MFI.

- The Right to Remember: Seeks to end involuntary electroconvulsive therapy by publicizing instances of forced electroconvulsive treatment and lobbying decision-makers to stop such practices.
- Oral Histories: Compiles and publicizes psychiatric survivor stories detailing the experiences of those who have been through the mental health system. The stories promulgated aim to document abuse by the mental health system and the success stories of individuals who attained a state of stable remission and were able to regain self-direction, usually by disengaging from traditional mental health treatment.
- Mad Pride: Advocates self-determination among those seemed "mad." The coalition has proclaimed July as "Mad Pride Month" and supports events around the world celebrating some of the myriad aspects of "madness," i.e., those aspects which are seen as positive.
- International Association for the Advancement of Creative Maladjustment (IAACM): Promotes the right to be nonviolently maladjusted. (Wikipedia, Nov. 30, 2008)

MindFreedom also has a "Shield Program" to prevent or stop forced treatment for specific individuals. Other consumer groups include Alliance for Human Research Protection <http://www.ahrp.org>; Public Citizen <http://www.citizen.org>; and Healthy Skepticism <http://www.healthyskepticism.org>.

36. ICSPP Newsletters, 2007, No. 1 (p. 2). Among accomplishments it claims are the following:

- The creation of a federal Psychosurgery Commission by Congress (1970's).
- Alerting professionals to the dangers of tardive dyskinesia in children (1983). Tardive dyskinesia is a potentially devastating neurological disorder caused by neuroleptic or antipsychotic drugs.
- Alerting professionals to the danger of dementia produced by long-term neuroleptic drug use (1983).
- Motivating the FDA to force the drug companies to put a new class warning of tardive dyskinesia on their labels for neuroleptic drugs (1985).
- Alerting the profession to danger of down-regulation and dangerous withdrawal reaction from the new SSRI antidepressants such as Prozac, Zoloft, and Paxil (1992–4).
- Encouraging the NIH Consensus Development Conference on Diagnosis and Treatment of Attention Deficit Hyperactivity Disorder to raise serious concerns about "ADHD" and stimulants for children. (ICSPP Newsletter, Fall 2004, p. 13)

37. A recent publication by the latter, *Branding the Cure: A Consumer Perspective on Corporate Social Responsibility*, Drug Promotion and the Pharmaceutical Industry in Europe, can be seen at <http://www.consumerinternational.org>. See also <http://SourceWatch.org>.
38. Tanne, 2007.
39. Specialized groups also form around specific topics. For example, in Spring 2007 a group of doctors in the United Kingdom accused the UK General Medical Council of failing children. It formed "to counter what they

described as the intimidation of child protection professionals" (Gornall, 2007, p. 765).
40. See also Kmietowicz, 2004. This article notes that there are over 200 patient groups in the United Kingdom, many of which rely on funding from Big Pharma. See also Common Cause Website, June 4, 2007. Wolves in sheep's clothing.
41. For example, see Hilts, 2000.
42. Devereaux, Choi, Lacchetti, Weaver, Schunemann, Hainer, et al., 2002.
43. Consider the following course description for a workshop on "Anxiety disorders:
Cognitive behavioral therapy and pharmacotherapy treatment approaches":

Anxiety disorders are among the most prevalent mental illnesses, [Note the assumption that anxiety is a mental illness] affecting approximately 40 million American adults annually. [Is this prevalence figure accurate?]... In order to optimally treat and manage patients with anxiety disorders, front-line practitioners require frequent updates of evidence-based treatments that are informed by cutting-edge research findings. [Is there any evidence for this?] Additionally, feedback from medically-trained practitioners [How many?] indicates a growing desire to acquire the skills necessary to integrate evidence-based [Are these really evidence-based–what does this mean?] psychosocial treatment approaches into medical management paradigms. (Brochure, Massachusetts General Hospital, Department of Psychiatry, May 2007).

(See chapter 3 for a description of the creation of "social anxiety disorder" as a mental illness.)
Questions here are: Will participants be informed about well-argued alternatives to a view of anxiety in social situations as mental illnesses? Will bogus prevalence estimates be made? Who is supporting the workshop?
44. See, for example, Reuben, 2002. See also Ethics in medicine, University of Washington School of Medicine, <http//depts.washington.edu/bioethx/topics>.
45. For example, see Stanford Study Calculates Cost of Pharmaceutical Marketing Efforts, Stanford School of Medicine, Office of Communication, Public Affairs, May 19, 2003. Retrieved Sept. 26, 2005, from <http://mednews.stanford.edu/relese/2003> (Gerth and Stolberg, 2000). Millions of dollars are spent by pharmaceutical companies on ghostwriters as described in chapter 3.
46. See also Feder, 2007b, C1.
47. See, for example, Ableson, 2006a, 2006b.
48. July 17, 2007, p. A9.
49. Proposed mergers are described in the business pages of our newspapers such as the planned merger as of May 21, 2007, of Cytye Corporation "a leader in diagnostics for cervical cancers and Hologic, Inc., a leader in breast cancer diagnostics." The resultant company, Hologic, would have a revenue of about $1.5 billion in 2007. Its products include screening, diagnostics, and treatments for breast and cervical cancer, prenatal health, osteoporosis, endometriosis, and contraception (Deutsch, 2007).
50. Fenton, et al., 2007. Screen for prostate cancer is also controversial.

51. Government regulators said yesterday that Medicare, the federal insurance program, planned to deny coverage for artificial disks implanted in the lower spines of older patients. . . .

    Yesterday's decision applies to patients over 60, which is most of the 43 million people Medicare covers.

    The Centers for Medicare and Medicaid Services, the agency that administers Medicare, said that none of the clinical trials used to gain F.D.A. approval of the devices included patients over 60, leaving Medicare with no basis for saying the devices were a reasonable or necessary therapy for such patients.

    Wall Street had foreseen the dawn of a major new orthopedics market when the Charité artificial disk received F.D.A. approval in October 2004. (Feder, 2007)

52. For example, see Capriccioso, 2009. See also Indigenous Peoples Council on Biocolonialsm. <http://www.ipcb.org>.
53. A recent estimate suggests that litigation costs amount to 1 to 1.5% of total medical costs, Baker, 2005.
54. See, for example, Gambrill & Shlonsky, 2001; Munro, 2010; Vincent, 2001.
55. <http://www.ahip.org>.
56. "WASHINGTON, MAY 14. In the first major investigation of Medicare marketing, the Oklahoma insurance commissioner has documented widespread misconduct by agents working for Humana and has ordered the company to take corrective action to protect consumers against high-pressure sales tactics" (Pear, 2007, p. A14).
57. For example, in UPDATE, Rogers Memorial Hospital 2005 Annual Newsletter, we read
    "Positive cognitive changes are necessary to maintain improvements in self image and behavior" (p. 3). (Is this true?) The Conners Scale is used as a key assessment measure. Is this a valid measure? We are told that an overseer of CBT is "a nationally recognized expert." Can we trust the "experts"? Do changes in aggressive behavior from pre (average levels of aggressive behavior of 6) to 4.4 at discharge make a difference in real-life settings? No follow-up data are presented.
58. BRUSSELS, Nov 21—The European Commission fined eight vitamin producers a total of just over 855 million Euros ($752 million) today for involvement in a number of cartels that fixed prices and market shares of vitamin products in the 1990's.

    Hoffmann-La Roche of Switzerland was singled out as the ringleader and ordered to pay 462 million Euros ($406 million), by far the biggest fine the European Union's competition authority has ever levied against a single company. **BASF** of Germany, which was also found to have helped coordinate the cartels, was fined 296 million Euros ($260 million).

    Both companies have also been fined by United States and Canadian agencies in connection with the same activities.

    This is the most damaging series of cartels the commission has ever investigated," said Mario Monti, the union's competition commissioner. "The companies" collusive behavior enabled them to charge higher prices, allowing them to pocket illicit profits. It is particularly unacceptable that this behavior concerned substances, which are vital elements for nutrition essential for normal growth and maintenance of life. (Meller, 2001, p. W1)

59. On the back cover we find: "What every woman should know . . ."

    - Does coffee give you high blood pressure? (No–but ANOTHER source of caffeine might. *SEE INSIDE* . . .)
    - Are the symptoms of a heart attack the same for women as for men? (NO! You must know this CRITICAL difference. *SEE INSIDE* . . .)
    - Is it dangerous to serve poultry for dinner? (Only if you SKIP these steps. *SEE INSIDE* . . .)
    - Do vitamin K creams make varicose veins vanish? (The truth may surprise you. *SEE INSIDE* . . . .)
    - What helps keep gallstones away? (You'll never guess! *SEE INSIDE* . . .)

    On the front of the oversize envelope we read:

    Many women have taken this harmless-looking capsule. DON'T BE ONE OF THEM!
    An urgent health message from the doctors at **Harvard Medical School**.

    (Notice the fear mongering and use of prestigious names.) Also inside:

    - The vaccine for women that will make history.
    - You should be "wide-awake" about Lunesta.
    - Once-a-month pill prevents osteoporosis.
    - The new light-therapy that smoothes wrinkles.
    - How to cool-down a "hot flash."
    - What you need to know about soy.
    - How overuse of a simple pain-reliever can be lethal."
    Notice the marketing language (e.g., "new," "need to know," "Make history").

60. *Psychotherapy Networker* is published bi-monthly. *The California Therapist* is published by the California Association of Marriage and Family Counselors. The March/April 1994 edition was 86 pages long. Conferences, workshops, books, CDs, and so on are advertised. *Bay Area Parent, East Bay Edition* is an 80-page monthly magazine. *MAMM: Women, Cancer and Community* is dedicated to serving women with breast and gynecological cancer. The magazine carries many pages of advertisements.
61. Doctors treating children with a rare and severe form of epilepsy were stunned by the news. A crucial drug, H.P. Acthar Gel, that had been selling for $1,600 a vial would now cost $23,000.

    The price increase, put in place over last Labor Day weekend, also jolted employers that provide health benefits to their workers and bear the brunt of drug costs.

As it turned out, the exclusive distributor of H.P. Achar Gel is **Express Scripts**, a company whose core business is supposed to be helping employers manage their drug insurance programs and get medicines at the best available prices.

But in recent years, drug benefit managers like Express Scripts have built lucrative side businesses seemingly at odds with that best-price mission. A growing portion of their revenue comes from acting as exclusive or semi-exclusive distributors of expensive specialty drugs that can cost thousands of dollars. And the prices of such medicines are rising much faster than for mainstream prescription drugs available through a wide variety of distributors. (Freudenheim, 2008, p. B1; see Ahmed, 2011)

62. In "Trust Us, We're the Experts," Sheldon Rampton and John Stauber (2001) note that Mathew Freud, the great grandson of Freud, owns and directs Freud Communications, a British PR firm.
63. Bernays (1928) viewed public relations "as an applied science, like engineering through which society's leaders would bring order out of chaos and muddle. 'If we understand the mechanism and motives of the group mind,' he argued, it would be possible to 'control and regiment the masses according to our will without their knowing it . . .'" (pp. 43–44). He viewed the use of this type of control as a duty. "It is certain that the power of public opinion is constantly increasing and will keep on increasing. It is equally certain that it is more and more being influenced, changed, stirred by impulses from below. . . . The duty of the higher strain of society—the cultivated, the learned, the expert, the intellectual—is therefore clear. They must inject moral and spiritual motives into public opinion." A public relations counsellor could accomplish this, Bernays said, because his special training and insight into human nature "permits him to step out of his own group to look at a particular problem with the eyes of an impartial observer and to utilize his knowledge of the individual and the group mind to project his client's point of view" (p. 44).
64. Examples from the Code of Professional Standards of the Canadian Public Relations Society include the following:

1. A member shall practice public relations according to the highest professional standards.

Member shall conduct their professional life in a manner that does not conflict with the public interest and the dignity of the individual, with respect for the rights of the public as contained in the Constitution of Canada and the Charter of Rights and Freedoms.

2. A member shall deal fairly and honestly with the communications media and the public.

Members shall neither propose or act to improperly influence the communications media, government bodies or the legislative process. Improper influence may include conferring gifts, privileges or benefits to influence decisions.

3. A member shall practice the lightest standards of honesty, accuracy, integrity and truth, and shall not knowingly disseminate false or misleading information.

Members shall not make extravagant claims or unfair comparisons, nor assume credit for ideas and words not their own.

65. Pratkanis & Aronson, 2001, note that Americans are exposed to 18 billion magazine and newspaper ads, 2.6 million radio commercials, 3,00,000 TV commercials, 5,00,000 billboards, and 40 million pieces of direct mail each day. Six percent of the world's population, the United States, accounts for 57% of the worlds' advertising. (See also Prakkanis, 2007.)
66. See Woloshin & Schwartz, 2006; Wilson, Bonevski, Jones, & Henry, 2009; Schwitzer, 2008.
67. These authors note that "By the 1990's, ... the tobacco industry itself was using the term 'junk science' to assail its critics. Its behind-the-scenes sponsorship of organizations purporting to defend sound science constitutes one of the great underreported stories of the past decade" (Rampton & Stauber, 2001, p. 225). (See also Oreskes & Conway, 2010.)
68. See, for example, Norcross, Santrock, Campbell & Smith, 2003.
69. The PsychCorp catalogue published by Harcourt Association is 208 pages long (2007). The 2008 catalogue of Psychological Assessment Research is 104 pages long. The 2005 catalogue from Western Psychological Service advertising tests, books, software and therapy material, is 256 pages long.
70. Levy & Luo, 2005.
71. Day, 2007.
72. E.g., see Giles, 2008; Edwards, 2009a. Consider other titles: "Huckster Targeting Elderly with False Claims Banned by FTC" (Jan. 4, 2006, <http://www.seniorjournal.com>) and "Online seller of breast enhancement products sued over false claims of being able to increase breast size without surgery" (July 14, 2007, <http://www.news-medical.net>). See also http:psychrights.org/articles and Pharmalot.
73. See, for example, Transparency International website (http://www.transparency.org). See also McNeil, 2007; Bogdanich, 2007; Parry, 2005.
74. See also Johnson, 2005.

VAST quantities of fake medicines are flooding into Britain every year and have almost certainly caused the deaths of patients, a leading expert claimed yesterday.

Last week it emerged that 1,20,000 packets of a bogus version of the heart drug Lipitor were sent to pharmacies. It was the third time in the past year that fake treatments were found in the healthcare system.

In Canada, the deaths of eight heart patients are being investigated after fake versions of the drug Norvasc–made of talcum powder–were found on sale in chemist shops.

75. "This company sold disinfectants that didn't deliver as promised, and did a disservice to doctors, staff, patients and the general public," said EPA Regional Administrator Alan J. Steinberg" (U.S. Environmental Protection Agency, Region 2). Newsroom EPA Cites Largest Hospital Disinfectant Manufacturer for False Claims, May 17, 2007, retrieved on July 14, 2007, from <http://Yosemite.epa.gov>).
76. See also Levy & Luo, 2005; Pear, 2007a, b.

77. See Levy, 2004; Grady, 2000; Olmos, 1997; Raab, 1996; Abelson, 2003; Hilts, 1995.
78. Harris & Berenson, 2009.
79. E.g., Lock, Wells, & Farthing, 2001.
80. Here is an example:

> In 1991, James Alderson, CFO at North Valley Hospital in Montana, was fired for refusing to participate in improper billing procedures. Alderson filed a wrongful termination suit against Quorum in 1991, which was settled in 1993. In 1993, he filed a civil suit under seal, alleging improper billing practices and Medicare fraud at North Valley Hospital. This suit led to federal investigations. (Retrieved on Aug. 8, 2011, from <http://www.whistleblowerprotection.com>)

CHAPTER 3

1. Titles of articles in journals and newspapers portray concerning examples: see Blumsohn, 2006; Saul, 2008a & b; Eichenwald & Kolata, 1998a & b; Greenhouse, 2008; Dyer, 2008.
2. See also Brody, 2007, Herzberg, 2009, Lo & Field, 2009; Petersen, 2008, Bass, 2008.
3. Berenson & Pollack (2007) suggest that:

> The explosion in the use of three anti-anemia drugs to treat cancer and kidney patients illustrates much that is wrong in the American pharmaceutical marketplace. Thanks to big payoffs to doctors, and reckless promotional ads permitted by lax regulators, the drugs have reached blockbuster status. Now we learn that the dosage levels routinely injected or given intravenously in doctors' offices and dialysis centers may be harmful to patients.
> . . .
> Aranesp and Epogen, from Amgen; and Procrit, from Johnson & Johnson–has been propelled by the two companies paying out hundreds of millions of dollars in so-called rebates. Doctors typically buy the drugs from the companies, get reimbursed for much of the cost by Medicare and private insurers, and on top of that get these rebates based on the amount they have purchased.
> . . .
> Although the drugs are deemed valuable in fighting severe anemia, there is scant evidence they help much in moderate cases and some evidence that high doses can be dangerous.
> Use of Procrit has also been fueled by television ads suggesting that it makes elderly cancer patients more energetic and, pushing all the emotional buttons, allows them to keep up with their grandchildren. That claim has not been established to the F.D.A.'s satisfaction. (Berenson & Pollack, 2007, p. A1/C4)

4. See <http://PharmedOut.org> or Nesi, 2008.
5. Quintiles acquires other companies in its pursuit of profits such as Bio-trials, a Central American research organization, and Eidetics, a decision-analysis and market research corporation. "NovaQuest, the managed partnership group of

Quintiles, received Eli Lilly and Company's highest award for its 'flawless execution' over four years in helping Lilly achieve strategic and operational objectives vital to its business success" in September of 2008 (retrieved Sept. 9, 2010, from <http://www.quintiles.com>).

6. See, for example, advertisement for the 15th Annual National Depression Screening Day, Oct. 1, 2005, published by NDSD, a program of the Non-Profit Screening for Mental Health, Inc. Is it really "non-profit?" Does it benefit professionals at clients' expense?
7. See, for example, Bentall, 2009.
8. There is no evidence for this serotonin theory (e.g., see Lacasse & Leo, 2005).
9. In the past decade, Dr. Biederman and his colleagues have promoted the aggressive diagnosis and drug treatment of pediatric bipolar disorder, a mood problem once thought confined to adults. They have maintained that the disorder was underdiagnosed in children and could be treated with antipsychotic drugs, medications invented to treat schizophrenia (p. C28). Many researchers strongly disagree over what bipolar looks like in youngsters, and some now fear the definition has been expanded unnecessarily, due in part to the Harvard group (Harris & Carey, 2008). Many of his studies were small and were often financed by drug companies. (See also Harris. 2009g; Harris & Carey, 2008.)
10. Kassirer (2005) described a particularly egregious practice called "shadowing."

    In this practice, physicians were paid $350 to $500 per day by a pharmaceutical company to allow its representatives to stay in the doctors' offices as patients came and went. In some instances the reps discussed the patient's treatment with the physician only after the patient was seen, but in others the drug representative was allowed to accompany the physician into the examining room. Some patients were not told who the visitor was. The doctors' collusion, while it may not be illegal, was certainly unethical. In 2003, a ruling by the Office of Inspector General makes it quite likely that shadowing is a practice of the past. (p. 48)

11. Harris & Roberts (2007b) point out that:

    The Minnesota records begin in 1997. From then through 2005, drug makers paid more than 5,500 doctors, nurses and other health care workers in the state at least $157 million. Another $40 million went to clinics, research centers, and other organizations. More than 20 percent of the state's licensed physicians received money. The median payment per consultant was $1,000; more than 100 people received more than $100,000.

    Doctors receive money typically in return for delivering lectures about drugs to other doctors. Some of the doctors receiving the most money sit on committees that prepare guidelines instructing doctors nationwide about when to use medicines. (p. A1/18)

12. Doctors "who have close relationships with drug makers tend to prescribe more, newer and pricier drugs—whether or not they are in the best interests of patients" (Harris & Roberts, 2007b, p. A1/18).

13. Drug company payments to psychiatrists in Vermont more than doubled last year, to an average of $45,692 for the highest paid psychiatrists.

    Antipsychotic medicines are among the largest expenses for the state's Medicaid program. Overall last year, drug makers spent $2.25 million on marketing payments, fees and travel expenses to Vermont doctors, hospitals and universities, a 2.3 percent increase over the prior year, the state said. The number most likely represents a small fraction of drug makers' total marketing expenditures to doctors since it does not include the costs of free drug samples or the salaries of sales representatives and their staff members. According to their income statements, drug makers generally spend twice as much to market drugs as they do to research them. (Harris, 2007)

14. It is legal for a doctor to use a drug off-label; however, it is illegal for a drug company to advertise a drug for any purpose other than the one or ones approved by the FDA. Angell (2004) notes that by recruiting physicians to discuss off-label uses, the drug companies avoid official channels and engage physicians in marketing efforts.
    Melody Petersen (2008), a reporter at the *New York Times*, noted that several physicians had been paid large sums to speak about "more than a dozen other medical uses of the anti-epilepsy drug, Neurontin, that were not approved by the Food and Drug Administration" (p. 27). In May 2004, Pfizer plead guilty to Medicaid fraud and agreed to pay fines of approximations $430 million.
    Kassirer (2005) notes that:

    As part of their campaign to market off-label uses of Neurontin, Warner-Lambert hired a for-profit medical education company that paid medical experts to be authors of ghostwritten articles about the beneficial effects of Neurontin for pain, migraine, and psychiatric disorders (at the time, it was approved only for certain kinds of seizures). Some doctors accepted $1,000 from the company to sign their names to medical articles on off-label uses of Neurontin for submission to neurology and psychiatry journals, even though the articles had been written by technical writers hired by the pharmaceutical company. (Kassirer, 2005, pp. 32–33)

15. Grouse (2008) notes that:

    In the United States more than 30,000 people are employed in the pharma funded CME industry. Until recently, they were reputedly crafting drug promotion disguised as education that focused on the advantages of the sponsor's product and minimizing discussion of dangerous side effects. The US Senate Committee on Finance recently wrote to the organization—Accreditation Council for Continuing Medical Education (ACCME)—that supervises US postgraduate education to express its concern about the conflict of interest when Pharma spends more than $1 billion a year for education about topics that highlight the use of their products. . . . ACCME replied that their policies and procedures for developing educational materials are sufficient for ensuring their objectivity. However, the Senate committee pointed out that although

ACCME surveyors review accredited organizations' procedures for ensuring the independence of certified CME, they do not analyze the actual content that is presented. (Grouse, 2008, pp. 7–8)

He reports that:

I've observed hundreds of CME-certified presentations sponsored by Pharma during my professional career, and in those content areas that I knew well enough to judge, it was clear to me that in the vast majority of instances, a bias was introduced in the communications in favor of the product produced by the sponsor of the CME. In some cases it was not so much that the information presented was false, but that the fair balance and clinical perspective that should have been present were predictably distorted by the proprietary interest. ACCME has recently introduced new procedures designed to eliminate some of the conflict of interest that has occurred in many CME activities. (pp. 7–8)

16. Detailed reports by 43 companies show that they spent more than $28m and attracted 3,85,221 people to the events, *British Medical Journal*, 336, 742 (April 5, 2008). (See also Healthy Skepticism website and Pharmedout website <http://www.pharmedout.org>.)
17. Dubovsky & Dubovsky (2007) point out that:

Participating in industry-sponsored education can be an effective marketing tool for speakers as well as manufacturers. The APA now requires that one speaker at an industry-sponsored symposium be a junior faculty member, and presenting at one of these events provides an opportunity for national exposure. At the same time, established senior investigators become even better known presenting at nationally prominent events such as the APA meeting. This kind of marketing of oneself may be a more enduring incentive than an honorarium for giving an exciting talk—and for being invited back. (p. 29)

18. Carey & Harris (2008) note that:

One of the doctors named by Mr. Grassley is the association's president elect, Dr. Alan F. Schatzberg of Stanford, whose $4.8 million stock holdings in a drug development company raised the senator's concern. In a telephone interview, Dr. Schazberg said he had fully complied with Stanford's rigorous disclosure policies and federal guidelines that pertained to his research.
. . .
In scientific publications, Dr. DelBello has reported working for eight drug makers and told universities officials that from 2005 to 2007 she earned about $100,000 in outside income, according to Mr. Grassley.
. . .
But AstraZeneca told Mr. Grassley it paid her more than $238,000 in that period. AstraZeneca sent some of its payments through MSZ Associates, an Ohio corporation Dr. DelBello established for 'personal financial purposes'. (Carey & Harris, 2008, p. A13)

19. Grouse (2008) argues that:

> Equally destructive is the fact the KOLs are chosen to be consultants to governments. They serve on the FDA and European Medicines Agency (EMEA) advisory panels to give advice on which drugs should be licensed and which rejected. They serve on National Institutes of Health (NIH) advisory panels to review grant applications. With this power, the KOLs can influence the entire direction of new research—competing ideas, directions, and the products that will or will not be used. These obvious conflicts of interest are finally beginning to be discovered. Experts are now often required to file disclosures about payments that they receive that could represent conflicts of interest. However, in most instances, these experts' opinions are still accepted regardless of their conflicts of interest. They should not be. (p. 8)

20. See reference in Grouse, 2008.
21. Grouse (2008) points out that:

> With today's new information technology, the AMA Masterfile is very valuable. Medical information services, such as Integrated Medical Services (IMS) (operating revenue in 1995, $1.75 billion), which track the prescriptions written in the United States and in most other countries worldwide, are able to match physician data and demographics with prescriptions tracked to individual regions and drug stores. In many cases their data can provide Pharma representatives with information about what drugs are and are not prescribed by individual physicians throughout the United States. These data allow drug detail representatives to provide negative information about competitors to specific physicians to promote their own products, knowing exactly what these physicians currently prescribe, and it allows them to punish and reward physicians for their prescribing decisions. More than a dozen states are considering laws to shield physician's prescription pads from Pharma. (p. 6)

22. Petersen (2008) notes that:

> At times the ghostwritten articles have turned out to be dangerously wrong. In the 1990s, Wyeth-Ayersttt paid tens of thousands of dollars to Exerpta Medica to ghostwrite articles promoting the use of Redux, a diet pill. The drug was part of the weight loss combination known as fen-phen. According to a copy of an invoice date in 1996, Excerpta Medica billed Wyeth more than twenty thousand dollars to write one article describing the 'therapeutic effects' of Redux, also known as dexfenfluramine. Dr. Richard Atkinson, a professor at the University of Wisconsin, was to receive fifteen hundred dollars of that amount to serve as 'author.'
>
> When the article was complete, Dr. Atkinson sent a letter to Excerpta, praising the ghostwriter's work. "Let me congratulate you and your writer on an excellent and thorough review of the literature, clearly written," the doctor wrote. "Perhaps I can get you to write all my papers for me! My only general comment is that this piece may make dexfenfluramine sound better than it really is."

A year later, the FDA pressed Wyeth to remove Redux and a similar diet drug called Pondimin from the market after doctors reported that they were injuring the heart valves of as many as a third of the patients who took them. By then millions of Americans had taken the drugs. The pills were later linked to dozens of deaths. (p. 190)

23. See Associated Press, "Judge orders Wyeth papers unsealed," July 25, 2009.
24. <http://www.fiercebiotech.com> is a daily monitor of the biotech industry.
25. An example is the oncogene test to predict risk of cancer recurrence.
26. In his book *On the Take*, Jerome Kassirer (2005) described that:

In 2002, doctors all over the country received a handy little book the size of a paperback novel entitled, *Quick Consult: Guide to Clinical Trails in Thrombosis Management*. More than half of the 450-page, inch-thick book is a summary of clinical trials in cardiovascular diseases, but most of the front section consists of monographs on the diagnosis and management of blood clots in veins. The book is a thinly veiled advertisement for Lovenox, a special kind of blood thinner (a form of heparin). Treatments with other blood thinners are given short shrift. Aventis Pharmaceuticals, which makes and sells Lovenox, paid the cost of having a for-profit medical-education company produce the book, and the project editor/author is on Aventis' speaker's bureau and reports having received royalties, commissions, and other compensation relating to the sale of textbooks, reprints of articles, and other written material from Pfizer, Genentech, Aventis, Pharmacia, and Bayer. Of the five other authors of the book, only two had a no financial conflicts, the others were all receiving money in one form or another from Aventis. (p. 100)

27. Harris, 2009d; Wilson, 2009a.
28. Lenzer, 2004b & c.
29. Harris, 2007b.
30. See Dutton, 1988.
31. Pharmaceutical companies contribute to support of the FDA. Concerns about lax oversight of trials, both in this country and abroad, continue to be raised (e.g., HHS (Health and Human Services) report confirming the rapid spread of unregulated drug trials abroad. <http://www.whistlelblower.org/blog/31-2010/622>.
32. Dubovsky & Dubovsky (2007) note that:

Industry has recently developed a rapidly growing liaison with potential consumers by providing educational materials and financial support for advocacy groups that is beginning to seem proportional to the support offered for professional societies. The national survey of patient attitudes toward their treatment ... by the Depression and Bipolar Support Alliance (Alliance, 2006) was supported by Wyeth Pharmaceuticals, and events by other support and advocacy groups have been able to rely on industry support of facilities, materials, and dinners, much as the APA [American Psychiatric Association] has been able to do over the years. (p. 38)

33. CHADD publishes a bi-monthly magazine (see chapter 2 for more detail).
34. A letter to the editor in the *BMJ* further comments on promotion of this drug.

> The small patient group 'Women Fighting for Herceptin' was supported by a leading marketing company. The ensuing national media campaign pushed politicians into supporting the unlicensed use of Herceptin and hence undermined the UK Medicines Act and the role of the National Institute for Health and Clinical Excellence (NICE). Many healthcare commissioners caved in under the subsequent pressure and agreed to early funding. (Letter to *British Medical Journal*)

35. See, for example, Krimsky, 2003; Washburn, 2005.
36. [W]hat 'everyone knows' about the science related to major public issues, then, often fails to reflect the actual state of scientific knowledge. In effect, there exists *knowledge monopolies* composed of international and national bureaucracies. Since those same organizations play large role in the funding of research as well as in the promulgation of findings, these monopolies are at the same time *research cartels*. Minority views are not published in widely read periodicals, and unorthodox work is not supported by the main funding organizations. Instead of *disinterested* peer review, mainstream insiders insist on their point of view in order to perpetuate their prestige and privileged positions. (Bauer, 2004, p. 651)
37. See Lang, 1998.
38. Harris (2008) reported in the *New York Times* that:

> Thousands of parents have sued AstraZeneca, Eli Lilly and Johnson & Johnson, claiming that their children were injured after taking the medicines; they also claim that the companies minimized the risks of the drugs.
>
> As part of the lawsuits, plaintiffs' lawyers have demanded millions of documents from the companies. Nearly all have been provided under judicial seals, but a select few that mentioned Dr. Biederman became public after plaintiffs' lawyers sought a judge's order to require Dr. Biederman to be interviewed by them under oath.
>
> In a motion filed two seeks ago, lawyers for the families argued that they should be allowed to interview Dr. Biederman under oath because his work had been crucial to the widespread acceptance of pediatric uses of antipsychotic medicines. To support this contention the lawyers included more than two dozen documents, among them e-mail messages from Johnson & Johnson that mentioned Dr. Biederman.
>
> The documents offer an unusual glimpse into the delicate relationship that drug makers have with influential doctors. (p. A18)

39. See "A.M.A. Joins Several States in Suing Aetna and Cigna," *New York Times International*, Feb. 11, 2008, B9.
40. Boyton, Shaw, & Callaghan (2004) report that:

> Rezulin a drug with effects on sugar metabolism different form the available drugs in the mid-1990s, seemed to be a promising addition to the medications then in use. Unfortunately, after only a little more than three years on the

market, it had been linked to 63 deaths from liver failure; hundreds more treated with the drug developed liver dysfunction. By the time it was withdrawn from the market, however, Warner-Lambert (now a division of Pfizer) had sales of several billion dollars. Financial conflict of interest was only one of the many factors that account for the misfortunes of the patients who were injured by the drug: pressure by Congress to speed up approval of new drugs, excessive kowtowing to industry by government officials, poor judgment by other officials in allowing conflicted scientists to participate in decision making, and aggressive attempts by the company to paper over the gravity of drug complications and to preserve sales all contributed. Nonetheless, financial arrangements between physicians and industry were important components. We owe the 'inside information' to the dogged investigations of David Williams of the *Los Angeles Times*. (Kassirer, 2005, p. 46)

41. See also Cook, Boyd, Grossman, & Pero, 2009.

Chapter 4

1. Cunningham (2002, p. 12) notes that academics have used the term "propaganda" for a variety of purposes: (1) to identify certain types of persuasive messages and slanted language; (2) to describe a variety of manipulative practices; (3) to refer to an object of study; and (4) as an interpretive concept in areas such as psychology, communication studies, political science, history, and sociology. Views of propaganda have been influenced by the research methods used to investigate related phenomenon such as the formation of public opinion.
2. Sproule (1994) suggests that when the focus is on groups that diffuse their ideas through propaganda channels, critics are less likely to overlook or dismiss propaganda that is personally appealing.
3. Rank (1984) reflects this view in his discussion of "the pitch," which involves attention getting (hi), confidence building (trust me), desire stimulating (you need—often to avoid threats), urgency stressing (hurry), and response seeking (buy). The "pitch" appeals to our interests in keeping the good (protect), getting the good (acquire), changing the bad (relieve), and avoiding the bad (prevent).
4. "Technique, in the form of psychotechnique, aspires to take over the individual, that is, to transform the qualitative into the quantitative. It knows only two possible solutions: the transformation or the annihilation of the qualitative" (Ellul, 1964, pp. 286–87). (See also Stivers, 2001, 2004.)
5. Consider the role of psychologists hired by industry to listen to worker complaints:

After it had been observed in certain industrial plants that the conditions of modern labor provoke psychological difficulties, psychologists were hired to act as 'safety valves' for employee grievances and dissatisfactions. Employees may express their feelings to these 'counselors' with the assurance that the counselors will say nothing to management. But the counselors never actually counsel anything. Their activities have nothing whatever to do with a positive care of the soul, a mission which would suppose at least the possibility of profound changes, new orientations, and an awakening consciousness on the worker's part, all of which are highly dangerous. Nor are the counselors concerned with investigations of concrete modifications that might be binding on the company. Their sole duty is to encourage the voicing of complaints and to listen to them. It is well-known that suffering expressed is suffering relieved. . . . To let people talk does them good and quashes revolt. It is dangerous to allow the workers to talk over their problems among themselves. It is far more prudent to give them a safety valve in the form of a discreet company agent, a psychological technician, than to let them air their grievances in public. (Ellul, 1964, p. 353) (See also Stivers, 2004; Double, 2006.)

6. Ellul (1965) argues that people today work more than slaves did in the past.
7. Propaganda furnishes objectives, organizes the traits of an individual's personality into a system, and freezes them into a mold. For example, prejudices that exist about any event become greatly reinforced and hardened by propaganda; the individual is told that he is *right* in harboring them; he discovers reasons and justifications for a prejudice when it is clearly shared by many and proclaimed openly. Moreover, the stronger the conflicts in a society, the stronger the prejudices, and propaganda that intensifies conflicts simultaneously intensifies prejudices in this very fashion. (Ellul, 1965, p. 162)
8. Diagnostic Related Groups for Medicare population.
9. Both anxiety and depression may result.
10. Ellul distinguishes between *covert* and *overt* propaganda. "Overt propaganda is necessary for attacking enemies. . . . But covert propaganda is more effective if the aim is to push one's supporters in a certain direction without their being aware of it" (Ellul, 1965, pp. 15–16). Sproule (1994) suggests that "If covertness is the first defining characteristic of propaganda, a second essential feature is the massive orchestration of communication" (p. 4).
11. Cunningham (2002) points out that:

    The propaganda process also exploits a wide range of para-epistemic structures, practices, and values [such as] . . . institutes, and research methodologies. In many texts and contexts, the propagandist will pose as an objective discussant and reasonable respondent who encouraged dialogue, but in such a way as to deflect audiences from harsher and more substantial truths . . . the term *propaganda* is really a handy place-marker because it summarizes this litany of epistemic deficits. (p. 98)

12. [O]ne needs to assess any message in the light of the existence or nonexistence of an adequate opportunity for rebuttal of the main arguments or sources of information at the base of the arguments. Few people will know adequately the details of most social and political questions of moment, but they can at least find other people who have more knowledge, and they can question those people as to whether a sufficiently representative range of facts and opinion have been presented to the public for debate. We can think of 'truth-reliability quotient' as related to the reliability of claims measured by their openness to critique. When facts or events are suppressed, it may well be because they are true but threatening to some established interests. (Marlin, 2002, p. 304)
13. Altheide & Johnson (1980) argue that "Bureaucratic propaganda is less a feature of the mass society, mass media, and government domination, than it is the

widespread belief in science, rationality, and objectivity . . . the subtle power of propaganda lies in its behind-the-scene power to influence decisions and define reality" (p. 18).

14. Ploys he suggests include the following:

- *Labeling and Euphemisms* which cast a positive or negative view with no explanatory details. The label "welfare reform" may refer to getting rid of family assistance programs.
- *Preemptive Assumption.* Assuming as given what needs to be argued [begging the question].
- *Face-Value Transmission.* Simply passing on assertions without critically examining them.
- *Framing.* Offering an appearance of objectivity for example "by bending the truth rather than breaking it and using emphasis." Other ways in which a message is framed includes how it is packaged, degree of exposure, placement (front page or buried within), tone (sympathetic or slighting), headlines, photographs, and visual and auditory effects. Newscasters "try to convey an impression of detachment." They affect a knowing tone designed to foster credibility, voicing what I call "authoritative ignorance," as in remarks like: "How will this situation end? Only time will tell." Sometimes trite truisms are palmed off as penetrating truths. "Unless the strike is settled soon, the two sides will be in for a long and bitter struggle."
- *Learning Never to Ask Why.* We are encouraged to see the world in terms of disconnected events, hiding structural influences such as class differences. . . . Related rhetorical devices include use of the passive voice and impersonal subjects. (Parenti, 1986, 2011)

15. The seven-devices format was not conducive to the mobilization of a unified wartime effort. Indeed, this required use of such devices. And, this simple, clear approach was not compatible with enhancing the scholarly reputations of academic social scientists. The Institute of Propaganda Analysis was disbanded in Oct. 29, 1941.
16. See *How to Detect Propaganda*. Propaganda Analysis 1, No. 2 (Nov. 1937): 5–7 (bound volume). Reprinted in Sproule, 2001, pp. 135–43.
17. Rather than addressing Wampold's arguments concerning the role of nonspecific effects of psychotherapy, Barlow (2010) implied that the reason Wampold contests the empirical status of "evidence-based practices" is because Wampold was once in therapy. (See also Wampold's reply, 2010.)
18. For example, Rising, Bacchetti, & Bero (2008) found biased reporting of trials:

Our findings extend those of others by demonstrating that reporting bias occurs across a variety of drug categories and that statistical significance of reported primary outcomes sometimes changes to give a more favorable presentation in the publications. These changes occur primarily in peer-reviewed, moderate impact factor journals that disclose funding sources and other financial ties. Thus, publication of trial data in peer-reviewed publications appears to be inadequate, supporting the need for reporting of full protocols and findings in a trial registry. (p. 1568)

Special interests of pharmaceutical companies encourage selective reporting of results. (See also Lexchin, et al., 2003; Melander, et al., 2003.)
19. Most books describing clinical assessment, diagnosis, and intervention do not describe competing views of alleged "disorders." For example, in Corcoran and Walsh (2009) we find no discussion or reference to books questioning the framing of anxiety in social situations as a mental disorder (e.g., Moynihan & Cassels, 2005). We find no discussion of Mary Boyle's (2002) critique in Corcoran & Walsh's chapter on "Schizophrenia and Other Psychotic Disorders." (See also Harris, 2004c; Steinbrook, 2005b.)
20. See, for example, Houts, 2002; Kirk & Kutchins, 1992; Kutchins & Kirk, 1997; Kirk, 2010.
21. See, for example, Paulos, 1998; Seife, 2010; Tufte, 1983.
22. See chapter 9.

Chapter 5

1. See, for example, Gamwell & Tomes, 1995; Valenstein, 1986; Sharpe & Faden, 1998; Whitaker, 2002; 2010.
2. This, as well as individual differences, render use of rigid rules that ignore variations that matter unwise.
3. See, for example, Gottlieb, 2000.
4. Vera Hassner Sharav argues that:

> those most responsible for the corruption of medicine are medicines' academic leaders, prestigious medical institutions, journal editors, experts charged with formulating practice guidelines and federal oversight agencies–in particular the FDA, the National Institute of Health and the Center for Disease Control where academia and government agencies become stakeholders in the business of medicine, promoting the commercial interests of manufacturers, rather than the public interest; they betrayed the public trust and their professional integrity. Retrieved on Nov. 13, 2010, from <http://veracare@ahrp.org>

See also *Conflicts of Interest* by V. H. Sharov, May 5–7, 2002, <http://www.ahrp/org/testimonypresentations/armymeddept>.
5. See history of medicine.
6. Or, questions may be ignored or answered in vague uninformative terms.
7. Bracken & Thomas (2008) argue that:

> In effect, *Defeat Depression* means that the patient's interpretation of his or her experiences must fall into place with the doctor's narratives about depression, which of course is located within the biomedical model. The campaign privileges the biomedical model with the result that other, culturally appropriate ways of interpreting distress are marginalized. . . . It also trivializes the importance of social and environmental factors in understanding the meaning of suffering. It implies that factors such as unemployment, bad housing, racial harassment, and poverty are of little value in helping us understand the origins of human distress. . ." <http://www.critpsynet.freeuk.com>

8. See, for example, "unemployment due to economic downturns increases risk of suicide (Wahlbeck & Awolin, 2009).

9. Failure to detect the causes of complaints may result in clients being called hypochondriacs or malingerers, as suffering from a psychosomatic illness, when there is a physical (but undetected) cause. An elderly confused client labeled as having dementia may be suffering from severe dehydration. As Vaughan (2009) argues, "'We don't know how many more physical conditions may be as yet unknown to the medical profession.' She ascribes an unjustified claim of 'psychosomatic illness' to 'the Dark Side of Freud's legacy'—the widespread belief that all symptoms that elude diagnosis are psychosomatic in origin."
10. The vagueness of labels get in the way of knowing when a label is no longer appropriate. Vague labels may reflect lack of conceptual knowledge regarding the phenomena labelled. The sociology of diagnosis is of increasing interest. See, for example, Busfield, 2001; Jutel, 2009.
11. See, for example, E. Pringle, 2007c.
12. See, for example, Moynihan & Cassels, 2005.
13. E. Munro, 2009; O'Connell et al., 2009.
14. References criticizing mainstream views include Boyle, 2002; Houts, 2002; Luyten et al., 2006; Horvich & Wakefield, 2007; Moncrieff, 2008a & b; Westen et al., 2002; Szasz, 1987; Francis, 2010.
15. See, for example, B. Meier, 2009; Harris, 2006a & b.
16. See "When Tough Love Is Too Traumatic," *New York Times*, Editorial, Oct. 16, 2007, A22.
17. "Boot camps as a whole have neither a greater nor a lesser effect on recidivism than all other alternatives combined. And, there is an indication, based on three studies, that boot camp participants are more likely to relapse into criminal behavior when compared solely to the alternative of probation" (Wilson, Mackenzie, Mitchell, 2005). (See also Lilienfeld, 2007).
18. Did staff have relevant knowledge and related skills regarding how to change behavior in positive ways? Were they trained in functional assessment and contingency management? A class action suit on behalf of youth in confinement was filed by the Legal Aid Society of New York ("Juvenile Injustice," *New York Times*, Editorial, Jan. 6, 2010, A.18).
19. See literature on applied behavior analysis. Parents may be seduced by propagandistic web advertisements for "boot camp like" programs that may not be licensed.
20. The occupational therapist was surprised by the results, but she agreed that the treatment was not beneficial for this child.
21. Ofshe & Watters (1994) suggest:

that recovered memory therapists like Herman should tout Freud's early work as 'brilliant' and 'compassionate' demonstrates how willingly these experts ignore the coercive nature of any procedure so long as the resulting memories confirm their beliefs. Herman makes no mention of the harsh nature of Freud's methods just as she ignores similar techniques today (and in doing so turns her back on the pain of women patients both past and present), for the apparent reason that the results confirm her ideological position. (p. 292)

22. For recent discussions and research regarding recovered memory, see McNally & Gergerts, 2009.
23. Ofshe & Watters (1994) note that:

at that time, the susceptibility of young children to the creation of false narratives because of investigators' beliefs was recognized in the United States because of the research by Stephen Ceci and Maggie Bruck into children's suggestibility. This research was key in overturning the conviction against Kelly Michaels in New Jersey who was accused of child abuse.

This should, at least, have alerted the team to the similarities between the cases on both sides of the Atlantic, but when the Abuse in Early Years report appeared, not only was the tainted police and social services investigation upheld, but the key material sent by the BFMS was denigrated as being 'unsolicited' and irrelevant. (Ofshe & Watters, 1994) <http://www.bfms.org.uk/site>

24. Sudbery, Shardlow, & Huntington (2010) suggest that holding therapy is effective, based on reports of a range of stakeholders including youth who experienced this and staff who implemented it.
25. See, for example, Kirsch, Deacon, Huedo-Medina, Scoboria, & Moore, 2008. For further discussion, see also Breggin, 2008; Healy, 2004; Moncrieff, 2007; Sessions, 2010. Drugs used to treat aggression such as haloperidol and Risperdone are no more effective than a placebo (Tyrer, Oliver-Africano, Ahmed, Bouras, Cooray, Deb, et al., 2008).
26. For example,

> In his editorial, Dr. Rennie described ondansetron, a drug that was being studied to prevent vomiting after surgery. Researchers analyzing the literature found 84 studies involving 11,980 patients–or so they thought. Some of the data had been published twice, and when the researchers sorted it out, they realized that there were really only 70 studies, involving 8,645 patients. The duplicated data, they concluded, would lead to a 23 percent overestimate of the drug's effectiveness.
>
> Studies of another drug, risperidone, used to treat schizophrenia, had been published multiple times in different journals, under different authors' names. The same thing had been done with studies of drugs to treat rheumatoid arthritis, with some having been published two or three times, and one published five times. (Grady, 1999, p. A18)

> Carefully hidden in advertisements is that a drug may be tested for only a few (8) weeks. In practice, doctors prescribe drugs for years. Violence toward others as a result of taking a drug may be hidden (e.g., Moore, Glenmullen, & Furberg, 2010).

27. FDA approved antipsychotic with a long history of failure, May 7, 2009, <http://www.ahrp.org>.
28. See, for example, testimony submitted for the record by Vera Hassner Sharav, June 8, 2008.
29. Wallace-Wells, 2009. See also Petersen, 2008.
30. See Harris, 2010b; Harris, 2010e; Harris, 2010h.
31. Harris, 2005.
32. D. Grady, 2007; Krumholz, Ross, Presler, & Egilman, 2007.

33. The Food and Drug Administration has determined that the treatment of behavioral disorders in elderly patients with dementia with atypical (second generation) antipsychotic medications is associated with increased mortality. Of a total of seventeen placebo controlled trials performed with olanzapine (Zyprexa), aripiprazole (Abilify), risperidone (Risperdal), or quetiapine (Seroquel) in elderly demented patients with behavioral disorders, fifteen showed numerical increases in mortality in the drug-treated group compared to the placebo-treated patients. These studies enrolled a total of 5106 patients, and several analyses have demonstrated an approximately 1.6–1.7 fold increase in mortality in these studies. Examination of the specific causes of these deaths revealed that most were either due to heart related events (e.g., heart failure, sudden death) or infections (mostly pneumonia). (FDA, public health advisory, Apr. 1, 2005).
34. This includes the possibility of death as with Ellen Liversidge's son who died from the side effects of Zyprexa. (See prior description in this chapter.) See also Wilson, 2010. Psychotropic medication is frequently prescribed to youth in foster care in spite of lack of substantive evidence concerning its effectiveness and safety (Zito et al., 2008).
35. E.g., see N. Angier (1997), "Critics of the widespread use of hysterectomies emphasize not only the dangers of major surgery, but the role of the uterus in a woman's lifelong physical, mental and sexual health" (p. 10).
36. See, for example, Moore, 2005.
37. "A study of more than 2,00,000 elderly heart attack patients indicates that invasive treatments like heart bypass operations and catheterizations may not increase long-term survival in many cases, Harvard University researchers said" (Leary (1994). See also Marchione, 2009.
38. Wennberg (2002) raised concerns about variations in practices.
39. See also previous discussion of unneeded cardiac implants (Harris, 2010a).
40. Baldwin & Oxland (1996) argues that surgical biopsies to detect breast cancer are overused. At the American Society of Breast Surgeons 10th Annual Meeting, San Diego, he described a study involving 4,465 breast cancer patients showing that private practice surgeons used surgical biopsy much more (36%) than breast surgeons in academic centers (10%). He said that "If an abnormality cannot be diagnosed by a needle biopsy, only then should we turn to surgical biopsy." He noted that lack of training in FN-biopsy was one reason for the high number of surgical biopsies. (See Mulcahy, 2009.)
41. Such advertisements can be used to hone propaganda-spotting skills.
42. Harms in group homes and institutional settings are often reported in our daily newspapers (e.g., "Firm faces large fine over death," *Oxford Times*, 2009). Scores of article titles reflect the variety of inquiries, for example, Badger et al., 2007.
43. See also Room, 2010; Hughes & Stevens (2010).
44. See, for example, Reason, 1997; Munro, 2005; Kohn, Corriqan & Donaldson, 2000).
45. Here too, newspaper reports illustrate these concerns (e.g. Dyer, 2009).
46. Efforts to hide evidence is a key form of propaganda often accompanied by assurances that excellent services are being provided; it seems the more grandiose the title ('Center of Excellence'), the more we should be cautious.

47. A blame culture in which staff are singled out and castigated for errors discourages a learning culture in which errors are viewed as inevitable and as opportunities to minimize avoidable ones.
48. Bogdanich, 2009.
49. See Greismann, 2009; Rew et. al, 2010.
50. About a million coronary angiograms are performed each year at a cost of $5,000 each (Altman, 1992).
51. See also Brenner & Hall, 2007.
52. A report from the U.S. National Academies of Science ("Preventing Mental, Emotional and Behavioral Disorders among Young People," O'Connell et al., 2009) recommended screening all children and adolescents for anxiety disorders, mood disorders, attention-deficit hyperactivity disorder, and schizophrenia.
53. Here is how AbleChild.org describes this.

> The Mother's Act, if passed, will mandate that all new mothers be screened by means of a list of subjective questions that will determine if each mother is mentally fit to take their newborn home from the hospital. Just imagine that after your child is born, you are told that you can't take them home since a multiple choice questionnaire wasn't answered correctly. Just imagine being told that the only way you can take your child home is if you or your spouse go into treatment or on anti-depressants which we know causes psychosis, delusions, and even homicidal thoughts. It just doesn't' make sense. Unfortunately, this bill is on a fast track—No public debate, no public disclosure of the broad impact on our society and that is why we need you to act now! (Retrieved on July 1, 2009, from <http://ablechild@mail.democracyinaction.org>)

54. See Coombes, 2009.
55. "[W]henever doctors look harder, they find more cancer. Second, most of the 'extra' cancers found are relatively small. Third, because they are small we can infer that many other small cancers are being missed. The reservoir of cancer is, therefore, potentially bottomless. So there you have it: all of us, at some point in our life, could probably be said to have cancer" (Welch, 2004, p. 88).
56. For a dissenting view, see Wald, Law, & Duffy, 2009.
57. Godlee, 2009.
58. See, for example, Whitbourne, 2010. Use of PET scans to detect plaques in the brain have also been recommended. One concern here is that one-third of the elderly have such plaques (Pimpliker, 2010).
59. Although psychiatrists have claimed otherwise, ECT seem[ed] to be used in the 1990s as a first-line treatment, in conjunction with pharmacological approaches.

> An analysis of these data confirms that at least in these instances, ECT was used as 'treatment of choice,' not a 'treatment of last resort.' Thus, although many children and adolescents had been given pharmacological therapies (often antidepressants and/or anti-psychotics) few had received other psychotherapeutic approaches. None had received a range of alternative treatments. In these published cases, at least, ECT was perceived as a beneficial 'treatment of choice,' not a 'treatment of last report.' Also, in these 217 cases, psychotherapy was only

offered as a treatment option, either before or after ECT in six cases. (Baldwin & Oxlad, 1996)

60. According to The Fair Foundation, $225,656 for research are budgeted per death for HIV/AIDS compared to $13,803 for diabetes, $11,595 for prostate cancer, $2,429 for cardiovascular diseases, and $811 for chronic obstructive pulmonary disease (retrieved June 21, 2010, from <http://www.fairfoundation.org>). Funds for family planning have been drastically cut over the past few years.
61. Effective interventions may not be offered because of conflicts of interests, lack of high profit, censorship in professional education programs, and misleading advertisements. Examples include parent training programs designed to prevent antisocial behavior (e.g., Hutchins et al., 2007), use of applied behavior analysis to maximize learning, self-management, and social skills of children and adults with developmental disabilities (e.g., Jacobson, Foxx, & Mulick, 2005), effective interventions to reduce falls and incontinence among the elderly (Oliver & Healy, 2009), and fine-needle biopsy rather than intrusive surgical biopsies of suspected breast tumors (ASBA 2009; Surgical biopsies for breast abnormalities overused, action needed. *Medscape Medical News*, Apr. 27, 2009). Other examples include use of social interventions rather than drugs and vaccines to control pandemic flu (Smith, 2007).
62. Fergusson and her co-authors (2007) note that such bednets will not break the transmission cycle in the most endemic parts of the world.
63. Such frames were invented by Josh Silver, who is the director of the Center for Vision in the Developing World. (www.vdwoxford.org).

CHAPTER 6
1. Entire books have been written describing this creation of fear (e.g., Altheide, 2002; Glassner, 1999).
2. Hadler, 2004; Illich, 1976; Payer, 1992; Szasz, 2005.
3. Sickness ideology is recycled under new euphemisms such as *clinical population*, considered to be qualitatively different from nonclinical populations (Bandura, 1978).
4. The biomedical industrial complex refers to all the players in the system.
5. See also Cottle, 1999; Lane, 1999.
6. For discussion of the complexity of causative factors in depression and measurement issues, see Luyten et al., 2006.
7. Anthony Burton wrote *The Anatomy of Melancholy* (1485) because he thought it might help him to get out of his depression. He described hundreds of variations.
8. "Edge-of-the-distribution illness" is a third model of disease suggested by Del Mar et al. (2006). Many risk factors have been converted into diseases. Obesity is now viewed as a disease. Is it? Many other areas can be mentioned such as the medicalization of menopause, breast implants, and cosmetic surgery. Consider, for example, the book by V. Pitts-Taylor (2007), *Surgery Junkies: Wellness and Pathology in Cosmetic Culture* published by Rutgers University Press.
9. For thousands of years the causes of diseases were thought to be related to disturbances in four humors: blood (related to the heart), phlegm (related to the

brain), yellow bile (related to the liver), and black bile (related to the spleen) (Hippocrates, c. 460–380 B.C.).
10. For guidelines for reviewing prevalence studies, see Boyle, 1998.
11. The medicalization of problems-in-living and risks is becoming a global problem. See, for example, the discussion by Schulz (2004) concerning the dramatic rise in the identification of "mild depression" in Japan and also in SSRI treatment since the pharmaceutical companies introduced and promoted the diagnosis.
12. See the website for Concerta to discover if you are an adult with ADHD. (See also earlier discussion of AndroGel.)
13. In the United Kingdom, there is a "surveillance studies network."
14. Personal beliefs about what is normal may encourage a focus on pathology. Some psychiatrists continue to believe that homosexuality is an illness despite the decision of the American Psychiatric Association that it is not in 1973.
15. Meader (1965) classified non-diseases into the following categories.
    1. Mimicking syndrome: e.g., non-Addison's disease (pigmentation and "low" blood pressure in the absence of abnormality of hormone secretion from the adrenal gland.)
    2. Upper-lower limit syndrome: (e.g., wrong diagnosis based on spurious borderline laboratory findings.)
    3. Normal variation syndrome: (e.g., non-dwarfism in familial short stature).
    4. Laboratory error syndrome: (e.g. John Smith who lives in Beckenham being treated as John Smith who lives in Dulwich).
    5. Radiological overinterpretation syndrome: (e.g., a tumor seen on an X-ray but no tumor found at surgery).
    6. Congenitally-absent-organ syndrome: (e.g., "nonfunctioning kidney" on X-way; absent kidney at surgery).
    7. Over-interpretation-of-physical-findings syndrome: (e.g., assuming that the liver is enlarged when it is displaced). (Described in Skrabanek & McCormick, 1998, p. 67).

Consider "gastroptosis."

The name means 'dropped stomach,' and was thought to be the explanation of epigastria pain in the late nineteenth century. Clinicians investigating such symptoms found people at barium swallow x-rays to have much lower stomachs than expected from autopsy examinations. An operation gastropexy was devised to hitch the stomach back up to the diaphragm where it 'should' be (at autopsy!). (p. 33.)

Examples of culturally specific "non-diseases" and their treatments Del Mar and his coauthors give include the following:

- "Off colour" (Britain): Over-use of iron replacements in the 1960s
- "Mal au foie" (France): Over-use of vitamins (to support the liver)
- Hypotension (Germany): Blood pressure raising drugs (such as pseudoephredrine)

- "Hot" and "cold" feelings (Vietnam): Eating compensating "cold" or "hot" foods to balance the ying and yang" (p. 34).

16. They believe that many class action lawsuits will be filed.
17. This dispositional bias is encouraged by the context in which most professional-client interactions take place—the office. Clients' real-life environments remain unknown. Most services are individually focused, for example, prescriptions of medications. The dispositional bias is compounded by the fact that most clinicians do not learn how to systematically observe environmental influences on behavior. Most do not know how to carry out a contingency analyses to identify environmental factors including behaviors of others, that contribute to client concerns (Layng, 2009). Not having such skills, the influence of environmental contingencies may be misunderstood or overlooked.
18. Renaud & Estess (1961) interviewed 100 men who were selected because there was no indication that they had any problems. They had no history of either mental or psychological conflict and did not complain of any problems. The men were functioning as normal or superior on all objective indices. They were in good health, had attained superior educational and occupational status, and had positive relationships with others both in their personal and work lives. The interviews held with these 100 men were similar to clinical intake interviews. These interviews revealed all kinds of traumatic events and experiences that could well be considered pathogenic and were at least as serious as experiences in the histories of psychiatric patients.
19. Paling (2006) suggests the following odds for different verbal descriptions (p. 13).

Verbal Description	Odds
Very High	1 in 1–1 in 10
High	1 in 10–1 in 100
Moderate	1 in 100–1 in 1,000
Low	1 in 1,000–1 in 10,000
Very Low	1 in 10,000–1 in 100,000
Minimal	1 in 100,000–1 in 1 million
Effectively Zero	1 in 1 million–1 in 1 billion (p. 13)

CHAPTER 7

1. Charles S. Pierce suggested four ways that we arrive at "ideas that settle down in the minds of people as habits, customs, traditions or commonly accepted opinions" (Pierce, 1958a, p. 91: the *method of tenacity*, the *method of authority*, the *a priori method* which rests on propositions that seem "agreeable to reason," and lastly *the method of science*).
2. See, for example, Ioannidis 2005.
3. For example, the findings of controlled in contrast to uncontrolled studies of the effects of facilitated communication (a method alleged to help nonverbal people to talk) "have been consistently negative indicating that FC is neither reliably replicable nor valid when produced" (Jacobson. Mulick, & Schwartz, 1995, p. 754). Controlled studies showed that the communication alleged to be from previously nonverbal people was actually determined by the facilitators.

4. A director of the Gates Foundation—a former practicing gastroenterologist—was so struck by his own prior failure to alter his practice based on the discovery that ulcers are caused by a bacteria, that he changed the Gates Foundation grant application policy to try to avoid the "circled wagons" mentality that protects dominant views from critical appraisal and consideration of alternative well-argued views.
5. Rudy, Coppin, Konefal, Shaw, Eyck, Harris, & Busch (2007).
6. The importance of specialized knowledge and skills is one of the major findings from research in problem solving and decision making, including professional decision making (Feltovich, Prietula, & Ericsson, 2006). *Performance knowledge* refers to knowledge about how and when to use *content knowledge* and how to automatize procedures so they can be used efficiently. *Inert knowledge* refers to content knowledge unaccompanied by procedural knowledge. Knowledge that decreases or reveals the degree of uncertainty about how to attain valued outcomes is emphasized in evidence-informed practice (Straus et al., 2005). Professionals differ in their percentage of inert and inaccurate knowledge compared to knowledge that could contribute to making sound decisions. This balance is influenced by their skill in detecting and avoiding influence by propaganda, for example, exaggerated claims of effectiveness in ads for drugs.
7. See A. Kerwin & M. Witte (1983). The Map of Ignorance. <http://www.ignorance.medicine.arizona.edu/ignorance.html>. Other domains of ignorance included on this map are errors (all the things you think you know but do not), taboos (dangerous forbidden knowledge), and denials (things too painful to know so you do not).
8. Popper (1994) suggests that we do not know more today than we did thousands of years ago because solving some problems creates new ones. For example, the invention of the automobile has created new problems such as pollution and congestion. Every technological advance has unanticipated consequences.
9. James Lind, a ship's surgeon, conducted what is now viewed as the first "controlled clinical trial" in 1747 to try to discover a remedy for scurvy.

   In his sick bay he had 12 men with scurvy 'as similar as I could have them,' kept them all on the standard 'sick' diet, and tested six different treatments—with two men in each treatment group—for a period of two weeks. I will just list three.
   1. Twenty-five drops of elixir of vitriol (diluted) three times per day.
   2. Two spoonfuls of vinegar, three times per day.
   3. Two oranges and one lemon per day—for six days only, when the supply ran out.

   The result was that those receiving the fruit were cured, and those receiving the other two acidic material were *not* cured, or even improved. (See James Lind Library (www.jameslindlibrary.org).)

10. Michalos (1971) identifies sixteen varieties of pseudoauthority.
11. A detailed citation analysis of a claim related to Alzheimer's disease revealed citation distortions including bias, amplification, and invention (Greenberg, et al. 2009). The author argues that such distortions can be used to create information cascades that result in an unfounded authority for claims.

12. Jane Jacobs refused to accept honorary degrees because of her rejection of credentialism (reliance on degrees and awards to confer status and indicate knowledge).
13. Here is my poem in response to Leo being referred to a "Nobody and nothing" because he and LaCasse raised questions:

    A Nobody and a Nothing or a Somebody and a Something?
    I'd rather be a nobody and a nothing
    And see what I can see,
    Than be a somebody and a something
    And hide what might be seen.
    I'd rather be a nobody and a nothing
    And learn what can be learned
    Than be a somebody and a something,
    And bury my head in the sand.
    I'd rather be a nobody and a nothing,
    And not as rich as I might be,
    Than be a somebody and a something,
    And fill my purse with tainted goods.
    I'd rather be a nobody and a nothing,
    And share with all who wish to see,
    Than be a somebody and a something,
    And hoard the truth for me.

14. Is it appropriate to use categories of mental disorder developed in the West in China, for example?
15. Consider the "Dr. Fox" effect demonstrated by Naftulin, Ware, & Donnelly (1973). An actor was hired to give a speech about application of mathematical theory to psychology, a subject about which he knew nothing. He used a polished, confidant manner of presentation. The audience viewed his presentation as very helpful.
16. Anecdotal case reports may be a valuable source of promising hypotheses, for example, regarding adverse events and possible causes, and may provide telling counterexamples that disprove an hypothesis (Aronson, 2003; see also Glasziou, Chalmers, Rawlins, & McCulloch, 2007).
17. New guidelines for expert testimony presented by the U.S. Supreme Court are as follows (Godden & Walton, 2006, p. 270):

    1. Testability: whether it [the evidence, theory or technique] can be (and has been) tested.
    2. Error Rate: the known or potential rate of error.
    3. Peer Review: whether the theory or technique has been subjected to peer review and publication.
    4. General Acceptance: the 'explicit identification of a relevant scientific community and an express determination of a particular degree of acceptance within that community.'

18. The report of the study was published in the *Journal of the American Medical Association* (Rosa, Rosa, Sarner, & Barrett, 1998).
19. Frazer (1925) suggested that there is a much closer relationship between magic and science, than between science and religion. For example, in both magic and science there is an interest in predicting the environment. Magic is a complex concept. It has been defined by anthropologists "as an intervention designed to reduce anxiety at times of uncertainty" (p. 364); for example, doing a rain dance.
20. My whole view of scientific method may be summed up by saying that it consists of these four steps:
    1. We select some *problem*—perhaps by stumbling over it.
    2. We try to *solve* it by proposing a *theory* as a tentative solution.
    3. Through the *critical discussion of our theories* our knowledge grows by the elimination of some of our errors, and in this way we learn to understand our problems, and our theories, and the need for new solutions.
    4. The critical discussion of even our best theories always reveals new problems.

    Or to put these four steps into four words: *problems–theories–criticisms–new problems.*
    Of these four all-important categories the one which is most characteristic of science is that of error-elimination through *criticism*. (Popper, 1994, pp. 158–59)

21. The Great Randi offers one million dollars to anyone who can demonstrate parapsychology effects (such as psychic predictions) via a controlled test. So far no one has won the prize. Will Daryl Bem win this? (See Bem, 2011.)
22. For critiques of Popper's view, see, for example, Schilpp, 1974.
23. In the physical sciences, there is a consensus about many of the phenomenon that need to be explained and some degree of consensus about explanations as Bauer notes. This consensus does not mean that a theory is accurate, for example, a popular theory may be overthrown by one that accounts for more events and makes more accurate predictions.
24. Tesh (1988) suggests that complex multifactual accounts give politicians and researchers free reign.
25. For a valuable website, see <http://healthyscepticism.org>. See also Carl Sagan's Baloney Detection Kit (Available on the Internet).
26. Misunderstandings and misrepresentations of science are so common that D. C. Phillips, a philosopher of science, entitled one of his books *The Social Scientist's Bestiary: A Guide to Fabled Threats to and Defenses of Naturalistic Social Science* (1992).
27. See, for example, Hook (2002), *Prematurity in Scientific Discovery* and Engelhart & Caplan (1987), *Scientific Controversies.*
28. Kuhn emphasized "conversion" and persuasion and argued that most investigators work within accepted (and often wrong) paradigms. They do "normal science."
29. For related discussion, see Young, Ioannidis, & Al-Ubaydli, 2008.
30. Bauer (2007b) asks how likely it is that scientists who question the causal relationship between HIV/AIDS will be selected to review grant applications.

As he suggests, only competent people are selected and questioning the HIV/AIDS connection is assumed to render one incompetent.
31. Consider a quote from Karl Popper: "I assert that the scientific way of life involves a burning interest in objective scientific theories—in the theories in themselves, and in the problem of their truth, or their nearness to truth. And this interest is a *critical* interest, an *argumentative* interest" (1994, p. 56).
32. Historians of science differ regarding how to demark the difference between pseudoscience and science. Some, such as Bauer (2001), argue that the demarcation is fuzzy as revealed by what scientists actually do, for example, fail to reject a favored theory in the face of negative results (e.g., perhaps a test was flawed) and the prevalence of pseudoscience within science (for example, belief in N rays and cold fusion). He contrasts Natural Science, Social Science, and Anomalists. He suggests that anomalists share some of the characteristics of all interdisciplinary search for knowledge, as well as searches for knowledge in fields that do not yet belong to any recognized discipline.
33. Popper (1994) argues that these "scientistic" tendencies "are in fact attempts to emulate what most people *mistakenly believe* to be the methods of the natural sciences, rather than the *actual* methods of the natural sciences" (p. 140).
34. Questioning related claims may result in threats of lawsuits as illustrated by threats to sue a physician who raised questions about the effectiveness of a cream claimed by the manufacturer to increase breast size (Laurance, 2010). Dr. Simon Singh was sued by the British Chiropractic Association as a result of questions he raised concerning the effectiveness of chiropractic practices for certain problems. This case was dropped.
35. E.g., *Health Letter* published by Public Citizens Health Research Group. (See also Transparency International web site.)
36. Max Planck (1949) suggested that "A new scientific truth does not triumph by convincing its opponents and making them see the light, but rather because its opponents eventually die, and a new generation grows up that is familiar with it" (quoted in Kuhn, 1970). (See also Planck, 1949.)
37. Consider, for example, the different criteria social workers want their physicians to rely on when confronted with a serious medical problem compared to criteria they say they rely on to select service method offered to clients. They rely on criteria such as intuition, testimonials, and experience with a few cases when making decisions about their clients but want their physicians to rely on the results of controlled experimental studies and demonstrated track record of success based on data collected systematically and regularly when making decisions about a serous medical problem of their own (Gambrill & Gibbs, 2002).
38. Tobacco Institute, Public Affairs Operating Plan—1991 (undated).

Chapter 8

1. Ellul (1965) suggests that there are four collective assumptions about the modern world: "that man's aim in life is happiness, that man is naturally good, that history develops in endless progress, and that everything is matter" (p. 39). He argues that such beliefs provide a sense of group belonging encouraged by years

of pre-propaganda in school. Indeed, Ellul (1965) believes that to be effective, the propagandist must appeal to these beliefs. Thus, we are complicit in being influenced by popular narratives because we ourselves embrace them.
2. A given view may be promoted to pursue certain goals even if it is not believed. For example, William Goode (1978) points out that "in class relations derogation can also be a nationally chosen program, a propaganda technique, by which one presents oneself or one's group as honorable and another as worthy of denigration—in order to justify a planned victimization. One can do this without at all believing the accusations made" (p. 367).
3. Costs of a particular view may not be apparent until many years later as illustrated by follow-up studies of antisocial children (Scott, Knapp, Henderson, & Maughan, 2001), as well as exposure of harmful treatments in the guise of helping as described in chapter 5. Consider also the "war on drugs." Billions of dollars have been spent on the "war on drugs" in the United States. What are the opportunity costs of such policies and are they working? Related laws in the United States have resulted in imprisonment of hundreds of thousands of (mostly) African American youth and men. Early marijuana policies were blatantly racist. Alexander (2010) describes current related police policies as the new Jim Crow laws. (See also Wacquant, 2009.) All drugs have been decriminalized since 2001 in Portugal based on the ineffectiveness of criminalization policies. Why does the success of this policy not receive more attention (e.g., Greenwald, 2009)? (See also Wood, Werb, Fischer, Hart, Wodak, Bastos, et al., 2010).
4. See Altheide, 2002; Glassner, 1999.
5. Fear is a key human reaction that has always been with us. It serves a vital cuing function in alerting us to danger.
6. See chapter 3.
7. Theories differ in a number of ways including their scope, evidentiary status (is there evidence that they are accurate), degree of optimism about potential for change, and kinds of behavior to which they apply. They are shaped by the particular time and place in which they develop including degree of understanding of our world. For example, scholars argue that Victorian culture influenced psychoanalytic theory.
8. See also Cottle, 1999; Lane, 2007; McDaniel, 2003.
9. For recent views, see *British Medical Journal*, September 2009. (For other views of the term disease, see chapter 6.)
10. Healing is a part of all religions. (See, for example, *Hospitals and Healing from Antiquity to the Later Middle Ages* (Hardon, 2008).
11. Consider this description:

The female possessed of masculine ideas of independence; the viragint [a masculine woman] who would sit in the public highways and lift up her pseudo-virile voice, proclaiming her sole right to decide questions of war and religion . . . the female who prefers the laboratory to the nursery . . . is a sad form of degeneracy. . . . The progeny of such human misfits are perverts, moral or physical. (William Lee Howard, "Effeminate Men and Masculine Women," *New York Medical Journal*, 1900, 21, 504–505; reprinted in Gamwell & Tomes, 1995, p. 126)

(See also Gibson, 1998, n 42.)

12. One view was that "Vapors originating from fermented menses could affect the nerves and circulatory system in much the same way that compacted excrement affected hypochondiacal men." (For other views of the term "disease," see chapter 6.)
13. Gosling (1987) characterizes the term "neurasthenia" as a "catch-all" one used in the nineteenth century to cover a variety of psychological and physical ills. The most common symptom was extreme fatigue (p. 125). (See also Taylor, 2001.)
14. Wolpe (1990) applied principles of learning to the treatment of anxiety, for example, using gradual exposure to feared events or objects to decrease fear. Anxiety was viewed as a learned reaction; different people had different learning histories and different arousal thresholds. Cultural values and related contingencies encourage particular anxieties, such as anxiety about how we look: Are we too fat? Are we too thin?
15. Nineteenth-century medical case books and professional journals frequently cited masturbation as a cause of insanity. In a discussion of a young man who had experienced a general loss of muscle control, seizures, and periods of delirium, one physician concluded:

> I was at no loss to ascribe all the symptoms to the habit of masturbation. On requesting a private interview, I drew from the unfortunate young man a full confession, which completely confirmed my diagnosis. . . . This was the first moment in his life that he had thought of harm or danger in the indulgence! While conversing with him, he seemed convinced of the cause of his ill health, and expressed, with a sort of despairing madness, his resolution to 'go and sin no more.' In view of the imbecile and delirious state of his mind, I expressed to his father my opinion of the cause of his sickness, and advised his immediate removal to the lunatic hospital. (A. Hitchcock, "Insanity and Death from Masturbation," *Boston Medical and Surgical Journal*, 1842, pp. 285–86) (Gamwell & Tomes, 1995, p. 111)

16. See discussion in Herzberg, 2009.
17. In a well-known 1880 case, inverted behavior was given as evidence of mental illness to obtain a certificate of insanity against Lucy Ann Lobdell, a woman who supported herself as a hunter from the 1850s to 1870s in upstate New York. The 'medical' reasons cited for committing Lobdell included that she wore men's clothing and called herself a hunter (see Gamwell & Tomes, 1995, p. 164). "Responding perhaps to the growing visibility of homosexual male subcultures in the late nineteenth-century city, George Beard viewed inversion as a form of sexual neurasthenia and attributed its epidemic rise to the nervous exhaustion caused by urban life (*Sexual Neurasthenia*, ed. A. D. Rockwell, New York, 1884, pp. 102–107)" (Gamwell & Tomes, 1995, p. 162). See also n 11.
18. See also "Bacteria Causes Ulcers? You're Kidding!" <http://people.ku.edu> (Jan. 26, 2011).
19. Eva Illouz (2008) suggests that economic capitalism has created *emotional capitalism*; it has changed the nature of intimate relationships and behavior and feelings in the workplace. She argues that it has created a new form of sociability, which decreases emotional connections. But the problem with consumer society is not that it encourages us to be discontent, but rather that it incites us to find contentment through things. Discontentment is historically a positive virtue

that has driven the human imagination. The problem with the consumer society is not that it makes us too ambitious but that is confines ambition to the sphere of consumption. (Really Bad Ideas: Environmentalism, spiked, Sept. 12, 2007).

Research suggests that materialistic-value-oriented consumers are less happy, less satisfied, and have overall poorer psychological health (Dittmar, 2008; Dittmar et al., 2011), not surprising when the consequences of healthism are considered, including the erosion of meaning and community (Ellul, 1965).

20. Illouz (2008), Cushman (1995), and Herzberg (2009) illustrate the complexity of the factors encouraging our pill-consuming culture and its reflection in the media and related class and gender factors.
21. See chapter 7.
22. The availability of a user-friendly translation of the Bible allowed the average person to read this for him or herself, something the church was not favorably disposed to; this would cut down (or out) the role of priests as the intermediaries between god and man. William Tyndale, to whom we owe the King James English translation of the Bible, knew his life would be in danger if the church authorities discovered what he was working on and fled from England to mainland Europe, where he remained until he was finally seized and burned at the stake for his heresy in translating the Bible into English.
23. California Clearing House of Child Welfare.
24. Pratkanis, 1995. "First you market the disease, then you push the pills to treat it" (Brendan Koerner, 2002 *Guardian*). <http://www.guardian.co.uk/Archives/Article/0,4273,4471963,oo.html>.

[At] the time the DSM-III was developed in 1980, thinking of mental illnesses as discrete disease entities . . . offered mental health professionals many social, economic, and political advantages. In addition, applying disease frameworks to a wide variety of behaviors and to a large number of people benefited a number of specific social groups including not only clinicians but also research scientists, advocacy groups, and pharmaceutical companies, among others. The disease entities of diagnostic psychiatry arose because they were useful for the social practices of various groups, not because they provided a more accurate way of viewing mental disorders. (Horwitz, 2002, p. 16)

25. To the question, "Is depression, or anxiety, or a narcissistic personality, or whatever, biological," the answer (assuming that dualism is false), is, "Of course. Everything is biological." To ask, "Is each psychopathological state biologically different from each healthy state," the obvious answer is, again, "Of course. Each sort of state is biologically different from each other sort of state." To prove that depression, say, has a different biology than non-depressive affect is to prove nothing that we did not already know. It is like saying, "since spaghetti has a different chemistry than ice cream, we know that spaghetti is not ice cream." But we knew that before we did the chemical assay of the spaghetti and of the ice cream. Discovering the precise biology of each state of an organism is truly a great thing, but that sort of discovery does not amount to a discovery of whether such states are to be understood as biological malfunctions. (Fancher, 2007, p. 268)

26. See critiques of neuroimaging (Leo & Cohen, 2003; Vul et al., 2009), as well as critiques of those who claim to have found localized brain functions (Uttal, 2001). See also Bentall, 2009.
27. Szasz's critics have dubbed him a "schizophrenic" for questioning a mental illness frame.
28. Zola (1972) argues that values intrude, especially regarding treatment. For example, those who do not seek and accept treatment for psychiatric or medical problems are often viewed as defective in some way. Even though the individual may not be held responsible for getting a problem, he or she is held responsible for doing something about it.
29. E.g., see Carey, 2009.
30. See Charlton (2009).
31. Erikson's (1980) proposed stages of development are a classic example. Attachment theorists emphasize the influence of early relationships on later behavior (see Cassidy & Shaver, 2008).
32. See also *The Triumph of the Therapeutic*, Reiff, 1985.
33. She draws on Weber's concept of discipline "as a set of cognitive practices through which social relationships are recoded" (p. 136).
34. See also discussion of self-surveillance in chapter 6.
35. Illouz (2003) raises the interesting point that the victim's appearance on Winfrey's show establishes a "trauma narrative" that "seems best to embody modern tragic narratives of the suffering self because it condenses the family narrative, the abhorrence for cruelty, and the moral demand that people be given a chance to develop unhindered" (Krasner, 2004).
36. Illouz (2003) suggests that this "objectification of emotions" is encouraged by literacy. "In this process, emotions are externalized in the sense that they become separate from the subjectivity of the speaker, with the aim of taking control of and transforming them. Literally this allows an emotion to become an object for the purpose of facilitating interpersonal transactions" (p. 140). We are invited to reflect on and discuss emotions disconnected from their original context (p. 141). The National Institute of Mental Health was formally established in 1949.
37. Victor Frankl (1967) suggests that each person is responsible for the fulfillment of the specific meaning of his or her own life. He contends that no matter what our circumstances (even if in a concentration camp), we cannot escape choosing among possibilities. He views this responsibility as the essence of human existence and suggests that our search for meaning is integral to how we live our lives and with what consequences.
38. See discussion of the relationship between the personal and political by Mills (1959), as well as related writings by Foucault, Illich, and Szasz.
39. See also Baughman, 2006; Timimi, 2002.
40. "The highest rates of 'idiocy and lunacy' in America were first among the millions of immigrant poverty-stricken Irish after the potato crop failure of 1845 then in successive waves of the poor Swedes, the Slavs and Russian Jews, then the Southern Italians, now the Blacks and Hispanics . . . as each group achieved good education and economic success their incidence of 'idiocy and lunacy' fell to the population average." <http://www.psychdiagnosis.net/GeorgeAlbee.html>.

41. Writers such as Jacque Ellul, Hannah Arendt, Ivan Ilich, Michael Foucault, C. Wright Mills, and Thomas Szasz (among others) interweave the psychological and sociological—the inner and the outer—in addressing suffering and its causes as does Paul Gilbert (1989) in his discussion of the importance of social ranking in understanding anxiety and depression. Hannah Arendt (1966) describes the interrelationships between psychological variables such as loneliness and depression and the creation of terrorist states such as the Soviet Union under Stalin and National Socialism under Hitler.
42. Yehudi Webster argues that racial and ethnic descriptions and events are "forms of propaganda, an indoctrination into a conviction that U.S. society has different racial and ethnic groups that are locked in a relationship of domination/oppression" (1992, p. 13). He argues that the view that certain physical differences imply a racial identify is propagated by social scientists, governmental institutions, and the media and suggests that racial classification was initiated as a justification for certain political and economic arrangements. Once persons are racially classified, there is no escaping the implications of racial motives (e.g., racism). Webster views racial classification itself as racism. (He notes that racism refers to many things, including "a belief system or ideology, discriminatory policies and behavior, theories of genetic inferiority, and socioeconomic inequality" [1992, p. 241]). He points out that the government, social scientists, and the media daily saturate us with the alleged validity of categories based on race, ethnicity, and class, which he considers bogus categories that do more harm than good (e.g., they underplay our shared humanness and, in so doing, make it easier for us to dehumanize others). Some of our most inspiring leaders such as Martin Luther King also emphasized our shared humanness. Use of race as a descriptor has been critiqued as incomplete and misleading (e.g., Hoffman, 2006; Braun, Fausto-Sterling, Fullwiley, Hammonds, Nelson, Quivers, et al., 2007).
43. Cushman suggests that this interior focus is reflected in healing practices throughout the last hundred years, including mesmerism, and argues that advertising and psychotherapy became the new therapeutic activities (p. 69).
44. For a discussion of the self-esteem fallacy, see Baumeister, Campbell, Krueger, & Vans, 2003; Foxx & Roland, 2005.
45. In the International Consensus Statement regarding ADHD (a striking example of propaganda) we find: "ADHD is a behavioral and emotional disorder this is based in the brain" (Barkley et al., 2002). What is in need of arguing is boldly asserted as fact. This consensus statement has two pages of text replete with propaganda stratagems such as ad hominem attacks and a notable absence of ad rem arguments. The other pages contain the signature of 86 professionals. There is an appeal to consensus.
46. In France, even today, psychiatrists are psychoanalytically oriented and are suspicious of cognitive behavioral therapy because this does not address the "meaning" of symptoms. This is also why they have little interest in the lists of symptoms in the DSM (2000).

Chapter 10

1. Burke (1969, 1966) argues that the negative (the act of saying that something is not something else) is one of the features inherent in language (symbol use).

We may say a psychologist is not a psychiatrist. He suggests that "the negative" results in moral actions (saying what is bad or good).
2. Helping professionals are "word smiths" in translating clients' words into words they value. Drinking alcohol may be labeled as an "addiction." If you hear voices, you may be called "schizophrenic" and placed on medication. (See for example Heritage & Clayman, 2010.)
3. See discussion of the importance of context regarding argument in chapter 12.
4. *The International Consensus Statement on ADHD* (Barkley et al., 2002) is a splendid example.
5. Consider, for example, terms that Firestone and Seiden (1987) present as similar to "microsuicide":

- indirect suicide or parasuicide
- masked suicide or slow suicide
- partial suicide or chronic suicide
- hidden suicide or embryonic suicide
- installment plan suicide.

6. Examples of rules suggested by Orwell (1958) include:

   1. Never use a metaphor, simile or other figure of speech which you are used to seeing in print.
   2. Never use a long word when a short one will do.
   3. If it is possible to cut a word out, always cut it out.
   4. Never use the passive when you can use the active.
   5. Never use a foreign phrase, a scientific word or a jargon word if you can think of an everyday English equivalent.
   6. Break any of these rules sooner than say anything outright barbarous p. 143).

7. For further discussion of the influence of metaphors, see Lakoff, 2001. (See also discussion of analogies in chapter 12.)
8. Ullmann (1962) suggests that vagueness is related to four factors: (1) the generic character of words; (2) the fact that meaning is never homogeneous (it is context related), (3) lack of clear-cut boundaries in the nonlinguistic world; and (4) lack of familiarity with what a word stands for (p. 6). Deese (1974) suggests "that vagueness of communication is inherent in the structure of our ideas, rather than in the language system" (pp. 7–8, cited in Channell, 1994). Channell (1994) argues that this just shifts the problem from linguistics into psychology in terms of how to deal with vagueness.
9. Consider the breakdown of bee colonies called "colony breakdown disorder," meaning that no one knew the cause (*New York Times*, Feb. 28, 2007).
10. See also discussion of bold assertions in chapter 13.
11. See, for example, Kolb, Gibb, & Robinson, 2003. Drury et al, 2011.
12. See <http://www.proveneffective.org> and <http://brody/hooked.blogspot.com>.
13. See also discussions of authority in chapters 7 and 12.

Chapter 11

1. See also website of Center for Media and Democracy <http://www.prwatch.org>.
2. See discussion of ghostwriting in chapter 2.
3. Skeptic's Dictionary.
4. See for example, Williams & Ceci (1997).
5. A recent review concluded, "In the condition most like the university classroom, where students were told before viewing the lecture that they would be tested on the materials and that they would be rewarded in accordance with the number of exam questions which they answered correctly . . . the Dr. Fox effect was not supported" (Marsh, 1987, p. 332).
6. The validity effect occurs when the mere repetition of information affects the perceived truthfulness of that information. It appears to be based on recognition memory and may be an automatic process. It occurs similarly for statements of fact that are true and false in origin, as well as political or opinion statements. Factors such as the belief that the information was heard previously or having some expertise in the content of the statement, prompts information to be rated as more valid, even if the information has not been repeated. The validity effect is not similar to the mere exposure effect, in that liking and validity are separate and distinct phenomena. And, the validity effect is not similar to attitude polarization, as shown by the fact that false statements demonstrate an increase in truth rating with repetition (the validity effect) rather than a stronger rating of being false (attitude polarization). (Adapted from Renner, 2004, pp. 211–12)
7. *Medical Hypotheses*, a journal published for decades was discontinued by Elsevier when the editor, Bruce Charlton planned to publish an article by Peter Duesberg (2010) questioning figures regarding AIDS in Africa.
8. Harlow (1964). See also recent literature on attachment.
9. See also discussions of groupthink, e.g. Janis, 1982.
10. Tousignant & DesMarchais (2002) compared medical students' performance in a number of situations to their self-perceptions of their performance. There was only a 0.36 correlation between their actual behavior and their self-rated performance, meaning that their self-estimates of their competence were inflated. Educators tend to overestimate the skills of their students (Whitfield & Xie, 2002).
11. Examples of excuses astrologers offered when they made a wrong statement about a client include the following (Dean, 1986–87, p. 173):
12. See literature on "neutralization" efforts—how we "neutralize" doing bad things to people. Doing evil is not as difficult as you may think. See, for example, Arendt, 1964 and Zimbardo, 2007. Here again, these sources highlight how we are influenced by our environments.

1. Client does not know himself.	This shifts the blame from astrologer to the participants.
2. Astrologer is not infallible.	This puts the blame on the ambiguity of the birth chart.
3. Another factor is responsible.	
4. Manifestation is not typical.	

13. See, for example, Batson, O'Quin, & Psych, 1982; Rosenhan, 1973.
14. As Ceci & Bruck (1995) point out, "Failure to test an alternative to a pet hunch can lead interviewers to ignore inconsistent evidence and to shape the contents of the interview to be consistent with their own beliefs" (p. 80).
15. This was a sell-out on the part of psychologists given the extensive literature in psychology describing how anxiety is created by environmental circumstances and, in turn, can be remedied by arranging new learning experiences—not by popping a pill. Included here are the discoveries by Joseph Wolpe (1990) and related clinical applications over the past decades (e.g., Brewin, 2006).

CHAPTER 12

1. Sales of Zyprexa generated $39 billion dollars in 1996, the year of its approval. Eli Lilly paid $1.4 billion to:

   > settle criminal and civil charges that it illegally marketed its blockbuster antipsychotic drug Zyprexa for unauthorized use in patients particularly vulnerable to its risky side effects....
   >
   > Among the charges, Lilly has been accused of a scheme stretching for years to persuade doctors to prescribe Zyprexa to two categories of patients—children and the elderly—for whom the drug was not federally approved and in whom its use was especially risky.
   >
   > In one marketing effort, the company urged geriatricians to use Zyprexa to sedate unruly nursing home patients so as to reduce "nursing time and effort," according to court documents. Like other antipsychotic drugs, Zyprexa increases the risks of sudden death, heart failure and life-threatening infections like pneumonia in elderly patients with dementia-related psychosis.
   >
   > The company also pressed doctors to treat disruptive children with Zyprexa, court documents show, even though the medicine's tendency to cause severe weight gain and metabolic disorders is particularly pronounced in children. (Harris & Berenson, New York Times, 2009, 1/15 B1)

2. See also discussion of medicalization in chapter 5, of metaphor in chapter 10, and inappropriate use of analogies in chapter 13.
3. Hobbs & Wynne, 1989.
4. See, for example, Jacobson et al., 2005; Lilienfled et al., 2003.
5. Some, such as Richard Smith (2003), past editor of the *British Medical Journal*, do not think so.
6. The book *Rival Hypotheses* (Huck & Sandler, 1979) presents 100 different claims and invites readers to evaluate these to sharpen their skills in identifying alternative hypotheses.
7. Contradictions are a type of implication. For example, to say that X contradicts Z, is to say that if X is true, Z must be false. A premise implies another premise when the second premise must be true if the first is true. Contractions involve a bidirectional relationship: if X contradicts Y, then Y contradicts X. However, this is not necessarily the case with implication—although X may imply Y, Y may not imply X.
8. For descriptions of how to analyze arguments, see, for example, Damer (2005), Kahane & Cavender (1998), and Walton (2008). Interactive training programs in argument analysis are available.

9. See, for example, the classic book by Huff (1954).
10. For other discussions of analyzing arguments see Halpern 2003; Toulmin, 2003.
11. As he notes, the U.S. Government removed limits on the length of commercials in 1984, allowing television stations and others to present infomercials of various lengths.
12. Questions include

    1. What type of dialogue is involved? What are the goals?
    2. In what stage of the dialogue did the alleged failure occur?
    3. Is more than one context of dialogue involved? Was there a dialectical shift that could affect the question of fallacy?
    4. Was a specific failure in argumentation alleged? What kind of failure or shortcoming was it? What type of argument was used? How was it deficient or used inappropriately?
    5. How bad was the failure? Was it a fallacy or more just a blunder [an error or lapse] or weakness? Should it be open to challenge or refutation?
    6. What rules of dialogue were violated? Was there a failure of relevance?
    7. What general technique of argumentation was used? How is the fallacy revealed in a profile of dialogue?
    8. Who are the parties and what are their roles in the dialogue? How was burden of proof distributed?
    9. How was the technique used by the one party against the other party as a tactic using deception [as indicated by the answer to questions 3]?
    10. Was the technique used as a calculated tactic of deception by its proponent? How aggressive was the use of the technique? How persistent?
    11. Which critical questions were not answered? Or was critical questioning diverted or shut off by the use of the technique? Was there a chance to reply? (above list slightly paraphrased).

13. "The counterpart of the weak argument is the *flawed argument*, which is a missing step or a gap in the sequence of moves required in order to carry out a successful sequence of moves in a dialogue. . . . The key difference between a fallacy and a flaw in an argument is this. In the fallacy type of case, there is an underlying systematic pattern of argument strategy that has been used in a way that goes strongly against the legitimate goals of dialogue in the given case. In the flawed argument, however, the main thrust and direction of the argument is consistent with the rules and aims of the dialogue, but gaps, missing parts, or questionable junctures make the argument fall short of its objective. Sometimes it is hard to prove whether a sequence of moves is fallacious or merely flawed. And sometimes it does not matter greatly, provided the flaw is noticed and understood as something that is a critical failure" (Walton, 1995, pp. 263–64).
14. Subtypes of fallacies from authority described by Schipper and Schuh (1959) include the following:

    1. Sweeping authority, where the source is not specified well enough, or identified. (See discussion of glittering generalizations in chapter 4.)
    2. Dogmatic authority, where the authority is held to be 'ultimate' or 'infallible' (bold assertions).

3. Misplaced authority where the field is wrong,
4. Misrepresented authority, where what the authority said is changed in meaning.
5. Venerable authority, where veneration or glamour is substituted for real authority (pp. 38–45. Quoted in Walton, 1997, p. 255).

CHAPTER 13

1. "Not the least of the merits of a really good classification of fallacies would be that it could be used in the formulation of appropriate points of order. It should be made possible in principle, as Bentham wished, that the perpetrator of fallacy be greeted with voices in scores crying aloud 'Stale! Stale! Fallacy of Authority! Fallacy of Distrust!' and so on" (Hamblin, 1970, p. 284). For descriptions of fallacies, see, for example, Engel, 1994; Kahane & Cavender, 1998; Thouless, 1974; Walton, 2008.
2. To determine disease rate divide the number of persons with a particular condition by the total number of individuals at risk.
3. For example, see Angell, 2005; Brody, 2007; Healy, 2004.
4. For further description of propaganda strategies used by the tobacco industry including the creation of doubt about the accuracy of research findings. See Orestees & Conway, 2010.
5. What is really at the heart of the *ad ignorantiam* fallacy is the idea that participants in argumentation in a dialogue have specific rights and obligations at local sequences or particular stages of the evolution of the dialogue, at junctures where they make particular types of moves, like making assertions, putting forward presumptions, or asking critical questions. A participant is obliged to take on commitment to a proposition urged by the other party only where appropriate conditions at that stage have been met.

   The other party, for example, must have allowed the participant sufficient room to ask critical questions, must have fulfilled an appropriate burden of proof by supplying arguments, and so forth. The *ad ignorantiam* fallacy is a characteristic sequence of moves that goes across these obligations and rights, interfering with the proper progress that a dialogue would presumably make were it not for the mischief of the fallacy. (Walton, 1996, p. 298)

6. Michalos (1971) has identified seven ways to beg the question, some of which overlap with improper appeals to authority.
7. See Table 12.1.
8. See, for example, Boyle, 2002.

CHAPTER 14

1. Reviews are prepared and maintained, based on standards described in *The Reviewers' Handbook*, which is revised often to ensure that it remains up-to-date. The Cochrane Library also includes a Controlled Trials Register and The Cochrane Review Methodology Database, which is a bibliography of articles concerning research synthesis and practical aspects of preparing systematic reviews.

2. For example, compare material on the web site of the American Psychiatric Association with material on the web site of the International Society for the Ethical Psychology and Psychiatry <http://www.psychintegrity.org> and <http://healthyskepticism.com>.
3. Resources to gain this information include Guyatt et al. (2008), Greenhalgh (2010), and Straus et al. (2005). The EBM (evidence-based medicine) tool kit is a Canadian-based collection of resources that includes critical appraisal checklists, methodological filters, and other resources, located at <http://www.ebm.medualberta.ca>. Workshops are available at a number of sources including the Critical Appraisal Skills Program (CASP) in Oxford (Institute of Health).
4. See also CAT bank, University of Michigan.
5. Other reporting guides include MOOSE (for observational studies), STARD (for diagnostic studies), and PRISMA (for reviews).
6. An example would be "The car was hit by Alice" versus "Alice hit the car."
7. See Bandolier worksheet for calculating NNT. We could compute the odds ratio comparing the percentage of people better in the control and better with treatment.
8. See, for example, Lauer & Betran, 2007; Smith, Trevana, Simpson, Barrett, Nutbeam, McCaffery, 2010; O'Connor, Wennberg, Legare, Llewellyn-Thomas, Moulton, Sepucha, Sodano, & King, 2007; O'Connor, Bennett, Stacey, Barry, Col, Eden, et al., 2009. Also available for professionals (e.g., Baysari, Westbrook, Braithwaite, & Ray, 2011), as well as for shared decision making (Woltmann et al., 2011). Formats include interactive videos, palm pilots, audiotapes, and audio-guided workbooks.
9. See, for example, Benedetti, 2009.
10. For example, predictions that the banks would fail created a rush on the banks to take out money, creating failure of the banks.
11. Helpful related books include: D. Huff, 1954; Huck, & Sandler, 1979; Skrabanek & McCormick, 1998; Michael, Boyce, & Wilcox, 1984, and Tufte, 1983, 1990, 1997, 2006. High quality reviews of research related to thousands of specific questions are available in the Cochrane and Campbell Libraries.
12. For example, see Baccaglini, Shuster, Cheng, Theriaque, Schoenbach, Tomar, & Poole, 2010; Ioannidis, 2005; Rubin & Parrish, 2007; Strasak, Zaman, Pfeiffer, Gobel, & Ulmer, 2007.

REFERENCES

Abbott, A. (1988). *The system of professions: An essay on the division of expert labor.* Chicago: University of Chicago Press.
Abbott, A. (2010). Varieties of ignorance. *American Sociologist*, 41, 174–89.
Abel, G. A., & Glinert, L. H. (2007). Chemotherapy as language: Sound symbolism in cancer medication names. *Social Science and Medicine*, 66(8), 1863–69. Published online Feb. 4, 2008.
Abel, G. A., Neufeld, E. J., Sorel, M., & Weeks, J. C. (2008). Direct-to-consumer advertising for bleeding disorders: A content analysis and expert evaluation of advertising claims. *Journal of Thrombosis and Haemostasis*, 6, 1680–84.
Abelson, R. (2003). Doctors are making a killing selling cancer drugs. *San Francisco Chronicle*, Jan. 26, A9.
Abelson, R. (2006a). New nerve test, a money maker divides doctors. *New York Times*, Oct. 20, C1/6.
Abelson, R. (2006b). The spine as profit center: surgeons invest in makers of hardware. *New York Times*, Dec. 30, A1/9.
Abelson, R. (2006c). Whistle-blower suit says device maker generously rewards doctors. *New York Times*, Jan. 24, C1/10.
Abraham, J. (1995). Science, politics, and the pharmaceutical industry: Controversy and bias in drug regulation. London: UCL Press.
Abramovitz, M. (1988). *Regulating the lives of women: Social welfare policy from colonial times to the present.* Boston: South End Press.
Adams, M. (2010). Breast cancer deception month: Hiding the truth beneath an area of print. Retrieved Aug. 1, 2011, from <http://www.naturalnews.com>.
Addley, E. (2008). Inventor's 20/20 vision: To help 1Bn of the world's poorest see better: Professor pioneers DIY adjustable glasses that do not need an optician. *Guardian*, Dec. 21, 11.
Ahmed, A. (2011). CVS Caremark agrees to buy a Medicare D Unit. *New York Times*, Jan. 1, 1/4.
Alberto, P. A., & Troutman, A. C. (1990). *Applied behavior analysis for teachers.* Columbus, OH: Merrill.
Alberto, P. A., & Troutman, A. C. (2008). *Applied behavior analysis for teachers* (8th ed.). Columbus, OH: Merrill.
Alderman, L. (2010). Getting a new knee or hip? Do it right the first time. *New York Times*, July 2, B5.
Alexander, B. K., Beyerstein, B. L., Hadaway, P. F., & Coambs, R. B. (1981). Effects of early and later colony housing on oral ingestion of morphine in rats. *Pharmacology, biochemistry, and behavior*, 15, 571–76.

Alexander, M. (2010). *The new Jim Crow laws: Mass incarceration in the age of colorblindness*. New York: New Press.

Ali, A., Sheringham, J., & Sheringham, K. (2008). Managing the curve downwards: A cross-sectional study of the use of management speak in public health. *Public Health*, doi:10.1016/j.puhe.2008.05.012.

Allan, S., Anderson, A., & Peterson, A. (2005). Reporting risk: Science journalism and the prospect in human cloning. In S. Watson & A. Moran (Eds.), *Trust, risk and uncertainty*. Basingstoke: Palgrave Macmillan.

Alliance for Human Research Protection. (2009). <http:www.ahrp.org>.

Alonso-Coello, P., Garcia-Franco, A. L., Guyatt, G., & Moynihan, P. (2008). Drugs for pre-osteoporosis: Prevention or disease mongering? *BMJ*, 336:126–29.

Altheide, D. L. (2002). *Creating fear: News and the construction of crises*. New York: Aldine de Gruyer.

Altheide, D. L., & Johnson, J. M. (1980). *Bureaucratic propaganda*. Boston: Allyn & Bacon.

Altman, D. G. (2002). Poor-quality medical research: What can journals do? *Journal of the American Medical Association*, 287, 2765–67.

Altman, D. G., Machin, D., Bryant, T. N., & Gardner, M. J. (Eds.) (2000). *Statistics with confidence: Confidence intervals and statistical guidelines*. London: BMJ Books.

Altman, L. K. (1992). Study calls many heart x-rays unnecessary. *New York Times*, Nov. 11, A7.

Altman, L. K. (1995). Health officials urge halt to routine eye operations. *New York Times*, Feb. 22, B7.

American Psychiatric Association. (2000). *Diagnostic and statistical manual of mental disorders* (4th ed.). Washington, DC: American Psychiatric Association.

American Psychiatric Association. (2009). The American Psychiatric Association phases out industry-supported symposia. News Release, Feb. 25. Arlington, VA.

Anderson, L. M., Scrimshaw, S. C., Fullilove, M. T., Fielding, J. E., Norman, D. J., and the Task Force on Community Preventive Services. (2003). Culturally competent health care systems: A systematic review. *American Journal of Preventive Medicine*, 24, 68–79.

Andre, L. (2009). *Doctors of deception: What they don't want you to know about shock treatment*. New Brunswick, NJ: Rutgers University Press.

Andreasen, N. C. (1997). What is psychiatry? *American Journal of Psychiatry*, 154, 591–93.

Andren, et al. (1978). *Rhetoric and Ideology in Advertising*. Liber: Stockholm.

Anesthesia journal retracts fluid paper over ethics concerns. Possible fraud—Anesthesiology News. Posted November 24, 2010 <http://roguemedic.com>.

Angell, M. (2004). The truth about the drug companies. *New York Review of Books*, 51(12), July 15, 5.

Angell, M. (2005). *The truth about drug companies: How they deceive us and what to do about it* (Revised and updated). New York: Random House.

Angell, M. (2008). Industry sponsored clinical research: A broken system. *Journal of the American Medical Association*, 300, 1069–71.

Angell, M. (2009). Drug companies & doctors: A story of corruption. *New York Review of Books*, Aug. 10, 1/15.

Angell, M. (2011). Illusions of psychiatry. *New York Review of Books*, July 14.

Angier, N. (1997). In a culture of hysterectomies, many question their necessity. *New York Times*, Feb. 17, A1/10.

Antman, E. M., Lau, J., Kupelnick, B., Mosteller, F., & Chalmers, T. C. (1992). A comparison of results of meta-analyses of randomized controlled trials and recommendations of clinical experts: Treatments for myocardial infarction. *Journal of the American Medical Association*, 268(2), 240–48.

Antonuccio, D. O., & Healy, D. (2009). Letter. Stealth advertising and academic stalking. *BMJ*, 338:968.

Antonuccio, D. O., Burns, D. D., & Danton, W. G. (2002). Antidepressants: A triumph of marketing over science. *Prevention & Treatment*, 5, 1–17.

Applbaum, K. (2000). Crossing borders: Globalization as myth and charter in American transnational consumer marketing. *American Ethnologist*, 27, 257–82.

Applbaum, K. (2009a). "Consumers as patients!" Shared decision-making and treatment non-compliance as business opportunity. *Transcultural Psychiatry*, 48, 107–30.

Applbaum, K. (2009b). Getting to yes: Corporate power and the creation of a psycho pharmaceutical blockbuster. *Culture and Medical Psychiatry*, 33, 185–215.

Arendt, H. (1958). *The human condition*. Chicago: University of Chicago Press.

Arendt, H. (1964). *Eichman in Jerusalem: A report on the banality of evil*. New York: Viking.

Arendt, H. (1966). *The origins of totalitarianism*. New York: Harcourt, Brace & World.

Arenson, K. W. (1995). Former United Way chief guilty in theft of more than $600,000. *New York Times*, Apr. 4, A1/8.

Ariely, D. (2009). *Predictably irrational: The hidden forces that shape our decisions*. New York: Harper.

A rip-off by health insurers? (2008). Editorial. *New York Times*, Feb. 18, A18.

Arkes, H. (1981). Impediments to accurate clinical judgment and possible ways to minimize their impact. *Journal of Consulting and Clinical Psychology*, 49, 323–30.

Arkin, R. M., & Oleson, K. C. (1998). Self-handicapping. In J. M. Darley & J. Cooper (Eds.), *Attribution and social interaction: The legacy of Edward E. Jones* (pp. 313–47). Washington, DC: American Psychological Association.

Armstrong, D., & Armstrong, E. M. (1991). *The great American medicine show*. New York: Prentice Hall.

Armstrong, J. C. (1980). Unintelligible management research and academic prestige. *Interfaces*, 10, 80–86.

Aronson, J. K. (2003). Anecdotes as evidence: We need guidelines for reporting anecdotes of suspected adverse drug reactions. *BMJ*, 326:1346.

Aronson, N. (1984). Science as claims-making activity: Implications for social problems research. In J. W. Schneider & J. I. Kitsuse (Eds.), *Studies in the sociology of social problems* (pp. 1–30). Northwood, NJ: Ablex Publishing.

ASBA. (2009). Surgical biopsies for breast abnormalities overused, action needed. *Medscape Medical News*, Apr. 27.

Asch, S. E. (1956). Studies of independence and conformity: Minority of one against a unanimous majority. *Psychological Monographs*, 70(9), Whole No. 416.

Asimov, I. (1989). The relativity of wrong. *Skeptical Inquirer*, 14, 35–44.

Associated Press. (2008). A.M.A. joins several states in suing Aetna and Cigna. *New York Times International*, Feb. 11, B9.

Averill, J. (1982). *Anger and aggression: Implications for theories of emotion*. New York: Springer-Verlag.

Baccaglini, L., Shuster, J. J., Cheng, J., Theriaque, D. W., Schoenbach, V. J., Tomar, S. L., & Poole, C. (2010). Design and statistical analysis of oral medicine studies: common pitfalls. *Oral Diseases*, 16, 233–41.

Bacon, F. [1620] (1985). *The essays (Appendix 4: Idols of the mind)*, ed. J. Pitcher. New York: Penguin Books.

Badger, W. J., Moran, M. E., Abraham, C., Yarlagadda, B., & Perrotti, M. (2007). Misdiagnosis by urologists resulting in malpractice payment. *Journal of Urology*, 178(6), 2537–39.

Baer, D. M. (1982). Applied behavior analysis. In G. T. Wilson & C. M. Franks (Eds.), *Contemporary behavior therapy: Conceptual and empirical foundations* (pp. 277–309). New York: Guilford.

Baer, D. M. (2004). *Program evaluation: Arduous, impossible, and political.* In H. E. Briggs & T. L. Rzepnicki (Eds.), *Using evidence in social work practice: Behavioral perspectives* (pp. 310–22). Chicago: Lyceum.

Bagdikian, B. H. (2004). *The new media monopoly.* Boston: Beacon Press.

Baird, J. W. (1974). *Mythical world of Nazi propaganda 1939-1945.* Minneapolis, MN: University of Minnesota Press.

Baker, T. (2005). *The medical malpractice myth.* Chicago: University of Chicago Press.

Baldwin, S., & Jones, Y. (1988). Is electroconvulsive therapy unsuitable for children and adolescents? *Adolescence*, Fall, 33, 645–55.

Baldwin, S., & Oxlad, M. (1996). Multiple case sampling of ECT administration with 217 minors: Review and meta-analysis. *Journal of Mental Health*, 5, 451–63.

Bandura, A. (1978). On paradigms and recycled ideologies. *Cognitive Therapy and Research*, 2, 79–103.

Bandura, A. (1999). Moral disengagement in the perpetration of inhumanities. *Personality and Social Psychology Review*, 3, 193–209.

Barkley, R. A., Cook, E. H., Diamond, A., Zametkin, A., Thapar, A., Teeter, A., et al. (2002). International consensus statement on ADHD. *Clinical Child and Family Psychology Review*, 5, 89–111.

Barlett, D. L., & Steele, J. B. (2002). Indian casinos: Wheel of misfortune—who gets the money? (PART 1), 12/16. Retrieved January 18, 2011, from <http://www.barlettandsteele.com>.

Barlett, D. L., & Steele, J. B. (2011). Deadly medicine. *Vanity Fair*, 122.

Barlow, D. H. (2010). The dodo bird—again—and again. *Behavior Therapist*, 33, 15–16.

Barnum, P. T. (1865). *Humbugs of the world* (autobiography). Whitefish, MT: Kessinger Pub. Rare Reprints.

Baron, J. (1994). *Thinking and deciding.* New York: Cambridge University Press.

Baron, J. (2005). Normative models of judgment and decision making. In D. J. Koehler & N. Harvey (Eds.), *Blackwell handbook of judgment and decision making* (pp. 19–36). Malden, MA: Blackwell.

Barrett, S., Jarvis, W. T., Kroger, M., & London, W. H. (2002). *Consumer health: A guide to intelligent decision* (7th ed.). New York: McGraw-Hill.

Barry, D., & Finkelstein, K. E. (2000). Stolen Medicaid millions stoke the boom in adult day care, officials say. *New York Times*, Feb. 7, A21.

Barsky, A. J., & Boros, J. F. (1995). Sommatization and medicalization in the area of managed care. *JAMA*, 274, 1931–34.

Basken, P. (2010). As he worked to strengthen ethics rules, NIMH director aided a leading transgressor. *Chronicle of Higher Education*, June 6. Retrieved July 1, 2010, from <http://chronicle.com>.

Bass, A. (2008). *Side effects: A prosecutor, a whistleblower, and a bestselling antidepressant on trial.* Chapel Hill, NC: Algonquin Books.

Bartholet, E. (2009). The racial disproportionality movement in child welfare: False facts and dangerous directions. *Arizona Law Review*, 51, 871–932.

Batson, C. D., O'Quin, K., & Pych, V. (1982). An attribution theory analysis of trained helpers' inferences about clients' needs. In T. A. Wills (Ed.), *Basic processes in helping relationships* (pp. 59–80). New York: Academic Press.

Bauer, H. (2001a). *Fatal attractions: The troubles with science*. New York: Paraview Press.

Bauer, H. (2001b). *Science and pseudoscience: Magnetic healing, psychic phenomena and other heterodoxies*. Urbana: University of Illinois Press.

Bauer, H. (2004). Science in the 21st century: Knowledge monopolies and research cartels. *Journal of Scientific Exploration*, 18, 643–60.

Bauer, H. (2007a). *The origin, persistence and failings of HIV/AIDS theory*. Jefferson, NC: McFarland.

Bauer, H. H. (2007b). Questioning HIV/AIDS: Morally reprehensible or scientifically warranted? *Journal of American Physicians and Surgeons*, 12, 116–20.

Baughman, F. A., Jr. (with C. Hovey) (2006). *The ADHD fraud: How psychiatry makes "patients" of normal children*. Victoria, BC: Trafford Publishing.

Baumeister, R. F., Campbell, J. D., Krueger, J. L., & Vohs, K. D. (2003). Does high self-esteem cause better performance, interpersonal success, happiness, or healthier lifestyles? *Psychological Science in the Public Interest*, 4, 1–44.

Bausell, R. B. (2007). *Snake oil science: The truth about complementary and alternative medicine*. New York: Oxford University Press.

Bayer, R. (1987). Politics, science and the problems of psychiatric nomenclature: A case study of the American Psychiatric Referendum on homosexuality. In H. T. Engelhart & A. L. Caplan (Eds.), *Case studies in the resolution and closure of disputes in science and technology* (pp. 381–400). New York: Cambridge University Press.

Baysari, M. T., Westbrook, J., Braithwaite, J., & Day, R. O. (2011). The role of computerized decision support in reducing errors in selecting medicines for prescription: Narrative review. *Drug Safety*, 34, 289–98.

Beaulieu, D. (2010). Medical testing out of control among U.S. patients. *FierceHealthcare*. March 12 <http://www.fiercehealthcare.com>.

Beck, A. T. (1976). *Cognitive therapy and the emotional disorders*. New York: International Universities Press.

Beck, U. ([1992] 2000). *Risk society: Towards a new modernity*. London: Sage.

Becker, H. S. (1996). The epistemology of qualitative research. In R. Jessor, A. Colby, & R. A. Shweder (Eds.), *Ethnography and human development: Context and meaning in social inquiry* (pp. 53–71). Chicago: University of Chicago Press.

Bekelman, J. E., Li, Y., & Gross, C. P. (2003). Scope and impact of financial conflicts of interest in biomedical research: A systematic review. *Journal of the American Medical Association*, 289, 454–65.

Bell, T., & Linn, M. C. (2002). Beliefs about science: how does science instruction contribute. In B. K. Hofer & P. R Pintrich (Eds.), *Personal epistemology: The psychology of beliefs about knowledge and knowing* (pp. 321–46). Mahwah, NJ: Erlbaum.

Bem, D. J. (2011). Feeling the future: Experimental evidence for anomalous retroactive influences on cognition and affect. *Journal of Personality and Social Psychology*, 100, 407–25.

Bender, L. (1947). 100 cases of childhood schizophrenia treatment with electroshock. Paper presented at the 72nd Annual Meeting of the American Neurological Association. June.

Benedetti, F. (2009). *Placebo effects: Understanding the mechanisms in health and disease*. New York: Oxford University Press.

Bennett, B. S., & O'Rourke, S. P. (2006). A prolegomenon to the future study of rhetoric and propaganda. In G. S. Jowett & V. O'Donnell (Eds.), *Readings in propaganda and persuasion: New and classic essays* (pp. 51–71). Thousand Oaks, CA: Sage.

Bentall, R. P. (2009). *Doctoring the mind: Is our current treatment of mental illness really any good?* New York: New York University Press.

Beral, V., & Peto, R. (2010). UK cancer survival statistics. *BMJ*, 341:c4112.

Berenson, A. (2006). Drug files show maker promoted unapproved use. *New York Times*, Dec. 18, A1.

Berenson, A. (2007a). Lilly settles with 18,000 over Zyprexa. *New York Times*. Jan. 5.

Berenson, A. (2007b). Medicare privatization abuses. *New York Times*, May 8.

Berenson, A. (2008). Lilly waited too long to warn about schizophrenia drug, doctor testifies. *New York Times*, Mar. 8.

Berenson, A., & Pollack, A. (2007). Doctors reaping millions for use of anemia drugs. *New York Times*, May 9, A1/C4.

Berger, J. (1971). *Ways of seeing*. London: British Broadcasting Corporation/Harmondsworth: Penguin.

Berlyne, D. E. (1960). *Conflict, arousal, and curiosity*. New York: McGraw Hill.

Bernays, E. L. (1923). *Crystallizing public opinion*. New York: Boni & Liverright.

Bernays, E. L. & Miller, M. C. (2005). *Propaganda*. Brooklyn, NY: Ig Pub.

Bernays, E. L. & Miller, N. C. (2005). *Propaganda*. New York: Ig Publishing.

Bero, L. A., & Rennie, D. (1996). Influences on the quality of published drug studies. *International Journal of Technology Assessment in Health Care*, 12, 209–37.

Bessant, J., Hil, R. & Watts, R. (eds.) (2005). *Violation of trust: How schools and welfare systems have failed our young people*. Aldershot: Ashgate Publishers.

Best, J. (2001). *Dammed lies & statistics: Untangling numbers from the media, politicians, & activists*. Berkeley: University of California Press.

Best, J. (2004). *More damned lies and statistics: How numbers confuse public issues*. Berkeley: University of California Press.

Best, J. (2008). *Stat-spotting: A field guide to identifying dubious data*. Berkeley: University of California Press.

Best, M., & Neuhauser, D. (2004). Heroes and martyrs of quality and safety: Ignaz Semmelweis and the birth of infection control. *Quality Safety and Health Care*, 13, 233–34.

Bets, J. W. (1944). Psychosurgery: An evaluation of 200 cases over seven years. *Journal of Mental Science*, 90, 532–37.

Beutler, L. E. (2000). Empirically based decision making in clinical practice. *Prevention & Treatment*, Vol. 3. Article 27, posted September 1, 2000.

Beyerstein, B. L. (1990). Brainscams: Neuromythologies of the new age. *International Journal of Mental Health*, 19, 27–36.

Bhandari, M., Busse, J. W., Jackowski, D., Montori, V. M., Schünemann, H., et al. (2004). Association between industry funding and statistically significant pro-industry findings in medical and surgical randomized trials. *Canadian Medical Association Journal*, 170, 477–80.

Biehl, J., Good, B., & Kleinman, A. (Eds.) (2007). *Subjectivity: Ethnographic investigations*. Berkeley: University of California Press.

Bikhchandani, S., Hirshleifer, D., & Welch, I. (1998). Learning from the behavior of others: Conformity, fads, and informational cascades. *Journal of Economic Perspectives*, 12, 151–70.

Black, N. (1994). Experimental and observational methods of evaluation. Letter. *BMJ*, 309:540.

Black, S. L. (2009). TYM test: Too many false positives. Reply to Brown, et al. June 11. Bloomberg <http://www.bloomberg.com>.

Bless, H. (2001). The consequences of mood on the processing of social information. In A. Tesser & N. Schwartz (Eds.), *Blackwell handbook of social psychology: Intraindividual processes* (pp. 391–421). Oxford: Blackwell.

Bloomberg News. (2010). Medtronic to settle lawsuits over devices tied to deaths. *New York Times*, Oct. 15, B5.

Blumsohn, A. (2006). Doctors as lapdogs to drug firms: The beast is ourselves. *BMJ*, 333:1121, doi:10:1136.

Bodenheimer, T. (2000a). Disease management in the American market. *BMJ*, 320:563–66.

Bodenheimer, T. (2000b). Uneasy alliance: Clinical investigators and the pharmaceutical industry. *New England Journal of Medicine*, 342, 1539–44.

Bodenheimer, T. (2006). Coordinating care—A perilous journey through the health care system. *New England Journal of Medicine*, 358, 1064–71.

Bogdanich, W. (2007). As FDA tracked poisoned drugs, a winding trail went cold in China. *New York Times*, June 17, A1/12.

Bogdanich, W. (2009). Oncologist defends his work at a V.A. hospital in Philadelphia. *New York Times*, June 30, A10.

Bogdanich, W. (2010a). After stroke scans, patients face serious health risks. *New York Times*, July 31. Retrieved Aug. 2, 2010, from <http://www.nytimes.com>.

Bogdanich, W. (2010b). California tightens oversight of CT scans. *New York Times*, Oct. 2, A12.

Bogdanich, W. (2010c). Radiation offers new cures, and ways to do harm. *New York Times*, Jan. 23. Retrieved Aug. 2, 2010, from <http://www.nytimes.com>.

Bogdanich, W. (2010d). Technology surges, radiation safeguards lag. *New York Times National*, Jan. 27, A1/A18.

Bok, D. (2003). Universities in the marketplace: The commercialization of higher education. Princeton, NJ: Princeton University Press.

Bok, S. (1978). *Lying: Moral choice in public and private life*. New York: Pantheon.

Bola, J., & Mosher, L. (2003). Treatment of acute psychosis without neuroleptics: Two year outcomes from the Soteria Project. *Journal of Nervous and Mental Diseases*, 191, 219–29.

Bonanno, G., & Lilienfeld, S. O. (2008). Let's be realistic: When grief counseling is effective and when it's not. *Professional Psychology: Research and Practice*, 39, 377–80.

Boom, W. (2010). Technology surges, radiation safeguards lag, *New York Times National*, Jan. 27, A1/A18.

Borchers, T. A. (2005). *Persuasion in the media age* (2nd ed.). New York: McGraw Hill.

Boren, J. H. (1972). *When in doubt, mumble: A bureaucrat's handbook*. New York: Van Nostrand Reinhold.

Boseley, S. (2010). Antidepressant reboxetine no better than a placebo, study finds. *The Guardian*, Oct. 13, 9.

Bosk, C. L. (1979). *Forgive and remember: Managing medical failure*. Chicago: University of Chicago Press.

Boyle, M. H. (1998). Guidelines for evaluating prevalence studies. *Evidence Based Mental Health*, 1, 37–39.

Boyle, M. (2002). *Schizophrenia: A scientific definition?* (2nd ed.). London: Routledge.

Boyton, P., Shaw, S., & Callaghan, W. (2004). How PR firms use research to sell products. *BMJ*, 328:530.

Bracher, M. (2009). *Social symptoms of identify needs: Why we have failed to solve our social problems and what to do about it*. Finchley Road, London: Karnac.

Bracken, P., & Thomas, P. (2004). Critical psychiatry in practice. *Advances in Psychiatric Treatment*, 10, 361–70.

Bracken, P., & Thomas, P. (2005). *Post psychiatry: Mental health in a post modern world.* New York: Oxford.

Braddock, C. H., Edwards, K. A., Hasenberg, N. M., Laidley, T. L., & Levinson, W. (1999). Informed decision making in outpatient practice: Time to get back to basics. *Journal of the American Medical Association,* 282, 2313–20.

Braun, L., Fausto-Sterling, A., Fullwiley, D., Hammonds, E. M., Nelson, A., Quivers, W., Reverby, S. M., & Shields, A. E. (2007). Racial categories in medical practice: How useful are they? *PloS Med,* 4(9):e271.

Breggin, P. R. (1991). *Toxic psychiatry: Why therapy, empathy, and love must replace the drugs, electroshock and biochemical theories of the new psychiatry.* New York: St. Martin's Press.

Breggin, P. R. (2008). *Brain-disabling treatments in psychiatry: Drugs, electroshock, and the psychopharmaceutical complex* (2nd ed.). New York: Springer.

Breggin, P. R., & Cohen, D. (2007). *Your drug may be your problem: How and why to stop taking psychiatric medications* (Rev. ed.). Philadelphia: DaCapo Life Long.

Brenner, D. J., & Elliston, C. D. (2004). Estimated radiation risks potentially associated with full-body CT screening. *Radiology,* 232, 735–38.

Brenner, D. J., & Hall, E. J. (2007). Computed tomography—an increasing source of radiation exposure. *New England Journal of Medicine,* 357, 277–84.

Brewin, C. R. (2006). Understanding cognitive behavior therapy: A retrieval competitive account. *Behavior Research and Therapy,* 44, 765–84.

Briesacher, B. A., Limcangco, R., Simoni-Wastila, L., Doshi, J. A., Levens, S. R., Shea, D. G., & Stuart, B. (2005). The quality of anti-psychotic drug prescribing in nursing homes. *Archives of Internal Medicine,* 165, 1280–85.

Broad, W., & Wade, N. (1982). *Betrayers of the truth.* New York: Simon & Schuster.

Brock, T. C., & Green, M.C. (Eds.) (2005). *Persuasion: Psychological insights and perspectives* (2nd ed.). Thousand Oaks, CA: Sage.

Broder, J. M. (2010). Developing nations to get clean-burning cookstoves. *New York Times,* Sept. 21, A8.

Brodkey, A. (2005). The role of the pharmaceutical industry in teaching psychopharmacology: A growing problem. *Academic Psychiatry,* 29, 222–29.

Brody, H. (2007). *Hooked: Ethics, the medical profession and pharmaceutical industry.* New York: Rowman & Littlefield.

Brody, J. E. (2009). More isn't always better in coronary care. *New York Times,* Jan. 6, D7.

Bromley, D. B. (1977). *Personality description and ordinary language.* New York: Wiley.

Bromley, D. B. (1986). *The case-study method in psychology and related disciplines.* New York: Wiley.

Broom, D. H., & Woodward, R. V. (1996). Medicalization reconsidered: Toward a collaborative approach to care. *Sociology of Health and Illness,* 18, 357–78.

Brown, J. (2006). Two ways of looking at propaganda. June 29. <http://uscpublicdiplomacy.org>.

Brown, J. (2009). Self administered cognitive screening test (TYM) for detection of Alzheimer's disease: Cross sectional study. *BMJ,* 338:b2030.

Brown, J., Pengas, G., Dawson, K., Brown, L. A., & Clatworthy, P. (2009). Self-administered cognitive screening test (TYM) for detection of Alzheimer's disease: Cross sectional study. *BMJ,* 338:b2030.

Brown, P., & Funk, S. C. (1986). Tardive dyskinesia: Barriers to the professional recognition of an iatrogenic disease. *Journal of Health & Social Behavior,* 27, 116–32.

Buettner, R. (2011). Reaping millions from Medicaid in nonprofit care for disabled. *New York Times*, Aug. 2, A1/18.
Buie, J. (1987). Newspaper's tone, errors irk sources. *APA Monitor*, 18, 23.
Buie, J. (1989). Psychologists defend reimbursement rights. *APA Monitor*, 20, 25.
Bunge, M. (1984). What is pseudoscience? *Skeptical Inquirer*, 9, 36–47.
Bunge, M. (2003). The pseudoscience concept, dispensable and professional practice, is required to evaluate research projects: A reply to Richard J. MacNally. *Scientific Review of Mental Health Practice*, 2, 111–14.
Burger, J. M. (2009). Replicating Milgram: Would people still obey today? *American Psychologist*, 64, 1–11.
Burke, K. (1966). *Language as symbolic action: Essays on life, literature and method*. Berkeley: University of California Press.
Burke, K. (1969). *A rhetoric of motives*. Berkeley: University of California Press.
Burke, K. (1972). *Dramatism and development*. Barre, MA: Clark University Press.
Burnham, J. C. (1987). *How superstition won and science lost: Popularizing science and health in the United States*. New Brunswick, NJ: Rutgers University Press.
Burns, D. D. (1999). *The feeling good handbook* (Rev. ed.). New York: Plume.
Burton, A. [1621] (1924). *The anatomy of melancholy*. London: Chatto & Windus.
Burton, B. (2008). Australian drug industry gives details of money spent courting doctors. *BMJ*, 336:742, doi:10.1136.
Busch, R. S. (2008). *Healthcare fraud: Auditing and detection guide*. Hoboken, NJ: John Wiley & Sons.
Busfield, J. (2001). Introduction. In J. Busfield & J. Gabe (Eds.), *Rethinking the sociology of mental health* (pp. 1–7). Oxford: Blackwell.
Bushman, B. J. (2002). Does venting anger feed or extinguish the flame? Catharsis, rumination, distraction, anger, and aggressive responding. *PSPB*, 28(6), 724–31.
Byrne, P. (2010). Challenging health care discrimination: Commentary on . . . Discrimination against people with mental illness. *Advances in Psychiatry and Psychiatric Treatment*, 61, 61–62.
Campbell, D. T. (1969). Reforms as experiments. *American Psychologist*, 24, 409–29.
Campbell, D. T., & Stanley, J. C. (1963). *Experimental and quasi-experimental design for research*. Chicago: Rand-McNally.
Campbell, E. G., Russell, L., Gruen, R. L., Mountford, J., Miller, L. G., Cleary, P. D., & Blumenthal, D. (2007). A national survey of physician–industry relationships. *New England Medical Journal*, 396, 1742–50.
Campbell, E. G., Weissman, J. S., Vogeli, C., Clarridge, B. R., Abraham, M., & Marder, J. E., et al. (2005). Financial relationships between institutional review board members and industry. *New England Journal of Medicine*, 355, 2321–29.
Caplan, P. J. (1995). *They say you're crazy: How the world's most powerful psychiatrists decide what's normal*. Reading, MA: Addison-Wesley.
Caplan, P. J. (2006). Psychiatric labels plague women's mental health. Retrieved Aug. 15, 2011, from <http://mindfreedom.org>.
Caplan, P. J., & Cosgrove, L. (2004). *Bias in psychiatric diagnosis*. Lanham, MD: Jason Aronson.
Capriccioso, R. (2009). Havasupas blood case lives on. *Indian Country Today*, Jan. 2.
Carey, B. (2007). Study says depression, grief often confused. *New York Times*, A1.
Carey, B. (2009). Report on gene for depression is now faulted. *New York Times*, June 17, A1/13.

Carey, B. (2010). Studies halted at brain lab over impure injections. *New York Times*, July 17, A1.

Carey, B. (2011). Drugs used for psychosis go to youths in foster care. *New York Times*, Nov. 21, A11.

Carey, B., & Harris, G. (2008). Psychiatric group faces scrutiny over drug industry ties. *New York Times*, July 12, A13.

Carlat, D. J. (2010). Unhinged: The trouble with psychiatry—A doctor's revelations about a profession in crisis. New York: Free Press.

Carlowe, J. (2010). Ghostwritten articles overstated benefits of HRT. *BMJ*, 341:c4894.

Carlowe, J. (2011). Investigation into home care of elderly people shows cases of "serious neglect." *BMJ*, 342:d3904.

Carpenter, K. J. (1986). *The history of scurvy & vitamin C*. New York: Cambridge University Press.

Carroll, D. W. (2001). Using ignorance questions to promote thinking skills. *Teaching of Psychology*, 28, 98–100.

Carroll, L. [1871] (1946). Through the looking glass, and what Alice found there. New York: Random House.

Cassell, E. (1986). Ideas in conflict: The rise and fall of new views of disease. *Daedalus*, 115, 19–42.

Cassels, A. (2009). Ponziceuticals within the medical industrial complex. *Canadian Medical Association Journal*, 181, 1–2.

Cassidy, J. (2009). *Whistleblowing*: Name and shame. *BMJ*, 339:b2693.

Cassidy, J. (2011). The international alliance of patients' organizations. *BMJ*, 342:d3485.

Cassidy, J., & Shaver, P. R. (Eds.) (2008). *Handbook of attachment: Theory, research, and clinical applications, 2nd ed.* New York: Guilford.

Ceci, S. J., & Bruck, M. (1995). *Jeopardy in the courtroom: A scientific analysis of children's testimony*. Washington, DC: American Psychological Association.

Chabris, C., & Simons, D. (2009). *The invisible gorilla: How our intuitions deceive us*. New York: Broadway Paperbacks.

Chadwick, D., & Smith, D. (2002). The misdiagnosis of epilepsy. *BMJ*, 324:495–96.

Chalmers, I. (1983). Scientific inquiry and authoritarianism in perinatal care and education. *Birth*, 10, 151–66.

Chalmers, I. (2003). Trying to do more good than harm in policy and practice: The role of rigorous, transparent, up-to-date evaluations. *Annals of the American Academy of Political and Social Science*, 589, 22–40.

Chalmers, I. (2007). The Alzheimer's Society and public trust. *BMJ*, 20, Sept.

Chan, S. (2006). City inquiry uncovers widespread fraud at Bronx charity. *New York Times*, Oct. 6, A23.

Channell, J. (1994). *Vague language*. New York: Oxford University Press.

Chapman, L. J. (1967). Illusory correlation in observational report. *Journal of Verbal Learning and Verbal Behavior*, 6, 151–55.

Chapman, L. J., & Chapman, J. P. (1967). Genesis of popular but erroneous diagnostic observations. *Journal of Abnormal Psychology*, 72, 193–204.

Chapman, L. J., & Chapman, J. P. (1969). Illusory correlation as an obstacle to the use of valid psychodiagnostic signs. *Journal of Abnormal Psychology*, 74, 271–80.

Charlton, B. G. (2009). Replacing education with psychometrics:How learning about IQ almost-completely changed my mind about education. *Medical Hypotheses*, 73, 273–277.

Charlton, B. R. (2010). The cancer of bureaucracy. *Medical Hypothesis*, 74(6), 961–1090.

Chauncey, G. (1995). *Gay New York: Gender, urban culture, and the making of the gay male world, 1890–1940.* New York: Basic Books.

Chesluk, B. J., & Holmboe, E. S. (2010). How teams work—or don't—in primary care: A field study on internal medicine practices. *Health Affairs, 29,* 874–79.

Choudhry, N., Stelfox, H., & Detsky, A. (2002). Relationships between authors of clinical practice guidelines and the pharmaceutical industry. *Journal of the American Medical Association, 287*(5), 612–17.

Cialdini, R. B. (1984). *Influence: The new psychology of modern persuasion.* New York: Quill.

Cialdini, R. B. (2001). *Influence: Science and practice.* Boston: Allyn & Bacon.

Cialdini, R. B. (2009). *Influence: Science and practice* (5th ed.). Boston: Pearson Education.

Ciliska, D., Thomas, H., & Buffett, C. (2008). *An introduction to evidence-informed public health and a compendium of critical appraisal tools for public health practice.* Na. Collaborating Centre for Methods and Tools (Feb.). School of Nursing McMaster University, Hamilton, Ontario.

Clark, T. (1997). *Art and propaganda in the twentieth century: The political image in the age of mass culture.* London: Weidenfeld & Nicolson.

Clarke, A. E., Mamo, L., Fosket, J. R., Fishman, J. R., & Shim, J. K. (Eds.) (2010). *Biomedicalization: Technoscience, health and illness in the U.S.* Durham, NC: Duke University Press.

Clay, R. A. (1998). Mental health professionals vie for position in the next decade. *APA Monitor,* Sept., 20.

Cohen, C. I., & Timimi, S. (Eds.) (2008). *Liberatory psychiatry: Philosophy, politics, and mental health.* New York: Cambridge University Press.

Cohen, D. (2009). Whither critical psychiatry? Keynote address, June 22, 2009, Critical Psychiatry Network Conference, Norwich, UK.

Cohen, D. (2010). Rosiglitazone: What went wrong? *BMJ,* 341:c4848.

Cohen, J. S. (2001). *Overdose: The case against the drug companies.* New York: Jeremy P. Tarcher.

Cohen, M. (2010). HHS IG report confirms the rapid spread of unregulated drug trials abroad. *The Whistleblogger,* June 22.

Cohen, M. R., & Nagel, E. (1934). *An introduction to logic and scientific method* (2nd ed.). New York: Harcourt, Brace & Company.

Cohen, N. (2009). A Rorschach cheat sheet on Wikipedia? *New York Times,* July 28, A1.

Coker, R. (2001). Distinguishing science and pseudoscience. Retrieved on Jan. 20, 2011, from <http://www.quackwatch.com>.

Combs, J. E., & Nimmo, D. D. (1993). *The new propaganda: The dictatorship of palaver in contemporary politics.* New York: Longman.

Confessore, N., & Kershaw, S. (2007). As home care booms, little oversight in New York. *New York Times,* Sept. 2, 25.

Conrad, P. (1975). The discovery of hyperkinesis: Notes on the medicalization of deviant behavior. *Social Problems, 32,* 12–21.

Conrad, P. (2005). The shifting engines of medicalization. *Health and Social Behavior, 46,* 3–14.

Conrad, P. (2007). *The medicalization of society: On the transformation of human conditions into treatable disorders.* Baltimore, MD: Johns Hopkins University Press.

Conrad, P. (2010). Pills and the pursuit of happiness and normalcy (book review). *Contexts, 9,* 78–80.

Conrad, P., & Leiter, V. (2004). Medicalization, markets and consumers. *Journal of Health and Social Behavior*, 45(Suppl), 158–76.

Conrad, P., & Leiter, V. (2008). From Lydia Pinkham to Queen Levita: DTCA and medicalization. *Sociology of Health and Illness*, 30, 825–38.

Conrad, P., & Schneider, J. W. (1992). *Deviance and medicalization: From badness to sickness*. Philadelphia: Temple University Press.

Conrad, P., Mackie, T., & Mehrotra, A. (2010). Estimating the costs of medicalization. *Social Science & Medicine*, 70(12), 1943–47.

Cook, D. M., Boyd, E. A., Grossmann, C., & Pero, L. A. (2009). Journalists and conflicts of interest in science: Beliefs and practices. *Ethics and Science and Environmental Politics*. Published online Apr. 28, 2009.

Cook, T. D., & Campbell, D. T. (1979). *Quasi-experimentation: Design and analysis issue for field settings*. Boston: Houghton & Mifflin.

Coombes, R. (2009). Evidence lacking for memory clinics to tackle dementia, say critics. *BMJ*, 338:b550.

Corcoran, J., & Walsh, J. (2009). *Clinical assessment and diagnosis in social work practice*. New York: Oxford University Press.

Cosgrove, L. (2010). Diagnosing conflict-of-interest disorder. *Academe*, 96(6). Online at <http://www.aaup.org>.

Cosgrove, L., Krimsky, S., Vijayaraghaven, M., Schneider, L. (2006). Financial ties between DSM-IV panel members and the pharmaceutical industry. *Psychotherapy and Psychosomatics*, 75, 154–60.

Cosgrove, L., Bursztajn, H. J., Krimsky, S., Anaya, M., & Walker, J. (2009). Conflicts of interest and disclosure in the American Psychiatric Association's clinical practice guidelines. *Psychotherapy and Psychosomatics*, 78, 228–32.

Cottle, M. (1999). Selling shyness. *New Republic*, Aug. 2, 24–29.

Coulter, A. (2002). *The autonomous patient: Ending paternalism in medical care*. London: Nuffield Trust.

Coyne, J. C., Thombs, B. D., & Hagedoorn, M. (2010). Ain't necessarily so: Review and critique of recent meta-analyses of behavioral medicine interventions in health psychology. *Health Psychology*, 29(2), 107–16.

Craig, D., with Richard Brooks of Private Eye (2006). *Plundering the public sector: How new labour are letting consultants run off with $70 billion of our money*. London: Constable.

Craven, P. A., & Lee, R. E. (2006). Therapeutic interventions for foster children: A systematic research synthesis. *Research on Social Work Practice*, 16, 287–304.

Creadick, A. G. (2010). *Perfectly average: The pursuit of normality in post war America*. Amherst: University of Massachusetts Press.

Cummings, N. A., & O'Donohue, W. T. (2008). *Eleven blunders that cripple psychotherapy in America: A remedial unblundering*. New York: Routledge.

Cunningham, S. B. (2002). *The idea of propaganda: A reconstruction*. Westport, CT: Praeger.

Cushman, P. (1990). Why the self is empty: Toward a historically situated psychology. *American Psychologist*, 45, 599–611.

Cushman, P. (1995). *Constructing the self, constructing America: A cultural history of psychotherapy*. Cambridge, MA: Persens.

Damer, T. E. (2005). *Attacking faulty reasoning: A practical guide to fallacy-free arguments* (3rd ed.). Belmont, CA: Wadsworth.

Darowski, A. (2009). Antidepressants and falls in the elderly. *Drugs & Aging*, 26, 381–94.

Daubert v Merrell Dow Pharmaceuticals Inc. 509 U.S. 113 S. Ct. 2786 (1993).

Davies, P. (2004). *Is evidence-based government possible?* Jerry Lee lecture, 4th Annual Campbell Collaboration Colloquium, Washington, DC, Feb. 19.

Davis, D., O'Brien, M. A., Freemantle, N., Wolf, F. M., Mazmanian, P., & Taylor-Vaisey, A. (1999). Impact of formal continuing medical education. *Journal of the American Medical Association*, 282 (9), 876–74.

Dawes, R. M. (1988). *Rational choice in an uncertain world*. Orlando, FL: Harcourt, Brace & Jovanovich.

Dawes, R. M. (1993). Prediction of the future versus an understanding of the past: A basic asymmetry. *American Journal of Psychology*, 106, 1–24.

Dawes, R. M. (1994). *House of cards: Psychology and psychotherapy built on myth*. New York: Free Press.

Dawes, R. M. (2001). *Everyday irrationality: How pseudoscientists, lunatics and the rest of us systematically fail to think rationally*. Boulder, CO: Westview Press.

Day, M. (2007). Would-be parents need safeguards for unscrupulous fertility clinics, says report. *BMJ*, 335:224–25.

Day, M. (2009). Misuse of ADHD drugs by young people is rising, US poisons data show. *BMJ*, 339:b3434.

Dean, G. (1986–87). Does astrology need to be true? Part 1: A look at the real thing. *Skeptical Inquirer*, 11(2), 166–85.

DeBord, G. (1983). *The society of the spectacle*. Detroit: Black and Red.

Del Mar, C., Droust, J., & Glasziou, P. (2006). *Critical thinking: Evidence, communication and decision making*. Malden, MA: Blackwell.

DePanfilis, D., & Salus, M. K. (2003). *Child protective services: A guide for caseworkers*. Washington, DC: U.S. Department of Health and Human Services, Administration for Children and Families, Children's Bureau, Office on Child Abuse and Neglect.

Deutsch, C. H. (2007). Deal to merge 2 health firms aimed at women. *New York Times*, May 21, C1/2.

Devereaux, P. J., Choi, P. T. L., Lacchetti, C., Weaver, B., Schunemann, H. J., Haines, T., et al. (2002). A systematic review and meta-analysis of studies comparing mortality rates of private for-profit and private not-for-profit hospitals. *Canadian Medical Association Journal*, 166, 1399–1406.

Deyo, R. A. (2002). Cascade effects of medical technology. *Annual Review of Public Health*, 23, 23–44.

Deyo, R. A., & Patrick, D. L. (2005). *Hope or hype: The obsession with medical advances and the high cost of false promises*. New York: American Management Association.

Deyo, R. A., Psaty, B. M., Simon, G., Wagner, E. H., & Omenn, G. S. (1997). The messenger under attack—Intimidation of researchers by special-interest groups. *New England Journal of Medicine*, 336, 1176–80.

Diaz, F. J., & de Leon, J. (2002). Excessive antipsychotic dosing in two US state hospitals. *Journal of Clinical Psychiatry*, 63, 998–1003.

Dichter, E. (1955). *A research study of pharmaceutical advertising*. Croton-on-Hudson, NY: Pharmaceutical Advertising Club.

Didi-huberman, G. (2003). *Invention of hysteria: Charcot and the photographic iconography of the Salpêtriere*. Cambridge, MA: Massachusetts Institute of Technology Press. (Originally published in 1982.)

Dillard, J. P., & Pfau, M. (Eds.) (2002). *The persuasion handbook: Developments in theory and practice*. Thousand Oaks, CA: Sage.

Diller, L. (1997). *Running on Ritalin*. New York: Bantum.

Diller, L. H. (2006). *The last normal child: Essays on the intersection of kids, culture and psychiatric drugs*. Westport, CT: Praeger.

Diller, L. (2008). Are our leading pediatricians drug industry shills? *San Francisco Chronicle*, July 13.

Dingwall, R., Eekelaar, J., & Murray, T. (1983). *The protection of children*. Oxford (UK): Basil Blackwell.

Dittmar, H. (2008). Consumer society, identity and well being: The search for the "good life" and the "body perfect." In R. Brown (Ed.), *European monographs in social psychology series*. New York: Psychology Press.

Dittmar, H., Bond, R., Casser, T., & Hurst, M. (2011). A meta-analysis of research on the link between materialism and well-being. In preparation.

Dixon, L. S. (Ed.) (2004). *In sickness and in health: Disease as metaphor in art and popular wisdom*. University of Delaware Press.

Djulbegovic, B., & Hozo, I. (2007). When should potentially false research findings be considered acceptable? *PLoS Med*, 4, e26.

Dobson, R. (2008). Atorvastatin advertising misled over benefits for women, study claims. *BMJ*, 337:a2209.

Doll, S. S., Gowers, S., James, A., Fazel, M., Fitzpatrick, R., & Pollock, J. (2009). Alternatives to inpatient mental health care for children and young people. *Cochrane Database SYST REV* (2009). Apr. 15(2), CD006410.

Doob, L. (1935). *Propaganda: Its psychology and technique*. New York: Henry Holt and Company.

Double, D. B. (2006). *Critical psychiatry: The limits of madness*. Basingstoke: Palgrave Macmillan.

Douglas, A. (1977). *The feminization of American culture*. New York: Knopf.

Douglas, M. (1992). *Risk and blame: Essays on cultural theory*. New York: Routledge.

Druckman, D., & Bjork, R. A. (Eds.) (1991). *In the mind's eye: Enhancing human performance*. Washington, DC: National Academy Press.

Drug trials outsourcing: Clinical concerns. (2009). Editorial. *Guardian*, Sept. 28, 34.

Drury, M. (1976). *The danger of words and writings on Wittgenstein*. Bristol: Thoemmes Press.

Drury, M. O'C., Berman, D., Fitzgerald, M., & Hayes, J. (1996). *The danger of words and writings on Wittgenstein*. Bristol, UK: Thoemmes Press.

Drury, S. S., Theall, K. A., Gleason, M. M., Smyke, A. S., Divito, I., Wong, J., et al. (2011). Telomere length and early social deprivation: linking early adversity and cellular aging. *Molecular Psychiatry* doi:10.1038/mp.2011.53.

Dubovsky, A. N., & Dubovsky, S. L. (2007). *Psychotropic drug prescriber's survival guide: Ethical mental health treatment in the age of Big Pharma*. New York: Norton.

Duesberg, P. H. (1996). *Inventing the AIDS virus*. Washington, DC: Regnery.

Duesberg, P., Mandrioli, D., McCormack, A., & Nicholson, J. M. (2011). Is carcinogenesis a form of speciation? *Cell Cycle*, 10, 2100–2114.

Dugger, C. W. (2009). As donors focus on AIDS, child illnesses languish. *New York Times*, Oct. 30, A8.

Duhl, L. J., Cummings, N. A., & Hynes, J. J. (1987). The emergence of the mental health complex. In L. J. Duhl & N. A. Cummings (Eds.), *The future of mental health services: Coping with crisis* (pp. 1–14). New York: Springer.

Duke University Medical Center. (2010). Nearly all depressed adolescents recover with treatment, but half relapse, study finds. *ScienceDaily*. Nov. 2. Retrieved Aug. 22, 2011, from <http://www.sciencedaily.com/releases>.

Dunning, D., Heath, C., & Suls, J. M. (2004). Flawed self-assessment: Implications for health, education and the work place. *Psychological Science in the Public Interest*, 5, 69–106.

Dutton, D. B. (1988). *Worse than the disease: Pitfalls of medical progress*. New York: Cambridge University Press.

Dyer, C. (2003). Sally Clark freed after appeal court quashes her convictions. *BMJ*, 326, 304.

Dyer, C. (2007a). King's fund accepts funding for seminars from U.S. insurance company. *BMJ*, 334:1294.

Dyer, C. (2007b). Lilly investigated in US over the marketing of olanzapine. *BMJ*, 334:171.

Dyer, C. (2008). Pfizer loses attempts to force journals to reveal peer review comments. *BMJ*, 336:743.

Dyer, C. (2009). Three elderly people died from inappropriate drugs, inquest finds. *BMJ*, 338:b1657.

Eagle, G. (2002). The political conundrums of post-traumatic stress disorder. In D. Hook & G. Eagle (Eds.), *Psychopathology and social prejudice* (pp. 75–91). Cape Town: University of Cape Town Press.

Eberstadt, N. (1995). *The tyranny of numbers*. Washington, DC: AEI Press.

Eddy, D. M. (1993). Three battles to watch in the 1990s. *Journal of the American Medical Association*, 270, 520–26.

Editorial (2007). *New York Times*, Mar. 23, A22.

Edmondson, R. (1984*). Rhetoric in sociology*. New York: Macmillan.

Edwards, A., Elwyn, G., & Mulley, A. (2002). Explaining risks: Turning numerical data into meaningful pictures. *BMJ*, 324:827–30.

Edwards, J. (2009a). AZ promoted Seroquel as superior to Haldol when company data said it wasn't. *New York Times*, Nov. 4.

Edwards, J. (2009b). Pfizer turned NAMI into "Trojan Horse" to push Geodon off-label to kids suit claims. Sept. 16. Retrieved August 20, 2011, from <http://www.bnet.com/blog/drug-business/Pfizer>.

Edwards, V. (1938). *Group leader's guide to propaganda analysis*. New York: Institute for Propaganda Analysis.

Ehrenreich, B. (2009). *Bright-sighted: How positive thinking is undermining America*. New York: Picador.

Ehrenreich, B., & English, D. (1973). *Complaints and disorders: The sexual politics of sickness*. Glass Mountain Pamphlet 2. New York: Feminist Press.

Eichenwald, K. (1995). Death and deficiency in kidney treatment. *New York Times*, Dec. 4, A1.

Eichenwald, K., & Kolata. G. (1999a). Drug trials hide conflicts for doctors. *New York Times*, May 16, A1.

Eichenwald, K., & Kolata. G. (1999b). When physicians double as business men. *New York Times*, Nov. 30, A1.

Eisenberg, T., & Wells, M. T. (2008). Statins and adverse cardiovascular events in modern-risk females: A statistical and legal analysis with implications for FDA preemption claims. *Journal of Empirical Legal Studies*, 5(3), 507–50.

El-hai, J. (2005). *The lobotomist: A maverick medical genius and his tragic quest to rid the world of mental illness*. Hoboken, NJ: John Wiley & Sons.

Elliott, C. (1998). The tyranny of happiness: Ethics and cosmetic psychopharmacology. In E. Parens (Ed.), *Enhancing human traits: Ethical and social implications* (p. 178). Washington, DC: Georgetown Press.

Elliott, C. (2003). *Better than well: American medicine meets the American dream*. New York: W. W. Norton & Company.

Elliott, C. (2011). Useless studies, real harm. Editorial. *New York Times*, July 28.

Elliott, C., & Abadie, R. (2008). Exploiting the research underclass in phase I clinical trials. *New England Journal of Medicine*, 358, 2316–17.

Elliott, D., & Chambers, T. (Eds.) (2004). *Prozac as a way of life*. Chapel Hill: University of North Carolina Press.

Ellis, A., & MacLaren, C. (1988). *Rational emotive behavior therapy: A therapist's guide*. Atascadero, CA: Impact Publishers.

Ellul, J. (1964). *The technological society*. New York: Vintage Books.

Ellul, J. (1965). *Propaganda: The formation of men's attitudes*. New York: Vintage.

Ellul, J. (1967). *The political illusion*, trans. Conrad Kellens. New York: Vintage.

Ellul, J. (1973a). *Hope in time of abandonment*, trans. Edward Hopkins. New York: Seabury.

Ellul, J. (1973b). *Propaganda: The formation of men's attitudes*, trans. K. Kellen & J. Lerner. New York: Random House/Vintage.

Ellul, J. (1985). *The humiliation of the word*, trans. Joyce Hanks. Grand Rapids, MI: Eerdmans.

Ellul, J. (1990). *The technological bluff*, trans. G. W. Bromiley. Grand Rapids, MI: William B. Eerdmans Publishing Company.

Elstein, A., & Schwartz, A. (2002). Clinical problem solving and diagnostic decision making: A selective review of the cognitive research literature. In J. A. Knottnerus (Ed.), *The evidence base of clinical diagnosis* (pp. 179–95). London: BMJ Books.

Elstein, A. S., Shulman, L. S., Sprafka, S. A., Allal, L., Gordon, M., Jason, H., Kagan, N., Loupe, M., & Jordan, R. (1978). *Medical problem solving: An analysis of clinical reasoning*. Cambridge, MA: Harvard University Press.

Ely, J. W., Osheroff, J. A., Maviglia, S. M. & Rosenbaum, M. E. (2007). Patient-care questions that physicians are unable to answer. *JAMA*, 14, 407–14.

Engel, S. M. (1982). *With good reason: An introduction to informal fallacies* (2nd ed.). New York: St. Martin's Press.

Engel, S. M. (1994). *With good reason: An introduction to informal fallacies* (5th ed.). New York: St. Martin's Press.

Englehardt, H. T., & Caplan, A. L. (1987). *Scientific controversies: Case studies in the resolution and closure of disputes in science and technology*. Cambridge: Cambridge University Press.

Epstein, S. S. (2010). American Cancer Society: The world's wealthiest "nonprofit" institution. Retrieved on Aug. 1, 2010, from <http://www.preventcancer.com>.

Erault, M. (1994). *Developing professional knowledge and competence*. London: Falmer Press.

Erickson, J. (2011). Air pollution near Michigan schools linked to poor student health, academic performance. *Michigan Today*, April.

Ericsson, L., Ohlsson, R., & Andren, G. (1978). *Rhetoric and ideology in advertising: A content analytical study of American advertising*. Stockholm: Grafiska Gruppen AB.

Erikson, E. H. (1980). *Identity and the life cycle*. New York: Norton.

Evans, I., Thornton, H., & Chalmers, J. (2006). *Testing treatments: Better research for better healthcare*. London: British Library.

Evetts, J., Mieg, H. A., & Felt, U. (2006). Professionalism, scientific expertise, and elitism: A sociological perspective. In K. A. Ericsson, N. Charness, P. J., Feltovich, & R. R. Hoffman (Eds.), *The Cambridge handbook of expertise and expert performance* (pp. 105–23). New York: Cambridge University Press.

Ewen, S. (1976). *Captains of conscientiousness: Advertising and the social roots of the consumer culture.* New York: McGraw Hill.

Ewen, S. (1999). *All consuming images: The politics of style in contemporary culture* (Rev. ed.). New York: Basic Books.

Fabrigar, L. R., Smith, S. M., & Brannon, L. A. (1999). Applications of social cognition: Attitudes as cognitive structures. In F. T. Durso (Ed.), *Handbook of applied cognition* (pp. 173–206). New York: John Wiley.

Fallowes, T. (1705). *The best methods for the cure of lunaticks.* London: [for the author].

False claims about fountain of youth oral spray. (2005). Federal Trade Commission, Nov. 18.

Fancher, R. T. (2007). *Health & suffering in America: The context and content of mental health care.* New Brunswick, NJ: Transaction.

Fanelli, D. (2009). How many scientists fabricate and falsify research? A systematic review and meta-analysis of survey data. *PLoS One,* 4:e5738.

Fanta, A. (2006). Jackson, Sharpton lead 1,500 in protest of Florida boot camp death. *Chicago Tribune,* Apr. 22.

Farrell, P. (2010). Book review. David Healy and Edward Shorter, *Shock therapy: A history of electroconvulsive therapy in mental illness. Canadian Bulletin of Medical history.*

Farrington, D. P. (2003). Methodological quality standards for evaluation research. *ANNALS of the American Academy of Political and Social Science,* 587, 49–68.

FDA approved antipsychotic with a long history of failure. (2009). Retrieved on May 7, 2009, from <http://www.ahrp.org/cms/content/view>.

Fearnside, W. W., & Holther, W. B. (1959*). Fallacy: The counterfeit of argument.* Englewood Cliffs, NJ: Prentice-Hall

Feder, B. J. (2007a). Medicare plans to deny coverage of artificial discs. *New York Times,* May 26, B9.

Feder, B. J. (2007b). A TheirSpace for drug sales reps. *New York Times,* June 11, C1.

Feeley, J., & Fisk, M. C. (2010). Johnson and Johnson must pay Louisiana $257.7 million over Risperdal marketing practices. *Bloomberg News,* Oct. 14. Retrieved Oct. 18, 2010, from <http://tinyurl.com/26awovg>.

Feinstein, A. (1967). *Clinical judgment.* Baltimore, MD: Williams & Wilkins.

Feller, C. P., & Cottone, R. R. (2003). Importance of empathy in the therapeutic alliance. *Journal of Humanistic Counseling, Education and Development,* 42, 53–61.

Feltovich, P. J., Ford, K. M., & Hoffman, R. R. (1997). *Expertise in context.* Cambridge, MA: MIT Press.

Feltovich, P. J., Prietula, M. J., & Ericsson, K. A. (2006). Studies of expertise from psychological perspectives. In K. A. Ericsson, N. Charness, P. J. Feltovich, & R. R. Hoffman (Eds.), *Cambridge handbook of expertise and expert performance* (pp. 39–68). New York: Cambridge University Press.

Feltovich, P. J., Sprio, R. J., & Coulson, R. (1993). The nature of conceptual understanding in biomedicine: The keep structure of complex ideas and the development of misconceptions. In D. Evans & V. Patel (Eds.), *Cognitive science in medicine: Biomedical modeling.* Cambridge, MA: MIT Press.

Fenton, J. J., Taplin, S. H., Carney, P. A., Abraham, L., Sickles, E. A., D'Orsi, C., et al. (2007). Influence of computer-aided detection on performance of screening mammography. *New England Medical Journal,* 356, 14.

Fergusson, H., Dornhaus, A., Beeche, A., Borgemeister, C., Gottlieb, M., Mulla, M. S., et al. (2007). It's ecology: A prerequisite for malaria elimination and eradication. *PLoS Med,* 4:e229; doi:10.1371.

Fiano, A. (2010). Sen. Grassley releases report on medical "ghostwriting." July 2. Retrieved July 10, 2010, from <http://www.dotmed.com/legal/print/story.html?nid=13151>.

Fingarette, H. (1988). *Heavy drinking: The myth of alcoholism as a disease*. Berkeley: University of California Press.

Firestone, R. W., & Seiden, R. H. (1987). Microsuicide and suicide threats in everyday life. *Psychotherapy*, 24, 31–39.

Fisher, B., Hall, W., Lenton, S., & Reutter, P. (2010). *Cannabis policy: Moving beyond stalemate*. Oxford: Oxford University Press.

Fisk, M. C., Feeley, J., & Voreacos, D. (2010). J & J pushed Risperdal for elderly after U.S. warning, files show. Retrieved on Mar. 10, 2010, from <http://Bloomberg.com>.

Fitzpatrick, M. (2001). *The tyranny of health: Doctors and the regulation of lifestyle*. London: Routledge.

Florini, A. (Ed.) (2007). *The right to know: Transparency for an open world*. New York: Columbia.

Folsom, C., Fesperman, S. F., Tojuola, B., Sultin, S., & Dahm, P. (2010). Direct-to-consumer advertising for urological pharmaceuticals: A cross-sectional analysis of print media. *Urology*, 75, 1029–33.

Fontanarosa, P. B., Rennie, D., & DeAngelis, C. D. (2004). Editorial. Post marketing surveillance—Lack of vigilance, lack of trust. *Journal of the American Medical Association*, 292, 2647–50.

Ford, J. (2003). Cures that harm: Unanticipated outcomes of crime prevention programs. *ANNALS of the American Academy of Political and Social Science*, 487, 16–30.

Forer, B. R. (1949). The fallacy of personal validation: A classroom demonstration of gullibility. *Journal of Abnormal Psychology*, 44, 118–21.

Forsetlund, L., Bjørndal, A., Rashidian, A., Jamtvedt, G., O'Brien; M. A., Wolf, F., et al. (2009). Continuing education meetings and workshops: Effects and professional practice and health care outcomes. *Cochrane Database of Systematic Reviews*. Issue 3.

Foster, E. M., & Bickman, L. (2000). Refining the costs analyses of the Fort Bragg evaluation: The impact of cost offset and cost shifting. *Mental Health Services Research*, 2(1), 13–25.

Foucault, M. (1965). *Madness and civilization: A history of insanity in the age of reason*. New York: Pantheon.

Foucault, M. (1970). *The Order of things: An archeology of the human sciences*. New York: Pantheon.

Foucault, M. (1973). *The birth of the clinic: An archeology of medical perception*. New York: Pantheon.

Foucault, M. (1977). *Discipline and punish: The birth of the prison*. New York: Pantheon.

Foucault, M. (1980). *Power/knowledge: Selected interviews and other writings, 1972–1977*. New York: Pantheon.

Foucault, M. (1982). *The archeology of knowledge & the discourse of language*. New York: Pantheon.

Foxcraft, L. (2009). *Hot flushes, cold science: A history of the modern menopause*. London: Granta.

Foxx, R. M., & Roland, C. E. (2005). The self-esteem fallacy. In J. W. Jacobson, R. M. Foxx, & J. A. Mulick (Eds.), *Controversial therapies for developmental disabilities: Fad, fashion, and science in professional practice* (pp. 101–10). Mahwah, NJ: Erlbaum.

Frances, A. (2009). A warning sign on the road to DSM-V: Beware of its unintended consequences. *Psychiatric Times*, 1–6.

Frances, A. (2010a). DSM5 suggests opening the door to behavioral addictions. *Psychiatric Times*, Apr. 23.

Frances, A. (2010b). DSM5 temper dysregulation—Good intentions, bad solution. *Psychiatric Times*, Apr. 21.

Frances, A. (2010c). The first draft of DSM-V: If accepted, will fan the flames of false positive diagnoses. Editorial. *BMJ*, 340:c1168.

Frances, A. (2010d). New guidelines for diagnosing Alzheimer's wishful thinking with dangerous consequences. *Psychiatric Times*, July 23.

Frances, A. (2010e). Normality is an endangered species: Psychiatric fads and overdiagnosis. *Psychiatric Times*, July 6. <http://www.psychiatrictimes.com/dsm-5>.

Frances, A. (2010f). Opening Pandora's Box: The 19 worst suggestions for DSM5. *Psychiatric Times*. Feb. 11. <http://www.psychiatrictimes.com>.

Frankfurt, H. G. (1986). On bullshit. *Raritan*, 6, 81–100.

Frankfurt, H. G. (2005). *On bullshit*. Princeton, NJ: Princeton University Press.

Frankl, V. (1967). *Psychotherapy and existentialism*. Harmondsworth: Penguin.

Frazer, J. G. (1925). *The golden bough: A study in magic and religion*. London: Macmillan.

Freeman, A. C., & Sweeney, K. (2001). Why general practitioners do not implement evidence: Qualitative study. *BMJ*, 323:1–5.

Freeman, W., & Watts, J. W. (1944). Psychosurgery: An evaluation of 200 cases over seven years. *Journal of Mental Science*, 90, 532–37.

Freire, P. (1973). *Education for critical consciousness*. New York: Seabury Press.

Freire, P. (1993). *Pedagogy of the oppressed*. New York: Continuum.

Freud, S. (1914). *Psychopathology of everyday life*. New York: Macmillan.

Freudenheim, R. (2008). The middleman's markup: Benefits managers earn profit with exclusive rights on specialty drugs. *New York Times*, Apr. 19, B1/4.

Friedan, B. (1963). *The feminine mystique*. New York: W. W. Norton.

Friedson, E. (Ed.) (1973). *Professions and their prospects*. Beverly Hills, CA: Sage.

Fritz, M. (1993). Evidence of abuse by psychiatric hospitals. *APA Monitor*, 24(1), 20.

Fritz, M. (2001). Forced drugging of outpatients is controversial. *Wall Street Journal*, Feb. 01.

Fromm, E. (1941). *Escape from freedom*. New York: Farrar & Rinehart.

Frosch, D. L., Krueger, P. M., Hornik, R. C., Cronholm, P. F., & Barg, F. K. (2007). Creating demand for prescription drugs: A content analysis of television direct-to-consumer advertising. *Annals of Family Medicine*, 5, 6–13.

Fugh-Berman, A. J. (2010). The haunting of medical journals: How ghostwriting sold "HRT." *PLoS Med*, 7(9):e1000335.

Fugh-Berman, A., & Ahari, S. (2007). Following the script: how drug reps make friends and influence doctors. *PLoS Med*, 4:e150.

Fuller, S. (2011). Beyond the dualism of the ADHD epidemic, Doctor of Education Symposia Conference: Culture and Literacies, School of Education, Flinders University, Australia.

Furedi, F. (2002). *Culture of fear: Risk-taking and the morality of low expectation* (Rev. ed.). New York: Continuum.

Furnham, A. F. (1988). *Lay theories: Everyday understanding of problems in the social sciences*. New York: Pergamon.

Furnham, A. F. (2004). The Barnum effect in medicine. *Complimentary Therapies in Medicine*, 2, 1–4.

Gabbay, D. M., & Woods, J. (2005). *A practical logic of cognitive systems*. Vol. 2. Amsterdam: Elsevier-North Holland.

Gabbay, D. M., & Woods, J. (2009). Games: Unifying logic, language, and philosophy. *Logic, Epistemology, and the Unity of Science*, 15, 57–98.

Gabbay, D. M., Woods, J., & Thagard, P. (Eds.) (2011). *Handbook of a philosophy of science*. Vol. 16, *Philosophy of medicine*. Edited by F. Gifford. Amsterdam: Elsevier North Holland.

Gagnon, M. A. (2010). Veblenian analysis of Big Pharma's intangible assets: Capitalizing medical bias. Presented at Association for Institutional Thought. Reno, NV, April.

Gagnon, M. A., & Lexchin, J. (2008). The cost of pushing pills: A new estimate of pharmaceutical promotion expenditures in the United States. *PLoS Med*, 5:e1.

Galik, M. (1996). Melancholy in Europe and China: Some observations of a student of intercultural process. *Asian and African Studies*, 5, 50–69.

Gambrill, E. D. (1982). Self-help books: Pseudoscience in the guise of science. *Skeptical Inquirer*, 16, 389–99.

Gambrill, E. (1997). Social work education: Possible futures. In M. Reisch & E. Gambrill (Eds.), *Social work in the 21st century* (pp. 317–27). Thousand Oaks, CA: Pine Forge Press.

Gambrill, E. (1999). Evidence-based practice: An alternative to authority-based practice. *Families in Society*, 80, 341–50.

Gambrill, E. (2001). Social work practice: An authority based profession. *Research on Social Work Practice*, 11, 166–75.

Gambrill, E. (2003). Evidence based practice: Sea change or the emperor's new clothes? *Journal of Social Work Education*, 39, 3–23.

Gambrill, E. (2006). Evidence-based practice: Choices ahead. *Research on Social Work Practice*, 16, 338–57.

Gambrill, E. (2011). Evidence-based practice and the ethics of discretion. *Journal of Social Work*, 11, 1–23.

Gambrill, E. (2012). *Critical thinking in clinical practice: Improving the quality of judgment and decisions* (3rd ed.). New Jersey: John Wiley & Sons, Inc.

Gambrill, E. D., & Gibbs, L. (2002). Making practice decisions: Is what's good for the goose good for the gander? *Ethical Human Sciences & Services*, 4(1), 31–46.

Gambrill, E., & Gibbs, L. E. (2009). *Critical thinking for the helping professions: A skills-based workbook* (3rd ed.). New York: Oxford University Press.

Gambrill, E., & Reiman, A. (2011). A propaganda index for reviewing articles and manuscripts: An exploratory study. *PLoS One*, 6, e19516.

Gambrill, E., & Shlonsky, A. (2001). The need for comprehensive risk management systems in child welfare. *Children and Youth Services Review*, 23, 79–107.

Gambrill, E., Shaw, T., & Reiman, A. (2006). A critical appraisal of master's students research projects in social work. Presented at Annual Program meeting of the Council on Social Work Education.

Gamwell, L., & Tomes, N. (1995). *Madness in America: Cultural and medical perceptions of mental illness before 1914*. Birmingham, NY: Cornell University Press.

Gandhi, A. G., Murphy-Graham, E., Petrosino, A., Chrismer, S. S., & Weiss, C. H. (2007). The devil is in the details: Examining the evidence for "proven" school-based drug abuse prevention programs. *Evaluation Review*, 31, 43–74.

Ganzach, Y. (2000). The weighing of pathological and non-pathological information in clinical judgment. *Acta Psychologia*, 104, 87–1091.

Garb, H. N. (1998). *Studying the clinician: Judgment, research and psychological assessment*. Washington, DC: American Psychological Association.

Garcia-Lizana, F., & Munoz-Mayorga, I. (2010). What about telepsychiatry?: A systematic review. Primary Care Companion, *J. of Clin.Psychiatry*, 12(2). <http://www.ncbi.nlm.gov/pmc/article>.

Gawande, A. (2010). *The checklist manifesto: How to get things right.* New York: Metropolitan Books.

Gelles, R. J. (1982). Applying research on family violence to clinical practice. *Journal of Marriage and the Family,* 44, 9–20.

Gellner, E. (1992). *Postmodernism, reason, and religion.* New York: Routledge.

Georgia psychologists use depression campaigns to strengthen referral network. (1993). *Practitioner Update,* 1(2), May, 3.

Gerth, J., & Stolberg, S. G. (2000). Drug makers reap profits on tax-backed research. *New York Times,* Apr. 23, A1/20.

Gever, J. (2008). Senator demands records of the American Psychiatric Association—Drug industry fiscal ties. *New York Times,* July 14, A1.

Geyman, J. P., Deyo, R. A., & Ramsey, S. D. (2000). *Evidence-based clinical practice: Concepts and approaches.* Boston: Butterworth Heinemann.

Gibbs, L. E. (1991). *Scientific reasoning for social workers: Bridging the gap between research and practice.* New York: Macmillan.

Gibbs, L., & Gambrill, E. (2002). Evidence-based practice: Counter-arguments to objections. *Research on Social Work Practice,* 12, 452–76.

Gibson, M. (1998). The masculine degenerate: American doctors' portrayals of the lesbian intellect, 1880–1949. *Journal of Women's History,* 9, 1042.

Giddens, A. (1990). *The consequences of modernity.* Stanford, CA: Stanford University Press.

Gigerenzer, G. (2002a). *Calculated risks: How to know when numbers deceive you.* New York: Simon & Schuster.

Gigerenzer, G. (2002b). *Reckoning with risk: Learning to live with uncertainty.* New York: Penguin.

Gigerenzer, G. (2005). Fast and frugal heuristics: The tools of bounded rationality. In D. J. Koehler & N. Harvey (Eds.), *The Blackwell handbook of judgment and decision making* (pp. 62–88). Malden, MA: Blackwell.

Gigerenzer, G. (2007). *Gut feelings: The intelligence of the unconscious.* New York: Viking.

Gigerenzer, G., & Brighton, H. (2011). Homo heuristicus: Why biased minds make better inferences. In G. Gigerenzer, R. Hertwig, & T. Pachur (Eds.), *Heuristics: The foundations of adaptive behavior* (pp. 2–27). New York: Oxford.

Gigerenzer, G., & Edwards, A. (2003). Simple tools to understand risks: From innumeracy to insight. *BMJ,* 327, 741–44.

Gigerenzer, G., Hoffrage, U., & Goldstein, D. G. (2008). Fast and frugal heuristics are plausible models of cognition: Reply to Dougherty, Franco-Watkins, & Thomas (2008), *Psychological Review,* 111, 230–39.

Gigerenzer, G., Gaissmaier, W., Kurz-Milcke, E., Schwartz, L. M., & Woloshin, S. (2008). Helping doctors and patients make sense of health statistics. *Psychological Science in the Public Interest,* 8, 53–96.

Gilbert, P. (1989). *Human nature and suffering.* New York: Guilford.

Giles, J. (2008). Did GSK [GlaxoSmithKline] trial mask Paxil suicide risk? *New Scientist.* Feb. 8.

Gill, S. S., Bronskill, S.E., Normand, S-L. T., Anderson, G. M., Sykora, K., Lam, K., et al. (2007). Antipsychotic drug use and mortality in older adults with dementia. *ANNALS of Internal Medicine,* 146, 775–86.

Gilovich, T. (1993). *How we know what isn't so: The fallibility of human reason in everyday life.* New York: Free Press.

Gilovich, T., & Griffin, D. (2002). Introduction—Heuristics and biases: Then and now. In T. Gilovich, D. Griffin, & D. Kahneman (Eds.), *Heuristics and biases: The psychology of intuitive judgement* (pp. 1–18). New York: Cambridge University Press.

Gilovitch, T., & Savitsky, K. (2002). Like goes with like: The role of representativeness in erroneous and pseudo-scientific beliefs. In T. Gilovich, D. Griffin, & D. Kahneman (Eds.), *Heuristics and biases: The psychology of intuitive judgment* (pp. 616–24). New York: Cambridge University Press.

Glassner, B. (1999). *The culture of fear: Why Americans are afraid of the wrong things.* New York: Basic Books.

Glasziou, P., Del Mar, C., & Salisgury, J. (2003). *Evidence-based medicine workbook.* London: BMJ.

Glasziou, P., Van den Broucke, J., & Chalmers, I. (2004). Assessing the quality of research. *BMJ*, 328:39–41.

Glasziou, P., Chalmers, I., Rawlins, M., & McCulloch, P. (2007). When are randomized trials unnecessary? Picking signal from noise. *BMJ*, 334:349–51.

Godden, D. M., & Walton, D. (2006). Argument from expert opinion as legal evidence: Critical questions in admissibility criteria of expert testimony in the American legal system. *Ratio Juris*, 19, 261–86.

Godlee, F. (2009). Less medicine is more. *BMJ*, 338:b2561.

Godlee, F. (2010). Are we at risk of being at risk? *BMJ*, 341:c4766.

Goffman, E. (1961). *Asylums: Essays on the social situation of mental patients and other inmates.* New York: Anchor Press.

Goffman, E. (1974). *Frame analysis: An essay on the organization of experience.* New York: Harper & Row.

Goffman, E. I. (1990). Stigma: Notes on the management of spoiled identity. London: Penguin.

Goldberg, L. R. (1959). The effectiveness of clinicians' judgments: The diagnosis of organic brain damage from the Bender-Gestalt Test. *Journal of Consulting Psychology*, 23, 25–33.

Goldenberg, I. I. (1978). *Oppression and social intervention: The human condition and the problem of change.* Chicago: Nelson Hall.

Gomory, T., Wong, S. E., Cohen, D., & LaCasse, J. R. (in press). Clinical social work and the biomedical industrial complex. *Journal of Sociology and Social Work.*

Goode, W. J. (1978). *The celebration of heroes: Prestige as a social control system.* Berkeley: University of California Press.

Goodman, S., & Greenland, S. (2007). Why most published research findings are false: Problems in the analysis. *PLoS Med*, 4(4):e165le168.

Goodnough, A. (2010). A wave of addiction and crime, with the medicine cabinet to blame. *New York Times National*, Sept. 24, A1/15.

Gorman, D. M. (1998). The irrelevance of evidence in the development of school-based drug prevention policy, 1986–1996. *Evaluation Review*, 22(1), 118–46.

Gorman, D. M. (2003a). The best of practices, the worst of practices: The making of evidence-based primary prevention programs. *Psychiatric Services*, 54, 1087–89.

Gorman, D. M. (2003b). Prevention programs and scientific nonsense. *Policy Review*, 17, 65–75.

Gorman, D. M. (2005). Drug and violence prevention: Rediscovering the critical rational dimension of evaluation research. *Journal of Experimental Criminology*, 1, 39–62.

Gorman, D. M. & Huber, J. C. (2009). The social construction of "evidence-based" drug prevention programs: A reanalysis of data from the Drug Abuse Resistance Education (DARE) Program. *Evaluation Review*, 33, 396–414.

Gornall, J. (2009). Industry attack on academics. *BMJ*, 338:b736.
Gosling. F. G. (1987). *Before Freud: Neurasthenia and the American medical community, 1870–1910*. Urbana: University of Illinois Press.
Gottlieb, S. (2000). Firm tried to block report on failure of AIDS vaccine, *BMJ*, 321:1173.
Gottman, J. M., & Rushe, R. H. (1993). The analysis of change: Issues, fallacies and new ideas. *Journal of Consulting and Clinical Psychology*, 61, 907–10.
Gotzsche, P. C. (2002). Commentary: Medicalization of risk factors. *BMJ*, 324, 890–891.
Gotzsche, P. C. (2004). On the benefits and harms of screening for breast cancer. *International Journal of Epidemiology*, 33, 56–64.
Gotzsche, P. C., & Nielsen, M. (2006). Screening for breast cancer with mammography. *Cochrane Database Syst. Rev.*, 4, CD001877.
Gotzsche, P. C., Liberati, A., Torri, V., & Rossetti, L. (1996). Beware of surrogate endpoints. *International Journal of Technology Assessment in Health Care*, 12, 238–46.
Gotzsche, P. C., Hartling, O. J., Nielsen, M., Brodersen, J., & Jørgensen, K. J. (2009). Analysis: Breast screening: The facts—or maybe not. *BMJ*, 338:b86.
Gould, P. (2009). Radiation overdose in 200 patients leads to FDA safety notice. *BMJ*, 339:b4217.
Goulding, R. (2004). One in twelve older people are prescribed the wrong drug. *Archives of Internal Medicine*, 164, 305–12.
Grady, C. (2000). Breast cancer study shows signs of more serious fraud. *New York Times*, Mar. 10, A13.
Grady, C. (2004). F.D.A. employee seeking help from whistle blower group. *New York Times*, Nov. 24, A21.
Grady, C. (2007). Studies find harm in 2 Parkinson's drugs. *New York Times*, Jan. 4, A15.
Grady, C. (2010). Hospitals make no headway in curbing errors, study says. *New York Times*, Nov. 25, 1/26.
Grady, D. (1999). Medical journal cites misleading drug research. *New York Times*, Nov. 10, A1/8.
Graebner, W. (1987). *The engineering of consent*. Madison: University of Wisconsin Press.
Gray, J. A. M. (2001a). *Evidence-based health care: How to make health policy and management decisions*. New York: Churchill Livingston.
Gray, J. A. M. (2001b). Evidence-based medicine for professionals. In A. Edwards & G. Elwyn (Eds.), *Evidence-based patient choice: Inevitable or impossible?* (pp. 19–33). New York: Oxford University Press.
Gray, W. D. (1991). *Thinking critically about New Age ideas*. Belmont, CA: Wadsworth.
Green, J., Czanner, G., Reeves, G., Watson, J., Wise, L., & Beral, V. (2010). Oral bisphosphonates and risk of cancer of oesophagus, stomach, and colorectum: Case-control analysis within a UK primary care cohort. *BMJ*, 341:c4444.
Greenberg, D. S. (2007). *Science for sale: The perils, delusions and rewards of campus capitalism*. Chicago: University of Chicago Press.
Greenberg, S. A. (2009). How citation distortions create unfounded authority: Analysis of a citation network. *BMJ*, 339:b2680.
Greenhalgh, T. (2010). *How to read a paper: The basis of evidence based medicine* (3rd ed.). London: BMJ Press.
Greenhouse, L. (2008). Justices shield medical devices from lawsuits. *New York Times*, Feb. 21, A1.
Greenhouse, S. (2010). Ex-worker says her firing was based on genetic tests. *New York Times*, Mar. 1, A12.

Greenwald, G. (2009). *Drug decriminalization in Portugal: Lessons for creating fair and successful drug policies.* Retrieved Jan. 28, 2011, from the CATO Institute website <http://www.cato.org/pub>.

Greismann, L. (2009). Direct to consumer genetic testing: Public right or public harm? *Intersect,* 2, 21–28.

Grice, H. P. (1975). Logic and conversation. In P. Cole & J. Morgan (Eds.), *Syntax and semantics* (Vol. 3, pp. 41–58). New York: Academic Press.

Grilli, R., Magrini, N., Penna, A., Mura, G., & Liberati, A. (2000). Practice guidelines developed by specialty societies: The need for a critical appraisal. *Lancet,* 355, 103–6.

Gross, P. R., & Levitt, N. (1994). *Higher superstition: The academic left and its quarrels with science.* Baltimore, MD: Johns Hopkins University Press.

Grouse, L. (2008). Physicians for sale: How medical professional organizations exploit their members. *Medscape J Med,* 10(7), 169.

Grove, W. M., & Meehl, P. E. (1996). Comparing efficiency of informal (subjective, impressionistic) and formal (mechanical, algorithmic) prediction procedures: The clinical-statistical controversy. *Psychology, Public Policy & Law,* 2, 293–323.

Guidelines for Environmental Risk Assessment and Management. Published Aug. 2, 2000, and page last modified Aug. 26, 2009. Parliamentary Office of Science and Technology in the U.K.

Gusfield, J. R. (1996). *Contested meanings: The construction of alcohol problems.* Madison: University of Wisconsin Press.

Gusfield, J. R. (2003). Constructing the ownership of social problems: Fun and profit in the welfare state. In J. D. Orcutt & D. R. Ruby (Eds.), *Drugs, alcohol, and social problems* (pp. 7–18). New York: Roman & Littlefield.

Gustafson, S., Nassar, S., & Waddell, D. (2011). Single-case design in psychophysiological research. Part I: Context, structure, and techniques.

Guyatt, G., & Rennie, D. (2002). Users' guides to the medical literature: A manual for evidence-based clinical practice. Chicago: American Medical Association.

Guyatt, G., Rennie, D., Meade, M. O., & Cook, D. J. (2008). *Users' guides to the medical literature: A manual for evidence-based clinical practice* (2nd ed.). Chicago: American Medical Association.

Guyatt, G. H., Oxman, A. D., Schunemann, H. J., Tugwell, P., & Knotterus, A. (2010). GRADE guidelines: A new series of articles in the Journal of Clinical Epidemiology, *Journal of Epidemiology.* <http://www.gradeworkinggroup.org>.

Hacking, I. (1991). The making and molding of child abuse, *Critical Inquiry,* 17, 264–74.

Hacking, I. (1992). Statistical language, statistical truth, and statistical reason: The self-authentification of a style of scientific reasoning. In E. McMullin (Ed.), *The Social Dimensions of Science* (pp. 148–49). Notre Dame, IN: Notre Dame University Press.

Hacking, I. (1995). The looping effect of human kinds. In D. Sperber, D. Premack, & A. J. Premack (Eds.), *Casual cognition: A multidisciplinary debate* (pp. 351–83). Oxford: Clarendon Press.

Hadler, N. M. (2004). *The last well person: How to stay well despite the health-care system.* Montreal and Ithaca: McGill-Queen's University Press.

Hadler, N. (2008). *Worried sick: A prescription for health in overtreated America.* Chapel Hill, NC: University of North Carolina Press.

Hall, C. C., Ariss, L., & Todorov, A. (2007). The illusion of knowledge: When more information reduces accuracy and increases confidence. *Organizational Behavior and Human Decision Processes,* 103, 277–90.

Hall, W. D., Mathews, R., & Morley, K. I. (2010). Being more realistic about the public health impact of genomic medicine. *PLoS Med*, 7(10):e1000347. doi:10.1371/journal.pmed.100347.

Halpern, D. F. (2003). *Thought & knowledge: An introduction to critical thinking* (4th ed.). Mahwah, NJ: Erlbaum.

Halpern, J. (2001). *From detached concern to empathy: Humanizing medical practice*. New York: Oxford University Press.

Halsted, W. (1894). The results of operations for the cure of cancer of the breast performed at the Johns Hopkins Hospital from June 1889 to January 1894. *Johns Hopkins Hospital Reports*, 297.

Hamblin, C. L. (1970). *Fallacies*. London: Methuen.

Hamilton, C. (2005). *Growth fetish*. Sterling, VA: Pluto.

Hammond, K. R. (1996). *Human judgment and social policy: Irreducible uncertainty, inevitable error, and unavoidable injustice*. New York: Oxford University Press.

Handler, J. F., & Hasenfeld, Y. (1991). *The moral construction of poverty: Welfare reform in America*. Newbury Park, CA: Sage.

Handler, J. F., & Hasenfeld, Y. (2007). *Blame welfare, ignore poverty and inequality*. New York: Cambridge University Press.

Hanks, H., Hobbs, C., & Wynne, J. (1988). Early signs and recognition of sexual abuse in the preschool child. In K. Browne, C. Davies, & P. Stratton (Eds.), *Early prediction and prevention of child abuse*. Chichester (UK): John Wiley.

Hanson, B. (2007). Michigan lawsuit uncovers psychiatry's dark secret: Psychiatric drug-induced movement disorders in young children. From Spring 2007 newslettter of the International Center for the Study of Psychiatry and Psychology (<http://www.iscpp.org>). Preventive Psychiatry E-Newsletter #237. Retrieved August 8, 2011, from <http://www.invisiblechildren.org>.

Hanson, F. A. (1993). *Testing, testing*. Berkeley: University of California Press.

Hare, E. H. (1962). Masturbatory insanity: The history of an idea. *Journal of Mental Science*, 108, 1–25.

Harlow, H. F. (1964). Early social deprivation and later behavior in the monkey. In A. Abrams, H. H. Gurner, & J. E. P. Tomal (Eds.), *Unfinished tasks in the behavioral sciences* (pp. 154–73). Baltimore, MD: Williams & Wilkins.

Harmon, A. (2010). Indian tribe wins fight to limit research of its DNA. *New York Times*, April 21.

Harmon, G. (1986). *Change in view: Principles of Reasoning*. Cambridge, MA: MIT Press.

Harmon, K. (2009). Designer focuses on marketing adjustable eyeglasses at $1 a pair. *Scientific American*, Feb. 24.

Harriet, A. (2006). *Medical apartheid: The dark history of medical experimentation on Black Americans from colonial times to the present*. New York: Doubleday.

Harris, G. (2004a). As doctor writes prescription, drug company writes a check. *New York Times*, A1/20.

Harris, G. (2004b). At F.D.A., strong drug ties and less monitoring. *New York Times*, Dec. 6.

Harris, G. (2004c). Expert kept from speaking at antidepressant hearing. *New York Times*, Apr. 16, A16.

Harris, G. (2005). Popular drugs for dementia tied to deaths. *New York Times*, Apr. 12, A15.

Harris, G. (2006a). Study condemns F.D.A.'s handling of drug safety: Sweeping changes urged. *New York Times*, Sept. 23, A1/A9.

Harris, G. (2006b). System said to fail to steer women from acne drug. *New York Times*, Feb. 11, A11.

Harris, G. (2007a). F.D.A. rule limits role of advisers tied to industry. *New York Times*, Mar. 22, A1/20.

Harris, G. (2007b). Potentially incompatible goals of F.D.A.: Critics say a push to approve drugs is compromising safety. *New York Times*, June 11, A16.

Harris, G. (2007c). Psychiatrists top list of drug maker gifts. *New York Times*, June 27, A14.

Harris, G. (2007d). Surgeon General says he is enduring political stress. *New York Times*, July 11, A1/16.

Harris, G. (2008a). In documents, ties between child psychiatric center and drug makers. *New York Times*, Nov. 25, A8.

Harris, G. (2008b). Research center tied to drug company. *New York Times*, November 25.

Harris, G. (2009a). Doctor's pain studies were fabricated, hospital says. *New York Times*, Mar. 10, A22.

Harris, G. (2009b). Drug makers are advocacy group's biggest donors. *New York Times*. Oct. 21, A25.

Harris, G. (2009c). Crackdown on doctors who take kickbacks. *New York Times*, Mar. 4, A11/12.

Harris, G. (2009d). In F.D.A. files: Claims of leniency and a rush to approve medical devices. *New York Times*, Jan. 13, A14.

Harris, G. (2009e). Pfizer pays $2.3 billion to settle marketing case. *New York Times*, Sept. 3.

Harris, G. (2009f). Report criticizes F.D.A. on device testing. *New York Times*, Jan. 16, A15.

Harris, G. (2009g). 3 researchers at Harvard are named in subpoena. *New York Times*, Mar. 28, A8.

Harris, G. (2010a). After many stent procedures, multiple lawsuits. *New York Times*, Dec. 6, A15.

Harris, G. (2010b). Caustic government report deals blow to diabetes drug. *New York Times*, July 10, A1/12.

Harris, G. (2010c). Controversial diabetes drug harms heart, U.S. concludes. February 19.

Harris, G. (2010d). Diabetes drug maker hid test data, files indicate. *New York Times*, July 13.

Harris, G. (2010e). F.D.A. disputes finding that Avandia is safe. *New York Times*, July 9.

Harris, G. (2010f). F.D.A. panel votes to restrict Avandia. *New York Times*, July 14.

Harris, G. (2010g). F.D.A. says it was urged to approve knee patch. *New York Times*, Oct. 15, A19.

Harris, G. (2010h). F.D.A. to restrict a diabetes drug, citing heart risk. Europe suspends sales. *New York Times National*, Sept. 24, A1/15.

Harris, G. (2011). Antipsychotic drugs called hazardous for the elderly. *New York Times*, May 9.

Harris, G., & Berenson, A. (2005). Ten voters on panel backing pain pills had industry ties. *New York Times*, Feb. 25.

Harris, G., & Berenson, A. (2009). Settlement called near on Zyprexa. *New York Times*, Jan. 15, B1.

Harris, G., & Carey, B. (2008). Researchers fail to reveal full drug pay. *New York Times*, June 8, C1/28.

Harris, G., & Roberts, J. (2007a). After sanctions, doctors get drug company pay. *New York Times*, June 3, A1.

Harris, G., & Roberts, J. (2007b). Doctors' ties to drug makers are put on close view. *New York Times*, Mar. 21, A1.

Harris, G., Carey, B., & Roberts, T. (2007). Psychiatrists, children and the drug industry's role. *New York Times*, May 10.

Hart, C., & Wellings, K. (2002). Sexual behavior and its medicalization: In sickness and in health. *BMJ*, 324, 7342.

Hastie, R., & Dawes, R. (2001). *Rational choice in an uncertain world: The psychology of judgment and decision making.* Thousand Oaks, CA: Sage.

Hathaway, S. R. (1948). Some considerations relative to nondirective counseling. *Journal of Clinical Psychology*, 4, 226–31.

Hawkes, N. (2009). Standing up for safety. *BMJ*, 338, b2286.

Hawthorne, F. (2005). *Inside the FDA: The business and politics behind the drugs we take and the food we eat.* Hoboken, NJ: John Wiley & Sons.

Hayakawa, S. I. (1978). *Language in thought and action* (4th ed.). New York: Harcourt Brace Jovanovich.

Hayek, F. A. (1976). *Law, legislation and liberty*, Vol. 2: *The mirage of social justice*. Chicago: University of Chicago Press.

Hayek, F. (1980). *The counter revolution of science: Studies in the abuse of reason.* Liberty Fund. June 1.

Health Letter. Public citizens research group, Federal Trade Commission, National Council Against Health Fraud, Center for Media Education.

Healy, D. (2001). *Psychopharmacology & the government of the self.* CBC National. Sept. 24. <http://pharmapolitics.com>.

Healy, D. (2002a). Conflicting interests in Toronto: Anatomy of a controversy at the interface of academia and industry. *Perspectives of Biology and Medicine*, 45, 250–63.

Healy, D. (2002b). *The creation of psychopharmacology.* Cambridge, MA: Harvard University Press.

Healy, D. (2004). *Let them eat Prozac: The unhealthy relationship between the pharmaceutical industry and depression.* New York: New York University Press.

Healy, D. (2006a). Did regulators fail over selective serotonin reuptake inhibitors. *BMJ*, 333:92–95.

Healy, D. (2006b). The latest mania: Selling bipolar disorder. *PLoS Med*, 3(4):e185.

Healy, D. (2006c). Manufacturing consensus. *Culture, Medicine and Psychiatry*, 30(2), 135–56.

Healy, D., & Thase, M. E. (2003). Is academic psychiatry for sale? *British Journal of Psychiatry*, 182, 388–91.

Heath, I. (2006). Combating disease mongering: Daunting but nonetheless essential. *PloS Med*, 3(4):e146.

Henriksen, K., & Dayton, E. (2006). Organizational silence and hidden threats to patients' safety. *Health Services Research*, 41, 1539–54.

Herbert, B. (2010). Too long ignored. *New York Times*, Aug. 21, A17.

Herer, J. (2000). *The emperor wears no clothes* (11th Ed.). Van Nuys, CA: AH HA Pub.

Heritage, J. & Clayman, S. (2010). *Talk in action: Interactions, identities and institutions.* Malden, MA: Wiley-Blackwell.

Hirsch, E. D., Jr. (1996). *The schools we need and why we don't have them.* New York: Doubleday.

Herzberg, D. (2009). *Happy pills in America: From Miltown to Prozac.* Baltimore, MD: Johns Hopkins University Press.

Heyman, G. M. (2009). *Addiction: A disorder of choice*. Cambridge, MA: Harvard University Press.

Higgins, J. P. T., & Greene, S. (Eds.) (2008). *Cochrane handbook for systematic reviews of interventions*. Chichester (UK): John Wiley & Sons.

Hilgartner, S. (2000). *Science on stage: Expert advice as public drama*. Stanford, CA: Stanford University Press.

Hilgartner, S., & Bosk, C. L. (1988). The rise and fall of social problems: A public arena's model. *American Journal of Sociology*, 94, 53–78.

Hilts, P. J. (1995). Drug maker admits it concealed test results that showed flaws. *New York Times*, Nov. 29, A1/C17.

Hilts, P. J. (2000). Company tried to bar report that H.I.V. vaccine failed. *New York Times*, Sept. 11, 26.

Hinds, P. J. (1999). The curse of expertise: The effects of expertise and debiasing methods on prediction of novice performance. *Journal of Experimental Psychology: Applied*, 5, 205–21.

Hobbs, C. J., & Wynne, J. M. (1989). Sexual abuse of English boys and girls: The importance of anal examination. *Child Abuse and Neglect*, 13, 195–210.

Hobbs, N. (1975). *The futures of children: Recommendations of the Project on Classification of Exceptional Children*. San Francisco: Jossey-Bass.

Hoffman, S. (2006). "Racially-tailored" medicine unraveled. *American University Law Review*, 55, 395–452.

Hoffrage, U., & Gigerenzer, G. (1998). Using natural frequencies to improve diagnostic inferences. *Academic Medicine*, 73, 538–40.

Hogarth, R. M. (2001). *Educating intuition*. Chicago: University of Chicago Press.

Holden, D. J., Jonas, D. E., Porterfield, D. S., Reuland, D., & Harris, R. (2010). Systematic review: Enhancing the use and quality of colorectal cancer screening. *Ann Intern Med*, 152, 668–76.

Holding, R. (2003). Medicare bilked for billions in bogus claims. *San Francisco Chronicle*, Jan. 12, A1.

Hook, D., & Eagle, G. (Eds.) (2002). *Psychopathology and social prejudice*. Cape Town: University of Cape Town Press.

Hook, E. B. (2002). *Prematurity in scientific discovery: On resistance and neglect*. Berkeley: University of California Press.

Horkheimer, M., & Odorno, T. (1972). The culture industry as mass deception. In *Dialectic of enlightenment*, trans. John Cummings. New York: Herder and Herder.

Horwitz, A. V. (2002). *Creating mental illness*. Chicago: University of Chicago Press.

Horwitz, A. V., & Wakefield, J. C. (2007). *The loss of sadness: How psychiatry transformed normal sorrow into depressive disorder*. New York: Oxford University Press.

Hotez, P. J. (2008). Neglected infections of poverty in the United States of America. *PLoS Neglected Tropical Diseases*, 2(6), e256.

Houts, A. C. (2002). Discovery, invention, and the expansion of the modern diagnostic and statistical manuals of mental disorders. In L. E. Beutler & M. L. Malik (Eds.), *Rethinking the DSM: A psychological perspective* (pp. 17–65). Washington, DC: American Psychological Association.

Howard, P. (1994). *The death of common sense*. New York: Random House.

Howard, W. L. (1900). Effeminate men and masculine women. *New York Medical Journal*, 71, 687.

Hrobjartsson, A., & Gotzsche, P. C. (2010). Placebo interventions for all clinical conditions. *Cochrane Database Syst Rev.*, Jan 20(1), CD003974.

Huber, R. B. (1963). *Influencing through argument*. New York: David McKay.

Huck, S. W., & Sandler, H. M. (1979). *Rival hypotheses: Alternative interpretations of data based conclusions*. New York: Harper & Row.

Hudson, K. (1978). *The jargon of the professions*. London: Macmillan.

Huff, D. (1954). *How to lie with statistics*. New York: W. W. Norton.

Hughes, C. E., & Stevens, A. (2010). What can we learn from the Portuguese decriminalization of illicit drugs? *British J. of Criminology*, 50, 999–1022.

Hughes, S. (2010a). Accusations of bias among FDA Rosiglitazone panel. *Heartwire*.

Hughes, S. (2010b). More evidence against GSK and FDA on rosiglitazone. Retrieved Aug. 8, 2011, from <http://www.theheart.org/article/1097979.do>.

Hutchins, J., Gardner, F., & Bywater, T. (2007). Parenting intervention in sure start services for children at risk of developing conduct disorder: Pragmatic randomized controlled trial. *BMJ*, 334, 678–82.

Huxley, A. [1932] (1969). *Brave new world*. New York: Harper/Perennial.

Huxley, A. (1958). *Tyranny over the mind: A shocking new look at today's world*. Long Island, NY: Newsday.

Huxley, A. (2005). *Brave new world and brave new world revisited*. New York: Harper Perennial.

Hyman, R. (1989). *The illusive quarry: A scientific appraisal of psychical research*. Amhurst, NY: Prometheus Books.

Illich, I. (1976). *Limits to medicine. Medical nemesis: The expropriation of health*. New York: Pantheon Books.

Illich, I., et al. (1977). *Disabling professions*. Salem, NH: M. Boyars.

Illouz, E. (2003). *Oprah Winfrey and the glamour of misery: An essay on popular culture*. New York: Columbia.

Illouz, E. (2008). *Saving the modern soul: Therapy, emotions, and the culture of self-help*. Berkeley: University of California Press.

Institute of Propaganda Analysis (1937). Seven rules of propaganda.

Institute for Propaganda Analysis. (1938). *Propaganda analysis*. New York: Columbia University Press.

Institute for Propaganda Analysis. (1939). *The fine art of propaganda*. New York: Harcourt, Brace, and Company.

Ioannidis, J. P. A. (2005). Why most published research findings are false. *PLoS Medicine*, 2, e124.

Ioannidis, J. P. A. (2008a). Some main problems eroding the credibility and relevance of randomized controlled trials. *Bull. NYU 3 Hosp Jt Dis*, 66, 135–39.

Ioannidis, J. P. (2008b). Why most discovered true associations are inflated. *Epidemiology*, 19, 640–48.

Isaacs, D., & Fitzgerald, D. (1999). Seven alternatives to evidence based medicine. *BMJ*, 319, 1618.

Isaacs, T. (2009). Breast cancer deception month: Hiding the truth beneath a sea of pink. Part II. Oct. 23. Retrieved Aug. 20, 2010, from <http://www.naturalnews.com>.

Jacobs, D. H. (1995). Psychiatric drugging: Forty years of pseudo-science, self-interest, and indifference to harm. *Journal of Mind and Behavior*, 16(4), 421–70.

Jacobs, D. H., & Cohen, D. (2004). Hidden in plain sight: DSM-IV's rejection of the categorical approach to diagnosis. *Review of Existential Psychology & Psychiatry*, 26(2–3), 81–96.

Jacobs, D. H., & Cohen, D. (2010). Does "psychological dysfunction" mean anything? A critical essay on pathology vs. agency. *Journal of Humanistic Psychology*, 50, 312–34.

Jacobs, P. (n.d.). How profits, research mix at Stanford. Available at: <http://www.matr.net/article_19768htm1-18K>.

Jacobson, J. W., Foxx, R. M., & Mulick, J. A. (Eds.) (2005). *Controversial therapies for developmental disabilities: Fad, fashion, and science in professional practice*. Mahwah, NJ: Erlbaum.

Jacobson, J. W., Mulick, J. A., & Schwartz, A. A. (1995). A history of facilitated communication: Science, pseudoscience and antiscience science. Working group on facilitated communication. *American Psychologist*, 50, 750–765.

Jacobson, M. F., & Mazur, L. A. (1995). *Marketing madness: A survival guide for a consumer society*. Boulder, CO: Westview Press.

Jacobson, N., & Gortner, E. (2000). Can depression be de-medicalized in the 21st century?: Scientific revolutions, counter-revolutions, and the magnetic field of normal science. *Behavior Research and Therapy*, 38, 103–17.

Jacoby, H. (1976). *The bureaucratization of the world*, trans. Eveline Kains. Berkeley: University of California Press.

Jadad, A. R., & Enkin, M. W. (2007). *Randomized controlled trials: Questions, answers and musings* (2nd ed.). Malden, MA: Blackwell Publishing.

James, W. (1975). *Pragmatism*. Cambridge, MA: Harvard University Press.

Janicek, M., & Hitchcock, D. L. (2005). *Evidence-based practice: Logic and critical thinking in medicine*. Chicago: American Medical Association.

Janis, I. L. (1982). *Groupthink: Psychological studies of policy, decisions and fiascos* (2nd ed.). Boston: Houghton Mifflin.

Janofsky, M. (2001). Therapists are sentenced in girl's "rebirthing" death. *New York Times*, June 19, A12.

Janson, D. (1988). End to suit denied in shooting death. *New York Times*, Apr. 22, AI, B2.

Jarvis, W. T.(1990). *Dubious dentistry: A dental continuing education course*. Loma Linda, CA: Loma Linda University School of Dentistry.

Jasti, A., Ojha, S. C., & Singh, Y. I. (2007). Mental and behavioral effects of parasitic infections: A review. *Nepal Medical College Journal*, 9(1), 50–56.

Jehl, D. (1994). Surgeon General forced to resign by White House. *New York Times*, Dec.10, A1/9.

Jensen, D. D. (1989). Pathologies of science, precognition and modern psychophysics. *Skeptical Inquirer*, 13, 147–60.

Jensen, R., & Burgess, H. (1997). Myth making: How introductory psychology texts present B. F. Skinner's analysis of cognition. *Psychological Record*, 47, 221–32.

Jesilow, P., Pontell, H. N., & Geis, G. (1993*). Prescription for profit: How doctors defraud Medicaid*. Berkeley: University of California Press.

Johnson, A. (2009). Cost-effectiveness of cancer drugs is questioned. *Wall Street Journal*. July 2.

Johnson, B., Kavanaugh, P., & Mattson, K. (Eds.) (2003). *Steal this university: The rise of the corporate university and the academic labor movement*. New York: Routledge.

Johnson, H. M. (2006). Alas for Tiny Tim, he became a Christmas cliche. *New York Times*, Dec. 25, A23.

Johnson. I. (2005). Lethal flood of fake prescription drugs. <http://www.Scotsman.com> News Update, paperboy@nevis.Scotsman.com (Aug. 2, 2005).

Johnson-Laird, P. N. (1985). Logical thinking: Does it occur in daily life? Can it be taught? In S. F. Chipman, J. W. Segal, & R. Glaser (Eds.), *Thinking and learning skills*. Vol. 2. *Research and open questions*. Hillsdale, NJ: Erlbaum.

Jolley, D. (2009). Memory clinics are all about stigma, not screening. *BMJ*, 338, b 860.

Jordan, M. (2009). From a visionary English physicist, self-adjusting lenses for the poor. *Washington Post*, Jan. 10.

Jørgensen, K. J., & Gøtzsche, P. C. (2004). Presentation on websites of possible benefits and harms from screening for breast cancer: Cross sectional study. *BMJ*, 328, 148–55.

Jørgensen, K. J., & Gøtzsche, P. C. (2009). Overdiagnosis in publicly organized mammography screening programs: A systematic review of incidence trends, *BMJ*, 339, b2587.

Jørgensen, K. J., Hrobjartsson, A., & Gøtzsche, P. C. (2009). Divine intervention? A Cochrane review on intercessory prayer gone beyond science and reason. *J Negat Results Biomed*, June 10, 8, 7.

Jørgensen, K. J., Brodersen, J., Hartling, O. J., Nielsen, M., & Gøtzsche, P. C. (2009). Informed choice requires information about both benefits and harms. *Journal of Medical Ethics*, 35, 268–69.

Jowett, G., & O'Donnell, V. (Eds.) (2006). *Readings in propaganda and persuasion: New and classic essays* (4th ed.). Thousand Oaks, CA: Sage.

Judson, H. F. (2004). *The great betrayal: Fraud in science*. New York: Harcourt.

Jüni, P., Altman, D. G., & Egger, M. (2001). Assessing the quality of controlled clinical trials. *BMJ*, 323, 42–46.

Jureidini, J. (2001). Oral testimony to the South Australia parliamentary committee's inquiry into attention deficit hyperactivity disorder. *Hansard*, Sept. 21, 119.

Jutel, A. (2009). Sociology of diagnosis: A preliminary review. *Sociology of Health & Illness*, 31(2), 278–99.

Juvenile injustice. (2010). Editorial. *New York Times*, Jan. 5, A18.

Kahane, H. (1995). *Logic and contemporary rhetoric: The use of reason in everyday life* (7th ed.). Belmont, CA: Wadsworth.

Kahane, H., & Cavender, N. (1998). *Logic and contemporary rhetoric: The use of reason in everyday life* (8th ed.). New York: Wadsworth.

Kahneman, D. (2003). A perspective on judgment and choice. *American Psychologist*, 9, 697–720.

Kahneman, D. (2011). *Thinking fast and slow*. New York: Farrar, Straus & Giroux.

Kahneman, D., & Krueger, A. B. (2006). Developments in the measurement of subjective well being. *Journal of Economic Perspectives*, 23, 2–24.

Kaid, L. L., & Holtz-Bacha, C. (Eds.) (2006). *The Sage handbook of political advertising*. Thousand Oaks, CA: Sage Publications.

Kalager, M., Zelen, M., Langmark, F., & Adami, H. (2010). Effects of screening mammography on breast-cancer mortality in Norway. *New England Journal of Medicine*, 363, 1203–10.

Kaminer, W. (1992). *I'm dysfunctional, you're dysfunctional: The recovery movement and other self help fashions*. Reading, MA: Addison-Wesley.

Kanishinsky, A. (1982). The effects of scarcity of material and exclusivity of information on industrial buyer perceived risk in provoking a purchase decision. Ph.D. Dissertation, Arizona State University.

Karan, L. (2010). *Medical ghostwriting: Tainting the integrity of medical research*, Apr. 14. Retrieved July 10, 2010, from <http://biotechpharmaceuticals.suite101.com>.

Kashima, Y., Fiedler, K., & Freytag, P. (Eds.) (2007). Stereotype dynamics: Language-based approaches to the formation, maintenance, and transformation of stereotypes. New York: Lawrence Erlbaum.

Kassirer, J. P. (1994). Incorporating patient preferences into medical decisions. *New England Journal of Medicine*, 330, 1895–96.

Kassirer, J. P. (2005). *On the take: How medicine's complicity with big business can endanger your health.* New York: Oxford University Press.

Kassirer, J. P., & Cecil, J. S. (2002). Inconsistency in evidentiary standards for medical testimony. *JAMA*, 288, 1382–1387.

Katz, D., Cartwright, D., Eldersveld, S., & Lee, A. M. (1954). *Public opinion and propaganda: A book of readings.* New York: Dryden Press.

Katz, J. (2002). *The silent world of doctor and patient.* Baltimore, MD: Johns Hopkins University Press.

Katz, M. B. (1989). *The undeserving poor: From the war on poverty to the war on welfare.* New York: Pantheon.

Kay, S., & Vyse, S. (2005). Helping parents separate the wheat from the chaff: Putting autism treatments to the test. In J. W. Jacobson, R. M. Foxx, & J. A. Mulick (Eds.), *Controversial therapies for developmental disabilities: Fad, fashion, and science in professional practice* (pp. 265–77). Mahwah, NJ: Lawrence Erlbaum.

Kazdin, A., & Weiez, J. (2003). *Evidence-based psychotherapies for children and adolescents.* New York: Guilford.

Keefe, R. (2000). *Theories of vagueness.* New York: Cambridge University Press.

Keiden, J. (2007). Sucked into the Herceptin maelstrom. *BMJ*, Jan. 6, 334, 18.

Kelly, I. W., Culver, R., & Loptson, P. J. (1989). Astrology and science: An examination of the evidence. In S. K. Biswas, D. C. V. Malik, & C. V. Vishveshwara (Eds.), *Cosmic perspectives.* New York: Cambridge University Press.

Kelly, R. E., Cohen, L. J., Semple, R. J., Bialer, P., Lau, A., Bodenheimer, A., Neustadter, E., et al. (2006). Relationship between drug company funding and outcomes of clinical psychiatric research. *Psychological Medicine*, 36, 1647–56.

Kennedy, N. J., & Sanborn, J. S. (1992). Disclosure of Tardiv Dyskinesia: Effect of written policy on risk disclosure. *Pharmacology Bulletin*, 28, 93–100.

Kenrick, D. T., & Gutierres, S. E. (1980). Contrast effects in judgments of attractiveness: When beauty becomes a social problem. *Journal of Personality and Social Psychology*, 38, 131–40.

Kerwin, A., & Witte, M. (1983). Map of ignorance (Q-Cubed Programs): What is ignorance? Retrieved Oct. 6, 2011, from <http://www.ignorance.medicine.arizona.edu/ignorance.html>.

Kessler, R. C., Chiu, W. T., Demler, O., & Walters, E. E. (2005). Prevalence, severity, and comorbidity of twelve-month DSM-IV disorders in the National Comorbidity Survey Replication (NCS-R). *Archives of General Psychiatry*, 62, 612–27.

Khatri, N., Brown, G. D., & Hicks, L. L. (2009). From a blame culture to a just culture in health care. *Health Care Management Review*, 34, 312–22.

Killeen, G. F., Smith, T. A., Ferguson, H. M., Mshinda, H., Abdulla, S., Lengeler, C., & Kachur, S. P. (2007). Preventing childhood malaria in Africa by protecting adults from mosquitoes with insecticide-treated nets. *PLoS Med*, 4, e229.

King, P. M., & Kitchener, K. S. (2002). The reflective judgment model: Twenty years of research on epistemic cognition. In B. K. Hoffler & P. R. Pintrich (Eds.), *Personal epistemology: The psychology of beliefs about knowledge and knowing* (pp. 37–61). Mahwah, NJ: Erlbaum.

Kirk, S. A. (2004). Are children's DSM diagnoses accurate? *Brief Treatment and Crisis Intervention*, 4, 255–70.

Kirk, S. (2010). Science and politics in the evolution of the DSM. Seabury Lecture. University of California, Berkeley, April.

Kirk, S. A., & Kutchins, H. (1992). *The selling of DSM: The rhetoric of science in psychiatry*. New York: Aldine de Gruyter.

Kirsch, I. (2010). *The emperor's new drugs: Exploding the antidepressant myth*. New York: Basic Books.

Kirsch, I., Scoboria, A., & Moore, T. J. (2002). Antidepresssants and placebos: Secrets, revelations, and unanswered questions. *Prevention & Treatment*, 5. Article 33, July 15.

Kirsch, I., Deacon, B. J., Huedo-Medina, T. B., Scorboria, A., Moore, T. J., & Johnson, B. T. (2008). Initial severity and antidepressant benefits: A meta-analysis of data submitted to the Food and Drug Administration. *PLoS Medicine*, 5(2), e45.doi:10.1371.

Kirwin, A., & Witte, M. (1983). The map of ignorance. <http://www.ignorance.medicine.arizona.edu/ignorance.html>.

Klein, G. (1998). *Sources of power: How people make decisions*. Cambridge, MA: MIT Press.

Kleinke, J. D. (2004). Access versus excess: Value-based cost sharing for prescription drugs. *Health Affairs*, 23, 34–47.

Kline, N. (1962). Factifuging. *Lancet*, June, 1396–99.

Kluger, M. P., Alexander, G., & Curtis, P. A. (2002). *What works in child welfare*. Washington, DC: CWLA Press.

Kmietowticz, Z. (2004). Tighter controls are needed to root out bogus patient groups. *BMJ*, 329, 1307.

Kmietowicz, Z. (2007). Computed tomography screening. Better safe than sorry? *BMJ*, 335, 1182–84.

Kmietowicz, Z. (2008a). Committee warms of risk of private computed tomography. *BMJ*, 336, 14–15.

Kmietowicz, Z. (2008b). GlaxoSmithKline to limit payments it makes to U.S. doctors to $150,000 a year. *BMJ*, 337, a2315.

Kmietowicz, Z. (2009). Eli Lilly pays record $1.4bn for promoting off-label use of olanzapine. *BMJ*, 338, b217.

Kmietowticz, Z. (2010). Family planning loses out to HIV and AIDS in development aid, shows analysis, *BMJ*, 341, c6460.

Kmietowicz, Z. (2011). "Harrowing accounts" show how NHS fails to meet basic standards of care of elderly people. *BMJ*, 342, d1064.

Knishinsky, A. (1982). The effects of scarcity of material and exclusivity of information on industrial buyer perceived risk in provoking a purchase decision. Doctoral dissertation, Arizona State University, Tempe.

Knerr, W., & Philpott, A. (2011). Strange bedfellows: Bridging the worlds of academia, public health and the sex industry to improve sexual health outcomes. *Health Research Policy Systems*, June 26, Supplement 1, S13.DLY.10.1186.

Koerner, B. (2002). First you market the disease, then you push the pills to treat it. *Guardian*. Retrieved on [date] from <http://www.guardian.co.uk/Archives/Article/0,4273,4471963,oo.html>.

Kohn, L. T., Corrigan, J. M., & Donaldson, M. S. (2000). *To err is human: Building a safer health system*. Washington, DC: National Academy Press.

Kolata, G. (1998). A child's paper poses a medical challenge. *New York Times*, Apr. 1. Retrieved May 19, 2009.

Kolata, G. (2001a). Costly emphysema surgery is challenged by researchers. *New York Times*, Aug. 15.

Kolata, G. (2008). A study revives a debate on arthritis knee surgery. *New York Times National*, Sept.11, A17.

Kolata, G. (2010a). In spinal test, early warning on Alzheimer's. *New York Times*, Aug. 10, A1, 14.

Kolata, G. (2010b). When drugs cause problems they are supposed to prevent. *New York Times*, Oct. 17.

Kolata, G. (2011a). First study of its kind shows benefits of providing medical insurance to poor. *New York Times National*, July 7, A14.

Kolata, G. (2011b). How bright promise in cancer testing fell apart. *New York Times National*, July 7, A1.

Kolb, B., Gibb, R., & Robinson, T. E. (2003). Brain plasticity and behavior. *Current Directions in Psychological Science*, 12, 1–5.

Kondro, W., & Sibbald, B. (2004). Drug company experts advise staff to withhold data about SSRI use in children. *Canadian Medical Association*, 170, 783.

Kozloff, M. A. (2005). Fads and general education: Fad, fraud, and folly. In J. W. Jacobson, R. M. Foxx, & J. A. Mulick (Eds.), *Controversial therapies for developmental disabilities: Fad, fashion, and science in professional practice* (pp. 159–74). Mahwah, NJ: Erlbaum.

Kramer, P. D. (1993). *Listening to Prozac*. New York: Viking.

Kramer, R. (1991). Ed school follies: The miseducation of America's teachers. New York: Free Press.

Krasner, D. (2004). Eva Illouz, Oprah Winfrey and the glamour of misery: An essay on popular culture. Book review. *African American Review*, 38, 539–41.

Kravitz, R. L., Epstein, R. M., Feldman, M. D., Franz, C. E., Azari, R., Wilkes, M. S., et al. (2005). Influence of patients' requests for direct-to-consumer advertised antidepressants: A randomized controlled trial. *JAMA*, 293, 1995–2002.

Krieger, L. M. (2009). Medical experts rethink routine screenings for breast and prostate cancer. Retrieved on [date] from <http://InsideBayArea.com>.

Krimsky, S. (2003). *Science in the private interest: Has the lure of profits corrupted biomedical research?* Lanham, MD: Rowman and Littlefield.

Krueger, A. B., Kahneman, D., Fischler, C., et al. (2009). Time use and subjective well-being in France and the U.S. *Social Indicators Research*, 93(1), 7–18.

Krumholz, H. M., Hines, H. H., Ross, J. S., Presler, A. H., & Egilman, D. S. (2007). What have we learnt from Vioxx? *BMJ*, 334, 120–23.

Kruskal, W., & Mosteller, F. (1981). Ideas of representative sampling. In D. Fiske (Ed.), *New directions for methodology of social and behavioral science: No. 9. Problems with language imprecision*. San Francisco: Jossey-Bass.

Kuhn, T. S. (1970). *The structure of scientific revolutions* (2nd ed.). Chicago: University of Chicago Press.

Kunin, M. M. (2007). Diagnosis: Conflict of interest. *New York Times*, June 13, Op-Ed.

Kunst, H., Groot, D., Latthe, P. M., Latthe, M., & Khan, K. S. (2002). Accuracy of information on apparently credible websites: Survey of five common health topics. *BMJ*, 324, 581–82.

Kutchins, H., & Kirk, S. A. (1997). *Making us crazy: DSM: The psychiatric bible and the creation of mental disorders*. New York: Free Press.

Lacasse, J. R. (2005). Consumer advertising of psychiatric medications biases the public against non-pharmacological treatment. *Ethical Human Psychology and Psychiatry*, 7(3), 175–79.

Lacasse, J. R., & Gomory, T. (2003). Is graduate social work education promoting a critical approach to mental health practice? *Journal of Social Work Education*, 39, 383–408.

LaCasse, J. R., & Leo, J. (2005). Serotonin and depression: A disconnect between the advertisements and the scientific literature. *PLoS Medicine*, 2, e392.

Lacasse, J. R., & Leo, J. (2010). Ghostwriting at elite academic medical centers in the United States. *PLoS Med, 7*(2); doi:10.1371/journal.pmed.1000230.

Lakoff, A. (2005*). Pharmaceutical reason*. Cambridge, MA: Cambridge University Press.

Lakoff, G., & Johnson, M. (1980). *Metaphors we live by*. Chicago: University of Chicago Press.

Lakoff, R. T. (2001). *The language war*. Berkeley: University of California Press.

Lambert, M. J. (Ed.) (2004). Bergen and Garfield's handbook of psychotherapy and behavior change (5th ed.). New York: Wiley.

Lane, C. (2007). *Shyness: How normal behavior became a sickness*. New Haven: Yale University Press.

Lang, S. (1998). *Challenges*. New York: Springer.

Langer, E. J. (1975). The illusion of control. *Journal of Personality and Social Psychology*, 32, 311–28.

Larson, M. S. (1977). *The rise of professionalism: A sociological analysis*. Berkeley: University of California Press.

Lasch, C. (1978). *The culture of narcissism: American life in an age of diminishing expectations*. New York: W. W. Norton.

Lasswell, H. D. ([1927] 1971). *Propaganda technique in World War I*. Cambridge, MA: MIT Press.

Lauer, J. A., & Betran, A. P. (2007). Editorial. Decision aids for women with a previous caesarean section. *BMJ*, 334, 1281–82.

Laurance, J. (2010). Doctor may be sued for criticism of breast cream. *The Independent*, Nov. 11.

Lavazza, A., & De Caro, M. (2010). Not so fast. On some bold neuroscientific claims concerning human agency. *Neuroethics*, 3, 23–41.

Law, M. R., Majumdar, S. R., & Sooumerai, S. B. (2008). Effect of illicit direct to consumer advertising on use of etanercept, mometasone, and tegaserod in Canada: controlled longitudinal study. *BMJ*, 337, a1055.

Layng, J. (2009). The search for an effective clinical behavior analysis: The nonlinear thinking of Israel Goldiamond. *Behavior Analysis*, 32, 163–84.

Leape, L. L. (2002). Reports on adverse events. *New England Medical Journal*, 347, 1633–38; *BMJ*, June 2009.

Leape, L. L., & Berwick, D. M. (2005). Five years after To Err Is Human: What have we learned? *Journal of the American Medical Association*, 293, 2384–90.

Leary, W. E. (1994). Study urges less heart surgery for elderly. *New York Times*, Sept. 26, A16.

Lebon, G. (1909). *The crowd*. London: T. F. Unwin.

Lee, A. M. (1952). *How to understand propaganda*. New York: Rinehart and Company.

Lee, A. M., & Lee, E. B. (Eds.) (1939). The fine art of propaganda: A study of father Coughlin's speeches. Harcourt, Brace & Co. Institute for Propaganda Analysis.

Lehmann-Haupt, C. (2005). Opal Petty, 86, patient held 51 years involuntarily in Texas. *New York Times*, Mar. 17, A27.

Leland, J. (2010). A battle against prescription drugs causes pain. *New York Times National*, Oct. 3, 17.

Lenzer, J. (2004a). Bush plans to screen whole U.S. population for mental illness. *BMJ*, 328, 1458.

Lenzer, J. (2004b). FDA is incapable of protecting US against another Vioxx. *BMJ*, 329, 1253.

Lenzer, J. (2004c). FDA's counsel accused of being too close to drug industry. *BMJ*, 329, 189.

Lenzer, J. (2004e). Secret US report surfaces on antidepressants in children. *BMJ*, 329, 307.

Lenzer, J. (2009). Watching over the medical device industry. *BMJ*, 338:b2321.

Leo, J. (2009). JAMA, free speech, and conflicts of interest. *Society*, 46, 472–76.

Leo, J., & Cohen, D. (2003). Broken brains or flawed studies? A critical review of ADHD Neuroimaging research. *Journal of Mind and Behavior*, 24, 29–56.

Leo, J., & Cohen, D. (2009). A critical review of ADHD neuroimaging research. In S. Timini & J. Leo (Eds.), *Rethinking ADHD: An international perspective*. London: Palgrave MacMillan.

Leo, J., & Lacasse, J. (2009a). Letter. Clinical trials of therapy versus medication: Even in a tie, Medication wins. *BMJ*, May 3, 2009.

Leo, J., & Lacasse, J. (2009b). A study of consumer advertisements. In S. Timini & J. Leo (Eds.), *Rethinking ADHD: An international perspective*. London: Palgrave MacMillan.

Lesser, L. I., Ebbeling, C. B., Goozner, M., Wypij, D., & Ludwig, D. S. (2007). Relationship between funding source and conclusion among nutrition-related scientific articles. *PLoS Medicine*, 4(1), e5.

Leucht, S., Kissling, W., & Davis, J. M. (2009). Second-generation antipsychotics or schizophrenia: Can we resolve the conflict? *Psychological Medicine*, 39, 1591–1602.

Leucht, S., Komossa, K., Rummel-Kluge, C., Corves, C., Hunger, H., Schmid, F., Lobos, C. A., Schwarz, S., & Davis, J. M. (2009). A meta-analysis of head-to-head comparisons of second-generation antipsychotics in the treatment of schizophrenia. *American Journal of Psychiatry*, 166, 152–63.

Levine, J. M., & Hogg, M. A. (Eds.) (2010). *Encyclopedia of group processes and intergroup relations*. London: Sage.

Levy, C. J. (2002). Voiceless, defenseless and a source of cash. *New York Times On the Web*, Apr. 30.

Levy, C. J. (2003). Doctor admits he did needless surgery on the mentally ill. *New York Times*, May 20.

Levy, C. J. (2004). Home for mentally ill settles suit on coerced prostate surgery for $7.4 million. *New York Times*, Aug. 5, A21.

Levy, C. J., & Luo, M. (2005). New York Medicaid fraud may reach into billions. *New York Times*, July 18, A1.

Lewis, L. (2008). Another state bans prone restraints. Retrieved from <http://www.youthtoday.org/publication/article>.

Lewontin, R. C. (1991). *Biology as ideology: The doctrine of DNA*. New York: Harper Collins.

Lewontin, R. C. (1994). *Inside and outside: Gene, environment, and organism*. Worcester, MA: Clark University Press.

Lewontin, R. (2009). Where are the genes? Retrieved Oct. 1, 2011, from <http://www.councilforresponsiblegenetics.org>.

Lexchin, J. (2006). Bigger and better: How Pfizer redefined erectile dysfunction. *PLoS Med*, 3, e132.

Lexchin, J., Bero, L. A., Djulbegovic, B., & Clark, O. (2003). Pharmaceutical industry sponsorship and research outcome and quality: Systematic review. *BMJ*, 326, 1167–70.

Li, Y., Berg, A., Woo, L. R., Wang, Z., Chang, G., & Woo, R. (2010). Modeling the aneuploidy control of cancer. *BMC Cancer*, 10, 1471–2407.

Liberman, P., & Pizarro, D. (2010). All politics is olfactory. *New York Times*. Oct. 23.

Lieberman, J. A., Stroup, T. S., McEvoy, J. P., Swartz, M.S., Rosenheck, R. A., & Perkins, D. O., et al. (2005). Effectiveness of antipsychotic drugs in patients with chronic schizophrenia. *New England Journal of Medicine*, 353, 1209–23.

Lieberman, T. (2007). The Medicare privatization scam. *Nation*, July 16.

Light, D. W., & Warburton, R. (2011). Demythologizing the high costs of pharmaceutical research. *BioSocieties Advance Online Publication*, Feb. 7, doi:10.1057/biosoc.2010.40.

Lilienfeld, S. O. (2002). When worlds collide: Social science, politics and the Rind et al. child sexual abuse meta-analysis. *American Psychologist*, 57, 176–88.

Lilienfeld, S. O. (2007). Psychological treatments that cause harm. *Perspectives on Psychological Science*, 2, 53–70.

Lilienfeld, S. O., & Landfield, K. (2008). Science and pseudoscience and law enforcement: A user-friendly primer. *Criminal Justice and Behavior*, 35, 1215–30.

Lilienfeld, S. O., Ammirati, R., & Landfield, K. (2009). Giving debiasing away: Can psychological research on correcting cognitive errors promote human welfare? *Perspectives on Psychological Science*, 4, 390–98.

Lilienfeld, S. O., Lynn, S. J., & Lohr, J. M. (2003). *Science and pseudoscience in clinical psychology*. New York: Guilford.

Lindsey, D., Martin, S., & Doh, J. (2002). The failure of intensive casework services to reduce foster care placements: An examination of family preservation studies. *Children and Youth Services Review*, 24(9/10), 743–75.

Liperoti, R., & Gambassi, G. (2010). Antipsychotics and the risk of venous thromboembolism. *BMJ*, 351, c4216.

Liptak, A. (2007). Fraud inquiry looking at lawyers in diet-drug case. *New York Times*, Mar. 24, 1/10.

Liptak, A. (2009). No legal shield in drug labeling. *New York Times*, Mar. 5.

Littell, J. (2005). Lessons from a systematic review of effects of multisystemic therapy. *Children and Youth Services Review*, 27, 445–63.

Littell, J. H. (2006). The case for multisystemic therapy: Evidence or orthodoxy? *Children and Youth Services Review*, 28, 458–72.

Littell, J. H. (2008). Evidence-based or bias? The quality of published reviews. *Children and Youth Services Review*, 30, 1299–1317.

Littell, J. H., & Girvin, H. (2002). Stages of change: A critique. *Behavior Modification*, 26, 223–73.

Littell, J. H., Corcoran, J., & Pillai, V. (2007). *Systematic reviews and meta-analysis*. New York: Oxford.

Littell, J. H., Popa, M., & Forsythe, B. (2005). Multisystemic therapy for social, emotional, and behavioral problems in youth age 10–17. *Cochrane Database of Systematic Reviews*, 4. Chichester, UK: John Wiley and Sons.

Ljung, B. M. (2007). Accuracy and usefulness of FNA vs Core needle biopsy in breast diagnosis. Presentation March 24, 2007, UCSF, USCAP PSC-companion meeting.

Lo, B., & Field, M. J. (Eds.) (2009). *Conflict of interest in medical research, education and practice*. Institute of Medicine. Washington, DC: National Academy Press.

Lock, M. (1993). *Encounters with aging: Mythologies of menopause in Japan and North America*. Berkeley: University of California Press.

Lock, S., Wells, F., & Farthing, M. (2001). *Fraud and misconduct in biomedical research* (3rd ed.). London: BMJ Books.

Loeske, D. R. (1999). *Thinking about social problems: An introduction to constructionist perspectives*. New York: Aldine de Gruyter.
Loftus, E. F. (1979). *Eyewitness testimony*. Cambridge, MA: Harvard University Press.
Loftus, E. F. (1980). *Memory: Surprising new insights into how we remember and why we forget*. Reading, MA.: Addison-Wesley.
Loftus, E. F. (1997). Creating false memories. *Scientific American*, 277, 70-75.
Loftus, E. F. (2004). Memories of things unseen. *Current Directions in Psychological Science*, 17, 145-47.
Loftus, E. F., & Guyer, M. J. (2002). Who abused Jane Doe? The hazards of the single case history Part 1. *Skeptical Inquirer*, 26(3), 22-32.
Loke, T. W., Koh, F. C., & Ward, J. E. (2002) Pharmaceutical advertisement claims in Australian medical publications:Is evidence accessible,compelling and communicated comprehensively? *Med. J. of Australia*,177, 291-93.
Lord, C., Ross, L., & Lepper, M. R, (1979). Biased assimilation and attitude polarization: The effects of prior theories on subsequently considered evidence. *Journal of Personality and Social Psychology*, 37, 2098-2109.
Lourenco, O. (2001). The danger of words: A Wittgensteinian lesson for developmentalists. *New Ideas in Psychology*, 19, 89-115.
Lumley, F. E. (1933). *The propaganda menace*. New York: Century Co.
Lundh, A., Barbateskovic, M., Hrobjartsson, A., & Gotzsche, P. C. (2010). Conflicts of interest at medical journals: The influence of industry-supported randomised trials on journal impact factors and revenue–Cohort study. *PLoS Med*, Oct. 10.
Luyten, S. J., Blatt, B., Van Houdenhove, B., & Corveleyn, J. (2006). Depression, research and treatment: Are we skating to where the puck is going? *Clinical Psychology Review*, 26, 985-99.
MacCoun, R. J. (1998). Biases in the interpretation and use of research results. *Annual Review of Psychology*, 49, 259-87.
MacCoun, R. J., & Reuter, P. (2001*). Drug war heresies: Learning from vices, times, & places*. New York: Cambridge University Press.
MacDonald, G. M., & Turner, W. (2008). Treatment foster care for improving outcomes. *Cochrane Database Systematic Review*, Jan. 23(1), CDOO5649.
MacGuyvers, R. (1982). *Evil in modern myth and ritual*. Athens: University of Georgia Press.
MacLean, E. (1981). *Between the lines: How to detect bias and propaganda in the news and everyday life*. Montreal: Black Rose Books.
MacLehose, R. R., Reeves, B. C., Harvey, I., Sheldon, T. A., Russell, I. T., & Black, A. M. (2000). A systematic review of comparisons of effect sizes derived from randomized and non-randomized studies. *Health Technology Assessment*, 4, 1-154.
Maclure, M. (1985). Popperian refutation in epidemiology. *American Journal of Epidemiology*, 12, 343-50.
Maddux, J. E., & Winstead, B. A. (2005). *Psychopathology: Foundations for a contemporary understanding*. Mahwah, NJ: Erlbaum.
Maestri, E. (2008). Letter to the Editor. Say "No to misleading advertising on osteoporosis." *BMJ*, Nov. 20.
Mahone, S., & Vaughn, M. (Eds.) (2007). *Psychiatry and empire*. New York: Palgrave MacMillan.
Maloney, M. E. (2009). "Up all night: The medicalization of sleeplessness." Dissertation. University of North Carolina, Chapel Hill.

Malpas, P. K. (2008). Predictive genetic testing of children for adult onset diseases and psychological harm. *Journal of Medical Ethics*, 34, 275–78.

Manning, N. P. (Ed.) (1985). *Social problems and welfare ideology*. Aldershot (UK): Gower.

Manning, P. (1977). *Police work*. Cambridge, MA: MIT Press.

Mansfield, P. R. (2003). Healthy skepticism's new ad. AdWatch: Understanding drug promotion. *Medical Journal of Australia*, 179, 644–45.

Marchand, R. (1985). *Advertising the American dream: Making way for modernity 1920–1940*. Berkeley: University of California Press.

Marchione, M. (2009). Stents overused in heart work new study finds. *San Francisco Chronicle*, Jan. 15.

Margo, C. E. (2003). A pilot study in ophthalmology of inter-rater reliability in classifying diagnostic errors: An underinvestigated area of medical error. *Quality and Safety Health Care*, 12, 416–20.

Margolin, L. (1997). *Under the cover of kindness: The invention of social work*. Charlottesville: University of Virginia Press.

Marlin, R. (2002). *Propaganda & the ethics of persuasion*. Orchard Park, NY: Broadview Press.

Marmot, M. (2010). Fighting the alligators of health inequalities. *BMJ*, 341, 76.

Marris, P. (1996). *The politics of uncertainty: Attachment in private and public life*. New York: Routledge.

Marsh, H. W. (1987). Students' evaluations of university teaching: Research findings, methodological issues and directions for future research. *International Journal of Educational Research*, 11 (Whole Issue No. 3).

Marshall, B. J., & Warren, J. R. (1983). Unidentified curved bacillus on gastric epithelium in active chronic gastritis. *Lancet*, 1, 1273–75.

Martin, A., Sherwin, T., Stubbe, D., Van Hoof, T., Scahill, L., & Leslie, D. (2002). Use of multiple psychotropic drugs by Medicaid-insured and privately insured children. *Psychiatric Services*, 53, 1508.

Martinic, M., & Leigh, B. (2004). *Reasonable risk: Alcohol in perspective*. New York: Routledge.

Mashta, O. (2009). Poor service provision is blamed for overuse of antipsychotics in dementia patients. *BMJ*, 339, b4818.

Masson, J. M. (1984). *The assault on truth: Freud's suppression of the seduction theory*. New York: Farrar, Straus & Giroux.

Masters, W. H., & Johnson, V. E. (1966). *Human sexual response*. New York: Bantam Books.

May, C. D. (1961). Selling drugs by "educating" physicians. *J. Med Ethics*, 36, 1–23.

Mayor, S. (2008). Low cost intervention reduces suicide rate in poorer countries, study shows. *BMJ*, 337, a1524.

Mayor, S. (2010). Critics attack new NHS breast screening leaflet for failing to address harms. *BMJ*, 341, c7267.

McCabe, D. P., & Castel, A. D. (2008). Seeing is believing: The effect of brain images on judgments of scientific reasoning. *Cognition*, 107, 343–52.

McCord, J. (2003). Cures that harm: Unanticipated outcomes of crime prevention programs. *ANNALS of the American Academy of Political and Social Science*, 487, 16–30.

McCormick, J. (1996). Health scares are bad for your health. In D. M. Warburton & N. Sherwood (Eds.), *Pleasure and quality of life* (pp. 189–99). New York: Wiley.

McCoy, R. (2000). *Quack! Tales of medical fraud from the museum of questionable medical devices*. Santa Monica, CA: Santa Monica Press.

McDaniel, T. A. (2003). *Shrinking violets and caspar milquetoasts*. New York: New York University Press.

McDowell, B. (2000). *Ethics and excuses: The crisis in professional responsibility*. Westport, CT: Quorum Books.

McFall, R. M. (1991). Manifesto for a science of clinical psychology. *Clinical Psychologist*, 44, 75–88.

McIntyre, N., & Popper, K. (1983). The critical attitude in medicine: The need for a new ethics. *BMJ*, 287, 1919–23.

McKie, R. (2011). British inventor's spectacles revolution for Africa: Joshua Silver shortlisted for an EU Award, hopes to supply children in a developing world with 200 million pairs of self-adjusting glasses. *The Observer*, May 22.

McKnight, J. L. (undated). *Do no harm: A policymaker's guide to evaluating human services and their alternatives*. Downloaded Nov. 25, 2011.

McLellan, D. (1986). *Ideology: Concepts in social thought*. Minneapolis: University of Minnesota Press.

McLuhan, M. (1951). *The mechanical bride: Folklore of industrial man*. Boston: Beacon Press.

McLuhan, M. (1962). *The Guttenberg galaxy: The making of topographic man*. Toronto: University of Toronto Press.

McLuhan, M. (1964). *Understanding media: The extensions of man*. New York: Mentor.

McLuhan, M., & Fiore, Q. (1967). *The medium is the message: An inventory of effects*. New York: Random House.

McNally, R. J., & Gergerts, E. (2009). A new solution to the recovered memory debate. *Perspectives in Psychological Science*, 20, 92–98.

McNeil, D. G., Jr. (2007). In the world of life-saving drugs, a growing epidemic of deadly fakes. *New York Times*, Feb. 20, D1.

McNeil, D. G., Jr. (2010). U.S. infected Guatemalans with syphilis in '40s. *New York Times*, Oct. 2, A1/6.

McNight, L., Stetson, P., Bakken, S., Curran, C., & Cimino, J. (2002). Perceived information needs and communication difficulties of inpatient physicians and nurses. *Journal of the American Medical Informatics Association*, 9, S64–S69.

Meador, C. K. (1965). The art and science of non-disease. *New England Journal of Medicine*, 272, 92–95.

Medawar, C., & Hardon, A. (2004). *Medicines out of control? Antidepressants and the conspiracy of goodwill*. The Netherlands: Aksant.

Medicare privatization abuses. (2007). Editorial. *New York Times*, May 8, A22.

Meehl, P. E. (1973). Why I do not attend case conferences. In P. E Meehl (Ed.), *Psychodiagnosis: Selected papers* (pp. 225–304). Minneapolis: University of Minnesota Press.

Mehta, S., & Farina, A. (1997). Is being sick really better? Effect of the disease view of disorder on stigma. *Journal of Social and Clinical Psychology*, 16(4), 405–19.

Meier, B. (2008). The evidence gap: A call for a warning system on artificial joints. *New York Times*, July 29, A1/17.

Meier, B. (2009). Medtronic links device for heart to 17 deaths. *New York Times*, Mar. 24, B1.

Meier, B. (2010a). Health system bears cost of implants with no warranties. *New York Times*, Apr. 3.

Meier, B. (2010b). The implants loophole. *New York Times*, Dec. 17, B1/8.

Meier, B. (1995). Dow Chemical in the center of a storm. *New York Times*, Nov. 1, Business Section.

Meier B. & Wilson, D. (2011). Spine experts repudiate Medtronic studies. *New York Times*, June 29, B1.

Meinhold, P., & Mulick, J. A. (1990). Counter-habilitative contingencies for mentally retarded people: Ecological and regulatory influences. *Mental Retardation*, 28, 67–73.

Meirer, B. & Singer, N. (2009). Drug ruling puts devices in spotlight. *New York Times*, Mar. 5, B1.

Meissner, C. A., Sporer, S. L., & Schooler, J. W. (2006). Person descriptions as eyewitness evidence. In R. Lindsay, D. Ross, J. Read, & M. Toglia (Eds.), *Handbook of eyewitness psychology: Memory for people*. Mahwah, NJ: Lawrence Erlbaum.

Melander, H., Ahlqvist-Rastad, J., Meijer, G., & Beermann, B. (2003). Evidence b(iased) medicine—Selective reporting from studies sponsored by pharmaceutical industry: Review of studies in new drug applications. *BMJ*, 326, 1171–73.

Meller, P. (2001). Vitamin products fined $752 million. *New York Times*, Nov. 22, W1 (World Business).

Mello, M. M. (2006). *Understanding medical malpractice insurance: A primer*. Robert Wood Johnson Foundation. In the Synthesis Project. <http://www.rwjf.org/pr/product.jsp?id=15091>.

Members will have an opportunity to submit content to the new website. (2005). *NASW News* (Washington, DC), 50, 3, Mar.

Merton, R. K., & Nisbet, R. A. (1976*). Contemporary social problems* (4th ed.). New York: Harcourt Brace & Jovanovich.

Metz, B., Mulick, J. A., & Butler, E. M. (2005). ASD: A late-twentieth-century fad magnet. In J. W. Jacobson, R. M. Foxx, & J. A. Mulick, *Controversial issues in developmental disabilities*.

Meyer, D. (1980). *The positive thinkers*. New York: Pantheon.

Meyer, H. (2009). Drugmakers' payments draw heat. *Bloomberg Businessweek*, Nov. 4. Retrieved Aug. 1, 2010, from <http://www.businessweek.com>.

MHS (Multi-Health Systems Incorporated). (2007). Catalogue.

Michael, M., Boyce, W. T., & Wilcox, A. J. (1984). *Biomedical bestiary: An epidemiologic guide to flaws and fallacies in the medical literature*. Boston: Little, Brown.

Michalos, A. C. (1971). *Improving your reasoning*. Englewood Cliffs, NJ: Prentice-Hall.

Midanik, L. (2006). *The biomedicalization of alcohol studies: Ideological shifts and institutional challenges*. New Brunswick, NJ: Aldine/Transaction.

Milgram, S. (1963). Behavioral study of obedience. *Journal of Abnormal and Social Psychology*, 67, 371–78.

Miller, D. (1994). *Critical rationalism: A restatement and defense*. Chicago: Open Court.

Miller, D. J., & Hersen, M. (1992). *Research fraud in the behavioral and biomedical sciences*. New York: John Wiley.

Mills, C. W. (1959). *The sociological imagination*. New York: Grove Press.

Miltenberger, R. G. (2008). *Behavior modification: Principles and procedures* (4th ed.). Belmont, CA: Thomson Wadsworth.

Mirowski, P., & Van Horn, R. (2005). The contract research organization and the commercialization of scientific research. *Social Studies of Science*, 205(35), 503–48.

Mirowsky, J., & Ross, C. E. (1989). *Social causes of psychological distress*. New York: Aldine de Gruyter. (See also 2nd ed. 2003.)

Mischel, W. (2003). *Introduction to personality: Toward an integration*. Hoboken, NJ: John Wiley & Sons.

Moher, D., Liberati, A., Tetzlaff, J., & Altman, D. G. (2009). The PRISMA Group. Preferred reporting items for systematic reviews and meta-analyses: The PRISMA statement. *PLoS Med*, 6, e1000097.

Moncrieff, J. (1999). An investigation into the precedents of modern drug treatment in psychiatry. *History of Psychiatry*, 10, 475–90.

Moncrieff, J. (2006). Psychiatric drug promotion and the politics of neoliberalism. *British Journal of Psychiatry*, 188, 301–2.

Moncrieff, J. (2007). Are antidepressants as effective as claimed? No, they are not effective at all. *Canadian Journal of Psychiatry*, 52, 96–97.

Moncrieff, J. (2008a). *The myth of the chemical cure: A critique of psychiatric drug treatment*. New York: Palgrave.

Moncrieff, J. (2008b). Neoliberalism and biopsychiatry: A marriage of convenience. In C. I. Cohen & S. Timimi (Eds.), *Liberatory psychiatry: Philosophy, politics and mental health* (pp. 235–56). New York: Cambridge University Press.

Moncrieff, J., & Cohen, D. (2006). Do antidepressants cure or create abnormal brain states? *PLoS Medicine*, July 3, e240.

Moncrieff, J., & Leo, J. (2010). A systematic review of the effects of antipsychotic drugs on brain volume. *Psychological Medicine*, Jan. 20, 1–14.

Mooney, H. (2011). Three out of 12 hospitals found to meet essential standards of care of older people, finds watchdog. *BMJ*, 342: d3346.

Moore, A., & McQuay, H. (2006). *Bandolier's little book of making sense of the medical evidence*. New York: Oxford University Press.

Moore, D. S. (2001). *The dependent gene: The fallacy of nature/ nurture*. New York Times Books.

Moore, K. D. (1986). *Inductive arguments: A field guide*. Dubuque, IA: Kendal/Hunt.

Moore, M. L. (2005). Increasing Cesarean birth rates: A clash of cultures? *Journal of Perinatal Education*, 14, 5–8.

Moore, T. J., Glenmullen, J., & Furberg, C. D. (2010). Prescription drugs associated with reports of violence towards others. *PLoS ONE*, 5(12), e15337; doi:10.1371/journal.pone.0015337.

Moran, G. (1998). *Silencing scientists and scholars in other fields: Power, paradigm controls, peer review and scholarly communication*. Grenwich, CT: Albex.

Morone, J. A. (1997). Enemies of the people: The moral dimension to public health. *Journal of Health Politics, Policy and Law*, 22, 993–1020.

Morrissey, J., & Monahan, J. (1999). *Coercion in mental health services: International perspectives*. Stanford, CT: JAI Press.

Mortberg, E., Clark, D. M., Sundin, O., & Wistedt, A. A. (2004). Intensive group cognitive treatment and individual cognitive therapy vs treatment as usual in social phobia: A randomized controlled trial. *Acta Psychiatrica Scandinavia*, 115, 142–54.

Moulan, P. (2005). *Remembering trauma. A psychotherapist's guide to memory and illusion*. London: Whurr.

Moynihan, R. (2003a). Claims by charity exaggerate dangers of osteoporosis. *BMJ*, 327, 358.

Moynihan, R. (2003b). The making of a disease: Female sexual dysfunction. *BMJ*, 326, 45–47.

Moynihan, R. (2008a). Doctors' education: The invisible influence of drug company sponsorship. *BMJ*, 336, 416–17.

Moynihan, R. (2008b). Key opinion leaders: Independent experts or drug representatives in disguise? *BMJ*, 336, 1402, doi:10.1136.

Moynihan, R. (2009). News. Court hears how drug giant Merck tried to "neutralize" and "discredit" doctors critical of Vioxx. *BMJ*, 338, b1432.

Moynihan, R. (2010a). US drug manufacturers will have to disclose payments to doctors. *BMJ*, 340, doi:10.1136/bmj.c1648.

Moynihan, R. (2010b). Who benefits from treating hypertension? *BMJ*, 341, c4442.

Moynihan, R., & Cassels, A. (2005). *Selling sickness: How the world's biggest pharmaceutical companies are turning us all into patients.* New York: Nation Books.

Moynihan, R., & Mintzes. B. (2010). *Sex, lies and pharmaceuticals: How drug companies plan to profit from female sexual dysfunction.* Vancouver (Canada): Greystone Books.

Moynihan, R., Heath, I., & Henry, D. (2002). Selling sickness: The pharmaceutical industry and disease mongering. *BMJ*, 324, 886–91.

Mulcahy, N. (2009). ABSA: Surgical biopsies for breast abnormalities overused, action needed. *Medscape Medical News*, April 27.

Multi-Health Systems Inc. (2007). Catalogue.

Munro, E. (2004). A simpler way to understand the results of risk assessment instruments. *Children and Youth Services Review*, 26, 873–83.

Munro, E. (2005). Snooper squad: New guidelines obliging professionals to pry into the sex lives of teenagers would do more harm than good. *Guardian*, May 31.

Munro, E. (2009a). Managing societal and institutional risk in child protection. *Risk Analysis*, 29(7), 1015–23.

Munro, E. (2009b). When families become enemies of the state. *Guardian*, Jan. 28.

Munro, E. (2010). Learning to reduce risk in child protection. *British Journal of Social Work*, 40(4), 1135–51.

Munz, P. (1985). *Our knowledge of the growth of knowledge: Popper or Wittgenstein.* London: Routledge & Kagan Paul.

Munz, P. (1992). What's postmodern, anyway? *Philosophy and Literature*, 16, 333–53.

Murphy, K. (2009). Bone health diagnostic tool under fire. *Globe & Mail*, Sept. 11, L–4.

Murray, T. L. (2009). The loss of client agency into the psychopharmaceutical-industrial complex. *Journal of Mental Health Counseling*, 31, 283–308.

Myron-Shatz, T., et al. (2009). Memories of yesterday's emotions. *Emotion*, 96, 885–91.

Naftulin, D. H., Ware, J. E., & Donnelly, F. A. (1973). The Dr. Fox lecture: A paradigm of educational seduction. *Journal of Medical Education*, 48, 630–35.

Narrow, W. E., Rae, D. S., Robins, L. N., & Regier, D. A. (2002). Revised prevalence estimates of mental disorders in the United States: Using a clinical significance criterion to reconcile 2 surveys' estimates. *Archives of General Psychiatry*, 59, 115–23.

Natale, J. A. (1988). Are you open to suggestion. *Psychology Today*, 22, 28–30.

Nathan, P. E., & Gorman, J. M. (2007). *A guide to treatments that work* (3rd ed.). New York: Oxford University Press.

National Science Foundation. (2006). *Surveys of public understanding of science and technology: 1979–2006.* Retrieved Aug. 22, 2011, from <http://www.ropercenter.uconn.edu>.

Nelson, T. D. (Ed.) (2009). *Handbook of prejudice, stereotyping, and discrimination.* New York: Psychology Press.

Nerlich, B., Elliott, R., & Larson, B. (Eds.) (2009). *Communicating biological sciences: Ethical and metaphorical dimensions.* Burlington, VT: Ashgate.

Nesi, T. (2008). *Poison pills: The untold story of the Vioxx drug scandal.* New York: St. Martin's Press.

Nettler, G. (1970). *Explanations.* New York: McGraw Hill.

Newman, M. (2010). Bitter pills for drug companies. *BMJ*, 341, c5095.

Newman, R. (1997). Promoting the profession is top priority. *APA Monitor*, Feb., 32.

Nickerson, R. S. (1986). *Reflections on reasoning*. Hillsdale, NJ: Lawrence Erlbaum.

Nickerson, R. S. (1998). Confirmation bias: A ubiquitous phenomena in many guises. *Review of General Psychology*, 2, 175–220.

Nickerson, R. S. (2008). *Aspects of rationality: Reflections on what it means to be rational and whether we are*. New York: Psychology Press.

Nickerson, R. S. (2009). Are social scientists harder on their colleagues than physical scientists were on theirs in the past? Comments on "Great Works of the Past." *Perspectives on Psychological Science*, 4, 79–83.

Nicole, R. M. (1991). Manifesto for science and clinical psychology. *Clinical Psychologist*, 44, 75–88.

Nisbett, R. E., & Ross, L. (1980*). Human inference: Strategies and shortcomings of social judgement*. Englewood Cliffs, NJ: Prentice Hall.

Nisbett, R. E., Borgida, E., Crandall, R., & Reed, H. (1976). Popular induction: Information is not necessarily informative. In J. S. Carroll & J. W. Payne (Eds.), *Cognition and social behavior*. Hillsdale, NJ: Erlbaum.

Nissen, S. E., & Wolski, K. (2007). Effect of Rosiglitazone on the risk of myocardio infraction and death from cardiovascular causes. *New England Journal of Medicine*, 356, 2457–71.

Norcross, J. C., Beutler, L. E., & Levant, R. F. (Eds.) (2006). *Evidence-based practices in mental health: Debate and dialogue on the fundamental questions*. Washington, DC: American Psychological Association.

Norcross, J. C., Santrock, J. W., Campbell, L. F., & Smith, T. P. (2003). *Authoritative guide to self-help resources in mental health* (Rev. ed.). New York: Guilford.

Notturno, M. A. (2000). *Science and the open society: The future of Karl Popper's Philosophy*. New York: Central European University Press.

Nugus, P., Greenfield, D., Travaglia, J., Westbrook, J., & Braithwaite, J. (2010). How and where clinicians exercise power: Interprofessional relations in health care. *Social Science & Medicine*, 71, 898–909.

Oakes, M. (1986). *Statistical inference: A commentary for the social and behavioral sciences*. New York: Wiley.

Oakley, A. (1976). *Women's work: The housewife, past and present*. New York: Vintage.

O'Connell, M. E., Boat, T., & Warner, K. E. (Eds.) (2009). *Preventing mental harm, emotional harm and behavioral disorders among young people: Progress and possibilities*. National Research Council and Institute of Medicine. Committee on the Prevention of Mental Disorders and Substance Abuse among Children, Youth, and Young Adults. Washington, DC: National Academy Press.

O'Connor, A. M., Wennberg, J. E., Legare, F., Llewellyn-Thomas, H. A., Moulton, B. W., Sepucha, K. R., Sodano, A. G., & King, J. S. (2007). Toward the "tipping point": Decision aids and informed patient choice. *Health Affairs*, 26, 716–25.

O'Connor, A. M., Bennett, C. L., Stacey, D., Barry, M., Col, N. F., Eden, K. B., Entwistle, V. A., Fiset, V., Holmes-Rovner, M., Khangura, S., Llewellyn-Thomas, H., & Rovner, D. (2009). Decision aids for people facing health treatment or screening decisions. *Cochrane Database of Systematic Reviews*, 3, CD001431.

Offit, P. A. (2009). *Autism's false prophets: Bad science, risky medicine, and the search for a cure*. New York: Columbia University Press.

Ofshe, R., & Watters, E. (1994). *Making monsters: False memories, psychotherapy, and sexual hysteria*. New York: Charles Scribner's.

Oldani, M. J. (2004). Thick prescriptions: Toward an interpretation of pharmaceutical sales practices. *Medical Anthropology Quarterly*, 18(3), 325–56.

Oliver, D. & Healey, F. (2009). Falls risk prediction tools for hospital inpatients: do they work? *Nursing Times*, 105, 18–21.

Oliver, J. E. (2006). *Fat politics: The real story behind America's obesity epidemic*. New York: Oxford University Press.

Olmos, D. R. (1997). Elaborate fraud scheme by plastic surgeons alleged. *San Francisco Examiner*, Oct. 26, D-5.

Oreskes, N., & Conway, E. M. (2010). *Merchants of doubt: How a handful of scientists obscured the truth and issues from tobacco smoke to global warming*. New York: Bloomsbury Press.

Orlowsky, J. P., & Wateska, L. (1992). The effects of pharmaceutical firm enticements on physician prescribing patterns. There is no such thing as a free lunch. *Chest*, 102, 270–73.

Orr, J. (2006). *Panic diaries: A geneology of panic disorder*. Durham, NC: Duke University Press.

Orr, J. (2010). Biopsychiatry and the informatics of diagnosis. In A. E. Clarke, L. Mamo, J. R. Fosket, J. R. Fishman, & J. K. Shim (Eds.), *Biomedicalization, technoscience, health, and illness in the U.S.* (pp. 352–79). Durham, NC: Duke University Press.

Orwell, G. ([1946] 1958). Politics and the English language. In S. Orwell & I. Angus (Eds.), *The collected essays, journalism and letters of George Orwell*. Vol. 4: *In front of your nose, 1945–1950* (pp. 127–40). London: Secker & Warburg.

Oskamp, S. (1965). Overconfidence in case-study judgements. *Journal of Consulting Psychology*, 29, 261–65.

Othman, N., Vitry, A., & Roughead, E. E. (2009). Quality of pharmaceutical advertisements in medical journals: A systematic review. *PLoS One*, 4, e6350.

Our Reporter. (2009). Firm faces large fine over death. *Oxford Times*, Oct.8, 16.

Overpromoted cholesterol drug. (2009). Editorial. *New York Times*, Apr. 2.

Oxlad, M., & Baldwin, S. (1995). Electroconvulsive therapy, children and adolescents: The power to stop. *Nursing Ethics*, 2, 333–46.

Oxman, A. D., & Guyatt, G. H. (1993). The science of reviewing research. In K. S. Warren & F. Mosteller (Eds.), *Doing more good than harm: The evaluation of health care interventions* (pp. 125–33). New York: New York Academy of Sciences.

Ozner, J. (2008). *The great American heart hoax: Life saving advice your doctor should tell you about heart disease prevention (but probably never will)*. Dallas, TX: Benbella Books.

Paling, J. (2006). *Helping patients understand risks: 7 simple strategies for successful communication*. Gainesville, FL: Risk Communication Institute.

Pam, A. (1995). Biological psychiatry: Science or pseudoscience? In C.A. Ross & A. Pam (Eds.), *Pseudoscience in biological psychiatry* (pp. 7–84). New York: John Wiley & Sons.

Parenti, M. (1977). *Democracy for the few*. New York: St. Martin's Press.

Parenti, M. (1986). *Inventing reality: The politics of the mass media*. New York: St. Martin's Press.

Parenti, M. (2011). Monopoly media manipulation. Retrieved Aug. 23, 2011, from <http://www.michaelparenti.org/monopoly/media>.

Parker, C., Coupland, C., & Hippisley-Cox, J. (2010). Antipsychotic drugs and risk of venous thromboembolism: Nested case-control study. *BMJ*, 341, c4245.

Parry, J. (2003). The art of branding a condition. *Medical Marketing and Media*, 38, 43–49.

Parry, J. (2005). WHO combats counterfeit malaria drugs in Asia. *BMJ*, 330, 10441.

Parry, J. (2008). Contaminated infant formula sickens 6200 babies in China. *BMJ*, 337, a1738.

Parsons, Talcott (1949). *Essays in sociological theory* (revised ed.). New York: Free Press.

Pashler, H., McDaniel, M., Rohrer, D., & Bjork, R. (2008). Learning styles. Concepts and evidence. *Psychological Science in the Public Interest*, 9, 105–19.

Passalacqua, R., Caminiti, C., Salvagni, S., Barni, S., Beretta, G. D., Carlini, P., et al. (2004). Effects of media information on cancer patients' opinions, feelings, decision-making process and physician–patient communication. *Cancer*, 100, 1077–84.

Patai, D., & Koertge, N. (2003). *Professing feminism: Education and indoctrination in women's studies* (New ed.). Lanham, MD: Lexington Books.

Patton, B. M. (2000). *Truth, knowledge or just plain bull: How to tell the difference*. Amherst, NY: Prometheus.

Paul, R. W. (1993). *Critical thinking: What every person needs to survive in a rapidly changing world* (3rd ed.). Santa Rosa, CA: Foundation for Critical Thinking. <http://www.criticalthinking.org>.

Paul, R. W., & Elder, L. (2004). *Critical thinking: Tools for taking charge of your professional and personal life*. Upper Saddle River, NJ: Prentice Hall.

Paul, R. W., Elder, L., & Bartell, J. (1997). *California teacher preparation for instruction in critical thinking: Research findings and policy recommendations*. Sacramento: California Commission on Teacher Credentialing.

Paulos, J. A. (1988). *Innumeracy: Mathematical illiteracy and its consequences*. New York: Vintage.

Payer, L. (1992). *Disease mongers: How doctors, drug companies, and insurers are making you feel sick*. New York: John Wiley & Sons.

Pear, R. (2004). U.S. finds fault in all 50 states' child welfare programs, and penalties may follow. *New York Times*, Apr. 26, A27.

Pear, R. (2007a). Audit cites overpaid Medicare insurers. *New York Times*, Sept. 10, A17.

Pear, R. (2007b). Insurer faces reprimand in Medicare marketing case. *New York Times*, May 15, A14.

Pear, R. (2007c). Oversight of nursing homes is criticized. *New York Times*, Apr. 22, A17.

Peck, P. (2007). FTC fines diet pill makers millions for bogus claims. Jan. 4, <http://medpagetoday.com>.

Peele, S. (1999). *Diseasing of America: How we allowed recovery zealots and the treatment industry to convince us we are out of control*. San Francisco: Jossey-Bass.

Peirce, C. S. (1934–48). *Collected papers* (4 vols.) Cambridge, MA: Harvard University Press.

Peirce, C. S. (1958). *Values in a universe of chance*, ed. P. P. Weiner. New York: Doubleday.

Penston, J. (2010). Stats.con: *How we've been fooled by statistics-based research in medicine*. London: London Press.

Pepper, C. (1984). *Quackery: A $10 billion scandal: Subcommittee on health ad long-term care of the Select Committee on Aging. U.S. House of Representatives*. Select Committee on Aging. U.S. House of Representatives. No. 98-435. Washington, DC: U.S. Government Printing House.

Pepper, S. (1981). Problems in the quantification of frequency experiences. In D. Fiske (Ed.), *New directions for methodology of social and behavioral science: No. 9. Problems with language imprecision* (pp. 25–42). San Francisco: Jossey-Bass.

Percy, W. (1991). *Signposts in a strange land*, ed. P. Samway. New York: Farrar, Straus & Giroux.

Perez-Alvarez, M., Sass, L. A., & Garcia-Montes, J. M. (2008). More Aristotle, less DSM: The ontology of mental disorders in constructivist perspective. *Philosophy, Psychiatry, & Psychology*, 15, 227–237.

Pérez-Peña, R. (2006). New York puts mental patients in homes illegally, group says. *New York Times*, Mar. 8, A23.

Pérez-Peña, R. (2010). New Jersey is sued over the forced medication of patients at psychiatric hospitals. *New York Times*, Aug. 4, A15.

Petersen, M. (2008). *Our daily meds: How the pharmaceutical companies transformed themselves into slick marketing machines and hooked the nation on prescription drugs*. New York: Picador.

Petrarca, F. (2003). *Invectives*, trans. D. Marsh. Cambridge, MA: Harvard University Press.

Petrosino, A., Turpin-Petrosino, C., & Buehler, J. (2003). Scared straight and other juvenile awareness programs for preventing juvenile delinquency: A systematic review of the randomized experimental evidence. *ANNALS of the American Academy of Political and Social Science*, 589, 41–62.

Petrosino, A., Turpin-Petrosino, C., & Finckenauer, J. O. (2000). Well-meaning programs can have harmful effects! Lessons from experiments of programs such as Scared Straight. *Crime & Delinquency*, 46, 354–79.

Petryna, A., Lakoff, A., & Kleinman, A. (Eds.) (2006). *Global pharmaceuticals: Ethics, markets, practices*. Durham, NC: Duke University Press.

Pfohl, S. (1994). *Images of deviance and social control: A sociological history* (2nd ed.). New York: McGraw Hill.

Phillips, C. B. (2006). Medicine goes to school: Teachers as sickness brokers for ADHD. *PloS Med*, 3, e182.

Phillips, D. C. (1987). *Philosophy, science and social inquiry: Contemporary methodological controversies in social science and related applied fields of research*. New York: Pergamon Press.

Phillips, D. C. (1992). *The social scientist's bestiary: A guide to fabled threats to, and defenses of, naturalistic social studies*. New York: Pergamon.

Phillips, D. C. (2000). *The expanded social scientist's bestiary: A guide to fabled threats to, and defenses of, naturalistic social science*. New York: Rowman & Littlefield.

Pignotti, M., & Mercer, J. (2007). Holding therapy and dyadic developmental psychotherapy are not supported in acceptable social work interventions: A systematic research synthesis revisited. *Research on Social Work Practice*, 17, 513–19.

Pimplikar, S. W. (2010). Alzheimer's isn't up to the tests. *Op Ed*, July 20, A21.

Pitts-Taylor, V. (2007). *Surgery junkies: Wellness and pathology in cosmetic culture*. New Brunswick, NJ: Rutgers University Press.

Planck, M. (1949). *Scientific autobiography and other papers*, trans. F. Gaynor. New York: Philosophical Library.

PLoS Medicine Editors. (2011). Let's be straight up about the alcohol industry. *PLoS Med*, 8, e1001041.

Poe, E. (2004). A simpler way to understand the results of risk assessment instruments. *Children and Youth Services Review*, 26, 873–83.

Poerksen, U. (1995). *Plastic words: The tyranny of a modular language*, trans. Jutta Mason and David Cayley. University Park: Penn State.

Pohl, R. F. (2004). *Cognitive illusions: A handbook on fallacies and biases in thinking, judgment and memory*. New York: Psychology Press.

Pollack, A. (2007). Studies show anemia drugs may harm cancer patients. *New York Times*, Feb. 27.

Popper, K. R. (1972). *Conjectures and refutations: The growth of scientific knowledge* (4th ed.). London: Routledge & Kegan Paul.

Popper, K. R. (1992). *In search of a better world: Lectures and essays from thirty years*. London: Routledge & Kegan Paul.

Popper, K. R. (1994). *The myth of the framework: In defense of science and rationality*, edited by M. A. Notturno. New York: Routledge.

Popper, K. (1998). *The world of Parmenides: Essays on the pre-Socratic enlightenment*. New York: Routledge.

Porter, R. (2002). *Quacks: Fakers & charlatans in English medicine*. Charleston, SC: Tempus.

Porter, T. (1995). *Trust in numbers: The pursuit of objectivity in science and public life*. Princeton, NJ: Princeton University Press.

Postman, N. (1976). *Crazy talk, stupid talk: How we defeat ourselves by the way we talk and what to do about it*. New York: Delacorte.

Postman, N. (1982). *The disappearance of childhood*. New York: Delacorte.

Postman, N. (1985a). *Amusing ourselves to death: Public discourse in the age of show business*. New York: Penguin.

Postman, N. (1985b). The parable of the ring around the collar. *Conscientious Objections*, 66–71.

Postman, N. (1992). *Technopoly: The surrender of culture to technology*. New York: Knopf.

Practitioner Update. (1996). American Psychological Association, 4/4, Dec., 3.

Pratkanis, A. R. (1995). How to sell a pseudoscience. *Skeptical Inquirer,* 19, 19–25.

Pratkanis, A. R., & Aronson, E. (2001). *Age of propaganda: The everyday use and abuse of persuasion* (Rev. ed.). New York: W. H. Freeman & Co.

Pratkanis, A. R. (2007). *The science of social influence: Advances and future progress*. New York: Psychology Press.

President of Missouri State U. threatens to shut social work school after scathing report. (2007). *Chronicle of Higher Education*, Apr. 20, A17.

President's new freedom commission on mental health. (2002).Retrieved Sept. 9, 2005, from <http://www.mentalhealthcommission.gov>.

Pringle, E. (2007a). No MedGuide for Zyprexa after eleven years of death and injury. June 18. Retrieved Aug. 25, 2011, from <http://psychrights.org>.

Pringle, E. (2007b). Lilly makes billions off Zyprexa. *Scoop Independent News*. Retrieved from <http://www.scoop.co/nz/stories/HL0711/S00248/lilly-makes-billions-off>.

Pringle, E. (2007c). Patients diagnosed schizophrenic and bipolar to boost Seroquel sales, Apr. 11, 3. Retrieved Nov. 26, 2008, from <http://psychrights.org>.

Proctor, R. N., & Schiebinger, L. (Eds.) (2008). *Agnotology: The making and unmaking of ignorance*. Palo Alto, CA: Stanford University Press.

Profession dominates mental health: There are more clinically trained social workers than members of other core mental health professions combined. (1999). *NASW News*, June.

Prounis, C. (2004). The art of advertorial. *Pharmaceutical Executive*, 24, 152–59.

Quinsey, V. L., Harris, G. T., Rice, M. E., & Cormier, C. A. (2006). *Violent offenders: Appraising the managing risks* (2nd ed.). Washington, DC: American Psychological Association.

Raab, S. (1996). New Jersey officials say mafia infiltrated health care industry. *New York Times*, Aug. 21, C19.

Raab, S. S., Meier, F. A., Zarbo, R. J., Jensen, D. C., Geisinger, K. R., Booth, C. N., et al. (2006). The "Big Dog" effect: Variability assessing the causes of error in diagnosis of patients with lung cancer. *Journal of Clinical Oncology*, 24(18), 2808–14.

Rabin, R. C. (2009). Benefits of mammogram under debate in Britain. *New York Times*, Mar. 31.

Rabin, R. C. (2010). Risks: Study looks at serotonin and SIDS deaths. *New York Times*, Feb. 9.

Raghunathan, R., & Pham, M. T. (1999). All negative moods are not equal: Motivational influences of anxiety and sadness on decision making. *Organizational Behavior and Human Decision Processes*, 79, 56–77.

Rampton, S., & Stauber, J. (2001). *Trust us, we're experts!: How industry manipulates science and gambles with your future*. New York: Penguin.

Randazzo, S. (1993). *Myth making on Madison Avenue*. Chicago: Probus.

Rank, H. (1984a). *The pep talk: How to analyze political language*. Park Forest, IL: Counter-Propaganda Press.

Rank, H. (1984b). *The pitch: A simple 1-2-3-4-5 way to understand the basic pattern of persuasion in advertising*. Park Forrest, IL: Counter-propaganda Press.

Ravitch, D. (2003). *The language police: How pressure groups restrict what students learn*. New York: Alfred A. Knopf.

Ravitch, D. R. (2000). *Left back: A century of failed school reforms*. New York: Simon & Schuster.

Read, J., van Os, J., Morrison, A. P., & Ross, C. A. (2005). Childhood trauma, psychosis, and schizophrenia: A literature review with theoretical and clinical implications. *Acta Psychiatrica Scandinavica*, 112, 330–50.

Reason, J. (1997). *Managing the risks of organizational accidents*. Aldershot (UK): Ashgate.

Reason, J. (2005). Understanding adverse events: The human factor. In C. Vincent (Ed.), *Clinical risk management: Enhancing patients safety* (2nd ed.) (pp. 9–30). London: BMJ Books.

Reiff, P. (1985). *The Triumph of the therapeutic: Uses of faith after Freud* (2nd Ed.) Chicago: University of Chicago Press.

Reiman, J. (2004). *The rich get richer and the poor get prison* (7th ed.). Boston: Allyn & Bacon.

Renaud, H., & Estess, F. (1961). Life history interviews with 100 normal American males: "Pathogenicity" of childhood. *American Journal of Orthopsychiatry*, 31, 796–802.

Renner, C. H. (2004). Validity effect. In R. F. Pohl (Ed.), *Cognitive illusions: A handbook on fallacies and biases in thinking, judgement and memory* (pp. 201–13). New York: Psychology Press.

Renstrom, L., Andersson, B., & Marton, F. (1990). Students' conceptions of matter. *Journal of Educational Psychology*, 82, 555–69.

Reuben, H. P. (2002). Effects of managed care and the length of time that elderly patients spend with physicians during ambulatory visits. National Ambulatory Medical Survey. *Medical Care*, July 40(7), 606–13.

Reverby, S. M. (2007). Racial categories in medical practice: How useful are they? *PloS Med*, e207.

Reverby, S. M. (2010a). Invoking "Tuskegee": Problems in health disparities, genetic assumptions and history. *Journal of Health Care for the Poor and Underserved*, 21(Supplement), 226–34.

Reverby, S. M. (2010b). "Normal exposure" and inoculation syphilis: A PHS "Tuskegee" doctor in Guatemala, 1946–48. *Journal of Policy History*, Jan.

Rew, L., Mandeep, K., McMillan, A., Mackert, M., & Bonevac, D. (2010). Systematic review of psychosocial benefits and harms of genetic testing. *Mental Health Nursing*, 31, 631–45.

Richtel, M. (2010). Growing up digital, wired for distraction. *New York Times*, Nov. 21, 1/29.

Ripkin, J. (1998). *The biotech century*. New York: Putman.

A Rip-off by health insurers? (2008). Editorial. *New York Times*, Feb. 18, A18.

Rising, K., Bacchetti, P., & Bero, L. (2008). Reporting bias in drug trials submitted to the Food and Drug Administration: Review of Publication and Presentation. *PLoS Med*, Nov.

Rivera, R. (2006). State fines clinic $16.54 million saying it overbilled Medicaid. *New York Times*, Oct. 2, A.19.

Roberts, G. (1994). *The mirror of alchemy: Alchemical ideas and images in manuscripts and books from antiquity to the seventeenth century*. London: British Library.

Roberts, S. (2008). Riff between dentist's groups illustrate power of the politically connected. *New York Times*, June 23, A22.

Roberts, S. (2010). Census figures challenge views of race and ethnicity. *New York Times*, Jan. 22, A13.

Rockoff, J. D. (2009). Analysis finds Vioxx's heart attack risk in 2001. *Health Industry*, Nov. 24.

Roehr, B. (2009). Pope claims that condoms exacerbate HIV and AIDS problem. *BMJ*, 338, b1206.

Roehr, B. (2010a). Medicalization costs $77 billion in US, study says. *BMJ*, 340, c2779.

Roehr, B. (2010b). US health lobbyists outnumbered members of Congress by eight to one in 2009. *BMJ*, 340, c1203.

Rogowski, S. (2010). *Social work. The rise and fall of a profession?* Bristol, UK: Policy Press.

Rokeach, M. (1960). *The open and closed mind*. New York: Basic Books.

Romme, M., & Escher, S. (1989). Hearing voices. *Schizophrenia Bulletin*, 15, 209–16.

Room, R. (2010). Prohibition of cannabis is not achieving its aims in the US, and may even worsen outcomes. *BMJ*, 341, 744.

Room, R., Fischer, D., Hall, W., Lenton, S., & Reuter, P. (2010). *Cannabis policy: Moving beyond stalemate*. New York: Oxford University Press.

Rosa, L., Rosa, E., Sarner, L., & Barrett, S. (1998). A close look at therapeutic touch. *Journal of the Medical Association*, 279, 1005–10.

Rose, S. C., Bisson, J., Churchill, R., & Wessely, S. (2002). Psychological debriefing for preventing post traumatic stress disorder (PTSD). (Cochrane Database of Systematic Review). Chichester: Wiley. (Published online November 21, 2009.)

Roseman, M., Milette, K., Bero, L. A., Coyne, J. C., Lexchin, J., Turner, E. H., & Thombs, B. D. (2011). Reporting of conflicts of interest in meta-analyses of trials of pharmacological treatments. *JAMA*, 305, 1008–17.

Rosen, G. R., & Lilienfeld, S. O. (2008). Post traumatic stress disorder: An empirical analysis of core assumptions. *Clinical Psychology Review*, 28, 837–68.

Rosenau, P. M. (1992). *Post-modernism and the social sciences: Insights, inroads, and intrusions*. Princeton, NJ: Princeton University Press.

Rosenhan, D. L. (1973). On being sane in insane places. *Science*, 179, 250–58.

Rosenthal, T. (1994). Science and ethics in conducting, analyzing, and reporting psychological research. *Psychological Science*, 5(3), 127–34.

Ross, J., Hill, K. P., Egilman, D. S., & Krumholz, H. M. (2008). Guest authorship and ghost writing in publications related to Rofecoxib. *JAMA*, 299, 1800–1812.

Ross, L., Lepper, M. R., & Hubbard, J. (1975). Perseverance in self perception and social perception: Biased attributional processes in the debriefing paradigm. *Journal of Personality and Social Psychology*, 32, 880–92.

Rossi, P. H., Lipsey, M. W., & Freeman, H. E. (2004). *Evaluation: A systematic approach* (7th ed.). Thousand Oaks, CA: Sage.

Rothfeld, M. (2010). Drug firms face bribery probe. *Wall Street Journal*, Oct. 5.

Rothman, D. J., McDonald, W. J., Berkowitz, C. D., Chimonas, S. C., DeAngelis, C. D., Hale, R. W., et al. (2009). Professional medical associations and their relationships with industry. *Journal of the American Medical Association*, 301, 1367–72.

Routzahn, E. G., & Routzahn, M. S. (1918). *The A B C of exhibit planning*. New York: Russell Sage.

Routzahn, M. S. (1920). *Traveling publicity campaigns*. New York: Russell Sage Foundation.

Rubin, A., & Parrish, D. (2007). Problematic phrases in the conclusions of published outcome studies: Implications for evidence-based practice. *Research on Social Work Practice*, 17, 592–602.

Rudy, A. P., Coppin, D., Konefal, J., Shaw, B. T., Eyck, T., Harris, C., & Busch, L. (2007). *Universities in the age of corporate science: The UC Berkeley–Novartis controversy*. Philadelphia: Temple University Press.

Rummel-Kluge, C., Komossa, K., Schwarz, S., Hunger, H., Schmid, F., Lobos, C. A., Kissling, W., Davis, J. M., Leucht, S. (2010). Head-to-head comparisons of metabolic side effects of second generation antipsychotics in the treatment of schizophrenia: A systematic review and meta-analysis. *Schizophr Res.*, 123(2–3), 225–33.

Ryan, W. (1976). *Blaming the victim* (Rev. ed.). New York: Vantage.

Rycroft, C. (1973). *A critical dictionary of psychoanalysis*. Towata, NJ: Littlefield, Adams.

Sackeim, H. A., Prudic, J., Fuller, R., Keilp, J., Lavori, P., & Olfson, M. (2007). The cognitive effects of electroconvulsive therapy in community settings. *Neuropsychopharmacology*, 32, 244–54.

Sackett, D. L. (1979). Bias in analytic research. *Journal of Chronic Disease*, 32, 51–63.

Sackett, D. L. (2002). The arrogance of preventive medicine. *Canadian Medical Association Journal*, 167, 363–64.

Sackett, D. L., & Oxman, A. D. (2003). Harlot pie: Amalgamation of the world's two oldest professions. *BMJ*, 327, 1442–45.

Sackett, D. L., Richardson, W. S., Rosenberg, W., & Haynes, R. B. (1997). *Evidence-based medicine: How to practice and teach EBM*. New York: Churchill Livingston.

Safety in numbers?—Risk Assessment and Environmental Protection. Available from POST at 7, Millbank, London SW1P 3JA (tel 0171-219-2840).

Sagan, C. (1987). The burden of skepticism. *Skeptical Inquirer*, 12, 38–74.

Sagan, C. (1990). Why we need to understand science. *Skeptical Inquirer*, 14, 263–69.

Sailor, W., & Paul, J. (2004). Framing positive behavior support in the ongoing discourse concerning the politics of knowledge. *Journal of Positive Behavior Intervention*, 6, 37–49.

Sailor, W., Dunlap, G., Sugai, G., & Horner, R. (Eds.). *Handbook of positive behavior support*. New York: Springer.

Sandblom, G., Varenhorst, E., Lofman, O., & Carlsson, P. (2011). Randomized prostate cancer screening trial: 20 year follow-up. *BMJ*, 342, d1539.

Sarbin, T. R. (1967). On the futility of the proposition that some people be labeled 'mentally ill'. *Journal of Consulting Psychology*, 31, 447–53.

Sarnoff, S. K. (2001). *Sanctified snake oil: The effect of junk science on public policy*. Westport, CT: Praeger.

Saul, S. (2008b). Heart group backs drug made by ally. *New York Times*, Jan. 24. B1

Saul, S. (2007a). Bristol-Myers pleads guilty and is fined in Plavix case. *New York Times*, June 12, C3.

Saul, S. (2007b). Doctors and drug makers: A move to end cozy ties. *New York Times*, C1.

Saul, S. (2007c). Doctor says he was assailed for challenging drug's safety. *New York Times*, June 12, C3.

Saul, S. (2008a). Drug executive is indicted on secret deal. *New York Times*, Apr. 24.

Saul, S. (2008b). Merck wrote drug studies for doctors. *New York Times*, Apr. 16, C1.

Saul, S. (2010). Prone to error: Earliest steps to find cancer. From tiniest samples to needless surgery. *New York Times National*, July 20, ___.

The scandal of social work education. (2007). National Association of Scholars. Retrieved on Aug. 19, 2011, from <http://www.nas.org>.

Scheff, T. J. (1984). *Labeling madness* (2nd ed.). Englewood Cliffs, NJ: Prentice Hall.

Schein, E. H. (1998). *Process consultation revisited: Building the helping 'relationship.'* Reading, MA: Addison Wesley.

Schemo, D. J. (2007). Report recounts horrors of youth boot camps. *The New York Times*, October 11.

Schetky, D. H. (2008). Conflicts of interest between physicians and the pharmaceutical industry and special interest groups. *Child and Adolescent Psychiatric Clinics of North America*, 17, 113–25.

Schilipp, P. A. (1974). *The philosophy of Karl Popper*. LaSalle, IL: Open Court.

Schipper, E. W., & Schuh, E. (1959). *A first course in modern logic*. New York: Henry Holt.

Schneeweiss, S., Setoguchi, S., Brookhart, A., Dormuth, C., & Wang, P. S. (2007). Risk of death associated with the use of conventional versus atypical antipsychotic drugs among elderly patients. *Canadian Medical Association Journal*, 176, 627–32.

Schneider, S. M. (2007). The tangled tale of genes and environment: Moore's *The dependent gene: The fallacy of "nature vs.nurture." Behav Anal*, 30(1), 91–105.

Schneider, W. H. (1965). *Danger: Men talking*. New York: Random House.

Schon, D. A. (1990). *Educating the reflective practitioner* (New Ed.). San Francisco, CA: Jossey-Bass.

Schooler, L. J., & Hertwig, R. (2005). How forgetting aids heuristic inference. *Psychological Review*, 111, 610–28.

Schopenhauer, A. (1942). The art of controversy. In A. Schopenhauer, *The essays of Arthur Schopenhauer*, trans. T. B. Saunders. New York: Wiley.

Schott, G., Pachl, H., Limbach, U., Gundert-Remy, U., Ludwig, W.-D., & Lieb, K. (2010). The financing of drug trials by pharmaceutical companies and its consequences. Part I: A qualitative, systematic review of the literature on possible influences of the findings, protocols, and the quality of drug trials. *Dtsch Arztebl Int.*, 107, 279–85.

Schulz, K. (2004). Did antidepressants depress Japan? *New York Times Magazine*, Aug. 22, 38–41.

Schulz, K. F., & Grimes, D. A. (2006). *The LANCET handbook of essential concepts in clinical research*. New York: Elsevier.

Schulz, K. F., Chalmers, I., Hayes, R. J., & Altman, D. G. (1995). Empirical evidence of bias. Dimensions of methodological quality associated with estimates of treatment effects in controlled clinical trials. *Journal of the American Medical Association*, 273(5), 408–12.

Schwartz, I. M. (1989). *(In)justice for juveniles: Rethinking the best interests of the child*. Lexington, MA: Lexington.

Schwartz, L. M., & Woloshin, S. (2011). The drug facts box: Making informed decisions about prescription drugs possible. In G. Gigerenzer & J. A. M. Gray (Eds.) (2011). *Better doctors, better patients, better decisions* (pp. 233–42). Cambridge, MA: MIT Press.

Schwartz, L. M., Woloshin, S., & Moynihan, R. (2008). Who's watching the watchdogs? *BMJ*, 337, a2535.

Schwartz, L. M., Woloshin, S., & Welch, H. G. (2007). Using a drug facts box to communicate drug benefits and harms: Two randomized controlled trials. *Medical Decision Making*, 27, 655.

Schwitzer, G. (2008). How do US journalists cover treatments, tests, products and procedures? An evaluation of 500 stories. *PLoS Med*, 5(5), e95.

Scott, I. (2009). Errors in clinical reasoning: Causes and remedial strategies. *BMJ*, 339, 22–25.

Scott, S., Knapp, M., Henderson, J., & Maughan, B. (2001). Financial cost of social exclusion: Follow-up study of anti-social children into adulthood. *BMJ*, 323, 191–94.

Scott, T., Stanford, N., & Thompson, D. R. (2004). Killing me softly: Myth in pharmaceutical advertising. *BMJ*, 329, 1484–87.

Scriven, M. (1976). *Reasoning*. New York: McGraw Hill.

Scull, A. (1989). *Social order/mental disorder: Anglo-American psychiatry in historical perspective*. London: Routledge.

Scull, A. (2005). *Madhouse: A tragic tale of megalomania and modern medicine*. New Haven, CT: Yale University Press.

Sedgwick, P. (1982). *Psychopolitics*. New York: Harper & Row.

Seife, C. (2010). *Proofiness: The dark arts of mathematical deception*. New York: Viking.

Senator Grassley's letter to the National Alliance for Mental Illness (NAMI). Apr. 26, 2010. Retrieved Aug. 8, 2011, from <http://grassley.senate.gov/about/upload/2010-04-26-letter to NAMI>.

Sennett, R. (1970). *The uses of disorder: Personal identity and city life*. New York: W. W. Norton.

Sessions, D. (2010). Psychotropic drug abuse in foster care costs government billions. *Politics Daily*, June 16.

Sexton, C. J. (2007). Florida: Settlement in boot camp death. *The New York Times*: March 15.

Severin, A. (2002). New York doctor charged with maiming mental patients at for-profit facilities *New York Times*, July 10.

Shadish, W. R., Cook, T. D., & Campbell, D. T. (2002). *Experimental and quasi-experimental designs for generalized causal inference*. Boston: Houghton-Mifflin.

Shaffer, V. A., & Hulsey, L. (2009). Are patient decision aids effective? Insight from revisiting the debate between correspondence and coherence theories of judgment. *Judgment and Decision Making*, 4, 141–46.

Shah, A. K., & Oppenheimer, D. N. (2008). Heuristics made easy: An effort-reduction framework. *Psychological Bulletin*, 134, 207–22.

Sharav, V. H. (2002). Conflicts of interest. 14th Tri-Service Clinical Investigation Symposium. The U.S. Army Medical Department and the Henry M. Jackson Foundation for the Advancement of Military Medicine, May 5–7.

Sharpe, V. A., & Faden, A. I. (1998). *Medical harm: Historical, conceptual, and ethical dimensions of iatrogenic illness.* New York: Cambridge University Press.

Shaw, A. (2008). Direct-to-consumer advertising (DTC) of pharmaceuticals. A pro quest discovery guide. <http://www.csa.com/discoveryguides/direct/review>.

Shaw, G. B. (1946). *The doctor's dilemma.* New York: Penguin.

Sheldon, T. (2008). Academics criticize suicide claims made in American Psychiatric Journal, *BMJ,* 1119.

Sheldon, T. (2010). Patient groups must reveal corporate sponsorship, urges campaign group. *BMJ,* 341, c4459.

Sheldon, T. A., Guyatt, G. H., & Haines, A. (1998). Getting research findings into practice: When to act on the evidence. *BMJ,* 317, 139–42.

Shenk, D. (1997). *Data smog.* New York: Harper Edge.

Sherdan, W. A. (1998). *The fortune tellers: The big business of buying and selling predictions.* New York: Wiley.

Shermer, M. (1997). *Why people believe weird things: Pseudoscience, superstition, and other confusions of our time.* New York: W. H. Freeman.

Shiv, B., Carmon, Z., & Ariely, D. (2005). Placebo effects of marketing actions: Consumers may get what they pay for. *Journal of Marketing Research,* 42, 383–93.

Shorter, E., & Healy, D. (2007). *Shock therapy: The history of electroconvulsive treatment in mental illness.* New Brunswick, NJ: Rutgers University Press.

Silverman, E. (2008). Erbitux prolongs life in lung cancer study. *Pharmalot.com,* May 31.

Silverman, E. (2010a). AstraZeneca pays $198 M for 17,500 Seroquel suits. Posted Aug. 9, 2010. Retrieved Aug. 20, 2011, from <http://www.pharmalot.com>.

Silverman, E. (2010b). Yale medical group tightens conflict policy. Sept. 16. Retrieved Sept. 17, 2010, from <http://www.pharmalot.com>.

Silverman, E. (2010). Healthcare Fraud, Whistleblowers & US Treasury. HYPERLINK "http://www.pharmalot.com" www.pharmalot.com Oct. 25.

Silverman, W. A. (1990). *Retrolental fibroplasia: A modern parable.* New York: Grune & Stratton.

Simes, R. J. (1986). Publication bias: The case for an international registry of clinical trials. *Journal of Clinical Oncology,* 4, 1529–41.

Simon, H. A. (1982). *Models of bounded rationality.* Cambridge, MA: MIT Press.

Simon, H. A. (1983). *Reason in human affairs.* Stanford, CA: Stanford California Press.

Simpson, E. L. (2002). Involving users in the delivery and evaluation of mental health services: Systematic review. *BMJ,* 325, 1260.

Sinclair, J. C., Cook, R. J., Guyatt, G. H., Pauker, S. G., & Cook, D. J. (2001). When should an effective treatment be used? Deviation of the threshold number needed to treat and the minimum event rate for treatment. *Journal of Clinical Epidemiology,* 54(3), 253–62.

Singer, N. (2009a). A birth control pill that promised too much. *New York Times,* Feb. 11.

Singer, N. (2009b). Doctor gifts to be public in Vermont. *New York Times,* May 20, B1/10.

Singer, N. (2009c). Forty year's war. In push for cancer screening, limited benefits. *New York Times,* July 16.

Singer, N. (2009d). Medical papers by ghostwriters pushed therapy. *New York Times,* Aug. 5.

Singer, N. (2009e). Senator moves to block medical ghostwriting. *New York Times,* Aug. 19. Retrieved June 10, 2010, from <http://www.nytimes.com>.

Singer, N. (2009f). Study raises questions about cholesterol drug's benefit. *New York Times*, Nov. 15.

Singer, N. (2010a). Drug suits raise questions for doctors, and juries. *New York Times*, Nov. 10.

Singer, N. (2010b). Hip implants are recalled by U. & J. unit. *New York Times*, Aug. 27, B1/5.

Singer, N. (2010c). Johnson & Johnson is accused of paying kickbacks. *New York Times*, Jan. 16, B2.

Singer, N. (2010d). Maker of Botox settles inquiry. *New York Times*, Sept. 1.

Singer, N. (2010e). Question for doctors, and juries. *New York Times*, Nov. 11, B1/6.

Singer, N., & Wilson, D. (2010a). Debate over industry role in educating doctors. *New York Times*, June 24, B1.

Singer, N., & Wilson, D. (2010b). Misgivings grow over corporate role in keeping doctors current. *New York Times*, June 24, B1/6.

Singh, I. (2002). Bad boys, good mothers, and the "miracle" of Ritalin. *Science in Context*, 15(4), 577–603.

Singh, I. (2004). Doing their jobs: Mothering with Ritalin in a culture of mother blame. *Social Science & Medicine*, 59, 1193–1205.

Singh, S., & Ernst, E. (2008). *Trick or treatment: The undeniable facts about alternative medicine*. New York: W. W. Norton.

Skeem, J. L., Douglas, K. S., & Lilienfeld, S. O. (2009). *Psychological science in the courtroom: Consensus and controversy*. New York: Guilford.

Skinner, B. F. (1953). *Science and human behavior*. New York: Macmillan.

Skinner, B. F. (1971). *Beyond freedom and dignity*. New York: Knopf.

Skinner B. F. (1974). *About behaviorism*. New York: Alfred A. Knopf.

Skrabanek, P. (1990). Reductionist fallacies in the theory and treatment of mental disorders. *International Journal of Mental Health*, 19, 6–18.

Skrabanek, P., & McCormick, J. (1998). *Follies and fallacies in medicine* (3rd ed.). Whithorn, UK: Tarragon Press.

Slife, B. D. (2008). *Taking sides: Clashing views on psychological issues*. Boston: McGraw-Hill Higher Education.

Sloman, L., & Gilbert, P. (2000). *Subordination and defeat: An evolutionary approach to mood disorders and their therapy*. Mahwah, NJ: Lawrence Erlbaum.

Slovic, P. (2000). *The perception of risk*. Sterling, VA: Earthscan.

Slovic, P., Finucane, M., Peters, E., & MacGregor, D. G. (2002). The affect heuristic. In T. Gilovich & D. Griffin (Eds.), *Heuristics and biases: The psychology of intuitive judgment* (pp. 397–420). New York: Cambridge University Press.

Smith, R. (2006). Peer review: A flawed process at the heart of science and journals. *Journal of the Royal Society of Medicine*, 99, 178–82.

Smith, R. (2007). Social measures rather than drugs and vaccines to control pandemic flu. *BMJ*, 334, 1341.

Smith, R. S. W. (2011). The chasm between evidence and practice: Extent, causes, and remedies. In G. Gigerenzer & J. A. M. Gray (Eds.) (2011). *Better doctors, better patients, better decisions* (pp. 265–80). Cambridge, MA: MIT Press.

Smith, S. K., Trevana, L., Simpson, J. M., Barrett, A., Nutbean, D., McCaffery, K. J. (2010). A decision aid to support informed choices about bowel cancer screening among adults with low education: Randomised controlled trial. *BMJ*, 341, c5370.

Snyder, C. R., Higgins, R. L., & Stucky, R. J. (1983). *Excuses: Masquerades in search of grace*. New York: Wiley.

Snyder, M., & Swann, W. B. (1978). Behavioral confirmation in social interaction: From social perception to social reality. *Journal of Experimental Social Psychology*, 14, 148–62.

Soares, H. P., Daniels, S., Kumar, A., Clarke, E. M., Scott, C., Swan, S., & Djulbegovic, B. (2004). Bad reporting does not mean bad methods for randomized trials: Observational study of randomized controlled trials performed by the radiation therapy oncology group. *BMJ*, 328, 22–24.

Sokol, D. K. (2008). Medicine as performance: What can magicians teach doctors? *J R Soc Med*, 101, 443–46.

Soman, D. (2005). Framing, loss aversion, and mental accounting. In D. J. Koehler & N. Harvey (Eds.), *Blackwell handbook of judgement and decision making* (pp. 379–98). Malden, MA: Blackwell.

Somerset, M., Weiss, M., & Fahey, T. (2001). Dramaturgical study of meetings between general practitioners and representatives of pharmaceutical companies. *BMJ*, 323, 22–29.

Sopory, P., & Dillard, J. P. (2002). The pervasive effects of metaphor: A meta-analysis. *Human Communication Research*, 28, 382–419.

Sorensen, R. A. (1988). *Blind spots*. Oxford: Clarendon.

Sorkin, A. R. (2006). Drug middleman plans hostile bid for larger rival. *New York Times*, Dec.18, A1/19.

Sparrow, M. (2000). *License to steal: How fraud bleeds America's health care system*. Boulder, CO: Westview Press.

Spence, M. A., Greenberg, D. A., Hodge, S. E., & Vieland, V. J. (2003). The emperor's new methods. *American Journal of Human Genetics*, 72, 1084–87.

Spitzer calls for passage of State False Claims Act. (2003). Press release, June 12. Office of the Attorney General, Media Center, State Capitol, Albany, New York. Retrieved Aug. 11, 2011, from <http://www.ag.ny.gov/media>.

Spock, B. (1945). *Baby and child care*. New York: Pocket Books.

Sproule, J. M. (1994). *Channels of propaganda*. ERIC Clearinghouse on Reading, English and Communication. Bloomington, IN.

Sproule, J. M. (1997). *Propaganda and democracy: The American experience of media and mass persuasion*. New York: Cambridge University Press.

Sproule, J. M. (2001). Rhetoric and public affairs. 41, 135–43.

Staats, A. W., & Staats, C. K. (1963). *Complex human behavior: A systematic extension of learning principles*. New York: Holt, Rinehart & Winston.

Stanford study calculates cost of pharmaceutical marketing efforts. (2003). Stanford School of Medicine, Office of Communication, Public Affairs. May 19.

Stange, K. C. (2007). Time to ban direct-to-consumer prescription drug marketing. *Annals of Family Medicine*, 5, 101–4.

Stanovich, K. E. (1986). *How to think straight about psychology*. New York: Harper Collins. (See also 7th ed. 2004.)

Stanovich, K. E., & West, R. F. (2002). Individual differences in reasoning: Implications for the rationality debate? In T. Gilovich, D. Griffin, & D. Kahneman (Eds.), *Heuristics and biases: The psychology of intuitive judgment* (pp. 421–40). New York: Cambridge University Press.

Starcevic, V. (2002). Opportunistic rediscovery of mental disorders by the pharmaceutical industry. *Psychotherapy and psychosomatics*, 71, 305–310.

Starker, S. (1989). *Oracle at the supermarket: The American preoccupation with self-help books*. New Brunswick, NJ: Transaction.

Staton, T. (2010). GSK settles Paxil suits for reported $1B. *Fierce Pharma*. Posted July 21, 2010. Retrieved Aug. 11, 2011, from <http://www.fiercepharma.com>.

Stein, R. (2007). Doctor says Avandia makers intimated him. *Washington Post*, June 7, A06.

Steinbrook, R. (2005a). Financial conflicts of interest in the Food and Drug Administration's advisory committees. *New England Journal of Medicine*, 353, 116–18.

Steinbrook, R. (2005b). Gag clauses in clinical-trial agreements. *New England Journal of Medicine*, 352, 2160–62.

Steinbrook, R. (2005c). Wall Street and clinical trials. *New England Journal of Medicine*, 353, 1091–93.

Steinbrook, R. (2008). Disclosure of industry payments to physicians. *NEMJ*, 359, 559–61.

Steinbrook, R. (2009). Controlling conflict of interest—Proposals from the Institute of Medicine. *New England Journal of Medicine*, 360, 2160–63.

Steinhauer, J. (1998). Agency fines hospital for fatal surgery, saying that salesman assisted. *New York Times*, Nov. 6, A27.

Sternberg, R. J. (1986). *Intelligence applied: Understanding and increasing your intellectual skills*. San Diego: Harcourt, Brace, Jovanovich.

Sternberg, R. J. (Ed.) (2002). *Why smart people can be so stupid*. New Haven, CT: Yale University Press.

Sterne, J. A., Egger, M., & Smith, G. D. (2001). Investigating and dealing with publication and other biases. In M. Egger, G. D. Smith, & D. G. Altman. (Eds.), *Systematic Reviews in Healthcare: Meta-analysis in Context* (2nd ed.). London: BMJ Books.

Steurer, J., Fischer, J. E., Bachmann, L. M., Koller, M., & ter Riet, G. (2002). Communicating accuracy of tests to general practitioners: A controlled study. *BMJ*, 324, 824–26.

Stivers, R. (1994). *The culture of cynicism: American morality in decline*. Cambridge, MA: Blackwell.

Stivers, R. (2001). *Technology as magic: The triumph of the irrational*. New York: Continuum Publishing Co.

Stivers, R. (2004). *Shades of loneliness: Pathologies of a technological society*. Lanham, MD: Roman & Littlefield.

Stivers, R. (2008). *The illusion of freedom and equality*. Albany, NY: State University of New York Press.

Stoesz, D., Karger, H. J., & Carrilio, T. (2010). *A dream deferred: How social work education lost its way and what can be done*. New Brunswick, NJ: Transaction Publishers.

Strasak, A. M., Zaman, Q., Pfeiffer, K. P., Gobel, G., & Ulmer, H. (2007). Statistical errors in medical research—a review of common pitfalls. *Swiss Med Wkly*, 137, 44–49.

Straus, S. E., Richardson, W. S., Glasziou, P., & Haynes, R. B. (2005). *Evidence-based medicine: How to practice and teach EBM* (3rd ed.). New York: Churchill Livingstone.

Strohman, R. (2003). Genetic determinism as a failing paradigm in biology and medicine: Implications for health and wellness. *Journal of Social Work Education*, 39, 169–91.

Strom, S. (2010). Lawmakers seeking cuts look at non-profit salaries. *New York Times*, July 26.

Sudbery, J., Shardlow, S. M, & Huntington, A. E. (2010). To have and to hold: Questions about a therapeutic service for children. *British Journal of Social Work*, 40, 1534–52.

Summerfield, D. (1995). Addressing human response to war and atrocity: Major challenges in research and practices and the limitations of Western psychiatric models. In R. J. Klever, C. R. Figley, & B. G. Gersons (Eds.), *Beyond trauma: Cultural and societal dynamics* (pp. 17–30). New York: Plenum.

Summerfield, D. (2001). The invention of post-traumatic stress disorder and the social usefulness of a psychiatric category. *BMJ*, 322, 95–98.

Summerfield, D. (2002). Selling sickness: The pharmaceutical industry and disease mongering. *BMJ*, 336, 992–94.

Sutton, A. (2010). School STD programs have limited influence on teens' sexual behaviors. *Health Behavior News Service*, Feb. 23.

Swazey, J. (1974). *Chlorpromazine in psychiatry: A study of therapeutic innovation*. Cambridge, MA: MIT Press.

Sweeney, H. M. (1997). Twenty-five ways to suppress truth: The rules of disinformation. Retrieved Oct. 1, 2007, from???.

Sweet, M. (2011). Doctor who complained to regulator about weight loss product is sued for libel. *BMJ*, 342, d3728.

Sykes, C. J. (1992). *A nation of victims: The decay of the American character*. New York: St. Martin's Press.

Szalavitz, M. (2010). Portugal's drug experience: New study confirms decriminalization was a success. *Time Magazine*, Nov. 30.

Szasz, T. S. (1961). *The myth of mental illness: Foundations of a theory of personal conduct*. New York: Harper & Row.

Szasz, T. S. (1970). *The manufacture of madness: The comparative study of the inquisition and the mental health movement*. New York: Harper & Row.

Szasz, T. S. (1987). *Insanity: The idea and its consequences*. New York: John Wiley.

Szasz, T. S. (1994). *Cruel compassion: Psychiatric control of society's unwanted*. New York: John Wiley.

Szasz, T. S. (2001). *Pharmocracy: Medicine and politics in America*. Westport, CT: Praeger.

Szasz, T. S. (2002). *Liberation by oppression: A comparative study of slavery and psychiatry*. New Brunswick, NJ: Transaction Press.

Szasz, T. S. (2007). *The medicalization of everyday life*. New York: Syracuse University Press.

Szasz, T. (2010). Psychiatry, anti-psychiatry, critical psychiatry: What do these terms mean? *Philosophy, Psychiatry, & Psychology*, 17, 229–32.

Tangirala, S., & Ramanujam, R. (2008). Employee silence on critical work issues: The cross level effects of procedural justice climate. *Personnel Psychology*, 61, 37–68.

Tanne, J. H. (2004). U.S. consumer group names "dirty dozen" dietary supplements. *BMJ*, 334, 115.

Tanne, J. H. (2007). Group asks US institutes to reveal industry ties. *BMJ*, 334, 115.

Tanne, J. H. (2008a). US medical schools should say no to pharma support. *BMJ*, 336, 1035.

Tanne, J. H. (2008b). U.S. psychiatrist steps down after questions about drug company payments. *BMJ*, 337, a2088.

Tanne, J. H. (2008c). Virginity pledge ineffective against teen sex despite government funding, US studies finds. *BMJ*, 337, a3168.

Tanne, J. H. (2010a). AstraZeneca to pay $198m to patients over diabetes claims. *BMJ*, 341, c4422.

Tanne, J. H. (2010b). Avandia panel member may be investigated for possible conflicts of interest. *BMJ*, 341, c4083.

Tanne, J. H. (2010c). U.S. drug companies paid $15bn in fines for criminal and civil violations over the last five years. *BMJ*, 341, c7360.

Tanne, J. H. (2011). U.S. Health Department recovers $4bn through antifraud action. *BMJ*, 342, d615.

Tarn, D. M., Heritage, J., Paternita, D. A., Hays, R. D., Kravitz, R. L., & Wenger, N. S. (2006). Physician communication when prescribing new medications. *Archives of Internal Medicine*, 166, 1855–62.

Tavris, C. (1992). *The mismeasure of women*. New York: Simon & Schuster.

Tavris, C. (2001). *Psychobabble & biobunk: Using psychology to think critically about issues in the news* (2nd ed.). Upper Saddle River, NJ: Prentice Hall.

Tavris, C., & Bluming, A. Z. (2008). Taking the scary out of breast cancer stats. *Los Angeles Times*, op. ed., April 17.

Taylor, P. M. (1992). Propaganda from Thucydides to Thatcher: Some problems, perspectives and pitfalls. Opening Address to the Social History Society of Great Britain Conference.

Taylor, R. E. (2001). Death of neurasthenia and its psychological reincarnation: A study of neurasthenia at the national hospital for the relief and cure of the paralysed and epileptic, Queens Square, London, 1870–1932. *British Journal of Psychiatry*, 179, 550–57.

Teigen, K. H., & Brun, W. (2003). Verbal expressions of uncertainty and probability. In D. Hardman & L. Macchi (Eds.), *Thinking: Psychological perspectives on reasoning, judgment and decision making* (pp. 125–45). New York: Wiley.

Tesh, S. N. (1988). *Hidden arguments of political ideology and disease prevention policy*. New Brunswick, NJ: Rutgers University Press.

Tetlock, P. E. (2005). *Expert political judgment: How good is it? How can we know?* Princeton, NJ: Princeton University Press.

Thomas, B., Dorling, D., & Smith, G. D. (2010). Inequities in premature mortality in Britain: observational study from 1921 to 2007. *BMJ*, 341, c3639.

Thomma, S. (2005). AARP opposed in bid for members, money. *Akron Beacon Journal*, Mar. 27, 5.

Thompson, Collum, McCaughan, Sheldon, & Raynor (2004). Nurses information use and clinical decision making. *Evidence Based Nursing*, 7, 68–72.

Thompson, J. B. (1987). Language and ideology. *Sociological Review*, 35, 517–536.

Thompson, J. W., & Blaine, J. D. (1987). Use of ECT in the United States in 1975 and 1980. *American Journal of Psychiatry*, 144, 557–62.

Thorne, A. (2010). The scandal of social work education: The scandal goes on. <http://www.nas.org/polupright/articles>.

Thornley, B., & Adams, C. (1998). Content and quality of 2000 controlled trials in schizophrenia over 50 years. *BMJ*, 317, 1181–84.

Thornton, H., Edwards, A., & Baum, M. (2003). Women need better information about routine mammography. *BMJ*, 327, 101–3.

Thouless, R. H. (1974). *Straight and crooked thinking: Thirty-eight dishonest tricks of debate*. London: Pan Books.

Thyer, B. A. (2005). The misfortunes of behavioral social work: Misprized, misread, and miscontrued. In S. A. Kirk (Ed.), *Mental health in the social environment: Critical perspectives* (pp. 330–43). New York: Columbia University Press.

Thyer, B. A., & Pignotti, M. (2010). Science and pseudoscience in developmental disabilities: Guidelines for social workers. *Journal of Social Work in Disability & Rehabilitation*, 9, 110–29.

Thyer, B. A., & Pignotti, M. (2012). *Pseudoscience in social work*. New York: Oxford.

Tice, K. W. (1998). *Tales of wayward girls and immoral women: Case records and the professionalization of social work*. Urbana: University of Illinois Press.

Tilly, C. (1998). How to hoard opportunities. In C. Tilly, *Durable inequality* (pp. 147–69). Berkeley: University of California Press.

Timimi, S. (2002). *Pathological child psychiatry and the medicalization of childhood*. London: Brunner Routledge.

Timimi, S. (2008). Children's mental health and the global market: An ecological analysis. In C. I. Cohen & S. Timimi (Eds.), *Liberatory psychiatry: Philosophy, politics and mental health* (pp. 163–82). New York: Cambridge University Press.

Timimi, S., & Leo, J. (2009). *Rethinking ADHD: An international perspective*. London: Palgrave/Macmillan.

Timimi, S., Leo, J., et al. (2004). A critique of the international consensus statement on ADHD. *Clinical Child and Family Psychology Review*, 7, 59–63.

Timimi, S., & Maitra, B. (Eds.) (2006). *Critical voices in child and adolescent mental health*. London: Free Association Books.

Timimi, S., & Taylor, E. (2004). ADHD is best understood as a cultural construct. *British Journal of Psychiatry*, 184, 8–9.

Timmermans, D. (1996). Lost for words? Using verbal terms to express uncertainty. *Making Better Decisions (an experimental newsletter by E. Gambrill & L. Gibbs)*. University of Wisconsin-Eau Claire, No. 3, 4–5.

Timmermans, D. (2008). Professions and their work. *Work and Occupations*, 35, 164–88.

Todd, J. T. (1992). Case histories and the great power of study misrepresentation. *American Psychologist*, 47, 1441–53.

Toulmin, S. E. (1990). *Cosmopolis: The hidden agenda of modernity*. New York: Free Press.

Toulmin, S. E. (2003). *The uses of argument*. Cambridge: Cambridge University Press (originally published 1958).

Toulmin, S. E., Rieke, R., & Janik, A. (1979). *An introduction to reasoning*. New York: Macmillan.

Tousignant, M., & DesMarchais, J. E. (2002). Accuracy of student self-assessment ability compared to their own performance. In Problem-Based Learning Medical Program: A correlational study. *Advances in Health Sciences Education*, 7, 19–27.

Transformative Neurodevelopmental Research in Mental Illness. (2008). Report of the National Advisory Mental Health Council's Workgroup on neurodevelopment distributed at Conference on Adolescent Psychopathology. Madison, WI, April 2009.

Trone, G. A. (1997). "You lie like a doctor!": Petrarch's attack on medicine. *Yale Journal of Biology and Medicine*, 70, 183–90.

Trotter, J. (2006). Violent crimes? Young people's experiences of homophobia and misogyny in secondary schools. *Practice*, 18, 291–302.

Trotter, W. (1916). *Instincts of the herd in peace and war*. London: T. F. Unwin.

Tuerkheimer, D. (2010). Anatomy of a misdiagnosis. *New York Times*, Sept. 21, A29.

Tuffs, A. (2004). Only 6% of drug advertising material is supported by evidence. *BMJ*, 328, 485.

Tuffs, A. (2008). Three jailed in Germany for selling a fraudulent cancer cure to terminally ill patients. *BMJ*, 337; doi: 10.1136/bmj.a875.

Tufte, E. (2006). *Beautiful evidence*. Cheshire, CT: Graphics Press.

Tufte, E. R. (1983). *The visual display of quantitative information*. Cheshire, CT: Graphics Press.

Tufte, E. R. (1990). *Envisioning information*. Cheshire, CT: Graphics Press.

Tufte, E. R. (1997). *Visual explanations*. Cheshire, CT: Graphics Press.

Turner, E. H., Matthews, A. M., Linardatos, E., Tell, R. A., & Rosenthal, R. (2008). Selective publications of antidepressant trials and its influence on apparent efficacy. *New England Journal of Medicine*, 358, 252–60.

Tversky, A., & Kahneman, D. (1973). Availability: A heuristic for judging frequency and probability. *Cognitive Psychology*, 5, 207–32.

Tversky, A., & Kahneman, D. (1974). Judgment under uncertainty: Heuristics and biases. *Science*, 185, 1124–31.

Tweed, R. G., & Lehman, D. R. (2002). Learning considered within a cultural context: Confucian and Socratic approaches. *American Psychologist*, 57, 89–99.

Tyrer, P., Oliver-Africano, P. C., Ahmed, Z., Bouras, N., Cooray, S., Deb, S., et al. (2008). Risperidone, haloperidol, and placebo in the treatment of aggressive challenging behavior of patients with intellectual disability: A randomized controlled trial. *Lancet*, 371, 57–63.

Ullman, S. (1962). *Semantics: An introduction to the science of meaning*. Oxford: Basil Blackwell.

UNAIDS/WHO. (2004). Joint United Nations programme on HIV-AIDS, World Health Organization (WHO).

Underhill, K., Operario, D. & Montgomery, P. (2007). Systematic review of abstinence plus HIV prevention in high-income countries. PLoS Med. September 18. Sexual abstinence only programs to prevent HIV infection in high income countries: Systematic review. *BMJ*, 335, 248.

Unemployment due to economic downturns increases risk of suicide by 20%. (2009). *BMJ*, 339, 1456–70.

Unsworth, C. (1987). *The politics of mental health legislation*. New York: Oxford University Press.

U.S. Federal Judge orders Wyeth documents unsealed. (2009). Associated Press, July 25. Alliance for Human Research Protection <http://www.ahrp.org>.

Uttal, W. R. (2001). *The new phenology: The limits of localizing cognitive processes in the brain*. Cambridge, MA: MIT.

Valenstein, E. S. (1986). *Great and desperate cures: The rise and decline of psychosurgery and other radical treatments for mental illness*. New York: Perseus Books.

Van der Weyden, M. B., Armstrong, R. M., & Gregory, A. T. (2005). The 2005 Nobel Prize in physiology or medicine. *Medical Journal of Australia*, 183, 612–14.

Van Voris, B. (2010). Merck Fosamax verdict cut to $1.5 million from $8 million. Posted Oct. 4, 2010. Retrieved Aug. 16, 2011, from <http:// www.blumberg.com>.

Vas, P., & Bruno, F. (2003). Types of self-surveillance: From abnormality to individuals "at risk." *Surveillance & Society*, 1, 272–91.

Vaughan, S. C. (2009). The dark side of Freud's legacy. *BMJ*, 338, b1606.

Veblan, I. ([1918] 1993). *The higher learning in America*. New Brunswick, NJ: Transaction.

Verhaeghe, M., Bracke, P., & Christiaens, W. (2010). Stigma and client satisfaction in mental health services. *Journal of Applied Social Psychology*, 40(9), 2295–2318.

Vincent, C. (2001). *Clinical risk management: Enhancing patient safety* (2nd ed.). London: BMJ Books.

Vrij, A., Granhag, P. A., & Porter, S. (2010). Pitfalls and opportunities in nonverbal and verbal lie detection. *Psychological Science in the Public Interest*, 11, 89–121.

Vul, E., Harris, C., Winkielman, P., & Pashler, H. (2009). Puzzlingly high correlations in fMRI studies of emotion, personality and social cognition. *Perspectives on Psychological Science*, 4, 274–90.

Wacquant, L. (2009). *Punishing the poor: The neoliberal government in social insecurity.* Durham, NC: Duke University Press.

Wahlbeck, K. & Awolm, M. (2009). *The impact of economic crisis on the risk of depression and suicide: A literature review.* Downloaded Nov. 24, 2011.

Wakefield, J. (1998). Foucauldian fallacies: An essay review of Leslie Margolin's *Under the cover of kindness. Social Service Review*, 72, 545–87.

Wakefield, J. C., Schmitz, M. F., First, M. B., & Horwitz, A. V. (2007). Extending the bereavement exclusion for major depression to other losses: Evidence from the national comorbidity survey. *Archives of General Psychiatry*, 64, 433–40.

Wald, N. J., Law, M. R., & Duffy, S. W. (2009). Lives saved by breast cancer screening. *BMJ*, Sept. 339.

Walker, S. (1994). *Sense and nonsense about crime and drugs: A policy guide* (3rd ed.). Belmont: Wadsworth.

Wallace-Wells, B. (2009). Bitter pill. *RollingStone.com* 1/28/09.

Walton, D. N. (1992). *Slippery slope arguments.* New York: Oxford.

Walton, D.N. (1995). *A pragmatic theory of fallacy.* Tuscaloosa: University of Alabama Press.

Walton, D. (1996a). *Arguments from ignorance.* University Park, PA: Pennsylvania State University Press.

Walton, D. (1997a). *Appeal to expert opinion: Arguments from authority.* University Park, PA: Pennsylvania State University Press.

Walton, D. (2000). *Scare tactics: Arguments that appeal to fear and threats.* Boston: Kluwer Academic Pub.

Walton, D. (2008a). *Informal logic: A pragmatic approach* (2nd ed.). New York: Cambridge University Press.

Walton, D. N. (1996b). *Fallacies arising from ambiguity.* Boston: Kluwer Academic.

Walton, D. N. (1997b). *Appeal to pity: Argumentum ad misericordiam.* Boston: Kluwer Academic.

Walton, D. N. (2002). *Legal argumentation and evidence.* University Park: Pennsylvania State University Press.

Walton, D. N. (2006). *Fundamentals of critical argumentation.* New York: Cambridge University Press.

Walton, D. N. (2008b). Witness testimony in evidence: Argumentation, artificial intelligence, and law. New York: Cambridge University Press.

Walton, D., & Macagno, F. (2009). Wrenching from context: The manipulation of commitments. *Argumentation*, 24, 283–317.

Walton, D. N., Reed, C., & Macagno, F. (2008). *Argumentation schemes.* Cambridge: Cambridge University Press.

Wampold, B. E. (2010). A letter to editors. I have an allegiance . . . to the research evidence. *Behavior Therapist*, 10, 137–38.

Wampold, B. E., Imel, Z. E., & Miller, S. D. (2009). Barriers to the dissemination of empirically supported treatment. Matching messages to the evidence. *Behavior Therapist*, 32, 144–55.

Wampold, B. E., Imel, Z. E., Laska, K. M., Benish, S., Miller, S. D., & Fluckiger, C. (2010). Determining what works in the treatment of PTSD. *Clinical Psychology Review*, 30, 923–33.

Warner, L. A., Pottick, K. J., & Bilder, S. M. (2005). Clinical and organizational correlates of psychotropic medication use among youths in outpatient mental health services in the U.S. *Social Service Review*, 79, 454–81.

Warner, T. D., & Roberts, L. W. (2004). Scientific integrity, fidelity, and conflicts of interests. *Current Opinion in Psychiatry*, 17, 381–85.

Washburn, T. (2005). *University, Inc.: The corporate corruption of American higher education*. New York: Basic Books.

Waters, R. (2007). Lilly's Zyprexa poised for approval for U.S. teens. *Bloomberg News*. Sept. 27. Available from <http://www.bloomberg.com>.

Watson, R. (2008). New law bans selling of products with unjustified health claims. *BMJ*, 336, 1150.

Watson, A. C., & Eack, S. M. (2011). Oppression and stigma and their effects. In N. R. Heller & A. Gitterman, *Mental health and social problems: A social work perspective* (pp. 21–43). New York: Routledge.

Watson, S., & Moran, A. (Eds.) (2005). *Trust, risk and uncertainty*. Basingstoke: Palgrave MacMillan.

Wazana, A. (2000). Physicians and the pharmaceutical industry: Is a gift ever just a gift? *Journal of the American Medical Association*, 283, 373–80.

Webster, Y. O. (1992). *The racialization of America*. New York: St. Martin's Press.

Webster, Y. O. (2002). A human-centric alternative to diversity and multicultural education. *Journal of Social Work Education*, 38, 17–38.

Wegwarth, O., & Gigerenzer, G. (2011). Statistical illiteracy in doctors. In G. Gigerenzer & J. A. M. Gray (Eds.) (2011). *Better doctors, better patients, better decisions* (pp. 137–51). Cambridge, MA: MIT Press.

Weisburd, D., Lum, C. M., & Yang, S.-M. (2003). When can we conclude that treatments or programs "Don't Work"? *Annals of the American Academy of Political and Social Science*, 587, 31–48.

Weiser, B. (2011). In New Jersey, sweeping shift on witness IDs. *New York Times*, Aug. 24, A1.

Weiss, R. (1969). *The American myth of success*. New York: Basic Books.

Welch, H. G. (2004). *Should I be tested for cancer? Maybe not and here's why*. Berkeley: University of California Press.

Welch, H. G. (2009). Editorial. Overdiagnosis and mammography screening. *BMJ*, 339, b1425.

Welch, H. G., Schwartz, L. M., & Woloshin, S. (2011). *Over-diagnosis: Making people sick in the pursuit of health*. Boston: Beacon Press.

Wen, P. (2010). Social worker warned that Rebecca Riley, 4, was overmedicated. *Boston Globe*. Jan. 21.

Wennberg, J. E. (2002). Unwarranted variations in health care delivery: Implications for academic medical centers. *BMJ*, 325, 961–64.

Westen, D., Novotny, C. N., & Thompson-Brenner, H. (2004). The empirical status of empirically supported psychotherapies: Assumptions, findings, and reporting in controlled clinical trials. *Psychological Bulletin*, 130, 631–63.

Wheelen, S. (2005). *Handbook of group research and practice*. Thousand Oaks, CA: Sage.

When tough love is too traumatic. (2007). Editorial. *New York Times*, Oct. 16, A22.

The Whistleblogger. (2010). HHS IG report confirms the rapid spread of unregulated drug trials abroad. June 22.

Whitaker, R. (2002). *Mad in America: Bad science, bad medicine and the enduring mistreatment of the mentally ill*. Cambridge, MA: Perseus Publishing.

Whitaker, R. (2010). *Anatomy of an epidemic: Magic bullets, psychiatric drugs, and the astonishing rise of mental illness in America*. New York: Crown.

Whitbourne, S. K. (2010). Medicalization of the mind. Retrieved Aug. 24, 2010, from *Psychology Today*, <http://www.psychologytoday.com>.

White, A. D. (1971). *A history of the warfare of science with theology in Christendom* (2 vols.). New York: Prometheus.

Whitfield, C. F., & Xie, S. X. (2002). Correlation of problem-based learning facilitators' scores with student performance on written exams. *Advances in Health, Science, Education, Theory, and Practice*, 7, 41–51.

Whittingham, R. B. (2004). *The blame machine: Why human error causes accidents*. New York: Elsevier.

Wilkes, M. S., & Hoffman, J. R. (2001). An innovative approach to educating medical students about pharmaceutical promotion. *Academic Medicine*, 76, 1271–77.

Wilkes, M. S., Doblin, B. H., & Shapiro, M. F. (1992). Pharmaceutical advertisements in leading medical journals: Experts' assessments. *Ann Intern Med*, 116, 912–19.

Williams, W. M., & Ceci, S. J. (1997). How am I doing? Problems with student ratings of instructors and courses. *Change*, 29, 12–23.

Williamson, J. (2002). *Decoding advertisements: Ideology and meaning in advertising*. New York: Marion Boyars.

Wilson, A. J., Bonevski, B., Jones, A. L., & Henry, D. (2009). Media reporting of health interventions: Signs of improvement, but major problems persist. *PLoS One*, 4(3), e4831.

Wilson, C. (1983). The rhetoric of consumption. In R. Foxx & T. J. Jackson Lears (Eds.), *The culture of consumption* (pp. 49–53). New York: Pantheon.

Wilson, D. (2008). Drug makers said to pay ghost writers for journal articles. *New York Times*, Dec. 12. Reported by the Alliance for Human Research Protection <http://www.ahrp.org>. Monday, July 27, 2009.

Wilson, D. (2009a). Challenge arises over an F.D.A. panels' approve of a Lilly drug. *New York Times*, Mar. 3, B6.

Wilson, D. (2009b). Medical schools quizzed on ghostwriting. *New York Times*, Nov. 18.

Wilson, D. (2009c). Poor children likelier to get antipsychotics. *New York Times*, Dec. 12.

Wilson, D. (2010a). A child's ordeal shows risks of psychosis drugs for young. *New York Times*, Sept. 1, A1/22.

Wilson, D. (2010b). Drug maker hired writing company for doctor's book, documents say. *New York Times Business*, Nov. 29, B3.

Wilson, D. (2010c). For $520 million AstroZeneca will settle case over marketing of a drug. *New York Times*, April 26.

Wilson, D. (2010d). Lilly moves closer to approval to market Cymbalta for chronic pain. *New York Times*, Business Section, Aug. 20.

Wilson, D. (2010e). Medical industry ties often undisclosed in journals. *New York Times*, Sept. 14, B1/6.

Wilson, D. (2010f). Novartis settles off-label marketing case over 6 drugs for $422.5 million. *New York Times*, Sept. 30.

Wilson, D. (2010g). Secret cable discusses Pfizer's actions in Nigeria Case. *New York Times Business*, Dec. 11, B2.

Wilson, D. (2010h). U.S. joins Pfizer suit over drug's marketing. *New York Times*, Sept. 22, B3.

Wilson, D. B., MacKenzie, D. L., & Mitchell, F. N. (2005). The effects of correctional bootcamps on offending. *Campbell Systematic Reviews*. The Campbell Collaboration. Retrieved from <http://www.campbellcollaboration.org>.

Wilson, J. M. G., & Jungner, G. (1968). Principles and practice of screening for disease. *WHO Public Health Papers No. 34.* Geneva, Switzerland: World Health Organization.

Winemiller, M. H., Billow, R. G., Laskowski, E. R., & Harmsen, W. S. (2003). Effect of magnetic vs sham-magnetic insoles on plantar heel pain: A randomized controlled trial. *JAMA*, 290, 1474–78.

Witte, C. L., Witte, M. H., & Kerwin, A. (1994). Suspended judgment: Ignorance and the process of learning and discovery in medicine. *Controlled Clinical Trials*, 15, 1–4.

Wittgenstein, L. (1953). *Philosophical investigations.* New York: Macmillan.

Wofford, J. L., & Ohl, C. A. (2005). Teaching appropriate interactions with pharmaceutical company representatives: The impact of an innovative workshop on students attitudes. *BMC Medical Education*, 5, 5.

Wolf, A. J. (1986). Individualization: The categorical imperative of behavior therapy practice. *Journal of Behavior Therapy and Experimental Psychiatry*, 17, 145–54.

Wolf, F. N. (2000). Summarizing evidence for clinical use. In J. P. Geyman, R. A. Deyo, & S. D. Ramsey (Eds.), *Evidence-based clinical practice: Concepts and approaches.* Boston: Butterworth Heineman.

Woloshin, S., & Schwartz, L. M. (2006). Giving legs to restless legs: A case study of how the media helps make people sick. *PLoS Med*, 3(4), e170.

Woloshin, S., & Schwartz, L. M. (2011). Think inside the box. *New York Times*, July 5, A19.

Woloshin, S., Schwartz, L. M., & Welch, H. G. (2008). *Know your chances: Understanding health statistics.* Berkeley: University of California Press.

Wolpe, J. (1990). *The practice of behavior therapy.* Elmsford, NY: Pergamon.

Woltmann, E. M., Wilkniss, S. M., Teachout, A., McHugo, G. J., & Drake, R. E. (2011). Trial of an electronic decision support system to facilitate shared decision making in community mental health. *Psychiatric Services*, 62, 54–60.

Wolves in sheep's clothing: Telecom industry front groups and astro turf. (2006). *Common Cause: Holding Power Accountable.* Washington, DC.

Wood, E., Werb, D., Fischer, B., Hart, C., Wodak, A., Bastos, F. I., Montaner, J., & Kerr, T. (2010). Tools for debate: U.S. Federal Government Data on Cannabis Prohibition. Report of the International Center for Science and Drug Policy, pp. 1–25. Available at <http://www.icsdp.org>.

Woods, D. D., & Cook, R. I. (1999). Perspectives on human error: Hindsight biases and local rationality. In F. T. Durso, R. S. Nickerson, R. W. Schzaneveldt, S. T, Dumais, D. S. Lindsay, & M. T. Chi (Eds.), *Handbook of Applied cognition* (pp. 141–71). New York: John Wiley.

Woodward, K. L. (2004). A political sacrament. *New York Times*, May 28, Sect. A, Column 2, p. 21.

Worthman, C. M., Plotsky, P. M., Schechter, D. S., & Cummings, C. A. (Eds.) (2010). *Formative experiences: The interaction of caregiving, culture and developmental psychobiology.* Cambridge: Cambridge University Press.

Wright, A., Sittig, D. F., Ash, J. S., Feblowitz, J., Meltzer, S., McMullen, C., Guappone, K., Carpenter, J., Richardson, J., Simonaitis, L., Evans, R. S., Nichol, W. P., & Middleton, B. (2011). Development and evaluation of a comprehensive clinical decision support taxonomy: Comparison of front-end tools in commercial and internally developed electronic health records systems. *J Am Med Inform Assoc*, 18, 232–42.

Wright, R. H. (2005). The myth of continuing education: A look at some intended and (maybe) unintended consequences. In R. H. Wright & N. A. Cummings (Eds.),

Destructive trends in mental health: A well-intentioned path to harm (pp. 143–51). New York: Routledge.

Wright, R. H., & Cummings, N. A. (Eds.) (2005). *Destructive trends in mental health: The well-intentioned path to harm.* New York: Routledge.

Yost, P. (2010). Stepped-up Medicare fraud enforcement snags $2.5B. *Washington Post*, May 13. Retrieved May 15, 2010, from <http://www.washingtonpost.com>.

Young, A. (1995). *The harmony of illusions: Inventing post-traumatic stress disorder.* Princeton, NJ: Princeton University Press.

Young, J. H. (1992). *American health quackery.* Princeton, NJ: Princeton University Press.

Young, J. H. (1992). *The medical messiahs: A social history of health quackery in twentieth century America.* Princeton, NJ: Princeton University Press.

Young, N. S., Ioannidis, J. P. A., & Al-Ubaydli, O. (2008). Why current publication practices may distort science. *PLoS Med*, 5(10), e201.

Zarocostas, J. (2007). Community care could prevent deaths of thousands of severely malnourished children. *BMJ*, 334, 1239 (June 16).

Zechmeister, E. B., & Johnson, J. E. (1992). *Critical thinking: A functional approach.* Pacific Grove, CA: Brooks/Cole.

Zerubavel, E. (2006). *The elephant in the room: Silence and denial in everyday life.* New York: Oxford University Press.

Zhang, J., Patel, V. L., Johnson, T. R., & Shortliffe, E. H. (2004). A cognitive taxonomy of medical errors. *Journal of Biomedical Informatics*, 37, 193–204.

Ziegler, M. G., Lew, P., & Singer, P. C. (1995). The accuracy of drug information from pharmaceutical sales representatives. *JAMA*, 273, 1296–98.

Ziman, J. (2000). *Real science: What it is and what it means.* New York: Cambridge University Press.

Zimbardo, P. (2007). *The Lucifer effect: Understanding how good people turn evil.* New York: Random House.

Zito, J. M., Safer, D. J., Sai, D., Gardner, J. F., Thomas, D., Coombes, P., Dubowski, M., & Mendez-Lewis, M. (2008). Psychotropic medication patterns among youth in foster care. *Pediatrics*, 121, e157–e163.

Zola, I. K. (1972). Medicine as an institution of social control. *Sociological Review*, 20, 487–504. Reprinted in P. Conrad (Ed.), (2009) *The sociology of health and illness: Critical perspectives* (8th ed.) (pp. 470–80). New York: Worth Publishing.

INDEX

Abbott Laboratories, 124
Abilify, 52, 87–88, 139, 141, 455n.33
AbleChild: Parents for Label and Drug Free Education, grassroots, 45
AbleChild.org, Mother's Act, 456n.53
Absolute risks
   definition, 186t
   reduction, 181, 182
   requesting, 191
Abstraction, levels of, 301
Academics
   helping professions, 34
   as "marketers," 77–78
   promoting new diagnoses, 63–66
Academy of General Dentistry, sponsors, 71
Acceptability, 363, 384t
Accreditation Council for Continuing Medical Education (ACCME), 444–445n.15
Accuracy
   estimating risk, 184–193
   no concern for, 230–231
Addiction
   treatable disease, 129
   treatment, 257
   word smiths, 469n.2
Ad hominem appeals, arguments, fallacies, questionable criteria, 207t, 209, 391–393, 402
Ad ignorantiam fallacy, 394, 473–474n.5
Administration on Aging, fraud, 59
Ad verecundiam fallacy, fallacious aspect, 215–216, 369, 370
Advertisements and professional literature
   ad illustrating appeal to fear, 286f
   appeal to authority, 284–285
   appeal to emotions, 285–287
   appeal to grand narratives, 294
   assumptions about consumers, 292
   card-stacking, 289
   distorted realities, 291–292
   exaggerated claims of knowledge, 289
   exaggerating differences, 292
   fallacies and flawed arguments, 292–293
   healer treating patient, 287f
   illusion of credibility and sincerity, 294
   lax standards of evidence, 287–288
   misleading figures, tables, and charts, 288
   newness, 294
   oversimplification, 289–291
   overwhelming with material, 288
   repetition, 293
   shared goals, 282–283
   shared strategies, 284–294
   similarity in goals, 282t
   transfer effects, 293
   treating constipation, 290f
   truthfulness, 294–295
   use of persuasive parables, 284
   vagueness, 288
Advertising. *See also* Advertisements and professional literature
   ad appealing to fear, 322f
   ad for AndroGel, 308f
   appeal to science for products, 201f, 237f
   appeal to scientific discoveries, 202f
   Concerta ad, 279, 280f
   direct to consumer advertising (DCA), 281
   disguising, as professional literature, 278–279, 295–296

Advertising (Cont'd)
    Dr. Miles Nervine product, 244, 246f
    Federal Trade Commission (FTC), 42
    Guilford Press, 44
    industry, 54–55
    Lovenox, 447n.26
    pharmaceutical, in professional
        journals, 79–80
    plethora of advertisements, 279–281
    shared goals with professional literature,
        282–283
    tonic for children, 243, 244f
    ubiquitous pharmaceutical ad, 281
Advice industry, players in, 29
Advocacy for Children in Therapy, 46
Advocacy groups
    conflict of interest with drug companies,
        84–85
    front groups, 46
    grassroots groups, 45
    pharmaceutical companies funding,
        44–45
    watchdog, 45–46
Affect heuristic, 337
Aging, medicalization, 161
Agitation propaganda, purpose, 95
AIDS test, dialogue between client and
    social worker, 180t
Alchemy, definition, 232
Alleged best practices, misleading, 155
Alliance for Human Research Protection,
    46, 139, 446n.35
Alzheimer's disease, 461n.11
Alzheimer's Society, alliance with drug
    manufacturing, 71
American Board of Mental Health
    Specialists, 37
American Cancer Society, 40, 204
American Civil Liberties Union, patient/
    client rights, 45
American College of Radiation Oncology,
    avoidable errors, 147
American Council on Science and Health, 61
American Heart Association, 204
American Iatrogenic Association, 46
American Medical Association, 36
American Nurses Association, 36
American Obesity Association (AOA),
    funding sources, 71
American Occupational Therapy
    Association, 36
American Psychiatric Association,
    35, 36
    and Big Pharma, 40–41
    brochures, 117–118
    education, 37
    pharmaceutical-company-sponsored
        lecturers, 75
    publication department, 44
    web site, 474n.2
American Psychological Association, 35–36
    best practice, 397
    privileges, 431–432n.5
    publication department, 44
American Speech-Language-Hearing
    Association, 36
Amusing Ourselves to Death, Postman, 105
Analogy
    inappropriate use of, 399–400
    reasoning from, 352–353
Analysis. *See* Argument analysis;
    Propaganda analysis
Analytic thinking, 216, 340, 376, 418
AndroGel, 167, 308f
Antidepressants, safety concerns, 42
Anti-psychotics, brochure, 116–117
Anti-Quackery Ring, 61
Antiscience
    definition, 232
    rejection of scientific methods, 229
    relativism, 229–230
Anxiety
    learning, 465n.14
    persuasion strategy, 321t
    psychological and sociological,
        468n.41
Anxiety Disorder Association of America
    (ADAA), 432n.7
Anxiety disorders
    brochure, 117–118
    treatment, 437n.43
Appraisal. *See* Critical appraisal
Argument, 356
    flawed, 472–473n.13
    forced analogy, 400
    foul ways to win an, 389t
    irrelevant conclusion, 399
    straw person, 398

Index

Argument analysis *See also* reasoning
  arguments, 355–360
  authority, 368–370
  avoiding propaganda influence, 360–364
  consistency, 375–376
  conversational maxims as guide, 364t
  corroboration, 375–376
  critical thinking, 375–376
  deductive arguments, 359
  deductive vs. inductive arguments, 359t
  deliberation, 367
  explanations, 378t, 379t
  fabrication, 370–371
  facts, beliefs and preferences, 375–376
  fallacies related to causal reasoning, 354t
  feeling about truth, 371–372
  hot and cold reasons, 355
  imaginary authority, 370–371
  importance of context, 364–370
  individual and cultural differences, 380
  inductive reasoning, 359–360
  information-seeking, 367
  inquiry, 366–367
  logical reasoning and creativity, 374–375
  logic and reasoning, 372
  negative rules in persuasion dialogue, 366t
  negotiation, 367
  premises and conclusions in valid logical argument, 358f
  quarrel, 367–368
  reasoning and truth, 374
  reasons, 352–355
  rebuttal, 361, 363–364, 450–451n.12
  Socratic questions, 361, 362t
  truth and credibility, 372
  types of dialogue, 365t
  types of statement in rational argument, 357t
  vulnerability to propaganda, 351–352
  what and how to think, 374
  widely accepted vs. true, 371
Argumentation
  persuasion dialogue, 366t
  process, 355–356
Aristotle, emotional appeals, 306t
The Arrogance of Preventive Medicine, Sackett, 177
Arthritis Foundation, sponsors, 71

Assertions
  arguments, 356
  exaggerated claims of effectiveness, 396–397
  language, 316–317
Assessments, self-inflated, 335–336
Association, language, 314
Association for the Treatment of Sexual Abusers (ATSA), 36–37
Association of Social Work Boards, 36
Assumptions, Socratic questions, 362t
AstraZeneca, 65, 72
  conflict, 445–446n.18
  lawsuits, 448n.38
Astroturfs, 46
Atkinson, Dr. Richard L., obesity researcher, 71
Atlas, Charles, photograph with friends, 282, 283f
Attachment theory, 139
Attention Deficit Hyperactivity Disorder (ADHD)
  case, 132–133
  Children and Adults with Attention Deficit Disorder (CHADD), 44–45
  choices, 23
  claims, 199
  diagnostic criteria, 131t
  funding, 84
  International Consensus Statement, 6, 468n.45
  labeling children, 123
  National Resource Center on ADHD, 43–44
  psychiatric drugs, 65, 142
Attrition bias, 421
Authority
  advertising and professional literature, 284–284
  arguments from, 368–370
  fallacies, 473n.1, 473n.14
  imaginary, 370–371
  method of, 459n.1
  persuasion, 321t, 324–325
  propaganda, 116
  questionable criteria, 206–209
  vulnerability to propaganda, 331
Avandia, 42, 77, 112, 140, 433n.11

Avoidable errors, propaganda contributing to, 146–147
Avoidable harms. *See also* Harms related to propaganda
　propaganda in helping professions, 123–124
Awareness-raising
　grand narratives, 238–239
　social anxiety disorder, 69

Babies, blinding of, 127, 147
Backing, rational argument, 357*t*
Bafflegarb, jargon, 304–305
Baloney Detection Kit, Sagan, 106
Bandwagon, propaganda, 102*t*, 111
Barnum effect, vague descriptions, 328–329
BASF, drug fines, 438–439*n*.58
Bayh–Dole
　Bayh–Dole Act of 1980, 85
　corporations and universities, 85
　research, 34
Begging the question, 395–397
Behavior modification, label, 310
Behaviors
　changing views, 249–251
　class, gender, culture and race, 269–271
　contextual views, 274–275
　demons carrying souls of sinners, 249–250
　demons causing bad, 235, 236*f*
　genetic explanations, 260–261
　grand narratives, 235–240
　labeling, 272–273
　social problems, 267–269
Belief encroachment, professionals becoming quacks, 33*t*
Belief perseverance, confirmation bias, 339–340
Beliefs
　facts, and preferences, 375–376
　views and consequences, 240–241
Benefits, describing risks and, 189–190
Bernays, Edward, public relations industry, 53–54, 97, 261, 440*n*.63
Best practices, misleading, 155
Bias
　confirmation, 338–340
　dispositional, 459*n*.17
　emotional leaning, 373
　observer, 416
　question of, 420–422
　publishing, 113, 412, 421–422
　reporting, 452*n*.18
　vulnerability to propaganda, 337–340
Bible, availability, 466*n*.22
Biederman, Dr. Joseph
　bipolar diagnoses, 63–64, 443*n*.9
　earnings, 71, 73
Big Pharma
　American Psychiatric Association and, 40–41
　influence, 78–79
　medical ghostwriting and, 326–328
　oversimplification, 302
Big Science, 204, 224–225
Biological psychiatry, grand narrative, 257–260
Biology, psychopathology, 466–467*n*.25
Biomedical Bestiary, faulty reasoning, 382
Biomedical industrial complex, 277, 344, 457*n*.4
Biomedical industry, disease mongering, 91
Biomedicalization, 56, 68, 156, 161
Biomedical research, false claims, 11
Biopower, 40
Biotech industry, health care, 48–49
Biotechnology corporations, medical devices, 81–82
Bipolar diagnoses, children, 63–64
Bipolar disorder, case, 133
Blinding, research design, 78
Bogus claims
　creating bogus risks, 159
　creation and promotion of nondiseases, 156
　influencing policy decisions, 125
　medication, 140
Bogus credential industry, 38–39
Bogus sickness
　depression, 164
　examples, 163–165
　irritable bladder, 163
　panic disorder, 164–165
　potential losses, 194–195
　pseudobulbar affect, 165
　social phobia, 164
Bold assertions, language, 316–317

Index

Bomdardier, Dr. Claire, University of Toronto, 86
Books. *See also* Professional books
　pharmaceutical companies and publication of, 82–83
　publishing industry, 44
Boot camps, juvenile, 135, 453n.17
Boredom, professionals becoming quacks, 33t
Boundary disputes, professions, 429n.9
Brain dysfunction, behaviors, 259
Brain images, allure of science, 329, 330f
Brave New World, Huxley, 105
Breast cancer
　Herceptin campaign, 84–85
　hormone replacement therapy, 183
　intrusive interventions, 169
　mergers, 437n.49
　natural frequencies, 185, 187
　radical mastectomy, 154–155
　risk, 183
　routine mammography screening, 150–152
　surgical biopsy, 455n.40
Bristol–Myers Squibb
　fraud, 59, 431n.24
　sponsor, 71, 72
　State of Florida, 87, 88
Britain, fake medicines, 441n.74
British Chiropractic Association, lawsuit, 463n.34
British False Memory Society (BFMS), 138
British Journal of Statistical Psychology, imaginary authority, 371
British Medical Association, 37, 44
Brochures, propaganda in guise of educational, 116–118
Brushing and joint compression therapy, interventions, 136, 137f
Bullshit. *See also* Palaver
　bluff, 230
　contemporary proliferation, 230–231
　notion, 105
Burden of proof, 363
Bureaucratic propaganda, 451n.13
　medium, 103–104
　purpose, 104
　target, 103
　truth, 104

Campbell collaboration, 334, 391, 407, 409, 410, 412, 428, 475n.13
Canadian Public Relations Society, Code of Professional Standards, 440–441n.64
Cancer
　advertising and Federal Trade Commission (FTC), 42
　biotech industry, 48–49
　doctors looking for extra, 456n.55
　drug rebates, 442n.3
　natural frequency, 188
　proposed mergers, 437n.49
Cancer Prevention Coalition, 433–434n.13
Capitalism
　emotional, 466n.19
　grand narrative, 251–252
Cardiac implants, unnecessary insertion, 124
Card-stacking
　advertising and professional literature, 289
　propaganda, 102t, 111
Case examples, questionable criteria, 207t, 213
Catholic Church, evolution theory, 225
Cause, reasoning by, 353–355
Celecoxib, Class Study, 86
Censorship
　education, 38
　missing language, 303
　propaganda, 112–114
Center for Bioethics, University of Pennsylvania, 77
Center for Media Literacy, 46
Center for Responsive Politics, lobbyists, 41
Center for Science in the Public Interest, 46
Centers for Disease Control, 43, 84, 204, 452n.4
Certification, "mad" by doctor, 434n.15
Chains of influence, propaganda in helping professions, 63, 64f, 89
Change, metaphors for, 307t
Charitable organizations
　bogus claims, 39–40
　public face of science, 204
Charity, 363
Charts, advertising and professional literature, 288

Children
  advertisement for tonic, 243, 244f
  biomedical explanations, 258
  Concerta ad, 279, 280f
  forced electroshock therapy (ECT), 153–154, 457n.59
  natural frequency of protection, 188
  suggestibility, 454n.23
Children and Adults with Attention Deficit Disorder (CHADD), funding, 44–45, 84
Children's Rights Group, 46
Chiropractic practice, lawsuit, 463n.34
Choices
  illusion of free, 7
  propaganda, 23–25
  rhetoric and propaganda, 9t
Chomsky, Noam, propaganda, 106
Church of Scientology, Citizens Commission on Human Rights, 46
Citizens Commission on Human Rights, 45, 46
Claims
  advertising and professional literature, 289
  false, 5
  rational argument, 357t
Clarification, Socratic questions, 362t
Clarity, 363
Class
  arbiter of one's fate, 245t
  behavior, 269–271
  differences, 380
Classification system
  claims about scientific base, 129–134
  clinical labels and illusion of knowledge, 129–130
  creation, 265
  helping professions, 15–16
  psychiatric labels, 130–134
  race and ethnicity as, 134
  technology, 254
Class Study, Celecoxib, 86
Clients, helping professions, 33–34
Clinical Endocrinology, ad for AndroGel, 308f
Clinical labels, illusion of knowledge, 129–130
Clinical psychology
  classification system, 265
  language of therapy, 264–265
  therapeutic grand narrative, 261–266
  therapeutic prescriptions, 263–264
Clinical trial, controlled, 460n.9
Closing, persuasion dialogue, 366t
Clozaril, side effects, 141
Cochrane collaboration, 334, 391, 406, 407, 409, 410, 412, 428, 474n.1, 475n.13
Code of Professional Standards, Canadian Public Relations Society, 440–441n.64
Coffee, problems with drinking, 271
Cognitive behavioral therapy, 468–469n.46
Cohn & Wolfe
  GSK hiring, for Paxil, 67–68
  public relations firm, 53
Commercial Free Childhood Organization, 46
Commercial research organizations (CROs), 35
Commission on Dietetic Registration, 36
Common misinterpretations, risk, 184
Common practice, appeal to, 394
Communication. *See also* Language
  facilitated, 7, 144–145, 460n.3
  jargon, 304–305
  rhetoric and propaganda of communicator, 9t
  using words for clear, 193
  vagueness, 469n.8
Communications industry
  Internet, 56
  media, 55–57
  psychological assessment, 57
  self-help, 57
Community mental health, helping professions, 13
Competing goals, helping professions, 16
Complexity, advertising and professional literature avoiding, 289–291
Computed tomography (CT), full body scan, 149
Concept Therapeutics, conflict of interest, 41
Concerta, 43, 45, 56, 279, 280f
Conclusion, irrelevant, 399
Conditional probabilities
  definition, 186t
  format, 187

Index

Conferences, masquerading as education, 75–77
Confidence, influence of, 331–332
Confirmation biases, vulnerability to propaganda, 338–340
Conflicts of interest
  chains of influence, 63, 64f, 89
  charitable and not-for-profit organizations, 39–40
  helping professions and industries, 29
  interventions, 457n.61
  medical devices, 81–82
  politicians, 40–41
  regulatory industry and funding sources, 83–85
  Rezulin, 449n.40
  state and local professional organizations, 432n.8
Conflicts of values, corporations and universities, 85
Confounders, 422, 424t
Confrontation, persuasion dialogue, 366t
Confusing representations, health statistics, 186t
Confusion
  fallacies by, 401–402
  propaganda, 115
Congenitally-absent-organ syndrome, 458n.15
Consensus
  persuasion, 324
  propaganda, 116
  questionable criteria, 207t, 209–210
Consistency
  corroboration and proof, 375
  persuasion, 321t, 322–323
Constipation, advertising and professional literature, 290f
Consumerism, grand narrative, 251–252
Consumer organizations
  front groups, 46
  funded by pharmaceutical companies, 44–45
  grassroots groups, 45
  watchdog groups, 45–46
Consumer Reports, watchdog, 46
Consumers
  advertising and professional literature, 292

  lawyers and state governments, 87–88
Consumers International, 46
Content knowledge, 460n.6
Contextual view, anecdote to propaganda, 274–275
Contingent truth, rhetoric and propaganda, 9t
Continuing education industry, 38
Contract-research organization (CRO), marketing, 77–78
Contrast effects, persuasion, 324
Controversies
  advertising and professional literature hiding, 289–291
  awareness of, 275–276
  research, 418–419
Conversational maxims, Grice's guide, 364t, 382, 388
Conversion phenomenon, professionals becoming quacks, 33t
Conviction, through repetition, 315–316
Corporate funding, not-for-profit organizations, 71–73
Corporate medicalizers, 166–167
Corporate science, research and knowledge, 203–204
Corroboration, consistency, and proof, 375
Corruption
  medicine, 452n.4
  propaganda, 23
Cotton, Joseph, focal sepsis theory of mental illness, 125–126
Council on Social Work Education, 36
Counterfeit drugs, 59
Covert propaganda, 450n.10
Creativity, logical reasoning and, 374–375
Credentials, bogus credential industry, 38–39
Credibility
  advertising and professional literature, 294
  lack of, 203f
  truth and, 372
Crime, labeling behavior, 248
Criminalization, drugs, 464n.3
Criteria. *See* Questionable criteria
Critical appraisal
  benefits vs. risks and costs, 414
  bias and validity, 421–422
  common errors and obstacles, 412

Critical appraisal (Cont'd)
    controversies, 418–419
    decision making, 415–416
    effectiveness of intervention, 414
    evaluating outcome, 416–417
    expert opinion, 415
    findings, 412
    levels of evidence, 427–428
    myths hindering, 419–420
    posing well-structured questions, 405–407
    preferences, 414
    quality filters, 407, 409t
    questioning research, 422–427
    question of bias, 420–422
    related research, 415
    relevant databases, 407, 409, 412
    research, 417–419
    searching related research, 407–409, 412
    sources, 409, 410t, 411t
    spotting propaganda, 405
    types of studies, 408t
    values, 414
    websites and tools, 410t, 411t
Critical discussion, definition, 232
Critical thinking,
    analysis, 106
    cultural differences, 380
    education, 96, 107, 292, 331
    lacking, 343–344, 382
    oversimplification, 289
    propaganda vs., 6, 17, 25, 90
    skills, 318, 329
    thinking for ourselves, 295
Criticism, self-correction, 218–219
The Crowd, Lebon, 54
CS-Chronic Comorbidity in CNS Medicine and Mental Fitness DDP, 52
Cuing effects, language, 314
Culture
    behavior, 269–271
    blame, 456n.47
    entitlement, 74
    facts, beliefs and preferences, 375–376
    of fear, 176
    pathology emphasis, 175
    personality, 284
    popular, 229, 238, 254, 256
    propaganda shaping, 104
    superiority of Euro-American, 258
    therapy, 251–252, 262–264
Curiosity, propaganda vulnerability, 334
CVS, 52
Cynicism, definition, 232

DARE (Drug Abuse Resistance Education), 155
Deception, history of, 202–203
Deceptive shifts, 380
Decision-making style
    critical appraisal, 415–416
    integrating findings and, 413–417
    vulnerability to propaganda, 342
Decriminalization of drugs, 145, 464n.3
Deductive arguments, 359
Defeat Depression, campaign, 128, 452–453n.7
Defiance, medicalization of, 144
Definitions, words, 301
Deliberation
    argument type, 367
    dialogue, 365t
DeMay, Dr. Charles, pharmaceutical industry and education, 76
Dementia
    antipsychotic medication, 141
    FDA treatment, 455n.33
    labels, 453n.9
Demons
    carrying condemned souls of sinners, 249f, 250
    causing bad behavior, 235, 236f
Dependent personality disorder, label, 269
Depression
    biology, 466–467n.25
    bogus sickness, 164
    history, 244, 247
    inflated claims of knowledge, 128
    psychological and sociological, 468n.41
Depression and Bipolar Support Alliance, 447–448n.32
DES (diethylstilbestrol), premature promotion, 148
Description, language, 300
Design Write, ghostwriting articles, 31
Detection bias, 421
Developmentally disabled youth, 307

Deviance, 172
    problems, 268
    social control of, 247–249
Deviants, 248
Device approaches, propaganda, 102*t*, 107–109
Diagnosis
    ADHD, 45, 84, 133
    Alzheimer's, 152
    bipolar, 443*n*.9
    computed tomography scans, 149
    confirmation biases, 338–339
    counseling session for AIDS patient, 180*t*
    false negatives, 46, 148, 149, 185, 390, 409*t*, 414
    false positives, 6, 46, 129, 146, 148, 171, 177–178, 180, 185, 257, 390, 406, 409*t*, 414
    hysteria, 293
    mammography screening, 150–152
    mental illness, 149–150
    overdiagnosis, 131, 150, 161, 162, 168, 177, 390
    prevalence, 114, 127–129, 160*t*, 166*f*, 168, 180*t*, 184, 188, 235, 238, 273, 398, 308, 409*t*
    schizophrenia, 291
    self-, 55, 166*t*
    sensitivity, 180*t*, 184, 188, 409*t*
Diagnostic and Statistical Manual of Mental Disorders, 69, 94, 114
    American Psychiatric Association, 57, 257
    consensus, 209–210
    creation of next edition, 254
    misbehaviors named diagnoses, 167–168
    misleading aura of credibility, 225
    panic disorder, 164–165
    problem creation, 273
    psychiatric labels, 130
Diagnostic Related Groups (DRGs), hospital admission, 94
Diagnostic tests, inflating need for and accuracy of, 148–149
Diapers, fraud, 58
Diarrhea, neglect, 156
Dichter study, process of rationalization, 74
Dietfraud.com, 61
Diet pills, 140, 434–435*n*.19

Differences, advertising and professional literature exaggerating, 292
Dilution effect, low-quality service, 157
Direct to consumer advertising (DCA), drugs, 281
Disabilities, facilitated communication, 144–145
Disabling professions, medicalization of life, 159
Disapproval, vulnerability to propaganda, 333
Discomfort, 172
Disease, 172
    definition, 161
    edge-of-the-distribution illness, 458*n*.8
    grand narrative, 255–261
    labeling risks as, 173–174
    propaganda ploy for use of word, 172–176
Disease mongering, 159
    creating fear, 169
    decreasing agency, 171–172
    encouraging intrusive interventions, 169
    frequency of key elements of, in newspaper articles, 166*f*
    ignoring real risks, 169–170
    method, 91
    self-medicalization, 170–171
    self-surveillance, 170–171
    stretching the boundaries, 165–168
    surveillance and privacy, 171
    tactics, 160*t*
Disinformation, history of, 202–203
Distortion, propaganda, 114
Diversion, propaganda, 114–115
Diversions, fallacies, 400–401
Down's syndrome, risk, 194*f*
Dramatism, 299
Drapetomania, label, 130
Dr. Fox Study, manner of presentation, 331–332, 461*n*.15
Drug companies
    advertising, 11, 12*f*
    conflict of interest with advocacy groups, 84–85
    counterfeit drugs, 59
    financial ties with researchers, physicians and professional organizations, 73–81
    fraud, 430*n*.21

Drugs
  abuse of Methadone, 31
  decriminalization, 145, 464n.3
  direct to consumer advertising (DCA), 281
  off-label, 444n.14
Drug war, United States, 145, 464n.3
Dubious Dentistry, 38-39, 51

Eclecticism, definition, 232
Ecological fallacy, risk factor, 178, 382
Economic inequities, neglect, 157
Edge-of-the-distribution illness, 458n.8
Education
  Accreditation Council for Continuing Medical Education (ACCME), 444-445n.15
  bogus credential industry, 38-39
  continuing, industry, 38
  continuing opportunities, 36
  DARE (Drug Abuse Resistance Education), 155
  effectiveness of propaganda, 95-96
  industry-sponsored, 445n.17
  marketing disguised as, 11-13
  marketing masquerading as, 75-77
  presenting propaganda as, 20-21
  professional programs, 37-38
  propaganda as brochures, 116-118
  Romantic-progressivist, 432-433n.10
  self-medicalization, 170-171
  sex, programs for teenagers, 145
Einstein, Albert, scientist, 225
Eiseley, Loren, scientist, 225
Elders, Surgeon General Joycelyn, 43, 250
Electric shock therapy, children and involuntary adults, 153-154, 457n.59
Eli Lilly
  conflict of interest, 41
  lawsuits, 448n.38
  marketing channels, 66
  Prozac, 87
  psychiatric drugs, 65
  Zyprexa, 6, 139-140, 471n.1
Ellul, Jacque, sociological analysis of propaganda, 90-99
Eloquence, manner of presentation, 317-318
Emotion, objectification of, 467n.36

Emotional appeals
  advertising and professional literature, 285-287
  Aristotle, 306t
  diversions, 401
  fallacies, 391
  language, 305-307
  predigested thinking, 303
  questionable criteria, 207t, 212-213
Emotional capitalism, 466n.19
Emotional culture, psychology, 263-264
Emotional vulnerability, propaganda, 332-335
Empathy, 16, 20, 33, 377, 378t, 379t
Empire State Association of Adult Homes & Assisted Living Facilities, 41
Empirical inquiry, 223, 377
Empiricism, definition, 232
Entertainment, vulnerability to propaganda, 335
Entertainment value, questionable criteria, 207t, 212
Entitlement culture, medical education, 74-75
Epilepsy, drugs, 439-440n.61
Equivocation, confusion, 402
Erectile dysfunction (ED), 161, 167, 172
Eristic, dialogue, 365t
Errors, propaganda contributing to avoidable, 146-147
Ethical Strategies Website, case studies, 65t
Ethics, Public Relations Association, 54
Ethnicity
  arbiter of one's fate, 245t
  classifications, 134
  propaganda, 468n.42
Euphemisms, language, 309
European Commission, drug fines, 438-439n.58
Evaluating outcome, interventions, 416-417
Evidence. *See also* Questionable criteria
  advertising and professional literature, 287-288, 289
  definition, 232
  doubtful, 388-389
  knowledge vs., 205-206
  levels of, 427-428
  partiality in the use of, 338-339, 351
  selective use of, 10

Socratic questions, 362*t*
standards of, 199–202
suppressed views and related, 389–391
Evidence-based medicine (EBM) tool kit, 474*n*.3
Evidence-based practice, 5, 185, 310, 311, 375
distortion, 114, 240, 291
education, 38, 201
misleading, 155
parables, 254
process and philosophy, 288, 315, 398, 405
propaganda, 25, 64*f*
Evil, neutralization efforts, 471*n*.12
Evolution, professions, 429*n*.9
Evolution theory, Catholic Church and, 225
Excerpta Medica, ghost writing, 446–447*n*.22
Exclusion, reasoning by, 355
Excuses, self-propaganda, 336–337
Expectations, grand narratives, 239–240
Experience, questionable criteria, 207*t*, 213–216
Expertise
expert testimony, 461–462*n*.17
helping professions claiming, 13–14
Explanations
different kinds of, 376–377, 378*t*, 379*t*
empathic, 377, 378*t*, 379*t*
ideological, 379–380
individual and cultural differences, 380
scientific, 377, 378*t*, 379
Expression, language, 300
Express Scripts, 52, 440*n*.61
Extensional meaning, word, 301
External validity, 422

Fabrication
distorting facts, 398–400
imaginary authority, 370–371
propaganda, 115
Facebook, 92
Facilitated communication
controlled and uncontrolled, 460*n*.3
development, 7
disabilities, 144–145
Factoids, 115, 315, 375
Facts
beliefs and preferences, 375–376

distorting, 398–400
evading the, 394–397
overlooking the, 397–398
Fad introduction, common script for, 113*t*
Failure, propaganda vulnerability, 334
Fairness & Accuracy in Reporting (FAIR), 46
Fallacies. *See also* Spotting fallacies
ad ignorantiam, 473–474*n*.5
advertising and professional literature, 292–293
argumentum ad ignoratium, 387
authority, 473*n*.1, 473*n*.14
causal reasoning, 354*t*
definition, 385
diversions, 400–401
examples containing, 383*t*
exchanges illustrating informal, 386*t*
importance of context, 385–388
informal, 384*t*, 385*t*
key properties, 387
questionable appeals and faulty inferences, 403*t*, 404*t*
use of confusion, 401–402
Walton's pragmatic view of, 383–388
Fallacy of accident, 397
Fallacy of alchemist, 298
Fallacy of appeal to will, 394
Fallacy of equivocation, 402
Fallacy of false cause, 398–399
Fallacy of golden mean, 382
Fallacy of hasty conclusion, 397
Fallacy of hasty generalization, 397–398
Fallacy of ignorance, 393–394
Fallacy of obfuscation, 382
Fallacy of special pleading, 393
Fallacy of sweeping generalization, 397
Fallibility, 363
False beliefs, propaganda, 17–18
False claims
charitable and not-for-profit organizations, 39–40
Federal Trade Commission (FTC), 42
history of, 202–203
propaganda, 5
False Claims Act, 22, 42, 430*n*.21
False epidemics, 168
False knowledge, 205, 233
Falsification approach to knowledge, 233

Fast and frugal heuristics, 215, 216, 324, 340
Fate, arbiters of one's, 245*t*
Faulty inferences, 403*t*, 404*t*
Fear
   ad appealing to, 319, 322*f*
   advertising and professional literature, 285–287, 286*f*
   creating, 169
   hopes for relief, 241–243
   persuasion strategy, 321*t*
Fear of appearing ignorant, vulnerability to propaganda, 333
Fear of failure, propaganda vulnerability, 334
Fear of social rejection, vulnerability to propaganda, 333
Federal Drug Administration (FDA)
   conflicts of interest with funding agencies, 83
   government agency, 42
   harmful drugs, 139
Federal government. *See also* Government agencies, 42–44
Federal Marijuana Tax Act of 1937, 271
Federal Trade Commission (FTC), 42, 82*t*, 431*n*.24, 435*n*.19
Feeling, truth, 371–372
Fen-phen, diet pill, 140
Figures, advertising and professional literature, 288
Financial ties
   corporations and universities, 85–86
   drug companies, professional organizations, researchers, and physicians, 73–81
Fine needle aspiration, 143
Flawed argument, 292–293, 472–473*n*.13
Flint Laboratories, commissioning University of California at San Francisco, 87
Focal sepsis theory, mental illness, 125–126, 128
Follies and Fallacies in Medicine, Skrabanek and McCormick, 156, 176, 382
Food, Drug, and Cosmetic Act (FDCA), 87–88
Food and Drug Administration (FDA)
   dementia treatment, 141–142, 455*n*.33
   direct to consumer advertising (DCA), 281

Forcing an extension, 398
Ford Foundation, 204
Forer Effect, vague descriptions, 328–329
Framing effects, vulnerability to propaganda, 337–338
Fraud
   appeal to science, 201*f*
   appeal to scientific discoveries, 202*f*
   billing procedures, 442*n*.80
   definition, 22, 57
   drug companies, 430*n*.21
   Galavit, 22
   identifying sources, 60–62
   Medicare, 430*n*.20, 431*n*.24
   propaganda, 21–23
   quackery, 227–228
   quacks and fraudsters, 57–60, 200
   whistleblowers, 60
Free choice, illusion, 7
Frequency statements, definition, 186*t*
Front groups, hidden sponsorship, 46
Fundamental attribution error, 128

Galavit, fraudulent treatment, 22
Gastroptosis, 458*n*.15
Gates Foundation, 460*n*.4
Gay rights movement, 248–249
Gender
   arbiter of one's fate, 245*t*
   behavior, 269–271
   differences, 380
Generalization
   fallacy of hasty, 397–398
   fallacy of sweeping, 397, 402
   unfounded, 396
Generalized anxiety disorder (GAD), 39, 164
Generational dysfunctions, pseudotechnical jargon, 305
Genetics, causes of behavior, 260–261
Genomic Health, OncotypeDX test, 48–49
Geodon, 87, 141
Gerontological Society of America, contributors, 71
Ghost writing
   Big Pharma and medical, 326–328
   Exerpta Medica, 446–447*n*.22
   product promotion, 80–81, 140–141
GlaxoSmithKline (GSK)

Avandia, 42, 77, 112, 140, 433n.11
  legal action against, 69–70
Paxil, 7, 53, 67–70, 83, 164, 436n.36
psychiatric drugs, 65
Glittering generality, propaganda, 102t, 110, 200
Good intentions, questionable criteria, 207t, 211
Government
  federal and state, departments, 43–44
  lobbyists, 41–42
  participation with helping professions, 40–44
  politicians, 40–41
  public face of science, 204
  state and federal regulation agencies, 42–43
The Grand Confounder, 382
Grand narratives
  advertising and professional literature appealing to, 294
  appeals to science, 237f
  awareness of, 238–239
  biological psychiatry, 257–260
  capitalism and consumerism, 251–252
  clinical psychology, 261–266
  consumerism, healthism and self-help, 272
  demons causing bad behavior, 235, 236f
  genes, 260–261
  health and disease, 255–261
  influencing expectations, 239–240
  mental health, 257–260
  popular beliefs influencing views, 235–240
  proposed causes for problems, 239t
  psychological, 261, 262f
  science and technology as, 252–255
  strategies promoting, 237–238
  transfer effects, 314
  views and consequences, 240–241
Granfalloon effect, persuasion, 321
Grasshopper mind, man with, 261, 262f
Grassley, Sen. Charles E., 40–41, 78
Grassroots groups, 45
Great and Desperate Cures, Valenstein, 126
Grice's maxims, conversation, 318, 364t, 382, 388
Group homes, avoidable harms, 143–144
Guidelines, pharmaceutical companies and publication of, 82–83

Guilford Press, advertising catalog, 44
Guilt by association, *ad hominem*, 392–393
Gullibility, vulnerability to propaganda, 344–347

Haldol, 43, 141
Harms related to propaganda
  attachment theory, 139
  avoidable, 123–124
  avoidable errors, 146–147
  blinding of 10,000 babies, 127
  boot camps and prison style juvenile facilities, 135
  brushing and joint compression therapy, 136
  facilitated communication, 144–145
  focal sepsis theory of mental illness, 125–126
  group homes and institutional settings, 143–144
  holding therapy, 139
  inflating claims of need for and accuracy of tests, 148–149
  knowledge claims hindering knowledge development, 154–156
  lobotomies, 126–127
  medication, 139–142
  neglecting common concerns, 156–157
  not offering effective methods, 157
  population-based screening, 149–152
  premature use of intrusive interventions, 152–154
  prevalence, nature and causes of problems, 127–129
  promoting harmful interventions, 135–139
  promoting ineffective practices and policies, 144–145
  promoting untested methods, 147–148
  rebirthing therapy, 139
  recovered memory movement, 136–138
  scientific base of classification systems, 129–134
  sex education for teenagers, 145
  unnecessary or unneeded interventions, 142–144
  Utica crib, 125, 126f
  violating right to make informed decisions, 124–127
  war on drugs in U.S., 145

Harris, William, diaper fraud, 58
Harvard Health Letter, 51
Harvard Women's Health Watch, 51
Hawthorne effect, 416
Healing, fear, suffering and hopes for, 241–243
Health
  consequences of enlarging territory of, 168–172
  helping professions, 14–15
Health care
  lobbyists, 41–42
  play of propaganda, 18–19
  politicians influence, 40–41
Health care industry
  biotech industry, 48–49
  grand narrative, 255–261
  health care publications, 51–52
  insurance industry, 50
  helping professions, 13–16
  laboratories, 52–53
  malpractice insurance industry, 50
  medical supply and device industry, 48
  middlemen, 52
  pharmaceutical industry, 47–48
  products industry, 51
  residential treatment center industry, 50
Healthism, 251, 272, 466n.19
Health statistics, confusing and transparent representations, 186t
Health Watcher, watchdog, 61
Healthy, 159
Healy, Dr. David, University of Toronto, 87, 203
Hearing Voices movement, grassroots, 45
Hello-goodbye effect, 416
Helping professions
  attention to hidden players, 29
  claimed and hidden roles, 14–16
  claim of expertise, 13–14
  classification, 15–16
  clients and patients, 33–34
  competing goals, 16
  consequences of propaganda, 19–21
  false claims of knowledge, 10
  marketing view, 30t
  occupations, 13
  professionalism, 16

social control, 15
social reform, 16
Herceptin campaign, breast cancer, 84–85, 448n.34
Heretical actions, 250
Hermeneutics, 233
Heuristics, 216, 324, 340
  affect, 337
  fast and frugal, 215, 216, 282, 324, 340
Hindsight bias, vulnerability to propaganda, 337–338, 417
History
  collaboration of industry and universities, 203–204
  dangers of scientific illiteracy, 228–229
  deception and disinformation, 202–203
Hitler, Adolph
  manner of presentation, 331
  Mein Kampf, 100, 355
  traditional propaganda, 103
HIV/AIDS, 224
  causal relationship, 463n.30
  Fair Foundation, 457n.60
  public issues, 204
Hoffman-La Roche, drug fines, 438–439n.58
Holding therapy, 139
Homosexuals, changing views, 251
Hopes for relief, fear, suffering and, 241–243
Hormone replacement therapy, risk of breast cancer, 183
H.P. Acthar Gel, epilepsy drug, 439–440n.61
Humana Europe, King's Fund and, 39
The Human Condition, Arendt, 127
Humbugs of the World, Barnum, 328
"Hush hush" fallacy, 382
Hypogonadism, AndroGel, 167
Hypothermia, neglect, 156

Identification. *See* Spotting fallacies
Ideology, 37, 128
  advertising, 289
  racism, 134, 468n.42
  science, 161, 204, 225, 227–228
  sickness, 457n.3
Ignorance
  domains, 460n.7
  fallacy of, 393–394

false claims, 5
fear of appearing, 333
inflated claims of, 7–8
Illness, behavior as, 248
Illness inflation, 172
Illusion of argument, 351
Illusion of certainty, 180, 192
Illusion of choice, vulnerability to propaganda, 335
Illusion of control, overestimation, 214
Illusion of credibility, advertising and professional literature, 294
Illusion of evidentiary status, 298
Illusion of knowing, knowing and, 374
Illusion of knowledge, pathology, 175
Illusions, advertising appeal, 282–283
Inconsistencies, evidentiary issues, 393
Indicators, propaganda, 8t
Inductive reasoning, 359–360
Inert knowledge, 460n.6
Inflated claims, avoidable errors, 146–147
Information
  advertising and professional literature, 288
  misleading, 340–341
  and propaganda, 96–97
  validity effect, 470n.6
Information-seeking, 365t, 367
Informed decisions, violating right to make, 124–127
Inquiry, argument type, 365t, 366–367
Insanity
  certificate against Lobdell, 465n.17
  masturbation, 465n.15
Institute for Motivational Research, collaboration, 74
Institute for Propaganda Analysis, 101, 102t
Institute for Safe Medicine, 46
Institutional settings, avoidable harms, 143–144
Integrated Medical Services (IMS), medical information, 446n.21
Integrating findings, 413–417
Integration propaganda, persuasive, 95, 98
Integrity of Science, website, 71
Intelligence traps, misleading, 340
Intentional meaning, words, 301
Internal validity, 421
International Center for the Study of Psychiatry and Psychology (ICSPP), 46

International Consensus Statement, ADHD (Attention Deficit Hyperactivity Disorder), 6
International Pauresis Association, 36
Internet
  communications industry, 56
  propaganda source, 6
Interventions
  attachment theory, 139
  boot camps and prison style juvenile facilities, 135
  brushing and joint compression therapy, 136, 137f
  comparing preferences and values, 414
  conflicts of interest, 457n.61
  diagnostic tests, 143
  effectiveness of, 199
  encouraging intrusive, 169
  evaluating outcome, 416–417
  group homes and institutional settings, 143–144
  holding therapy, 139
  inflating need for and accuracy of tests, 148–149
  premature use of intrusive, 152–154
  promoting untested methods, 147–148
  rebirthing therapy, 139
  recovered memory movement, 136–138
  source and treatment of problems, 272–273
  types of studies, 408t
  unnecessary or unneeded, 142–144
Intuition
  guide, 420
  questionable criteria, 207t, 216–217
Irrelevant appeals, fallacies, 391–394
Irrelevant conclusion, argument, 399
Irritable bladder, bogus sickness, 163

Janssen, psychiatric drugs, 65
Jargon, pseudotechnical, 304–305
Johnson & Johnson
  conflict of interest, 41, 73
  lawsuits, 448n.38
  rebates, 442n.3
Journalists, interactions with for-profit companies, 88
Journal of the American Medical Association (JAMA), addiction, 129

Journals. *See also* Professional journals
  interactions with for-profit
    companies, 88
Judgment, suspension of, 363
Judicial Watch, 46
Jumping to conclusions, misleading, 340
Junk science, 56, 441*n*.67
Justification approach to knowledge, 233
Juvenile facilities, boot camps and
  prison style, 135

Ketek, safety concerns, 42
Key opinion leaders (KOLs), 78, 79, 446*n*.19
King, Martin Luther, 134, 468*n*.42
King's Fund, British charity, 39–40
Knoll Pharmaceutical, obesity, 71
Knowing, and illusion of, 374
Knowledge
  advertising and professional literature,
    289
  claims of, and hopes for relief, 241–243
  clinical labels and illusion of, 129–130
  definition, 233
  evidence vs., 205–206
  importance of specialized, 460*n*.6
  inflated claims hindering development,
    154–156
  inflated claims of, 7–8
  logic and reasoning, 372
  personal and objective, 373
  standards of evidence, 199–202
  vulnerability to propaganda, 343–344
  ways of knowing, 205–206
Knowledge monopolies, research cartels
  and, 85–86, 203–204, 431*n*.3, 448*n*.36
Ku Klux Klan (KKK), 326

Labels, naming, 309–310
Laboratories, health care, 52–53
Laboratory error syndrome, 458*n*.15
Language. *See also* Persuasion strategies
  association, 314
  assumption of one word, one meaning,
    310
  bafflegarb, 304–305
  bold assertions, 316–317
  censorship, 303
  constructing reality, 299
  conviction through repetition, 315–316
  emotional or buzz words, 305–307
  euphemisms, 309
  functions, 300
  grand narratives, 238
  levels of abstraction, 301
  making effective use of, 318
  manner of presentation, 317–318
  metaphors, 307–309
  metaphors for change, 307*t*
  misleading effects, 298–299
  misleading use of scientific discourse,
    303–304
  misuse of verbal speculation, 315
  naming, 309–310
  newsspeak, 317
  oversimplifications, 301–303
  predigested thinking, 301–303
  problematic descriptions, 311, 312*t*
  propaganda ploys, 301
  pseudotechnical jargon, 304–305
  psychology, 263–264
  questions about use of words, 313–314
  reification, 313–314
  role in helping professions, 297
  semantic linkages and cuing effects, 314
  slogans, 315
  sources of error, 298*t*
  synecdoches, 315
  transfer of effects, 314
  vagueness, 310–311, 312*t*
  weasel words, 297
  word magic, 313–314
Laswell, Harold, *Propaganda Technique in
  World War I*, 19
Lawyers
  consumers and state governments,
    87–88
  pharmaceutical companies, and
    researchers, 86–88
  settlements, 32–33
Learning theory, 457*n*.61, 465*n*.14
  associative, 92
  difficulty, 419
  disorder, 271
  from experience, 214, 218
  illusion of, 296
  principles, 344, 364–365
  questions about life-long, 406–407
  recognizing propaganda, 239

social view, 265
style, 342
vulnerability to propaganda, 342
Lebon, Gustav, *The Crowd*, 54
Legislation, politicians, 40–41
Leon, D. Martin, physician and educator, 63
License to Steal, Sparrow, 58
Liking rule, persuasion, 319, 321
Lobbyists, health care, 41–42
Lobdell, Lucy Ann, certificate of insanity, 465n.17
Lobotomies, harm from past, 126–127
Logic, reasoning and, 372
Logical argument, premises and conclusions, 358f
Logical positivism, definition, 233
Logical reasoning, and creativity, 374–375
Lovenox, 77, 447n.26

Magic
　relationship with science, 462n.19
　symbolic nature of, 255
　technology as, 255
Major Depressive Disorder, case, 133
MalAM, medical lobby, 41
Malpractice insurance industry, 50
Mammography screening, routine, 150–152
Manner, conversational maxim, 364t
Manner of presentation
　language, 317–318
　questionable criteria, 207t, 211
　vulnerability to propaganda, 331–332
Marijuana, 10, 271
Marketing
　academics and researchers as "marketers," 77–78
　advertising, 11, 12f
　creation and control of channels, 66
　disguising as education, 11–13
　grand narratives, 238–239
　helping professions, 30–31
　illegal, 59–60
　masquerading as education, 75–77
　pharmaceutical industry, 47–48, 49f
　post-marketing surveillance, 42
　sales representatives, drugs to professionals, 73–74

Marticles, 282
Mastectomy, radical, for breast cancer, 154–155
Masturbation, 43, 250, 290, 465n.15
Medco Health, 52
Medeva Pharmaceuticals, obesity, 71
Media
　communications industry, 55–57
　false claims, 5
　lawyers advertising, 32
　propaganda, 8, 100–101
Medicaid, overbilling, 60
Medical devices, 48
　appeals to science in advertising, 237f
　manufacture and marketing, 81–82
　Medicare, 438n.51
Medical education
　culture of entitlement, 74–75
　promoting pharmaceutical products, 76–77
Medicalization, 159
　aging, 161
　bogus diseases and risks, 161–163
　creating fear, 169
　decreased agency, 171–172
　decreased privacy, 171
　disease mongering tactics, 160t
　encouraging intrusive interventions, 169
　enlarging territories of health and risk, 168–172
　global problem, 458n.11
　ignoring real risks, 169–170
　increased surveillance, 171
　risk factors, 177–178
　self-, and self-surveillance, 170–171
　society, 256
Medicalization of defiance, mental illness, 144
Medical malpractice, insurance industry, 50
Medical products, ghost writing, 80–81
Medical professional organizations (MPOs), 78–79
Medical supply and device industry, 48
Medical technology, influences on use of new, 82f
Medicare
　devices and trials, 438n.51
　fraud, 430n.20, 431n.24
　overbilling, 58, 60

Medication
　avoidable harms, 139–142
　biomedical explanations, 258
　brochures, 116–117
Medicine
　corruption, 452n.4
　play of propaganda, 18–19
Medivai, 63
Medscape, Schizophrenia Resource Center, 56
Mein Kampf, Hitler, 100, 355
Mental disorders, brochure, 117
Mental Fitness, 52
Mental health, grand narrative, 257–260
Mental health services, helping professions, 13
Mental illness, 313
　biochemical changes, 258–259
　certificate of insanity, 465n.17
　disease entities, 466n.24
　focal sepsis theory of, 125–126, 128
　inappropriate use of analogies, 399
　label, 172, 173, 309–310
　medicalization of defiance, 144
　propaganda classification, 106t
　screening entire populations, 149–150
　views and consequences, 240–241
Merck, Vioxx, 63, 80, 81, 83, 86, 112, 140, 191
Mergers, cancer products, 437n.49
Metaphors
　drugs, 238, 307
　language, 307–309
Meta-analysis, 407, 409t, 433n.10
Meta-reasoning, 215
Methadone, drug abuse, 31
Method of authority, 459n.1
Method of science, 459n.1
Method of tenacity, 459n.1
Microsuicide, 469n.5
Middlemen, 52, 66
Mimicking syndrome, 458n.15
Mind Freedom, 45, 436n.35
Miniscule differences, exaggerating, 292
Minnesota, money for lectures, 443n.11
Misconceptions, science, 223
Misleading
　effectiveness of claims, 5
　figures, tables and charts, 288
　shortcuts to decisions, 340–342

The Mismeasure of Women, Tavris, 131, 269
Misrepresentations, science, 223–226
Misunderstandings
　science, 223–226
　words, 310
Moms Rising Organization, grassroots, 45
Moniz, Dr. Egas, Nobel Prize in medicine, 127
Moral views, psychoanalysis, 266–267
Mortality rates, definition, 186t
Mother's Act, 456n.53
Motivational vulnerability, propaganda, 332–335
MRI (magnetic resonance imaging) scans, full body, 149
Myths
　advertising and professional literature appealing to, 294
　hindering critical appraisal, 419–420
　propaganda, 17–18

Naive trust, vulnerability to propaganda, 342
Name calling, propaganda, 102t, 109
Naming, language, 309–310
Narratives. *See* Grand narratives
National Alliance for Research on Schizophrenia and Depression (NARSAD), 39
National Alliance for the Mentally Ill (NAMI)
　corporate funding, 72t
　funding, 44, 84, 114
National Association for Rights Protection and Advocacy (NARPA), 46
National Association of Alcoholism & Drug Abuse Counselors, 36
National Association of Cognitive-Behavioral Therapists (NACBT), 36
National Association of Social Workers, 36
National Board for Certified Counselors, 36
National Coalition of Mental Health Professionals and Consumers, 298–299
National Council Against Health Fraud (NCAHF), 46
National Council on Family Relations, 36
National Health and Social Life Survey, 167
National Health Service (NHS), 39

Index

National Institute of Health (NIH), 4, 222, 436n.36, 452n.4
  Bayh-Dole Act, 85
  ghost writing, 80
  research, 34
  science, 204
National Institute of Mental Health (NIHM), agency, 43–44
National Institute on Drug Abuse, *NIDA Notes*, 43
National Medical Enterprises (NME), kickbacks, 58–59
The National Panic/Anxiety Disorder Newsletter, 52
National Resource Center on ADHD, 43–44
National Science Foundation (NSF), 204
Natural frequencies, 186t, 187–188
Nature, publishing, 44
Negotiation
  argument type, 367
  dialogue, 365t
Nerves, 243–244, 247
Nervine, Dr. Miles, tonic advertisement, 244, 246f
Nervous tension, 244
Neurasthenia, 465n.13
New Freedom Commission on Mental Health, 124
New Freedom Initiative, screening for mental illness, 149–150
The New Jim Crow Laws, Alexander, 145
Newness
  advertising and professional literature, 294
  questionable criteria, 207t, 210
Newsletters, health care publications, 51–52
Newspaper articles, frequency of elements of disease mongering, 166f
Newspapers, persuasiveness of propaganda, 10
Newsspeak, language, 317
New York State Department of Mental Health, *Treatment of Children with Mental Disorders*, 43
Nobel Prize for medicine, Dr. Egas Moniz, 127
NOLVADEX, benefits and side effects, 189t, 190t
Nondiseases
  categories, 458n.15
  creation and promotion, 156
  culturally specific, 459n.15
  labeling risks as diseases, 173–174
  potential losses, 194–195
Nonjustificationist epistemology, definition, 233
Nonprofit organizations, 35, 36
Normal variation syndrome, 458n.15
Not-for-profit organizations
  bogus claims, 39–40
  corporate funding, 71–73
Numerator Monster, 382
Nutrition and health, differences in opinion, 223–224

Obedience, authority, 331
Objectification, emotions, 467n.36
Objectivity, scientists striving for, 221–222
Obscure terms, jargon, 304–305
Observer bias, 416
Occupations, helping professions, 13
OCD Newsletter, 52
Odds, verbal descriptions, 459n.19
Office of the Inspector General, hotline for fraud, 59
Off-label drugs, 444n.14
Omission, propaganda, 112–114
Ondansetron, literature, 454n.26
One word-one meaning fallacy, language, 313
Open Exchange: Healthy Living Magazine, 51
Operational definitions, words, 301
Opinion
  factors influencing public, 179
  study of nutrition and health, 223–224
Opinion leader, 65, 73, 78, 100, 109, 113, 319, 325, 347
Optimizing, 340
Organized Research Units (ORUs), University of California at Berkeley, 34
Osteoporosis, 7, 39
Overconfidence, illusion of control, 214
Overinterpretation, confirmation bias, 339
Over-interpretation-of-physical-findings syndrome, 458n.15
Oversimplification
  advertising and professional literature, 289–291
  language, 301–303
Overt propaganda, 450n.10

Palaver. *See also* Bullshit
  new propaganda, 105
Panic disorder, bogus sickness, 164–165
Parables, advertising and professional literature, 284
Paradigm, definition, 233
Parasitic infections, neglect, 156
Parenti, Michael, propaganda, 106–107
Parkinson's Disease, drugs for, 141
Parsimony, science, 221
Pathology, factors encouraging overemphasis, 175–176
Patients, helping professions, 33–34
Pattern matching, 215
Pattern recognition, 215
Patterns, search for, 221
Paxil, 7, 53, 67–70, 83, 164, 436*n*.36
Peele, Norman Vincent, positive psychology, 272
People with disabilities, facilitated communication, 144–145
Perceptions, lack of credibility, 203*f*
Performance bias, 421
Performance knowledge, 460*n*.6
Personal persuasion, 324–325
Persuasion
  critical discussion, 365–366
  dialogue, 365*t*
  emotive language, 305–307
  language, 300
  negative rules of dialogue, 366*t*
  reasoning, 372
Persuasion strategies. *See also* Language
  advertisement appealing to fear, 322*f*
  by affect, 319
  appeals to consistency, 322–323
  appeal to authority, 325
  contrast effects, 324
  creating fear or anxiety, 321*t*
  Granfalloon effect, 321
  making it personal, 324–325
  principle of liking, 319, 321
  principle of social proof, 324
  promoting false scarcity, 323–324
  reciprocity rule, 323
  social psychology, 318–325
  tactics for manipulating physicians, 319, 320*t*

Persuasive parables, advertising and professional literature, 284
Pervasive propaganda, 95
Pfizer, Viagra, 12*f*, 167
Pharma, opinion leaders and, 78
Pharmaceutical Advertising Club, collaboration, 74
Pharmaceutical companies
  advertising, 11, 12*f*
  ghost writing, 80–81
  lawyers and researchers, 86–88
  marketing channels, 66
  medical professional organizations (MPOs), 78–79
  publications, 82–83
Pharmaceutical industry
  advertising, 48, 49*f*
  advertising raising awareness, 161, 162*f*
  groups funded by, 44–45
  health care, 47–48
  interactions with journalists and journals, 88
  lobbyists, 41–42
  medical education promoting products, 76–77
  play of propaganda, 18–19
  Psychiatric Industry Watch, 435–436*n*.35
  shadowing, 443*n*.10
  social anxiety disorder creation, 67–71
  state and federal regulation agencies, 42–43
Phenomenology, definition, 233
Phrenology, grand narrative, 252, 253*f*
Physicians
  financial ties with drug companies, professional organizations and researchers, 73–81
  medical devices, 81–82
  money for lectures, 443*n*.11
  tactics for manipulating, 319, 320*t*
Placebo effect, 416
Plain folks, propaganda, 102*t*, 110–111, 116
Plaintiffs, lawyers cheating, 32–33
Planck, Max, scientific truth, 463*n*.36
Play therapy, acting-out, 206
PLoS Medicine, 140
PloS Neglected Tropical Diseases, 156
Plundering the Public Sector, Craig, 56
Point of view, interests, 373

Index 561

Political correctness, science and, 224
Political propaganda, 92
Politicians, policies and legislation, 40–41
Politics
  contextual views, 275
  problem creation, 273–274
Pope Gregory XV, Sacra Congredatio de Propaganda Fide, 6
Popper, Karl
  critical attitude, 226
  falsification, 219
  objectivity of science, 221–222
  openness to criticism, 222
  science, 463n.31
  truth and credibility, 372
Popularity
  propaganda, 116
  questionable criteria, 207t, 209–210
Population-based screening
  Alzheimer's disease, 152
  full body computed tomography (CT) and MRI scans, 149
  mental illness, 149–150
  routine mammography, 150–152
Portugal, 145, 464n.3
Post-marketing surveillance, 42
Postmodernism, definition, 233
Postpositivism, definition, 233
Preconceived notion, influence, 326, 327f
Preconceptions, misleading, 340–341
Prediction, 337, 376
  contradictory, 218–219, 220t, 221
  incorrect, 184, 185
  intuition, 216
  questions, 406, 408t
Predictive accuracy, 185
Predigested thinking, language, 301–303
Preferences, facts, beliefs and, 375–376
Premarin, 140
Prempro, 76, 80, 140
Pre-propaganda, conditioning the mind, 95
Prevention
  comparing, and cure, 176–177
  exaggerated claims of healing and, 242–243
Principle of social proof, persuasion, 324
Prison-style juvenile facilities, 135
Problems
  changing views of, 249–251
  class, gender, ethnicity and race as arbiters of fate, 245t
  creation and definition of, 271–272
  hiding politics of, creation, 273–274
  historical perspective, 243–251
  moral, existential views, 266–267
  proposed causes, 239t
  social control of deviance, 247–249
  views and consequences, 240–241
Procrit, cancer, 442n.3
Professional books
  pharmaceutical companies and, 82–83
  publishing industry, 44
Professional education, programs, 37–38
Professionalism, appeal, 16
Professional journals
  false claims, 5
  interactions with for-profit companies, 88
  pharmaceutical advertising in, 79–80
  publishing industry, 44
Professional literature. See also Advertising and professional literature
  persuasiveness of propaganda, 10
  propaganda, 8
  shared goals with advertising, 282–283
  shared strategies with advertising, 284–294
Professional organizations, 35–37
  financial ties with drug companies, researchers and physicians, 73–81
  lobbyists, 41–42
Professionals
  becoming quacks, 33t
  examples, 32t
  helping professions, 32–33
Profit motive, quackery, 33t
Progress and Freedom Foundation, think tank, 35
Project Censored, 46
Proof, 219
  consistency, corroboration and, 375
Propaganda. See also Advertisements and professional literature; Harms related to propaganda; Psychological vulnerabilities
  aims of, 17–19
  awareness of controversies as antidote for, 275–276

Propaganda (Cont'd)
  bureaucratic, 103–104
  chains of influence in helping
      professions, 63, 64f, 89
  choices, 23–25
  conflicts and prejudices, 450n.7
  consequences of, 19–21
  construction of realities, 10
  contextual views, 274–275
  corruption, 21
  definitions, 8–9, 429n.3, 449n.1, 450n.11
  description, 6–13
  device-based approaches, 107–109
  encouraging beliefs and actions, 373
  examples of ploys, 108t
  false claims, 5
  fraud, 21–23
  hiding of context, 6–7
  illusion of free choice, 7
  indicators, 8t
  inflated claims of knowledge, 7–8
  information and, 96–97
  integral to technological society, 92–95
  key figures, 106–107
  marketing as education, 11–13
  media and professional literature, 8
  methods, 97–99
  myths about, 17–18
  palaver, 105
  play of, 18–19
  presenting as education, 11–12
  public relations industry, 53–54
  quackery, 21
  racial and ethnic, 468n.42
  repetition, 315–316
  rhetoric and, 9t
  rules of thumb for decreasing
      vulnerability, 345–347
  selective use of evidence, 10, 111–116
  suppression of information, 10–11
  ten commandments of, 91t
  use of information, 238–239
  whistleblowers, 60
Propaganda analysis
  contexts, 101–102
  devices and symbols, 102t
  effects, 102
  fairness, 103
  media for, 101t
  message, 100
  methods and media, 100–101, 118–119
  organization, 100
  source, 99
  target audience, 100
  who stands to gain?, 99
The Propaganda Menace, Lumley, 112
Propaganda ploys, 451n.14
  altering definition, 396
  bandwagon, 102t, 111
  card-stacking, 102t, 111
  examples, 107, 108t
  glittering generalities, 102t, 110
  Institute of Propaganda Analysis, 109–111
  language, 301
  name calling, 102t, 109
  plain folk, 102t, 110–111
  testimonial, 102t, 110
  transfer, 102t, 110
  use of word "disease", 172–176
Propaganda Technique in World War I,
      Lasswell, 19
Prophet motive, 21, 23, 33t
Provincialism, tradition, 210
Pseudobulbar affect, bogus sickness, 165
Pseudo-diseases, creation and promotion,
      156
Pseudo-explanations, language, 313
Pseudonutrition industry, 51
Pseudoscience
  confusing science with, 225
  definition, 233
  difference between science and, 225–226
  hallmarks of, 226
  publications, 431n.22
  quackery, 227–228
  and science, 463n.32
Pseudotechnical jargon, language, 304–305
Psychiatric Industry Watch, pharmaceutical
      industry, 435–436n.35
Psychiatric labels
  classification, 130–134
  personal stories of harm, 132–134
Psychiatric Services, American Psychiatric
      Association publication, 36
Psychiatry
  brain diseases and behavior, 259–260
  moral, existential views, 266–267
Psychiatry Drug Alert, 51

Psychiatry Industry Watch, 46
Psychic deficiencies, pseudotechnical jargon, 305
Psychoanalytic, 97, 209, 219, 261, 464n.7, 468n.46
Psychological assessment industry, 57
Psychological grand narratives, 261, 262f
Psychological vulnerabilities
  allure of science and technology, 329, 330f
  apparent truth of vague descriptions, 328–329
  Barnum effect, 328–329
  biases, 337–340
  Big Pharma and medical writing, 326–328
  confirmation biases, 338–340
  contentment with illusion, 335
  decreasing gullibility, 344–347
  disapproval, 333
  Dr. Fox study, 331–332, 461n.15
  fear of failure, 334
  fear of social rejection, 333
  Forer effect, 328–329
  helpful rules of thumb for decreasing, 345–347
  influenced by overconfidence, 331–332
  influence of propaganda, 326–328, 347
  lack of critical thinking values, knowledge and skills, 343–344
  lack of curiosity, 334
  learning and decision-making style, 342
  low tolerance for uncertainty, 342–343
  misleading shortcuts, 340–342
  misplaced trust, 342
  motivational and emotional, 332–335
  obedience to authority, 331
  preconceived notion, 327f
  preference for entertainment, 335
  rationalizations or excuses, 336–337
  reluctance to assume responsibility, 334
  reluctance to hold others responsible, 334–335
  self-deception, 335–337
  self-inflated assessments, 335–336
  validity effect, 332
Psychologists, industrial plants, 449–450n.5
Psychology, therapeutic prescriptions, 263–264
Psychopathic traits, professionals becoming quacks, 33t

Psychopathology, biology, 466–467n.25
Psychopathology, Maddux and Winstead, 271
Psychopharmacology Bulletin, 52
Psychotechnique, 449n.4
Psychotherapy
  brochure, 117
  configuration of self, 252
  history, 244, 247
Psychotherapy Networker, 439n.60
Psychotropic drugs, 46, 134, 142, 168, 206, 269
PsychRights, 45–46
Publications
  bias, 422
  evidence, 390–391
  health care, 51–52
  pharmaceutical companies, 82–83
  pseudoscience, 431n.22
Public Citizens Health Research, 46
Public funding, research, 34
Public health, politics, 434n.17
Public health regulations, helping professions, 15
Public opinion, factors influencing, 179
Public Relations Association, code of ethics, 54
Public relations industry
  Bernays, 53–54, 97, 261, 440n.63
  marketing and propaganda, 53–54, 63–66
  social anxiety disorder creation, 67–70
Publishing industry, professional journals and books, 44

Quack, 57
  appeal to science in advertising, 201f, 237f
  appeal to scientific discoveries, 202f
  professionals becoming, 33t
Quackery
  Anti-Quackery Ring, 61
  definition, 33, 233
  hallmarks of, 226
  propaganda, 21, 22f
  pseudoscience, 227–228
  quacks and fraudsters, 57–60
  taking advantage of lack of understanding, 200

Quackwatch, 56
Qualifier, rational argument, 357t
Quality, conversational maxim, 364t
Quantity, conversational maxim, 364t
Quarrel, argument type, 367–368
Questionable appeals, examples, 403t, 404t
Questionable criteria
 ad hominem appeals, 207t, 209
 appeal to authority, 206–209
 appeal to Vatican, 208f
 case examples, 207t, 213
 characteristics of person, 207t, 209
 consensus, 207t, 209–210
 emotional appeals, 207t, 212–213
 entertainment value, 207t, 212
 experience, 207t, 213–216
 good intentions, 207t, 211
 intuition, 207t, 216–217
 manner of presentation, 207t, 211
 newness, 207t, 210
 popularity, 207t, 209–210
 testimonials, 207t, 213
 tradition, 207t, 210
 what makes sense, 207t, 211–212
Question begging, 395–397
Questions
 about research, 422–427
 answers with a, 401
 begging the, 395–397
 bias, 420–422
 dialogue, 472n.12
 ignoring, 397
 posing well-structured, 405–407
 taxonomy of Socratic, 362t
Quintiles, conflicts of interest, 63, 443n.5

Race
 arbiter of one's fate, 245t
 behavior, 269–271
 classifications, 134
 propaganda, 468n.42
Radiation, avoidable errors, 147
Radical behaviorism, 240
Radical mastectomy, breast cancer, 154–155
Radiological overinterpretation syndrome, 458n.15
Rational argument, types of statements in, 357t
Rationality, definition, 233

Rationalization
 process of, in Dichter study, 74
 self-propaganda, 336–337
Rationalizing, reasoning compared to, 373–374
Realities
 advertising and professional literature distorting, 291–292
 language constructing, 299
 propaganda and constructing, 10
Reality shock, professionals becoming quacks, 33t
Reasoning. See also Argument analysis
 from analogy, 352–353
 by cause, 353–355
 comparison to rationalizing, 373–374
 by exclusion, 355
 fallacies related to causal, 354t
 hot and cold reasons, 355
 logical, and creativity, 374–375
 logic and, 372
 persuasion, 372
 propaganda and, 9t
 from samples, 353
 from signs and symptoms, 353
 Socratic questions, 362t
 truth and, 374
Rebates, drugs, 442n.3
Rebirthing therapy, 139
Rebuttal
 argument analysis, 361, 363–364
 arguments, 450–451n.12
 fallacies violating, 385t
 rational argument, 357t
Reciprocity rule, persuasion, 321t, 323
Reconsideration, 364
Recovered memory movement, intervention, 136–138, 453–454n.21
Red herring, 401
Redux, 71, 446–447n.22
Refutationist, philosophy of science, 219, 220f
Regression effects, 416–417
Regularities, search for, 221
Regulatory agencies, conflicts of interest with funding, 83–85
Reification, language, 313–314
Relative risk reduction, 181, 182
Relative risks, definition, 186t

Index

Relativism, 229, 233
Relevance, 363
  conversational maxim, 364*t*
  fallacies violating, 384*t*
Repetition
  advertising and professional literature, 293
  language, 315–316
  vulnerability to propaganda, 332
Research
  academics, 34
  accuracy of claims, 427
  commercial research organizations (CROs), 35
  critical appraisal, 417–419
  data analyses, 426–427
  evaluating findings, 413–414
  findings, 427
  integrating information and decision making, 413–417
  levels of evidence, 427–428
  measures, 425–426
  questions to ask about, 422–427
  sample size and source, 425
  study design, 424–425
  think tanks, 35
  universities, 34
Research cartels, knowledge monopolies and, 85–86, 203–204, 431*n*.3, 448*n*.36
Researchers
  consensus appeal, 200–201
  evaluating claims, 201–202
  financial ties with drug companies, professional organizations and physicians, 73–81
  helping professions, 34
  lawyers, pharmaceutical companies and, 86–88
  as "marketers," 77–78
  skepticism, 222
Research funding, decisions about source, 29
Residential treatment center industry, 50
Resolution, 363
Resource hoarding, politicians, 40
Responsibility
  actions and decisions of others, 334–335
  assuming, for decisions, 334
  propaganda vulnerability, 334–335
Retrospective accuracy, 185
Rezulin, 83, 449*n*.40

Rhetoric, 9*t*, 318
Risk
  absolute, 191
  absolute risk reduction, 181
  accurately estimating, 184–193
  alleged factors, 176–178
  base-rate information, 184–185
  challenges in understanding, 191–192
  challenges of assessing, 178–184
  consequences of enlarging territory of, 168–172
  describing, and benefits, 189–190
  Down's syndrome, 194*f*
  ignoring real, 169–170
  inaccurate estimates of, 179–183
  labeling, as diseases, 173–174
  medicalization of, factors, 177–178
  natural frequencies, 185, 187–188
  prevention vs. cure, 176–177
  relative risk reduction, 181
  using test results, 184
  visual aids, 191, 192*f*, 193, 194*f*
Risk chart, benefits and side effects, 189*t*, 190*t*
Risperdal, 7, 87, 88, 141, 455*n*.33
Risperidone, literature, 454*n*.26
Rival hypotheses, science, 218
Roche Laboratories, obesity, 71
Rockefeller Foundation, 204
Rofecoxib, ghost writing, 80–81, 86
Rosenthal effect, 416
Routinization, 429*n*.8
Rule of optimism, 398
Rules of thumb, vulnerability to propaganda, 345–347

Sacra Congredatio de Propaganda Fide, Pope Gregory XV, 6
Sagan, Carl, 106, 225
Samples, reasoning from, 353
Sandplay certificate, 433*n*.12
Satisfice, 340
Scams, whistleblowers, 60
Scarcity principle, persuasion, 321*t*, 323–324
Schizophrenia, 72, 114, 257, 352, 399
  brochure describing, 116
  electroshock therapy, 153
  fabrication, 115
  heredity, 261

Schizophrenia (*Cont'd*)
   language, 300, 301
   propaganda, 116, 291, 304
   research funding, 39, 65
   treatment and medication, 52, 139–141, 443*n*.9, 454*n*.26
Schizophrenia: A Scientific Delusion?, Boyle, 313, 390
Schizophrenia Resource Center, Medscape, 56
Scholarly inquiry, inflated claims of knowledge, 11
Science
   advertisement illustrating appeal to, 201*f*, 237*f*
   allure of, 329, 330*f*
   antiscience, 229–230
   appeal to scientific discoveries, 202*f*
   contrasts between philosophies, 219, 220*f*
   criticism as essence of, 218–219
   dangers of scientific illiteracy, 228–229
   definition, 233
   difference between, and pseudoscience, 225–226
   evaluating true and false, 201–202
   glossary, 232–234
   grand narrative, 252–255
   knowledge and evidence, 205–206
   method of, 459*n*.1
   misrepresentations, 223–226
   misunderstandings, 223–226
   parsimony, 221
   phrenology, 252, 253*f*
   pseudoscience and, 463*n*.32
   refutationist, 219, 220*f*
   relationship with magic and religion, 462*n*.19
   researchers and consensus, 200–201
   rigorous testing, 219–220
   and scientific criteria, 217–218
   scientific method, 462*n*.20
   search for patterns and regularities, 221
   self-correction, 218–219
   skeptical attitude, 222
   solving problems, 223
   standards of evidence, 199–202
   striving for objectivity, 221–222
   verificationist, 219, 220*f*
Scienticism, authority, 226–227

Scientific criteria, science and, 217–218
Scientific discourse, misleading use of, 303–304
Scientific explanations, 377, 378*t*, 379
Scientific illiteracy, dangers of, 228–229
Scientific method, 462*n*.20
Scientific objectivity, definition, 233
Scientific research, inflated claims of knowledge, 11
Scientism
   confusing science with, 225
   definition, 233–234
Screening
   Alzheimer's disease, 152
   populations for mental illness, 149–150
   routine mammography, 150–152
Searching for answers. *See* Critical appraisal
Selection bias, 421
Selective use of evidence
   authority, 116
   censorship, 112–114
   common script for introduction of fad, 113*t*
   confusion, 115
   consensus, 116
   distortion, 114
   diversion, 114–115
   fabrication, 115
   omission, 112–114
   popularity, 116
   propaganda, 10, 111–116
   tradition, 116
Self-correction
   criticism, 218–219
   research lacking, 11
Self-deception, self-propaganda, 335–337
Self-help industry, 57
Self-interests, professionals, 32
Self-medicalization, encouraging self-surveillance, 170–171
Self-propaganda
   rationalization and excuses, 336–337
   self-deception as, 335–337
   self-inflated assessments, 335–336
Self-surveillance, self-medicalization, 170–171
The Selling of DSM, Kirk and Kutchins, 131
Semantic linkages, language, 314
Senility, allure of science, 329, 330*f*

Sense, questionable criteria, 207t, 211–212
Sensory integration therapy, 136, 137f
Seroquel, 52, 87, 141, 455n.33
Sex education program, teenagers, 145
Shadowing, 443n.10
Shape Up America!, obesity, 71
Shrinking Violets and Casper Milquetoasts, McDaniel, 175
Sickness, historical perspective, 243–244, 247
Sick-sick fallacy, pathology, 175
Signs, reasoning from, 353
Sincerity, advertising and professional literature, 294
Single-event probabilities, definition, 186t
Skepticism
    definition, 234
    healthy, and propaganda, 6
    scientists, 222
Slogans, 238–239, 315
Social anxiety disorder
    bogus sickness, 164
    creation of, 67–71
    definition, 68
    Rickey Williams raising awareness, 69
    symptoms, 68
Social Anxiety Disorder Coalition, 68
Social control
    deviance, 247–249
    helping professions, 15
Social desirability effect, 416
Social phobia, bogus sickness, 164
Social problems
    behaviors, 267–269
    marketing in industry, 31
    social definitions, 267
Social proof, persuasion, 321t, 324
Social psychology, persuasion strategies, 318–325
Social reform, helping professions, 16
Social rejection, vulnerability to propaganda, 333
Social Work, journal, 282
Social workers
    criteria, 463n.37
    Under the Cover of Kindness, 16
Society ills, historical perspective, 243–244, 247
Sociological analysis

information and propaganda, 96–97
integrative propaganda, 95–96
Jacque Ellul, 90–99
propaganda integral to technological society, 92–95
propaganda methods, 97–99
Sociological perspective
    big picture, 267–272
    class, gender, culture and race, 269–271
Sociological propaganda, 92, 104
Socrates, 380
Socratic questions, taxonomy, 361, 362t
Sound science, 56
Speculation, language, 315
Spitzer, Elliot, NY Attorney General, 42, 69–70
Spotting fallacies. *See also* Fallacies
    ad hominem arguments, 391–393
    appeal to emotion, 401
    distorting facts and positions, 398–400
    diversions, 400–401
    doubtful evidence, 388–389
    emotional appeals, 391
    evading the facts, 394–397
    fabrication, 398–400
    false even when valid, 388–391
    foul ways to win an argument, 389t
    inappropriate use of analogies, 399–400
    irrelevant appeals, 391–394
    irrelevant conclusion, 399
    overlooking the facts, 397–398
    related evidence, 389–391
    suppressed views, 389–391
    use of confusion, 401–402
Staging, propaganda, 18–19
Standardization, 429n.8
Standards of evidence, advertising and professional literature, 287–288
Stanford, conflict of interest, 41
State government. *See also* Government
    agencies, 42–44
    lawyers, consumers and, 87–88
State Medicaid Programs, Abilify, 87–88
State of Louisiana v. Janssen, 88
State of New Jersey, group homes and institutional settings, 143
Status offenders, 143
Stereotyping, fallacy of, 341–342
Stockholders, medical devices, 81–82

Stratagem, 382
Straw person arguments, 398
Structural frame of reference,
	pseudotechnical jargon, 305
Study designs
	questions, 408*t*
	research method, 424–425
Subjectivism, 380
Substance abuse and addiction, brochure, 118
Substance Abuse and Mental Health Service Administration, *SAMHSA News*, 43
Suffering, hopes for relief, 241–243
Sufficient grounds, 363, 384*t*, 385*t*
Suppression, important information, 10–11
Surveillance
	decreasing privacy, 171
	self-medication encouraging self-, 170–171
Surveillance society, 171
Survival, 401
Survival rates, definition, 186*t*
Suspension of judgment, 363
Sweeping generalization, fallacy of, 397, 402
Symbols, propaganda, 102*t*
Symptoms, reasoning from, 353
Synecdoches, language, 315
Systematic review, 474*n*.1
	conflicts of interest, 73
	effectiveness, 428
	filter, 407, 409, 410*t*
	good intentions, 211
	haphazard, 113
	multi-systemic therapy, 291
	obstacles, 412, 419
	over-diagnosis, 151

Tables, advertising and professional literature, 288
Tamoxifen, benefits and side effects, 189*t*, 190*t*
Tardive dyskinesia, 116–117, 141
Technological society, propaganda integral to, 92–95
Technology
	allure of science and, 329, 330*f*
	grand narrative, 252–255
	as magic, 255
	measures of emotion, 254

Teenagers, sex education programs, 145
Ten commandments, propaganda, 91*t*
Testimonials
	expert testimony, 461–462*n*.17
	propaganda, 102*t*, 110
	questionable criteria, 207*t*, 213
Test materials, 57
Test publishing industry, 57
Test sensitivity, risk, 184
Test specificity, risk, 184
Texas Medication Algorithm Project (TMAP), 150
Textbooks, false claims, 5
Thalidomide, premature promotion, 148
Theory, definition, 234
Theory ladenness of perception, 234
Therapeutic prescriptions, psychology, 263–264
Think, what and how to, 374
Thinking, intuitive and analytic, 376
Think tanks, research, 35
Third Reich, traditional propaganda, 103
Thorazine, 434*n*.18
Tolerance, low, for uncertainty, 342–343
Tradition
	propaganda, 116
	questionable criteria, 207t, 210
Transfer, propaganda, 102t, 110
Transfer effects
	advertising and professional literature, 293
	language, 314
Transparency, organizations for, 46
Transparency International, 46
Transparent representations, health statistics, 186*t*
Treatment of Children with Mental Disorders, New York State Department of Mental Health, 43
Trends in Evidence-Based Neuropsychiatry, 52
Trick, 382
Troubled-persons industry, marketing, 31
Trust, vulnerability to propaganda, 342
Truth
	advertising and professional literature, 294–295
	bureaucratic propaganda, 104
	credibility and, 372
	definition, 234

feeling of, vs. what is true, 371–372
reasoning and, 374
vague descriptions of, 328–329
Truth seeking, 363
Twin studies, oversimplification, 302–303
Twitter, 92

UNAIDS, 204
Uncertainty, low tolerance for, 342–343
Under the Cover of Kindness, Margolin, 16
Unfounded generalizations, 396
United Seniors Association (USA Next), corporate funding, 72*t*
United States
   idiocy and lunacy rates, 468*n*.40
   preventable medical errors, 146–147
   war on drugs, 145, 464*n*.3
Universities
   administrators, 34
   financial ties with corporations, 85–86, 203–204
   ghost writing, 80
University of California at Berkeley, 34, 85
University of California at San Francisco (UCSF), 87
University of Michigan, 29
University of Pennsylvania, Center for Bioethics, 77
University of Toronto, VIGOR study, 86–87
Upjohn, alprazolam (Xanax), 69, 165
Upper-lower limit syndrome, 458*n*.15
USA Next (United Seniors Association), corporate funding, 72*t*
U.S. Center for Science in the Public Interest, 46
Utica crib, harm from past, 125, 126*f*

Vagueness
   advertising and professional literature, 288
   arguments, 356
   Barnum effect, 328–329
   communication, 469*n*.8
   labels, 453*n*.10
   language, 310–311
Validity, bias and, 421–422
Validity effect
   information, 470*n*.6
   vulnerability to propaganda, 332

Values
   advertising and professional literature appealing to, 294
   scientific findings, 267
   vulnerability to propaganda, 343–344
Vatican, appeal to authority, 208*f*
Verbal descriptions, odds, 459*n*.19
Verbal overshadowing, language, 299
Verbal speculation, language, 315
Verificationist, philosophy of science, 219, 220*f*
Vermont, drug company payments, 444*n*.13
Vesicare, ad appealing to fear, 319, 322*f*
Viagra, 12*f*, 167
VIGOR study, University of Toronto, 86–87
Violation, right to make informed decisions, 124–127
Vioxx, 63, 80, 81, 83, 86, 112, 140, 191
Vulnerabilities. *See also* Psychological vulnerabilities
   rules of thumb for decreasing, 345–347

War on drugs
   metaphor, 238, 307
   United States, 145, 464*n*.3
Warrants, rational argument, 357*t*
Watchdog groups, consumer organizations, 45–46
Weasel words, 156, 278, 288–289, 296, 297, 311, 324, 356, 369
Wellness, helping professions, 14–15
Whistleblower Protection Acts, 60
Whistleblowers, scams and propaganda, 60, 430*n*.21
Williams, Rickey, public awareness of social anxiety disorder, 69
Winfrey, Oprah, trauma narrative, 263, 467*n*.35
Wishful thinking, hope, 329
Women's Health Initiative, breast cancer, 183
Woozle Effect, Gelles, 316
Word magic, reification, 313–314
Words
   assumption of one word, one meaning, 310
   clear communication, 193
   functions of language, 300
   vagueness, 310–311, 312*t*
   word smiths, 469*n*.2

World Health Organization (WHO), 204
Wyeth
  hormone therapy drugs, 140
  medical writing, 80
  obesity, 71
  Redux, 71, 446–447*n*.22

Xanax, 69, 165
Xenadrine, 434–435*n*.19

YouTube, 92

Zoloft, 53, 67, 81, 133, 163, 281, 409, 436*n*.36
Zyprexa
  adverse effects, 141, 351
  avoidable harm, 139–140
  Eli Lilly, 6, 471*n*.1
  marketing channels, 66
  side effects, 125, 455*n*.34
  state lawsuit, 87

BAKER COLLEGE LIBRARY
3 3504 00573 2708

HD 8038 .A1 G36 2012
Gambrill, Eileen D., 1934-
Propaganda in the helping
 professions

PROPERTY OF
BAKER COLLEGE
Owosso Campus